Unfolding Destiny

The Guardian's grave set in the peaceful surroundings of the New Southgate Cemetery, London.

THE UNFOLDING DESTINY OF THE BRITISH BAHÁ'Í COMMUNITY

The Messages from the Guardian of the Bahá'í Faith to the Bahá'ís of the British Isles

"... this community can do no better than to gird up afresh its loins, turn its back upon the clamour of the age, its fears, confusion and strife, step resolutely forward on its chosen path, unshakably confident that with every step it takes, should it remain undeflected in its purpose and undimmed in its vision, a fresh outpouring of Divine grace will reinforce and guide its march on the highroad of its destiny."

Shoghi

Bahá'í Publishing Trust

FIRST PUBLISHED 1981

© BAHÁ'Í PUBLISHING TRUST 1981
27 RUTLAND GATE
LONDON SW7 1PD

Designed by Stocks and Chow Designs.
now of Hongkong

Typeset in 11/12 pt Bembo
by Clowes Computer Composition
Text printed on
Glastonbury Antique Laid paper
and illustrations on
Basingwerk Parchment.
Bound in Skivertex.

All rights reserved. No part of this publication may be reproduced, stored in a retrieval system, or transmitted in any form or by any means, electronic, mechanical, photocopying, recording or otherwise, without the prior permission of the Bahá'í Publishing Trust of the United Kingdom.

ISBN 0 900125 43 8

B169

*Printed and bound in Great Britain
by William Clowes (Beccles) Limited
Beccles and London*

". . . The annals of the British Bahá'í community, small in numbers, yet unconquerable in spirit, tenacious in belief, undeviating in purpose, alert and vigilant in the discharge of its manifold duties and responsibilities, have in consequence of its epoch-making achievements been vastly enriched.

"The process set in motion and greatly accelerated through the successive formulation of the Six Year Plan, the Two Year Plan and the Ten Year Plan, must continue unabated and unimpaired. Nay with every passing day it must gather momentum. Every individual believer must, henceforth, encouraged and inspired by all that has already been achieved, contribute to its future and speedy unfoldment.

"That the entire community may befittingly respond to the call of the present hour and bring to a final consummation the Mission with which it has been entrusted is the deepest yearning of my heart and the object of my unceasing prayers."

Shoghi

FOREWORD

It is with a profound feeling of humble, inexpressible gratitude and untold joy that I write these few lines—gratitude for the loving care particularly bestowed by the Guardian of the Bahá'í Faith on the Bahá'ís of the British Isles to guide them along their destined road and to evoke from them the effort which would set them on the path to their high destiny, joy for the loyal response by a community, very small in numbers, to the guidance of him, who was the 'Sign of God on Earth'.

These letters and cables of Shoghi Effendi tell their own story. No words can better relate the story of the creative impulse received and the heroic endeavour made by the British Bahá'í community than the words of the beloved Guardian himself.

Those of us, who read, at the conclusion of the Six Year Plan, the following cables of Shoghi Effendi, can not forget to our dying day the thrill of life that they contained, the exhilaration that they brought:

"OVERJOYED DEEPLY GRATEFUL IMMENSELY PROUD SIGNAL VICTORY ACHIEVED BAHÁ'Í COMMUNITY BRITISH ISLES SHEDDING LUSTRE OPENING YEARS SECOND BAHÁ'Í CENTURY...."

"HEARTILY CONGRATULATE NATIONAL ELECTED REPRESENTATIVES TRIUMPHANT COMMUNITY INDEFATIGABLE NATIONAL TEACHING COMMITTEE ALL SUBSIDIARY AGENCIES PARTICULARLY SELF-SACRIFICING PIONEERS WHO SO OUTSTANDINGLY CONTRIBUTED SIGNAL VICTORY REVERBERATING BAHÁ'Í WORLD."

H.M. Balyuzi
London, April 1979

PREFACE

The period covered by these letters and cables is unique in more ways than one. It covers the first thirty-six years of the Formative Age of the Faith of Bahá'u'lláh, an Age inaugurated by the accession of Shoghi Effendi to the Guardianship of that Faith. It is a period which has witnessed, in human society, the greatest upheavals, the most destructive war, the most widespread disruption of any comparable period in human history. It has witnessed the rise and establishment of the Administrative Order of Bahá'u'lláh throughout the earth.

What an appalling prospect faced the young Guardian in 1921 as he came face to face with his destiny. The unimaginably powerful forces released through more than seventy-five years of almost continuous Divine Revelation were now to be conserved by him and directed to their appointed task—the spiritual regeneration of the entire human race. His sole instrument was a small, widely-scattered community, wholly unconscious of the social implications of its faith, largely unorganised, untrained in collective action, containing within itself all the historic elements of strife, unaware even of the fundamental verities of its religion.

These messages record how the Guardian nurtured and educated one of the national elements in that primitive Bahá'í community, showering it with love and encouragement, training it, raising its vision beyond the confines of its own place and time, forging it into an instrument of spiritual receptivity and action and eventually fusing it into the single, world-wide brotherhood of the embryonic World Commonwealth of Bahá'u'lláh.

The Guardian himself, as well as the Guardianship, are seen in perspective through these successive messages. The *"youthful branch"*, *"blest, tender"*, is seen in the early days, eagerly responsive, with all the ardour of *"his radiant nature"*, to any and every effort made for the service of the Cause. As the heroic tasks of his life develop, as he unfolds to the believers the sublime vision of Bahá'u'lláh's Kingdom, the majesty of his station and of his person becomes more apparent until it is seen by all that *"he is the blest and sacred bough that hath branched out from the Twin Holy Trees. Well is it with him that seeketh the shelter of his shade that shadoweth all mankind."*

The Bahá'í community of the British Isles, the fortunate recipient of these messages, can only express its gratitude, its joy, its pride in the love and confidence showered upon it by its "true brother", by pursuing relentlessly the "long, steep and thorny", but glorious path assigned to it. Its beloved Guardian, even in death, conferred upon this country the incalculable privilege of receiving his mortal remains and becoming the custodian of his resting place.

To those of us who have lived through the stirring times when these messages were received they have caused an uplifting of the spirit and a divine joy. To the generations of the future they will be a never-ending source of inspiration, guidance and incitement to service.

David Hofman

ACKNOWLEDGEMENTS

It is almost impossible adequately to acknowledge all the work which has gone into this publication. Many believers, over a long period of time, have made important contributions.

Our gratitude must first be expressed to David Hofman, who devoted many valuable hours in 1962–1963 making the original collection. Marion Hofman later proof-read the copy, looked out much additional material and made invaluable suggestions for the other workers during the great number of hours she lovingly gave to the task. As the years slipped by and as the work of the Cause increased, busy people spent an enormous amount of time correcting and searching. These included such National Spiritual Assembly members as Elizabeth Chapman, Richard Backwell, Owen Battrick, Joe Jameson and Adib Taherzadeh. Betty Reed, whose copious notes indicate a most thorough examination of each of the paragraphs which formed the first collection, actually saw it through to a page-proof stage. Here it rested for some years as it was realised that more material might be found for there were some important gaps in the record. It was also felt that although the British Bahá'í community, and indeed the Bahá'ís of the world, had a right to, and were eagerly awaiting these messages, it was better to make further searches and present them finally with footnotes and brief biographical notes as a more complete work.

In October, 1972 Philip Hainsworth was released from some of his other national commitments to carry out the search, prepare the footnotes and biographies, and produce the book ready for the printer. It was found that much material had been overlooked or left out and although it is possible that in the future a few more letters may come to light, all the sources available to the National Spiritual Assembly have been utilised. We now believe that there are no gaps of major significance and we place on record our deep appreciation for all those who have made this book possible. Above all we acknowledge with the utmost humility our debt to Shoghi Effendi, that Sign of God on earth, whose words are now preserved for posterity, whose guidance and encouragement led the British Bahá'í community on the "highroad of its destiny" and to whose sacred memory this compilation is dedicated.

National Spiritual Assembly of the Bahá'ís
of the United Kingdom 1979

CONTENTS

Foreword Ḥasan M. Balyuzi	Page	vii
Preface David Hofman		ix
Acknowledgements National Spiritual Assembly of the Bahá'ís of the United Kingdom		xi
Introduction Philip Hainsworth		xv
The seeds are tended (1922–1944)		1
"Their first collective enterprise" The Six Year Plan (1944–1950)		167
"The threshold of a new and glorious epoch" The Africa Plan (1950–1953)		243
"World-wide mission entrusted British Bahá'í community": The British rôle in the Ten Year Crusade (1953–1957)		295
Letters to local Spiritual Assemblies		389
Excerpts from letters to individuals		419
Biographical Notes		465
Indexes		491

LIST OF ILLUSTRATIONS

The Guardian's resting place

Shoghi Effendi. A photograph taken two years before the commencement of his ministry — 14

Examples of Shoghi Effendi's handwriting in 1923, 1924 — 30

Typical receipts given by Shoghi Effendi — 46

First letter to the British Isles written by Amatu'l-Bahá Rúḥíyyih Khanum as the Guardian's secretary — 142

Examples of receipt cards given by Shoghi Effendi — 286

The Guardian. The last photograph of Shoghi Effendi taken a few months before he passed away — 302

Shoghi Effendi's handwriting from the later days of his Guardianship — 318

INTRODUCTION

With his very first letter to the British Bahá'í community Shoghi Effendi Rabbaní, the Guardian of the Bahá'í Faith, established the relationship which was to characterise all his subsequent messages. His opening words, "*My dearest brethren and sisters in the faith of God!*" reflected his deep personal regard for those early British believers with whom he had so recently been associated. As the years went by and the struggling little group expanded, this same loving consideration was extended to each and every new believer. In over eight hundred letters and cables the theme is developed and now this compilation shares with its readers a most precious love story.

For the Bahá'í there is painted a picture of care, patience and encouragement, of inspiration and guidance and of fine attention to detail. For the historian there is a wealth of material not to be found elsewhere.

The reader, as he progresses through the book, will see how, gradually and almost imperceptibly, the picture changes. In the early days of the Guardianship, Shoghi Effendi, knowing personally almost all of those who would read his letters, having met them in London or Manchester, guided them gently along the pathway towards full recognition of the principles of Bahá'í administration which he was then developing through the American Bahá'í community. "Unity in essentials but diversity in the non-essentials" was the pattern. As the membership of the Bahá'í community changed and as the believers began to understand the Institution of the Guardianship, so was he able to pour out more of his infallible guidance to them. The recognition of the Faith as an independent religion, the emancipation of the Bahá'ís from their old allegiances, the incorporation of the National Assembly and the establishment of its own Publishing Trust, as well as the unity of the friends and later his intense concern for the safety of the believers during the Second World War, emerge as the outstanding features of the first twenty-two years covered by these messages.

As the first Centenary approached the Guardian called upon

the British community to "... *ensure unprecedented expansion pioneer teaching activities*" befittingly to celebrate the first hundred years of Bahá'í history and obtain for it the widest publicity. This community, then comprising five local Spiritual Assemblies and fewer than one hundred believers, received, while commemorating Naw-Rúz, 1944, a letter which concluded, "*I feel proud of their record of service, and will pray with increasing fervour for their protection and success*". This was followed by a cable, "... *praying great victories opening century*".

The "Seeds" sown by the Master, 'Abdu'l-Bahá, had indeed been lovingly "tended".

It was at the National Convention held a few weeks later, in war-torn London, on the eve of the Allied invasion of Europe, that a handful of British believers took stock, decided to have their own "Six-Year Plan" and cabled the Guardian asking him to set them some goals. Instantly, as was his wont, Shoghi Effendi seized upon this positive evidence of movement within the Cause and wrote, "*The English believers stand identified with this Plan. The immediate destinies of the entire community depend upon it.*" It was from this turning point that the character of the Guardian's messages changed. The community had evolved in their understanding so their guidance became more specific. As they learned to turn to him so was he able to pour out his love for them. Encouragement, detailed instructions, the pin-pointing of individual goals, the financial support which always seemed to arrive just at the most crucial time, advice in difficult situations and tantalising glimpses of the great future which lay ahead were the characteristics of the period of their "... *first collective enterprise*".

After an eleventh hour victory the radiant delegates, now aware of the power which came to them through their dedication to the Centre of the Covenant, met at Convention in 1950 and with thankful hearts received the Guardian's cable which so vividly conveyed his reaction. "*Heart flooded joy* ... *Historic pledge* ... *nobly redeemed* ... *tribute Martyr Prophet Faith worthily paid* ..." Their reward, however, was not to be allowed to rest on their laurels for in that same cable he then announced the goals for their next, their Two Year, Africa, Plan. The overseas rôle of the British Bahá'í community had begun and once again the reader will become conscious of the increasing strength and

INTRODUCTION   xvii

authority with which the Guardian was able to guide this community in its growing maturity.

When the Two Year Plan was triumphantly concluded, the British responsibilities in the Ten Year Crusade were confidently accepted and the community's efforts in Africa were attended by a *"swift and spectacular success"*. Yet even so, the Guardian, in his last long letter written to the British National Spiritual Assembly less than three months before his passing, made reference to a still more glorious future. *"The splendid work achieved, in such a short space of time, in a field so distant, and amongst a race so alien in background, outlook and customs must . . . be regarded as only a prelude to the series of future campaigns . . ."* to be launched in the years ahead. To the end of his life he continued to sustain and surround with his prayers the members of that community whose African victories had given him so much joy.

It has been to present this picture as faithfully as possible that the letters and cables have been printed verbatim. Prior to April 1941 when Amatu'l-Bahá Rúḥíyyih Khánum began to write to the British Bahá'ís on behalf of the Guardian, he had had few helpers and his secretaries had caused him much suffering. Their names are not mentioned in this book and only their letters which carried the Guardian's handwriting as a footnote or contained words which indicated they were writing as instructed by him have been used. A number of strictly personal items have been omitted, the omissions being noted by (. . .)

In the early years the Guardian would type a few copies of his general letters and most of these were published in the American "Bahá'í Administration". Where there are copies in the British files which carry his corrections and signature, they are printed in this book in their original format, and the titles in "Bahá'í Administration", added by the editor, the late Hand of the Cause, Horace Holley, have not been used.

The footnotes, indicated by asterisk (★) have been added only to throw light on some word or message which otherwise would not be understood; they are not intended as commentary.

The biographical notes, noted by (†) make only brief reference to those who were at the time of mention members of the British Bahá'í community; they are listed in the order in which they first appear in the text.

The extracts from letters to individuals represent only a small fraction of the vast amount of guidance and encouragement which the beloved Guardian poured out on all who turned to him. They have been selected because of their permanent value and as they are printed strictly in chronological order some idea is given of the differing problems which from time to time exercised the minds of the believers; they frequently reflect a mood or condition of the community itself.

The full import of all the letters and cables reproduced in this book, not only to the privileged few who received them, but to the entire British people, may well be left to a future generation to appreciate. We of this day and age, about to embark upon yet another in that series of future campaigns, "... *campaigns which in their range and significance, must throw into shade the feats performed in the African Continent* ..." can only turn again and again with humility and gratitude to the inspiration which flows so abundantly from its pages.

Philip Hainsworth
Naw-Rúz, 1979

THE SEEDS ARE TENDED
1922-1944

5 March 1922*

Dear Fellow-workers in the Cause of Bahá'u'lláh,

It is with words of regret and disappointment that I desire to open this letter because of my inability, in view of my manifold and pressing duties, to respond individually and in writing to the many messages of love and sympathy and of hope that you have so affectionately sent me since our Beloved's passing from this World. I am sure I am voicing the sentiments of the bereaved ladies of the Household when I say that however desirous we may be to correspond separately with every one of you, the grave responsibilities and manifold duties now devolved upon us make it regrettably impossible to express in written messages to every friend what we constantly feel in our hearts, and pray for when visiting His sacred Shrine.

At this grave and momentous period through which the Cause of God in conformity with the Divine Wisdom is passing, it is the sacred duty of every one of us to endeavour to realise the full significance of this Hour of Transition, and then to make a supreme resolve to arise steadfastly for the fulfilment of our sacred obligations.

Great as is the love and paternal care which our beloved Master is extending to us from on High, and unique as is the Spirit that animates today His servants in the world, yet a great deal will depend upon the character and efforts of His loved ones on whom now rests the responsibility of carrying on His work gloriously after Him. How great is the need at this moment when the promised outpourings of His grace are ready to be extended to every soul, for us all to form a broad vision of the mission of the Cause to mankind, and to do all in our power to spread it throughout the world. The eyes of the world, now that the sublime Personality of the Master has been removed from this visible plane, are turned with eager anticipation to us who are named after His name, and on whom rests primarily the responsibility to keep burning the torch that He has lit in this world. How keenly I feel at this challenging hour in the history of the Cause the need for a firm and definite determination to subordinate all our personal likings, our local interests, to the interests and requirements of the Cause of God! Now is the time to set aside, nay, to forget altogether, minor considerations regarding our internal relationships, and to present a solid united front to the world animated by no other desire but to serve and propagate His Cause.

*Printed also in "Bahá'í Administration". (See para. 3, page xvii.)

It is my firm conviction which I now express with all sincerity and candour, that the dignity and unity of the Cause urgently demands—particularly throughout the American continent—that the friends should in their words and conduct emphasise and give absolute prominence to the constructive dynamic principles of Bahá'u'lláh, rather than attach undue importance to His negative Teachings. With hearts cleansed from the least trace of suspicion and filled with hope and faith in what the spirit of love can achieve, we must one and all endeavour at this moment to forget past impressions, and with absolute goodwill and genuine co-operation unite in deepening and diffusing the spirit of love and service that the Cause has thus far so remarkably shown to the world. To this attitude of goodwill, of forebearance and genuine kindness to all, must be added, however, constant but unprovocative vigilance, lest unrestricted association with the peoples of the world should enable the very few who have been definitely pronounced by the Master as injurious to the body of the Cause, to make a breach in the Movement. Not until, however, an unmistakable evidence should appear, manifestly revealing the evil motives of a certain individual or groups of individuals, is it advisable to make the matter public; for an untimely declaration that shall give rise to open differences among the friends is far more detrimental than forbearing still further with those who are suspected of evil intentions. As the Master so fully and consistently did throughout His lifetime, we must all make a supreme effort to pour out a genuine spirit of kindness and hopeful love to peoples of various creeds and classes, and must abstain from all provocative language that may impede the effect of what true and continued kindness can produce.

Does not 'Abdu'l-Bahá wish us, as He looks down upon us with loving expectation from His glorious Station, to obliterate as much as possible all traces of censure, of conflicting discussions, of cooling remarks, of petty unnecessary observations that impede the onward march of the Cause, that damp the zeal of the firm believer and detract from the sublimity of the Bahá'í Cause in the eyes of the inquirer? In order, however, to insure fair and quick and vigorous action whenever such an evil activity is revealed and has been carefully ascertained, the best and only means would appear to be, for the careful observer, once he is assured of such an evil action, and has grown hopeless of the attitude of kindness and forbearance, to report it quietly to the Spiritual Assembly representative of the friends in that locality and submit the case to their earnest and full consideration. Should the majority of the members of that Assembly be conscientiously convinced of the case—and this being a national issue affecting the body of the friends in America—it should, only through the intermediary of that Assembly, be cautiously communicated to that greater body representing all the Assemblies in America, which will in its turn obtain all the available data from the local Assembly in question, study carefully the situation and reserve for itself the ultimate decision. It may, if it decides so, refer to the Holy Land for further consideration and consultation.

This clearly places heavy responsibilities on the local as well as national Assemblies, which in the course of time will evolve, with the Master's power and guidance, into the local and national Houses of Justice. Hence the vital necessity of having a local Spiritual Assembly in every locality where the number of adult declared believers exceeds nine, and of making provision for the indirect election of a Body that shall adequately represent the interests of all the friends and Assemblies throughout the American Continent.

A perusal of some of the words of Bahá'u'lláh and 'Abdu'l-Bahá on the duties and functions of the Spiritual Assemblies in every land (later to be designated as the local Houses of Justice), emphatically reveals the sacredness of their nature, the wide scope of their activity, and the grave responsibility which rests upon them.

Addressing the members of the Spiritual Assembly in Chicago, the Master reveals the following:—"Whenever ye enter the council-chamber, recite this prayer with a heart throbbing with the love of God and a tongue purified from all but His remembrance, that the All-powerful may graciously aid you to achieve supreme victory:—'O God, my God! We are servants of Thine that have turned with devotion to Thy Holy Face, that have detached ourselves from all beside Thee in this glorious Day. We have gathered in this spiritual assembly, united in our views and thoughts, with our purposes harmonised to exalt Thy Word amidst mankind. O Lord, our God! Make us the signs of Thy Divine Guidance, the Standards of Thy exalted Faith amongst men, servants to Thy mighty Covenant. O Thou our Lord Most High! Manifestations of Thy Divine Unity in Thine Abhá Kingdom, and resplendent stars shining upon all regions. Lord! Aid us to become seas surging with the billows of Thy wondrous Grace, streams flowing from Thy all-glorious Heights, goodly fruits upon the Tree of Thy heavenly Cause, trees waving through the breezes of Thy Bounty in Thy celestial Vineyard. O God! Make our souls dependent upon the Verses of Thy Divine Unity, our hearts cheered with the outpourings of Thy Grace, that we may unite even as the waves of one sea and become merged together as the rays of Thine effulgent Light; that our thoughts, our views, our feelings may become as one reality, manifesting the spirit of union throughout the world. Thou art the Gracious, the Bountiful, the Bestower, the Almighty, the Merciful, the Compassionate.'"

In the Most Holy Book is revealed:—"The Lord hath ordained that in every city a House of Justice be established wherein shall gather counsellors to the number of Bahá, and should it exceed this number it does not matter. It behoveth them to be the trusted ones of the Merciful among men and to regard themselves as the guardians appointed of God for all that dwell on earth. It is incumbent upon them to take counsel together and to have regard for the interests of the servants of God, for His sake, even as they regard their own interests, and to choose that which is meet and seemly. Thus hath the Lord your God commanded you. Beware lest ye put away that which is clearly revealed in His Tablet. Fear God, O ye that perceive."

Furthermore, 'Abdu'l-Bahá reveals the following:— "It is incumbent upon every one not to take any step without consulting the Spiritual Assembly, and they must assuredly obey with heart and soul its bidding and be submissive unto it, that things may be properly ordered and well arranged. Otherwise every person will act independently and after his own judgment, will follow his own desire, and do harm to the Cause."

"The prime requisites for them that take counsel together are purity of motive, radiance of spirit, detachment from all else save God, attraction to His Divine Fragrances, humility and lowliness amongst His loved ones, patience and long-suffering in difficulties and servitude to His exalted Threshold. Should they be graciously aided to acquire these attributes, victory from the unseen Kingdom of Bahá shall be vouchsafed to them. In this day, assemblies of consultation are of the greatest importance and a vital necessity. Obedience unto them is essential and obligatory. The members thereof must take counsel together in such wise that.no occasion for ill-feeling or discord may arise. This can be attained when every member expresseth with absolute freedom his own opinion and setteth forth his argument. Should any one oppose, he must on no account feel hurt for not until matters are fully discussed can the right way be revealed. The shining spark of truth cometh forth only after the clash of differing opinions. If after discussion, a decision be carried unanimously well and good;

but if, the Lord forbid, differences of opinion should arise, a majority of voices must prevail."

Enumerating the obligations incumbent upon the members of consulting councils, the Beloved reveals the following:—"The first condition is absolute love and harmony amongst the members of the assembly. They must be wholly free from estrangement and must manifest in themselves the Unity of God, for they are the waves of one sea, the drops of one river, the stars of one heaven, the rays of one sun, the trees of one orchard, the flowers of one garden. Should harmony of thought and absolute unity be non-existent, that gathering shall be dispersed and that assembly be brought to naught. The second condition:—They must when coming together turn their faces to the Kingdom on High and ask aid from the Realm of Glory. They must then proceed with the utmost devotion, courtesy, dignity, care and moderation to express their views. They must in every matter search out the truth and not insist upon their own opinion, for stubbornness and persistence in one's views will lead ultimately to discord and wrangling and the truth will remain hidden. The honoured members must with all freedom express their own thoughts, and it is in no wise permissible for one to belittle the thought of another, nay, he must with moderation set forth the truth, and should differences of opinion arise a majority of voices must prevail, and all must obey and submit to the majority. It is again not permitted that any one of the honoured members object to or censure, whether in or out of the meeting, any decision arrived at previously, though that decision be not right, for such criticism would prevent any decision from being enforced. In short, whatsoever thing is arranged in harmony and with love and purity of motive, its result is light, and should the least trace of estrangement prevail the result shall be darkness upon darkness.... If this be so regarded, that Assembly shall be of God, but otherwise it shall lead to coolness and alienation that proceed from the Evil One. Discussions must all be confined to spiritual matters that pertain to the training of souls, the instruction of children, the relief of the poor, the help of the feeble throughout all classes in the world, kindness to all peoples, the diffusion of the fragrances of God and the exaltation of His Holy Word. Should they endeavour to fulfil these conditions the Grace of the Holy Spirit shall be vouchsafed unto them, and that assembly shall become the centre of the Divine blessings, the hosts of Divine confirmation shall come to their aid, and they shall day by day receive a new effusion of Spirit."

So great is the importance and so supreme is the authority of these assemblies that once 'Abdu'l-Bahá after having Himself and in His own handwriting corrected the translation made into Arabic of the Ishráqát (the Effulgences) by Shaykh Faraj, a Kurdish friend from Cairo, directed him in a Tablet to submit the above-named translation to the Spiritual Assembly of Cairo, that he may seek from them before publication their approval and consent. These are His very words in that Tablet:—"His honour, Shaykh Faraju'lláh, has here rendered into Arabic with greatest care the Ishráqát and yet I have told him that he must submit his version to the Spiritual Assembly of Egypt, and I have conditioned its publication upon the approval of the above-named Assembly. This is so that things may be arranged in an orderly manner, for should it not be so any one may translate a certain Tablet and print and circulate it on his own account. Even a non-believer might undertake such work, and thus cause confusion and disorder. If it be conditioned, however, upon the approval of the Spiritual Assembly, a translation prepared, printed and circulated by a non-believer will have no recognition whatever."

This is indeed a clear indication of the Master's express desire that nothing whatever should be given to the public by any individual among the friends, unless fully considered and approved by the Spiritual Assembly in his locality; and if this (as is undoubtedly the case) is a matter that pertains to the general interest of the Cause in that land, then it is incumbent upon the Spiritual Assembly to submit it to the consideration and approval of the national body representing all the various local assemblies. Not only with regard to publication, but all matters without any exception whatsoever, regarding the interests of the Cause in that locality, individually or collectively, should be referred exclusively to the Spiritual Assembly in that locality, which shall decide upon it, unless it be a matter of national interest, in which case it shall be referred to the national body. With this national body also will rest the decision whether a given question is of local or national interest. (By national affairs is not meant matters that are political in their character, for the friends of God the world over are strictly forbidden to meddle with political affairs in any way whatever, but rather things that affect the spiritual activities of the body of the friends in that land).

Full harmony, however, as well as co-operation among the various local assemblies and the members themselves, and particularly between each assembly and the national body, is of the utmost importance, for upon it depends the unity of the Cause of God, the solidarity of the friends, the full, speedy and efficient working of the spiritual activities of His loved ones.

Large issues in such spiritual activities that affect the Cause in general in that land, such as the management of the "Star of the West" and any periodical which the National Body may decide to be a Bahá'í organ, the matter of publication, or reprinting Bahá'í literature and its distribution among the various assemblies, the means whereby the teaching campaign may be stimulated and maintained, the work of the Ma<u>sh</u>riqu'l-A<u>dh</u>kar, the racial question in relation to the Cause, the matter of receiving Orientals and associating with them, the care and maintenance of the precious film exhibiting a phase of the Master's sojourn in the United States of America as well as the original matrix and the records of His voice, and various other national spiritual activities, far from being under the exclusive jurisdiction of any local assembly or group of friends, must each be minutely and fully directed by a special board, elected by the National Body, constituted as a committee thereof, responsible to it and upon which the National Body shall exercise constant and general supervision.

The time is indeed ripe for the manifold activities, wherein the servants and handmaidens of Bahá'u'lláh are so devoutly and earnestly engaged, to be harmonised and conducted with unity, co-operation and efficiency, that the effect of such a combined and systematised effort, through which an All-powerful Spirit is steadily pouring, may transcend every other achievement of the past, however glorious it has been, and may stand, now that, to the eyes of the outside world the glorious Person of the Master is no more, a convincing testimony of the potency of His everliving Spirit.

Your brother and co-worker in His Cause,
Shoghi

16 December 1922

To my spiritual brethren and sisters in Great Britain.
Care of the members of the Spiritual Council.*

My dearest brethren and sisters in the faith of God!
May I at the very outset of this, my very first letter to you, convey

---

*Dr. Esselmont† and E. T. Hall† were "chosen" to represent Bournemouth and Manchester respectively and they met with seven others representing "The London Groups" to form the first "All-England Bahá'í Council" which met at the London home of Mrs. Thornburgh-Cropper† 6 June, 1922. Mr. G. P. Simpson† was elected Chairman.

to your hearts in words, however inadequate but assuredly deeply felt and sincere, a measure of my burning impatience, during my days of retirement, to return speedily and join hands with you in the great work of consolidation that awaits every earnest believer in the Cause of Bahá'u'lláh.

Now that happily I feel myself restored to a position where I can take up with continuity and vigour the threads of my manifold duties, the bitterness of every disappointment felt, time and again, in the course of the past weary months at my feeling of unpreparedness, have been merged in the sweetness of the present hour, when I realise that spiritually and bodily I am better equipped to shoulder the responsibilities of the Cause. The thought, so often comforting and sustaining, that in the counsels of my British co-workers of that land, I shall find spontaneous and undiminished support as well as wise and experienced assistance, is surely one of those forces which will hearten me in the midst of my future labours for the Cause.

That in every one of you our departed Master reposed His future and truest hopes for an able and convincing presentation of the Cause to the outside world, is abundantly revealed in His spoken and written words to you, as well as in His general references to the spirit of sincerity, of tenacity and devotion that animates His friends of that land.

The fierce tests that have raged over that island in the past; the calm and determination with which they have been so bravely faced and surmounted; the seeds of loving fellowship that the Beloved in person has more than once scattered in its soil; the rise, as its result, of a few but indeed capable, reliable, devoted and experienced followers and admirers of the Cause; the splendid and in many instances unique opportunities that are yours—these indeed are cherished thoughts for a land that illumines its past and should cheer its future.

I need hardly tell you how grateful and gratified I felt when I heard the news of the actual formation of a National Council whose main object is to guide, co-ordinate and harmonise the various activities of the friends, and when I learned of its satisfactory composition, its harmonious procedure and the splendid work it is achieving.

My earnest prayer is that the blessing of the Almighty may rest upon all its deliberations, that it may be divinely guided, inspired in its work, may smooth speedily and definitely all differences that may arise, may promote the all-important work of Teaching, may widen the sphere of its correspondence and exchange of news with the distant

THE SEEDS ARE TENDED (1922–1944)

parts of the Bahá'í world, may secure through its publications a dignified and proper presentation of the Cause to the enlightened public, and may in every other respect prove itself capable of distinct and worthy achievements.

With abiding affection and renewed vigour I shall now await the joyful tidings of the progress of the Cause and the extension of your activities, and will spare no effort in sharing with the faithful, here and in other lands, the welcome news of the progressive march of the Cause and the unceasing labours of our British friends for the Cause of Bahá'u'lláh.

Your brother,
Shoghi

23 December 1922

To my beloved brethren and sisters throughout Great Britain.
Care of the members of the Bahá'í Council.

Dearest Friends,

I have during the last few days been waiting eagerly for the first written messages of my Western friends, sent to me since they have learned of my return to the Holy Land. How great was the joy when dear Miss Rosenberg's† letter—the very first that reached me from the West—was handed to me this evening, bearing the joyful news of the safety, the unity and the happiness of my British friends across the seas! I read it and re-read it with particular pleasure and felt a thrill of delight at the welcome news of the harmonious and efficient functioning of your Spiritual Assembly.

I very sincerely hope that now that I have fully re-entered upon my task, I may be enabled to offer my humble share of assistance and advice in the all-important work which is now before you. I fervently pray to God that the field of your activities may go on expanding, that your zeal and efforts may never diminish, and that new souls, active, able and sincere, may soon join with you in bearing aloft the Glorious Standard of the Cause in that land. . . .

Ere long, an able and experienced teacher recently arrived from Persia will visit your shores and will, I trust, by his thorough knowledge of the Cause, his wide experience, his fluency, his ardour and his devotion, reanimate every drooping spirit and inspire the active worker to make fresh and determined efforts for the deepening as well as the spreading of the Movement in those regions. His forthcoming book, which he has patiently and laboriously written on the history of the Movement and which has been partly revised by the Pen of our Beloved Master is beyond any doubt the most graphic, the most reliable and comprehensive of its kind in all Bahá'í literature. I am sure he will considerably enrich the store of your knowledge of the various phases and stages of the Bahá'í Movement. Our beloved Dr. Esslemont will, I trust, be particularly pleased to meet him, as he is eminently qualified to offer him valuable help in connection with various aspects of his (Dr. Esslemont's) book. I am enclosing various suggestions of Mr. Dreyfus-Barney and of Mr. Roy Wilhelm made by them at my request, during their last sojourn in the Holy Land. I submit them to Dr. Esslemont's consideration as well as to that of the Spiritual Assembly. I very deeply regret my inability to give the attention I desire to this admirable work of his, but will assuredly do all in my power to aid him in the final stages of his work. I am certain however that the book as it now stands gives the finest and most effective presentation of the various aspects of the Cause to the mind of the Oriental as well as to that of the Westerner. May it arouse a genuine and widespread interest in the Cause throughout the world.

I am now starting correspondence with every Bahá'í local centre throughout the East and will not fail to instruct and urge the believers everywhere to send directly through their respective spiritual local Assemblies the joyful tidings of the progress of the Cause, in the form of regular detailed reports, to the various assemblies of their spiritual brethren and sisters in the West. England, I am confident, will regularly and consistently receive, directly, and indirectly through the "Star of the West" and the "Bahá'í News" of India, a large share of such tidings from Persia, Caucasus, Turkestan, India, Turkey and Mesopotamia, North Africa and Egypt. It would be most gratifying and encouraging to all earnest workers for the Cause of Bahá'u'lláh if every now and then a report on the spiritual activities of the friends in Great Britain, as well as articles on spiritual matters, would be submitted for publication to the above-mentioned periodicals. It would, I feel very strongly, react very favourably on the Cause in England, and would serve to draw closer the ties that bind all spiritual centres together at the present time.

I would be pleased and grateful if the members of the Spiritual Assembly would at any time inform me of their needs, wants and desires, their plans and activities, that I may through my prayers and brotherly assistance contribute, however meagrely, to the success of their glorious mission in this world.

To my extreme regret, I feel unable in view of my manifold and pressing duties, and owing to the extraordinary extension of the Movement in recent times, to correspond with the friends individually and express to them in writing what I always feel in the depth of my heart of brotherly affection and abiding gratitude for their love and sympathy for me. I shall, however, await with eager expectation their individual letters and assure them of my readiness and wish to be of any service to them in their work for the Cause.

Remembering every one of you in these hallowed surroundings and fervently praying at the three sacred Thresholds that the blessings of the Lord may rest upon your individual and collective efforts,

I am as ever your devoted brother,
Shoghi

17 February 1923

The beloved of the Lord and the handmaids of the Merciful throughout London, Manchester and Bournemouth.
Care of the members of the National Spiritual Assembly.*

Dearest brethren and sisters in 'Abdu'l-Bahá,
The letters that I have recently received from the friends in London and Manchester have been to me a source of great hope and encouragement, and have served to strengthen the ties that bind me to my dearly-beloved friends in that great country.

I am much pleased and gratified to hear of the wonderful progress of the work of our able and devoted brother, Jináb-i-Ávárih, and my earnest hope and prayer is that he may, by his zeal, patience, experience and knowledge, set ablaze the fire that the Master has kindled in the heart of that land.

The supreme necessity, and the urgent need of the Cause of God at present, is the unity of the friends, and their sustained and wholehearted

---

*The first meeting of the elected "National Spiritual Assembly" took place in London on 13 October 1923.

co-operation in their task of spreading the Divine Teachings throughout the world. It is the sacred duty of all believers to have implicit confidence in, and support heartily, every decision passed by their Spiritual Assemblies, whether local or central; and the members of these Assemblies must, on their part, set aside their own inclinations, personal interests, likes and dislikes, and regard only the welfare of the Cause and the well-being of the friends. This is surely the foundation which must be firmly laid in the hearts of all believers the world over, for upon this only can any constructive and permanent service be achieved, and the edifice of the Beloved's last instructions, as revealed in His Will and Testament, be raised and established.

The all-conquering Spirit of Bahá'u'lláh cannot prove effective in this world of strife and turmoil, and cannot achieve its purpose for mankind, unless we, who are named after His Name, and who are the recipients of His Grace, endeavour, by our example, our daily life and our dealings with our fellow-men, to reveal that noble spirit of love and self-sacrifice of which the world stands in need at present.

I have been reading lately some of the oldest Tablets of 'Abdu'l-Bahá and am enclosing for your perusal the translation of various selections from His soul-stirring words, revealed some twenty-five years ago, during the darkest days of His incarceration in the prison city of 'Akká. You will realise as you read them the unshakable confidence of the Master in the future growth of the Movement, the significance of the Cause in this age, and the glorious privilege of the friends to labour for its spread in every land.

I am enclosing also my revised translation of the Hidden Words, both Persian and Arabic, a copy of which I have sent to the friends in the United States in response to their cable, requesting me to authorise circulation of my version among the friends in America.

I have recently received a message from our beloved brethren and sisters in Germany, who, in the midst of their sufferings and trials, yearn to receive a word of sympathy and comfort from their fellow-workers in France and England. I am sure you will gladly respond to their request, and cheer them with the glad-tidings of the wonderful progress of the Cause in your land and elsewhere.

I am always looking forward to receiving your letters and hear from you personally in all matters pertaining to the Cause. It is my earnest prayer whenever I visit the Sacred Shrines, that the friends in England may be always protected, guided and blessed in their work of service to the Cause, and may soon witness the fulfilment of the glorious promises

SHOGHI EFFENDI
A photograph taken two years before the commencement of his ministry

of the Master regarding the future of that land and the spiritual re-awakening of its people.

Your brother and fellow-worker,
Shoghi

24 February 1923

Dear Spiritual Brother,

Your letter to Shoghi Effendi has been received and was read by him with keen delight and satisfaction for it bespoke of the new spirit of ardent devotion that has enkindled the hearts of the faithful followers of Bahá, and of their loyal and active endeavours in the parth of service. Should the friends continue in their labours of love and service their activities will yield glorious results and they shall witness the realisation of the promises of the Beloved regarding the spiritual achievements of the friends in that land.

Shoghi Effendi is highly gratified and encouraged to know that the friends have carried out so efficiently his directions regarding the establishment of National and local Spiritual Assemblies; and he feels confident that the co-ordinated and unified efforts of its members, blessed by the unfailing assistance and guidance of the Beloved Master, will mark the dawn of a new era of spiritual activity and enlightenment.

He is very pleased to know that you are faithfully working for peace and harmony amongst the friends; and he prays that you may be blessed in your endeavours and be inspired and guided to clear all misunderstandings that may arise; and may help bring about that spirit of unity which is so essential to the life and growth of the Cause. There is no doubt that difficulties will always arise; but if met in the spirit of earnest and selfless devotion and purity of motive all problems will be solved and we shall emerge from every difficulty spiritually stronger and wiser.

Shoghi Effendi wishes to extend to you his thanks for your giving him the report of the activities of the friends there. He will soon write a letter to the Assembly based on their report. He wishes you to rest assured that his thoughts and prayers are with you wishing you all success in your labours for the promulgation of the Blessed Cause.

Although unable to write individual letters he will gladly welcome all letters that you will send him in the future...

29 November 1923

To the members of the English National Spiritual Assembly

My dearly-beloved fellow-workers in the Vineyard of God!
  I am in receipt of your letter dated Nov. 17th 1923, and forwarded to me by our active and devoted brother, Mr. Simpson. I have read it with the utmost pleasure and satisfaction. I feel happy and encouraged to learn that those few, yet earnest and promising, servants of Bahá'u'lláh in that land are, despite the vicissitudes and obstacles that confront the rapid rise of the Movement, wholeheartedly striving and co-operating for the fulfilment of His divine Promise.

  You, surely, have laid a firm foundation for the future development of the Cause in those regions, and my hope is that the National Assembly of Great Britain may, by full, frequent, and anxious consultation, protect the Cause, maintain and promote harmony amongst the friends, and initiate and execute ways and means for the diffusion of its spirit and the promotion of its principles.

  I welcome with keen and genuine satisfaction the active participation of our beloved sister, Mrs. Thornburgh-Cropper, in the affairs of the Cause, and feel confident that her wisdom, her experience, her influence, and her unparalleled opportunities for the service of the Movement will pave the way for the wholesome growth of the Cause in that land.

  I am sure you all realise the seemingly unsurmountable difficulties in the way of individual correspondence with the ever-increasing multitude of Bahá'ís throughout the world, and I need hardly tell you how tremendously difficult it is, and how reluctant I feel, to discriminate at all between the many letters of varying importance which I daily receive from almost every corner of the globe. Realising however that direct and intimate individual correspondence, in some form or other, is most urgent and vital to the interests of the Cause, I am, I assure you, giving it these days again my careful and undivided attention, and pray God that to this problem may soon be found a satisfactory and feasible solution. In the meantime, I wish to emphasise the fact that I eagerly await, and would welcome, and would assuredly have time to peruse, most carefully and <u>in person</u>, every individual letter you may wish to send me, and my readiness and wish to attend, in the very best way I can, to every matter raised in those letters. No written message, however unimportant, will first be opened and read by any one save myself.

Regarding the proposed conference on "Living Religions within the British Empire", I feel that such a great opportunity for the Movement should not be neglected, and I am glad to know that it has been seized by the members of the National Assembly, and is being closely examined by them. I would welcome further particulars as to who has conceived the idea, under whose auspices it will be conducted, and whether it is being supported by government authorities, and what conditions are imposed on its proceedings. I am discussing the matter with some of the Bahá'í representatives of India and America as to what friends would be most competent to represent the Cause at this conference. I shall communicate on this subject with the National Assemblies of India and America, and will inform you immediately I receive definite information from them.

As to the raising of funds to provide for the expenses of the Bahá'í representatives, I am sure the friends in England will find in the National Assemblies of India and America and in myself ready and generous supporters of a step that will undoubtedly prove of immediate and universal value for the ultimate recognition of the Cause by the world.

It is my ardent prayer that we may all be inspired to adopt the most effective measures for the successful achievement of this great undertaking.

I was much impressed by the charm and force of Major Moore's article, published recently in T. P. Cassell's weekly, and I would much desire to know whether his action was spontaneous, or whether he was urged or requested by someone to write it. I strongly urge the friends, and particularly the members of the National Assembly, to do all in their power to make of this able and highly-minded admirer of the Cause, a zealous and true Bahá'í. I am looking forward with keen anticipation to his spiritual development and his taking a more active part in the affairs of the Cause.

I am enclosing for the friends recent translations of the wonderful prophetic utterances of Bahá'u'lláh, and I trust you will find them of great value in your work of teaching and spreading the Cause.

Awaiting eagerly your letters, individually as well as collectively,

I am your brother,
Shoghi

9 December 1923

My dear Mr. Simpson,

Your short yet encouraging letter was gladly received by our dear Shoghi Effendi just yesterday evening. He felt very pleased indeed with that spirit of hopefulness which your letter conveyed, and he eagerly hopes that in the days to come nothing will mar the brightness and optimism of his English brethren and sisters over in the West.

Your references to the commemoration meeting held in London, brought back with all its painful sadness recollections of that one night. In a calm and quiet night, brightened by the silvery rays of the moon, gathered 'Abdu'l-Bahá's sorrow-stricken faithful ones, to commemorate the night of His last farewell. On the cistern by the Tomb sat His fervent servants; below them flickered the dying lights of Haifa, and above head shown in full magnificence the star bespangled heavens. It was in the mid-watches of such a night that with sorrow and fervour the servants turned unto their dear Master so near and yet so far away; and with a deep feeling of that bitter loss they supplicated help and guidance from their Lord. A word or two from Shoghi Effendi made them feel the Master nigh, and made them realise as never before that it was only in following in His steps, and in living the life that He had, that we can prove our faithfulness to our Master's Cause. It was indeed a night of meditation and prayer and we missed you all so much.

We are receiving encouraging news from almost everywhere, such as Italy, Germany, China and Australia; and as you will have them more fully in the circulars of the Spiritual Assembly, I had hardly need make mention of them here.

Shoghi Effendi's earnest hopes in England are very great, and I am sure that the sincere and true-hearted efforts of his fellow-workers, will spread the principles of this great Revelation as never before. Hard though it be to get access to the more intellectual circles in England, he firmly believes that through persistence, the obstacles will be soon overcome and they, with their own accord, will welcome you in their midst, turning a sympathetic ear to all that you have to share with them. May these high hopes be realised. . . .

My beloved brother,
My deepest admiration for your indefatigable exertions for the success of the Cause. I will always remember you in my prayers and await eagerly your personal letters. I welcome any suggestions and further particulars regarding the conference on the Living Religions within the British Empire.

Your brother,
Shoghi

6 January 1924

Dear Bahá'í Brother,

Your letter of Dec. 23rd furnishing necessary information concerning the Conference on Religions arrived and made our dear Guardian highly pleased and delighted.

As he has quite recently written to the friends in England, he has instructed me to answer your letter and inform you that he has written and directed the National Spiritual Assembly of America to have a comprehensive article written by the ablest pen among the American friends—to be excellent both in style and in representation.

After this essay is written, it will be sent to our dear Shoghi Effendi who will send it to your N.S. Assembly for your perusal and consideration. You will add your remarks and suggestions and return it to him for final approval.

Shoghi Effendi is also thinking of selecting someone among the Indian friends to represent India. This Conference and a worthy and dignified representation of the Holy Cause therein, are under his serious consideration. We hope that through his wise instruction and powerful prayers your activities in this respect will be crowned with glorious success and that it will be known to the public that the Cause is not a movement collateral with other movements such as the Brahma Somaj or Aḥmadí movements.

Here at the Holy Shrine of our Beloved we remember all the dear friends in England and supplicate humbly for their happiness.

Shoghi Effendi is sending you his love and affection together with his deep appreciation towards your noble labours and sacrifical efforts in the service of the Holy Cause . . .

My dear friend,
 I enclose a copy of my recent letter to the National Spiritual Assembly of America regarding the Conference as well as copies of my recent translation of some of the most remarkable and prophetic utterances of Bahá'u'lláh and 'Abdu'l-Bahá which might interest the friends in Great Britain. Pray convey my love to all of them.
Shoghi

4 January 1924 (Enclosure)

To the members of the American National Spiritual Assembly.

My dearest friends!
 On Nov. 28th I received the following communication from the President of the National Spiritual Assembly of Great Britain!
"I have now to bring to your notice, though possibly you are already aware of it, a matter which is of the first importance in the opinion of the National Spiritual Assembly as you will see from one of the paragraphs of the enclosed minutes of its first meeting, which was held on October 13th. So far the programme of the conference on the 'Living Religions within the British Empire' is in a somewhat nebulous condition, but I have ascertained from Miss Sharples, the honorary secretary of the committee of organisation, that the conference has been approved by the authorities of the British Empire Exhibition, 1924 and will last for ten days, covering the last week of the month of September and the first three days of October. It is proposed that all religions taught and practised throughout the British Empire shall be represented at the conference, including the Christians, Muhammadans, Buddhists, Brahma Somaj, Theosophists and others, and that each one in turn shall have at its disposal a day or part of a day for a meeting to expound its principles and deal with its organisation and objects."
 In their last letter, the members of the National Spiritual Assembly of Great Britain further inform me that the idea of the above-mentioned conference has originated with the Theosophical Society,

but these having later dropped its management the organisation of the conference passed into the hands of the School of Oriental Studies and the Sociological Society. You will also note from the enclosed copy of a letter addressed by the same Miss Sharples to the President of the British National Spiritual Assembly that the time offered to the Bahá'í representatives will be very limited, and that most probably the allotted time will be just sufficient to read their papers or deliver their address and engage in the discussion that might arise after their formal presentation of the Cause.

As the British Empire Exhibition, of which this conference forms a part, is itself a semi-official undertaking, and receives actually the generous support and active participation of the government authorities throughout the British Empire, I feel that the opportunities now offered to the Bahá'í world should not be missed, as this chance, if properly utilised, might arouse and stimulate widespread interest among the enlightened public.

As so much will depend upon the nature and general presentation of the theme, rather than upon the personality of the reader or speaker, I feel that first and foremost our attention should be concentrated on the choice and thorough preparation of the subject matter as well as on the proper drafting and the form of the paper itself, which might possibly have to be submitted afterwards to the authorities of the conference.

I feel the necessity of entrusting this highly important and delicate task to a special committee, to be appointed most carefully by the National Spiritual Assembly of America, and consisting of those who by their knowledge of the Cause, their experience in matters of publicity, and particularly by their power of expression and beauty of style will be qualified to produce a befitting statement on the unique history of the Movement as well as its lofty principles.

I am enclosing an article on the Bahá'í Movement which I trust might serve as a basis and example of the paper in question. An account of the most salient features of the history of the Cause, a brief but impressive reference to its many heroes and martyrs, a convincing and comprehensive presentation of the basic principles, and a characteristic survey of the Master's life, as well as a short but graphic description of the present position and influence of the Movement both in the East and the West, should, in my opinion, be included and combined into one conclusive argument. Its length should not surpass that of the enclosed article, and its general tone, expression and language should be at once dignified, sober and forceful.

The greatest care and caution must be exercised in choosing those who can best provide and fulfil the above-mentioned requisites and conditions.

I shall be most pleased to offer my views and suggestions once the paper has assumed its final shape, and wish you to obtain the assistance and advice of those whom you think able to judge amongst the friends in England and elsewhere.

Mr. Simpson, the President of the British National Spiritual Assembly, writes that Miss Grand from Canada has suggested the names of Dr. Watson and Mr. J. O. McCarthy of Toronto to represent the Canadian Bahá'ís. I would be pleased to receive your views as to who should represent Canada at the Conference. India is the only other country within the British Empire that can send a native Bahá'í representative to the conference, and it is rather unfortunate that the United States of America should have to be excluded, as the speakers at the conference must necessarily be subjects of the British Empire.

I am enclosing recent translations of the prophetic and most remarkable words of Bahá'u'lláh and 'Abdu'l-Bahá which I trust you will all find of great value and interest in the great work you are doing for the Cause.

May this great project yield an abundant harvest for the Cause, and your efforts be richly blessed by the guiding Spirit of 'Abdu'l-Bahá.

Your fellow-worker,
Shoghi

18 January 1924

My dear Mr. Simpson,

Shoghi Effendi was glad to hear from you again and hopes that the activities of the friends in England are progressing day after day. There is really so much to be done in almost every country that the more the friends accomplish, the larger does the field of service become. As a matter of fact in many countries we can hardly claim to have fully represented the Cause and to have declared its strong and sublime principles to all classes of men. It is with a vision of greater accomplishments among higher and higher circles of society, that our Guardian wishes his fellow-workers to feel inspired; and in these dark and dismal days it is the proclamation of Bahá'u'lláh's great Message for which the faithful servant must strive with heart and soul.

Concerning the sum which Shoghi Effendi has sent to the National Assembly as a personal gift; he would like to inform you that in case you feel in great need of funds for the activities of the Cause in England, you might take from the sum which he sent you, and at the time of the Exposition Shoghi Effendi might be able to help you in case you cannot collect the necessary expense. Shoghi Effendi attaches great hopes to the activities of the friends in London, and may they some day be realised.

The copies of the "Hidden Words" you had published were received and Shoghi Effendi thinks that they are quite well printed. He is glad that he can share these comforting thoughts from Bahá'u'lláh with his brothers and sisters in the West....

My dear fellow-worker,

I always look forward with keen anticipation to any news from England indicating the progress and advancement of the Cause so dear to our hearts. I pray ardently for every one of you and assure you personally of my affection, esteem and gratitude,

Your brother,
Shoghi

6 February 1924

My dear Mr. Simpson,

I wish to acknowledge receipt of your letter to our dear Guardian and assure you that he is always most glad to hear from you in person and to know still more of the activities of his fellow-workers in that country. At a time when the whole work and administration of the Cause with all its overpowering intensity and extent has devolved upon the shoulders of our youthful Guardian, I am sure you quite well realise what every single expression of the progress of the Cause he stands for would mean to him as our leader and captain; and at a time when the varied questions and problems that the Bahá'í Movement, on its way to the spiritual reconquest of the world, is confronted with, seem endless in number, I hardly need mention what effect the personal assurance and the undying enthusiasm of his fellow-workers would bear upon the tender heart of Shoghi Effendi.

Concerning the passing away of Mr. Hall's father, he wishes me to ask you to extend to him a full measure of his grief at the bereavement of such a radiant brother as Mr. Hall, although he briefly conveyed his sentiments to him through a short telegram. He was, however, quite pleased with Mr. Hall's work and the measure of success which he has met with. He shared this good news with his friends here with a view to inspire all to action. You should assure Mr. Hall that the deep sense of love and gratitude that Shoghi Effendi feels toward him is perhaps too great for me to put into words, but I feel that the success which he has attained is an ample proof of Shoghi Effendi's ardent prayers for him.

My esteemed brother:—

Just a word of appreciation on my part of your devoted and persistent efforts in the service of the Cause. Do please convey to our precious Mr. Hall my condolences and sentiments of undying affection as well as the assurance of my ardent prayers for the welfare and spiritual happiness of his dear family and the Manchester Bahá'í Group.

Shoghi

11 June 1924

To Mr. Simpson, President of the Bahá'í National Spiritual Assembly of England.

My dear and revered Bahá'í Brother,

As I do not have your address with me I am writing and forwarding this to you through our dear brother, Mr. Asgarzadeh.† Some time ago I received a letter addressed to our beloved Guardian from Miss Mabel M. Sharples, the Hon. Secretary of the Conference on Living Religions within the Empire, giving him some information concerning the time of the Conference, and conditions covering the submission of papers to be read at the Conference. I forwarded this letter to our beloved Shoghi Effendi.

Yesterday I received a letter from him instructing me to

answer in his behalf Miss Sharples' letter. Yesterday I answered her letter and told her that Shoghi Effendi hopes to be able to attend the Conference and deliver an address on the Cause in person and in case circumstances prevent him from doing so, a paper will be sent to the Conference through Mr. Simpson, the President of the Bahá'í Spiritual Assembly, to be read on that occasion. I told her also that we will appreciate any further information or suggestion she thinks necessary in regard to this matter. This information or suggestion will be communicated by her to your National Spiritual Assembly.

This morning a cablegram was communicated by the Greatest Holy Leaf to Mr. Roy Wilhelm in New York, instructing the committee in charge of the desired article to hasten its despatch. This article should be handed towards the end of July. The time is short. If the American friends have already sent that article, I mean if it is on the way, and we receive it in time, we shall immediately forward it to our dear Shoghi Effendi for his approval and then mail it to you. If it, however, arrives late, we will directly mail it to you so that you may modify it if necessary and hand it over to the Secretary of the Conference. In the latter case, it is not necessary to submit it to Shoghi Effendi for his approval, for he authorises you, the members of the National Spiritual Assembly to make any correction which you think advisable.

Shoghi Effendi has also instructed me to enclose a cheque for thirty pounds in this letter as contribution towards the Conference. If the English friends are to add something to this sum and offer it to the Conference, it will be highly appreciated by Shoghi Effendi.

The cheque is drawn by the Anglo-Palestine Bank at Haifa on the Jewish Colonial Trust, London, payable to your order. It is dated June 15th and No. F077834/34224. Today we received the answer to our cablegram to Mr. Wilhelm, stating that the article was mailed on the 11th, both to Haifa and England and that Mr. Mills would gladly act at the Conference.

As we understand Mr. Mountfort Mills may go from America to England at the time of the Conference. Shoghi Effendi will be very glad, if Mr. Mills read the Paper. This desire of Shoghi Effendi was also mentioned in to-day's cablegram which was communicated to Mr. Wilhelm.

Through the many cablegrams and letters which have arrived from different centres of the Cause, promising the maintenance of harmony, union and love among the dear friends, the grief and sorrow of our beloved Guardian has been greatly lightened and so we have great hope that when the hot season of the Holy Land is over, we will have the pleasure and joy of his return.

The members of the Holy Family are all sending you and your dear co-workers their tender love and assure you of their ardent prayers at the Holy Shrines in your behalf. They are always awaiting heart-refreshing glad tidings from you. My humble greeting and warm love to yourself and the dear friends too.

Your humble brother and co-worker in His service,

(Enclosure)
Bahíyyih Khánum, Haifa
ARTICLE MAILED ELEVENTH BOTH HAIFA LONDON GLADLY ACT CONFERENCE.

MILLS

16 July 1924

My dear Bahá'í Brother,
    ... I have to write you and inform you that only yesterday I had the privilege of receiving a letter from our dear Guardian who is still away from Haifa ... he wishes me to write you, in answer to your letter to him, that he very much regrets to be unable to be present in London and represent a Cause to which he has ... dedicated his heart and soul. Were it at all possible for me to send you his short note, you would see for yourself with what a spirit he expresses his deep regret.... Although he realises your disappointment at his inability to go to London, he wishes me to assure every one of you that his eager prayers for you all is unfailing and that it is with a glad heart that he cherishes the fondest hopes in the effort that the proceedings of the religious Conference shall have on the audience. May I also add that this is a hope in which everybody shares especially the Greatest Holy Leaf and the members of the family.

I presume by now you have already received a copy of the address that is to be read ...

You might be interested to know that the news of the progress of the Cause among the Kadiani sect in India is quite surprising and two of their chief leaders have not only become Bahá'ís, but have started an admirable little weekly, I think, through which they hope to bring many of their colleagues over. By the way, I believe the leader of the sect who is himself a young man is coming over to London to represent his sect at the Conference.

The confusion and disorder in Persia which had aroused so much apprehension on the part of the helpless Bahá'ís and had even led in one case to actual martyrdom, has apparently subsided for the moment.

Here in Haifa everybody is in good health. With heartfelt greetings to all the friends in London....

23 September 1924

MAY WEMBLEY (sic CONFERENCE) FULFIL YOUR FONDEST HOPES PRAY CONVEY AUTHORITIES MY SINCERE REGRET AT INABILITY TO BE PRESENT I WISH THEM FULL SUCCESS IN THEIR NOBLE ENDEAVOURS.

SHOGHI

24 September 1924★

The beloved of the Lord and the hand-maids of the Merciful in Great Britain.

Care of the National Spiritual Assembly.

Dear Friends,
I return to the Holy Land with an overpowering sense of the gravity of the spiritual state of the Cause in the world. Much as I deplore the disturbing effect of my forced and repeated withdrawals from the field of service, I can unhesitatingly assure you that my last and momentous step was taken with extreme reluctance and only after

★Also addressed to America and published in "Bahá'í Administration".

mature and anxious reflection as to the best way to safeguard the interests of a precious Cause.

My prolonged absence, my utter inaction should not, however, be solely attributed to certain external manifestations of unharmony, of discontent and disloyalty—however paralysing their effect has been upon the continuance of my work—but also to my own unworthiness and to my imperfections and frailties.

I venture to request you to join me in yet another prayer, this time more ardent and universal than before, supplicating with one voice the gracious Master to overlook our weaknesses and failings, to make us worthier and braver children of His own.

Humanity, through suffering and turmoil, is swiftly moving on towards its destiny; if we be loiterers, if we fail to play our part surely others will be called upon to take up our task as ministers to the crying needs of this afflicted world.

Not by the force of numbers, not by the mere exposition of a set of new and noble principles, not by an organised campaign of teaching—no matter how worldwide and elaborate in its character—not even by the staunchness of our faith or the exaltation of our enthusiasm, can we ultimately hope to vindicate in the eyes of a critical and sceptical age the supreme claim of the Abhá Revelation. One thing and only one thing will unfailingly and alone secure the undoubted triumph of this sacred Cause, namely, the extent to which our own inner life and private character mirror forth in their manifold aspects the splendour of those eternal principles proclaimed by Bahá'u'lláh.

Looking back upon those sullen days of my retirement, bitter with feelings of anxiety and gloom, I can recall with appreciation and gratitude those unmistakable evidences of your affection and steadfast zeal which I have received from time to time, and which have served to relieve in no small measure the burden that weighed so heavily upon my heart.

I can well imagine the degree of uneasiness, nay of affliction, that must have agitated the mind and soul of every loving and loyal servant of the Beloved during these long months of suspense and distressing silence. But I assure you such remarkable solicitude as you have shown for the protection of His Cause, such tenacity of faith and unceasing activity as you have displayed for its promotion, cannot but in the end be abundantly rewarded by 'Abdu'l-Bahá, who from His station above is the sure witness of all that you have endured and suffered for Him.

And now as I look into the future, I hope to see the friends at all times, in every land, and of every shade of thought and character, voluntarily and joyously rallying round their local and in particular their national centres of activity, upholding and promoting their interests with complete unanimity and contentment, with perfect understanding, genuine enthusiasm, and sustained vigour. This indeed is the one joy and yearning of my life, for it is the fountain-head from which all future blessings will flow, the broad foundation upon which the security of the Divine Edifice must ultimately rest. May we not hope that now at last the dawn of a brighter day is breaking upon our beloved Cause?

Shoghi

10 October 1924

My dear good brother,

Your letter of Sept. 30th written to our beloved Guardian, Shoghi Effendi, arrived and rejoiced his dear heart with its very interesting contents.

Yesterday he instructed me to translate a great part of it into Persian so that it may be inserted in the circular of the Haifa Spiritual Assembly and also to convey to you his great affection for you and the dear English friends who so splendidly laboured towards the dignified representation of the Cause of God at the Conference on Religions.

We have already the reports given in "The Times" from the two sessions of the Conference allotted to the Aḥmadíyyih people and to us. Both are very interesting indeed. . . .

Shoghi Effendi prays for the success and confirmation of you and all the dear and noble English friends whose earnestness of efforts towards the welfare of the Cause of God he highly admires and appreciates with profound love. . . .

10 October 1924

My dearly-beloved brother,

I am highly gratified with your splendid achievements and deeply appreciative of your painstaking efforts. More power to your elbow! You are rendering our precious Cause a splendid service in its hour of need! Lady Blomfield's † idea of a reception was undoubtedly inspired and was admirably executed. It has indeed rejoiced my heart. My love and my gratitude for her wise, patient and fruitful efforts.

Your brother,
Shoghi

25 October 1924

My dear Bahá'í Brother,

Your very interesting letter of Oct. 15th. written to our beloved Guardian together with the printed copy of the sermon of Dr. Walsh arrived the day before yesterday and imparted great joy to his dear heart. He cherishes great hopes for the bright future of the Cause in England. Of course his hopes are partly based on the intrinsic mighty power of the Cause of God and partly on the dignified way the dear friends in England are presenting the Cause of God to the public.

Yesterday afternoon he instructed me to write this informing you of the safe arrival of your letter and assure you that he appreciates with great love your distinguished services to the Cause of God. He prays at the Holy Shrines that fresh confirmations may reach you from the Abhá Kingdom day by day so that you may have material comfort and spiritual success. He is sure that the holy spirit of our beloved Lord, 'Abdu'l-Bahá is watching over you and guiding your steps in life.

The members of the Holy Family and the friends in Haifa are thinking of you and the other dear friends in England with love and admiration, joining all in prayers for your happiness.

My dearest friend,

I wish to add a few words of assurance and sympathy in view of the heavy burden of responsibility that rests on your shoulders in these difficult and trying times. My fervent and increasing prayer is that 'Abdu'l-Bahá may show you the way that will enable you to continue your splendid pioneer work effectually, peacefully, free from every earthly care and anxiety. Dr. Walsh's sermon is astonishingly good. I wish you would send me about 50 copies of the same. I pray unceasingly for my friends in England.

Shoghi

> My dear friend:
> I enclose a copy of my recent letter to the National Spiritual Assembly of America regarding the Conference as well as copies of my recent translation of some of the most remarkable *prophetic utterances of Bahá'u'lláh & 'Abdu'l-Bahá which might interest the friends in Great Britain. Pray convey my love to all of them.
> Shoghi

> My beloved brother:
> My deepest admiration for your indefatigable exertions for the success of the Cause. I will always remember you in my prayers & await eagerly your personal letters. I welcome any suggestion & further particulars regarding the Conference on the Living Religions within the B. Empire.
> Your brother,
> Shoghi

Examples of Shoghi Effendi's handwriting in the early days of his Guardianship, from letters dated 6 January 1924 and 9 December 1923 (*slightly reduced size*)

4 November 1924

My dear Mr. Simpson,

It is always a pleasure to acknowledge receipt of your letters to our dear Guardian, and he was deeply interested in the minutes of the last meeting of the N.S.A. which you were so kind as to enclose.

Your own letter, however, brought up a very interesting and vital question in regard to the future progress of the Cause in England, especially now that through the efforts of you all the spread of the Bahá'í Movement has been well placed on the road to our ultimate victory. Now is the time to take all necessary measures against a slacking in our pace and it is truly unfortunate that just when the individual endeavours of every single member is most needed and necessary, age and earthly cares deprive us of some of our experienced and able co-workers. It would, I believe, be a great service if just as few as possible could manage to deny themselves of the joy and enthusiasm of serving as noble a Cause.

I am sure it would interest you to know that Mr. and Mrs. Mills are now in Haifa and all that they have to say proves well the energy and efforts of the London friends. We already have about ten pilgrims and are expecting some more. I suppose Dr. Esslemont who would have much to tell us and whose arrival Shoghi Effendi is eagerly awaiting, is among those who will soon arrive. . . .

My dear fellow-worker,

I trust that the prolonged visit of Dr. Esslemont will prove to be in future pregnant with far-reaching possibilities for the service of the Cause in England. To yourself I send my imperishable love and brotherly greetings.

Affectionately,
Shoghi

22 November 1924

My dear Mr. Simpson,

The letter you had sent through Dr. Esslemont to Shoghi Effendi has arrived and it gave him very great pleasure to read it. Although it is quite beyond me to express to you just what thoughts and sentiments your frank expressions of loyalty and love aroused in his heart, this I feel I can assure you that it made him hopeful of the future and added to his great confidence in you.

The Bahá'í Cause has a great mission to the people of England but the field of service though immensely vast presents innumerable difficulties, and it needs the able hand of a staunch and true Bahá'í primarily and the dexterity of a good supervisor, to overcome every confronting difficulty and to carry His Message to millions of people. This responsibility has been entrusted to you by the guided decision of the Bahá'ís in England and our Guardian finds great pleasure in confiding the same duty in you and in endorsing the happy decision of the friends there.

In regard to your contemplated withdrawal from the presidency of the N.S.A. and the London Assembly, it made him very happy to know that even the thought of it has totally vanished. The hopes that he cherished in you are far too many to permit you a more quiet part in Bahá'í activities in England, and the hopeful signs of progress in the past year has made the prospects of the coming year very bright and it all depends upon the efforts of the friends in England and the guidance of our Master from on high just how bright it shall turn out to be.

We still have Mr. Mills with us in Haifa and I assure you, we miss you very much. The photograph you had sent to Shoghi Effendi has been received and it shall be framed and placed in the Persian Pilgrim House . . .

. . . just of late we had the very sad news of the martyrdom of a Bahá'í woman expecting to be soon a mother, and although she was related to very influential officers in the army, nothing could make the criminals, who sought refuge in the house of one of the Mullas, arrested. Though such cases of untold carnage prove with much more force than mere words just what the spirit of Bahá'u'lláh infused into every such Bahá'í has been, and exactly what it means in Persia to try and become one, the horrors of such a murder are truly beyond words. All that we have to do is to seek His Grace and to beg and implore for God's mercy.

May I also write a further assurance of Shoghi Effendi's reliance upon you and with an expression of his heartfelt love for you. . . .

My most precious fellow-worker,
But for your unremitting labours, your sound and selfless efforts, the burden that weighs upon me would prove well-nigh unbearable. I am sure your heart responds to the sentiments that surge in my heart. I have a profound admiration for the heroic manner in which you are rendering such pioneer service to the Cause in England. May the Master sustain you, comfort you and uphold you in your great task. Be assured of my brotherly, unfailing prayers.
I am your true and affectionate brother,
Shoghi

24 November 1924*

To my dearly beloved brothers and sisters in 'Abdu'l-Bahá.
Care of the English National Spiritual Assembly.

Dearest friends!
The day is drawing near when for the third time we shall commemorate the world over the passing of our well-beloved 'Abdu'l-Bahá. May we not pause for a moment, and gather our thoughts? How has it fared with us, His little band of followers, since that day? Whither are we now marching, what has been our achievement?
We have but to turn our eyes to the world without to realise the fierceness and the magnitude of the forces of darkness that are struggling with the dawning light of the Abhá Revelation. Nations, though exhausted and disillusioned, have seemingly begun to cherish anew the spirit of revenge, of domination, and strife. Peoples, convulsed by economic upheavals, are slowly drifting into two great opposing camps with all their menace of social chaos, class hatreds, and world-wide ruin. Races, alienated more than ever before, are filled with mistrust, humiliation and fear, and seem to prepare themselves for a fresh and fateful encounter. Creeds and religions, caught in this whirlpool of conflict and passion, appear to gaze with impotence and despair at this spectacle of increasing turmoil.
Such is the plight of mankind three years after the passing of Him from Whose lips fell unceasingly the sure message of a fast-approaching Divine salvation. Are we by our thoughts, our words, our deeds,

*Printed also in "Bahá'í Administration".

whether individually or collectively, preparing the way? Are we hastening the advent of the Day He so often foretold?

None can deny that the flame of faith and love which His mighty hand kindled in many hearts has, despite our bereavement, continued to burn as brightly and steadily as ever before. Who can question that His loved ones, both in the East and the West, notwithstanding the insidious strivings of the enemies of the Cause, have displayed a spirit of unshakable loyalty worthy of the highest praise? What greater perseverance and fortitude than that which His tried and trusted friends have shown in the face of untold calamities, intolerable oppression, and incredible restrictions? Such staunchness of faith, such an unsullied love, such magnificent loyalty, such heroic constancy, such noble courage, however unprecedented and laudable in themselves, cannot alone lead us to the final and complete triumph of such a great Cause. Not until the dynamic love we cherish for Him is sufficiently reflected in its power and purity in all our dealings with our fellowmen, however remotely connected and humble in origin, can we hope to exalt in the eyes of a self-seeking world the genuineness of the all-conquering love of God. Not until we live ourselves the life of a true Bahá'í can we hope to demonstrate the creative and transforming potency of the Faith we profess. Nothing but the abundance of our actions, nothing but the purity of our lives and the integrity of our character, can in the last resort establish our claim that the Bahá'í spirit is in this day the sole agency that can translate a long cherished ideal into an enduring achievement.

With this vision clearly set before us, and fortified by the knowledge of the gracious aid of Bahá'u'lláh and the repeated assurances of 'Abdu'l-Bahá, let us first strive to live the life and then arise with one heart, one mind, one voice, to reinforce our numbers and achieve our end. Let us recall, and seek on this sad occasion the comfort of the last wishes of our departed yet ever watchful Master:

> "It behoveth them not to rest for a moment, neither to seek repose. They must disperse themselves in every land, pass by every clime, and travel throughout all regions. Bestirred, without rest, and steadfast to the end, they must raise in every land the triumphal cry, Yá Bahá'u'l-Abhá! (O Thou the Glory of Glories). . . . The disciples of Christ forgot themselves and all earthly things, forsook all their cares and belongings, purged themselves of self and passion,

and with absolute detachment scattered far and wide and engaged in calling the peoples of the world to the divine guidance; till at last they made the world another world, illumined the surface of the earth, and even to their last hour proved self-sacrificing in the pathway of that beloved one of God. Finally in various lands they suffered glorious martyrdom. Let them that are men of action follow in their footsteps!"

Having grasped the significance of these words, having obtained a clear understanding of the true character of our mission, the methods to adopt, the course to pursue, and having attained sufficiently that individual regeneration—the essential requisite of teaching—let us arise to teach His Cause with righteousness, conviction, understanding and vigour. Let this be the paramount and most urgent duty of every Bahá'í. Let us make it the dominating passion of our life. Let us scatter to the uttermost corners of the earth; sacrifice our personal interests, comforts, tastes and pleasures; mingle with the divers kindreds and peoples of the world; familiarise ourselves with their manners, traditions, thoughts and customs; arouse, stimulate and maintain universal interest in the Movement, and at the same time endeavour by all the means in our power, by concentrated and persistent attention, to enlist the unreserved allegiance and the active support of the more hopeful and receptive among our hearers. Let us too bear in mind the example which our beloved Master has clearly set before us. Wise and tactful in His approach, wakeful and attentive in His early intercourse, broad and liberal in all His public utterances, cautious and gradual in the unfolding of the essential verities of the Cause, passionate in His appeal yet sober in argument, confident in tone, unswerving in conviction, dignified in His manners—such were the distinguishing features of our Beloved's noble presentation of the Cause of Bahá'u'lláh.

If we all choose to tread faithfully His path, surely the day is not far distant when our beloved Cause will have emerged from the inevitable obscurity of a young and struggling Faith into the broad daylight of universal recognition. This is our duty, our first obligation. Therein lies the secret of the success of the Cause we love so well. Therein lies the hope, the salvation of mankind. Are we fully conscious of our responsibilities? Do we realise the urgency, the sacredness, the immensity, the glory of our task?

I entreat you, dear friends, to continue, nay, to redouble your efforts, to keep your vision clear, your hopes undimmed, your determination unshaken, so that the power of God within us may fill the world with all its glory.

In this fervent plea joins me the Greatest Holy Leaf. Though chagrined in the evening of her life at the sorrowful tales of repression in Persia, she still turns with the deepest longings of her heart to your land where freedom reigns, eager and expectant to behold, ere she is called away, the signs of the universal triumph of the Cause she loves so dearly.

Shoghi

13 February 1925

"I have read with the deepest pleasure the Minutes of the meeting of your National Assembly and am deeply gratified to note the constancy, devotion and thoroughness with which you are conducting your affairs."

(Copied from National Spiritual Assembly Minutes, 28 February 1925)

26 March 1925

My dear Bahá'í Brother,

Your interesting letter of March 12th written to our beloved Guardian together with the draft minutes of the 12th meeting of your National Spiritual Assembly has been received. The draft on Haifa for the sum of thirty-three pounds sterling which is the joint contribution of the English friends for the relief of their suffering brothers at Nayríz, and enclosed in your letter, has also been received. This sum has been added to contributions received from other centres and will be sent by next mail to the National Spiritual Assembly of Persia. From Persia they shall acknowledge the receipt of this sum directly and for the present, our Guardian acknowledges its receipt gratefully and wishes you to kindly convey his gratitude to all the dear friends who have so kindly and generously contributed.

Our dear brother, Dr. Esslemont, was not well for some time, but now I am glad to tell you that he is better and we are expecting him to come out of the hospital to-day.

We have nowadays the pleasure of having among us the first group of our beloved New Zealand and Australian believers. They are of great sincerity and devotion. From here they are intending to visit England where I am sure you will enjoy their acquaintance and company very much. . . .

My precious fellow-worker,

The prompt and generous contribution of the British friends for the relief of the sufferers in Nayríz is deeply appreciated and I wish to offer through you to them all in the name of the victims of that great catastrophe my deep and grateful thanks. May the All-Bountiful reward and bless them a hundred fold! The sum of approximately 1000 pounds has been until now collected from various parts of the Bahá'í world and more is expected. What an admirable and convincing testimony of the reality of the Bahá'í bond that binds the East with the West. Regarding the historical compilation suggested by the Persian friends, I think your plan is suitable and correct. The English N.S.A. will I trust collect all the data and exercise its discretion and judgment in collating all the material received from the friends and assemblies throughout Great Britain, and, after having given it a definite and final shape, will forward it direct to Persia. I would welcome a copy of it myself. Assuring you of my gratitude and prayers,

Your true brother,
Shoghi

2 November 1925

'IRÁQ'S SUPREME COURT UNEXPECTEDLY PRONOUNCED VERDICT AGAINST US IN BAGHDÁD CASE STRONGLY ADVISE NATIONAL AND EVERY LOCAL ASSEMBLY COMMUNICATE BY CABLE AND LETTER WITH 'IRÁQ HIGH COMMISSIONER APPEALING ARDENTLY FOR ACTION TO ENSURE THE SECURITY OF BAHÁ'U'LLÁH'S SACRED HOUSE.
SHOGHI.

6 November 1925*

To the beloved of the Lord and the handmaids of the Merciful throughout the East and throughout the West.

Dearly-beloved friends:

The sad and sudden crisis that has arisen in connexion with the ownership of Bahá'u'lláh's sacred house in Baghdád has sent a thrill of indignation and dismay throughout the whole of the Bahá'í world. Houses that have been occupied by Bahá'u'lláh for well nigh the whole period of His exile in 'Iráq, ordained by Him as the chosen and sanctified object of Bahá'í pilgrimage in future, magnified and extolled in countless Tablets and Epistles as the sacred centre "round which shall circle all peoples and kindreds of the earth"—lie now, due to fierce intrigue and ceaseless fanatical opposition, at the mercy of the declared enemies of the Cause.

I have instantly communicated with every Bahá'í Centre in both East and West, and urgently requested the faithful followers of the Faith in every land to protest vehemently against this glaring perversion of justice, to assert firmly and courteously the spiritual rights of the Bahá'í community to the ownership of this venerated house, to plead for British fairness and justice, and to pledge their unswerving determination to ensure the security of this hallowed spot.

Conscious of the fact that this property has been occupied by Bahá'í authorised representatives for an uninterrupted period of not less than thirty years, and having successfully won their case at the Justice of Peace and the Court of First Instance, the Bahá'ís the world over cannot believe that the high sense of honour and fairness which inspired the British Administration of 'Iráq will ever tolerate such grave miscarriage of justice. They confidently appeal to the public opinion of the world for the defence and protection of their legitimate rights now sorely trampled under the feet of relentless enemies.

Widespread and effective publicity along these lines, in well-conceived and carefully-worded terms, is strongly recommended for it will undoubtedly serve to facilitate the solution of this delicate and perplexing problem.

Having exerted ourselves to the utmost of our ability, let us rest assured in the power of the Lord, Who keepeth watch over His house, and Who will, no matter how dark present prospects appear, assure for generations yet unborn His cherished and holy edifice.

Your brother and fellow-worker,
Shoghi

*Printed also in "Bahá'í Administration".

11 November 1925

Dear Friends,
I have been asked to enclose for your kind attention the following papers:—

1. Circular letter concerning the residential house of Bahá'u'lláh in Baghdád.
2. Circular letter concerning the purchase of land around the Holy Shrines in Haifa.
3. The system of transliteration to be used in all Bahá'í references.
4. A plan of the immediate neighbourhood of the Shrines in Haifa showing in approximate proportions the different plots around it.

In view of the extreme importance of the aforementioned papers, Shoghi Effendi trusts that all necessary measures will be taken to insure their prompt distribution among all the different assemblies and among all such recognised Bahá'ís as your distinguished assembly deems fit and advisable....

12 November 1925

Dear Bahá'í Brother,
Our dear Guardian was very glad to receive your letter of Nov. 4th through which you acquaint him with the steps you have already taken in carrying out his instruction concerning the Baghdád House.

He is highly pleased with what you have done. In other Bahá'í Centres also the friends have in a similar way followed promptly his telegraphic instruction. Up to this time we have received no further information regarding the actual situation of the House.

Shoghi Effendi will let you know of any fresh development as soon as he receives information. He sends you his warm affection and extends to you his appreciation for your noble services to the Cause of God. He prays for your health and success in service. He wishes you to kindly convey his loving greeting to all the dear friends in England....

My dear self-sacrificing brother,

The wise and prompt measures you have taken have given me the utmost satisfaction. I trust your devoted endeavours will be crowned with full success. I have sent you a few days ago various circulars, a list of transliterated terms and the plan of the surroundings of the Holy Shrine, copies of all of which I earnestly request you to place in the hands of every recognised believer.

Your grateful brother,
Shoghi

23 November 1925

BELOVED ESSLEMONT PASSED AWAY, COMMUNICATE FRIENDS AND FAMILY DISTRESSING NEWS URGE BELIEVERS DEDICATE SPECIAL DAY FOR UNIVERSAL PRAYER AND REMEMBRANCE.

SHOGHI

27 November 1925

My dear Bahá'í Brother,

I find it very hard to be able to express in adequate words our deep feelings and sorrow at the loss of our dearly-beloved brother Dr. Esslemont. Those of us who had known him only since his sojourn in Haifa, had even in that short period of time, learnt to admire and love him. How much more so those of you to whom he was an old friend and fellow-worker.

I have been ordered by Shoghi Effendi to relate in as simple words as possible for the information of his friends in England, the sufferings of his last days and yet words fail me in that painful task.

The chronic disease from which he had suffered in the past had very much undermined his weak constitution and his eagerness to serve the Cause he so dearly loved, despite all advice to the contrary, was a great tax upon his failing strength. His stay at the Black Forest in Germany all through the summer had improved his health, but upon his return to Haifa he felt rather weak and he was frequently in bed for a few days. Not until a fortnight ago was Dr. Esslemont seriously ill and even then the doctors thought that in spite of the fact that the trouble from which he had suffered in the past was now more active there was no reason for great anxiety. His health was slowly improving and everything was being done to give him the best medical advice obtainable here in Haifa, when suddenly and unexpectedly at about midnight of November 21st the doctor had a severe stroke of "cerebral embolus". The next day a second stroke followed and he at last succumbed to the third which he had at about seven o'clock of the next evening. The attending doctors were both European—one Italian and the other German. Our two Bahá'í doctors Yunis Khán and Mírzá Arastú, whom you must have met in London very gladly put themselves at his disposal.

Hard as it was for everyone who had known Dr. Esslemont to see him pass away and to realise what a great loss it means to the friends the world over, we can find no greater consolation than in the happy thought that he now lies in peace and his soul where it so loved to be. Beyond all earthly cares, all pains and sorrows his soul dwells forever.

The funeral service was both simple and touching. His body was washed by two of the friends, dressed and wrapped in white silk cloth and perfumed by attar of roses. On his finger Shoghi Effendi placed his own Bahá'í ring which he had worn for a good many years. Laid in a simple casket of walnut and placed in the hall of the Pilgrim House, the friends gathered together and said their funeral prayer over him. The casket was carried for a short distance by Shoghi Effendi and then placed in the Master's carriage and accompanied by the sons-in-law of the Master it slowly wound its way, followed by eleven other cabs carrying the friends, to the foot of Mt. Carmel. There it was laid to rest in that beautifully-situated cemetery, and flowers from the garden of the Master's home were scattered over his grave. Simple as he was in his life and character, equally simple was his funeral service. And yet just as in the simplicity of his character lay his many virtues, in like manner did the simplicity of that service sink into every heart and fill every eye with tears.

In case you think it would please them you are perfectly welcome to communicate to the family of Dr. Esslemont the particulars of his death and burial. Enclosed you will please find a letter from Shoghi Effendi addressed to the family and relations of the deceased. You will please have it read by his wife, who I believe is in London, and then sent over to his father and sister who are in Aberdeen.

Due to the reason that Shoghi Effendi hopes to build in the near future the grave of Dr. Esslemont on his behalf and on behalf of all the friends, our Guardian would like very much to have the design chosen by the family of the deceased. Of course you would let them know that through certain considerations it would be best to have the design devoid of any cross as that in this country would particularise it to the Christian faith. You would let the family know that the expense would be defrayed by the friends all over the world and by Shoghi Effendi himself.

Shoghi Effendi would also like you to send the picture of Dr. Esslemont to the countries where the friends have published magazines with a request to have it published. They are America, India, Germany and Australia. He wants you also to write a comprehensive biographical sketch of the life of Dr. Esslemont for "The Star" in America laying most stress on his life since he became a Bahá'í. This of course does not necessarily mean that you should write it yourself but anyone in London. You should also make mention of him in your circular letter in detail. . . .

*30 November 1925**

To the beloved of God and the handmaids of the Merciful in the East and in the West.

Dear fellow-workers,

It is with feelings of overwhelming sorrow that I communicate to you the news of yet another loss which the Almighty, in His inscrutable wisdom, has chosen to inflict upon our beloved Cause. On the 22nd of November, 1925—that memorable and sacred day in which the Bahá'ís of the Orient celebrated the twin Festivals of the Declaration of the Báb and the Birthday of 'Abdu'l-Bahá—Dr. John E. Esslemont passed on to the Abhá Kingdom. His end was as swift as it was unexpected. Suffering from the effects of a chronic and insidious disease, he fell at last a victim to the inevitable complications that ensued, the fatal course of which neither the efforts of vigilant

*Printed also in "Bahá'í Administration".

physicians nor the devoted care of his many friends could possibly deflect.

He bore his sufferings with admirable fortitude, with calm resignation and courage. Though convinced that his ailments would never henceforth forsake him, yet many a time he revealed a burning desire that the friends residing in the Holy Land should, while visiting the Shrines, implore the All-Merciful to prolong his days that he may bring to a fuller completion his humble share of service to the Threshold of Bahá'u'lláh. To this noble request all hearts warmly responded. But this was not to be. His close association with my work in Haifa, in which I had placed fondest hopes, was suddenly cut short. His book, however, an abiding monument to his pure intention, will, alone, inspire generations yet unborn to tread the path of truth and service as steadfastly and as unostentatiously as was trodden by its beloved author. The Cause he loved so well he served even unto his last day with exemplary faith and unstinted devotion. His tenacity of faith, his high integrity, his self-effacement, his industry and painstaking labours were traits of a character the noble qualities of which will live and live forever after him. To me personally he was the warmest of friends, a trusted counsellor, an indefatigable collaborator, a lovable companion.

With tearful eyes I supplicate at the Threshold of Bahá'u'lláh—and request you all to join—in my ardent prayers, for the fuller unfolding in the realms beyond of a soul that has already achieved so high a spiritual standing in this world. For by the beauty of his character, by his knowledge of the Cause, by the conspicuous achievements of his book, he has immortalised his name, and by sheer merit deserved to rank as one of the Hands of the Cause of God.

He has been laid to rest in the heart of that beautifully situated Bahá'í burial ground at the foot of Carmel, close to the mortal remains of that venerable soul, Hájí Mírzá Vakílu'd-Dawlih, the illustrious cousin of the Báb and chief builder of the Mashriqu'l-Adhkár of 'Ishqábád. Pilgrims visiting his grave from far and near will, with pride and gratitude, do honour to a name that adorned the annals of an immortal Cause.

May he eternally rest in peace.

Shoghi

5 December 1925

My dear Mr. Simpson,

I write to acknowledge receipt of your two letters of Nov. 25 and 28th to Shoghi Effendi and to thank you on his behalf for all the trouble you have taken in communicating to the friends and to his family the sad news of the passing away of Dr. Esslemont. Shoghi Effendi cannot but appreciate the many evidences of your devotion and love.

We are very glad to know that Mr. Mills is as successful in his endeavours and we trust that it should end with a decisive victory on our part. Mr. Mills has kept us briefly in touch with what he has been doing in London but we still await more detailed news from him. He is probably too busy to write.

Shoghi Effendi has already heard from Miss Esslemont.

Everybody is well here. Shoghi Effendi and the family send you their heartfelt greetings. . . .

My dear indefatigable co-worker,

Knowing what the urgency and multiplicity of pressing activities mean to a person who pursues his task almost single-handed, I can well understand, sympathise, and admire your noble endeavours and the splendid work you are doing for the Cause of God. I wish to renew the expression of my deep confidence in, and great appreciation of, the part you play at this highly-important and difficult stage of our work. Your communications regarding the houses in Baghdád have been highly satisfactory and I trust will yield the long-desired fruit. Regarding the position of . . ., 'Azízu'lláh Khán Bahádur will immediately after my decision let you know on my behalf what I feel to be the most suitable way of meeting this difficult situation. I feel too overwhelmed with work to write more.

Shoghi

9 December 1925

URGE FRIENDS INQUIRE IN COURTEOUS TERMS BY CABLE AND LETTER FROM 'IRÁQ HIGH COMMISSIONER RESULTS OF INVESTIGATIONS.

SHOGHI

14 December 1925

My dear Mr. Simpson,

I am sending you enclosed a copy of the pamphlet written by Dr. Esselmont.

Last year Dr. Esslemont sent you a similar copy of the pamphlet fully revised for you to publish. Shoghi Effendi would like very much to have a copy of his revised edition and is sending the enclosed only as a reminder of some of the corrections and revisions he had made in the copy he sent you. In case you have published copies of the revised edition, Shoghi Effendi would like to have a number of copies sent to him and in case you have not published it, he would like you to send him a correct copy of the revised form of the edition as you have it. He could have it published himself. In any case, however, he wishes you to send back to him the enclosed copy.

We received last night news that the keys of the houses in Baghdád have been given to the Shí'ites and they had made a regular demonstration on the occasion. We await to see what will be done at last. . . .

23 January 1926

My dear Bahá'í Brother,

I take pleasure in thanking you on behalf of our dear Guardian for your letters of Dec. 9th and 13th and of Jan. 4th which he was very glad to receive. He appreciates immensely your many efforts and although so far away, you are to him, I assure you, a great and indispensable helper. It is always with confidence in its thoroughness that he refers to you anything of importance.

He is so glad to learn that the friends in England have in the different centres held memorial meetings for our departed brother. He was to us all a great friend and fellow-worker and to the Cause a faithful servant—his memory will help us to follow an equally righteous path.

The biographical sketch which you have written for the different Bahá'í magazines and a copy of which you had sent to our Guardian was received and read. He fully approves of it and feels sure that the different publications will welcome your article and will be glad to devote some of their pages to the memory of one whose name and writings were often to be seen in those same magazines.

With regard to the design of the grave of Dr. Esslemont, a picture of which you had sent enclosed, Shoghi Effendi wishes to inform you that although he himself liked the design and would have been glad to follow it altogether, up till the present the tombs of the Bahá'ís have been very simply built and the custom has been to have them as beautiful and at the same time as simple as possible. This general custom holds true even in the case of the tombs of the Master's mother and brother. The graves are built of white marble stones but the designs have in every case been simple, and he wishes you very much to make the family of Dr. Esslemont understand that although Shoghi Effendi will not be able to follow the design strictly he will try to make the tomb as near it as possible, while keeping within the range of the customary simplicity. Even the tomb of the cousin of the Báb which is close to that of Dr. Esslemont and which Shoghi Effendi also intends to build will be very simple.

In connection with the leaflet of Dr. Esslemont, Shoghi Effendi feels that if you intend to publish a new edition you would do well to keep it until you are through with it, but if you already have many copies of the last issue and the Assembly does not intend to bring out a new edition in the near future, he wants you to send him the leaflet so as to be able to send it to America where he wants to have it translated into Hebrew and other languages. At any case he wants you to send him a copy of it or the original as soon as possible.

Our Guardian has been very glad to receive a wire of late from Baghdád telling him that everything was hopeful. As yet we do not have any particulars but we trust that we can soon regain our rights in the houses. It is perhaps very fortunate that the High Commissioner himself will be in Baghdád and will be able to help us very much....

P.S. With regard to the accent in the letter *a* in the transliteration of Persian names and words and the difficulty of the publishers in having a vertical mark, Shoghi Effendi feels that in case having the regular vertical mark means too much trouble and expense it would be justified to replace it by the horizontal dash on the *a*, but if the trouble and expense would

I gratefully acknowledge the receipt of the sum of seventeen pounds from my dear friends the Bahá'ís of England as their much appreciated contribution for the purchase of land around the holy Shrines on Mt. Carmel.

Shoghi

Haifa, Palestine.
April 11, 1926.

Typical receipts given by Shoghi Effendi

I gratefully acknowledge the receipt of the sum of three hundred pounds from the Bahá'ís of the British Isles, to be expended for the construction of the Shrine of the Báb on Mt. Carmel.

Shoghi

Sept. 19, 1951.

not be much, for the sake of uniformity throughout transliterations everywhere, it would be best to have the regular vertical mark.

My dear fellow-worker,
I am sure you will understand, and explain my motive and reasons to dear Esslemont's relatives in connexion with the design of the tomb. Much as I love and esteem my departed friend, I feel I must pay due consideration to the general practice prevailing in Haifa and 'Akká particularly as it is applied even to the resting places of the Master's nearest relations. I will however follow the design as closely as it is consistent with simplicity, without altering in any way the shape and general outline presented by the architect. Please assure his relatives of my keen desire to do everything possible that will enhance and preserve the memory of such a staunch and precious friend.
Shoghi

1 April 1926

My dear Mr. Simpson,
Many thanks for your letter of Feb. 21, and I am so sorry I could not answer you earlier.

I am sending you enclosed the plan that you had sent and behind it I have marked the approximate prices of the plots. You realise that the exact price cannot be determined because they fluctuate and various causes bring about this change in price. For this reason I have given two figures one being the minimum and the other the maximum. There are no probabilities that under any conditions the maximum and the minimum will change. However, I have sent you the price for the so called region rather than the individual plots, the latter being due to many reasons quite impossible.

Shoghi Effendi is quite well though as usual very busy with an overwhelmingly vast correspondence. The family are all well and send you their love and best wishes. . . .

My esteemed and valued friend:
I understand from your recent cable to me that Miss . . . has at last complied with my request and written the London Assembly acknowledging their authority. I have immediately cabled you my

heartfelt appreciation of her act. If that is the case I wish to urge you and the London Council to exercise the utmost care, consideration and vigilance that this new step taken in the right direction may gradually lead to a definite solution of this painful problem. I am as usual terribly overwhelmed with my unceasing work and this cable of yours has been a most welcome relief. I have received your letter dated Feb. 7. I am returning one of the leaflets for future publication in London. I wish to remind you of the necessity of close co-operation on the part of the English National Spiritual Assembly with 'La nova Tago' published in Hamburg.

Shoghi

11 April 1926

My dear Bahá'í Brother,

I thank you very much indeed on behalf of our dear Guardian for your kind letters of March 29th and 31st.

The news of the reconciliation of ... with the National Assembly has been the source of immeasurable joy to the heart of Shoghi Effendi and he appreciates the spirit of both parties in trying to forget all past misunderstandings and in starting anew with genuine love and goodwill. This has relieved Shoghi Effendi of a very heavy weight of thought and distress and this itself gives you as much satisfaction as it does to us all.

Shoghi Effendi has gladly received the names of the elected body for the London Assembly and he wishes them all success from the bottom of his heart. That they may all help to vindicate still more strongly the great claim of our dear Cause in England, that they may succeed to increase daily the numbers of earnest Bahá'í workers and that they may mirror forth the great spirit of our beloved Master, is the fondest hope and the fervent prayer of our dear Guardian.

As I write you these lines we are all sorely distressed with the ghastly news of the martyrdom of twelve Bahá'ís in one of the towns of southern Persia. . . .

My dear and valued friend:

I have received with feelings of deep satisfaction the welcome news of . . . compliance with my request. I wish to impress upon all those who come in contact with her the necessity of exercising forbearance, kindness and loving consideration while adhering closely to the established principles of the Cause. I will inform you if any action is necessary regarding the martyrdom in Jahrum in Southern Persia— a monstrous crime that has deeply afflicted us all. Concerning the membership of the Spiritual Assembly, I have already communicated with America to the effect that the members who are entitled to vote must be strictly limited to nine. Additional members may attend only in a consultative capacity. I realise fully the delicacy and difficulty of your position but it must be made clear to all that nine and only nine can vote. All other subsidiary matters are left to the Assemblies.

Lovingly,
Shoghi

11 April 1926*

I gratefully acknowledge the receipt of the sum of seventeen pounds from my dear friends the Bahá'ís of England as their much appreciated contribution for the purchase of land around the Holy Shrines on Mt. Carmel.

Shoghi

22 April 1926**

To the beloved of the Lord and the handmaids of the Merciful throughout the West.

Fellow-labourers in the Divine Vineyard:
In the midst of the many vicissitudes which the creative Word of God is destined to encounter in the course of its onward march towards the redemption of the world, there breaks upon us the news of still another loss, more bewildering in its character, yet more inspiring in its challenge, than any of the gravest happenings of recent times. Once again the woeful tale of unabated persecution, involving this time the martyrdom of twelve of our long-suffering brethren in Jahrum, southern Persia, has reached our ears, and filled us with a gloom which all the joys and ennobling memories of Riḍván have failed to dispel.

---

*This is the first example of a receipt from the Guardian. A few such receipts appear in this book as they illustrate his meticulous attention to detail. They do not, however, represent the total contributions made by members of the British Bahá'í community during the thirty-five years covered by the book.

**Printed also in "Bahá'í Administration".

From the meagre reports which have thus far been received from that distracted country it appears that this shameful and atrocious act, though the outcome of a number of obscure and complex causes, has been chiefly instigated by that ever-present factor of fierce and relentless impulse of religious hostility. Persia—long-neglected and sorely-tried—continues, despite the revival of recent hopes, to be the downtrodden victim of unscrupulous personal rivalries and factious intrigue, of tribal revolt, political dissensions and religious animosities—all of which have in times past brought in their wake the shedding of the blood of so many of its innocent and choicest sons.

Fully alive to the gravity of the occasion, and realising the urgency of my sacred duty, I have, upon the receipt of the news, transmitted telegraphically through the National Spiritual Assembly of the Bahá'ís of Persia a special message addressed in the name of the Bahá'ís in every land to the supreme Authority in the State, expressing our profound horror at this outrageous act as well as our earnest entreaty to inflict immediate punishment on the perpetrators of so abominable a crime. And as this sad event involved chiefly the welfare and security of the Bahá'í residents in Persia, I have specially requested all local Assemblies in that land to address a similar message to the highest authorities concerned appealing for full protection and justice. Should future developments necessitate direct and foreign intervention, I shall acquaint the national Bahá'í representatives in every land to take in cooperation with all local Assemblies such measures as will effectually conduce to a fuller recognition of the dynamic force latent in the Bahá'í Faith and ensure the betterment of the lot of the heroic supporters of our Cause.

Pending the opening of official and direct communication with recognised authorities whether in Persia or elsewhere, I strongly feel that the time has assuredly come when it is incumbent upon every conscientious promoter of the Cause to bestir himself and undertake in consultation with the friends in his locality such measures of publicity as will lead to the gradual awakening of the conscience of the civilised world to what is admittedly an ignominious manifestation of a decadent age.

I would specially request all National Assemblies to give their anxious and immediate consideration to this grave matter, and to devise ways and means that will secure the fullest publicity to our grievances. I would remind them that whatever is published should be couched in terms that are at once correct, forceful and inoffensive. I *would particularly stress the importance of making every effort to secure the sympathy and hospitality of the leading journals and periodicals of the Western world, and of sending to the Holy Land any such references in papers that will arise to champion the cause of Righteousness and Justice. I greatly deplore the fact that owing to the remoteness and the unstable conditions in Persia, details and particulars regarding this ugly incident are not as yet available, but will be duly communicated to the various centres immediately upon their receipt. I would however ask the believers throughout the West to arise without any further delay and supplement the publication of the news conveyed in this message with an account of previous happenings of a similar character, combined with an adequate survey of the aim, the principles, and history of the Bahá'í Cause.*

It is to you, dearly beloved friends of the West, who are the standard-bearers of the emancipation and triumph of the Bahá'í Faith, that our afflicted brethren of the East have turned their expectant eyes, confident that the day cannot be far-distant when, in accordance with 'Abdu'l-Bahá's explicit utterance, the West will "seize the Cause" from Persia's fettered hands and lead it to glorious victory.

Though grief-stricken and horrified at this cruel blow, let us be on our guard lest we give way to despair, lest we forget that in the Almighty's inscrutable Wisdom this sudden calamity may prove to be but a blessing in disguise. For what else can it do but to stir the inmost depths of our souls, set our faith ablaze, galvanise our efforts, dissolve our differences, and provide one of the chief instruments which the unhampered promoters of the Faith can utilise to attract the attention, enlist the sympathy, and eventually win the allegiance of all mankind?

Ours is this supreme opportunity; may we fulfil our trust.

Your true brother,
Shoghi

11 May 1926*

To the beloved of the Lord and the handmaids of the Merciful throughout the West.

Dearly beloved brothers and sisters in 'Abdu'l-Bahá!

Grave and manifold as are the problems confronting the struggling Faith of Bahá'u'lláh, none appear more significant nor seem more

*Printed also in "Bahá'í Administration".

compelling in their urgency than the incredible sufferings borne so heroically by our down-trodden brethren of the East. Recent reports confirming the news which I have lately communicated to you have all emphasised the barbarous severity practised on the innocent followers of our Cause. They reveal the possibility of the extension of this agitation, partly instigated for political purposes and selfish motives, to neighbouring towns and provinces, and dwell upon the traditional slackness of the local authorities to inflict prompt and severe punishment upon all the perpetrators of such abominable crimes. It has been ascertained that in the town of Jahrum women have suffered martyrdom in a most atrocious manner, that the knife of the criminal has mercilessly cut to pieces the body of a child, that a number have been severely beaten and injured, their bodies mutilated, their homes pillaged, their property confiscated, and the homeless remnants of their family abandoned to the mercy of a shameless and tyrannical people. In other parts of Persia, and particularly in the province of Ádhirbáyján, in the town of Marághih, the friends have been pitilessly denied the civic rights and privileges extended to every citizen of the land. They have been refused the use of the public bath, and been denied access to such shops as provide the necessities of life. They have been declared deprived of the benefit and protection of the law, and all association and dealing with them denounced as a direct violation of the precepts and principles of Islám. It has even been authoritatively stated that the decencies of public interment have been refused to their dead, and that in a particular case every effort to induce the Moslem undertaker to provide the wood for the construction of the coffin failed to secure the official support of the authorities concerned. Every appeal made by these harassed Bahá'ís on behalf of their brethren, whether living or dead, has been met with cold indifference, with vague promises, and not infrequently with severe rebuke and undeserved chastisement.

The tale of such outrageous conduct, such widespread suffering and loss, if properly expressed and broadcast, cannot fail in the end to arouse the conscience of civilised mankind, and thereby secure the much-needed relief for a long-suffering people. I would, therefore, renew my plea, and request you most earnestly to redouble your efforts in the wide field of publicity, to devise every possible means that will alleviate the fears and sorrows of the silent sufferers in that distracted country.

Surely these vile wrong-doers cannot long remain unpunished for *their ferocious atrocities, and the day may not be far distant when we shall witness, as we have observed elsewhere, the promised signs of Divine Retribution avenging the blood of the slaughtered servants of Bahá'u'lláh.*

Your true brother,
Shoghi

20 May 1926

My dear Mr. Simpson,
I thank you on behalf of Shoghi Effendi for your letter of May 8th.
He was very glad indeed to learn the names of the newly elected London Spiritual Assembly and he wishes them success from the bottom of his heart. He earnestly trusts that throughout the coming year they will succeed to give a fresh impetus to the progress of the Cause in England and will not be satisfied with only mediocre efforts and endeavours.
With regard to the election of the Assemblies and your desire to have substitutes in order to ensure a steady and easy-to-obtain quorum for business, Shoghi Effendi would not like to give you any further special regulations but would prefer you to communicate with America and follow the method they have adopted. He has a keen desire that uniformity should exist in the regulations. I am sure you would gladly communicate with Mr. Horace Holley on the subject.
He is so gratified that the case of . . . is settled permanently and he hopes that in future no such petty misunderstandings will come in the way of the steady growth of the Movement, which is of the utmost necessity not only in England but throughout the world.
Shoghi Effendi is well but as usual very busy. The recent atrocities in Persia have been a source of deep grief to his heart. . . .

My dear fellow-worker,
In order to avoid misunderstandings and confusion and ensure uniformity of method and action I have requested you to conform to the

principle adopted by the American friends and Mr. Holley will inform you of the method they pursue. I realise the special and peculiar difficulties that prevail in London and the nature of the obstacles with which they are confronted. I feel however that an earnest effort should be made to overcome them and that the members must arrange their affairs in such a way as to ensure their prompt attendance at 9 meetings which are held in the course of the year. This surely is not an insurmountable obstacle.

I will remember their needs and difficulties in my prayers at the Holy Shrines and will continue to supplicate for them Divine guidance and blessings.

Shoghi

28 June 1926

Dear Mr. Simpson,

Shoghi Effendi wishes me to acknowledge the receipt of your letter dated June 22nd, 1926. He is most appreciative of the many and continuous services you are rendering to the Cause in that land. Your efficiency, sincerity and untiring zeal are great assets for the friends in England. . . .

Shoghi Effendi fully approves of your suggestion to put a royalty on the translations of Dr. Esslemont's book equal to what he had arranged for the original. Not only is that a fair thing to do but also it is incumbent upon us to show our appreciation of Dr. Esslemont's services to the Cause by safeguarding the interests of his family, especially as his wife is an invalid and in need of help. Shoghi Effendi specially wants me to ask you to show utmost consideration to her interests.

My dear fellow-worker,

I hope you will assure Mrs. Esslemont on my behalf and express to her my warm approval of your suggestion which would safeguard her interests and prove of some assistance to her. . . .

Assuring you of my earnest prayers for your continued and unsparing efforts for the promotion of the Cause you serve so well,

I am your grateful brother,

Shoghi

16 July 1926

Dear Mr. Simpson,

This is to acknowledge the receipt of your letter to Shoghi Effendi dated June 20, 1926. He is very thankful for what you are trying to do for the friends in Persia. I hope the efforts of the whole western friends combined will alleviate this great burden which rests upon them, and at least give them the peace and comfort which they have been for so long desiring.

As to the translation or rather revision of the translation of the "Hidden Words". A year ago, I believe, the American friends wrote to Shoghi Effendi and asked him to do it. Complying with their wish he revised his translation and they have published it both in paper and leather bound. Shoghi Effendi believes that another edition in England will be useless and perhaps will not find the necessary market. You could buy from America all the copies you need. Nevertheless, if you want to have a new English edition you can procure a copy from America. Shoghi Effendi does not believe it necessary to give it a still other revision....

My dear and able friend,

I am in correspondence with Rev. Townshend† in connexion with various alterations in my rendering of the Hidden Words. I have just received his second letter containing suggestions which I greatly appreciate and value. I am hoping to revise it for a third time after my correspondence with Mr. T. is over. I feel you can postpone it for the present. I hope and pray you will succeed in giving wide and effective publicity to the atrocities perpetrated in Persia, in the British Press. It is so necessary and important. We must at all costs capture the heights and the British friends have in this connexion a unique and splendid opportunity in their own country and amid their own people. Difficult though it be we must persevere and not relax in our efforts. What Martha* has achieved is a great incentive and example. Your own splendid efforts are deeply and lovingly appreciated by me.

Shoghi

*Martha Root.

17 October 1926*

To the beloved of the Lord and the handmaids of the Merciful throughout the West.

Dearly-beloved brothers and sisters in 'Abdu'l-Bahá!

In the course of the few months that have elapsed since my last communication to you regarding the appalling circumstances that have culminated in the martyrdom of our Persian brethren in Jahrum, events of the highest importance to the future welfare of our beloved Cause have transpired, and with startling suddenness conferred abiding solace upon those who still have to face the pains and terrors of unmitigated and shameless tyranny.

You have, most of you I presume, read with thrilling joy in one of the recent issues of the "Star of the West" that illuminating account given by our beloved sister, Miss Martha Root, wherein she tells with her characteristic directness and modesty the story of her moving interview with Her Majesty Queen Marie of Rumania and of the cordial and ready response which her gentle yet persuasive presentation of the principles of the Bahá'í Faith has evoked in the heart of that honoured Queen. One of the visible and potent effects which this historic interview proved capable of achieving was the remarkable appeal in the form of an open letter which Her Majesty freely and spontaneously caused to be published to the world at large testifying in a language of exquisite beauty to the power and sublimity of the Message of Bahá'u'lláh.

It was indeed a never-to-be-forgotten occasion when, on the eve of the day commemorating the passing of Bahá'u'lláh, a handful of us, His sorrowing servants, had gathered round His beloved Shrine supplicating relief and deliverance for the down-trodden in Persia, to receive in the midst of the silence of that distressing hour the glad-tiding of this notable triumph which the unbending energy and indomitable spirit of our beloved Martha has achieved for our sacred Cause.

With bowed heads and grateful hearts we recognise in this glowing tribute which Royalty has thus paid to the Cause of Bahá'u'lláh an epoch-making pronouncement destined to herald those stirring events which, as 'Abdu'l-Bahá has prophesied, shall in the fullness of time signalise the triumph of God's holy Faith. For who can doubt but that the deeds of those valiant pioneers of the Faith, unexampled though

*Printed also in "Bahá'í Administration".

they have been in the abundance of their number and unexcelled in their sublime heroism, are but a faint glimmer of what, according to the Divine Promise, its steadfast followers are destined to perform? Those heroic exploits that have immortalised the names of its primitive adherents will continue to adorn and illuminate the pages of its blood-stained history; yet we cannot forget that the period of its full fruition with all its promise of world felicity and undreamt-of-achievements is yet to be realised, its golden Age yet to unfold. Indeed, how chastening to our pride, how challenging to our enthusiasm, if we but pause for a moment amidst the world's many distractions and ponder in our hearts the vastness, the compelling urgency, the ineffable glory of what still remains unachieved.

But let us all remember, in this connexion, that prior to every conceivable measure destined to raise the efficiency of our administrative activities, more vital than any scheme which the most resourceful amongst us can devise, far above the most elaborate structure which the concerted efforts of organised Assemblies can hope to raise, is the realisation down in the innermost heart of every true believer of the regenerating power, the supreme necessity, the unfailing efficacy of the Message he bears. I assure you, dear friends, that nothing short of such an immovable conviction could have in days past enabled our beloved Cause to weather the blackest storms in its history. Naught else can today vitalise the manifold activities in which unnumbered disciples of the Faith are engaged; naught else can provide that driving force and sustaining power that are both so essential to the success of vast and enduring achievements. It is this spirit that above all else we should sedulously guard, and strive with all our might to fortify and exemplify in all our undertakings.

Moved by an irresistible impulse, I have addressed to Her Majesty in the name of the Bahá'ís of both the East and the West a written expression of our joyous admiration and gratitude for the queenly tribute which Her Majesty has paid to the beauty and nobility of the Bahá'í Teachings. I have, moreover, assured Her Majesty of the far-reaching effect which her superb testimony will inevitably produce, and of the welcome consolation it has already brought to the silent sufferers in that distracted country. To my message of appreciation and gratitude there has come lately a written response, penned by Her Majesty, profoundly touching, singularly outspoken, and highly significant in the testimony it bears, from this queenly tribute to a Divine Ideal I quote these penetrating words:

"Indeed a great light came to me with the Message of Bahá'u'lláh and 'Abdu'l-Bahá. It came as all great messages come at an hour of dire grief and inner conflict and distress, so the seed sank deeply. . . . We pass on the Message from mouth to mouth and all those we give it to see a light suddenly lighting before them and much that was obscure and perplexing becomes simple, luminous and full of hope as never before. That my open letter was balm to those suffering for the Cause is indeed a great happiness to me, and I take it as a sign that God accepted my humble tribute. . . . With bowed head I recognise that I too am but an instrument in greater Hands and rejoice in the knowledge. . . ."

Dear friends, with feelings of profound emotion we recall the glowing promises that have so often fallen from the lips of our departed Master, and with throbbing hearts rejoice in the gradual realisation of His most cherished desire.

And as we call to mind the circumstances that have led to such a notable advance, we are filled with admiration for that unique and great-hearted apostle of Bahá'u'lláh, our dearly-beloved Martha Root, who under trying circumstances and almost single-handed in her efforts, has so wonderfully paved the way for the universal recognition of the Cause of God. In her case we have verily witnessed in an unmistakable manner what the power of dauntless faith, when coupled with sublimity of character, can achieve, what forces it can release, to what heights it can rise.

Let such remarkable revelations of the reality and continuity of the Divine Purpose, made manifest from time to time to us His feeble children serve to fortify our faith in Him, to warm the chill which fleeting misfortunes may leave behind, and fill us with that Celestial potency which alone can enable us to withstand the storm and stress that lives dedicated to His service must needs encounter.

Your true brother,
Shoghi

23 October 1926

My dear Mr. Simpson,

Shoghi Effendi wishes me to acknowledge the receipt of your letters dated October 3rd and 10th, 1926. He wishes me especially to mention how appreciative he is of your many services so efficiently and devotingly rendered. He will pray for you and for the other members of the London Group that through your combined efforts an unprecedented progress be made there and numerous persons attracted to the precepts of the Cause.

Concerning the attendance of certain individuals at the meeting of the Assemblies and at the invitation of that body. This, Shoghi Effendi considers, to be as expert advice which is absolutely necessary for good administration. The members of the Assembly are not supposed to know everything on every subject, so they can invite a person, versed in that question, to attend their meetings and explain his views. But naturally he will have no right to vote. . . .

My dear and precious co-worker,
I am glad and grateful to feel that the joint efforts of Martha and Mountfort* have given a fresh impetus to the promotion of the Cause in Great Britain. I trust that the collective and individual efforts of the members of the British Spiritual Assemblies will serve to consolidate the work already achieved. I should be pleased to receive if available full copies of any newspapers in Great Britain that may have published the appreciations broadcast by the Queen of Rumania. The entire issue of the papers—not clippings—will be of great significance to the friends in Persia. Ten copies of each would be sufficient. I wish also to request you to urge all the friends in Great Britain to subscribe to the "Messager Bahá'í" published by Mrs. Stannard in Geneva. It is essential and valuable.
Your true brother,
Shoghi

29 October 1926**

To the beloved of the Lord and the handmaids of the Merciful throughout the West.

Dear fellow-workers in the Divine Vineyard!
It will gladden and rejoice every one of you to learn that from

*Martha Root and Mountfort Mills.
**Printed also in "Bahá'í Administration".

various quarters there has of late reached the Holy Land tidings of fresh developments that are a clear indication of those hidden and transforming influences which, from the source of Bahá'u'lláh's mystic strength, continue to flow with ever-increasing vitality into the heart of this troubled world.

Both in the wider field of its spiritual conquests, where its indomitable spirit is forging ahead, capturing the heights, pervading the multitude; as well as in the gradual consolidation of the administrative structure which its avowed followers the world over are labouring to raise and fortify, the Faith of Bahá'u'lláh, we can increasingly discern, bids fair to become that force which, though not as yet universally recognised, none can afford to belittle or ignore.

In the bold and repeated testimonies which Her Majesty, Queen Marie of Rumania, has chosen to give to the world—a copy of whose latest pronouncement I enclose—we truly recognise evidences of the irresistible power, the increasing vitality, the strange working of a Faith destined to regenerate the world. Her Majesty's striking tribute paid to the illuminative power of the Teachings of Bahá'u'lláh and 'Abdu'l-Bahá is bound to effect an entire transformation in the attitude of many to a Faith the tenets of which have often been misunderstood and sorely neglected. It will serve as a fresh stimulus to the enlightened and cultured to investigate with an open mind the verities of its message, the source of its life-giving principles.

From Baghdád, moreover, where the sacred habitation of Bahá'u'lláh has been violated by a relentless enemy and converted into a rallying centre for the corrupt, the perverse, and the fanatical, there comes the news, highly reassuring to us all, of the satisfactory progress of the negotiations which, we are informed on high authority, will soon lead to the expropriation of the property by the State, culminating in the fullness of time in its occupation by the triumphant followers of God's holy Faith. The case of the houses, so ably presented, so persistently pursued, above all reinforced by the vigilant and protecting power of our departed Master, will eventually triumph, and by its repercussions in Persia as in the world at large, will lend a powerful impetus to the liberation of those forces which will carry the Cause to its ultimate destiny. I will, when the occasion presents itself, inform the believers through their respective National Spiritual Assemblies to address messages of appreciation and gratitude to the Authorities concerned in view of their unrelaxing efforts for the triumph of Right and Justice.

For the present, we cannot but rejoice and feel profoundly thankful as we witness in so many directions the welcome signs of the gradual emancipation of the struggling Faith of Bahá'u'lláh, of the increasing recognition on the part of both the high and lowly of its universal principles—all so rich in their promise of ultimate victory.

Your true brother,
Shoghi

29 November 1926

Dear Mr. Simpson,

Shoghi Effendi wishes me to acknowledge the receipt of your letter dated November 14th, 1926, together with the minutes of the 18th meeting of the National Assembly, held on October 23rd 1926. He has received the 200 copies of the 4th edition of the folder and desires to thank you for them.

The question of incorporating the National Assembly is very important for though at present there may not be any important business which necessitates that, one may arise at any time. There is also some advantage in being ready for any future developments. But naturally such a step should be taken after consultation with competent lawyers lest some defect may in the future cause some inconveniences.

What Shoghi Effendi desires to have are clippings of any article written by the Queen of Rumania on subjects referring to the Cause and published in England. He has received such declarations or open letters from America and wishes to know what she is doing along those lines in England which is her own native home. It is really wonderful how boldly she is advocating this Cause absolutely regardless of what others may say. This is a very good lesson for those who being Bahá'ís keep in the dark so as not to be criticised and perhaps ostracised by so called society people.

We are eagerly awaiting to meet Miss Rosenberg and Mrs. Slade† to obtain a first hand information of the condition of the Cause in England and the extent to which Mr. Mills and Miss Root have succeeded to improve it.

My dearly-beloved co-worker:
I am hoping that our deliberations with our English Bahá'í visitors

will assist and aid the work in which you are engaged and prove beneficial to the Cause in general. I feel that the opportunities now open to the friends are greater than ever before and I will pray that the measures they undertake will redound to the glory, the power and effectiveness of the Cause. The utterances of the Rumanian Queen should be given the fullest possible publicity and be fully utilised as I feel they are of great significance and value. More power to your elbow!

Shoghi

29 January 1927

Dear Bahá'í Friend, Mr. Simpson,

Thank you so very much for your clear good letter of Jan. 16th—Shoghi Effendi bids me say how much pleasure he always derives from the perusal of your letters—which are always expressed with such admirable clearness, and to the point. He has just now been discussing with me the various matters you mention.

He says that in one way we are not quite correct in the way we manage our elections for the National Assembly—Shoghi Effendi says that the intention is, that when once the 19 delegates have been elected by the friends of the respective centres in the proportions you mention, i.e. 12 delegates from among the London friends, five from the Manchester friends, and two from the Bournemouth group, that then, these 19 delegates assembled should choose by secret ballot from the whole body of the believers in Gt. Britain and Ireland, the nine friends they consider most suitable as members of the National Assembly. Heretofore, as I understand it, it has rather been our practice that the 12 London delegates elected six from the London friends—the Manchester five delegates elected two from Manchester and the Bournemouth delegates elected one from Bournemouth. But, Shoghi Effendi says, all the 19 delegates must clearly understand that they must select from the whole body of the believers in Gt. Britain and Ireland those 9 whom they consider the most fit and suitable members to constitute the National Assembly. Therefore it will be necessary to supply each of the 19 delegates with a complete list of all those believers in Gt. Britain and Ireland. From that complete list of course must be eliminated all those who from one cause or another are unable to serve on the

National Assembly. Also—Shoghi Effendi says that those 19 elected delegates should if possible meet during the Feast of Riḍván in London thus forming as it were a baby Convention! I had not realised before that the annual Bahá'í Convention in the U.S.A. consists solely of those delegates who had been chosen by their respective Centres in order that they may elect the 9 to form the National Assembly of that country. Did you understand this? I certainly did not. As Shoghi Effendi points out—it is quite possible that—e.g. in the future—7 members might be elected from the Manchester friends and only two from London! On the other hand—it is quite possible that all nine members chosen by the 19 delegates might be from the London group. Of course, on reflection one sees clearly that the proceedings must be as now described because in the future there may be 21 or 53 separate local Assemblies in Gt. Britain just as is now the case in the U.S.A.—and it would obviously be impossible for each of these Assemblies to elect one of their number to sit as their representative on the National Assembly. No doubt I ought to have understood this before—but I must confess I did not! . . .

It is very grievous that our dear Mrs. Cropper should have been so ill—we have all been praying for her recovery since we knew of it and I am thankful to hear she is now making steady progress.

Since writing to you I too have had a bad influenza cold that swept through our house. But I am now quite recovered I am glad to say.

With all best wishes to yourself.

Your sincere friend in His service,
Ethel Rosenberg

P.S. I have just remembered I have said nothing about the London area that should be included—Shoghi Effendi thinks it would save trouble if you drew your circle widely enough to include Mrs. Slade and her daughter! At first he inclined to agree with you that it would be best to take the middle one—the Postal Area—and make exceptions in favour of Mrs. Haybittel and her daughter. (Mrs. Ginman† I hear from my brother has moved into town now) but it seemed to him that you might possibly have other friends residing or moving out to Surbiton etc., so that it might save you trouble in the future if you selected the widest area? This is merely a suggestion on his part—as it will no doubt be decided at the meeting of the London Assembly. But with regard to the choosing by the 19 delegates of the nine members of the National Assembly, his instructions are quite definite and must not be departed from—as these instructions are as laid down by the Master in the Testament and other Tablets. Shoghi Effendi says you can even now soon select the day for the 19 delegates to come to London during Riḍván. By the way Riḍván begins exactly 31 days after the New Year so it starts almost always on April 21st and lasts for 12 days. I have recorded my notes on list enclosed.

Yours ever,
E. Rosenberg

*Shoghi Effendi emphatically urges that the 19 friends elected as delegates should meet together during Riḍván—Shoghi Effendi has sent you three copies of the Bahá'í Year Book, one for London, one for Manchester and one for Bournemouth.

Read and approved. Shoghi

Editor's Note:

From December 1926 to April 1927, while the secretary who was then helping with the English correspondence was away from Haifa, Miss Ethel J. Rosenberg (addressed in letters by the Guardian as "My dear Rosa"), was on pilgrimage and kept up a lengthy and repetitive correspondence with George P. Simpson. In these letters from Miss Rosenberg are many instructions from the Guardian to the British National Assembly. The letter reproduced in this compilation, dated January 29th, 1927 is important for many reasons:

1. It is the only one from Miss Rosenberg which carried the handwriting of Shoghi Effendi where he "Approved" what had been written.
2. It outlined the principle for the election of the National Spiritual Assembly by delegates which the British N.S.A. had not then appreciated from the earlier letters of the Guardian (of 1923, 1924, 1925, later published in "Bahá'í Administration").
3. It insisted upon Convention being held in London during Riḍván.
4. It clarified the need to have a recognised voting area for London but left the final decision to the local Spiritual Assembly of London.

As a result of this letter 13 delegates attended Convention and 4 voted by post; ten members were elected to the National Assembly (Guardian's letter of May, 13th, 1927 refers), and the London area was defined as having a radius of 36 miles.

*In a different handwriting from Miss Rosenberg's.

12 February 1927*

To the beloved of the Lord and the handmaids of the Merciful throughout the West.

Dearly-beloved brothers and sisters in 'Abdu'l-Bahá:
The trend of various events, affecting directly and indirectly the interests of the Bahá'í Cause, have of late served to bring into further prominence the character as well as the significance of a Faith destined to regenerate the world.

Of all the diverse issues which today are gradually tending to consolidate and extend the bounds of the Revelation of Bahá'u'lláh, the decision of Egypt's religious Tribunal regarding the Bahá'ís under its jurisdiction appears at the present moment to be the most powerful in its challenge, the most startling in its character, and the most perplexing in the consequences it may entail. I have already alluded in my letter of January 10, 1926, addressed to the National Spiritual Assembly of the Bahá'ís of the United States and Canada, to a particular feature of this momentous verdict, which after mature deliberation has obtained the sanction of Egypt's highest ecclesiastical authorities, has been communicated and printed, and is regarded as final and binding. I have stressed in my last reference to this far-reaching pronouncement the negative aspect of this document which condemns in most unequivocal and emphatic language the followers of Bahá'u'lláh as the believers in heresy, offensive and injurious to Islám, and wholly incompatible with the accepted doctrines and practice of its orthodox adherents.

A closer study of the text of the decision will, however, reveal the fact that coupled with this strong denunciation is the positive assertion of a truth which the recognised opponents of the Bahá'í Faith in other Muhammadan countries have up to the present time either sedulously ignored or maliciously endeavoured to disprove. Not content with this harsh and unjustifiable repudiation of the so-called menacing and heretical doctrines of the adherents of the Bahá'í Faith, they proceed in a formal manner to declare in the text of that very decision their belief, that the Bahá'í Faith is a "new religion", "entirely independent" and, by reason of the magnitude of its claim and the character of its "laws, principles and beliefs," worthy to be reckoned as one of the established religious systems of the world. Quoting various passages judiciously

---

*Printed also in "Bahá'í Administration".

gleaned from a number of Bahá'í sacred Books as an evidence to their splendid testimony, they proceed in a notable statement to deduce the fact that henceforth it shall be regarded as impossible for the followers of such a Faith to be designated as Muslim, just as it would be incorrect and erroneous to call a Muhammadan either Christian or Jew.

It cannot be denied that in the course of the inevitable developments of this present situation the resident Bahá'ís of Egypt, originally belonging to the Muslim Faith, will be placed in a most humiliating and embarrassing position. They, however, cannot but rejoice in the knowledge that whereas in various Muhammadan countries and particularly in Persia the overwhelming majority of the leaders of Islám are utterly opposed to any form of declaration that would facilitate the universal recognition of the Cause, the authorised heads of their co-religionists in one of the most advanced communities in the Muhammadan world have, of their own initiative, published to the world a document that may justly be termed as the first charter of liberty emancipating the Bahá'í Faith from the fetters of orthodox Islám. And in order to insure the complete rupture of Bahá'í official relations with Muslim Courts they lay down in unmistakable terms the condition that under no circumstances can the marriage of those Bahá'ís who have been required to divorce their Muslim wives be renewed by the Muslim Court unless and until the husbands formally recant their faith by solemnly declaring that the Qur'án is the "last" Book of God revealed to man, that no law can abrogate the Prophet's Law, no faith can succeed His Faith, no revelation can claim to fulfill His Revelation.

While unwavering in their belief in the Divine station of the Author of the Qur'án and profoundly convinced of the necessity and worldwide influence of His Divine mission, Bahá'ís in every land stand undeterred and unabashed in the face of the strong condemnation pronounced against their brethren in Egypt. Indeed, they together with their fellow-workers in all Muslim countries welcome with gladness and pride every opportunity for further emancipation that they may set forth in a truer light the sublime mission of Bahá'u'lláh.

In the face of such an outspoken and challenging declaration, the Bahá'ís of the West cannot but feel the deepest sympathy with their Egyptian brethren who, for the sake of our beloved Cause and its deliverance, have to face all the embarrassments and vexations which the severance of old-established ties must necessarily entail. They will, however, most certainly expect every staunch and loyal believer in the

Faith who resides in that land to refrain in view of the grave warning uttered expressly by our opponents, from any practice that would in any manner constitute in the eyes of a critical and vigilant enemy a repudiation of the fundamental beliefs of the people of Bahá. They will most assuredly, whenever the moment is opportune, step forth with eager hearts to offer every support in their power to their fellow-workers who, with stout hearts and irreproachable loyalty, will continue to hold aloft the standard of God's struggling Faith. They will not fail to come to the rescue of those who with joyous confidence will endure to the very end such vicissitudes as this New Day of God, now in its birth-throes, must needs suffer and surmount.

We cannot believe that as the Movement grows in strength, in authority and influence, the perplexities and the sufferings it has had to contend with in the past will correspondingly decrease and vanish. Nay, as it grows from strength to strength, the fanatical defendants of the strongholds of orthodoxy, whatever be their denomination, realising the penetrating influence of this growing Faith, will arise and strain every nerve to extinguish its light and discredit its name. For has not our beloved 'Abdu'l-Bahá sent forth His glowing prophecy from behind the prison walls of the citadel of 'Akká—words so significant in their forecast of the coming world turmoil, yet so rich in their promise of eventual victory:—

"How great, how very great is the Cause; how very fierce the onslaught of all the peoples and kindreds of the earth! Erelong shall the clamour of the multitude throughout Africa, throughout America, the cry of the European and of the Turk, the groaning of India and China be heard from far and near. One and all they shall arise with all their power to resist His Cause. Then shall the Knights of the Lord, assisted by grace from on high, strengthened by faith, aided by the power of understanding and reinforced by the legions of the Covenant, arise and make manifest the truth of the verse: 'Behold the confusion that hath befallen the tribes of the defeated!'"

Dearly beloved friends, upon us devolves the supreme obligation to stand by His side, to fight His battles and to win His victory. May we prove ourselves worthy of this trust.

Your true brother,
Shoghi

26 February 1927

... quite in order to utilise the Bahá'í Fund for the payment of at least half of the travelling expenses of the Friends who come to London from a distance, *"one chief object of the Fund should be to help the Friends in these difficulties".*

(Quoted in National Spiritual Assembly Minutes)

22 March 1927

LOVING APPRECIATION AFFECTIONATE REMEMBRANCE.

SHOGHI

27 April 1927*

Dearly-beloved friends:

With feelings of horror and indignation I communicate to you the tale of yet another tragedy involving the shedding of the blood of a martyr of the Faith on Persia's sacred soil. I have before me, as I pen these lines, the report of the local Spiritual Assembly of Ardibíl, a town on the north-east confines of the province of Adhirbáyján, not far distant from those hallowed spots where the Báb suffered His last confinement and martyrdom. Addressed to the National Spiritual Assembly of the Bahá'ís of Persia, this report recounts in simple but moving language the circumstances that have led to the cowardly crime committed in the darkness of the night at the instigation of the fanatical clergy—the deadliest opponents of the Faith in that town.

Our martyred brother, Aminu'l-'Ulamá' by name, had for some time past become notorious in the eyes of the Muslim inhabitants of Ardibíl for his tenacity of faith by openly refusing at every instance to vilify and renounce his most cherished convictions. In the latter part of Ramaḍán—the month associated with prayer, pious deeds and fasting—his use of the public bath—that long-established institution the amenities and privileges of which are as a rule accorded only to the adherents of the Muslim Faith—had served to inflame the mob, and to provide a scheming instigator with a pretext to terminate his life. In the market-place he was ridiculed and condemned as an apostate of the

*Printed also in "Bahá'í Administration".

Faith of Islám, who, by boldly rejecting the repeated entreaties showered upon him to execrate the Bahá'í name, had lawfully incurred the penalty of immediate death at the hands of every pious upholder of the Muslim tradition.

In spite of the close surveillance exercised by a body of guards stationed around his house, in response to the intercession of his friends with the local authorities, the treacherous criminal found his way into his home, and on the night of the 22nd of Ramadán, corresponding with the 26th of March 1927, assailed him in a most atrocious and dastardly manner. Concealing within the folds of his garment his unsheathed dagger, he approached his victim and claiming the need of whispering a confidential message in his ears plunged the weapon hilt-deep into his vitals, cutting across his ribs and mutilating his body. Every attempt to secure immediate medical assistance seems to have been foiled by malicious devices on the part of the associates of this merciless criminal, and the helpless victim after a few hours of agonising pain surrendered his soul to his Beloved. His friends and fellow-believers, alarmed at the prospect of a fresh outbreak that would inevitably result were his mortal remains to be accorded the ordinary privileges of a decent burial, decided to inter his body in one of the two rooms that served as his own dwelling, seeking thereby to appease the fury of an unrelenting foe.

He leaves behind in desperate poverty a family of minors with no support but their mother, expectant to bring forth her child, and with no hope of relief from their non-Bahá'í relatives in whose eyes they deserve to be treated only with the meanest contempt.

It appears from the above-mentioned report that the merciless assailant has been arrested, waiting, however, as has been the case with similar incidents in southern Persia, to be sooner or later released under the pressure of bribery and intimidation sedulously exercised by an impenitent enemy.

Dearest friends! Any measure of publicity the concerted efforts of the Bahá'í Spiritual Assemblies of the West, on whom almighty Providence has conferred the inestimable benefits of religious toleration and freedom, can accord to this latest manifestation of unbridled barbarism in Persia will be most opportune and valuable. It will, I am certain, confer abiding solace to those disconsolate sufferers who with sublime heroism continue to uphold the traditions of their beloved Faith. Our one weapon lies in our prayerful efforts, intelligently and persistently pursued, to arouse by every means at our disposal the conscience of unheeding humanity, and to direct the attention of men of vision and authority to these incredibly odious acts which in their ferocity and frequency cannot but constitute in the eyes of every fair-minded observer the gravest challenge to all that is sacred and precious in our present day civilisation.

Your true brother,
Shoghi

29 April 1927

MAY DELIBERATIONS FIRST BRITISH BAHÁ'Í CONVENTION BE DIVINELY GUIDED AND BLESSED.

SHOGHI

13 May 1927

My dear Mr. Simpson,

I thank you on behalf of our dear Guardian for your welcome letter of the 2nd.

It was with unbounded joy and great hopes for the future that we learnt of the success of your first National Convention. May it prove to be the beginning of a new era of achievement and expansion in the field of service. Time was when individually we had to drink deep from the all-satisfying teachings of the Bahá'í Faith, and although this is far from being accomplished yet it is time for us to share with many others what we firmly believe. . . .

Miss Rosenberg left only a few days ago and I suppose she will arrive back home earlier than this letter.

As she will have plenty of news to give you I hardly need add any. . . .

My dear and valued co-worker:

Although I rejoice at your appointment as member of the National and local Assemblies, I fully sympathise with you in your arduous work and responsibilities, for all of which you are so distinctly equipped and qualified. I feel that next year, the number of members should be strictly confined to nine, and a second ballot is quite proper and justified.* I trust that the choice of Rev. Biggs signifies his unreserved acceptance of the Faith in its entirety—a condition that we must increasingly stress in the years that come. Please assure the elected members of my love, my best wishes and of my ardent prayers for them all individually and collectively that the Beloved may guide them, and reinforce their efforts for the spread of our beloved Cause.

Your true brother,
Shoghi

22 May 1927

My dear Mr. Simpson,
    I thank you on behalf of Shoghi Effendi for your short letter of the 8th giving the name of the occupants of the various offices.
    He is glad to see the well chosen members each undertaking his suitable task with the chairman shining amongst them. However he trusts that the coming year may be one of renewed activity and greater accomplishment. Let us not be loiterers in a fast-flying world especially when we know to what grave and universal ills this Cause is a divine remedy. . . .

With loving greetings and apologies for inability to write more due to mental fatigue and strain.

Your true brother,
Shoghi

25 May 1927

NATIONAL ASSEMBLY AFFECTIONATELY REMEMBERED HOLY SHRINES.

SHOGHI

8 October 1927
17 October 1927
Referred to in Minutes; no text available.

*As there were two believers with an equal number of votes for the ninth place it had been decided to have all ten on the National Assembly!

15 November 1927

LOVING APPRECIATION REMEMBRANCE.

SHOGHI

28 November 1927

LOVING APPRECIATION TENDEREST REMEMBRANCE.

SHOGHI

5 January 1928

"... Nothing should be attempted that would, in the least and however indirectly, interfere with the unqualified freedom of local and national elections..."

(Quoted in National Spiritual Assembly Minutes)

16 January 1928

My dear Mr. Simpson

I am instructed by our dear Shoghi Effendi to thank you for your letter of Dec. 31st with enclosures all of which he was very glad and interested to read.

With regard to Miss Pinchon's† book, Shoghi Effendi feels that if she herself and the Assembly in London feel that the arrangement with the London branch of Brentano's is really to her advantage, he would then be glad to endorse it. The arguments you had brought were really very favourable and that might help the success of the book in America. Moreover, he would wish you to thank Asgarzadeh for his commitment in helping the Assembly to promise a sum of fifty pounds. Shoghi Effendi has liked the book immensely and trusts that it may render great services and fulfil all our hopes.

He has taken notice of your solicitor's answer with regard to official recognition by the Board of Trade and thinks your view of the subject perfectly sound. Will the answer of the Board of Trade prove a stimulus to the friends in England and help to multiply their numbers and establish the Faith?...

My dear and valued co-worker:
  I am so glad to have the opportunity of reaffirming in person my deep affection for, and unshaken confidence in, you as well as my growing appreciation of your ability and constancy in service. I am delighted at the prospect of the joint publication of Miss Pinchon's admirable book in London and in New York, and I would leave all subsidiary matters in this connexion to the National Assembly and Miss Pinchon herself. I wish to order beforehand 50 copies of her book at whatever price the publishers will fix the rate of its sale, and will gladly send through you the amount whenever seems to you the most suitable time. Kindly assure the friends of my continued prayers at the Holy Shrines for their welfare and the success of their arduous yet noble task.
Affectionately,
Shoghi

8 February 1928

My dear Mr. Simpson,
  I am instructed by our dear Guardian to thank you for your letter of Jan. 29th with the minutes of the regular meeting of the English N.S.A. enclosed.
  He has read both your letter and the minutes with interest and pleasure. He trusts that your next list of electors will show marked progress and your weekly meetings at Lindsay Hall will attract new and enlightened people. It is strange that the English Bahá'ís have really contributed a great deal to the Cause, and in the form of books and publications given us works of real and permanent value—perhaps proportionately more than America, and yet it is such a Herculean affair to bring in new fellow-workers. Perhaps just that difficulty is a sign of their merit—staunch and unflinching adherence once they believe in something.
  In connection with the form in which new electors are to be admitted into the Cause, our Guardian will personally append his suggestions if any. You would do well to see what the American system is.
  Shoghi Effendi hopes very much that Miss Pinchon's book will prove a "good-seller" in England also. Perhaps in being less scholarly it might prove more popular and widely read. . . .

My very dear and valued co-worker:

Pressure of cares and anxieties, most of them sudden and unforeseen, has caused the delay in mailing this letter to you. Although immersed in an ocean of preoccupations and work, I can always find the time to turn my heart in prayer at the Holy Shrines and supplicate for you as well as for your fellow-workers in that land the Beloved's unfailing Guidance, sustaining strength and imperishable blessings. May He assist you to persevere in your task, and enable you to achieve in the various fields of your activity your heart's desire.

Your true brother,
Shoghi

22 March 1928

LOVING APPRECIATION.

SHOGHI

15 April 1928

My dear and valued co-worker:

I am glad to learn of your sustained activity, your undiminished enthusiasm and vigour in the service of our beloved Cause. I will, on my part, continue to pray for you from the very depths of my heart, that the Beloved may guide you in every step you take, help you to remove misunderstandings and difficulties amongst the friends and grant you strength and long life to consolidate and extend the bounds of the splendid pioneer work you are engaged in at present.

Your true brother and well-wisher,
Shoghi

24 April 1928

BROTHERLY GREETING LOVING APPRECIATION.

SHOGHI

24 May 1928

NATIONAL ASSEMBLY TENDERLY REMEMBERED HOLY SHRINES.

SHOGHI

13 November 1928

CONVEY NATIONAL ASSEMBLY LOVING APPRECIATION.

SHOGHI

29 November 1928

LOVING REMEMBRANCE.

SHOGHI

6 December 1928*

To the beloved of the Lord and the handmaids of the Merciful throughout the West.

Dearly-beloved brothers and sisters in 'Abdu'l-Bahá,

Events of a startling character and of the utmost significance to the Faith of Bahá'u'lláh, have recently transpired throughout the Near and Middle East in such rapid succession, that I feel moved to write about them to those who, in distant lands and with eager hearts, are waiting to witness the fulfilment of the prophecies of Bahá'u'lláh. You will, I am certain, rejoice with me to learn that the quickening forces of internal reform are swiftly awakening from their age-long slumber of negligence those lands which, trodden by the feet of Bahá'u'lláh and wherein are enshrined the memorable scenes of His birth, His ministry, His exiles, His banishments, His suffering and His ascension, are destined in the fullness of time to play a pre-eminent rôle in the regeneration of the East—nay of all mankind.

From Persia, the cradle of our Faith and the object of our tenderest affections, there breaks upon us the news of the first stirrings of that social and political Reformation which, as we firmly believe, is but the direct and unavoidable consequence of that great spiritual Revival ushered in by the Revelation of Bahá'u'lláh. These social and political forces now released by the Source of such a tremendous Revival are bound in their turn to demolish one by one the barriers that have so long impeded its flow, sapped its vitality and obscured its radiance.

*Printed also in "Bahá'í Administration".

From a communication addressed to me recently by the National Spiritual Assembly of the Bahá'ís of Persia, as well as from reliable reports submitted by the local representatives of the Persian believers, and confirmed by the vivid narrative of visiting pilgrims, it is becoming increasingly manifest that the glowing promises so many times uttered by our departed Master are, with extraordinary exactitude and remarkable swiftness, being successively fulfilled. Reforms of a revolutionary character are, without bloodshed and with negligible resistance, gradually transforming the very basis and structure of Persia's primitive society. The essentials of public security and order are being energetically provided throughout the length and breadth of the <u>Sh</u>áh's domain, and are hailed with particular gratification by that much harassed section of the population—our long-suffering brethren of that land. The rapidity, the incredible ease, with which the enlightened proposals of its government, in matters of education, trade and finance, means of transportation and travel, and the development of the country's internal resources, are receiving the unqualified sanction of a hitherto reactionary Legislature, and are overcoming the resistance and apathy of the masses, have undoubtedly tended to hasten the emancipation of our Persian brethren from the remaining fetters of a once despotic and blood-stained regime. The severely repressive and humiliating measures undertaken on the initiative of progressive provincial Governors, and with the connivance of State officials in the Capital, aiming at the scattering and ultimate extinction of a rapidly waning clergy, such as degradation, detainment, deportation and in some cases pitiless execution, are paving the way for the entire removal of the shackles imposed by an ignorant and fanatical priesthood upon the administration of State affairs. In matters of dress; in the obligatory enforcement of a uniform style of national head-gear; in the strict limitation of the number, the rights and the prerogatives of high ecclesiastical officials; in the growing unpopularity of the veil among almost every section of society; in the marked distinction which unofficially and in various phases of public life is being made by an enlightened and pressing minority between the tottering forms of a discredited Ecclesiasticism and the civil rights and duties of civilised society; in the general laxity in religious observances and ceremonies; in the slow and hidden process of secularisation invading many a Government department under the courageous guidance of the Governors of outlying provinces—in all of these a discerning eye can easily discover the symptoms that augur well for a future that is sure to witness the formal and complete separation of Church and State.

To this uplifting movement, various external factors are being added that are tending to hasten and stimulate this process of internal regeneration so significant in the life of renascent Persia. The multiplicity and increasing facilities in the means of transportation and travel; the State visit of energetic and enlightened reformers to Persia's capital; the forthcoming and widely-advertised journey of the Sháh himself to the progressive capitals of Western Europe; the repercussion of Turkey's astounding reforms among an essentially sensitive and receptive people; the loud and persistent clamour of a revolting order in Russia against the evil domination and dark plottings of all forms of religious sectarianism; the relentless vigour with which Afghánistán's ambitious Ruler, reinforced by the example of his gracious Consort, is pursuing his campaign of repression against a similar order of a corrupted clergy at home—all tend to lend their force in fostering and fashioning that public opinion which can alone provide an enduring basis for the reform Movement destined to usher in that golden Era craved for by the followers of the Faith in Bahá'u'lláh's native land.

As a direct consequence of the birth of this new consciousness in the life of the nation, as evidenced by these early stirrings in the minds of the people, both high and low, meetings of an elaborate character, unprecedented in the number of their attendants, in the tone of the public addresses, in the undisturbed atmosphere of their proceedings, and the general impressiveness of their organisation, have been publicly held in Ṭihrán, under the auspices of the National Spiritual Assembly of the Bahá'ís of Persia. Particularly significant and impressive were those that were held in the Ḥaẓíratu'l-Quds, the administrative and spiritual centre of the Faith in the Capital, on the occasion of the twin Festivals commemorating the declaration of the Báb and the birth of 'Abdu'l-Bahá, at the chief of which no less than two thousand representative Bahá'ís and non-Bahá'ís, leaders of public opinion, State officials and foreign representatives were officially invited. The addresses stressing the universality of the Teachings of the Cause, the formal and ordered character of the proceedings so unusual a feature to a gathering of such proportions, the mingling of the Bahá'ís with the recognised representatives of progressive thought in the Capital who, by virtue of their high office and stately appearance, lent colour and weight to the concourse of attending believers, have all contributed to enhance the brilliance and spiritual significance of that gathering on that memorable occasion.

Moreover, reports of a highly encouraging nature are being

continually received from local Assemblies and individual believers, giving the names and stating the numbers of influential Persians who, hitherto reluctant to declare openly their faith in Bahá'u'lláh, are as a result of this reassuring and promising state of affairs emerging from the obscurity of their concealment and enlisting under the erected banner of Bahá'u'lláh. This has served to embolden the followers of the Faith to take the necessary steps, under the direction of their local Assemblies, for the institution of Bahá'í schools, for the holding of public gatherings, for the establishment of Bahá'í hostels, libraries and public baths, for the construction of official headquarters for their administrative work, and for the gradual execution among themselves, within the limits imposed upon them by the State, of the laws and ordinances revealed in the Kitáb-i-Aqdas. Words fail me to describe the feelings of those patiently suffering brethren of ours in that land, who, with eyes dim with tears and hearts overflowing with thanksgiving and praise, are witnessing on every side and with increasing force the unfoldment of a Faith which they have served so well and love so dearly. Accounts pathetic and inspiring in their tone are being received from that steadfast and cheerful band of exultant believers, and are being shared with the resident friends in the Holy Land who, having had the privilege of close and continued association with the person of 'Abdu'l-Bahá, cannot but marvel at the range, the potency and accuracy of the prophecies of their departed Master.

From Turkey, on whose soil, for well nigh three score years and ten, were enacted some of the sublimest and most tragic scenes in the annals of the Cause; Turkey, under whose rule Bahá'u'lláh twice proclaimed Himself, was thrice exiled and banished, and finally ascended to the Abhá Kingdom, and where 'Abdu'l-Bahá spent more than fifty years of His Life, in incarceration and suffering; has of late been rudely awakened to a Call which it has so long obstinately despised and ignored. Following on the overthrow of that effete theocracy, resting on the twin institutions of the Caliphate and Sultanate—those two sinister forces that have combined to inflict the deadliest blows to our beloved Faith in the earliest stages of its infancy and growth—an uncompromising policy aiming at the secularisation of the State and the disestablishment of Islám was initiated and carried out with exemplary vigour. Religious institutions and monastic orders which under the guise of religious propaganda were converted into hotbeds of political intrigue and sedition were peremptorily closed, their adherents scattered and banished, their funds confiscated, their privileges and *prerogatives abolished. None, save the little band of Bahá'u'lláh's devoted followers, escaped the trenchant axe of the pitiless reformer; all, without fear or favour, had to submit to his searching investigations, his dictatorial edicts, his severe and irrevocable judgment. Lately, however, the Turkish Government, faithful to its policy of ceaseless vigilance, and fearful of the growing activities of the Bahá'ís under its rule, decided to order the Police in the town of Smyrna to conduct a close investigation into the purpose, the character and the effects of Bahá'í activity in that town. No sooner were the representative Bahá'ís in that locality arrested and conducted to the Law Courts for purposes of investigation, than the President of the Bahá'í Spiritual Assembly of Constantinople who, having read in the morning papers the report of the Smyrna incident, had resolved unsummoned to offer the necessary explanations to the authorities concerned, was in his turn arrested and taken to the Police Headquarters where he soon afterwards was joined by the other members of the Assembly. The official searching of their homes, the seizure of whatever Bahá'í literature they had in their possession, their twenty-four hours' detention at the Police station, the searching severity of the cross-examination to which they were subjected—all proved powerless to alarm and shake the faith of those intrepid champions of the Cause, or to evince anything detrimental to the best interests of the State. On the contrary, they served to deeply impress upon the minds and hearts of the officials concerned the sublimity, the innocence, and the dynamic force of the Faith of Bahá'u'lláh. So much so that their books were returned, a genuine desire to deepen their knowledge of the Cause was expressed by their examiners, and widespread publicity, as reflected in the articles of about a dozen leading newspapers of Turkey, was accorded by the Government, proclaiming the innocence of the Cause and lifting up the ban that now so oppressively weighs upon religious institutions in Turkey.*

From Constantinople in European Turkey to the eastern confines of Anatolia, on the banks of the river Euphrates, where a small and flourishing Bahá'í Community has been recently established, a wave of public interest, criticism and inquiry has been sweeping over the surface of the land, as witnessed by the character and number of the leading articles, the illustrations and caricatures that have appeared in the most prominent newspapers of the capital and the provincial towns of Asiatic Turkey. Not only Turkey, but its neighbouring countries of the East and the West, have lifted up their voice in the vindication of the Bahá'í truth. From information thus far gathered we learn that in Hungary, in 'Iráq, Egypt and Syria, and as far west as France and England, newspapers have, of their own accord, with varying degree of accuracy, and in more or less detail, reported this incident in their columns, and have given, unasked and unaware, such publicity to our beloved Faith which no campaign of teaching, however elaborately organised by the believers themselves, could ever hope to achieve at the present time. Surely the invincible arm of Bahá'u'lláh, working through strange and mysterious ways, will continue to guard and uphold, to steer the course, to consolidate, and eventually to achieve the world-wide recognition and triumph of His holy Faith.

And while the East, through suffering and turmoil, is moving on in its slow and toilsome march towards the acceptance of God's holy Faith, let us turn for a moment our gaze to the Western Hemisphere, and particularly to the American continent, and attempt to visualise the possibilities of the future spread of the Cause, and to estimate afresh those golden yet swiftly passing opportunities which Bahá'u'lláh in those far-away lands has accorded to His chosen people. I feel thoroughly convinced, and am moved to share this firm conviction within me with that great company of western believers, that in the speedy resumption of the sorely-neglected construction of the Mashriqu'l-Adhkár at Wilmette lies our undoubted privilege, our primary obligation, our most vital opportunity to lend an unprecedented impetus to the advancement of the Cause, not only throughout the West but in every country of the world. I would not stress at this moment the prestige and good name of the Cause, much as they are involved in this most pressing issue, I would not dwell upon the eager expectancy with which the unnumbered followers of the Faith as well as the vast number of the non-believers in almost every section of society throughout the East are awaiting to behold that noble structure rear its head in the heart of that far-western continent; nor would I expatiate on the ineffable beauty of this holy Edifice, its towering glory, its artistic design, its unique character, or its functions in the organic life of the Bahá'í community of the future. But I would with all the strength of my conviction emphasise the immeasurable spiritual significance of an Edifice, so beauteous, so holy, erected solely by the concerted efforts, strained to the utmost degree of self-sacrifice, of the entire body of the believers who are fully conscious of the significance of the Revelation of Bahá'u'lláh. In this vast endeavour, unparalleled in modern times, its world-wide range, its spontaneity, its heroic and holy character, the American believers, on the soil of whose country Bahá'u'lláh's first universal House of Worship is to be built, must, if they be faithful to their trust, claim and fulfil a pre-eminent share in the collective contributions offered by the Bahá'ís of the world.

For this reason do I feel impelled to direct my incessant plea in particular to the followers of the Faith in the United States and Canada to arise and play their part, while there is yet time, and not to allow their earnest strivings to be swamped and superseded by the self-sacrificing heroism of the multitude of their brethren in Persia. Again I feel the urge to remind you one and all of the necessity of keeping ever in mind this fundamental verity that the efficacy of the spiritual forces centering in, and radiating from, the first Mashriqu'l-Adhkár in the West will in a great measure depend upon the extent to which we, the pioneer workers in that land will with clear vision, unquenchable faith, and inflexible determination, resolve to voluntarily abnegate temporal advantages in our support of so meritorious an endeavour. The higher the degree of our renunciation and self-sacrifice, the wider the range of the contributing believers, the more apparent will become the vitalising forces that are to emanate from this unique and sacred Edifice; and the greater, in consequence, the stimulating effect it will exert upon the propagation of the Faith in the days to come. Not by the abundance of our donations, not even by the spontaneity of our efforts, but rather by the degree of self-abnegation which our contributions will entail, can we effectively promote the speedy realisation of 'Abdu'l-Bahá's cherished desire. How great our responsibility, how immense our task, how priceless the advantages that we can reap!

I cannot refrain, however, from giving expression to my gratification and appreciation of the substantial and continued support already accorded, and in particular during the past year by the believers in the United States and Canada, under the wise and judicious direction of their elected national representatives, to the Plan of Unified Action, whose declared purpose is to insure, ere the present Bahá'í year comes to a close, the raising of the funds required for the building of the first Unit of the Mashriqu'l-Adhkár. The vigilance and fidelity with which the National Assembly of the United States and Canada has observed its pledge in connection with the limitation of the current administrative expenses of the Cause, and the zeal and ready response manifested by local Assemblies and individual believers to curtail their local and personal expenditures in order to concentrate on the Temple Fund, are worthy of the highest praise, and will deservedly attract the manifold blessings of a loving and bountiful Master. Much indeed has been accomplished during this past year of concentrated and consecrated self-sacrifice for so glorious a purpose. Much more still remains unachieved if we are to vindicate, in the eyes of an expectant world, the honourable name, the inexhaustible and miraculous vitality of the Revelation of Bahá'u'lláh.

In the mid-watches of the night, commemorating the passing of Him Who with His own hands laid the head-cornerstone of His Father's House of Worship in that land, seated within the hallowed precincts of His shrine, and keeping vigil in the company of His closest companions, I have more than once in the midst of my devotions prayerfully remembered those chosen ones of God on whose shoulders has fallen so weighty a responsibility, whose destiny is to bring to full fruition so excellent a heritage. I have recalled on that peaceful and moonlit night, with much emotion and gratitude, the inestimable bounties He lavished while on earth upon you. I have revived in my memory the glowing promises that His unfailing guidance and gracious assistance would continue from His station on high to be showered upon you. I have pictured in my mind that beauteous vision of a Cause unfolded in all its glory which in His immortal writings He has revealed unto you. And with my head upon His threshold, I have prayed and prayed again that we may all prove ourselves worthy disciples of so gracious a Master, that we may, when called unto Him, transmit, undiminished and unimpaired, our share of the immeasurably precious heritage bequeathed by Him to us all.

And in closing, dearly-beloved friends, what more appropriate thought with which to conclude my fervent plea than these pregnant words fallen from the lips of Bahá'u'lláh: "O My friends! I bear witness that the Divine Bounty has been vouchsafed unto you, His Argument has been made manifest, His Proof has been revealed and His Guidance has shone forth upon you. Let it now be seen what your endeavours in the path of renunciation can reveal."

Your true brother,
Shoghi

6 December 1928*

To the beloved of the Lord and the handmaids of the Merciful throughout the East and West.

*Printed also in "Bahá'í Administration".

Dear fellow-workers,

I desire to convey to you in a few words my impressions of the recently published "Bahá'í World", copies of which, I understand, have already, thanks to the assiduous care and indefatigable efforts displayed by the Publishing Committee of the American National Spiritual Assembly, been widely distributed among the Bahá'í countries of East and West.

This unique record of world-wide Bahá'í activity attempts to present to the general public, as well as to the student and scholar, those historical facts and fundamental principles that constitute the distinguishing features of the Message of Bahá'u'lláh to this age. I have ever since its inception taken a keen and sustained interest in its development, have personally participated in the collection of its material, the arrangement of its contents, and the close scrutiny of whatever data it contains.

I confidently and emphatically recommend it to every thoughtful and eager follower of the Faith, whether in the East or in the West, whose desire is to place in the hands of the critical and intelligent inquirer, of whatever class, creed or colour, a work that can truly witness to the high purpose, the moving history, the enduring achievements, the resistless march and infinite prospects of the Revelation of Bahá'u'lláh. Eminently readable and attractive in its features, reliable and authoritative in the material it contains, up-to-date, comprehensive and accurate in the mass of information it gives, concise and persuasive in its treatment of the fundamental aspects of the Cause, thoroughly representative in the illustrations and photographs it reveals—it stands unexcelled and unapproached by any publication of its kind in the varied literature of our beloved Cause. It will, without the slightest doubt, if generously and vigorously supported, arouse unprecedented interest among all classes of civilised society.

I earnestly request you, dearly-beloved friends, to exert the utmost effort for the prompt and widespread circulation of a book that so faithfully and vividly portrays, in all its essential features, its far-reaching ramifications and most arresting aspects, the all-encompassing Faith of Bahá'u'lláh. Whatever assistance, financial or moral, extended by Bahá'í Spiritual Assemblies and individual believers, to those who have been responsible for such a highly valuable and representative production will, it should be remembered, be directly utilised to advance the interests and reinforce the funds that are being raised in behalf of the Ma*sh*riqu'l-A*dh*kár, and will indirectly serve to exert a most powerful stimulus in removing the malicious misrepresentations and unfortunate misunderstandings that have so long and so grievously clouded the luminous Faith of Bahá'u'lláh.

Your true brother,
Shoghi

21 December 1928*

To the beloved of the Lord and the handmaids of the Merciful throughout the West.

Dearly-beloved brothers and sisters in 'Abdu'l-Bahá!

With feelings of profound sorrow I am moved to address you these few lines mourning the loss which the Cause has undoubtedly sustained by the passing of one who, for many years and in circumstances of exceptional significance, rendered the sacred Threshold distinctive and inestimable services. The hand of Divine Decree has removed, by the death of our talented and dearly-beloved friend, Mr. Hippolyte Dreyfus-Barney, yet another outstanding figure in the Cause of Bahá'u'lláh, who, by his brilliant gifts of mind and heart as well as by the divers achievements of his life, has truly enriched the annals of God's immortal Faith.

A pioneer of the Cause of Bahá'u'lláh ever since its celestial light first warmed and illuminated the West, he has, by his close association with the person of 'Abdu'l-Bahá, by his contact with all sections of society, by his scholarly presentation of the history and fundamentals of the Faith, and lastly by his unforgettable share in the settlement of the complex and pressing issues that called for expert assistance in the days following 'Abdu'l-Bahá's passing, achieved a standing which few have as yet attained.

The days of his spiritual communion with 'Abdu'l-Bahá and His household within the walls of the prison-city of 'Akká, wherein he imbibed the principles which he later so ably expounded to the peoples of the West; his pre-eminent role on his return to Paris in kindling the torch which is destined to shed eternal illumination upon his native land and its people; the links of abiding fellowship which he forged with our Persian brethren in the course of the historic mission entrusted

---

*Printed also in "Bahá'í Administration".

to his charge by our Beloved; the seeds which he scattered far and wide during his subsequent travels to the heart of Asia, throughout India, beyond the remotest villages of Burma and as far as the eastern confines of Indo-China; the able support he lent in its initial and intermediary stages to the case of Bahá'u'lláh's house in Baghdád; his unhesitating intervention with State officials in paving the way for the ultimate emancipation of our Egyptian brethren from the yoke of orthodox Islám; the stimulating encouragement his visit caused to the Bahá'í community of Tunis on the northern shores of Africa; and last but not least the ability and diligence with which he applied himself to the solution of the delicate and vexing problems of the Holy Land in the critical years following 'Abdu'l-Bahá's ascension—all stand out as memorable landmarks in a life that was as varied in its international aspects as it was rich in its spiritual experience.

His gifts of unfailing sympathy and penetrating insight, his wide knowledge and mature experience, all of which he utilised for the glory and propagation of the Message of Bahá'u'lláh, will be gratefully remembered by future generations who, as the days go by, will better estimate the abiding value of the responsibilities he shouldered for the introduction and consolidation of the Bahá'í Faith in the Western world.

Suffering as he did in his last days from the effects of a slow and painful illness, he bore heroically his share of the afflictions of the world, and is now in the realms of blissful deliverance partaking his full share of the goodly reward which he certainly deserved. To me, and particularly amid the storm and stress that have agitated my life after 'Abdu'l-Bahá's passing, he was a sustaining and comforting companion, a most valued counsellor, an intimate and trusted friend.

With much emotion and the deepest sense of gratitude I supplicate at the holy Threshold—and request you to join with me in my prayers—for the spiritual advancement in the realms above of a soul who by the sheer merit of the signal services he rendered already deserves to rank highly among the departed faithful.

May he forever rest in peace.

Shoghi

31 December 1928

Not until harmony and concord are firmly established among the friends of London and Manchester will the Cause advance along sound and progressive lines.

May they be guided and inspired to do His Will and achieve His Purpose.

Shoghi

29 August 1929

My dear Mr. Simpson,

I write on behalf of the Guardian with reference to a subject that has lately been raised by the N.S.A. of America, and referred to him—the publication of a revised edition of the "Hidden Words" in England.

Shoghi Effendi has asked me to write to America that in view of the alterations that were lately introduced through the assistance of Miss Rosenberg and Canon Townshend, a new edition of the "Hidden Words" is fully justified and he approves of it. However he does advise that such a publication should not be taken up privately but wholly undertaken by the English N.S.A. and in view of the large stock which the American N.S.A. now holds of the present edition, he would urge that the new edition should be deferred until the American N.S.A. has sold off the bulk of its present stock. In general he would greatly desire and keenly advise better co-operation and co-ordination in the work of the American and English N.S.A. with regard to publication. London, despite its small group has done great work in Bahá'í publications but they must never forget that their market lies unfortunately mainly across the Atlantic. . . .

. . . I hope you have been able to go to Geneva with Mr. Mills. Yours will be an Englishman's sober and matter of fact talk. . . .

27 September 1929*

GUARDIAN WIRES DEEPLY REGRETS INABILITY PARTICIPATE PERSON-

---

*On the occasion of the opening of the new Bahá'í Centre on 19 September, at Walmer House, Regent St., London.

ALLY DEDICATION GATHERING OVERJOYED BRIGHT PROSPECTS LOVING GOOD WISHES, SHOGHI.

BAHÁ'ÍYYIH

(taken from National Spiritual Assembly Minutes of 16 November.)

29 November 1929

My dear Mr. Simpson,
Thank you so much for your letter of Sept. 19th and for the copy of the "Hidden Words" you sent me later.

Evidently enough I kept them until our Guardian's arrival and I now hasten to reply.

While he is well pleased with the booklet as it is now produced, Shoghi Effendi wishes me to express his regret that by appearing so soon, it has rendered the sale of a few thousand copies now in the hands of the American Publications Committee, extremely difficult, if not impossible.

Of course the Guardian appreciates your efforts and understands perfectly your desire to have a more correct and a better printed copy of the work on hand. It is with that view that he is sending enclosed a cheque to the value of £19 for which kindly send him leather bound copies exactly like the specimen you sent.

Shoghi Effendi has returned much refreshed and has again taken up his work with renewed strength. He is much hopeful of your new centre in Regent Street or thereabouts, and he trusts that it will mark a turning point in the history of the Cause in England—from happy tea-parties at individual homes, into a group of less personal but eager, active and thoughtful workers co-operating in a common service. It is a basis upon which healthy progress is possible. . . .

26 December 1929

EARNESTLY APPEAL ENGLISH FRIENDS REINFORCE HEROIC EXERTIONS AMERICAN BRETHREN IN BEHALF MA<u>SH</u>RIQU'L-A<u>DH</u>KÁR.

SHOGHI

January 1930 (Circa)

Through Mrs. Coles†:—

"... I am delighted with your new centre, and will pray at the Holy Shrines from the depths of my heart for its progress. Kindly assure my dear English friends of my heartfelt appreciation of their staunchness, their renewed activity, their self-sacrificing endeavours. I will continue to pray for their individual, as well as their collective efforts, from the bottom of my heart."

Shoghi

Through Miss Challis†:—

"I rejoice to hear of the new centre in London. I will pray for its extension and growth and for the success of your manifold activities..."

Shoghi

Through his Secretary to Sister Challis:—

"Now that the London centre has been transferred to a better locality we hope it will attract more attention and add to the number of attendants at the meetings. We should however, bear in mind that no matter how important the hall may be—the talks given and the unity manifested are of far greater significance."

"Shoghi Effendi has a special affection for the English friends, for he has been in their midst and knows most of them personally. He therefore wishes and prays fervently that their number may increase, and that they may render distinguished services to the Cause. Please assure them all of his prayers and extend to them his loving greetings."

(Taken from National Spiritual Assembly Minutes of 8 January 1930)

31 January 1930

With regard to change in the official title of the N.S.A. he is pleased that the matter has been definitely decided.

(i.e.—"National Spiritual Assembly of the Bahá'ís of the British Isles.")

In connection with the important question of collating and editing the Master's Tablets to the friends in the British Isles . . . Shoghi Effendi has already wired his reply.

(i.e.—Cablegram Haifa February 3 1930—
"WELCOME TOWNSHEND'S SPLENDID SUGGESTION REGARDING COLLECTION TABLETS, ADVISE SEND ORIGINALS TO HIM FOR PRESENT.")

Shoghi Effendi wants me to express his pleasure over such an undertaking, and he sincerely trusts that it will result into a splendid achievement for posterity—a mine of endless knowledge, illumination, and insight into Bahá'í teachings and outlook.

He wishes me to add that whereas he welcomes the work on the Tablets the friends have received from the Master he does not wish anything done on notes taken or personal accounts of visits.

The reason for this is the fear that a set of conflicting accounts of the same topic may crop up in various parts of the world from friends who have drawn largely from their memory, or have based their understanding of the Master's opinion or words, upon the imperfect, not to say faulty, renderings of the interpreters of those days.

Such accounts are not only impossible to verify but may lead to much perplexity and constitute a set of traditions that may not prove healthy. . . .

29 April 1930

CONVEY CONVENTION DELEGATES AND FRIENDS ASSEMBLED FEAST OF RIḌVÁN LOVING APPRECIATION REMEMBRANCE HOLY SHRINES.

SHOGHI

20 September 1930

The work of collecting and publishing the Tablets is one of the most important tasks that this generation has undertaken, for upon it depends our true understanding of the Cause and its principles. The more we put it off, the more we are apt to lose some of the original writings. Yet important as this task may be, it is fraught with difficulties. The early translations are far from being accurate, no matter who the translator may be. Shoghi Effendi firmly believes that only Tablets with the Master's signature and in the original tongue should be recognised. Any translations or copies of them fail from having real authority. This shows the importance of collecting the original Tablets that bear the Master's signature.

November 1930

(on the death of Miss Ethel J. Rosenberg, 17 November 1930)

DEEPLY GRIEVED PASSING ROSENBERG ENGLAND'S OUTSTANDING BAHÁ'Í PIONEER WORKER. MEMORY HER GLORIOUS SERVICE WILL NEVER DIE 'ABDU'L-BAHÁ'S FAMILY JOIN ME IN EXPRESSING HEARTFELT CONDOLENCES HER BROTHER RELATIVES URGE FRIENDS HOLD BEFITTING MEMORIAL SERVICE.

SHOGHI

Editor's Note:

From the end of 1930 until early 1934 there are no records of cables or letters from the Guardian. Indeed there are very few references to the Guardian in the scanty Minutes of the National Assembly of that period. These brief Minutes indicate that only five or six short meetings were held each year.

At the meeting of the National Assembly on 12 June, 1932 it was reported that a reply had been received from Shoghi Effendi in answer to a request from a Mr Wren for some confirmation of the Lambeth Resolution on Peace. Another letter from the Guardian was read during the September 11 meeting and it was recorded that the Assembly endorsed Resolution 26 of the Lambeth Conference, 1930 "with the full sanction of Shoghi Effendi".

24 January 1934*

Dear Bahá'í Friend,

At the request of the Guardian I am sending you enclosed the programme of "The New Commonwealth", a society for the promotion of international law and order, having its headquarters in London, and which seems to have a wide and well selected membership. The Guardian wishes the British N.S.A. to consider the possibility of their joining this organisation, and to carefully investigate whether any affiliation with that body involves any political allegiance or may indirectly and eventually lead to participation in any form of political activity. In the contrary case, he strongly advises the N.S.A. to join that organisation, as he feels that in this way the friends can give a wide and effective publicity to the teachings of the Cause. Membership in non-political organisations of this type is, indeed, the best method of teaching indirectly the Message by making useful and frequent contacts with well-known and influential persons who, if not completely won to the Faith, can at least become of some effective use to it.

Trusting that you are in the best of health, and with the assurance of Shoghi Effendi's ardent prayers on your behalf and on behalf of all the friends in London,

Yours in His Service,

11 February 1934

Dear Bahá'í Friend,

Shoghi Effendi wishes me to acknowledge on his behalf the receipt of your letters dated Jan. 20th and Feb. 2nd, 1934, all of which he read with deep interest. He has also received the text of the High Commissioner's reply to your petition.

With regard to the "New Commonwealth" society he would advise the N.S.A. to join it as soon as possible after having carefully ascertained that affiliation with such a body does not involve any political allegiance to any doctrine or group. As you have already stated this organisation is run on non-party lines. It would be, however, advisable that you should find out the real

*Addressed to Mrs. Slade.

aims and objectives of the society and specially the methods it advocates for the carrying out of its ideals before definitely joining it.

The Guardian hopes that this will give the friends a further opportunity to make new contacts, and to draw more competent and sincere people to the Cause. He is fully alive to the difficulties facing the friends at the present time. But he would urge each and all to work harder than ever, and to persevere in order that the Faith may be better appreciated and understood by the public.

He will continue to supplicate on behalf of you all at the Holy Shrines, so that Bahá'u'lláh may sustain you in your efforts to spread His message.

With best wishes for Mr. Slade and yourself,
Yours in His Service,

May the Almighty bless richly your continued and self-sacrificing endeavours, restore your health, cheer your heart, and enable you to promote effectively the vital interests of our beloved Faith.
Your true and grateful brother,
Shoghi

5 May 1934

Dear Bahá'í Friend,

I wish to thank you in the name of the Guardian for your deeply appreciated letter of April 24th, as well as for the article on Jerusalem which appeared in "Time and Tide", all of which he greatly enjoyed reading.

In regard to Mr. Townshend's book* he wishes me to renew his request that your N.S.A. should seriously consider the ways and means for the speedy publication of this highly valuable work, the spread of which cannot but give an unprecedented publicity to the Faith. He values the efforts that have thus far been exerted to this end and particularly appreciates the careful attention you have given the matter and hopes that as a result of these combined efforts something truly substantial will be achieved.

*"Promise of All Ages"

Shoghi Effendi feels rather surprised that no acknowledgment has thus far been made of his last general letter, Feb. 8,* to the believers in the West, a copy of which was forwarded to you as secretary of the N.S.A. Will you please be kind enough to inform him whether the said document has reached you safely.

With the renewed assurance of his best wishes and of his continued supplications for the speedy development of the Cause in your country.

Yours in His Service,

With the assurance of my continued prayers for the extension of the range of your splendid activities and for the success of your constant and high endeavours,
Your true brother,
Shoghi

15 May 1934

Dear Bahá'í Friend,

The Guardian has received and deeply appreciated your message dated May 7th, and was gratified to learn of the results of your national Bahá'í elections. He wishes me to convey to you, and to the remaining officers of the N.S.A. his hearty greetings, and his best wishes for the success and continued expansion of your Bahá'í activities in this year. He is fervently praying for your guidance and assistance in all the various and historic steps you are taking for the spread and the consolidation of the Movement throughout Great Britain.

What the Guardian would strongly urge your National Assembly to do in the next few months is a renewed and decisive effort for the speedy publication of Mr. Townshend's recent book on the Cause. Through the reading of such a challenging and scholarly work many will, undoubtedly, be awakened and stimulated, while others will be infuriated to the extent of virulently attacking the Faith. The unprecedented publicity which the Cause will be thus receiving will in itself constitute an important step towards a wider and fuller recognition of the Movement by distinguished personalities, in both intellectual and social circles. Mr. Townshend's book is, indeed, very timely,

*Published under the title, "The Dispensation of Bahá'u'lláh".

and through it the friends and the non-believers will be given a new vision of the Cause. Shoghi Effendi is hoping that, as a result of his repeated requests, your N.S.A. will be stimulated to renew and persevere in their efforts in this vitally important matter.

With the renewed assurance of his prayers on your behalf and on behalf of the friends in London.

Yours in His Service,

Dear and valued co-worker,

I will fervently pray that the obstacles that stand in your way and which hinder the publication of Canon Townshend's splendid work will be completely and speedily surmounted. I anticipate an outburst of interest and an unprecedented revival of activity as a direct result of the circulation of this notable work—a work which I trust will prove a landmark in the history of the Faith in your land.

Shoghi

2 July 1934

Dear Mrs. Slade,

Shoghi Effendi is pleased to learn, from your letters of June 11th, and 16th, of the new possibilities for the publication of Canon Townshend's book. Realising the number and force of the difficulties which have thus far stood in your way, he cannot indeed but feel gratified that you have at last been able to overcome some of them. He hopes that through your determination to have this valuable booklet published without any further delay some valuable and permanent result will be achieved, and that a few people of capacity and influence will be attracted to the Faith.

In case no publishing firm accepts your offer for the printing of the booklet, the Guardian approves that the N.S.A. should undertake the publication.

Hoping to hear very soon some more definite and encouraging news about this matter, and with the Guardian's best wishes for you and for your collaborators in the N.S.A.

Yours in His Service,

With the renewed assurance of my loving and continued prayers for the success of your unsparing efforts for the spread of His Faith and the consolidation of its institutions,
                              Your true brother,
                                        Shoghi

11 July 1934

Dear Mrs. Slade,

On behalf of the Guardian I wish to acknowledge the receipt of your letter, and to assure you once more of his deepfelt appreciation of your highly-valued efforts for the publication of Canon Townshend's booklet on the Cause. He hopes that the believers the world over will co-operate with your N.S.A. for giving the work the widest publicity possible, and by ordering as many copies as they can for distribution in their own communities. They will surely appreciate, and draw great benefit from, this original and beautifully-written essay of Mr. Townshend, and they will certainly do their best to make it known by the outside world.

Shoghi Effendi wishes you to send him, as soon as the book is published, 150 copies for his library. He will also place some of them in Bahá'u'lláh's Mansion at Bahjí for the benefit of the Bahá'í as well as non-Bahá'í visitors.

With the renewed assurance of his best wishes and of his continued prayers on your behalf.
                              Yours in His Service,

May the Almighty bless your incessant and meritorious endeavours and crown them with unprecedented success,
                              Your true and grateful brother,
                                        Shoghi

2 September 1934

Dear Mrs. Slade,

The Guardian has received and read with much interest your letter of August 9th. It gives him pleasure to learn that the agreement for the publication of Canon Townshend's book has already been signed, and he is looking forward to see the book out of the press within the next few weeks. He hopes that your communications with the American N.S.A. for bringing out an American edition of this same book are proceeding satisfactorily, as he has every reason to believe that the friends in America will do their best to secure for that important publication the widest demand and publicity possible.

Shoghi Effendi would advise that you should also communicate with the N.S.A. of the Bahá'ís of Australia and New Zealand, and with other English speaking Assemblies, groups and individuals, informing them of this new publication, and asking for their assistance in creating for it as wide a demand as possible.

With his renewed greetings and best wishes to you and to all the friends in London,

Yours in His Service,

Dear and valued co-worker,

I have read your letter of May 22 and Aug. 9 with joy and thankfulness as both eloquently testify to your inflexible resolve to promote by every means in your power the best interests of our beloved Cause. I trust and pray that the effect of the publication of the "Promise" will be such as to gladden your heart and reinforce the constant efforts which you have so devotedly exerted in recent years for the propagation of the Faith. I will soon send the cheque for the books I have asked you to send me and which I will distribute as widely as I possibly can.

Your true and grateful brother,
Shoghi

30 September 1934

Dear Mrs. Slade,

The Guardian has directed me to thank you for your welcome letter dated September fifth. The news of the passing away of Mr. Simpson has deeply grieved his heart. He hopes and fervently prays that the Beloved may fully reward him for all the services which he has rendered the Faith in Great Britain, and particularly for the active part which he took during the early days of his association with the Movement, in establishing the Cause of the Administration in that land. May the Almighty enable his soul to progress spiritually in the other world, and may the memory of his earlier services to the Faith sustain and encourage the friends in their labours for the propagation of the Cause in Great Britain.

The Guardian has already written Mr. . . . concerning Mr. . . . gift to the Cause and has expressed his profound appreciation of the suggestion made by him to have his property registered in the name of your National Assembly. This step, he is convinced, would be of great help to your Assembly, in that it would assist in enabling it to obtain full legal recognition from the authorities and thus become an effective and powerful organ for the administration of Bahá'í affairs throughout the British Isles. But, if your Assembly feels that such a step would be premature, he suggests that you should have the property registered in the name of the Palestine Branch of the American N.S.A., until such time as your own Assembly would be in a position to acquire full legal recognition from the British authorities, and will be entitled to hold property in Palestine. In the meantime the American N.S.A. can issue a statement testifying that this property is registered only temporarily in their name, and that as soon as the incorporation is effected they will have it transferred to the name of the National Assembly of the British Isles.

Concerning the material which your Assembly has been requested to provide for the writing of a history of the Cause in England, the Guardian feels the advisability of making as few references to individuals as possible. He further suggests that emphasis be placed on two major events, the Master's visit to England, and the publication of Dr. Esslemont's "New Era" which, indeed, constitutes a real landmark in the history of the Faith in that country.

There is another point to which the Guardian wishes to draw the attention of your N.S.A. It is the importance which national Bahá'í summer schools are acquiring in the development and spread of the Cause. Two of these, as you know, have already been established and are now regularly functioning, that of America with its three branches in Green Acre, Lou-Helen Ranch and Geyserville, and that of Esslingen in Germany which in the last two years has considerably developed, and has attracted the attention of non-German believers throughout the Bahá'í world. The Guardian suggests that pending the establishment of a similar Bahá'í Summer School in England, your Assembly should take into consideration the most effective way in which it can co-operate with the German friends in furthering the interests of their summer school at Esslingen. Meanwhile an effort should be made by our English believers to take the necessary steps for the formation of a similar institution in Great Britain. Many Bahá'í travellers in Europe, mostly American, have had this summer the opportunity of attending meetings and classes of the friends in Esslingen. Mr. and Mrs. Greven, Mrs. Collins, Mr. and Mrs. Bishop representing the Bahá'í Bureau at Geneva. Bahá'ís from Austria and Persia attended. Miss Jack and Mrs. Gregory came specially from the Balkans, and gave detailed reports on the conditions of the Cause in the Balkans. In view of this international importance which the Esslingen summer school is thus acquiring, at least in Europe, the Guardian feels the advisability of your National Assembly being represented at these important gatherings.

In closing I wish to ask you to convey the Guardian's greetings and love to Mr. Aṣgharzádeh who, as you write, seems to be suffering from ill-health. Will you kindly assure him of Shoghi Effendi's prayers for his complete recovery, and express his appreciation of his continued labours for the Cause in London.

With warmest greetings to you and to all the friends,
Yours in His Service,

Dear and valued co-worker:

The utmost effort, I feel, should be exerted to ensure the incorporation of the British National Assembly. Should the authorities require a document setting forth the laws and principles governing the activities of the community, the text of the Declaration of Trust and By-laws now operating in America and adopted by the National Assemblies of Egypt, India and 'Iráq should be presented to them. The text is published in Vol. IV of the "Bahá'í World" and constitutes a pattern for all national Bahá'í constitutions. I would also greatly welcome close collaboration by the believers in England in the development of the very useful and promising summer school recently initiated in Esslingen and which has served this summer as a meeting place of teachers and representatives in Europe.

Your true brother,
Shoghi

22 November 1934

Dear Bahá'í Sister,

Your letters dated September 21st and November 16th have been received and their contents carefully noted by the Guardian.

He has also received the one hundred and fifty copies of "The Promise of All Ages" and wishes me to thank you for them, and to renew his appreciation of your painstaking efforts for the publication of this most timely and singularly penetrating book on the Cause. He hopes and prays that your labours in this connexion may be abundantly rewarded. He has already sent Mr. Townshend a cheque of thirty-five pounds on account of the 150 copies of his book. He hopes the sum will reach him very soon. He would deeply appreciate if you kindly send him copies of the letters of acknowledgment which you receive from those to whom the book has been offered, as in this way he can more or less know of the reaction which the book has produced on the mind of the intellectual public in London and elsewhere.

With regard to Mr. Townshend's suggestion to procure the copyright of the portraits of the Master taken in Paris, Shoghi Effendi fully approves the idea, and would advise you to write the Paris Assembly about it and to try to enlist their co-operation and help in this matter.

The Guardian also wishes to express his whole-hearted approval of the steps your National Assembly is taking for incorporating their Assembly as a duly recognised religious body in England and throughout the British Isles. He would suggest that in case the authorities refuse to recognise the N.S.A. as a religious society you should insist on having it temporarily registered as a commercial body or under any other designation. He requests you to send him copies of the registration documents as soon as they are ready, as he intends to take the necessary steps for the establishment of a Palestine Branch of your National Assembly similar to that which the American N.S.A. now possesses in Palestine.

With his fervent prayers and loving greetings to you and to all the friends in London,

Yours in His Service,

Dear and valued co-worker:
The books you have sent me are being widely distributed and I am

sure they will serve to stimulate genuine interest in the fundamentals of the Faith. A special and sustained effort, I feel, should be exerted by your National Assembly in order to ensure that copies of this brilliant production may reach most, if not all the Bahá'í centres throughout the East and West and may be made accessible to the most influential leaders and organisations in every continent of the Globe. The success it can achieve largely depends upon the publicity which the continued and organised endeavours of your Assembly can now accord it.
      Praying for your success and protection.
               Your true brother,
                  Shoghi

17 December 1934

Dear Mrs. Slade,
 The Guardian has directed me to thank you for your welcome letter dated December 8th, and also for the undated one just received.
 In regard to his money order for the 150 copies of the "Promise of All Ages", he wishes you to offer the remaining sum to your National Assembly for the purposes of their national fund.
 He is pleased to learn that the editor of "The Times' Literary Supplement" has accepted to have Canon Townshend's book reviewed in his paper. He trusts that the result will be such as to stimulate many people to buy this volume, and to carefully and seriously study and meditate upon its contents.
 With reference to Mr. . . . property on Mt. Carmel, the Guardian specially requests you to proceed quickly in the matter of your National Assembly's incorporation so as to enable him to establish a branch of that Assembly in Palestine and thus make possible the registration of the land in question in the name of the British N.S.A. The land is completely safe-guarded at present.
 He would deeply appreciate if you send him photostatic copies of the registration documents as soon as they will be ready.
 In this connection, the Guardian wishes me to draw once more your attention to the importance of following, in the adoption of your Assembly's constitution, complete and exact wording of the text of the Declaration of Trust and By-Laws of

the American N.S.A., with due consideration however to all local conditions which may necessitate some minor departure from the original American copy.

It will interest you to know that the N.S.A. of the Bahá'ís of India and Burma have carefully followed the constitutions adopted by the American believers, both in the local and the national sphere, and have succeeded in registering their National Assembly as a legal body empowered to administer the affairs of the Cause throughout India and Burma. The Guardian is now engaged in establishing a branch of the Indian N.S.A. in Palestine. The National Assemblies of Egypt, 'Iráq and Persia have likewise adopted without any alteration whatever the text of the American constitution as a pattern for their local as well as national regulations and by-laws.

Yours in His Service,

May the Almighty enable you to surmount all the obstacles that stand in your path and accomplish the great project which you are initiating, and establish your manifold administrative activities on a sound, permanent and unassailable basis.

Your true and grateful brother,
Shoghi

27 December 1934

Dear Mrs. Slade,

The Guardian has directed me to send you enclosed a copy of the Declaration of Trust and By-Laws of the National Spiritual Assembly of the Bahá'ís of India and Burma.

You will find, after going carefully over the text, that except for Article VIII which is being amended, it is fully identical with the constitution adopted by the American N.S.A., and as such is in close conformity with the principles laid down by the Guardian concerning national Bahá'í constitutions throughout the world.

He feels it his duty, now that your N.S.A. is taking steps for its formal registration in the Government, to earnestly request you to adopt, in its entirety and without any alteration, the full text of the constitution of the American N.S.A. so as to maintain the necessary uniformity in the essential principles of the Administrative Order. Whatever is not specified in the text of this national constitution, the Guardian has already explained to the National Assemblies of America, India, Egypt, 'Iráq and Persia, is to be left to the discretion of these Assemblies. He does not object if there be any differences in these secondary matters, but he feels that he should insist on uniformity in essentials. Diversity in unity—which is so vital and basic a principle of the Movement—would thereby be maintained.

With heartiest greetings to you and to all the friends,
Yours in His Service,

15 February 1935

Dear Mrs. Slade,

I am directed by the Guardian to thank you for your letters of the fourth of January last and of the seventh of this month, all of which he has read with deepest interest.

He was, however, grieved to learn of the slight indisposition in your health, and particularly of the serious illness of Miss Elsie Lea. He is praying for you both at the Holy Shrines that you may be given the necessary strength to resume your work for the Cause in London.

With regard to the situation in Persia, it is pretty bad indeed. Conditions have not improved in the slightest degree, and the friends are still suffering from the intolerable burden of restrictions imposed upon them by the Authorities. The Guardian does not advise your Assembly to enter into detailed correspondence with any of the friends there, but sees no objection if you send them copies of your News Letters. . . .

The friends will no doubt appreciate the possibilities which the admission of so distinguished a person as . . . in their midst will have for the Cause. This new development should, indeed, encourage and stimulate them to persevere, nay to redouble their efforts for the extension of their teaching activities throughout Great Britain. The future of the Cause in that country is, indeed, bright. But the friends should also exert their utmost, lest through neglect and apathy its progress be impeded. Now that such a wonderful opportunity has presented itself to them, it is their responsibility to take their full chance and to make a renewed attempt to extend and further consolidate their teaching work in London and throughout the British Isles.

Shoghi Effendi is fervently praying that through the confirmations and blessings of Bahá'u'lláh you may all be assisted in effectively attaining this objective.

Yours in His Service,

Dear and valued co-worker:
I am so pleased to learn of the splendid response of . . . to the call of our Faith, and would urge you to make a special effort, in conjunction with the friends and Assemblies in England, to aid him to deepen his faith and extend the scope of his valued activities. I will pray for the success of your efforts and the realisation of your highest hopes.
Your true and grateful brother,
Shoghi

7 April 1935

Dear Mrs. Slade,
   Shoghi Effendi has received your letters dated March 8th and April 1st, and wishes me to thank you for them.
   With regard to the incorporation of the British N.S.A., he is sorry, indeed, that the authorities have definitely refused your application. He is, nevertheless, confident that your Assembly's efforts in this connection will, in due time, bear fruit, and that the officials concerned will gradually come to alter their views regarding the nature and significance of the Movement.
   In the meantime, the Guardian can have . . . property on Mt. Carmel transferred to the name of the Palestine Branch of the American N.S.A.
   With the renewed expression of Shoghi Effendi's deepfelt appreciation of your services, and with his loving greetings and best wishes to you and to the friends in London. . . .

Dear co-worker,
I grieve to learn of the refusal of the Board of Trade to incorporate the National Assembly, but I feel certain that the friends will not allow this setback to damp their zeal or to weaken their determination

to prosecute the work they have so devotedly undertaken. It may indeed prove a blessing in disguise, and I would urge the friends to persevere and not to lose heart and to rest assured that our beloved Faith will ultimately conquer.

With my best wishes for all of you,
Shoghi

9 December 1935

Dear Mrs. Slade,

The Guardian has just received letters from Sir Herbert Samuel and Sir Francis Younghusband inviting him to attend and present a paper on the subject: How to promote the spirit of World Fellowship through religion at the projected conference of the "World Fellowship Through Religion" to be held in London this coming July.

As he is unable to be present at this meeting, he has thought best to ask the British N.S.A. to act as his representatives, and to appoint someone to read this paper which he is asking Mr. Townshend to prepare for that occasion. He is specially writing Mr. Townshend about it, and urging him to have the statement ready by the end of January, when it has to be handed by your N.S.A. to Sir Francis Younghusband according to his request from the Guardian.

He also thinks it necessary for your Assembly to communicate as promptly as you can with Sir F. Younghusband, and to express your readiness and pleasure to participate in the activities and deliberations of the World Fellowship conference.

In view of the vital importance of this gathering, at which representatives of various religious organisations will be present, and specially as Sir Herbert Samuel has himself expressed the desire that the Cause should be authoritatively and adequately represented there, Shoghi Effendi would urge the British N.S.A. to make every effort to fully avail themselves of this splendid opportunity for giving the Faith in England a fresh and unprecedented impetus.

Wishing you complete success in your labours in this connection, and awaiting the news of the progress of the action that you will take in this matter,

Yours in His Service,

26 December 1935

Dear Mrs. Slade,

This letter is to confirm the one I wrote you nearly two weeks ago at the direction of the Guardian regarding the projected World Congress of Faiths to be held in London next summer.

As stated in that letter, the Guardian has whole-heartedly accepted the Committee's invitation, as expressed through both Sir Herbert Samuel and Sir Francis Younghusband, to have the Cause authoritatively represented at the above-mentioned Congress.

He now wishes to urge again your N.S.A. to speed up the matter of preparing the address which he has requested Mr. Townshend to prepare for that occasion. He is also urging Mr. Townshend to have the address ready for presentation to the Committee towards the end of next January.

The Guardian hopes that the N.S.A. will do its very best to speed up this matter.

With his renewed thanks to you and to the friends,

Yours in His Service,

13 March 1936

Dear Mrs. Slade,

The Guardian has just sent you a cable asking you to send him, as soon as you can, two copies of the photograph of the N.S.A. of the British Isles of the year 1935–36 for publication in Volume Six of the "Bahá'í World". He hopes there will be no delay in forwarding to him these photographs.

Thanking you in anticipation,
Yours in His Service,

16 March 1936

Dear Mrs. Slade,

The Guardian has been very pleased to learn, from the report you have submitted for the next issue of the "Bahá'í World" regarding the activities of the Cause in England, that the centre in London has been given by the authorities the status of a place of worship, and that the Movement has been registered as a definite religious community.

If there are any documents or any letters you have obtained from the Government in connection with such a registration will you kindly send him reproductions of them as promptly as you can for publication in the next issue of the "Bahá'í World" (Vol. VI).

With many thanks and warmest greetings,

Yours in His Service,

April 1936

The National Teaching Committee of the N.S.A. of the British Isles.

Dear Bahá'í Friends,

The Guardian has read with profoundest interest the second number of the "Teaching Bulletin" issued by the N.S.A. of the Bahá'ís of the British Isles, and feels highly gratified at the steps your committee is taking for the inauguration of a new teaching campaign throughout England. This is surely a clear evidence of the new spirit animating the friends in that country, and a further revelation of their intense desire to give the cause of teaching a fresh and unprecedented stimulus. There is undoubtedly no higher call than that of bringing the Message to a world tormented and torn on every side by the forces of destructive materialism. It is for us to realise the full measure of responsibility that has been laid upon our shoulders in this matter, and having attained full consciousness of our responsibility to unitedly arise to contribute all that we can towards its discharge.

It is Shoghi Effendi's hope that under the guidance and encouragement of the N.S.A. your committee's work will steadily progress, and that the results achieved will be such as to create further confidence and arouse fresh hopes in your activities among all the friends throughout the British Isles. He is looking eagerly forward to learn more of your activities, and to witness further signs of the effectiveness, unity and power with which

you are striving to diffuse the Teachings and principles of the Cause.
May the Almighty ever bless and sustain you in your labours....

27 April 1936 (Convention)

DEEPLY APPRECIATE MESSAGE FERVENTLY PRAYING SUCCESS DELIBERATIONS LOVE.

SHOGHI

3 May 1936

The National Teaching Committee of the N.S.A. of the British Isles.

Dear friends and co-workers,

The Guardian has instructed me to convey to you his deep gratitude for your welcome message of April 21st. He has been made truly happy by its perusal and wishes me to express once more his genuine appreciation of the remarkable work which your committee is accomplishing for the spread of the Message throughout England. He wishes you full success in your labours, and is praying to Bahá'u'lláh to guide and assist you in every step you are taking for the dissemination of His Teachings and the establishment of His Faith in your country.

His chief advice to you is perseverance without which, he strongly feels, no success is attainable. The difficulties in your way are undoubtedly manifold and not always easy to overcome. But provided you persevere, and face with courage, full faith and confidence such obstacles you can be sure of attaining the goal you have set yourselves to achieve.

Now is the beginning of your work. And as in the beginning of every task you are bound to meet all sorts of difficulties. The more you strive to overcome these, the greater will be your reward, and the nearer you will get to that glorious success which, as repeatedly promised by Bahá'u'lláh, must needs crown the efforts of all those who, whole-heartedly and with pure detachment, strive to work for the spread and establishment of His Cause.

With cordial greetings and every good wish ...

With the renewed assurance of my loving and constant prayers for the extension of your meritorious activities and services,
Your true brother,
Shoghi

9 May 1936

Dear Mr. Hofman†,

The Guardian has duly received your letter of April 29th written at the direction of the N.S.A. of the British Isles, and he wishes me to thank you for it.

He has learned with deep satisfaction of the result of your national elections, and has instructed me to convey to each and every member of your newly elected assembly his hearty congratulations and sincere good wishes. He hopes that the officers of the N.S.A. will be fully guided in the discharge of their manifold and heavy responsibilities, and that through their collective and sustained efforts the Cause will receive a fresh and unprecedented impetus throughout England. He is praying from the very depth of his heart on behalf of you all, entreating Bahá'u'lláh to ever bless, sustain and guide you in your labours.

The Guardian would deeply appreciate receiving the minutes of the N.S.A. meetings, and hopes that you will send these to him as regularly as you can.

With his renewed and most loving greetings, also to the members of the N.S.A....

Wishing you the fullest success in your high and deeply appreciated endeavours,
Your true brother,
Shoghi

3 September 1936

Beloved Bahá'í Brother,
   Your welcome letter of August 7th together with the enclosed programme of the English Bahá'í Summer School and Mrs. Bishop's notes on the Bahá'í session of the World Fellowship of Faiths Congress have all duly arrived and been read with sustained interest and deepest appreciation by our beloved Guardian.
   He has been particularly pleased to read Mrs. Bishop's report which is truly illuminating and highly encouraging. The Cause has no doubt been well represented at the Congress, and the attendants must have surely been deeply impressed by the manner in which the Message was introduced and presented by both the Bahá'í and non-Bahá'í speakers.
   The Guardian feels particularly grateful for the share which your N.S.A., as well as your distinguished and able co-workers Mrs. Bishop and Madame Orlova have contributed towards the success of the Bahá'í meeting. May the noble efforts which you all have so unitedly and so successfully exerted in this connection serve to attract, even as a magnet, the blessings of God and His favours upon the entire community of the believers throughout the British Isles.
   With every good wish and hearty greetings to you, and to your fellow-members in the N.S.A....

Dearest co-workers,
   I rejoice to learn of the splendid work that has recently been achieved. Your accomplishments should spur you on to achieve still greater results in both the teaching and administrative spheres of Bahá'í service. My prayers will be offered on your behalf. The work in which you are so devotedly engaged is near and dear to my heart. Persevere and never feel disheartened.

Affectionately,
Shoghi

17 October 1936

Dear Mr. Hofman,
   I am directed by our beloved Guardian to acknowledge with thanks the receipt of your letter dated August 25th with the

enclosed minutes of the British N.S.A.'s last meeting. He has read them all with utmost care and profoundest appreciation.

Regarding your Summer School; he is indeed grateful to your Assembly for the great success that has attended your efforts for the formation of this institution, the teaching value of which for England cannot be overestimated. He wishes, in particular, to offer his most sincere thanks to the Bahá'í youth group in London for their remarkable share in making the school such an outstanding success this year. This has been certainly a bold undertaking, considering the limited number and resources of the believers in England. But the results obtained are highly encouraging and augur well for the future of this first English Bahá'í Summer School. The unity, courage and whole-hearted loyalty of the friends have enabled them to boldly face and successfully overcome the difficulties and obstacles which may have first appeared, to many at least, to be quite unsurmountable. The Guardian would, therefore, urge all the believers to persevere in their efforts for raising the standard, both intellectual and spiritual, of their Summer School and to heighten its prestige in the eyes of the friends, and of the general non-Bahá'í public outside. The institution of the Summer School constitutes a vital and inseparable part of any teaching campaign, and as such ought to be given the full importance it deserves in the teaching plans and activities of the believers. It should be organised in such a way as to attract the attention of the non-believers to the Cause and thus become an effective medium for teaching. Also it should afford the believers themselves an opportunity to deepen their knowledge of the Teachings, through lectures and discussions and by means of close and intense community life.

As regards the N.S.A.'s request concerning Mrs. Bishop's teaching services in England, the Guardian wishes you to assure your fellow-members of his hearty approval of their suggestion that she should extend her stay in your country for another year. He is advising her to visit Geneva for a brief period and then return immediately back to England. . . .

Dearest co-worker,
I wish to congratulate in person the English believers, and particularly the members of the youth group, on their splendid achievements. The activities they have initiated, the perseverance, zeal

and fidelity they have increasingly manifested, the plans they have conceived and the obstacles they have already overcome, rejoice my heart and arouse fresh hopes and expectations within me. I will continue to pray for their success. Rest assured and persevere.

Affectionately,
Shoghi

2 December 1936

Dear Bahá'í Friend,

Your kind letter of November 22nd with enclosures have been read with deep interest and profound gratitude by our beloved Guardian, and their contents have imparted fresh encouragement to his heart. He has also received your communication of the 28th September with the accompanying minutes of the British N.S.A. and the report of your Summer School, and is indeed sorry for the long delay in thanking you for them.

Regarding Mr. Townshend, the Guardian is pleased to hear that he has written you, and offered a method whereby he could be freed to serve the Faith. He is confident that your N.S.A. will give this matter their most careful and sympathetic consideration, and fervently hopes that they will, as a result, be able to find some way that would relieve Mr. Townshend of his many domestic cares and troubles which, as you know only too well, seriously impede the progress and expansion of his activities for the Faith.

It is a matter of deep regret, indeed, that our dear friend's material position is such as to make it quite impossible for him to devote his full time and energies to the Cause. The friends in Great Britain, who are in special need of his able assistance in their teaching work, should, therefore, consider it their responsibility to find some solution to this urgent problem facing one of their most distinguished and competent fellow-workers.

Any suggestion which your N.S.A. could offer would certainly be deeply appreciated by Mr. Townshend, and the Guardian would be only too pleased to assist your Assembly in insuring the success of any plan you may propose and decide upon in this matter.

Wishing you full and continued success in your work, and assuring you again of Shoghi Effendi's fervent prayers on your behalf and on behalf of your fellow-members in the N.S.A....

Dear and prized co-worker,
Your splendid collaboration with the English believers is, as I am gradually and increasingly realising it, infusing a new life and a fresh determination into individuals and assemblies which will prove of the utmost benefit to our beloved Cause. Persevere in your remarkable efforts and historic achievements. With the aid of Mrs. Bishop an unprecedented and most powerful impetus will I am sure be given to the onward march of the Cause of God. I am deeply grateful to you.
Your true brother,
Shoghi

10 January 1937

Beloved Bahá'í Brother,
The Guardian has instructed me to inform you of the receipt of your communications of the 6th and 24th December and of the 1st January, all of which he has read, together with their enclosures, with sustained interest. Kindly convey to your fellow-members in the N.S.A. his appreciation and gratitude for the truly valuable work they are accomplishing for the promotion of the Faith in Great Britain. He is continually and fervently praying for the guidance and success of the plans they have recently initiated for the extension of the teaching work and for the consolidation of the administrative institutions of the Cause in their land.

The Guardian is specially praying for the success of your N.S.A.'s project in connection with Mr. Townshend's problem. Much as he realises the financial difficulties involved in such a plan, he is nevertheless convinced that if every individual believer, no matter how limited his resources, pledges himself to give it his whole-hearted and continued support it will eventually, though after considerable effort and self-sacrifice, become effective and successful. The opportunity has now come for the friends in Great Britain to demonstrate the measure of their devotion to the Cause, as well as their capacity to maintain, consolidate and extend its nascent administrative institutions in that land. The occasion calls for a tremendous amount of sacrifice, of perseverance and united labour on the part of the friends, and for the self-same devotion that characterised the nation-wide efforts of the American believers for the building up of their beloved Temple at Wilmette. May the friends in Great Britain, despite their limited numbers and resources, be guided and assisted to successfully meet this challenge. Their triumph will assuredly draw upon them the blessings and confirmations of Bahá'u'lláh, and may prove to be the signal for fresh conquests and unprecedented developments in the Cause throughout the British Isles.

Regarding the New Commonwealth Society, the Guardian does not wish the friends, whether individually or collectively, to affiliate themselves with this and other kindred organisations, in view of the fact that the aims and ideals upheld by such bodies do not entirely conform to the Teachings, and hence there is always the possibility of creating complications for the Cause by accepting membership in them.

However, as the New Commonwealth Society is nearer to the Cause than perhaps any other organisation of its kind, the Guardian would advise the friends to participate, occasionally and in an informal manner, in its activities, to attend some of its meetings, and to contribute articles to its publications. Association, as you certainly realise, is quite different from affiliation, and it is the latter which the Guardian wishes the friends to strictly avoid.

With his warmest greetings and sincere good wishes to you and your fellow-members in the N.S.A. . . .

With the renewed assurance of my continued, my loving and ardent prayers for the expansion and the consolidation of the splendid work which the English believers are unitedly accomplishing for the furtherance of the Cause of Bahá'u'lláh,
Your true brother,
Shoghi

24 February 1937

Beloved Bahá'í Brother,

I am directed by the Guardian to acknowledge the receipt of

your welcome communications of the 19th January and the enclosed latest number of the "Bahá'í Journal" issued by the British N.S.A., and to transmit to you, and through you to your distinguished collaborators in that body, his admiration and gratitude for the quick action you have been prompted to take in connection with the formation of a Publishing Company under the direction of your National Assembly.

The plan you have conceived is certainly bold, knowing how limited are the number and resources of the believers in England. But it nevertheless offers great possibilities of development and success, provided your Assembly gives it full moral and financial support, and succeeds in stimulating the interest and obtaining the assistance of the believers outside Great Britain for its immediate and effective prosecution.

In this connection, he wishes you to assure the N.S.A. of his whole-hearted and full approval of their suggestion to solicit subscriptions from the Bahá'ís of those countries who normally order literature from them. He feels it, indeed, to be the duty of every believer who has the means, and has also the interest of the Cause at heart, to assist in any capacity, and to any extent he can, in carrying out the British N.S.A.'s project. Nothing can demonstrate more effectively the spirit of solidarity and self-sacrifice which should animate the friends than their response to this call. Aside from the fact that London is the heart of the British Empire, and as such commands an importance which few other centres in the world can equal and should consequently be raised to the status of one of the leading outposts of the Faith, it should be stated that now that the Administrative Order has at last been firmly established and is being increasingly consolidated in that centre, it is the supreme obligation of all the believers, both in Great Britain and other European countries, to assist by every means in hastening this internal development and growth. And it is quite evident that the formation of a Publishing Company along the lines suggested by the British N.S.A. is the greatest asset to such a development and expansion of the Cause in London and throughout England as a whole.

It is the Guardian's hope that the response which the friends will make to this project will be such as to mark the inauguration of a new era of expansion of the Cause throughout the British Isles, and the rest of the far-flung British Empire. He would appeal to every believer to carefully ponder upon the responsibilities which he is called upon to shoulder in order to meet this supreme and vital obligation.

5 March 1937*

Dear and prized co-worker,
  Your subsequent letters dated Jan. 29th enclosing the minutes of the National Assembly meeting, and February 26th enclosing copy of the Bahá'í Journal No. 5 have also reached me and have filled my heart with joy and gratitude for the splendid services of your Assembly and the efforts they are systematically and vigorously exerting for the initiation, the expansion and consolidation of Bahá'í administrative activities and enterprises at this auspicious stage in the evolution of the Faith in your country. I fully approve the publication in your Journal of the passages quoted in your letter of February 26th. I am enclosing the sum of £50 as my contribution towards the Fund which is being raised for the establishment of the Publishing Company for the success of which I cherish the brightest hopes. I will especially pray for the removal of every obstacle that may impede its formation and development, and for the realisation of your highest hopes in this connection. Persevere in your great enterprise, and rest assured that the almighty power of Bahá'u'lláh will, if you remain steadfast in your purpose, enable you to attain your goal.
  Your true and grateful brother,
  Shoghi

25 March 1937

ANNOUNCE ASSEMBLIES CELEBRATION MARRIAGE BELOVED GUARDIAN IMPERISHABLE HONOUR BESTOWED UPON HANDMAID OF BAHÁ'U'LLÁH RUḤÍYYIH KHÁNUM MISS MARY MAXWELL.
  (Sgd. ZÍAIYYIH, MOTHER OF THE GUARDIAN)

2 April 1937

GREATLY VALUE MESSAGE ABIDING LOVE.
  SHOGHI

*Added as footnote to letter of February 24th.

1 May 1937

Dear Mr. Hofman,

I am charged by our beloved Guardian to acknowledge the receipt of your communications of March 21st, 31st and of April 22nd with enclosures.

He has received and read with particular interest the latest issue of the Journal issued by the British N.S.A. and is indeed happy to realise that the teaching work, now so ably reinforced by the valuable support extended to it by dear Mrs. Bishop, is steadily progressing in England. He is most pleased over the progress of the Devonshire Group, and wishes you to assure its members, and particularly Mrs. Stevens†, of his deep appreciation of their efforts for the propagation of the Message in that highly promising centre from which, he hopes, the light of the Cause will radiate throughout South Western England which has heretofore remained closed to the Faith. He would urge your N.S.A. to continue giving your attention to the problem of finding ways and means to further widen the interest that has been aroused, and is fervently praying that your efforts in this connection may bear the richest and most satisfactory results.

Concerning the N.S.A.'s Publishing Fund; the Guardian has learned with satisfaction that the friends are gradually awakening to the realisation that it constitutes an invaluable support to the extension of the teaching work throughout the British Isles. He hopes that the flow of contributions will steadily increase, so as to enable your Assembly to carry out its important project. He is rejoiced to hear that you have taken the necessary steps to have the Company legally established—which step, he hopes, will pave the way for the registration of the N.S.A. as an independent religious organisation. . . .

With the assurance of my continued prayers for the realisation of your highest hopes, and for the uninterrupted progress and consolidation of your teaching and administrative activities,

Your true brother,
Shoghi

3 May 1937 (Convention)

ASSURE DELEGATES FRIENDS LOVING APPRECIATION REMEMBRANCE HOLY SHRINES SUPPLICATING UNPRECEDENTED SUCCESS TEACHING FIELD ADMINISTRATIVE ACTIVITIES.

SHOGHI

10 July 1937

Dear Mr. Hofman,

I am charged by our beloved Guardian to acknowledge the receipt of your communications of May 3rd and 29th written on behalf of the British N.S.A.

The enclosed copy of the Annual Report, as well as the minutes of the N.S.A. meeting of the 13th May have also reached him and he has read their contents with deepest satisfaction.

With regard to your Assembly's request for permission to publish in the "Bahá'í Journal" an extract from his letter of April 24th addressed to Miss Baxter†, he wishes you to assure your fellow members of his approval of their request.

With his loving Bahá'í greetings and with his renewed and abiding appreciation of your labours for the Cause....

Dear and valued co-worker,

Your letter of June 24th has also been received. I feel the urge to add these few words in person in order to assure you afresh of my deep appreciation of the remarkable spirit of constancy, devotion and loyalty which you and your fellow workers, in both the teaching and administrative spheres of Bahá'í service are ably and continually manifesting. My heart overflows with unspeakable gratitude. I will continue to pray for all of you from the depths of my heart.

Shoghi

7 September 1937

Dear Bahá'í Brother,

On behalf of our beloved Guardian I acknowledge with thanks the receipt of your letter of the 17th August enclosing the minutes of the meeting of the British N.S.A. held at the Summer School on August 8th. . . .

May the Beloved bless your persistent efforts and enable you to consolidate still further the manifold interests of the Faith of God.
Your true and grateful brother,
Shoghi

16 November 1937

Beloved Bahá'í Brother,

I am charged by the Guardian to acknowledge the receipt of your communications of September 26th and November 6th with enclosures, all of which he has read with deepest interest and appreciation.

He very much regrets indeed the departure of Mrs. Bishop and Madame Orlova from England, as the services they rendered all through their stay in that country have been truly outstanding. The teaching force, in particular, will feel the loss of these two of its most capable and promising supporters. Every effort should now be exerted by the N.S.A. however, to carry on the teaching work through every means possible, and every believer should be made to realise that he has an added and most grave responsibility to shoulder in this matter.

The Guardian has also learned with deep regret of . . . resignation from the membership of the N.S.A. and trusts that the new member who will be elected to replace her will be able to contribute as much as she did to the growth and further consolidation of the National Assembly.

He will continue to pray for the confirmation and guidance of all the members, that they may befittingly discharge their manifold and weighty obligations toward the Faith throughout the British Isles.

With his loving greetings and deepest appreciation of your efforts. . . .

Wishing you the fullest success in the efforts which you are exerting in conjunction with the believers for the protection, the promotion, and the consolidation of the Cause of God.
Your true and grateful brother,
Shoghi

22 April 1938 (Convention)

DEEPEST LOVING APPRECIATION FERVENT SUPPLICATION SUCCESS DELIBERATIONS.

SHOGHI

24 April 1938 (Convention)

DELIGHTED URGE INCOMING NATIONAL ASSEMBLY PERSEVERANCE SUBORDINATE ALL ACTIVITIES TEACHING OBJECTIVE.

SHOGHI

28 April 1938

BAHÁ'Í WORLD MOURNS LOSS HOLY MOTHER MUNIRIH KHÁNUM STOP RIḌVÁN FESTIVITIES SUSPENDED. ADVISE ALL CENTRES HOLD MEMORIAL GATHERINGS COMMEMORATE HER OUTSTANDING SERVICES RENDERED DURING ONE OF MOST CRITICAL STAGES IN EVOLUTION BELOVED FAITH.

SHOGHI

17 May 1938

Dear Mr. Hofman,

I am instructed to acknowledge the receipt of your communications addressed to our beloved Guardian dated December 24th, January 10th, February 13th and March 22nd together with the enclosed minutes of the meetings of the British N.S.A., as well as the copies of the "Bahá'í Journal", all of which he has read with closest attention and keenest interest.

He has noted with gratification that the Teaching Conference held in Manchester during last December was successful, and that the meetings were all pervaded with a spirit of unity and of fellowship. He has read with deep satisfaction the report of the above Conference which you had sent, and indeed trusts that the decision and plans that have been adopted will, through their faithful application in the course of this year, serve to greatly accelerate the expansion of the teaching work throughout the British Isles....

P.S. Shoghi Effendi has just received your letter of May 16th and wishes your Assembly to make strenuous efforts in connection with the incorporation of the N.S.A. He would advise you to approach Lady Blomfield, Major Tudor-Pole and Lord Lamington.

The Guardian wishes me to inform you that you have been appointed by him a member of the International staff of editors of the "Bahá'í World". He wishes you to start from now collecting the necessary material for the next edition and to send them gradually and directly to Mrs. French.

Dear and valued co-worker,

I greatly welcome the determination of the English believers to concentrate their energies on the teaching work, and I pray from all my heart for the success of their high endeavours in this all-important field of Bahá'í service. Individuals as well as local Assemblies must arise and co-operate and persevere and refuse to allow any obstacle, however formidable, to dim their hopes or to deflect them from the course they have so spontaneously chosen to pursue. Kindly assure them of my constant prayers for their success.

Shoghi

30 June 1938

Dear Bahá'í Brother,

I am instructed by the Guardian to acknowledge the receipt of your communication dated May 31st, enclosing two copies of the newly published booklet prepared by the British N.S.A. for teaching purposes, and also the latest issue of the "Bahá'í Journal", and the report of the Convention proceedings for this year.

He has read with keenest interest and with deep gratification the Annual Report of your Assembly and has been very much impressed indeed by its comprehensiveness, and by your ability in presenting the facts in such a lucid and effective language. He has sent the text to Mr. Holley for reproduction in the next "Bahá'í World", as an appendix to the International Survey of activities.

Although the range of Bahá'í activities throughout Great Britain during this past year has been considerably restricted as a result of the departure of many travelling and visiting Bahá'í teachers, yet the fact that the friends were, in spite of that and other handicaps, able to maintain the course of their activities constitutes a clear evidence that the English Bahá'í Community is at last able to stand on its own feet, and has sufficient resources, both moral and material, to enable it to carry on, without any external help, the heavy task that has been committed to its charge.

The Guardian wishes you to assure your fellow members on the N.S.A. and through them the friends throughout Great Britain, of his fervent prayers that throughout the course of this new year they may evince such a unity, zeal and renewed consecration to their task as to further demonstrate the strength of their position as a self-supporting and ever-growing national Bahá'í community....

Wishing you and your dear co-workers the utmost success in your high and meritorious endeavours,
Your true and grateful brother,
Shoghi

October 1938 (Third Summer School)

ASSURE YOU PRAYERS HEARTILY RECIPROCATE GREETINGS.

SHOGHI

24 October 1938

Dear Bahá'í Brother,

Your communications written on behalf of the British N.S.A. and dated June 23rd, July 8th and September 15th with their enclosures have all been duly received and their contents noted with interest and satisfaction by our beloved Guardian.

Regarding the papers you had enclosed in your last letter relating to the N.S.A.'s application for incorporation, he has read these with the closest attention, and has already communicated to you his approval by cable, and wishes me now to urge your Assembly to proceed with this matter without delay and to make every effort to have the whole thing completed in the course of the next few months, preferably before the termination of your Assembly's term of office next April. . . .

The Guardian has read with considerable interest Mr. Balyuzi's† booklet on "Bahá'u'lláh", and hopes that the two companion essays on the Báb and the Master on which he is working will be soon completed and ready for distribution, as he feels they can be of a valuable help to the friends in their teaching work.

With the renewed assurances of his prayers for the confirmation of your services, and reciprocating your greetings. . . .

Dear co-worker,

The energy, loyalty and resourcefulness with which your Assembly is conducting and extending the manifold activities of the Faith in these days of stress and trial deserve the highest praise. Your achievements constitute indeed a landmark in the history of the Faith in that land. I urge you, with all earnestness and with feelings of abounding gratitude, to redouble your efforts and to persevere until your highest hopes and plans in both the spiritual and administrative spheres are realised and fulfilled. My prayers are always with you.

Shoghi

27 November 1938

Dear Bahá'í Brother,

I am directed by our beloved Guardian to express his thanks for your letter of the 2nd inst. written on behalf of the N.S.A.

He has noted your Assembly's request for his advice as to what forms of national service friends may volunteer for in times of emergency. While the believers, he feels, should exert every effort to obtain from the authorities a permit exempting them from active military service in a combatant capacity, it is their duty at the same time, as loyal and devoted citizens, to offer their services to their country in any field of national service which is not specifically aggressive or directly military. Such forms of national work as air raid precaution service, ambulance corps, and other humanitarian work or activity of a non-combatant nature, are the most suitable types of service the friends can render, and which they should gladly volunteer for, since in addition to the fact that they do not involve any violation of the spirit or principle of the Teachings, they constitute a form of social and humanitarian service which the Cause holds sacred and emphatically enjoins.

The Guardian has noted with genuine satisfaction what you had written about your recent visit to . . . and his earnest desire to become of increasing service to the Faith. We will certainly pray that he may fully avail himself of the manifold opportunities that now lie before him of spreading the knowledge of the Cause in hitherto closed and conservative circles, and of thus drawing to it the attention of thoughtful and responsible people throughout Britain.

With the renewed assurances of his prayers for you and for your dear fellow members of the N.S.A. . . .

Dear and trusted co-worker,

The marvellous zeal, unity, understanding and devotion exemplified by the English believers in recent months, individually as well as through their concentrated efforts, constitute a landmark in the progressive development of the Faith in that land. They who have risen to the height of their present opportunities stand at the threshold of unprecedented achievements. They must labour continually, exercise the utmost vigilance, proclaim courageously, and cling tenaciously to the principles of their Faith, spiritual as well as administrative, and resolve to endure every sacrifice and hardship, however severe, for the vindication, the consolidation and recognition of the Faith they profess and are now so admirably serving.

With a heart filled with pride and gratitude I pray continually for their triumph.

Shoghi

29 November 1938

RAḤMATU'LLÁH 'ALÁ'Í OUTSTANDING PROMOTER FAITH ÍRÁN SOON ARRIVING LONDON FOR TREATMENT EXTEND CORDIAL WELCOME EVERY POSSIBLE ASSISTANCE.

SHOGHI

15 January 1939

URGE 'ALÁ'Í FOLLOW WHATEVER TREATMENT PRESCRIBED DOCTOR PRAYING.

SHOGHI

10 February 1939

Dear Bahá'í Brother,

At the direction of our beloved Guardian I acknowledge with thanks the receipt of your communications dated November 28th, December 5th, January 5th and 14th written on behalf of the British N.S.A., all of which he has read, together with their enclosures, with earnest and fullest attention.

Regarding the matter of the N.S.A.'s incorporation, he has noted with real satisfaction that in spite of the difficulties raised by the officials in the Board of Trade in connection with your application, the contacts you have formed with these officials have been of such a friendly nature as to give your Assembly an opportunity to further press your case, and also to impress the authorities concerned with the true nature and significance of the Faith.

The Guardian would urge your Assembly to strain every nerve to bring this task to speedy completion, and wishes me to reassure you and your fellow-members that he will continually and most fervently pray that your renewed efforts in this connection may be crowned with full success.

He also wishes me to express his feelings of deep satisfaction at the efforts of your Assembly in connection with the publication of "New World Order", which paper, he hopes, will prove of increasing value as a medium for the spread of the Cause throughout England.

In closing I feel I must also convey his loving thanks to your Assembly for the very cordial welcome and warm hospitality which you have, in response to his telegram, kindly extended to our well beloved and highly esteemed brother Mr. 'Alá'í. The love and consideration he has been shown by the friends, and by the members of your Assembly in particular, will, he feels certain, help to a marked degree in counter-acting the painful effects of the insidious disease from which he is so severely, yet so uncomplainingly suffering. The spirit of courage and fortitude which he is displaying surely cannot but create a profound impression upon all those friends, doctors and patients who come in contact with him. May his presence in your midst, however temporary, serve as an opportunity of further spreading the knowledge of the Faith, and also be the means of encouragement and inspiration to the believers. . . .

Dear and valued co-workers,
I am delighted with the work which is being so energetically conducted, and so faithfully extended and consolidated by the English believers, and particularly by their national elected representatives whose magnificent efforts, courage and perseverance deserve the highest praise. A splendid beginning has been made. A firm foundation has been established. Perseverance is now required to bring these devoted, painstaking and concerted efforts to full and speedy fruition. The path you are treading is beset with formidable obstacles, but the invincible power of the Faith will, if you remain faithful and steadfast, enable you to surmount them. My prayers will continue to be offered on your behalf. May Bahá'u'lláh fulfil every hope you cherish in the service of His Faith.
Your true and grateful brother,
Shoghi

22 March 1939

LOVING APPRECIATION PRAYING UNPRECEDENTED TRIUMPHS.
SHOGHI

March 1939

". . . Under no circumstances should any local Assembly be given the right to criticise and much less oppose, the policy duly adopted and approved by the N.S.A."
(Bahá'í Journal 17—cited in an article).

30 April 1939 (Convention)

DELIGHTED NOTABLE ACHIEVEMENTS*, GRATEFUL PRAYING RICHEST BLESSINGS DELIBERATIONS DEEPEST LOVE.

SHOGHI

31 May 1939

Dear Bahá'í Brother,

At our beloved Guardian's direction I gratefully acknowledge the receipt of your communications dated February 19th, March 7th and 27th, May 3rd with enclosures, written on behalf of the British N.S.A.

He has noted with considerable satisfaction the report of the progress recently achieved in Bradford and Torquay where, he is most delighted to know, the friends, and particularly the newly enrolled young believers, are displaying great enthusiasm in their activities and have obtained many openings of presenting the Cause.

The news of the confirmation of Mr. Frank Hurst† is specially gratifying and should prove of deep encouragement to all the friends who should indeed avail themselves of the opportunity of his presence in the community to give intensive publicity to the Faith.

Regarding the new prayer book which the N.S.A. is proposing to publish; the manuscript has already been returned to your address and the suggestions and recommendations of the Guardian on the matter duly conveyed to your Assembly in a recent letter. He would advise that on the inside cover mention should be made only of the British Reviewing Committee's approval, as it is invariably done in the case of all official Bahá'í publications.

In connection with the problem of Bahá'í refugees, the Guardian feels this is a matter which concerns the N.S.A., who would be justified in taking any action they deem appropriate,

---

*In reply to the Convention's cable stating that two new Assemblies—Bradford and Torquay—were represented, and the incorporation documents were completed.

provided the state of the National Fund permits it, and only after the particular case of each individual applicant has been thoroughly investigated, and his status as a believer duly ascertained.

With reference to your suggestion as to the advisability of your approaching Mr. Eden, and through him possibly Lord Halifax, with the view to obtaining from them statements for the "Bahá'í World", Shoghi Effendi would approve of your seeing Mr. Eden only, and would leave it to the N.S.A.'s discretion whether you should approach him as his representative or as the representative of the British National Assembly.

Concerning Mrs. Basil Hall's† paper which she had prepared for last year's Summer School; the N.S.A.'s approval sanctioning its publication would be sufficient. You need not, therefore, send the manuscript to Haifa. But as to the passages she had quoted from Myron Phelps' book, the Guardian does not advise that these quotations be included in the pamphlet, as Phelps' book is full of inaccuracies that are misleading, and for this reason should be ignored by the believers.

The Guardian is inexpressibly delighted at the news of the completion of the N.S.A.'s incorporation certificate, and would appreciate your sending him three photostat reproductions of the original, one of which he will arrange to be placed in the Mansion at Bahjí, and the second he will include in the next issue of "Bahá'í World", and the third he will keep in his own files.

The Guardian wishes me in closing to urge your Assembly to make a special effort during this year to concentrate on furthering the teaching work in Birmingham, Leeds, Newcastle, Brighton, Sheffield and Bournemouth, in view of the teaching opportunities that these centres, as indicated in your letter, seem to offer at present. He welcomes the recommendation made to this effect at the last Annual Convention and would urge the newly elected N.S.A. to give this task its continued and fullest attention. However stupendous the plan now confronting your Assembly may be, you should resolutely and relentlessly endeavour to carry it through, ever confident in the promised assistance and unfailing guidance of Bahá'u'lláh.

To you and your distinguished fellow-members I beg to convey the assurances of his profound and loving appreciation of your loyal and affectionate greetings....

Dear and valued co-workers,

The extension, along sound lines and with such memorable swiftness and harmony, of the activities in which the believers of the United Kingdom are so earnestly and devotedly engaged, merits the highest praise and is a source of constant encouragement and satisfaction to me in my arduous work. They are taking a momentous step forward and are launching enterprises that will no doubt shed fresh lustre on their beloved Faith and leave a distinct mark on Bahá'í history. I will continue to pray on their behalf, and feel certain that if they persevere the Beloved will richly bless their concentrated and highly meritorious efforts.

Shoghi

4 June 1939

Dear Bahá'í Brother,

I am charged by our beloved Guardian to inform you of the receipt of your letter of May 9th written on behalf of the British N.S.A. on the subject of the Bahá'í attitude towards war.

His instructions on this matter, conveyed in a letter addressed to your Assembly during last November, were not intended for that particular occasion, but were meant for present conditions, and for any such emergency as may arise in the immediate future.

It is still his firm conviction that the believers, while expressing their readiness to unreservedly obey any directions that the authorities may issue concerning national service in time of war, should also, and while there is yet no outbreak of hostilities, appeal to the government for exemption from active military service in a combatant capacity, stressing the fact that in doing so they are not prompted by any selfish considerations but by the sole and supreme motive of upholding the Teachings of their Faith, which make it a moral obligation for them to desist from any act that would involve them in direct warfare with their fellow-humans of any other race or nation. The Bahá'í Teachings, indeed, condemn, emphatically and unequivocally, any form of physical violence, and warfare in the battlefield is obviously a form, and perhaps the worst form which such violence can assume.

There are many other avenues through which the believers can assist in times of war by enlisting in services of a non-combatant nature—services that do not involve the direct shedding of blood—such as ambulance work, anti-air raid precaution service, office and administrative works, and it is for such types of national service that they should volunteer.

It is immaterial whether such activities would still expose them to dangers, either at home or in the front, since their desire is not to protect their lives, but to desist from any acts of wilful murder.

The friends should consider it their conscientious duty, as loyal members of the Faith, to apply for such exemption, even though there may be slight prospect of their obtaining the consent and approval of the authorities to their petition. It is most essential that in times of such national excitement and emergency as those through which so many countries in the world are now passing that the believers should not allow themselves to be carried away by the passions agitating the masses, and act in a manner that would make them deviate from the path of wisdom and moderation, and lead them to violate, however reluctantly and indirectly, the spirit as well as the letter of the Teachings.

The N.S.A., in this and similar issues that may arise in future, should act with firmness and vigilance and with such wisdom and tact as would make them an example worthy of the confidence and admiration of all the believers....

May the beloved bless and guide you in collaboration with your fellow members, to uphold the integrity, vindicate the truth, demonstrate the power, and promote the spirit of the exalted teachings of Bahá'u'lláh.

Your true and grateful brother,
Shoghi

26 June 1939

Dear Bahá'í Brother,

On behalf of our beloved Guardian I beg to acknowledge with grateful thanks the receipt of your Assembly's communications of May 26th and June 1st, together with the accompanying copy of the minutes of your meeting held on May 20th–21st, and the latest issue of the "Bahá'í Journal" containing your Annual Report and the account of the Convention proceedings for this year.

He found the Annual Report published in the Journal so encouraging that he decided to have certain sections of it translated into Persian, and sent through the Haifa Assembly's news letter, to different Bahá'í centres throughout the East.

In response to your request for one copy of each of the printed translations of Dr. Esslemont's book which the N.S.A. wishes to include as part of the Bahá'í exhibit at the forthcoming "Sunday Times" Book Exhibition to be held in London during next Autumn, the Guardian has directed me to mail to your address thirty-one printed translations of that book, which are the only ones available at present. There are a few more translations in process of publication, among which, it will surely interest the friends to know, is the Icelandic version which, it is hoped, will be off the press sometime in the course of this Summer. The new revised edition of the German translation, which is being published under the auspices of the International Bahá'í Bureau in Geneva, will be soon ready, and you can obtain a copy of that new edition by applying to Mrs. Lynch.

The Guardian does not want these books to be returned to Haifa after the closing of the Exhibition, but wishes you to accept them as his gift to the National Bahá'í Library at the Centre in London, and would suggest that you keep them for any future Bahá'í exhibit which the N.S.A. may propose to hold in other parts of England.

He wishes me, in this connection, to express the hope that the exhibition you have arranged for this coming Autumn will prove highly successful and a most useful and effective medium of teaching the Cause. The idea of a Bahá'í display, chiefly of publications, he feels, is indeed excellent, and he will specially pray therefore that the one you are now preparing will achieve such results as to encourage and stimulate the N.S.A. to arrange for similar exhibits in the future.

Regarding the originals of Tablets revealed in honour of the late Miss Rosenberg, there are only one or two of them, here in Haifa, and these were sent by Miss Rosenberg herself. The

Guardian is keeping them for the present as they contain important references concerning the practice of monogamy in the Cause.

To you and your dear fellow-members I seize this opportunity of renewing the assurances of his abiding and loving gratitude, and of wishing you continued guidance for the further promotion of the Faith in England....

Dear and valued co-workers,

The determination of the English believers to extend rapidly and systematically the range of their teaching and administrative activities is a welcome evidence of the genuineness of their faith, the nobility of their purpose and the depth of their devotion. That such a determination may yield the richest fruit is my special and constant prayer. What they have already achieved fortifies my hopes and confidence in them. They have laid a firm and unassailable basis for their future work. Perseverance, co-ordination, fearlessness, vigour and wisdom will enable them to gradually rear on this basis the majestic structure of Bahá'u'lláh's administrative order, which in the fulness of time must yield, on the soil of their country a harvest unexampled in its abundance and glory. May His Spirit guide and sustain them to hasten that hour and consummate that task.

Your true brother,
Shoghi

2 July 1939

Dear Bahá'í Brother,

Enclosed please find a draft for fifteen English pounds issued in your name which the Guardian has directed me to forward to you with the request that you send him for that sum copies of Mr. Townshend's "Heart of the Gospel", which he understands will be off the press in the course of this month.

May I take this opportunity of expressing his hope that this little volume may fulfil the author's purpose, namely to attract the attention of the orthodox Christian element in England to the Cause, and stimulate many thoughtful and spiritually minded individuals to seriously investigate the Teachings....

26 July 1939 (Summer School)

CONGRATULATE ATTENDANTS NOTABLE PROGRESS GRATEFUL PRAYING FRESH ADVANCES DEEPEST LOVE.

SHOGHI

7 August 1939

HEARTIEST CONGRATULATIONS OUTSTANDING SUCCESS.

SHOGHI

6 November 1939

OVERJOYED THANKFUL PERSEVERANCE ENGLISH BELIEVERS ATTESTED RECENT COMMUNICATIONS ASSURE THEM SPECIAL PRAYERS ABIDING APPRECIATION.

SHOGHI RABBANÍ*

20 November 1939

Dear Bahá'í Brother,

On behalf of our beloved Guardian I beg to acknowledge with grateful thanks the receipt of your communications dated July 11th, 20th, August 14th (2 letters) and October 19th with enclosures written on behalf of the British N.S.A.

He also wishes me to inform you that the photostatic reproductions of the incorporation papers of your Assembly have safely reached him, and he has placed one copy in Bahá'u'lláh's Mansion in Bahjí, and is keeping the other for inclusion in the next issue of the "Bahá'í World".

The copies of Mr. Townshend's latest book, "The Heart of the Gospel", which you have forwarded at his request have likewise been received and a number of volumes distributed among the

---

*The Guardian only used his full name in cables when the censorship regulations during states of emergency made it obligatory.

various Bahá'í libraries established in the Holy Land. He feels confident the N.S.A. is sparing no effort to bring this valuable production to the attention of leading personalities throughout the British Isles, and will pray that the interest aroused may be such as to lead to the full spiritual awakening and confirmation of a number of thoughtful individuals in various parts of the country.

As regards the projected prayer book; he does not know whether the N.S.A. has been able to proceed with the printing of this work. But in case it is published, he would like you to mail to him twenty copies, some of which he needs for distribution among various Bahá'í libraries here.

The Guardian feels most truly delighted to know that the outbreak of war has, in general, stimulated the friends to greater teaching effort, and that the newly established communities such as those of Bradford and Torquay are showing particular enthusiasm in carrying on the teaching work in their respective centres. He will earnestly supplicate the Almighty that He may bless and reinforce these steadfast and self-sacrificing exertions of the English believers, and that He may, in these days of storm and stress, vouchsafe unto them all an increasing measure of His unfailing protection and guidance. . . .

Dear and valued co-worker,

I wish to reaffirm clearly and emphatically my deep sense of gratification and gratitude for the recent and truly remarkable evidences of the devotion, courage and perseverance of the English Bahá'í community in the face of the perils that now confront it. Its members have abundantly demonstrated their profound attachment to their Cause, their unshakable resolution to uphold its truth and defend its interests, and their unfailing solicitude for whatever may promote and safeguard its institutions. However great and sinister the forces with which they may have to battle in future, I feel confident that they will befittingly uphold the torch of Divine Guidance that has been entrusted to their hands and will discharge their responsibilities with still greater tenacity, fidelity, vigour and devotion.

Shoghi

5 December 1939

REMAINS PUREST BRANCH AND 'ABDU'L-BAHÁ'S MOTHER PERMANENTLY LAID REST CLOSE NEIGHBOURHOOD SHRINE GREATEST HOLY LEAF HEARTS REJOICING.

SHOGHI RABBANÍ

7 December 1939

Dear Bahá'í Brother,

The Guardian has just received your letter of the 20th November last, and feels indeed deeply encouraged at the report of the teaching activities of our dear English believers. He is unspeakably grateful to you all, and in particular to the members of your Assembly, for the determination, resourcefulness and the spirit of absolute consecration with which you are prosecuting the teaching campaign throughout England, and he will ardently pray that, in spite of the smallness of your numbers and means, and notwithstanding the various obstacles you may encounter in the course of your future activities for the Faith, you may, individually and collectively, receive such confirmations from Bahá'u'lláh as would enable you each and all to befittingly and completely acquit yourselves of this high task you have undertaken to accomplish in service of His Faith.

In connection with your application for exemption from active military service, the Guardian trusts that the authorities will give careful consideration to this matter, and will find it possible to relieve the Bahá'í friends from the necessity of serving in the army in a combatant capacity. Should they, however, refuse to grant such exemption, the believers should unhesitatingly assure them of their unqualified obedience and of their readiness to join and serve in the army in whatever manner the government deems best.

Renewing to you and to all the friends his warmest good wishes and greetings....

Dear and valued co-workers,

The various and compelling evidences of the unquenchable enthusiasm, the unbreakable resolution and the inflexible purpose of

the English believers, in these days of stress, of turmoil and danger, have cheered my heart and fortified me in the discharge of my arduous and multitudinous duties and responsibilities. I feel truly proud of them all, and will, with increasing gratitude and redoubled fervour, supplicate the Beloved whose Cause they are so valiantly serving, to bless, sustain, guide and protect them under all circumstances, and aid them to establish firmly the institutions of His Faith throughout the length and breadth of their country.
                    Your true and grateful brother,
                                            Shoghi

29 December 1939

Dear Bahá'í Brother,

I am instructed by our beloved Guardian to acknowledge with thanks the receipt of your communication of the 19th December, sent through the care of our very dear brother Dr. 'Alí, and of the twenty copies of the newly-published prayer book, as well as the last copy of the "Bahá'í Journal" and the Christmas number of "New World Order".

He has also received and read with deep satisfaction the statement on 'Bahá'ís and War' recently issued by the N.S.A., together with the teaching report prepared by your Assembly, both of which he will consider for incorporation in the next issue of the "Bahá'í World", the manuscript of which he hopes to receive in the course of January or February next....

The Guardian welcomes the plan suggested by Mr. Townshend to republish "The Promise of All Ages" under his own name, and trusts this will serve to attract wider publicity to the Cause, and in particular to fully awaken the church officials to the significance of such direct and vigorous presentation of the Faith by so well-known and long-standing a Christian divine.

Renewing to you and your dear fellow-members and to all the friends in London, the assurances of his prayers for your welfare and protection in these perilous days, and with his warmest greetings to you all....

Dear and valued co-workers,
The news of your persistent activities, your safety and protection, and above all of your unyielding resolve and undisturbed confidence in

the face of the uncertainties and perils that face and surround you, have greatly cheered and heartened me in my duties and responsibilities which are now heavily pressing upon me. You are often in my thoughts and prayers at this grave hour. I cherish the brightest hopes for you, and will continue to supplicate the Almighty on your behalf.
Be assured, persevere and be happy,
Shoghi

1 January 1940*

PROFOUNDLY GRIEVE PASSING DEARLY BELOVED OUTSTANDING CO-WORKER SITÁRIH KHÁNUM MEMORY HER GLORIOUS SERVICES IMPERISHABLE ADVISE ENGLISH COMMUNITY HOLD BEFITTING MEMORIAL GATHERINGS ASSURE RELATIVES MY HEARTFELT SYMPATHY LOVING FERVENT PRAYERS.

SHOGHI RABBANÍ

2 January 1940 (Teaching Conference)

WELCOME NOBLE RESOLVE PROSECUTE ENERGETICALLY TEACHING CAMPAIGN PRAYING ARDENTLY SIGNAL SUCCESS.

SHOGHI RABBANÍ

18 February 1940

Dear Mr. Hofman,

The Guardian wishes me to write and thank you for your welcome communication of January 29th with its various enclosures, all of which he was indeed most gratified and encouraged to read.

As you have not mentioned having received his general letter of December 21st written in connection with the transfer of the sacred remains of the Purest Branch and of 'Abdu'l-Bahá's mother to Mt. Carmel, I am taking the liberty of sending you on his behalf another copy which, I trust, will reach you safely....

The Guardian welcomes your suggestions to send a memorial of the late Lady Blomfield for publication in the next issue of the

---

*Lady Blomfield passed away 31 December 1939.

THE SEEDS ARE TENDED (1922–1944) 137

"Bahá'í World", Vol. VIII, and wishes you to send him in addition a good photograph of her for reproduction in the same volume.

Also he would appreciate your sending him a brief account of Mrs. Thornburgh-Cropper's Bahá'í life and services together with her photograph for publication in the same issue of the Biennial.

The passing away of these two long-standing believers has indeed robbed the Cause in England of two of its most distinguished members, and the English Bahá'í Community is certainly the poorer now that it has been deprived of their ready and invaluable support.

The departure of Sitárih Khánum in particular is to be deeply mourned, not only by the members of the Faith throughout England, but by so many of her fellow-believers abroad, and the Guardian himself feels most keenly the loss of so precious and faithful a co-worker, who, in the early days following 'Abdu'l-Bahá's ascension, had proved of such invaluable assistance to him in the discharge of his heavy duties and responsibilities....

Dear co-workers,

I wish to reaffirm my deep sense of gratitude and admiration for the splendid manner in which the English believers are discharging their duties and responsibilities in these days of increasing peril, anxiety and stress. Their tenacity, courage, faith and noble exertions will as a magnet attract the undoubted and promised blessing of Bahá'u'lláh. They have, at a time when the basis of ordered society itself is rocking and trembling, laid an unassailable foundation for the Administrative Order of their Faith. Upon this basis the rising generation will erect a noble structure that will excite the admiration of their fellow countrymen. My prayers for them will continually be offered at the Holy Shrines.

Gratefully,
Shoghi

27 March 1940

Dear Mr. Hofman,

Your letter dated March 13th has safely reached our beloved Guardian together with the following enclosures:

In Memoriam: Lady Blomfield.
Minutes N.S.A. March 2nd and 3rd.
"Bahá'í Journal" No. 21.
Introduction to "The Chosen Highway."
Preface to "The Chosen Highway."

He has also received by registered post the photographs of Lady Blomfield and Mrs. Thornburgh-Cropper which you had kindly sent at his request for reproduction in the "Bahá'í World"....

The Guardian has noted with satisfaction that the arrangements for the publication of "The Chosen Highway" are complete, and hopes that by the time you receive this letter it will be well on the way to printing.

Concerning the question you have asked as to whether in elections for Spiritual Assemblies the electors should cast exactly nine votes, or may cast less than this number. Inasmuch as Spiritual Assembly membership, according to the principles of Bahá'í Administration, has been limited for the present to nine members, it follows that no electoral vote can be effective unless it is cast for exactly that number. It is, therefore, the sacred duty of every Bahá'í elector to cast nine votes, neither more nor less, except under special circumstances, so as to ensure that the results of the elections for the Spiritual Assembly will be effective and on as wide a basis of representation as possible....

P.S. The Guardian has noted with surprise in reading over the Minutes of your N.S.A. that the British Annual Convention is to be held this year on the 12th May. He wishes you from now on to hold that gathering on any day during the period of Riḍván (21 April–2 May)

May the Almighty bless, sustain and protect the English believers, who in these days of unprecedented turmoil, stress and danger, are holding aloft so courageously the banner of the Faith, and who will, in the days to come, contribute, through His grace and power, a notable share to its establishment and recognition in the West.
Your true and grateful brother,
Shoghi

12 May 1940 (Convention)

GREATLY ADMIRE DEEPLY THANKFUL UNDAUNTED COURAGE INFLEXIBLE RESOLUTION ENGLISH BELIEVERS REPRESENTED CONVENTION INTENSIFY EFFORTS EXTEND ACTIVITIES NOTWITHSTANDING GRAVITY HOUR PRAYING ARDENTLY PROTECTION SUCCESS.

SHOGHI RABBANÍ

14 August 1940

DELIGHTED NEWS SAFETY ENGLISH BELIEVERS PROGRESS TEACHING WORK ASSURE THEM EACH ALL LOVING CONTINUED PRAYERS.

SHOGHI RABBANÍ

10 October 1940

Dear Mr. Hofman,

I beg to acknowledge the receipt of your letter of May 7th addressed to our beloved Guardian, and of the enclosed memoir of Lady Blomfield which you have condensed at his request for use in the "Bahá'í World", Vol. VIII.

The size of the memoir in question makes it now quite suitable for reproduction in the Biennial, and it will be forwarded to the U.S.A. for incorporation in the manuscript, as the latter has been already mailed to America for printing.

The material regarding the Bahá'í wedding recently held in London has been also received and noted with interest and appreciation by our beloved Guardian. He is keeping it for possible use in the forthcoming or future editions of the "Bahá'í World".

Renewing to you and your dear co-workers the assurances of his prayers, and of his deep gratitude for your painstaking and devoted exertions in service to the Cause in England, and with greetings. . . .

Dear and valued co-worker,
Our anxiety for the safety of the English believers is deepening every day, as it is fully realised how dangerous the situation has

become in recent months, and how manifold and pressing are the problems that confront them in the faithful discharge of their sacred and vital responsiblities. The perusal of the reports, minutes and periodicals received lately from that country has served to deepen my sense of admiration and my feelings of gratitude for the wisdom, the staunchness and fidelity with which the elected representatives of the English believers are conducting in these critical times the activities of their Faith. My fervent and constant prayer is that Bahá'u'lláh may ever keep them safe and protected under the shadow of His wings and aid them to play a worthy and memorable part in these tragic days of the Formative Period of our beloved Cause.

Shoghi

19 October 1940

ANXIOUS WELFARE ENGLISH BELIEVERS PRAYING PROTECTION CABLE ASSURANCE DEEPEST LOVE.

SHOGHI RABBANÍ

22 November 1940

Dear Mr. Hofman,

On behalf of the Guardian I beg to acknowledge the receipt of your communications dated May 28th, June 20th, July 5th and August 30th with enclosures, written at the direction of the British N.S.A.

He has noted with satisfaction the results of the elections for the new N.S.A. and wishes you to convey to your fellow members the assurances of his prayers for the success of their work during this year. Notwithstanding the storm and stress raging around them, the friends in England should more than ever, firmly united behind their National Assembly, and strengthened by an unshakable conviction in the ultimate triumph of their Faith, earnestly and resolutely endeavour to foster the cause of teaching. The trials and tribulations facing them should but serve to steel their resolve to leave no stone unturned until their goal has been fully accomplished. The

Guardian's prayers are being ardently offered that whatever the immediate repercussions of the war may be on the British Bahá'í Community, its members may, through the Divine aid and protection of Bahá'u'lláh, receive such guidance and strength as would enable them to face confidently and courageously the sufferings and vicissitudes of the present hour, and to arise as one body for the promulgation and wider establishment of the Faith throughout Great Britain.

Concerning your Assembly's request for lantern slides of the Shrines on Mt. Carmel which you propose to use in your teaching campaign, the Guardian much regrets that no such slides are at present available here.

As regards the question of what procedure the Bahá'í Assemblies should adopt when dissatisfied with the services of any of their officers, should such dissatisfaction involve the loyalty of an Assembly officer to the Faith, he should, following a majority vote be dismissed. But in case the dissatisfaction is due to the incompetence of a member, or simply to a neglect on his part to discharge his duties, this does not constitute sufficient justification to force his resignation or dismissal from the Assembly. He should be kept in office until new elections are held.

The Guardian fully approves that, in view of the National Secretary's key position in the Cause at the present time, he should apply for complete exemption. He hopes that the representations the N.S.A. will make will meet with success.

In closing he wishes me to acknowledge with thanks the receipt of two copies of Lady Blomfield's book presented to him by the N.S.A., one of which he has already placed in the Library of Bahá'u'lláh's Mansion in Bahjí. . . .

Dear and valued co-worker,
I was greatly relieved to learn of the safety of the English believers and was filled with admiration through the assurance you have given me of their steadfastness, their unwavering determination to labour for the spread of our beloved Faith and the defence and protection of its interests in spite of the unprecedented calamities and confusion that now afflict their country. Bahá'u'lláh from His station on high is watching over them, is pleased with them, and will, I feel certain,

guide their steps, cheer their hearts, bless their efforts, protect their lives, and fulfil the desire of their hearts.
Gratefully and affectionately,
Shoghi

27 December 1940

WIRE SAFETY LONDON MANCHESTER FRIENDS CONSTANTLY PRAYING LOVING ADMIRATION.
SHOGHI RABBANÍ

24 February 1941

LETTERS JUNE JULY AUGUST ENCLOSING MINUTES ARRIVED ANSWER MAILED NOVEMBER LETTER DECEMBER NINTH JUST RECEIVED ALSO BLOMFIELD'S BOOKS CABLING HUNDRED POUNDS MY CONTRIBUTION RELIEF BELIEVERS INCESSANTLY PRAYING DEEPEST LOVE.
SHOGHI RABBANÍ

19 April 1941

REJOICE SAFETY ADMIRE DAUNTLESS COURAGE MARVEL UNQUENCHABLE SPIRIT ENGLISH BELIEVERS SHARING JOYFUL NEWS NOBLE PERSEVERANCE WITH PILGRIMS ARRIVING IN INCREASING NUMBERS FROM NEAR AND MIDDLE EAST ALL PRAYING CONTINUED SAFETY EXTENSION ACTIVITIES SORE TRIED EXEMPLARY SERVANTS FAITH BAHÁ'U'LLÁH THROUGHOUT BRITISH ISLES URGE PERSISTENT EFFORTS UTILISE UTMOST LIMIT PRICELESS SPIRITUAL OPPORTUNITIES PRESENT HOUR.
SHOGHI RABBANÍ

30 April 1941 (Convention)

EXHILARATED RESOLUTION INTENSIFY TEACHING ADMIRATION HEIGHTENED PRAYING REDOUBLED FERVOUR.
SHOGHI RABBANÍ

Haifa,
April 30th,
1941

Dear Bahá'í friends:

Shoghi Effendi has instructed me to answer your letter to him of Dec. 7th, 1940.

He was greatly relieved to hear from your letter and cables that all the dear friends in the U.S. etc. are well and safe, as his thoughts have been so constantly with them during these dangerous and tragic days.

The extreme devotion to the Faith of Bahá'u'lláh which the English friends are evincing at such a time of trial and

[last page:]

...dearly loved co-workers — have recently founded with the assistance of quite a number of devoted & quite unknown to him amidst the indirect fruit the suffering inflicted in these days of increasing hardships are manifesting itself & these, though only West – yet qualities which the house-holders duty, though your duty & the arduous task of fending aloft & the cause of God & its numerals of the oppressed are very great, their children, all to revival. They are by its vocations, above all by the funds & sanctions of their faith, laying foundations of the magnificent foundations of a [illegible]...

for the spiritual edifice their hands are destined to raise in their native land. My prayers for them all will surround them wherever they labour & in every sphere...

[side margin:]
assuring you of the guardian's ardent love and prayers,
with Bahá'í greetings,
Yours in His service,
R. Rabbani

[signed:] Shoghi

First and last pages of the first letter received by the National Spiritual Assembly in which the secretarial part was written by Amatu'l-Bahá Rúḥíyyih Khanum (*reduced size*)

30 April 1941*

Dear Bahá'í Friends,
Shoghi Effendi has instructed me to answer your letter to him of December 9th, 1940.

He was greatly relieved to hear from your letter and cables that all the dear friends in the British Isles are well and safe, as his thoughts have been so constantly with them during these dangerous and tragic days.

The extreme devotion to the Faith of Bahá'u'lláh which the English friends are evincing at such a time of trial and suffering not only sets a truly heroic example to their fellow Bahá'ís the world over, but greatly cheers and encourages the Guardian himself, at a time when he has every reason to long to see the Bahá'ís stand out as luminous examples to their fellow-men—thus leading them out of the valley of spiritual death into the glorious plains of the future World Order of Mankind.

The recently received news of the Convention's resolve to teach the Faith as never before in those islands, and to achieve new victories in this all-important field, meets not only with Shoghi Effendi's whole-hearted approval, but also evokes his profound gratitude and admiration. His ardent and loving prayers continually surround you all and all the sorely tried Bahá'ís, who with you are toiling for the triumph of our Faith.

He was deeply touched at the spirit which impelled Lord Lamington to wish to place in the hands of the Guardian that ring which he had for so long treasured as a gift of the beloved Master. He feels that it is only befitting that this historic relic should be the property of the British Bahá'ís and wishes it to be kept in your National Archives. If you could send a copy of Lady Lamington's letter the Guardian would very much like to have it. Assuring you of the Guardian's ardent love and prayers....

Dearly beloved co-workers,
The message I have recently received, with the assurance it gives me and the spirit it conveys, merits indeed the highest praise. The English believers in these days of increasing peril and stress, are manifesting

---

*This was the first letter received by the British N.S.A. in which the secretarial part was written by, and signed, "R. Rabbani" (Amatu'l-Bahá Rúḥíyyih <u>Kh</u>ánum).

those qualities which only those who have deeply imbibed the transforming spirit and the ennobling principles of the Cause of God are able to reveal. They are by their very acts, their sufferings and exertions, and above all by the superb staunchness of their faith, laying a magnificent foundation for the spiritual edifice their hands are destined to raise in their native land. My prayers for them all will surround them wherever they labour and in every sphere of their meritorious activities.

Gratefully and affectionately,
Shoghi

15 May 1941*

INFORMING MOTHER PRAYING HIS SOUL FERVENTLY SUPPLICATING PROTECTION DEVOTED MUCH LOVED ENGLISH BELIEVERS.

SHOGHI RABBANÍ

22 May 1941

Dear Bahá'í Friends,

Shoghi Effendi instructs me to answer your letter to him of March 10th, 1941 together with the minutes of your meeting held March 1st, 2nd and 3rd, and your Feb. "Bahá'í Journal" and the "World Congress of Faiths" programme, all of which he was very pleased indeed to receive.

I cannot adequately express to you all the warm love and profound admiration for the Bahá'ís of those islands which Shoghi Effendi feels. At such a time of personal danger and anguish the spirit of pure love and devotion to the Faith and Order of Bahá'u'lláh which they manifest, and which is so typified by the zeal and wisdom with which your National Spiritual Assembly is handling the affairs of the Cause in that country, is a source of great comfort to the Guardian himself.

Indeed he feels that the N.S.A. members are bearing their load of responsibility in a manner which lifts partially the weight of cares from his own shoulders, and sets a noble example to all Bahá'í administrative bodies.

*In reply to cable sent to the Guardian 13 May 1941 FU'ÁD AFNÁN FIRST BAHÁ'Í AIR RAID VICTIM ENGLAND KILLED EARLY SUNDAY MORNING GRATEFUL IF YOU INFORM MOTHER.

THE SEEDS ARE TENDED (1922–1944)

In reference to your question contained in minute 208* of the recent N.S.A. meeting: Shoghi Effendi feels that while all Bahá'ís should be encouraged to turn to their Assembly for the solution of their various problems, thus enabling the Spiritual Assembly to fulfil one of its most important functions, yet they are quite free to write to him if they feel the urge to do so....

He was also very pleased to note the teaching plans undertaken by your body at this time, particularly in respect to Manchester. He hopes the believers there are all well and safe, and will pray for the confirmations of Bahá'u'lláh in their contemplated teaching campaign.

Indeed, dear friends, his thoughts and prayers are constantly with you and the beloved flock of English believers over whom you are so faithfully watching through these dark days.

He wishes you at all times to turn to him for any advice or help you may need.

With assurances of his abiding love ...

Dearly beloved co-workers,

As the dangers confronting the believers in the British Isles increase in number and gravity, my admiration, as well as the admiration of the Bahá'ís in East and West, for the spirit that animates those who face them, grows deeper and acquires added intensity and fervour. Though their numbers be small, and their activities restricted, and their trials and anxieties manifold and oppressive, yet their spiritual contribution through their fortitude, valour and self-sacrifice, to the progressive unfoldment of the Faith's latent potentialities in the Western World is both notable and constantly increasing. As the clouds of war dissipate, and the horrors of this universal carnage fade away, it will become increasingly evident, to both the friends and foes of the Faith, how solid has been the foundation which their indomitable spirit has laid, and how rich the harvest which their incessant labours have yielded.

With a heart brimful with love and gratitude, I will, when visiting the Holy Shrines, recall their signal acts, and supplicate increasing blessings on the historic work, which, in their hour of trial, they are so magnificently achieving, for the glory, for the honour, the extension and the establishment of the invincible Faith of Bahá'u'lláh.

Shoghi

*This Minute recorded that: "Personal problems should not be referred to the Guardian without the advice or direction of the National Spiritual Assembly ..."

30 May 1941

PRAYING FERVENTLY GUIDANCE ASSEMBLY'S DELIBERATIONS PROTECTION BELIEVERS SUCCESS ACTIVITIES FAITH LOVING APPRECIATION.

SHOGHI RABBANÍ

9 July 1941

ASSURE JOSEPHS† APPROVAL PROFOUND APPRECIATION BUILDING SCHEME. THESE FURTHER EVIDENCES GROWING VITALITY CONTINUALLY AFFLICTED BELIEVERS BRITISH ISLES ENHANCE PRESTIGE CAUSE BAHÁ'U'LLÁH HEIGHTEN ADMIRATION INCREASE DEBT GRATITUDE HIS FOLLOWERS OWE VALIANT BRITISH COMMUNITY PRAYING CONTINUALLY SAFETY INCREASING SUCCESS.

SHOGHI RABBANÍ

18 July 1941

Dear Bahá'í co-worker,

The Guardian has instructed me to answer your letter to him of May 6th, and to acknowledge the receipt of the minutes of the N.S.A. meetings held on April 25th and 27th.

He was very happy to receive your letter, and his heart rejoiced at the good news which it conveyed. The holding of a successful Bahá'í Convention during days of such stress and strain as the English believers are passing through, he considers as a triumph of the spirit of their faith in Bahá'u'lláh. They are increasingly demonstrating their right to be called champions of the Cause of God, and manifesting their ability to follow in the footsteps of the early heroes of their religion. The Guardian feels truly proud of them.

In accordance with the request you made in connection with the generous proposal of . . ., Shoghi Effendi cabled your Assembly his approval of their plan for establishing a building fund for a future Bahá'í property to be built in. . . . He feels that this demonstrates a most notable donation to the Cause of God on their parts, and wishes you to convey to them both the expression of his profound gratitude for this service they are rendering the Faith in England.

These evidences of growth, in spite of the universal destruction that is holding the planet in its grip at the present time, should greatly hearten the believers. They bear witness to the future harvests which their increasing labours are sure to reap, and demonstrate the great and God-given strength which flows and will flow ever more abundantly from the springs which Bahá'u'lláh has unsealed in these days.

Shoghi Effendi assures you all of his unceasing prayers on your behalf, that God may strengthen, bless, and guide you in your great work for His Faith.

He wishes you to please convey his love to all the British believers and to assure them of his prayers for their protection and for the triumph of their labours. . . .

Dear and prized co-workers,

I am thrilled by the recent evidences of the noble determination of the English believers to extend the range of their activities in these days of grave danger and widespread and ever deepening anxiety and stress. The report of your Convention sessions, of your teaching activities and of your Bahá'í publications, and other administrative undertakings, enhances my admiration and deepens my gratitude for the historic work you are achieving in these days. This feeling is shared by all those of your co-workers, both in the East and the West, who follow the progress of your work despite the formidable obstacles in your path. We all pray for your safety, for the realisation of all your hopes, and the fulfilment of the plans you have so boldly conceived and are so energetically carrying out.

Your true brother,
Shoghi

1941 *(Summer School)*

OVERJOYED SUCCESS ATTENDING EVER EXPANDING INSTITUTIONS FAITH. CONTINUALLY SUPPLICATING UNFAILING PROTECTION EVER-INCREASING BLESSINGS ETERNAL GRATITUDE.

SHOGHI RABBANÍ

20 *August 1941*

Dear Bahá'í Friend,

The Guardian has instructed me to answer your letters to him dated June 6th and 30th respectively, also the minutes of the N.S.A. meetings of May 24th and 25th and June 14th were safely received.

He is happy to see that, in spite of the great physical and nervous strain which the believers of England are at present being subjected to—especially in centres like London—they yet persevere with the work of the Cause and the attraction of new souls.

The Guardian does not feel that the friends should for a moment feel discouraged if they do not succeed in having large meetings or the public do not regularly attend, this is easily understandable in view of the severe ordeal which their present sufferings subject them to. However, the importance of broadcasting the seeds of the Cause far and wide can never be sufficiently stressed. It is the right and privilege of organised humanity to hear of the Faith and the Plan of Bahá'u'lláh in these days, and in this holy duty to their fellow men the Bahá'ís must not fail whatever may be the sadness of their personal plight, for they alone can truly see the future in the tragic present, and possess hope and strength to go on with the spiritual battle for the victory of the New Day.

Regarding the question you have put to the Guardian concerning minute No. 259, whatever is not laid down in "Bahá'í Administration" is left to the judgement of the National Spiritual Assembly to decide. These are purely secondary details and as the Guardian wishes to avoid introducing into the administration a labyrinth of rules and regulations he leaves the friends in authority to decide such matters as they arise.

He hopes the Summer School will be a success. In all your undertakings you may rest assured of his constant and most loving prayers, not only for the National Assembly members, but for each and every member of the flock they are watching over and guiding. . . .

Dear and valued co-workers,
  The report of your continued activities, conducted amid the turmoil

that oppresses and afflicts the English believers, is a source of continual joy and inspiration to me, as well as those who, in distant parts of the Bahá'í world are made to realise the unwavering constancy with which you are all upholding the vital interests of the Faith of God. That the teaching work is speedily expanding, that the institutions of the Faith are functioning with vigour and in accordance with the principles of the Administrative Order, testify to the solidity of the foundations that have been established. On this foundation you will as the present hindrances are removed, and the tremendous reactions of this conflict are made apparent, rear an edifice worthy of the name, and attesting the glory of the Faith, of Bahá'u'lláh. Persevere in your present labours and be ever confident.

Your true and grateful brother,
Shoghi

3 November 1941

RUHI AFNÁN'S SISTER MARRIED SECRETLY COVENANT BREAKER HER MOTHER AND BROTHERS ALL CONCURRED ALL MANNER COMMUNICATION WITH THEM ACCORDING MASTER'S WILL FORBIDDEN.

SHOGHI RABBANÍ

29 December 1941

SISTER MEHRANGIS FOLLOWED EXAMPLE RUHI'S SISTER JUSTICE DEMANDS ANNOUNCE BELIEVERS HER EXPULSION.

SHOGHI RABBANÍ

28 February 1942

Dear Bahá'í Sister,

The Guardian has instructed me to answer your letters dated June 30th, Aug. 20th, Sept. 5th, Oct. 20th and 28th (duplicates of both received) and December 23rd and to acknowledge the receipt of the various minutes, programmes, etc., which they enclosed.

Regarding . . ., Shoghi Effendi is writing him direct, advising him to sever his membership in the Synagogue, but to continue to maintain friendly association with the members of its community.

The Guardian was very happy indeed to hear of the success of the Summer School and the enthusiasm that prevailed. He has received news of it from some of the friends, as well as the N.S.A., and feels that the English Bahá'ís have every reason to feel encouraged and proud of the way their tireless efforts are being rewarded.

The good news of the increase in Bahá'í membership is yet another evidence of the vitality of the community and the activity of the friends, in spite of the gloom of the times, which increasingly prevails. Indeed as material affairs go from bad to worse in the world, the confidence, optimism, love and hope of the believers will, by force of contrast, shine out as an ever brighter beacon, leading the people to the Path of Truth, the way laid down by God, which alone can guide them to the promise of the future.

Now that the British Isles have a respite from intense aerial warfare, no doubt the friends, especially in London and other cities, find themselves more refreshed and consequently better able to carry on the work of the Cause. They should not lose any time in consolidating the teaching work, reinforcing new centres, and enlarging their numbers.

The Guardian is urging the American friends, also, to redouble their efforts and not lose their precious opportunities. The value of work accomplished at present is inestimable, and opportunities lost are in a way quite irretrievable, as the agony of mankind moves forward to a climax. . . .

The many activities undertaken by the English friends, their determined efforts to bring the Cause before a wider public and reach people of outstanding importance, their new centres and study groups, are all signs which should greatly encourage them and demonstrate to them that the Holy Spirit is ever ready to sustain and reinforce the believers in all work for the good of our precious Faith.

The Guardian assures the members of the National Assembly of his most loving prayers on their behalf and his deep and abiding appreciation of their tireless services. They are helping the friends to build an edifice which neither time nor tide shall undermine and which needs must become the sole refuge for their sorely tried countrymen. . . .

Dear and valued co-workers,

I wish to assure you again of my feelings of profound gratitude for the manner in which you are performing your sacred task and discharging, individually and collectively, your pressing and manifold responsibilities. I rejoice and am deeply thankful to learn that the trials and tribulations that so fiercely assailed you in the past have lessened and have failed to interfere with the progress of your activities. Bahá'u'lláh will no doubt continue to guide, sustain and protect you in the days to come and is well pleased with the marvellous evidences of your perseverance, unity, loyalty and devotion. I will continue to supplicate His abundant blessing for you all, that your numbers may steadily increase, your community life be continually enriched, your institutions flourish and multiply, and the foundation of your individual spiritual lives be strengthened. Persevere in your high labours.

Your true and grateful brother,
Shoghi

27 April 1942 (Convention)

MAGNIFICENT SPIRIT ENGLISH BELIEVERS CHEERS STRENGTHENS ME ARDUOUS TASK THANKFUL THEIR MESSAGE ADMIRE THEIR ACHIEVEMENTS PRAYING THEIR PROTECTION CHERISH GREAT HOPES TRIUMPHANT ATTAINMENT THEIR GOAL.

SHOGHI RABBANÍ

20 June 1942

Dear Bahá'í Sister,

The Guardian has instructed me to answer your letters written on behalf of the National Assembly, and dated Feb. 6th, March 17th and April 6th, and to acknowledge the receipt of the minutes of the Jan. and March meetings of your Assembly together with other enclosures.

In pursuance of your request the Guardian wrote to Mr. and

Mrs. Hill about the tragic and unexpected passing of their daughter. He also felt moved to cable them his condolences and the assurance of his prayers. This must have been for them a very grievous blow; but he feels sure the deep assurances concerning the future life, which have been given us by Bahá'u'lláh, have comforted and sustained them throughout.

He was pleased to read the sympathetic letter you received from ex-President Benes of Czechoslovakia, as well as that of Sir Ronald Storrs. Many men in high positions are aware now of the existence and aims of our Faith, but they do not yet reckon it to be a movement worthy of more profound interest on their part. As time goes by, however, we may rest assured their interest will grow.

That is perhaps what is most glorious about our present activities all over the world, that we, a band not large in numbers, not possessing financial backing or the prestige of great names, should, in the name of our beloved Faith, be forging ahead at such a pace, and demonstrating to future and present generations that it is the God-given qualities of our religion that are raising it up and not the transient support of worldly fame and power. All that will come later, when it has been made clear beyond the shadow of a doubt that what raised aloft the banner of Bahá'u'lláh was the love, sacrifice and devotion of His humble followers and the change that His teachings wrought in their hearts and lives.

It is just such exemplary devotion and perseverance that the British Bahá'ís are showing at present, and their reward cannot but be great and lasting. The laying of the foundation is a slow process, but the most important one in the erection of any structure. The Guardian feels that your Assembly, as well as the friends in England, have every reason to feel proud of, and encouraged by, the way the work is progressing there.

He hopes that your Summer School this year will be even more successful than last year, in spite of being held in two parts. You may be sure he will pray for its success.

He fully realises the difficulties you are undergoing enhanced by the war and its hardships, yet he sees, perhaps even more clearly than you yourselves can, that these very difficulties and the surmounting of them are deepening and strengthening the ties that bind you all to our beloved Faith, and enabling you to do a work which only future generations of your countrymen will be able to properly appreciate and assess.

Please convey to all the dear friends the assurances of his love and his prayers for their service in these days, and his high hopes for the future that awaits them in the days to come, when the Cause of God begins to emerge above the waves of the old order and shines forth in all its strength and beauty.

Assuring you and all your fellow-members of his deep appreciation of your tireless work and his ardent prayers for your guidance and strength. . . .

Dearly beloved co-worker,
The steady progress and extension of Bahá'í activities in the British Isles is, no doubt, the direct consequence of the unswerving loyalty, the high courage, the incorruptible spirit and the exemplary devotion and steadfastness of the British believers, who have, simply and strikingly, demonstrated the quality of their faith and the soundness of their institutions in these days of unprecedented commotion, stress and peril. I feel proud of their record of service and of the evidence of their noble faith. The Beloved watches over them from the Abhá Kingdom. The Concourse on High extols their achievements and will reinforce their endeavours. They should confidently, gratefully, joyously and unitedly redouble their efforts, extend the range of their activities, rededicate themselves to their historic task and anticipate a renewed outpouring of Bahá'u'lláh's promised blessings and favours.
Your true and grateful brother,
Shoghi

28 July 1942

MAGNIFICENT SPIRIT ANIMATING STEADFAST ENGLISH BELIEVERS NOTABLE ACCOMPLISHMENTS TEACHING FIELD PROMPT ME CONTRIBUTE TWO HUNDRED POUNDS FURTHERANCE THEIR HISTORIC TEACHING ACTIVITIES URGE REDOUBLE EFFORTS PRAYING SIGNAL VICTORIES LOVING GRATITUDE.
SHOGHI RABBANÍ

8 August 1942 (Summer School)

DELIGHTED SUCCESSFUL SCHOOL APPRECIATE SPIRIT BELIEVERS ASSURE ALL CONTINUED PRAYERS.

SHOGHI RABBANÍ

8 August 1942

Dear Bahá'í Sister,

Your letters of May 14th and June 10th together with their enclosures reached the Guardian safely, and he has instructed me to answer you on his behalf.

He has been very gratified to hear of the successful Summer School sessions, news of the Buxton one having just recently reached him in your latest cable. He feels that you must all be very encouraged that this new way of holding them in different places, which circumstances made imperative, has proved so successful in the end. It presages the day when the friends in England will see the institutions of their Faith rising from various flourishing centres.

Regarding minute No. 507, the Guardian feels that it would be better for either the mothers of Bahá'í children—or some committee your Assembly might delegate the task to—to choose excerpts from the Sacred Words to be used by the child rather than just something made up. Of course prayer can be purely spontaneous, but many of the sentences and thoughts combined in Bahá'í writings of a devotional nature are easy to grasp, and the revealed Word is endowed with a power of its own....

Shoghi Effendi fully realises the strain which those who are so actively bearing the weight of Bahá'í responsibility are subjected to in these days, when already, as private individuals, the events of the world are affecting their lives and drawing on their strength. It makes the quality of Bahá'í service so much finer, that it should entail on the part of all definite self-sacrifice.

Though the friends may not be fully aware of it, their staunch perseverance in carrying out their Bahá'í activities in the face of war conditions, is really in itself of historic importance. Convention, Summer Schools, meetings, all are not only demonstrating the calibre of their faith, but also evincing marked progress, all of which greatly cheers and delights the Guardian.

He assures you and your fellow-members of the National Spiritual Assembly, of his continued prayers on your behalf, that you may be guided, protected and sustained in your devoted services to the Faith. . . .

P.S.—Shoghi Effendi is deeply interested in the plans you are developing to aid and attract more young people to the Faith. He feels this is both praiseworthy and a valuable method of teaching the Cause.

Dear and valued co-worker,

The work so splendidly initiated by the English believers and so devotedly and energetically pursued and consolidated in these days of peril, uncertainty and turmoil, establishes beyond any doubt their right to claim to be the true upholders and custodians of the Faith of Bahá'u'lláh. They have, ever since the outbreak of this world wide conflict, abundantly demonstrated the high quality of their faith, the soundness of their institutions, the intensity of their devotion, and their capacity to defend and promote the interests of their beloved Cause. Impelled by admiration and gratitude for the work they have already accomplished, I have contributed a sum which I trust will enable them to extend the range of their teaching activities throughout the British Isles. May the Beloved graciously assist them to achieve such victories in this field as shall truly befit the conclusion of the first century of the Bahá'í Era.

Your true and grateful brother,
Shoghi

12 November 1942

CABLING TWO HUNDRED POUNDS CARE COOKS THANKSGIVING PROTECTION COMMUNITY BELIEVERS BRITISH ISLES AND FURTHERANCE ALL-IMPORTANT TEACHING ACTIVITIES PRAYING CONTINUALLY EPOCH MAKING VICTORIES.

SHOGHI RABBANÍ

13 January 1943

CONVEY GLAD TIDINGS ENGLISH BELIEVERS COMPLETION EXTERIOR

EDIFICE MOTHER TEMPLE WEST ADVISE CABLE CONGRATULATIONS
REPRESENTATIVES AMERICAN BAHÁ'ÍS SUPERB ACHIEVEMENT AND
WIDE PUBLICITY BRITISH PRESS.

SHOGHI RABBANÍ

20 January 1943

ASSURE ATTENDANTS CONFERENCE LOVING APPRECIATION PRAYERS.

SHOGHI RABBANÍ

9 March 1943

Dear Bahá'í Sister,

Your letters dated July 19th 1942, Aug. 20th 1942, Sept. 15th 1942, and Dec. 8th 1942 have all reached the Guardian safely, as well as their enclosures, and he has instructed me to answer them on his behalf.

This last year he has been greatly overburdened with work, and that is why he so frequently has to delay the answering of his many letters.

The good news you conveyed of the marked success of the various Summer Schools held last year pleased him greatly. When the English friends remember that it is not many years since they ventured on their first Summer School and now, during war time, they have managed to hold four successful ones, they should feel very encouraged and proud! It shows that when the determination is strong and the faith firm, the friends can work wonders and surprise even themselves!

He was also delighted to hear of the successful teaching work and public meetings undertaken in Bradford and Manchester, and that the advertisements and publicity which you are sponsoring are meeting with a certain amount of response from the public.

He hopes that some of the friends will find it possible to move, at least temporarily, to centres where sufficient believers, or interested enquirers exist to enable a Spiritual Assembly to be formed by 1944. If such work is feasible it is, indeed, of great importance and well worth the sacrifices involved. This policy of settlement has been fruitful in both India and the United States, and as soon as a determined and active Assembly is started it is, of course, much easier to teach and carry on the work of the Cause.

The burdens everyone has to bear these days are heavy, and the way often seems long and hard which we and our fellow-men in general, are called upon to tread; but we know where it leads and what our work is and what that work must ultimately mean to not only the Bahá'ís but the whole world. This knowledge strengthens us and enables us to go on with a faith and confidence which cannot but help and inspire others. We are Bahá'u'lláh's army and we cannot fail, as He leads us on.

The Guardian assures you and all the N.S.A. members of his most loving prayers. The English friends are increasingly dear to him, and he has great hopes for their future achievements.

Dear and valued co-workers,

The evidences of renewed activity in the teaching field are most encouraging and the spirit which animates the English believers in these days of stress and peril is highly inspiring. As the first Bahá'í century draws to a close, a supreme effort should be exerted by the believers in order to consummate befittingly the task they have arisen to achieve. I will pray with all my heart that the hopes they cherish may be realised, and their continued labours be crowned with glorious success.

Your true and grateful brother,
Shoghi

Naw-Rúz, 1943

APPRECIATE MESSAGE RECIPROCATE LOVING GREETINGS THANKFUL DIVINE PROTECTION PRAYING UNPRECEDENTED VICTORIES LAST YEAR FIRST BAHÁ'Í CENTURY.

SHOGHI RABBANÍ

21 April 1943 (Convention)

APPEAL DELEGATES ASSEMBLED CONVENTION DELIBERATE PROMPT

EFFECTUAL MEASURES ENSURE UNPRECEDENTED EXPANSION PIONEER TEACHING ACTIVITIES LAST YEAR CENTURY AND BEFITTING CELEBRATION MAY 1944 CENTENARY FAITH ADVISE PREPARE SURVEY OUTSTANDING EVENTS FORTY-FIVE YEAR HISTORY FAITH BRITISH ISLES ASSURE FRIENDS FERVENT CONTINUED PRAYERS ABUNDANT BLESSINGS SUCCESS TWO-FOLD TASK CABLING THREE HUNDRED POUNDS CONTRIBUTION TOWARDS FULFILMENT PROJECTED UNDERTAKINGS DEEPEST LOVE.

SHOGHI RABBANÍ

26 April 1943

DELIGHTED RESPONSE HIGH RESOLVE ASSURE ASSEMBLY PRAYERS MAGNIFICENT VICTORIES.

SHOGHI RABBANÍ

12 May 1943

KINDLY AIR MAIL IMMEDIATELY FULL LIST NAMES ALL LOCALITIES BRITISH ISLES WHERE ONE OR MORE BELIEVERS RESIDE SPECIFYING THOSE POSSESSING SPIRITUAL ASSEMBLIES.

SHOGHI RABBANÍ

17 June 1943

CABLING TWO HUNDRED POUNDS THROUGH COOKS CONTRIBUTION ASSIST YOUR ASSEMBLY CELEBRATE BEFITTINGLY CENTENARY BELOVED FAITH WRITING.

SHOGHI RABBANÍ

17 June 1943

Dear Bahá'í Sister,

Your letters, written on behalf of the National Spiritual Assembly, and dated Oct. 22nd 1942, Feb. 18th 1943 and April 12th and May 11th, have all been received, and the Guardian has instructed me to answer them on his behalf.

He was very pleased to hear that the publicity you are giving the Faith is meeting with a wider response than has hitherto been the case, and he hopes that the N.S.A. and local Assemblies will organise their efforts in such a way as to enable them to draw enquirers closer to the Cause and, if possible, meet with them and include them in suitable teaching classes.

Regarding the matter of Fuád Afnán's grave, the Guardian has no objection to its being built.

He feels that Bahá'ís who, though still considering themselves believers, omit attending the 19 Day Feasts for long periods, should not be deprived of their voting rights; they should, however, be encouraged to attend these Feasts as often as possible.

In less than a year the Bahá'ís the world over will be celebrating the 100th anniversary of their Faith, and the Guardian is very anxious that the British believers should commemorate this historic occasion befittingly. He would, therefore, suggest that your Assembly take up the following points for deliberation as soon as possible:

1. The holding of a large and representative gathering, attended by the Bahá'ís and the public alike, in a hired hall in London on the 23rd May 1944. He feels that prominent friends and sympathisers of the Faith should be invited to speak on this occasion, as well as Bahá'ís, and that every effort should be made to make the gathering both festive and dignified, as befits so blessed and solemn an occasion.
2. The publication of a Centenary Pamphlet outlining the important events of the Faith, and with a special emphasis placed on the rise and development of the Cause in England, its early history in that country, the achievements of the friends in spreading the Teachings there and establishing the administration, the formation of the Publishing Trust, and so on.
3. He wishes your Assembly to call the annual Bahá'í Convention for days that will include the 22nd May, so that all the assembled friends may be present at a special Bahá'í meeting to be held at 2 hours and 11 minutes after sunset on May 22nd as this is the exact time at which the Báb made His first historic declaration of His mission to Mullá Ḥusayn.

In order to aid the dear English believers in their befitting celebration of so glorious an occasion the Guardian is forwarding to your Assembly the sum of two hundred pounds sterling to be used for the arrangements you deem fit to make, and the publication of the above mentioned pamphlet. The Bahá'í communities all over the world—wherever free to do so—will also be celebrating this memorable day, each according to its capacity, and he is very anxious that the British Bahá'ís should, as befits their increasingly prominent position in the Bahá'í World, demonstrate to the public and to their fellow believers, the vitality of their community and the marked advancement it has made of late. He leaves all details to the discretion of your Assembly.

Mr. Yool of Manchester was recently able to spend his leave in Haifa at the Western Pilgrim House, and the Guardian was so happy to welcome one of the English friends here. He hopes that after the war many will be able to make the pilgrimage. They will be most welcome.

Assuring you and all the members of the N.S.A. of his loving prayers and his ardent hopes for the success of this great celebration which you will now be planning. . . .

P.S. The Guardian recently cabled asking you to forward a complete list of all Spiritual Assemblies in the British Isles and the name of every locality where one or more believers reside.

Dear and valued co-workers,

I pray that the celebration of the Centenary of our beloved Faith by the English believers may be a remarkable success. The committee that will have to be appointed for this purpose must strain every nerve, explore every avenue, and lose no time in order to ensure the unqualified success of this undertaking. I will supplicate the Beloved to guide every step you take, to aid you to surmount all obstacles, and to inspire you to undertake the measures that are most conducive to the proper discharge of your noble task. The widest possible publicity should be given to the Faith by every means at your disposal.

Your true and grateful brother,
Shoghi

4 August 1943

Dear Bahá'í Sister,

Your letters, written on behalf of the National Spiritual

Assembly and dated May 14th and June 6th have been received, together with the minutes of the April and May N.S.A. meetings, and the Guardian has instructed me to answer them on his behalf.

He was very encouraged to see the number of places where there are now one or two registered Bahá'ís residing, as these are beacons of the Faith—however lonely and however, as yet, feeble the light they are able to radiate.

The Guardian feels that it would be an excellent plan if some way could be found to raise Bournemouth and Torquay to Assembly status; either through some self-sacrificing souls moving to these places and thus giving them the required number, or through the efforts of the local and visiting teachers. With the Centenary of the Faith so rapidly approaching it seems a great pity that England should be deprived of these two Assemblies, when each one of them only requires one person to bring it to Assembly status.

Regarding the questions you asked in connection with the following minutes of the N.S.A. meetings:

753. The Guardian advises you to consult Canon Townshend, and if he considers it advisable to compile a pamphlet for distribution to the clergy you could get one out along the lines he might suggest as suitable.
754. He would not advise any special contact being made with the Swedenborgians as the Master's reference is not sufficiently clear and emphatic to warrant it.
775. The Guardian does not believe you should ask the Russian Embassy for help in locating Mde. Grinevskaya's play about the Báb, as he believes they could be of no help in the matter. You might ask the American N.S.A. if they have this material available.

The Guardian's prayers are offered on behalf of the N.S.A. members, that you, one and all, may be aided and guided in your labours during the coming months, to prepare the way for a befitting and glorious Centenary celebration of our beloved Faith during May of 1944.

Dearly beloved friends,
I was so pleased and encouraged to witness the recent evidences of

the determination of the English believers to arise, as never before, during this concluding year of the first Bahá'í century, and ensure the extension of the teaching activities of the Faith, the consolidation of its interests, and a better understanding and wider recognition of its aims, its principles, and accomplishments. The efforts they must exert during these remaining months must be unprecedented in their range and character. The blessings that will be vouchsafed to them, if they unitedly persevere and vigorously prosecute their urgent task, will alike be unprecedented. The preparation for a befitting celebration of the forthcoming Centenary must likewise be carefully and energetically carried out. May the Almighty sustain and guide them in their vast and meritorious endeavours.

Shoghi

10 August 1943 *(Summer School)*

CONCENTRATION TEACHING AND CENTENARY PREPARATIONS MOST VITAL MATTERS FERVENTLY PRAY ALL MAY BECOME RADIANTLY ACTIVE GREETINGS DEEPLY APPRECIATED.

SHOGHI RABBANÍ

25 October 1943

ADVISE CONTACT HERBERT SAMUEL RONALD STORRS TUDOR POLE AND OTHER SYMPATHISERS WHICH NATIONAL ASSEMBLY MAY SUGGEST VIGOROUS ACTION NECESSARY SAFEGUARD INTERESTS FAITH INSURE SUCCESS CELEBRATION.

SHOGHI RABBANÍ

2 November 1943

CABLING FIVE HUNDRED POUNDS TO BE EXPENDED DISCRETION YOUR ASSEMBLY FURTHERANCE TEACHING ACTIVITIES AND BAHÁ'Í PUBLICATIONS DEEPEST LOVE ASSURANCE CONTINUED PRAYERS.

SHOGHI RABBANÍ

5 January 1944*

KINDLY CABLE DATE FORMATION FIRST BAHÁ'Í NATIONAL ASSEMBLY.

SHOGHI RABBANÍ

13 March 1944

Dear Bahá'í Sister,
Your letters dated July 15th, Aug. 12th, Oct. 3rd, Nov. 1st and 10th and Dec. 5th together with various enclosures have been received, and the Guardian has instructed me to answer them on his behalf.

Regarding the article by Mrs. Thornburgh-Cropper, the Guardian does not place such material in the archives, but it might possibly be either stored with past documents or have been returned to the "Bahá'í World" Committee. He regrets his inability to forward it to you in time to be of any use in preparing the Centenary Pamphlet.

He would like you to assure Mr. St. Barbe Baker† that the Bahá'ís would be happy to avail themselves of his connections in Africa and his assistance and advice in the future teaching work there. Tremendous tasks lie ahead of the believers during the opening years of the second Bahá'í century, and undoubtedly spreading the Faith in Africa will be one of them.

He considered the Diary gotten out by the Publishing Trust to be in excellent taste, and is very pleased it has proved a medium of spreading the news of the existence of our beloved Faith and its nature. He appreciated receiving the copies forwarded to him. He is also very pleased to hear that the publication of the Centenary Pamphlet is now assured.

He sees no objection to getting out a compilation of Tablets of Bahá'u'lláh and 'Abdu'l-Bahá (as per minute No. 906) providing the source is authentic and the translations faithful and presentable.

He was very pleased to see that new and better headquarters for the Assembly and meetings in London have been found, and trusts this foreshadows the development of a national administrative headquarters there in England in the not too distant future.

*The cabled reply was "First meeting thirteenth October, 1923."

In spite of the burden the Bahá'ís, in common with their countrymen, are bearing these days, they are showing marked progress in their activities, and he feels confident that the friends, so loyal and devoted to the beloved Faith, will arise unitedly, in so important a country as England—one of the first to receive the Divine Message in the West—and will ensure that the Centenary is befittingly celebrated in spite of the many difficulties to be overcome.

Assuring you one and all of his ardent prayers for the success of your work, for your strength and protection....

P.S. Your letter of Jan. 18th has been received and the Guardian wishes to state that in connection with the royalties on "Paris Talks" that, as Mrs. Hall and her sister wish to turn them over to the Cause, the Assembly should accept and the money in future go to the National Fund there in England....

Any royalties on the works of the Master, as one of the Central Figures of our Faith, are naturally the property of the Cause and not of His heirs.

Dear and valued co-workers,

I am delighted to hear of the steps that have been taken by your Assembly in preparation for the forthcoming celebration of the centenary of our beloved Faith, and I pray that success may crown your devoted efforts. The English believers are in every field of Bahá'í activity and service demonstrating the quality of their faith and the keen sense of responsibility which animates them in their organised and concerted endeavours for the promotion of the vital interests of the Faith. I feel proud of their record of service, and will pray with increasing fervour for their protection and success.

Shoghi

Naw-Rúz, 1944

APPRECIATE GREETINGS PRAYING GREAT VICTORIES OPENING CENTURY.

SHOGHI RABBANÍ

22 April 1944

CABLING ONE THOUSAND POUNDS MY LOVING CONTRIBUTION FURTHER EXTENSION BAHÁ'Í PUBLISHING ACTIVITIES AND INITIATION ADDITIONAL MEASURES ENSURE BRILLIANT SUCCESS CENTENARY CELEBRATIONS PRAYING ARDENTLY SUCCESS BOTH FIELDS.

SHOGHI RABBANÍ

1 May 1944

DELIGHTED PRAYING FERVENTLY SUCCESS.

SHOGHI RABBANÍ

3 May 1944*

ADVISE SHARE FOLLOWING FACTS WITH BELIEVERS AT CONVENTION CELEBRATING HUNDREDTH ANNIVERSARY FAITH BAHÁ'U'LLÁH. BAHÁ'ÍS ESTABLISHED RESIDENCE SEVENTY EIGHT COUNTRIES FIFTY SIX OF WHICH ARE SOVEREIGN STATES. BAHÁ'Í LITERATURE TRANSLATED PUBLISHED FORTY ONE LANGUAGES. TRANSLATIONS UNDERTAKEN TWELVE ADDITIONAL LANGUAGES. THIRTY ONE RACES REPRESENTED BAHÁ'Í WORLD COMMUNITY. FIVE NATIONAL ASSEMBLIES AND SIXTY ONE LOCAL ASSEMBLIES BELONGING TEN COUNTRIES INCORPORATED LEGALLY EMPOWERED HOLD PROPERTY. BAHÁ'Í INTERNATIONAL ENDOWMENTS HOLY LAND ESTIMATED HALF MILLION POUNDS. NATIONAL BAHÁ'Í ENDOWMENTS UNITED STATES ESTIMATED ONE MILLION SEVEN HUNDRED THOUSAND DOLLARS. AREA LAND JORDAN VALLEY DEDICATED BAHÁ'Í SHRINES OVER FIVE HUNDRED FIFTY ACRES. SITE PURCHASED FUTURE BAHÁ'Í TEMPLE PERSIA COMPRISES THREE AND HALF MILLION SQUARE METERS. COST STRUCTURE FIRST BAHÁ'Í TEMPLE WEST ONE MILLION THREE HUNDRED THOUSAND DOLLARS. IN EVERY STATE PROVINCE NORTH AMERICA BAHÁ'Í ASSEMBLIES FUNCTIONING. IN THIRTEEN HUNDRED LOCALITIES UNITED STATES CANADA BAHÁ'ÍS RESIDING. BAHÁ'Í CENTRES ESTABLISHED EVERY REPUBLIC LATIN AMERICA FIFTEEN OF WHICH POSSESS SPIRITUAL ASSEMBLIES. FAITH WESTERN HEMISPHERE NOW STRETCHES FROM ANCHORAGE ALASKA TO

---
*Printed also in "Messages to America (1932–1946)".

MAGALLANES WORLD'S SOUTHERN-MOST CITY. SIXTY TWO CENTRES ESTABLISHED INDIA TWENTY SEVEN WITH SPIRITUAL ASSEMBLIES. AMONG HISTORIC SITES PURCHASED PERSIA ṬIHRÁN HOME BAHÁ'U'LLÁH BÁB'S SHOP BÚSHIHR BURIAL PLACE QUDDÚS PART VILLAGE CHIHRIQ THREE GARDENS BADASHT PLACE CONFINEMENT ṬÁHIRIH. BAHÁ'Í NATIONAL ADMINISTRATIVE HEADQUARTERS FOUNDED ṬIHRÁN DELHI CAIRO BAGHDÁD WILMETTE SYDNEY. BAHÁ'Í ENDOWMENTS HOLY LAND AND UNITED STATES EXEMPTED TAXES BY CIVIL AUTHORITIES. CIVIL RECOGNITION EXTENDED BAHÁ'Í ASSEMBLIES IN FIVE STATES UNITED STATES SOLEMNISE BAHÁ'Í MARRIAGES. SUGGEST UTILISE ABOVE INFORMATION PUBLICITY PURPOSES WHEREVER ADVISABLE.

SHOGHI RABBANÍ

22 May 1944

REJOICE MAGNIFICENT SUCCESS CENTENARY CELEBRATIONS VALIANT LOYAL BELOVED COMMUNITY ENGLISH BELIEVERS. CONVEY SIR RONALD STORRS LOVING APPRECIATION HIS NOBLE ACT. ASSURE ALL ATTENDANTS CONVENTION PARTICIPANTS CELEBRATION LOVING REMEMBRANCE FERVENT PRAYERS SHRINES BÁB 'ABDU'L-BAHÁ. CONFIDENT UNQUENCHABLE SPIRIT ANIMATING WELL-TRIED STOUT-HEARTED FIRMLY KNIT FOLLOWERS BAHÁ'U'LLÁH BRITISH ISLES WILL ENABLE THEM SURMOUNT ALL OBSTACLES SCALE NOBLER HEIGHTS ACHIEVE GREATER VICTORIES OPENING YEARS SECOND BAHÁ'Í CENTURY.

SHOGHI RABBANÍ

23 May 1944

ANNOUNCE FRIENDS JOYFUL TIDINGS HUNDREDTH ANNIVERSARY DECLARATION MISSION MARTYRED HERALD FAITH SIGNALISED BY HISTORIC DECISION COMPLETE STRUCTURE HIS SEPULCHRE ERECTED BY 'ABDU'L-BAHÁ ON SITE CHOSEN BY BAHÁ'U'LLÁH. RECENTLY DESIGNED MODEL DÔME UNVEILED PRESENCE ASSEMBLED BELIEVERS. PRAYING EARLY REMOVAL OBSTACLES CONSUMMATION STUPENDOUS PLAN CONCEIVED BY FOUNDER FAITH AND HOPES CHERISHED BY CENTRE HIS COVENANT.

SHOGHI RABBANÍ

"Their first collective enterprise"

THE SIX YEAR PLAN
1944-1950

25 May 1944*

WELCOME SPONTANEOUS DECISION ADVISE FORMATION NINETEEN SPIRITUAL ASSEMBLIES SPREAD OVER ENGLAND WALES SCOTLAND NORTHERN IRELAND AND EIRE PRAYING SIGNAL VICTORY.

SHOGHI RABBANÍ

26 May 1944

OVERJOYED SUCCESS CELEBRATIONS. PRAYING EVER INCREASING FLOW DIVINE OUTPOURINGS.

SHOGHI RABBANÍ

8 July 1944

PREPARE CONDENSED REPORT NOT EXCEEDING THIRTY PAGES REGARDING ACTIVITIES ACHIEVEMENTS BAHÁ'Í FAITH DURING PAST FOUR YEARS. MAIL ONE COPY AMERICA ANOTHER HAIFA PROMPT ACTION NECESSARY.

SHOGHI RABBANÍ

11 August 1944

APPRECIATE GREETINGS PRAYING BLESSINGS SUMMER SCHOOL AND TEACHING PLAN LOVE.

SHOGHI RABBANÍ

12 August 1944

Dear Bahá'í Sister,
  Your letters dated March 3rd and 25th, April 23rd, May 18th

*In response to cable from Convention announcing adoption of a six year plan and requesting the Guardian to set the goals.

and July 6th together with their enclosures have all been received, and the beloved Guardian has instructed me to answer them on his behalf.

He was most deeply gratified over the way the Centenary was conducted in London and feels that it has adequately demonstrated the vitality of the faith which animates the British Bahá'í community. They may well look upon this as their major achievement since the visits to their shores of the beloved Master. He was also very pleased to hear of the celebrations successfully held by the Manchester and Torquay Bahá'ís in their respective communities.

"The Centenary of a World Faith" he found most excellently gotten out and not only well written but calculated to arouse the interest of the reader and impress him with the true stature of our World Faith. He has distributed copies among the friends and placed some in the library of the Mansion, at Bahjí. He was also pleased with the programme of the London Meetings—so you can see that the patient efforts and sacrifices of the members of the N.S.A. and all those who contributed to the marked success of the Centenary celebrations in England, have met not only with his approval and admiration but brought happiness to his often heavily over-burdened heart!

Regarding your question concerning minute No. 1050; this is entirely a matter of conscience; if the individual feels for some reason justified in voting for himself, he is free to do so. Regarding your question of the proper time to celebrate or hold our meetings of commemoration, the time should be fixed by counting after sunset; the Master passed away one hour after midnight, which falls a certain number of hours after sunset; so His passing should be commemorated according to the sun and regardless of daylight saving time. The same applies to the ascension of Bahá'u'lláh who passed away about 8 hours after sunset.

The Guardian has already cabled you regarding your Six Year Teaching Plan, and he hopes that events in the future will be more favourable to carrying it out than they are at present. He often thinks of and prays for the English friends during these days of ordeal they are again passing through and he feels confident Bahá'u'lláh will strengthen their work and bless their efforts for this Holy Cause. . . .

THE SIX YEAR PLAN (1944–1950)

Dear and valued co-workers,
  The Six Year Plan which the national elected representatives of the English believers have spontaneously launched is a further evidence of their unquenchable faith and noble and unyielding determination to prosecute energetically the teaching work in the British Isles and to exploit to the full the notable advantages derived from the successful celebrations of the Bahá'í Centenary in London. Attention should be focussed in the course of the opening year of the second Bahá'í Century on the needs and requirements of this Plan. The multiplication of Bahá'í centres and the dissemination of Bahá'í literature should be regarded as the chief objectives of the prosecutors of the Plan. Every sacrifice should be made, every effort should be exerted and every avenue should be explored to ensure the success of the Plan. The English believers stand identified with this Plan. The immediate destinies of the entire community depend upon it. I will pray for its success, will watch its progress and pledge every assistance within my power for its promotion. May the Beloved bless all those who have embarked upon it and crown their enterprise with brilliant and total victory.
  Your true and grateful brother,
  Shoghi

14 August 1944

ANXIOUS SAFETY LONDON BELIEVERS KINDLY CABLE.
  SHOGHI RABBANÍ

5 January 1945

APPRECIATE VERBATIM REPORTS ADDRESSES DELIVERED OPENING CENTENARY EXHIBITION AND PUBLIC MEETING DENISON HOUSE.
  SHOGHI RABBANÍ

27 January 1945

KINDLY CABLE ADDRESS TUDOR-POLE MAIL THREE COPIES EVERY PHOTOGRAPH TAKEN CENTENARY.
  SHOGHI RABBANÍ

27 March 1945

Dear Bahá'í Sister,

Your letters, written on behalf of the National Spiritual Assembly, and dated Aug. 2nd, 21st and 31st (airgraph) and Oct. 9th, Nov. 16th (airgraph) and Nov. 23rd (duplicate copy also received), Dec. 19th (duplicate copy also received) all of 1944, and Jan. 25th 1945 (duplicate copy also received) have arrived safely with any enclosures they contained, and the beloved Guardian has instructed me to answer them.

He fully realises the many handicaps the English Bahá'ís are labouring under, and appreciates all the more deeply their perseverance and devotion shown in such activities as the National Centenary in London and local exhibitions and meetings held elsewhere, as well as the successful Summer School, the various printing undertakings and the renewed efforts to establish new centres and strengthen older ones. In this connection he would like you to please convey to Miss Young* and all other pioneers the expression of his loving appreciation of this historic service they have arisen to render the Faith in England.

The tasks facing the believers everywhere are great, for they see only too clearly that the only permanent remedy for the many afflictions the world is suffering from, is a change of heart and a new pattern of not only thought but personal conduct. The impetus that has been given by the Manifestation of God for this Age is the sole one that can regenerate humanity, and as we Bahá'ís are the only ones yet aware of this new force in the world, our obligation towards our fellow men is tremendous and inescapable! Therefore he hopes that many more of the friends there will arise to do pioneering work and help achieve the important goals set by the Six Year Plan. When once a few bold, self-sacrificing individuals have arisen to serve, their example will no doubt encourage other timid would-be pioneers to follow in their footsteps. The history of our Faith is full of records of the remarkable things achieved by really very simple,

---

* Miss Jessica Young†; Mrs. Kathleen Brown (later Lady Hornell)†; Miss Ursula Newman (later Mrs. Samandarí)† were the first to arise to pioneer in the British Isles.

insignificant individuals, who became veritable beacons and towers of strength through having placed their trust in God, having arisen to proclaim His Message. The stamina and fortitude shown by the people at large during all these hard and bitter years of war should surely find a nobler example in the deeds of the Bahá'ís who are connected with the Divine Source! He urges your Assembly to do all in its power, through financial and moral assistance, to get more pioneers into the field.

Mr. Hofman has just written him about his meeting with the Paris believers, and he feels that as most of the friends there are elderly people and have suffered many privations, the British N.S.A. should keep in close touch with them and help and inspire them all it can. . . .

Also concerning your question about the prayers and changing the pronouns: This cannot be done, even in the long Obligatory Prayer or the healing prayers. Either we must ignore this mere detail or say a prayer that applies to our sex or number. . . .

You may be sure that you, and your fellow members of the N.S.A., are very often in his thoughts and prayers. He deeply appreciates your steadfast and persevering labours and hopes that the believers of England will arise to fulfil their high duties and discharge the debts they owe their countrymen through the privilege of being the followers of Bahá'u'lláh in these dark yet historic days. . . .

P.S. The following is a copy of the cable the Guardian sent you in answer to your request for his advice as to the Six Year Plan the British believers resolved to undertake:

"WELCOME SPONTANEOUS DECISION. ADVISE FORMATION NINETEEN BAHÁ'Í SPIRITUAL ASSEMBLIES SPREAD OVER ENGLAND WALES SCOTLAND NORTHERN IRELAND AND EIRE. PRAYING SIGNAL VICTORY."

He will, you may be sure, do everything in his power to assist the friends to achieve this objective.

Dear and valued co-workers,
The Six Year Plan which the English believers have conceived and are now energetically prosecuting constitutes a landmark in the history of the Faith in the British Isles. It is the first collective enterprise undertaken by them for the spread of the Faith and the consolidation

of its divinely appointed institutions. The national elected representatives of the Bahá'í community in those islands must watch carefully every phase in its development, provide whatever is required for its systematic and steady extension, encourage the believers to disperse, to settle, to persevere, and to appeal more directly and effectively to the masses who are waiting for this Divine Message, and on whose ultimate response the triumph of the Cause of Bahá'u'lláh must depend. Obstacles, however formidable, should be surmounted. Setbacks, however discouraging at first, must not, under any circumstances, cause them to deviate from the path they are so devotedly and determinedly pursuing. That glorious success may eventually crown their concerted and historic endeavours is my fervent and constant prayer at the Holy Shrines. May the Beloved aid them to achieve their noble end.

Shoghi

11 April 1945

BAHÁ'Í PERSIAN NATIONAL ASSEMBLY EXPELLED . . . FAMILY OWING REPUDIATION VITAL PROVISIONS MASTER'S WILL AND LONG-STANDING DISOBEDIENCE. POSITION ANY MEMBER THIS FAMILY IN LONDON SHOULD BE IMMEDIATELY ASCERTAINED BY YOUR ASSEMBLY. CABLE RESULTS. UTMOST FIRMNESS VIGILANCE REQUIRED OTHERWISE CONTACT BREAKERS COVENANT WILL ENDANGER FAITH.

SHOGHI RABBANÍ

25 April 1945

APPRECIATE CABLE RECEIVED FROM. . . . FEEL HOWEVER OWING DEFECTION HIS ENTIRE FAMILY NECESSITY FORMAL ASSURANCE BEFORE YOUR ASSEMBLY HIS DETERMINATION CEASE COMMUNICATION WITH HIS FAMILY AWAITING ASSEMBLY'S REPLY.

SHOGHI RABBANÍ

1 May 1945

LOVING APPRECIATION CONVENTION MESSAGE. ENGLISH BELIEVERS LOVINGLY REMEMBERED SHRINES FERVENTLY SUPPLICATING

THE SIX YEAR PLAN (1944–1950)

SUCCESS SIX YEAR PLAN URGE REDOUBLED EFFORTS CABLING FIVE HUNDRED POUNDS MY CONTRIBUTION PLAN.

SHOGHI RABBANÍ

3 May 1945

ASSURE... APPRECIATE RESPONSE. CONCERNING MEDIUM DO NOT ADVISE ACCEPTANCE MEMBERSHIP.

SHOGHI RABBANÍ

9 May 1945*

FOLLOWERS BAHÁ'U'LLÁH THROUGHOUT FIVE CONTINENTS UNANIMOUSLY REJOICE PARTIAL EMERGENCE WAR TORN HUMANITY FROM TITANIC UPHEAVAL UNERRINGLY PREDICTED SEVENTY YEARS AGO BY PEN AUTHOR THEIR FAITH. CESSATION HOSTILITIES EUROPEAN CONTINENT SIGNALISES CLOSING YET ANOTHER CHAPTER TRAGIC TALE FIERY TRIALS PROVIDENTIALLY DECREED BY INSCRUTABLE WISDOM DESIGNED ULTIMATELY WELD MUTUALLY ANTAGONISTIC ELEMENTS HUMAN SOCIETY INTO SINGLE ORGANICALLY UNITED UNSHATTERABLE WORLD COMMONWEALTH. GRATEFULLY ACCLAIM SIGNAL EVIDENCE INTERPOSITION DIVINE PROVIDENCE WHICH DURING SUCH PERILOUS YEARS ENABLED WORLD CENTRE FAITH ESCAPE WHAT POSTERITY WILL RECOGNISE AS ONE OF GRAVEST DANGERS EVER CONFRONTED NERVE CENTRE ITS INSTITUTIONS. PROFOUNDLY AWARE BOUNTIFUL GRACE VOUCHSAFED BY SAME PROVIDENCE ENSURING UNLIKE PREVIOUS WORLD CONFLICT UNINTERRUPTED INTERCOURSE BETWEEN SPIRITUAL CENTRE AND VAST MAJORITY COMMUNITIES FUNCTIONING WITHIN ORBIT FAR FLUNG FAITH. IMMEASURABLY THANKFUL MIRACULOUS PRESERVATION INDIAN PERSIAN EGYPTIAN BRITISH 'IRÁQÍ COMMUNITIES LONG THREATENED DIRE PERILS OWING PROXIMITY THEATRE MILITARY OPERATIONS. DEEPLY CONSCIOUS PROGRESS ACHIEVED DESPITE SIX TEMPESTUOUS YEARS IN BOTH EASTERN WESTERN HEMISPHERES THROUGH COLLECTIVE ENTERPRISES LAUNCHED BY THESE COMMUNITIES OUTSHINES SUM TOTAL ACCOMPLISHMENTS SINCE INCEPTION FORMATIVE AGE FAITH. SEVEN YEAR PLAN

* Printed also in "Messages to America (1932–1946)".

INAUGURATED BY AMERICAN BAHÁ'Í COMMUNITY UNDER LOWERING CLOUDS APPROACHING CONFLICT VICTORIOUSLY COMPLETED EXTERIOR ORNAMENTATION MOTHER TEMPLE WEST ESTABLISHED STRUCTURAL BASIS FAITH EVERY STATE PROVINCE NORTH AMERICAN CONTINENT AND HOISTED ITS BANNER EVERY REPUBLIC LATIN AMERICA. INDIAN BELIEVERS SIX YEAR PLAN LAUNCHED EVE HOSTILITIES MORE THAN QUADRUPLED CENTRES FUNCTIONING WITHIN PALE ADMINISTRATIVE ORDER. EDIFICES CONSECRATED ADMINISTRATIVE AFFAIRS EVER ADVANCING CAUSE INVOLVING EXPENDITURE OVER HUNDRED THOUSAND DOLLARS ERECTED PURCHASED OR COMPLETED CAPITAL CITIES INDIA 'IRÁQ EGYPT AS WELL AS SYDNEY AUSTRALIA. ACQUISITION NUMEROUS PROPERTIES BAHÁ'U'LLÁH'S NATIVE LAND MT. CARMEL AND JORDAN VALLEY AS WELL AS PURCHASE SEVERAL IMPORTANT HISTORIC SITES ASSOCIATED LIVES BOTH HERALD AUTHOR FAITH SWELLED UNPRECEDENTED DEGREE BAHÁ'Í ENDOWMENTS. PRELIMINARY STEPS COMPLETION BÁB'S SEPULCHRE AND ESTABLISHMENT WORLD ADMINISTRATIVE CENTRE THROUGH REMOVAL REMAINS BROTHER MOTHER 'ABDU'L-BAHÁ UNDERTAKEN. TERMINATION FIRST CENTURY BAHÁ'Í ERA SYNCHRONISING CLIMAX RAGING STORM PUBLICLY BEFITTINGLY CELEBRATED DESPITE MULTIPLICATION RESTRICTIONS. ABOVE ALL UNITY INTEGRITY INCORRUPTIBLE WORLD COMMUNITY CONSISTENTLY SAFEGUARDED IN FACE INSIDIOUS OPPOSITION AVOWED ENEMIES WITHOUT AND COVENANT BREAKERS WITHIN. SUCH SPLENDID VICTORIES OVER SO VAST FIELD AMIDST SUCH TRIBULATIONS DURING SO PROLONGED ORDEAL AUGUR WELL COLLOSSAL TASKS DESTINED BE ACCOMPLISHED COURSE PEACEFUL YEARS AHEAD BY BUILDERS EMBRYONIC WORLD ORDER BAHÁ'U'LLÁH AMIDST WRECKAGE DISTRACTED DISRUPTED DISILLUSIONED SOCIETY.

SHOGHI

10 May 1945

Dear Bahá'í Sister,

The beloved Guardian has instructed me to forward you the enclosed copy of his message* to the Bahá'ís of East and West on the happy occasion of the termination of the European war.

*Cable 9 May 1945.

He would appreciate your sharing it not only with all the British friends but with the Paris believers too.

Please inform him of the safe receipt of this message as soon as it reaches you.

We all send you our loving greetings and are greatly relieved to know your lives will now assume a more normal course after all these years of suffering. . . .

9 August 1945

Dear Bahá'í Sister,

Your letters dated March 8th and 12th, April 17th, May 10th and 18th and July 8th and June 9th have been received, as well as the various enclosures you mention in them, and the photographs, sent under the separate cover. The beloved Guardian has instructed me to answer them on his behalf.

He was very pleased to hear you are now in touch with the French believers and able to help them morally, and also with some physical assistance too! It is only right that England, the first country whose Bahá'í community is in a position to reach out a helping hand to its sister communities in Europe, should do so, and should have this privilege and honour.

He realises the many difficulties that stand in the way of the British Bahá'ís in regard to fulfilling the important Six Year Teaching Plan they have undertaken. But he hopes that now the European war is over, and conditions are returning to a more normal way of life, that the friends, conscious of their very great spiritual responsibility, will arise and, in spite of everything, accomplish the work they have chosen for themselves and which is of such great spiritual importance to their countrymen.

The more we study the present condition of the world, the more deeply we become convinced that there just cannot be any way out of its problems except the way of God, as given by Him, through Bahá'u'lláh. The early Persian Bahá'ís gave their lives for the Cause; the Western believers have been spared this necessity, but their comfort, to some extent, they must sacrifice if they are going to discharge their moral obligation to tortured humanity, and bring to it the message of the Father. Once the friends start out to win the goals set in their Plan, they will find the Divine confirmation sustaining them and hastening its consummation. This is what happened in the American Seven Year Plan and the Indian Six Year Plan, and the same spiritual assistance will certainly be vouchsafed the English believers, once they arise with faith and confidence, to do their work.

In regard to the question you raise in your letter of June 9th about the "Paris Talks", the Guardian does not advise your putting the suggested footnote, as we cannot be absolutely sure, unless we see the Persian text, that what you propose is really what the Master means. The present translation cannot be considered accurate in all its details, obviously, and as at the moment the Persian text is not available, he suggests you either put no footnote at all, or one stating that the meaning is obscure and future re-translation will clear up such passages.

You may be sure that his ardent prayers will be offered on behalf of all the British Bahá'ís, that Bahá'u'lláh may aid them to fulfil His work and may open the doors of servitude and guide them on their way. He will also pray for you and your fellow N.S.A. members, for your strength, protection and guidance in fulfilling your many important tasks.

P.S. Regarding Mr. . . . . financial affairs; there is naturally no objection to his receiving his own money, but he should have no communication with his family, and should arrange for your N.S.A. to receive his money and deliver it to him. The Guardian is very pleased that he has taken the right, courageous, Bahá'í course of action in his life, and will certainly pray for his happiness and protection.

There is no ambiguity about the Master's attitude towards psychic forces; He very strongly warned the believers against using them.

Dear and valued co-workers,

I grieve to learn of the slow progress of the Six Year Plan which the English believers have so nobly conceived, and which, I pray and hope, will be triumphantly consummated. The Plan constitutes a direct and grave challenge to the English Bahá'í community in its entirety. It should be regarded as the greatest collective enterprise ever launched by the followers of the Faith of Bahá'u'lláh in the British Isles. It is thus far one of the most significant undertakings embarked upon by the members of Bahá'í National Assemblies during the opening years of

THE SIX YEAR PLAN (1944–1950)

the second Bahá'í century. To it, as already observed, the immediate destinies of the community of the English believers are linked, and on it must depend the future orientation and evolution of the institutions which the members of that community are labouring to erect for the diffusion of the principles and the establishment of the Faith of Bahá'u'lláh in their country. It must not, it cannot, fail. The attention of the entire body of the believers must be continually focussed upon it. No sacrifice can be deemed too great for its successful prosecution. All must arise harmoniously, co-operate and lend their share of assistance. May the spirit of Bahá'u'lláh enable them to achieve signal success.

Shoghi

18 December 1945

Dear Bahá'í Sister,

The beloved Guardian has instructed me to acknowledge the receipt of your two letters dated Aug. 11th and Nov. 9th and to answer them on his behalf. Their enclosures were also received. . . .

He was very pleased to hear that you have had eight new Bahá'ís since Convention and hopes that this is only a foretaste of the conversion of souls in far greater numbers in the years lying ahead of us.

The Six Year Plan is of the umost importance, and he urges your Assembly to continually keep reminding the friends of the necessity for sustaining their efforts through arising personally to serve and through giving generously that others may serve in their place.

In this connection he hopes you will use the services of Marion Holley, now Mrs. David Hofman†, to the full. She is a gifted speaker and writer, and has had invaluable experience in America as a member of the National Teaching Committee, during the Seven Year Plan. Both she and Mr. Hofman are wholly dedicated to the service of the Cause, and eager to do all in their power to help accomplish the goals of your Six Year Plan.

He was happy to hear that the Summer School was held successfully. Now that the war is over, and conditions gradually returning to normal, he hopes that the British believers will exert their utmost in serving the Cause and spreading its message.

Although from time to time they will receive the help of outside Bahá'ís, the major responsibility is theirs, and the lion's share of the work will naturally fall to them as both their privilege and their duty.

He assures you one and all that his ardent prayers sustain you in your labours for the Faith and he feels sure that with sufficient effort on the part of all, and the Power of God which inevitably sustains self-sacrificing service in His Path, the goals can be gloriously achieved....

P.S. He was delighted to hear of the welfare of the German believers. Reports of a similar nature had already reached him, but no figures had been given.

Dearly beloved co-workers,

I am anxiously waiting for the news of the progress of the Six Year Plan, upon which the future orientation of the collective activities of the English believers depends, and with which the immediate destinies of their Faith are interwoven. No sacrifice is too great to ensure its success. The utmost effort, vigilance, perseverance and self-sacrifice are required to carry it to a successful conclusion. If the friends, individually and collectively, play their part and exert their utmost, the abundant blessings of Bahá'u'lláh will be fully vouchsafed, and the strength of the Plan will mark a glorious chapter in the history of the Faith. I appeal to the entire community to dedicate itself to this sacred and urgent task, the greatest collective enterprise ever undertaken by the followers of Bahá'u'lláh in the British Isles.

Your true and grateful brother,
Shoghi

21 February 1946

ASSEMBLY SHOULD EXPLAIN TO... OWING HIS BROTHER'S SECESSION FAITH ADHERENCE ISLÁM PARTICIPATION POLITICS AND ASSOCIATION WITH HIS OTHER BROTHERS AND MOTHER WHO HAVE FLAGRANTLY DISOBEYED MASTER'S WILL COMMUNICATION WITH HIM AND THEM FORBIDDEN. ASSEMBLY SHOULD EXERCISE UTMOST VIGILANCE THIS VITAL MATTER OTHERWISE AS MASTER REPEATEDLY WARNED CONTAMINATING INFLUENCE WILL SPREAD AND IMPERIL STRUCTURE FAITH. CABLE HIS RESPONSE SHOW UTMOST FIRMNESS.

SHOGHI

5 March 1946

OVERJOYED RECENT DECISIONS TEACHING CONFERENCE ARDENTLY PRAYING SPEEDY REALISATION CHERISHED HOPES URGE SUPREME UNITED CONTINUOUS EFFORT CABLING ONE THOUSAND POUNDS FURTHERANCE NOBLE AIMS SIX YEAR PLAN DEEPEST LOVE.

SHOGHI

12 March 1946

INFORM . . . APPRECIATE HIS ASSURANCE PRAYING STEADFASTNESS BLESSINGS.

SHOGHI

22 March 1946

Dear Bahá'í Sister,
Your letters dated Sep. 6th and Nov. 6th 1945 and Jan. 2nd, Feb. 8th and 19th 1946, have been received together with their enclosures, and the beloved Guardian has instructed me to answer them on his behalf.

He has been delighted to see, through your letter and reports sent by other Bahá'ís, that the Teaching Conference in Manchester was such a success, and he feels this marks a turning point in your Six Year Plan. Now that goal towns have been chosen, the friends must concentrate all their forces and resources on establishing Assemblies in them as soon as possible. He feels sure that once the signs of success become evident all the believers, tired and depressed after so many years of war and privation, will become vitalised with optimism and enthusiasm and drive forward unitedly towards the complete victory of their plans.

He was delighted to hear that Miss Townshend† and Mr. Lee† have arisen as pioneers, and he wishes you to please assure them of his special prayers for the success of their devoted labours.

He was also very happy to hear you have found a place to hold your Summer School; this is such an important Bahá'í activity that even if the expenses are such as to necessitate its being subsidised by the National Fund it does not matter.

He advises you to send half of the Russian books in your possession to the Bahá'í Bureau in Geneva. Mrs. Lynch can distribute them from there, as required, to other centres.

He feels it would be an excellent means of serving the Cause and enhancing the prestige of the British Bahá'ís if you can send a delegate to the Spiritual World Congress to be held in Brussels.

We are sending ... the Haifa News Letter direct from here; thank you for sending his address. The Guardian suggests if you have not already done so, that you send the address of the Dutch Bahá'í to Mrs. Lynch, so that travelling believers can be put in touch with him.

He is eagerly awaiting more good news of the progress of your Six Year Plan, and assures you all that he will ardently pray for its speedy and complete success in the Holy Shrines.

Your Assembly's labours are very deeply appreciated. . . .

Dear and valued co-workers,

The enterprise launched by the English Bahá'í community in the opening years of the second Bahá'í Century is of tremendous significance, and will, if successful, mark not only the inception of a glorious chapter in the history of the Faith in the British Isles, but will constitute a landmark in the spiritual awakening of its people. The forces which such a consummation will release none can estimate sufficiently at present. The task is colossal, but the reinforcing power of Bahá'u'lláh, who is watching over it and is ready to bless and sustain it if its prosecutors arise to play their part, is likewise immeasurable. The recent Teaching Conference is but the initial stage in this mighty, this collective, and indeed historic undertaking. The goal towns which have been selected should be regarded as the chief objectives requiring the immediate and concentrated attention of its zealous promoters. Every consideration should be subordinated to the paramount need of establishing at any cost and by every means possible, vigorously functioning assemblies at these centres. No effort should be wasted, all must arise to lend their assistance; no sacrifice is too great to ensure the completion of the first stage of this noble enterprise. Unity, perseverance, self-sacrifice, will guarantee its success. Obstacles may arise, set-backs will no doubt occur, but the unconquerable spirit animating the English believers must ultimately triumph.

Your true and grateful brother,
Shoghi

24 April 1946

ADVISE NOT PURCHASE AT PRESENT. RENT IF POSSIBLE BEFITTING ROOMS CENTRAL POSITION.

SHOGHI

24 April 1946

KINDLY AIRMAIL TWO PHOTOGRAPHS NATIONAL ASSEMBLY FOR "BAHÁ'Í WORLD".

SHOGHI

26 April 1946

URGE FOCUS ATTENTION SIX YEAR PLAN SUBORDINATE EVERY ACTIVITY PARAMOUNT ISSUE TEACHING FACING ENGLISH BELIEVERS.

SHOGHI

30 April 1946 (Convention)

DEARLY BELOVED ENGLISH BELIEVERS REMEMBERED SHRINES PRAYING ARDENTLY SUCCESS DELIBERATIONS CONVENTION SUPREME CONTINUOUS EFFORT REQUIRED ENSURE SUCCESS PLAN CONCENTRATION ATTENTION RESOURCES ENTIRE COMMUNITY PROMOTION PARAMOUNT AIM INDISPENSABLE GREATER SACRIFICES DEMANDED ENSURE ULTIMATE VICTORY EAGERLY AWAITING NEWS PROGRESS HISTORIC ENTERPRISE.

SHOGHI

8 May 1946

WHATEVER NOT SPECIFIED ARTICLES ASSOCIATION LEFT DISCRETION NATIONAL ASSEMBLY.*

SHOGHI

10 May 1946

APPRECIATE MAIL HAIFA PHOTOGRAPH ALL MEMBERS LAST YEAR'S NATIONAL ASSEMBLY FOR BAHÁ'Í WORLD.

SHOGHI

22 May 1946

APPROVE DROP CARDIFF SUBSTITUTE ANY TOWN DEEMED ADVISABLE PRAYING SPEEDY SUCCESS URGE PERSEVERANCE LOVING APPRECIATION.

SHOGHI

29 May 1946

Dear Bahá'í Brother,

Your letters (and those previously written by Mrs. Ferraby† as secretary) dated March 19th and 21st; April 12th and 23rd; and May 2nd and 11th, as well as their enclosures, have all been received, and the Guardian has instructed me to answer them on his behalf.

Regarding the various points which have been raised in these letters.

As he already informed you by cable, he sees no objection to substituting some other town for Cardiff if that has proved too unpromising . . . .

People who for years have ceased to either attend meetings or show the slightest interest in the Cause can be dropped from the voting list; but any who are unable to attend meetings, but still

---

*In answer to cabled request for guidance about tied vote at Convention.

consider themselves to be Bahá'ís and are desirous of keeping up their contact with the Faith, should naturally be kept on the voting list.

He feels at the present stage of the Cause's development in England it is perhaps wiser not to make any hard and fast rules about the boundaries of towns for assembly purposes. However, you should bear in mind that in the future some proper delineation will be necessary.

As to the question of the Publishing Trust about quoting excerpts from some of the Meditations; there is no objection to this at all.

He hopes you will be able to find some suitable quarters in London for your Bahá'í Centre; he considers that at the present time, with the heavy and essential teaching programme you have undertaken, it is out of the question to purchase headquarters.

The Guardian takes the keenest interest in your Six Year Plan, and he wishes me to point out to you certain things in this connection: if the important goals of new Assemblies are to be achieved, he feels you will have to organise the work on a new basis. England now stands, one might say, on the brink of a new phase of its Bahá'í life; the long years of war are over, the friends are not only awakened to a sense of their responsibilities, but have increased in numbers, in zeal, and in unity; there is a growing number of people who are anxious to do pioneer work. What is needed is a planned and consistent form of teaching and administrative support of the activities your Assembly is inaugurating.

He feels the time has come when the British Bahá'ís' resources are sufficient to enable them to embark on their teaching campaign in a manner similar to that already followed by the American and Indian Bahá'ís. In other words pioneers who volunteer for work, if they are not able to support themselves, should be supported by the National Fund until they either find work or their task is completed.

Likewise travelling teachers should be assisted financially to carry out the "projects" assigned to them. The friends should not for a moment confuse this type of support with the creation of a paid clergy. Any Bahá'í can, at the discretion of the N.S.A., receive this necessary assistance and it is clearly understood it is temporary and only to carry out a specific plan. Bahá'u'lláh

Himself has not only enjoined on everyone the duty of teaching His Faith, but stated if you cannot go yourself, to send someone in your stead. The National Assembly, through and with its Teaching Committee, should take immediate steps to get pioneers out into the goal towns and teachers circulating about, to not only support and inaugurate the new work, but to stimulate the existing Assemblies and groups, and help them to expand.

He hopes that your Assembly, unitedly and with complete dedication to the great work that lies ahead of you, will concentrate all your forces on the teaching work. You may be sure he will pray for your success in the Holy Shrines, and that all the British Bahá'ís may realise to the full their historic responsibilities and arise to discharge them. . . .

P.S. Your letter of May 29th has since been received and the extra photos of N.S.A. members will be forwarded to America.

Dear and valued co-workers,
The activities of the English Bahá'í community in pursuance of the Plan, which in its scope and potentialities is wholly unprecedented in the history of the Faith in the British Isles, are now approaching a critical stage, and will, if not relentlessly expanded and consolidated, fall far short of their ultimate objective. They have now entered the third year of their Plan, and the work that still remains unaccomplished is considerable, but not beyond what their united and sustained endeavours can accomplish. The utmost support, if the Plan is to yield its promise, should be continually and increasingly extended to every pioneer, both moral and financial, who will arise to contribute his or her share to its success. All the institutions of the Faith so laboriously erected since the inception of the Formative Age, most of the financial resources of the community that have been accumulated, the deliberations of the elected representatives of the entire body of the believers, both local and national, should henceforth be dedicated to the vital requirements and noble aims of an enterprise which, if successful, will pave the way, and provide the necessary agencies, for the proclamation of the Faith to the masses throughout the British Isles.

The Faith is too circumscribed at present, its resources too limited, its range too restricted, and the number of its active supporters too few, to allow a systematic and nation-wide campaign designed to awaken the masses, to be effectively inaugurated. The present Plan is but a stepping stone that must lead eventually the English believers to execute so tremendous and meritorious an undertaking. The duties and responsibilities now facing them must, however, be fully discharged. No time or effort should be wasted. All, young and old, must be aroused to a new consciousness of their collective responsibilities. A greater measure of self-sacrifice, a greater audacity, a greater reliance on the sustaining grace of Bahá'u'lláh, are required to lend the necessary impetus to the progressive unfoldment and ultimate fruition of this dynamic process which the followers of Bahá'u'lláh, labouring in the heart of a world encircling empire, have set in motion. May signal success crown their historic labours.

Shoghi

7 June 1946

National Youth Committee

Dear Bahá'í Sister,

Your letter dated May 16th and written on behalf of the National Youth Committee, was received, and the beloved Guardian has instructed me to answer it on his behalf.

He is very happy to see that the Bahá'í Youth of the British Isles are now organised and working with enthusiasm for the spread of the Faith there. He feels that they have a great and important rôle to play during the next few years in fulfilling the objectives of the Six Year Plan.

Young people, being, for the most part, freer than the older believers, are in a position to arise as pioneers and move to new towns as settlers. A great number of the pioneers in America, who left their native cities, and often their native land, in order to fulfil the Seven Year Plan, were young people—some of them so young that the Spritual Assemblies they helped to establish they were themselves not yet old enough to be elected to!

The Guardian has enjoyed very much meeting Capt. Philip Hainsworth†, who had the unique privilege of being in Haifa for over a month, and he feels sure that upon his return to England he will lend great impetus to both the Youth and teaching work.

He heartily approves of your "Youth Bulletin" project and urges you to place special emphasis on articles that are of pertinent interest to young people, such as those dealing with the economic, social and moral aspects of society.

Assuring you, and all the members of your Committee, of his loving prayers for the success of your labours....

May the Beloved bless your meritorious endeavours, guide every step you take in the path of service, aid you to extend the range of your activities, and enable you to promote, by every means in your power, and in a most effective manner, the vital interests of a Plan with which the immediate destinies of the members of the English Bahá'í Community, both young and old, are so inextricably interwoven.

Your true brother,
Shoghi

18 June 1946

Dear Bahá'í Brother,

The beloved Guardian has instructed me to send you the following copy of a cable he sent the N.S.A. on the 7th of this month: "DELIGHTED LATEST REPORT TEACHING ACTIVITIES. PRESENT YEAR CRUCIAL FORTUNES PLAN. CONCENTRATE 5 MOST PROMISING GOAL TOWNS, ALSO EXERT UTMOST RE-ESTABLISH TORQUAY, BOURNEMOUTH ASSEMBLIES. SUCCESS IMMEDIATE PLAN WILL NECESSITATE INCREASE CONVENTION DELEGATES BRITISH ISLES TO TWICE 19. UPON CONSUMMATION ENTIRE PLAN FURTHER INCREASE TO THREE TIMES 19 WILL BECOME ESSENTIAL. CABLING FIVE HUNDRED POUNDS FOR TRAVEL SETTLEMENT PIONEERS. PROSPECTS BRIGHT, REDOUBLED EFFORTS ABSOLUTELY ESSENTIAL, EXERTION YOUTH VITAL. FORTHCOMING GATHERING SUMMER SCHOOL SHOULD DEVOTE SPECIAL ATTENTION REQUIREMENTS PLAN. ARDENTLY PRAYING TRIUMPHANT SUCCESS FIRST STAGE COLLECTIVE EFFORT DEARLY BELOVED ENGLISH BELIEVERS."

In the first draft of this cable sent you a word was left out, namely "twice" before the "19" in reference to the first increase of the number of convention delegates. This was corrected the same day by cable.

The Guardian has so far received no acknowledgment of the

receipt of this long cable and he is anxious to know if it reached you safely? Also the five hundred pounds which was forwarded by cable, through Barclays Bank, to your name? Assuring you of his loving prayers on your behalf. . . .
P.S. He was very happy to hear that the N.S.A. is now united, and that sources of misunderstanding and uneasiness have been entirely cleared up.

6 July 1946

DELIGHTED BRIGHT PROSPECTS ACHIEVEMENT THIS YEAR'S GOAL WILL CONSTITUTE TURNING POINT FORTUNES PLAN LANDMARK BRITISH BAHÁ'Í HISTORY SUSTAINED CONCENTRATION ESSENTIAL CONVEY PIONEERS TRAVELLING TEACHERS ASSURANCE LOVING APPRECIATION ABIDING GRATITUDE NOBLE RESPONSE URGE EXERT SIMULTANEOUSLY EFFORTS ESTABLISH THIS PIVOTAL YEAR NUCLEUS FUTURE ASSEMBLY BOTH SCOTLAND IRELAND PRAYING CONTINUALLY INCREASING EVIDENCES NATION-WIDE EXPANSION PROGRESSIVE CONSOLIDATION DEARLY BELOVED ENGLISH BAHÁ'Í COMMUNITY.

SHOGHI

2 August 1946 (Summer School)

OVERJOYED PRAYING EVER INCREASING SUCCESS DEEPEST APPRECIATION HIGH ENDEAVOURS.

SHOGHI

25 August 1946

DELIGHTED URGE UTMOST SACRIFICE PROVIDE REQUIREMENTS GOAL TOWNS PRAYING SUCCESS.

SHOGHI

12 October 1946

Dear Bahá'í Brother,
Your letters dated June 1st and 26th and July 20th and 25th,

together with their enclosures, have been received, and our beloved Guardian has instructed me to answer you on his behalf.

Regarding the various points you raised.

Unless the Russian "New Era" is hopelessly bad, the Guardian advises it nevertheless be made use of, as it will be some time before the funds of the Cause can be used for a new edition. If the mistakes are mostly in the nature of mistranslations of certain important terms it might be possible for you, in conjunction with Mrs. Lynch, to have printed or mimeographed a list of errata, and stick it in the book, in this way Russian-speaking people will not be denied some literature on the Faith, however inadequate.

The attitude of the friends towards orientals should be one of great caution, according to the Master's own often-repeated and explicit instructions and warnings. Any believer in good standing would not leave his home community without a letter of credential, and certainly no Persians, claiming to be Bahá'ís, but lacking credentials, should be accepted until the Persian N.S.A. has clarified their status. They can, naturally, attend public meetings, but should not be permitted to come to the 19-Day Feasts; the friends may associate with them, but should be very cautious, bearing in mind that many orientals, who scorned or were even actively against the Cause while living in the East, now find it convenient to pose as believers or friends of the Faith in a Western community where they are strangers.

As regards your question about Bahá'í procedure; the present statement can certainly be amplified to include the United Nations Organisation.

He feels that your Assembly should constantly, through its communications to the friends and its committees, and in every way possible, stir the British Bahá'í community to a sense of the great urgency of their pioneer activities; and the need for more pioneers. They now have a golden opportunity to arise and fulfil their own cherished plans before it is too late. In the future we may well look back upon these present days and see that in them lay our greatest chance to build for the future and to call people to the Faith while they were still deeply impressed with the tragedy and futility of war; and before they become too engulfed in post war problems, or too bitterly disillusioned by the trend of world affairs to even seek a solution. More believers must arise, and, putting their trust in Bahá'u'lláh, do their duty to the Faith they believe in and love so dearly. The youth in particular should be encouraged to enter this field of service, for the spread of the Cause is their only hope for a stable world in which to live and establish families of their own.

His loving prayers are with you all in your many services to the Cause of God, and he is greatly encouraged by the way the work is going forward in England. . . .*

Dear and valued co-workers,

The evidences of intensified activity and of notable progress on the part of the English believers in recent months have rejoiced my heart and deepened my feelings of admiration and gratitude for the manner in which they are discharging, individually and collectively, their high responsibilities. I long to hear of the steady progress of their Plan, and will continue to pray for the removal of every obstacle in their path. However considerable their recent achievements, they are still in the initial stage of their great unfolding mission, and are not even capable as yet of visualising the possibilities or of estimating the consequences of their present-day labours. The consummation of their present task will mark the opening of a new era in the development of their community and will signalise the inauguration of a great epoch in the history of the Faith in their land—an epoch that must witness the universal recognition of their Cause and the proclamation of its truths, its claims and tenets, to the masses of their countrymen throughout the British Isles. The Plan they are now prosecuting will provide the machinery and establish the basic structure that will enable them to arouse the people, among all sections of the population, and aid them, systematically and gradually, to recognise Bahá'u'lláh, and support the nascent institutions of this World Order. Now it is their duty to lay an unassailable foundation for the great work that is to be undertaken in the future. There is no time to lose. Theirs is a priceless opportunity and a great privilege. They must neither vacillate nor falter. They

---

* Although some pioneer settlement had been attempted, at the time this letter was being written only the first nine pioneers had actually become established: Ursula Newman (later Samandarí) and Kathleen Brown (later Lady Hornell) in October 1945; Walter Wilkins† in July 1946; Alma Gregory† in August 1946; Robert Cheek† and Una Townshend in September 1946; David Hofman, Marion Hofman and Philip Hainsworth in October 1946.

must determinedly persevere until their immediate and distant goals have been attained.

Shoghi

15 November 1946

OVERJOYED MARVEL MAGNIFICENT SUCCESS URGE AFTER ATTAINMENT THIS YEAR'S GOAL CONCENTRATION IRELAND SCOTLAND WALES LONGING FORMATION NUCLEI THESE VIRGIN TERRITORIES ARDENTLY PRAYING LOVING ADMIRATION.

SHOGHI

21 November 1946*

APPROVE LOVING APPRECIATION PRAYING SUCCESS.

SHOGHI

26 December 1946

National Youth Committee

Dear Bahá'í Sister,

Your letter of September 19th was received, and our beloved Guardian has instructed me to answer it on his behalf, and to congratulate you and the other members of your committee on the excellent first issue of your Bahá'í Youth Bulletin.

This is an important new undertaking, and must be established as a firm innovation on the part of the British Bahá'í community. He hopes it will gradually become the means of interesting and attracting many new souls to the Faith.

In fact the Youth work everywhere in the Bahá'í World is dear to his heart, and he attaches great importance to it. The young people, who will inevitably grow up to shoulder all the work of the Cause, are really its hope, and should be one of the most active factors in its propagation. Through their courageous

---

* Approving Teaching Conference to be dedicated to the 25th Anniversary of the Guardianship.

adherence to the high moral and ethical standards set out by Bahá'u'lláh, and through gaining a mastery of His many, diversified, and profound teachings, they can shape, to a great extent, the development and aid in the rapid expansion of their beloved Faith in the various countries in which they labour. They should be made to realise their responsibility is heavy and their privilege very precious.

He wishes to assure you and all the other members of the National Youth Committee, of his most loving prayers for your progress, and for the success of the work you have so enthusiastically and devotedly undertaken. . . .

May the Beloved bless abundantly the work which your Committee has so nobly initiated, remove all obstacles from your path, aid you to realise every hope you cherish, and carry out every plan you conceive, for the furtherance of the interests of our beloved Faith and of its God-given institutions.

Your true brother,
Shoghi

30 December 1946

PRAYING FERVENTLY REMOVAL ALL OBSTACLES IMPEDING PROGRESS PLAN AND RECOVERY. SUPPLICATING RICHEST BLESSINGS TEACHING CONFERENCE DEEPEST LOVING APPRECIATION.

SHOGHI

1 January 1947*

REJOICE SUCCESS PRAYING RICHEST BLESSINGS.

SHOGHI

12 January 1947 (To Teaching Conference)

PROFOUNDLY MOVED MESSAGE. GREATLY APPRECIATE NOBLE SENTIMENTS PRAYING DEPTHS GRATEFUL HEART CONTINUED SUCCESS MAGNIFICENT COLLECTIVE EFFORTS DEEPEST LOVE.

SHOGHI

* At news of move to new National Bahá'í Centre.

20 January 1947

CONSULTATION BETWEEN DELEGATES COMMUNITY ADVISABLE PRESENTATION COMMUNITY VIEWS TO CONVENTION ADVISABLE MANNER CONSULTATION LEFT DISCRETION N.S.A. DOUBLING NUMBER DELEGATES CONDITIONED ACHIEVEMENT NINE GOAL TOWNS.

SHOGHI

29 January 1947

ASSURE JOAN GIDDINGS† DEEPEST LOVING APPRECIATION.

SHOGHI

8 February 1947

DELIGHTED PROGRESS NOTTINGHAM BIRMINGHAM RESPONSE MCKINLEYS† URGE SUPREME EFFORT AS CRUCIAL YEAR DRAWS CLOSE ENSURE ATTAINMENT OBJECTIVE LOVING ARDENT PRAYERS.

SHOGHI

26 February 1947

Dear Bahá'í Friends,

Your communications dated Sept. 12, Oct. 4th and 17th, Nov. 19th, 18th and 21st and Dec. 29th 1946 have all been received together with their enclosures and our beloved Guardian has instructed me to answer you on his behalf....

He was very happy to see the marked success of your Summer School this past year and also to receive very encouraging reports of the Manchester Teaching Conference; a great change has come over the work in England during the past year and one which must certainly rejoice the hearts of the older Bahá'ís in particular as they compare the present state of the Cause with the decades that passed when it had two or three spiritual Assemblies and seemed to be practically standing still! It seems, indeed, as if an important corner had been turned and that the Faith in the

British Isles is at last showing its true stature and casting a portentous shadow of future events before it!

He is particularly happy to see the way the Bahá'í young people are arising and serving in the pioneer field with such courage, determination and success.

Regarding the question you asked him about the sentence from the "Aqdas" for the marriage certificate: he feels that the following is a suitable translation of this passage: "Enter into wedlock, O people, that ye may bring forth one who will make mention of me."

The very good news of Nottingham and Birmingham achieving Assembly status was most welcome and he hopes the friends will redouble their efforts in connection with the remaining goal towns. Likewise the establishment of pioneers in both Eire and Scotland is of historic importance and they should receive every assistance from the National Teaching Committee and from your Assembly.

Now that the British believers see tangible results of their labours and perseverance taking shape, they should feel encouraged to make new sacrifices; a little effort on our part is so richly blessed by Bahá'u'lláh—we can only wonder what the rewards would be for a great, concerted, truly inspired effort by all members of the community.

He assures you all of his most loving prayers for your guidance and the success of your historic enterprises. . . .

P.S. Shoghi Effendi would like your Assembly to make every effort to help Dr. Lotfullah Hakim† to come to England from Persia; he wishes to continue his study of massage etc. and he could be of great help in the teaching work as he is a devoted and fine Bahá'í. Shoghi Effendi suggested he might investigate the possibility of carrying out his studies in Edinburgh or some other goal town and thus help with the Six Year Plan at the same time.

Dear and valued co-workers,

The present crucial year, now drawing to a close, may well be regarded as one of the most memorable in the annals of British Bahá'í history. The magnificent, spontaneous and collective response of almost the entire community of the English believers to the imperative call of teaching; the support lent by individuals, groups and Assemblies to the

Plan set in motion by its national elected representatives; the success attending the Teaching Conference; the multiplication of Bahá'í centres in England; the initial steps taken to establish the structure of the Administrative Order of the Faith, in Ireland, Scotland and Wales—all these have combined to raise the stature of the community, and to prepare it for the still greater tasks that must be faced by its members after the successful prosecution of the present Plan.

The Bahá'ís of the British Isles are now, slowly, laboriously and in strict accordance with the principles of a steadily expanding, divinely appointed Administrative Order, building up the essential and primary institutions which are destined to act as the chief and most powerful instruments for the proclamation of the Faith to the masses of their countrymen, at a subsequent stage in the development of the Faith in their land. As these institutions expand and are consolidated, the community will find itself equipped, not only to carry the Message of the New Day to the multitudes throughout the length and breadth of its homeland, but prepared and fortified to initiate teaching campaigns beyond the shores of its native land, and in distant territories and various parts of the Empire of which that land is the heart and centre.

Theirs is the duty, during these coming years, to lay patiently, assiduously and unitedly the foundation on which the structure of their future international services to their beloved Faith can be firmly and unassailably established. Upon the success of the Plan they are now so diligently and devotedly prosecuting, must depend the scope and effectiveness of their two-fold task of proclaiming the verities of their Faith to their fellow countrymen at home, and of implanting its banner abroad amidst the peoples and races of a far-flung Empire.

That they may carry out, in a befitting manner and by the appointed time, the preliminary steps so essential for the fulfilment of their high destiny is my dearest wish and constant prayer.

Shoghi

20 March 1947 (To First Regional Youth Conference)

PROFOUNDLY APPRECIATE MESSAGE CONFERENCE URGE CONCENTRATE NEEDS PLAN PRAYING GREAT VICTORIES.

SHOGHI

21 March 1947

OVERJOYED PROSPECTS PRAYING ARDENTLY CONSUMMATION CHERISHED HOPES APPEAL ENTIRE COMMUNITY EXERT SUPREME EFFORT ENSURE TOTAL SUCCESS MIGHTY ENTERPRISE DEEPEST LOVING APPRECIATION ABIDING GRATITUDE.

SHOGHI

28 March 1947

ADVISE APPORTION DELEGATES COMING CONVENTION IN STRICT ACCORDANCE NUMBER BELIEVERS ACTUALLY RESIDING IN FOUR COMMUNITIES MENTIONED LETTER FEBRUARY 24TH.

SHOGHI

7 April 1947

National Youth Committee

Dear Bahá'í Friends,

Your letters dated August 10th (from the secretary) and December 19th and March 18th (from the Business Manager of the Editorial Committee) were received, and as our beloved Guardian is greatly overburdened by his steadily expanding correspondence, he has instructed me to answer these communications all in one.

He was very pleased to receive copies of "Youth Bulletin," which he thinks is starting out in the right direction; he would like to receive this publication regularly.

The work you are doing is very important, and the British Bahá'í Youth should feel very encouraged to see the way some of their members have arisen and gone forth to pioneer. He hopes others will follow this example in order to ensure the success of the Six Year Plan.

You may be sure his loving prayers are offered for you all in the Holy Shrines. . . .

May the Spirit of Bahá'u'lláh sustain, bless and guide you in your notable, meritorious, and deeply appreciated activities, aid you to extend the range of your services, and lend a great impetus to the progress of the Plan which the English believers are so devotedly and assiduously prosecuting.

Your true and grateful brother,
Shoghi

16 April 1947

OVERJOYED HISTORIC SUCCESS APPROVE MINUTE 590 PRAYING STILL GREATER VICTORIES HEARTFELT CONGRATULATIONS ABIDING GRATITUDE.

SHOGHI

29 April 1947

ACCLAIM PRIDE GRATITUDE VICTORY ACHIEVED REVITALISED TRIUMPHANT DEARLY BELOVED BRITISH BAHÁ'Í COMMUNITY MARVELLOUS CONSUMMATION ARDUOUS TASK CRUCIAL YEAR HISTORIC PLAN UNPRECEDENTED ANNALS FIFTY YEARS BRITISH BAHÁ'Í HISTORY SISTER COMMUNITIES EAST WEST NORTH SOUTH HAIL SIGNIFICANT VICTORY WON NOTWITHSTANDING PROLONGED STRAIN FORMIDABLE OBSTACLES SMALLNESS NUMBERS DIVERSITY TRIALS CONFIDENT ALL MEMBERS COMMUNITY YOUNG OLD TEACHERS PIONEERS ADMINISTRATORS WILL RESOLUTELY SAFEGUARD PRIZES WON FORGE AHEAD UNDIMINISHED ZEAL ATTAIN GOALS WITHIN REACH CABLING ONE THOUSAND POUNDS PROMOTION GREAT TASKS AHEAD TOKEN MY ABIDING GRATITUDE SIGNAL SERVICE RENDERED FOLLOWERS FAITH BAHÁ'U'LLÁH BRITISH ISLES.

SHOGHI

8 May 1947

Dear Bahá'í Brother,

Your letters dated Jan. 19th and 23rd; Feb. 16th, 27th and 28th; March 8th and 25th; and April 4th, 19th, 20th, 22nd and 23rd, 1947, have all been received, together with their enclosures and the material sent under separate cover, and our beloved Guardian has instructed me to answer you on his behalf.

Regarding the various questions you have raised.
He has already informed the American N.S.A. that he feels Mr. Townshend's services to the Faith can best be rendered by his writing about it, as he obviously has an outstanding ability in this direction, combined with knowledge and zeal, and can render a very valuable service this way; he also feels that Mr. Townshend, now that his church association seems about to be broken, could be used as part of the pioneer force in Eire. It is his own land, he knows his own people, and the need for workers there is very particularly great this year. . . .

If Mr. Townshend has not as yet been registered as a voting believer he certainly should be immediately. Everyone knows he has been a most devoted Bahá'í for many years and his contributions should certainly be considered those of a voting Bahá'í.

He would appreciate receiving, for the files here in Haifa, a copy of the revised Articles of Association.

Regarding the prayer translated by Dr. Khán and his daughter: although he has not taken time to compare it with the original, he assumes it is a faithful translation. Unfortunately it is not a style which in our language can convey the richness and power of the original, and he would not recommend that this version of it be printed. There is no objection, however, to its circulation among the friends if they want it.

As to certain of your voting members who have long been inactive, and whose conduct you disapprove of, he suggests you make an effort to find out if they still believe in the Faith, and if they do, and wish to be members of it, then they should be helped to mend their ways. If this patient and loving method does not prove successful and they refuse to identify themselves with the Faith, they should be removed from the voting list.

Miss . . . should be advised, for the sake of better serving the Cause she loves so dearly, to take care of her health; also she should be made to realise that a pessimistic and critical approach (although perhaps fully justified by the situation) produces no results. We, having the power of the Faith to draw on, must always be constructive in our efforts, as this will produce results and attract Divine blessings upon them.

Concerning the membership of . . . in the synagogue: as this concerns his non-Bahá'í Jewish wife and means a great deal to her—even involving the place of her burial—the Guardian does not feel it is right to request him to take a step which would deprive her of her own religious rights. On the other hand, he sees no reason why . . . should not write a letter to the appropriate authority in this synagogue, explaining that he is a practising Bahá'í but is keeping his synagogue membership for the benefit of his wife and children. Some similar action should be taken by . . . , or he should give up his synagogue membership.

He realises the difficult position of the London community, but the goals of the Plan, and its success, justify any temporary weakening of the work in the capital, which in the end will be greatly strengthened by the national spread of the Faith. He certainly will specially pray for this work in London.

The achievement of all goals during this crucial year has been very great, and brought him a conviction that the Cause in the British Isles is now operating on an entirely new footing, and that the community of believers there has thrown off once and for all time a certain lethargy which seemed to have retarded its progress in the past. Although so much still remains to be accomplished, the combination of the new zest for work and the determination of the friends to succeed, and the unfailing assistance of Bahá'u'lláh, promised to all who arise and put their faith in Him, will surely mow down all obstacles and carry the British believers through to victory.

He feels that the way your assembly is working, with its many and active committees, and the plans you have outlined in your report, are excellent. Any suggestions he has to make, as the work unfolds, he will communicate to you.

The Summer School, he feels, is of great importance, and he hopes gradually believers from the continent will visit it and be helped and inspired by their contact with the now active and flourishing British Bahá'í community!

You may be sure in the prayers he offers in the Holy Shrines you and your assembly's work are often remembered. . . .

Dear and valued co-workers,
The success that has crowned the strenuous efforts exerted by the entire British Bahá'í community in the course of this crucial year, has raised immensely its prestige in the estimation of its sister communities in East and West, and has demonstrated in a very striking manner, the vitality, resourcefulness and determination of its members, and

merits the praise and blessings of the concourse on high, and particularly of our beloved Master, who in the course of two successive visits showered His loving kindness on the English believers, and chose the capital city of their country as the scene of His first public appearance before a western audience. This remarkable exploit, unparelleled since the inception of the administrative order in that land, and unsurpassed by any achievement associated with the followers of Bahá'u'lláh in the British Isles since the introduction of His Faith into their country, augurs well for the successful termination of the Initial Phase of the Plan, and fills me with hope that total victory will ultimately be achieved, at the appointed time, by the prosecutors of this bold, this historic and far-reaching enterprise.

The Plan itself when consummated will signalise the opening of a new epoch in British Bahá'í history, an epoch which must witness, simultaneously with the vigorous initiation of subsequent Plans designed to broaden the basis, and multiply the institutions, of a steadily evolving administrative order, the inauguration of systematic undertakings, jointly launched by the English, the Scottish, the Irish and Welsh believers, and aiming, on the one hand, at the proclamation of the Divine Message to the masses of their respective countrymen, and, on the other, at the establishment of the structural basis of a divinely appointed Administrative Order throughout the far-flung dependencies of the British Crown.

For the present, however, and as an essential preliminary to the vast and challenging tasks that await them beyond the shores of their homeland, the eyes of the prosecutors of the present Plan must be focused on the vital and urgent requirements in England, and particularly Scotland, Wales and Ireland, wherein the nuclei that have been recently formed, should, ere the expiry of the present year, be converted into full-fledged assemblies. The erection of the administrative institutions of the Faith of Bahá'u'lláh in these virgin territories will no doubt befittingly mark the termination of the initial phase of the Plan, and proclaim to the entire Bahá'í world the resolution, as well as the ability, of its valiant promoters to create the indispensable agencies required for an intensive propagation of the Faith at home, and the planting of its banner overseas.

Theirs is an unspeakably thrilling task, an awe-inspiring obligation, a priceless opportunity. Their recent victories inspire a confident hope that a no less outstanding success will mark their future endeavours.

Your true and grateful brother,
Shoghi

14 May 1947

DEEPLY APPRECIATIVE PLEDGE PRAYING ABUNDANT BLESSINGS DELIBERATIONS.

SHOGHI

24 May 1947

TOWNSHEND'S RESIGNATION IMPERATIVE. ALLOCATION FIVE HUNDRED POUNDS FROM NATIONAL FUND EXCESSIVE. ADVISE USE PART RELIEF FUND THIS PURPOSE PRAYING SOLUTION PROBLEM.

SHOGHI

18 June 1947

OVERJOYED TOWNSHEND'S MEMORABLE DECISION NOBLE EXAMPLE COMMENDABLE DETERMINATION SETTLE DUBLIN ARDENTLY PRAYING SUCCESS PROTECTION REMOVAL DIFFICULTIES DELIGHTED STAHLER'S† GEORGE'S† PIONEERING SUPPLICATING ABUNDANT BLESSINGS CHERISH BRIGHT HOPES FRUITION ASSEMBLY'S HISTORIC TASK DEEPEST LOVE APPRECIATION.

SHOGHI

28 June 1947

National Youth Committee

Dear Bahá'í Sister,

Your letter, with enclosures, to our Beloved Guardian, on behalf of the National Youth Committee, and dated February 26th, was received and he has instructed me to answer it on his behalf. He did not reply sooner because he is so very busy and overworked, and feels sure you understand the reason for the delay.

The services which the Bahá'í young people are rendering the Cause, not only in England but in Scotland and in Eire, please him greatly, as the Youth are the ones who perforce, in the near future, will find themselves carrying on the administrative and teaching work of the Faith, and the sooner they prepare themselves for this heavy responsibility through actual experience in the pioneer field, the better.

He is delighted to see the steady progress of your activities and the way your Bulletin is progressing, and he assures you all of his loving prayers for the success of all your undertakings....

May the Beloved bless continually your meritorious efforts, guide and sustain you in your activities, and aid you to fulfil your heart's desire in the service of His glorious Faith.

Your true brother,
Shoghi

19 July 1947

ADVISE TOWNSHEND TRANSFER RESIDENCE OUTSIDE IRELAND IF NECESSARY APPROVE PROVISION COAL AMERICAN BELIEVERS.

SHOGHI

20 August 1947

OVERJOYED MAGNIFICENT PROGRESS SUMMER SCHOOL ASSURE ATTENDANTS LOVING PRAYERS GRATEFUL ADMIRATION CONGRATULATE ENTIRE BRITISH COMMUNITY ASTOUNDING ACHIEVEMENTS BAHÁ'ÍS WORLD PROUD UNFORGETTABLE VICTORIES BRITISH ISLES.

SHOGHI

12 September 1947

DELIGHTED TOWNSHEND SETTLEMENT MAGNIFICENT SUCCESS SUMMER SCHOOL BELOVED MASTER ABHÁ KINGDOM WELL PLEASED CONSTRUCTIVE HISTORIC MANIFOLD ACHIEVEMENTS VIRILE BRITISH BAHÁ'Í COMMUNITY PRAYING INCREASING FERVOUR DIVINE GUIDANCE SURMOUNT OBSTACLES RESOLVE PROBLEMS WIN STILL GREATER VICTORIES HEARTFELT GRATITUDE ABIDING LOVE.

SHOGHI

25 September 1947

The National Bahá'í Youth Committee of the British Isles

Dear Bahá'í Friends,

Your letter to our beloved Guardian, dated August 21st, as well as the note of your Secretary, Miss Howes, dated August 29th, have been received, together with the copy of your Youth Letter, and I have been instructed to answer you on his behalf.

He is very happy to hear of the formation of the new Youth Groups you mention, as this will not only greatly stimulate the Bahá'í Youth and enable them to attract new young people to the Faith, but will also do the general work of the Cause in these cities a great deal of good. He urges your Committee to make every effort to establish youth groups wherever there are Spiritual Assemblies, and circumstances permit. He would like to receive five copies of your Youth Letter if this is convenient.

Your services are very deeply valued, and he assures you all of his loving prayers for the success and expansion of your activities. . . .

Dear and valued co-workers,

The activities initiated and diligently pursued by the members of your committee deserve the highest praise. The devotion, the perseverance, the loyalty, the assiduous care with which you are striving to promote the interests of the Bahá'í Youth throughout the British Isles rejoice my heart, and will no doubt act as a magnet that will attract the blessings of the Almighty. Persevere in your historic labours, and rest assured that the Beloved is well pleased with your splendid accomplishments. I will continue to pray from the depths of my heart for the extension of your valued activities.

Your true and grateful brother,
Shoghi

9 October 1947

Assembly Development Committee

Dear Bahá'í Friends,

Your letter to our beloved Guardian dated Aug. 4th, has been received and he has instructed me to answer it on his behalf.

He is very pleased to see the work your Committee is undertaking and feel that it is of the greatest importance. The unity, love, harmony and proper understanding of the administration of the Cause which exists in a community are the measure of its progress, and on them depend directly the expansion of the Faith.

He wishes you every success, and assures you of his prayers in support of your labours. . . .

P.S. He has received your bi-monthly news letter and thinks it is very well written and excellent in every way.

May the Almighty bless continually your valued activities, aid you to overcome all obstacles in your path, promote effectively the vital interests of our beloved Faith, and contribute, in a notable manner, to the multiplication of its nascent institutions.

Your true and grateful brother,
Shoghi

9 October 1947

Child Education Committee

Dear Bahá'í Friends,

Your letter to our beloved Guardian, dated Sept. 1st, has been received by him, and he has instructed me to answer it on his behalf.

He was very pleased to see the enthusiasm and devotion with which you have entered into this important branch of Bahá'í activity, and he hopes your labours will be richly rewarded with success.

He would suggest that wherever classes for Bahá'í children are held, liberal minded parents be invited to send their children too, so that their minds may receive the broad, basic and tolerant doctrines of our glorious Faith.

He assures you of his loving prayers for the success of your activities.

With warmest greetings,

May the Spirit of Bahá'u'lláh guide and sustain you in your highly important and vital undertaking, enable you to extend continually the range of your meritorious activities, and lend a great impetus to the consolidation of the institutions of our glorious Faith.

Your true brother,
Shoghi

10 October 1947

HIGHLY APPROVE ARRANGE MARION HOFMAN RESUME SECRETARYSHIP TEACHING COMMITTEE URGE ENTIRE COMMUNITY PERSEVERE UNITED STRENUOUS EFFORTS ENSURE TRIUMPHANT TERMINATION PRESENT PHASE PLAN STATUS NEWLY FORMED ASSEMBLIES MUST BE MAINTAINED AT ALL COSTS ATTENTION SHOULD MOREOVER BE FOCUSED ESTABLISHMENT FIRM FOUNDATIONS HISTORIC ASSEMBLIES SCOTLAND WALES EIRE ERE TERMINATION CURRENT YEAR CABLING FIVE HUNDRED POUNDS ASSIST ASSEMBLY VIGOROUS PROSECUTION MIGHTY ENTERPRISES CONFERRING IMPERISHABLE LUSTRE DIVINELY SUSTAINED VICTORIOUSLY ADVANCING DEARLY BELOVED BRITISH BAHÁ'Í COMMUNITY.

SHOGHI

16 October 1947

DELIGHTED EVIDENCES PROGRESS EDINBURGH DUBLIN BLACKPOOL HEARTFELT ABIDING APPRECIATION.

SHOGHI

24 October 1947

Dear Bahá'í Brother,

Your letters to our beloved Guardian, dated May 18th and 27th; June 4th, 9th and 16th; July 5th, 8th (two of this date), 12th and 14th; August 9th and September 15th, 20th and 29th; and October 6th and 13th, have all been received, as well as their enclosures, and he has instructed me to answer you on his behalf....

He received a letter direct from the World Congress of Faiths, and wrote them offering full Bahá'í co-operation, and informing them he was ready to appoint a Bahá'í representative to attend any conference they may hold.

The discovery of the Master's letter to Andrew Carnegie is very interesting, in spite of the very poor translation of this Tablet, and he will be very pleased to receive a photostat of the original, or at least a faithful copy of the text in Persian.

He would be pleased to continue receiving the reports of the Assembly Development Committee.

Regarding the question you asked him: he feels that in the case of a believer who will be 21 years old on April 22nd, there is no objection, at this time, when the work of the Cause is so urgent and the workers so few, in permitting him to vote on April 21st.

The conduct of ... is an excellent example of why he, (and 'Abdu'l-Bahá before him), feels it so necessary to be very strict about the admission of Orientals into the communities of the Western world. The British people, being shrewd by nature and having had considerable experience with Orientals and peoples of all races, are far less vulnerable to the insidious influence of the insincere than are the more naive and less experienced Americans. People such as this young man, Bahá'í in name whenever it suits their convenience to be so, caring really nothing about the Faith at heart, and ready to abandon it at a moment's notice if the pleasures to be gained outweigh the humiliation of ostracism, are a real menace to the Cause, especially to the faith of young and untried believers. It is to protect the Cause against such individuals that the Guardian is at present so strict about not permitting Persians to visit America at this time.

In regard to your question about qualifications of delegates and assembly members: the qualifications which he outlined are really applicable to anyone we elect to a Bahá'í office, whatever its nature. But those are only an indication, they do not mean people who don't fulfil them cannot be elected to office. We must aim as high as we can. He does not feel the friends should attach so much importance to limitations—such as people perhaps not being able to attend assembly or convention meetings, because if they do, then the fundamental concept of everyone being willing to do Bahá'í service on administrative bodies will be weakened, and the friends may be tempted to vote for those who, because of independent means or circumstances in their lives, are freer to come and go but less qualified to serve.

Regarding "'Abdu'l-Bahá in London". Nothing can be considered scripture for which we do not have an original text. A verbatim record in Persian of His talks would of course be more reliable than one in English because He was not always accurately interpreted. However such a book is of value, and certainly has its place in our literature.

He assures you all of the deep appreciation of your valiant labours and his loving prayers on your behalf....

Dear and valued co-workers,

The gigantic task, now being so energetically and successfully carried out by the consecrated and firmly knit British Bahá'í community, constitutes a glorious landmark in recent Bahá'í history, and will, when viewed in proper perspective, deserve to be regarded as one of the most outstanding enterprises launched by the followers of Bahá'u'lláh in the opening years of the second Bahá'í century. Alike in its magnitude and significance, this momentous undertaking is unprecedented in the annals of the Faith in the British Isles, and deserves to rank as one of the most compelling evidences of the creative power of its Author, marking the rise and establishment of His institutions on the European continent. It is yet too early to assess the potentialities of this present Plan and those destined to follow it, or estimate their future benefits. The blessings they will confer, as the forces latent within them are progressively revealed, on the people dwelling within those Islands, and subsequently, as their sphere is enlarged and their implications are fully disclosed, on the diversified peoples and races inhabiting the widely scattered dependencies of a far-flung empire, in both the East and the West, are unimaginably glorious.

A staggering responsibility rests on the shoulders of those who have been called upon to assist in the operation of the initial stages of this heroic colossal enterprise, and to participate in the privilege of directing its course, and nursing its infant strength. Setbacks and reverses are inevitable as this mighty Plan progresses and expands. Critical stages in its unfoldment must be encountered with unswerving resolution and confident hope. Whatever hardships and sacrifices its future prosecution may involve must be borne with courage, pride and thankfulness. To insure its speedy advancement every issue must be subordinated to its vital requirements, and every individual effort co-ordinated with the agencies designed for its execution.

Its present and pressing needs in the virgin territories of Eire, Northern Ireland, Wales and Scotland must be met with concentrated attention, continuous, systematic effort and the utmost self-sacrifice. The goals to be achieved in the capitals and chief cities of these newly opened territories must be relentlessly pursued, no matter how hard and stony the path that must be trodden. The prizes already won in other towns in those islands must at all costs be preserved and subsequently further enriched by fresh spiritual conquests in neighbouring counties and farther afield. Indeed the steps preliminary to the formation of a Bahá'í administrative centre in every county throughout the British Isles, must sooner or later be taken, as an essential prelude to the effective proclamation of the Faith to the masses. That the English Bahá'ís, aided and reinforced gradually by fresh recruits from among their Irish, Welsh and Scottish countrymen, may hasten the advent of such a glorious day in British Bahá'í history is the dearest wish of my heart and the object of my constant supplication at the Threshold of Bahá'u'lláh.

Shoghi

10 December 1947

DEEPLY TOUCHED ASSEMBLY'S SOLICITUDE ALL SAFE HEARTFELT APPRECIATION.

SHOGHI

7 January 1948

FERVENTLY PRAYING SIGNAL SUCCESS TEACHING CONFERENCE URGE CONCENTRATED UNRELAXING EFFORT ENSURE GLORIOUS TERMINATION INITIAL PHASE HISTORIC PLAN DELIGHTED SETTLEMENT CARDIFF DEEPEST LOVE.

SHOGHI

20 January 1948

CHEERED HEARTENED MAGNIFICENT SUCCESS TEACHING CONFERENCE. GREATLY WELCOME VALUABLE ASSISTANCE EXTENDED

DISTINGUISHED TEACHER DOROTHY BAKER. INITIAL PHASE PLAN DRAWING TRIUMPHANT CLOSE. SIGNAL SERVICES RENDERED SOUND BLESSED FIRMLY KNIT WIDE AWAKE BRITISH BAHÁ'Í COMMUNITY EVOKING ADMIRATION SISTER COMMUNITIES EAST WEST SETTING STIRRING EXAMPLE RISING GENERATION CONFERRING INESTIMABLE BLESSINGS POSTERITY MERITING APPLAUSE CONCOURSE ON HIGH AUGMENTING MY DEBT GRATITUDE. PRAYING ARDENTLY SUCCESS NEWLY LAUNCHED CO-ORDINATED TEACHING PLAN SUPPLICATING RICHEST BLESSINGS NEWLY ARISEN PIONEERS DEEPEST LOVE.

SHOGHI

6 February 1948

DEPLORE LOSS VALIANT SOUL JOHN MARSHALL† PRAYING FOR HIM. PRAYING CONTINUALLY EVER INCREASING SUCCESS GREATLY ADMIRED DEEPLY LOVED HIGH SPIRITED BRITISH BAHÁ'Í COMMUNITY.

SHOGHI

25 February 1948

INCREASINGLY ADMIRE DEEPLY THANKFUL PROGRESS HISTORIC ACHIEVEMENTS BLESSED COMMUNITY DELIGHTED RESPONSE EDINBURGH ASSURE OLGA MILLS† ALFRED SUGAR† LUCY† BEST WISHES LOVING APPRECIATION PRAYING REMOVAL DIFFICULTIES.

SHOGHI

3 March 1948

ASSURE YOU PRAYERS SUMMER SCHOOL DEEPEST LOVE.

SHOGHI

4 April 1948

KINDLY AIR MAIL AFTER APRIL ELECTIONS SEPARATE UP TO DATE ALPHABETICAL LISTS ASSEMBLIES GROUPS ISOLATED BELIEVERS BRITISH ISLES.

SHOGHI

4 April 1948*

ASSURE DEARLY LOVED ALFRED SUGAR FERVENT PRAYERS RECOVERY HEARTILY WELCOME NEW BELIEVERS EDINBURGH DUBLIN GREATLY APPRECIATE SUPPORT NEW PIONEERS ADDRESS LAST MINUTE APPEAL VALIANT BRITISH BAHÁ'Í COMMUNITY INTENSIFY EFFORT FILL REMAINING GAPS ENSURE TOTAL VICTORY INITIAL PHASE MOMENTOUS PLAN ARDENTLY PRAYING FULFILMENT DEAREST HOPES.

SHOGHI

25 April 1948

ACCLAIM TRIUMPHANT CONCLUSION INITIAL STAGE EPOCH MAKING PLAN INITIATED BAHÁ'Í COMMUNITY BRITISH ISLES OPENING YEAR SECOND BAHÁ'Í CENTURY SUSTAINED PRODIGIOUS EFFORT CULMINATING LAYING STRUCTURAL BASIS RISING ADMINISTRATIVE ORDER LEADING CITIES EIRE SCOTLAND WALES UNPRECEDENTED BRITISH BAHÁ'Í HISTORY CONSTITUTES LANDMARK ANNALS WORLD BAHÁ'Í COMMUNITY SIGNALISES COMMENCEMENT SIGNIFICANT PHASE SPIRITUAL HISTORY IRISH SCOTTISH WELSH PEOPLES POTENT SEEDS SOWN 'ABDU'L-BAHÁ'S TWICE REPEATED VISITS UNITED KINGDOM LONG LAST GERMINATING CONCOURSE ON HIGH APPLAUDS BRILLIANT FEAT UNITEDLY ACHIEVED BRITISH FOLLOWERS FAITH BAHÁ'U'LLÁH SISTER COMMUNITIES EAST WEST MARVEL VICTORY WON SUCH MAGNITUDE SO SHORT PERIOD BY COMMUNITY SO SORELY AFFLICTED SO SMALL NUMERICALLY SO CIRCUMSCRIBED IN RESOURCES YET SO ALIVE SO SOUND SO RESOLUTE PLEAD URGE VALIANT PROMOTERS SO MOMENTOUS PLAN GUARD AGAINST DISSIPATION RESOURCES RELAXATION EFFORT DISTRACTION ATTENTION FORFEITURE HARDWON PRIZES APPEAL FURTHER SACRIFICES NOBLER DEDICATION GREATER INTENSIFICATION LABOURS UNTIL LAST ACT FINAL PHASE DIVINELY SUSTAINED PLAN GLORIOUSLY CONSUMMATED.

SHOGHI

*Pioneers referred to were Charles Dunning† who had arrived in Belfast, and Evelyn Baxter, Ata'o'lláh K͟hochbine, Claire Gung†, Lizzie Hainsworth†, and Margaret Sullivan†, for whom projects were completed.

29 April 1948

Dear Bahá'í Brother,

Your letters to our beloved Guardian, written on behalf of the British N.S.A., and dated as follows: Oct. 20th, 22nd, 24th and 29th, Nov. 10th and 17th, Dec. 1st and 15th of 1947, and Jan. 13th, Feb. 8th, 9th, 13th, and 27th, and March 1st and 4th of 1948 and April 5th, 1948, together with various enclosures, have been received, and he has instructed me to answer you on his behalf.

A number of matters referred to in them have been answered by cable, so I will not go into them again.

He was specially pleased to receive the copies of the Tablet of the Master to Andrew Carnegie, as this is yet another authentic and interesting Bahá'í document.

He was, likewise, very pleased to receive the statement of Sir A. Ramaswami Mudaliar testifying to his appreciation of the Faith, and he will use it in the appropriate section of "Bahá'í World" in the forthcoming edition.

The instruction he gave to the effect that committees should elect their own officers, he feels, is universal in scope and should, therefore, apply to Great Britain as well. . . .

Regarding the matter of the budget of the N.S.A. he feels that both wisdom and courage is required in this matter. You should not fix a budget which is too heavy for the community to meet, even with sacrifice. Both the pressing needs of the Cause and your Plan, as well as the foreseeable possibilities of your income should guide you.

He has no objection to extracts from his letters to . . . being published. He feels that in the future it is not necessary to ask his permission to publish such extracts. As long as the person who has received a letter, such as he would wish to share with others, from the Guardian, has no objection to its publication, he has no objection either. Anything confidential he always specifies as being such.

He feels that the question of Mrs. Hofman giving up the secretaryship of the National Teaching Committee, and who is to be chairman of it, etc. is something to be decided there by those responsible for the work.

In one of your letters you mentioned some . . . who have

visited the London Centre and their attitude: great patience must be used in dealing with the child-like members of some of these primitive races. They are innocent in heart and have certainly had a very bad example, in many Christians, of a purely mercenary approach to religion, but if their hearts and minds once become illumined with the Faith they could make very fine believers.

Regarding the matter of believers who have been deprived of their voting rights: just as no one should ever be deprived of his voting right lightly, it should likewise be realised that to be deprived of it is a grave matter, and involves heavy penalties spiritually. People who have been so deprived should not be permitted to attend any meetings involving the administration of the Cause, such as an election or a 19 Day Feast. They can attend the 9 Holy Days, however; they should not be married by Bahá'í law, no money should be accepted from them, they should not be given credentials (which imply a member of the community in good standing) nor should they be used officially as teachers or speakers.

He has no objection to your getting out a book on Bahá'í Procedure similar to the synopsis you enclosed for his information. He wishes you, however, to stick to essentials and, as far as possible, avoid—not only in the book but in your Assembly's decisions—binding the friends by a lot of procedure on minor matters which he always urges should be, as much as possible, dealt with according to each case that comes up. He wishes to keep the administration of the Cause as flexible as possible and not impede the work by a codified set of rules.

As to the attitude of the Bahá'ís in the British Isles towards the World Government Movement: he thinks that as this Movement, so far, seems to be working for what we believe in, and not for anything we do not subscribe to, the Bahá'ís should by all means support it, vote for the representatives to be sent to its constituent Assembly in 1950, and stand for election if they wish to. However, he feels your Assembly should keep a careful watch on this Movement, and if it becomes in any way imperialistic, anti-Russian, or in any other field starts sponsoring attitudes partizan or political in nature, the believers should be advised to withdraw their support and help. He does not think your Assembly should take any initiative in this Movement outside of its jurisdiction, such as in the Middle East, through asking the friends to send in non-Bahá'í names, etc.

He does not advise you to try and create more than one Assembly, i.e. the present one, in the London area.

The work being accomplished in the British Isles is not only a source of pride to him, but is increasingly being recognised and admired by the Bahá'í communities throughout the World, and is greatly encouraging them in their own struggles. For people are prone to thinking that the American Bahá'ís accomplish so much solely because of the great advantages they enjoy in their very fortunate country, whereas now the friends, knowing full well how much England suffered during the war, and is still suffering, are forced to acknowledge that it is spirit, determination, faith and devotion which bring victories into being, one after another, in Britain, and not luxury and leisure. Your achievements are heartening the friends in many places where their numbers are few, and the obstacles to be overcome great! In fact the American Bahá'ís who have visited England feel there is much to be copied at home in your spirit and methods.

He, therefore, urges you all to persevere courageously, knowing what you are accomplishing is infinitely precious and great. You are witnessing with your own eyes the fruition of your plans, the nearing of the moment when your hopes will be fully realised.

He assures you all of his very loving prayers on your behalf, and for the speedy progress of your work.

Dear and valued co-workers,

The successful conclusion of the Initial Phase of the first collective enterprise launched by the followers of Bahá'u'lláh in the British Isles during the first year of the second Bahá'í century constitutes a milestone of the utmost significance on the road leading the British Bahá'í community to the glorious destiny ordained for them by Divine Providence. The efforts exerted, the magnitude of the success which has been achieved, the spirit of consecration that has been demonstrated, the solidarity, determination and perseverance evinced by individuals, groups and assemblies during the opening years of this century are indeed unprecedented in British Bahá'í history, and may be regarded next to 'Abdu'l-Bahá's twice repeated visit to the British Isles, as the most potent period in the annals of the British Bahá'í community.

The establishment of the structural basis of the Administrative Order of the Faith in Scotland, Wales and Eire—an accomplishment of tremendous spiritual significance in itself—has greatly enhanced the momentous character of this period, and will lend a mighty impetus to the evolution of the Faith in the days to come.

The Final Phase of the Plan must now be carried forward with still greater energy, with still nobler self-sacrifice, with a clearer vision of the historic import of the work which is to be accomplished, with a mightier determination to bring it to a successful conclusion. The resources at the disposal of the community must, as a result of its expansion, be continually augmented and carefully extended. The prizes so painstakingly won must, at all costs, be safeguarded and consolidated. The newly enrolled believers must be constantly encouraged to assume an increasing share of the responsibilities and of the administrative functions devolving upon the members of the community. The pioneer activities undertaken by its members must, however great the sacrifices involved, be increasingly developed, systematised and accelerated. The needs of the Faith in the newly opened territories in the west, in the north, and in the south, must, while the specific goals of the Plan are being pursued, be given special attention, in order to enrich the life of the entire community, to increase the diversity of its constituent elements, to demonstrate the welding and assimilative power of the Faith, and to stimulate the processes now set in motion for the spiritual regeneration of all the ethnic elements within the British Isles.

In token of my gratitude for the work already accomplished, as a recognition of the status achieved by the British Bahá'í community in the Western Hemisphere, in anticipation of the tasks that still remain to be undertaken, I feel moved to initiate, as soon as the situation here permits, measures that will enable me, through the institution of a Palestine Branch of the British Bahá'í National Assembly, to register in the name of the body of the elected representatives of the followers of Bahá'u'lláh throughout the British Isles, a portion of Bahá'í international endowments dedicated to the Shrine of the Báb on Mount Carmel. May this step, associating it with its sister national assemblies in the United States and India in the possession of so sacred a trust, lend its share to the consolidation and distinction of the central institution of the Administrative Order of the Faith of Bahá'u'lláh in the British Isles.

Shoghi

2 May 1948

HAPPILY TRANSMIT REJOICING NEWS BELOVED GUARDIAN'S SAFETY HAIFA.

BAHABUREAU

5 May 1948

GREATLY WELCOME DEEPLY APPRECIATE CONVENTION'S RESPONSE SUCCESSFUL CONCLUSION INITIAL PHASE PLAN ENCOURAGES ME INITIATE AS SOON AS CIRCUMSTANCES PERMIT MEASURES ESTABLISH HOLY LAND PALESTINE BRANCH BRITISH NATIONAL ASSEMBLY ENABLE IT LEGALLY OWN PORTION BAHÁ'Í INTERNATIONAL ENDOWMENTS MT. CARMEL TOKEN MY ABIDING GRATITUDE SHINING ACHIEVEMENTS.

SHOGHI

9 May 1948

KINDLY CABLE NUMBER ASSEMBLIES GROUPS ISOLATED BELIEVERS BRITISH ISLES.

SHOGHI

13 May 1948

LOULIE MATHEWS PROCEEDING SOUTH AFRICA THIS SUMMER ADVISE SEND HER CARE HORACE HOLLEY ADDRESSES CONTACTS AFRICA ALSO INTRODUCTION FROM BARBE BAKER PRAYING ARDENTLY SUCCESS NEWLY ELECTED NATIONAL ASSEMBLY TEACHING COMMITTEE.

SHOGHI

10 June 1948

ASSURE GRACE CHALLIS ARDENT PRAYERS DEEPEST LOVING APPRECIATION SERVICES ALSO PRAYING ... SUCCESS HOFMAN'S VISIT DEEPEST LOVE.

SHOGHI

7 July 1948

PRAYING REMOVAL DIFFICULTIES URGE STEADFASTNESS INCREASING SELF SACRIFICE ALSO WISDOM EXPENDITURE PRIZES PAINSTAKINGLY WON MUST AT ALL COSTS BE SAFEGUARDED WORK INITIATED GOAL TOWNS ENERGETICALLY PURSUED DEEPEST LOVE APPRECIATION.

SHOGHI

7 September 1948 (Summer School)

ASSURE ATTENDANTS SUMMER SCHOOL LOVING FERVENT PRAYERS SUCCESS SESSIONS DEEPER UNDERSTANDING DISTINGUISHING FEATURES FAITH CLOSER ASSOCIATION MEMBERS VICTORIOUSLY ADVANCING STEADILY CONSOLIDATING COMMUNITY.

SHOGHI

2 October 1948*

ASSURE THREE NEW SETTLERS FERVENT PRAYERS DEEPEST LOVING APPRECIATION DELIGHTED WELSH PUBLICATION EAGERLY AWAITING COPIES SUPPLICATING ALMIGHTY'S BLESSING FORTHCOMING REGIONAL MEETINGS. CABLE WHETHER FIVE HUNDRED POUNDS ARRANGE BE SENT YOU FROM ṬIHRÁN REACHED YOU.

SHOGHI RABBANÍ

27 October 1948

DR. YÚNIS AFRÚKHTEH STAUNCH DISTINGUISHED SERVANT FAITH PROCEEDING ENGLAND MEDICAL TREATMENT EXTEND ASSISTANCE ADVISED HIM HELP TEACHING WORK BRITAIN.

SHOGHI RABBANÍ

---

*Walter Wilkins, Cyril Jenkerson†, and Zara Warman had settled in Norwich, Blackpool, and Brighton, respectively.

29 October 1948

ASSURE MILLS BACKWELL† LOVING APPRECIATION GRIEVE PASSING CHALLIS PRAYING PROGRESS SOUL SERVICES FAITH GRATEFULLY REMEMBERED.

SHOGHI RABBANÍ

5 November 1948

APPROVE TOWNSHEND'S ADMIRABLE STATEMENT CONVEY CONGRATULATIONS PRAYING SIGNAL SUCCESS APPROVE APPEAL FUNDS OVERSEAS.

SHOGHI RABBANÍ

5 November 1948

Dear Bahá'í Brother,

Your letters to our beloved Guardian, dated July 14th and of July 20th, August 6th and 30th and September 11th and October 8th, have been received, as well as various enclosures forwarded, and he has instructed me to answer you on his behalf.

... There are always bound to be some human complications cropping up in the work, but with love and patience these can usually be smoothed out, and he feels your assembly invariably shows these qualities in helping the friends to overcome their problems.

He believes that people such as ... have no real idea of what the New History Society stands for, and can therefore be taught the Faith, and converted to it, by the right handling. All the friends must do in such cases is to make quite sure that the person in question is sincere and grasps the Will and Testament. There are, of course, some individuals in whom the subversive spirit of Sohrab has taken root, and these should be carefully guarded against, but they are more the exception than the rule.

He feels that the local Assemblies should be encouraged to realise that the National Committees are constituted to serve their needs, not to dictate arbitrarily to them, and to unify the work of the Cause which is now spreading so rapidly in the

British Isles. The committees in question should be very tactful in dealing with a young assembly which is beginning to "feel its oats", as this spirit of independence, if properly handled, can lead it to be strong and independent rather than weak and always relying on other bodies to carry it forward. Assemblies, however, should certainly co-operate with National Committees and not refuse their assistance.

Dr. Yúnis Khán Afrúkhteh is planning to go to England for medical treatment, and the Guardian would appreciate your Assembly's giving him every assistance possible. He has been ill for some time, and Shoghi Effendi hopes he will recover his health, as he is a wonderful believer, full of wisdom and devotion, and his services are much needed in the Cause. He has advised him to assist you in your teaching work as soon as his health permits this exertion.

He also hopes dear Dr. Loṭfulláh Ḥakím will be of valuable assistance in your teaching work.

He has recently asked Mr. Varqá, his representative, to transfer to your Assembly five hundred pounds to assist you in your manifold activities connected with your Six Year Plan. Unfortunately it is not possible to send any money out of Palestine at present, even from Persia it is difficult to transfer funds, but he trusts this sum will be of assistance to you.

The Guardian feels that the assemblies of Cardiff, Dublin and Edinburgh must receive sustained support, as they are the three most important assemblies formed under the Plan, and must be built into strong and flourishing communities, free from any danger of relapse.

He is very happy about the general progress of the work in the British Isles, and the remarkable, sustained, and self-sacrificing work the believers are doing, guided and assisted by the devoted efforts of your Assembly.

You may be sure you are all remembered in his prayers in the Holy Shrines, and he eagerly awaits news of fresh victories in the teaching field.

Dearly-beloved friends and co-workers,
The opening of the Final Phase of the First Collective Enterprise undertaken in the history of the British Bahá'í community marks the closing of a stage of tremendous historic significance in the evolution

of that community and, indeed, in the spiritual history of the British Isles. Well nigh fifty years after the inception of that community, almost a quarter of a century after the birth of the Administrative Order, and on the morrow of the world-wide celebrations of the centenary of the Faith, a Plan, ambitious in its scope and endowed with vast potentialities, was nobly and spontaneously conceived by the small band of its devoted adherents in those islands. An effort, extending over a period of no less than four years, nation-wide in its range, sustained, systematic, prodigious has been exerted. A victory unparalleled in British Bahá'í annals has been achieved. Towards its consummation newly won recruits to the ranks of this growing community, representative of the English, the Scottish, the Irish and Welsh races have notably contributed. The seeds sown, with such lavish hands by the Founder of that community in the course of two successive visits to the United Kingdom, have at last germinated. The machinery of the Administrative Order, slowly and laboriously taking shape, on the morrow of His ascension, has, as destined by Him who delineated its features in His Will and Testament, been put to the service of this newly conceived Plan, and is now yielding its first fruits. Born at the turn of the last century, its nucleus formed in the heart and nerve centre of a far-flung Empire, gestating for over a decade whilst confined to the narrow limits of the English territory whence it first sprang, energised, after having lain dormant for no less than ten years, through the twice repeated journeys of the Centre of Bahá'u'lláh's Covenant to both the English and Scottish capitals, shaped and trained through the processes of a divinely conceived, slowly evolving Administrative Order, propelled along the broad highroad of its destiny in direct consequence of the initial operation of the First Plan set in operation for its further unfoldment, emerging as a truly representative and firmly-knit community, at the conclusion of the Initial Phase of that Plan through the spread of its ramifications among the peoples of Scotland, Wales and Ireland, the organised band of the followers of the Faith of Bahá'u'lláh throughout the British Isles, within sight of the conclusion of the Final Phase of the Six Year Plan, stands on the threshold of a door which when opened will disclose to the eyes of its members a vista of vast dimensions, of majestic beauty, of infinite promise.

Theirs is the unrivalled opportunity, should they bestir themselves, to carry forward to a triumphant conclusion this first corporate effort to which they have consecrated themselves and their nascent institutions, to embark, in the course of subsequent Plans, on enterprises destined to safeguard and consolidate, in all parts of the motherland, the achievements so hardly won, to proclaim, unequivocally, systematically and effectively, to the masses throughout the length and breadth of the British Isles the verities enshrined in their Faith, to initiate the establishment of a befitting National Ḥaẓíratu'l-Quds in either the capital of the United Kingdom or further north in the very heart of the British Isles, to inaugurate national and local endowments, to incorporate the newly constituted assemblies, to undertake the preliminary measures for the erection of the first Mas͟hriqu'l-Ad͟hkár in the British Empire, and to launch crusades designed to implant the banner of the Faith and lay the structural basis of its Administrative Order throughout the diversified, the numerous and widely scattered colonies of the British Crown.

Not theirs, however, while the present tasks remain as yet unaccomplished, to dwell upon, or even visualise, however dimly, the course which the progress of their subsequent labours must assume in a world whose stability is so lamentably shaken, and whose immediate future is so dark. Theirs is the duty to derive from this fleeting glimpse of the glories which their future destiny holds in store for them fresh inspiration and added stimulus for a befitting performance of the work that lies immediately ahead.

Two brief years separate them from the hour destined to witness the total triumph of their first organised, nation-wide collective enterprise. Every minute of this interval is infinitely precious. The gloom overhanging the entire planet is deepening ominously every day. The American followers of the Faith of Bahá'u'lláh, through the ever-swelling army of their pioneers and settlers, on the northern, the western and southern fringes of the European Continent, as well as the newly resuscitated German and Austrian Bahá'í communities labouring in its very heart, have nobly arisen, and are doing their part in paving the way for the spiritual awakening and the ultimate redemption of the teeming millions of its war-torn, discordant, fear-stricken and spiritually famished inhabitants.

They who man the North-Western outpost of the Faith in Europe must, whilst pursuing their chartered course, play a distinctive part in this threefold crusade launched, almost simultaneously, from three directions, in conformity with specifically laid out plans, at so critical an hour, in so vast a field, amidst such diversified and conflicting races and nations of what may well be regarded as the cradle of a civilisation, and the mother of a Faith, whose fate now hangs so perilously in the balance.

That the valiant community of the British followers of the Faith of Bahá'u'lláh may assume an ever-increasing share in this gloriously unfolding, this herculean, this Divinely propelled enterprise is the dearest wish of my heart and the object of my constant prayers.

Shoghi

25 November 1948

ASSURE ADA WILLIAMS† ... DEEPEST LOVING APPRECIATION DELIGHTED ENROLMENT NEW BELIEVERS PRAYING REMOVAL DIFFICULTIES NOTTINGHAM DEEPEST LOVE.

SHOGHI RABBANÍ

22 December 1948

ASSURE HOFMANS BOB CHEEK LOVING ARDENT PRAYERS SUCCESS MERITORIOUS EFFORTS SUPPLICATING SATISFACTORY SOLUTION SECRETARIAT PROBLEM DEEPEST LOVING APPRECIATION ASSEMBLY'S NOBLE EXERTIONS.

SHOGHI RABBANÍ

2 January 1949

APPEAL BRITISH BAHÁ'Í COMMUNITY FOCUS ATTENTION CRITICAL STAGE PIONEER ACTIVITY SO ESSENTIAL STEADY UNFOLDMENT PLAN ATTAINMENT GOALS. PLEAD PARTICULARLY NUMERICALLY LARGER COMMUNITIES ARISE PLAY DECISIVE RÔLE VITAL URGENT TASK SUBSTANTIAL INCREASE NUMBER ACTIVE PIONEERS DEDICATED MERITORIOUS LABOUR AIMED SAFEGUARDING MULTIPLICATION PRIZES WON SO LABORIOUSLY OVER SO SHORT PERIOD DESPITE FORMIDABLE OBSTACLES BY MEMBERS SO VALIANT RESOLUTE HIGH SPIRITED COMMUNITY URGE APPROACHING CONFERENCE DELIBERATE VITAL ISSUE ROUSE PIONEER SPIRIT INDISPENSABLE SUCCESS

PLAN INVOKING ALMIGHTY'S BLESSINGS ANXIOUSLY AWAITING BEFITTING RESPONSE.

SHOGHI RABBANÍ

12 January 1949

DELIGHTED IMMEDIATE ACTION INITIAL RESPONSE PIONEERS ARDENTLY PRAYING TEACHING CONFERENCE MAY LEND POWERFUL DECISIVE IMPETUS PARAMOUNT VITAL URGENT PIONEER UNDERTAKING CONSTITUTING SUPREME CHALLENGE CONFRONTING STEADILY CONSOLIDATING IRRESISTIBLY ADVANCING BRITISH BAHÁ'Í COMMUNITY.

SHOGHI RABBANÍ

19 January 1949

APPEAL ALL MEMBERS COMMUNITY RESOLUTELY ARISE ATTAIN GREATER HEIGHTS HEROISM THROUGH DEMONSTRATION FURTHER MEASURE SELF-SACRIFICE IN SUPPORT PIONEER FUND URGE NEWLY ENROLLED BELIEVERS PARTICULARLY AS SIGN GRATITUDE INESTIMABLE BENEFITS NEWLY CONFERRED BAHÁ'Í MEMBERSHIP AND EVIDENCE SOLIDARITY RAPIDLY EXPANDING COMMUNITY EXTEND FINANCIAL ASSISTANCE FULLEST MEASURE POSSIBLE PIONEER ACTIVITIES ON WHICH HINGE FORTUNES PLAN SUPPLICATING DIVINE OUTPOURINGS MUCH NEEDED MERITORIOUS ENDEAVOURS.

SHOGHI RABBANÍ

20 February 1949*

APPROVE DRASTIC MEASURES PRAYING ARDENTLY SUCCESS.

SHOGHI RABBANÍ

*This was in reply to a cable from the N.S.A. which ended "ASSEMBLY READY CONTINUE PLAN INTENSIVE TEACHING OTHER COMMUNITIES DESIGNED RELEASE KNOWN WILLING PIONEERS. INVOLVES DRASTIC REDUCTION ADMINISTRATIVE WORK FREE CAPABLE TEACHERS. SUSPEND UNTIL CONVENTION A.D.C., YOUTH, PUBLISHING TRUST, REDUCE SUMMER SCHOOL, TOWNSHEND COMMITTEES, DELAY NUMERICAL INCREASE VIRGIN TERRITORIES NEW ASSEMBLIES. READY OPERATE DESPERATE MEASURES IMMEDIATELY RECEIPT YOUR APPROVAL. BEGS PRAYERS GUIDANCE."

1 April 1949*

ASSURE NEWLY DECLARED BELIEVERS WELCOME PRAYERS. CONVEY NEW PIONEERS DEEPEST LOVING ADMIRATION PRAYING RICHEST BLESSINGS ASSEMBLY'S STRENUOUS ENDEAVOURS. APPEAL FURTHER SACRIFICE CONTINUED RESPONSE CALL PIONEERS . . . DEEPEST LOVE.

SHOGHI RABBANÍ

9 April 1949

Dear Bahá'í Brother,

Your letters to our beloved Guardian, with their various enclosures, and dated October 4, 20; November 2, 7, 17, 18, 27; December 19, 22, 25, 28; of 1948, and January 4, 19; February 3, 17; and March 1, 1949, have been received, and he has instructed me to answer you on his behalf. . . .

Please assure Mr. Walter Wilkins that the Guardian was aware of his pioneer labours through various reports forwarded to him, and that he deeply appreciates them and is praying for his success.

He considers that Final Phase day must be April 21st, and not in July.

He feels that, although precedence must be given to the new goal assemblies, this does not mean the older assemblies like Bournemouth can afford to be neglected. They must be maintained, but the first call on pioneers must be from the critical goal assemblies who—at least theoretically—need help more urgently! He has just cabled you about this.

He sees no objection to your printing excerpts from his "Dispensation" and "God Passes By" in your compilation on the Covenant. Although he strongly feels that the Master's writings, the revealed Word of Bahá'u'lláh and the Báb, and his own writings should, out of respect for the difference in their relative stations, be published whenever possible in separate volumes,

---

*Louise Charlot, Constance Langdon-Davies†, and Cyril Jenkerson were pioneering to Oxford.

this must not be fanatically adhered to where an educative compilation on a certain subject is conceived.

A vacancy can be recognised, under the circumstances you outlined in your letter of December 22, 1948, and a new assembly member be elected. But of course this in no way implies the retiring member of the Assembly is not a full voting believer, and a member of the community in good standing.

He deeply sympathises with the struggles of the British Bahá'ís at present to perform their task, now reaching the crucial stage, in spite of financial difficulties and shortage of pioneers. It would seem as if all of our tasks, all over the world, including here at the World Centre, are becoming increasingly more of a challenge to us. As the time approaches for the ending of the various Plans, Six Year ones, Seven Year, Five Year, etc., the obstacles seem to become greater, and the friends are made to realise that very real, hard, often back-breaking effort and sacrifice is involved! The The American Bahá'ís here-to-fore so relatively easily victorious(!), are now feeling a very real squeeze on their resources and determination. The same is true of India, Persia, and the other countries with goals to accomplish within a fixed and rapidly diminishing period! He himself, having undertaken at such a disturbed time to raise at least the first story or arcade of the new part of the Báb's Shrine, finds himself beset with worries, problems and complications which have not only doubled his work, but exhaust and harass him all the time. So at least, let the British friends know that when they struggle and feel hard beset, they are not struggling and worrying alone! Far from it!!

We must expect these things: It is becoming evident that the world is not yet through with its labour, the New Age not yet fully born, real Peace not yet right round the corner. We must have no illusions about how much depends on us and our success or failure. All humanity is disturbed and suffering and confused; we cannot expect to not be disturbed and not to suffer—but we don't have to be confused. On the contrary, confidence and assurance, hope and optimism are our prerogative. The successful carrying out of our various Plans is the greatest sign we can give of our faith and inner assurance, and the best way we can help our fellow-men out of their confusion and difficulties.

He assures you he feels that the British Bahá'ís have got what it takes (to be a trifle slangy) to be successful and accomplish their goals. Let them therefore demonstrate it to the rest of the Bahá'í World....

P.S.—Your letter of April 4th has just been received. The Guardian is too busy to undertake at present the revision of Bahá'u'lláh's Tablet to the Christians, but he has no objection to a committee doing it.

Dear and valued co-workers:

The British Bahá'í community, now embarked on the final phase of the first historic collective enterprise undertaken in British Bahá'í history, stands at the parting of the ways. Only a brief interval separates it from the fateful date when its first experiment in a collective nation-wide effort to achieve a definite goal in the path of service to its beloved Faith will have ended. Five years of stupendous effort, of magnificent self-sacrifice, of marvellous dedication and of splendid cooperation have marked the progressive evolution of the Plan to its present stage. What has been achieved during this short span of years, despite the smallness of numbers, the paucity of resources and the exhaustion resulting from a prolonged and severely devastating conflict, has, beyond the shadow of a doubt, eclipsed the brightest achievements recorded in the course of more than half a century in the annals of the Faith of Bahá'u'lláh in that country.

The Bahá'í world, in its entirety, is struck with amazement at the quality of the work performed, at the extent and number of the victories achieved by this community. Its sister-community in the great Republic of the West, already laden with many and splendid trophies gathered in distant fields and over a long period of time cannot regard this resurgence of the Bahá'í spirit, this manifestation of Bahá'í solidarity, these ennobling evidences of Bahá'í achievement, amidst so conservative a people, within so short a time, under such trying circumstances, and by so small a band of workers, except with feelings compounded of envy, of admiration and respect. Its sister-communities throughout the East, venerable by reason of their age, and the sacrifices they have made, and fully aware of the long period of incubation this community has undergone, recall, with feelings of delight, 'Abdu'l-Bahá's prediction, forecasting the germination, at their appointed time, of the potent seeds His loving hands have sown in the course of His twice-repeated visit to that Island, and marvel at the rapidity with which its soil is now manifesting the potentialities with which it has been endowed. He Who blessed it with His footsteps, Who called into being, and fostered the growth of, the community labouring in that Island, hails, from His station on high, the exploits which immortalise the small band of His present-day consecrated and resolute followers, who are carrying on the torch which He Himself had entrusted to their immediate predecessors. Bahá'u'lláh Himself lauds the conspicuous victories being won in His Name, in the dawning years of the Second Bahá'í Century, at the very heart and centre of the greatest Empire the world has ever seen, whose Sovereign Monarch He Himself had addressed and whose deeds He, with His Own pen, had commended.

The one remaining year, ere the present Plan of this blessed, this radiant and spiritually potent community, is scheduled to draw to a close, cannot, must not, be allowed to jeopardise the prizes so painstakingly won during five memorable years of British Bahá'í history. The newly-enrolled believers, on whom the mantle of the first generation of 'Abdu'l-Bahá's British disciples has now fallen, and are now summoned to participate in a Plan, whose scope and potency their predecessors could have never visualised and whose initial success must thrill and rejoice their souls in the Abhá Kingdom, have a distinct, a sacred, a peculiar and urgent responsibility to discharge in ensuring the consummation of this mighty enterprise. Through active and constant participation with their veteran co-workers, in filling swiftly the still remaining gaps in the pattern of the Plan, now in its concluding stage; in displaying systematic and sustained activity in the pioneer field now stretching before them; in sacrificing, in as great a measure as possible, their resources, to facilitate the attainment of all its goals, they can best discharge their immense debt of gratitude to the Cause of the Most Great Name, Who has singled them out, at so critical an hour, and from among such a vast multitude of their slumbering countrymen, to serve and glorify His Faith.

I entreat them, and plead as well with their older brethren who have set so momentous a Plan in motion, to arise as one soul, to exert one more superhuman effort, to fix steadily their gaze on the pinnacle they are visibly approaching and to disencumber themselves of any burden impeding their arduous climb, in a last and determined attempt to scale and conquer the summit, from which alone they can catch a glimpse of the future glory of their destiny.

Shoghi

15 April 1949

Bahá'í Public Relations, Mr. Richard Backwell, sec.

Dear Bahá'í Brother:
Our Guardian thanks you very kindly for the excellent piece of publicity you forwarded to him with your letter of March 31. It should bring the Cause to the attention of many, and is sober, and very encouraging, in tone.
He hopes your committee will have many more triumphs along this line! . . .
P.S. Please convey to Mr. George Marshall† a cordial welcome into the service of our beloved Faith from our Guardian.

Assuring you of my loving prayers for the success of your constant and meritorious efforts in the service of our beloved Faith, and for the realisation of your heart's desire in its service,
Your true and grateful brother,
Shoghi

18 April 1949

APPROVE ELECTION LOCAL ASSEMBLIES BEFORE APRIL.

SHOGHI

19 April 1949

BE NOT DISTRESSED REDOUBLE EXERTIONS PERSEVERANCE WILL ENABLE PROSECUTORS PLAN ATTAIN GOAL ARRANGING CONTRIBUTION TERMINATION PLAN APRIL ASSEMBLIES MAY BE FORMED DURING YEAR ARDENTLY PRAYING REALISATION DEAREST HOPES.

SHOGHI

27 April 1949

ACCLAIM HISTORIC OCCASION PARTICIPATION DOUBLE NUMBER DELEGATES BRITISH BAHÁ'Í CONVENTION TESTIFYING RAPID UN-

THE SIX YEAR PLAN (1944–1950)

PRECEDENTED HIGHLY PROMISING EXPANSION DEARLY BELOVED COMMUNITY FOLLOWERS FAITH BAHÁ'U'LLÁH BRITISH ISLES THOUGH IMMEDIATE GOALS UNATTAINED AMOUNT WORK ACHIEVED STANDARD EFFORT EXERTED RANGE TASK PERFORMED QUALITY SPIRIT DEMONSTRATED SINCE INCEPTION PLAN HAVE CONTRIBUTED RAISING STATURE ENTIRE COMMUNITY ENHANCING ITS PRESTIGE PROCLAIMING ITS FAME DEMONSTRATING ITS VIRILITY ESTABLISHING BEYOND SHADOW DOUBT ITS RIGHT OCCUPY FRONT RANK ONWARD MARCHING ARMY FAITH BAHÁ'U'LLÁH APPEAL ASSEMBLED DELEGATES AROUSE ENTIRE COMMUNITY EXERT REMAINING TWELVE MONTHS EFFORT SURPASSING NOBLEST ENDEAVOURS AS YET MADE SERVICE PLAN VICTORY WITHIN SIGHT INTERVENING PERIOD RAPIDLY SHRINKING RESPONSIBILITY EVERY SINGLE MEMBER COMMUNITY GROWING GRAVER HOURLY MY PRAYERS LONGING TOTAL SUCCESS LIKEWISE INCREASING INTENSITY BAHÁ'U'LLÁH'S SUSTAINING UNFAILING GRACE MORE EFFICACIOUS READIER BLESS LAST ATTEMPTS MADE SAVE FORTUNES PLAN SO INEXTRICABLY INTERWOVEN DESTINY BRITISH BAHÁ'Í COMMUNITY.

SHOGHI

8 July 1949

HIGHLY APPROVE ASSEMBLY'S PROGRAMME ACTION DELIGHTED ENERGETIC HOPEFUL MEASURES AS CONCLUDING YEAR FINAL PHASE SIX YEAR PLAN RAPIDLY EBBS AWAY ATTENTION ALL MEMBERS BRITISH BAHÁ'Í COMMUNITY ALREADY FULLY AROUSED ACTION HIGHLY CONSCIOUS GLORIOUS OPPORTUNITY UNFLINCHINGLY DETERMINED ATTAIN GOAL SHOULD BE UNWAVERINGLY FOCUSSED ENERGIES MUSTERED ALL AVAILABLE RESOURCES MOBILISED ONE LAST FORWARD CHARGE ENABLING THEM ERE FINAL HOUR STRIKES SEIZE LAURELS VICTORY HANGING WITHIN THEIR REACH CONCERTED EFFORT SUSTAINED CONSECRATED NATION WIDE SCOPE TRANSCENDING INTENSITY MIGHTY EFFORTS ALREADY EXERTED PAST FIVE YEARS BY COMMUNITY WILL UNFAILINGLY ENSURE WORTHY CONSUMMATION INITIAL MEMORABLE STAGE FIRST HISTORIC CRUSADE LAUNCHED BY BAHÁ'U'LLÁH'S SPIRITUAL BATTALIONS LENGTH BREADTH BRITISH ISLES PLEAD AFRESH DIRECTING PARTICULAR APPEAL FEW REMAINING INACTIVE PARTICIPANTS WHO THROUGH INEXPERIENCE TIMIDITY OR OVER-

BURDENING CIRCUMSTANCES STILL HESTITATE FLING THEMSELVES ARENA WHEREIN STRUGGLING COMMUNITY BEING CALLED UPON THIS FATEFUL HOUR DISPLAY BEFORE EYES BAHÁ'Í WORLD ITS PROWESS DEMONSTRATE THE INTRINSIC WORTH ITS STEWARDSHIP FAITH BAHÁ'U'LLÁH IMPELLED IN RECOGNITION BRILLIANT RECORD PAST SERVICES AND TOKEN CONFIDENCE INSPIRED LATEST EXPLOITS FIELD SERVICE PLEDGE THOUSAND POUNDS FURTHERANCE SACRED TASK NOW MOST ACUTE PHASE STEADILY APPROACHING CULMINATION INTENSE PRAYERS ASCENDING FROM LONGING HEART THRONE LORD HOSTS SUPPLICATING VICTORY WHICH WILL BEFITTINGLY CROWN STRENUOUS EXERTIONS WHOLLY UNPARALLELED ANNALS FAITH BAHÁ'U'LLÁH BRITISH ISLES.

SHOGHI

9 July 1949

CENTENARY MARTYRDOM SHOULD HAVE NO PUBLIC COMMEMORATION NON-BAHÁ'ÍS MAY PARTICIPATE PUBLICITY PRESS PERMISSIBLE.

SHOGHI

19 July 1949

ADVISE SHOW UTMOST CONSIDERATION TUDOR-POLE INVITE HIM SUMMER SCHOOL PARTICIPATION OTHER ACTIVITIES.

SHOGHI

24 July 1949

DELIGHTED NEWS OXFORD ASSURE JENKERSON FAMILY LOVING PRAYERS.

SHOGHI

6 September 1949

Dear Bahá'í Friends:
Your letters dated April 8, 22, 27; May 13, 17, 24; June 7, 10,

23 (two of this date), 25, 28; July 19, 22, and 30; and August 10th, together with various enclosures, have been received by our beloved Guardian, and he has instructed me to answer them on his behalf.

He has already informed you by cable of his views regarding. . . . He realises that, of course, it is very difficult for him to renounce his plan of educating his son . . . in England, and the Guardian hopes that the boy can find a way, either through doing agricultural work or gaining a scholarship, or through the help his father might himself obtain from Persia for him, to go on with his studies. But it is obviously out of the question for your Assembly to shoulder this financial burden.

He already cabled you about the appropriate manner for commemorating the Centenary of the Báb's martyrdom, so I will not go into the subject again here.

The fine spirit of co-operation shown by . . . pleased him immensely. He has since received from her a letter full of joy and devotion to the Cause, which pleased him greatly. . . .

Now that the Cause is spreading so rapidly throughout the world, the National Assemblies must be vigilant, and do all they can to protect and assert its independent status, and to give assistance to isolated or repressed Assemblies, when they are turned to for help or advice.

He has recently received enthusiastic letters from Mrs. Preston† in Kenya and informed her that when she needs advice or assistance she should turn to your Assembly, while, of course, keeping in close contact with him as well.

He realises that your Assembly, and all the British Bahá'ís, are facing the most difficult and critical months of your Plan. The friends must be made to realise that the urgency of the task during these few months which lie ahead, is not only acute but temporary. Once they make this final effort, and clamber to the top of their goal, they can rest. The opportunity for achievement is absolutely unique, for this is their first Plan, and consequently the most historic one of the many they will, no doubt, carry out in future decades. To fail, so near to victory, would indeed be sad, and he cannot but suppose, would be a severe blow to that stubborn British pride which is so famous for its tenacity of purpose! However he himself is not thinking in terms of their failure, but rather believes they can, by one last determined drive, be successful, even if they feel some exhaustion at the end of their race against time. They must, likewise, at this crucial hour, remember that failure or success are never confined to the immediate community concerned, but have wide repercussions. Their success will not only greatly enhance their prestige in the Bahá'í World, but will inspire the often flagging efforts of the believers in the East, who have so many obstacles to overcome, and are by nature and experience more prone to become disheartened in the execution of fixed tasks.

It was the success of America's first Seven Year Plan which so stimulated the British community that it, in its turn, was determined to have a Plan and a victory of its own. Now it really cannot lose; it has gone too far, laboured too brilliantly, shown too much courage and high sacrifice, to let, at the last minute, the prize fall from its grasp!

His prayers and thoughts are with you all, constantly, and with all the believers, toiling so devotedly all over the British Isles. . . .

Dear and valued co-workers,

As the Plan, to which the entire British community has pledged its support, approaches its end, my heart turns with increasing longing and expectation, towards those who so spontaneously initiated it, so enthusiastically set it in motion, so valiantly overthrew the barriers that confronted them in the initial stage of its unfoldment, who so unitedly consecrated their efforts to its subsequent development, and who are now within sight of its final consummation. I cannot believe that a community which, motivated by so noble an impulse, capable of such prodigious efforts, dedicated so whole-heartedly to so gigantic a task, blessed by so many evidences of Divine assistance and guidance, enriched by the first fruits garnered in the course of the execution of a splendidly conceived enterprise, will allow, at the very moment when final victory is, at long last, within sight, through a momentary relaxation of effort, the magnificent prize of total success, to slip from its grasp, and the fortunes of such a potentially powerful undertaking to be marred by any feelings of impotence or exhaustion which might well, at the eleventh hour, assail those who have for so long and in such a great measure, expended their energies for the prosecution of so weighty and far-reaching a Plan.

THE SIX YEAR PLAN (1944–1950)

The required number of pioneers who must arise, while there is yet time, and stop the dangerous breaches which a fate-laden Plan, now in the last stages of its development, reveals to the eyes of its prosecutors must, however costly the sacrifice, be instantly found, and rushed without delay to the scene of action. The funds, which must enable these last minute pioneers to adjust their affairs and settle down wherever most needed, must, under no circumstances, and particularly on the part of the well-to-do, be withheld, as the present critical situation moves towards its climax.

Great and overpowering as these sacrifices may now appear, they will, when viewed in their proper perspective, be adjudged as inconsiderable, and pale into insignificance when balanced against the inestimable advantages which must accrue to a community that has achieved total and complete victory for a Plan so epoch-making in character, and so charged with undreamt of potentialities. The sacrifices which this fateful hour calls for, are by their very nature, individual; the loss or inconvenience they entail are at most transitory in their effect, and might well be fully compensated for in the days ahead, whereas the blessings that must irresistibly flow out, as the result of the integral success of a nation-wide, historically unprecedented Plan, will enrich and ennoble the life of an entire community, exert an abiding influence on its fortunes, and empower it to launch still mightier crusades in the course of subsequent stages in its organic spiritual development. How bountiful, moreover, will be the rewards which He who watches from on high the varying fortunes of the Plan and presides over its destinies, must either in this world or in the next— and it may well be in both—choose to confer upon those, who, at the hour of the Plan's greatest need, will fly to its succour, exhibit the rarest evidences of courage and heroism, and choose to subordinate their personal interests to the immediate needs and future glory of the community to which they belong.

The interval during which a decision so momentous, so rich in promise, must be taken is steadily and inexorably shrinking. The golden opportunity which such a decision offers will never again recur. The issues hinging on such a decision can neither be over-estimated nor visualised while the fate of the First Plan embarked upon by the British Bahá'í community still hangs in the balance. The invisible hosts of the Kingdom are ready and eager to rush forth to the assistance of such as will have the courage to weigh the issues involved and to take the decision commensurate with these issues. To such as take it, while there is yet time, the present generation as well as those who will succeed it will be eternally grateful, for theirs will have been the privilege of sealing on the one hand, the fate of the First Historic Plan in British Bahá'í annals, and on the other of paving the way for the initiation of the successive enterprises that must follow in its wake.

To reach such a decision, to face willingly and cheerfully its consequences, will, above all, earn the good-pleasure and commendation of the One Who, well nigh a hundred years ago, so gloriously made the supreme sacrifice of laying down His life that the Cause for which the present prosecutors of the Plan have so wholly dedicated themselves might live, prosper and bear, in the fullness of time, its fairest fruit in both the East and the West.

Dear friends! As the tale of the woes and trials He endured is called to mind, during the months preceding the centenary of His martyrdom, and destined to witness the conclusion of the Six Year Plan sponsored by the British Bahá'í community, a resolution, born of the love and admiration which the memory of His heroic life and tragic death must evoke in every Bahá'í heart, should seize, and galvanise into action, the little band of His lovers and followers, who, of their own accord, and at the dawn of the second Bahá'í century, have risen to launch the first collective enterprise in British Bahá'í history, and chosen to associate its consummation with the centenary of the death of the martyr Prophet and co-founder of their Faith. The centenary of the inception of His Mission has witnessed the initiation of so praiseworthy, so vast and potent an enterprise, extending its ramifications over the entire territory of the British Isles. The observances, commemorating the hundreth anniversary of the last act of His life, must, as pledged by its initiators, synchronise with the successful termination and glorious triumph of that same enterprise throughout the length and breadth of that same territory.

Your true brother,
Shoghi

29 September 1949

DEARLY BELOVED DISTINGUISHED CO-WORKER AMELIA COLLINS ARRIVING LONDON EN ROUTE POLAND SHOW GREAT CONSIDERATION PRAYING UTMOST BENEFIT VISIT.

SHOGHI

29 September 1949

OVERJOYED SUCCESS SUMMER SCHOOL ASSURE NEWLY ENROLLED NEWCASTLE LIVERPOOL LOVING WELCOME PRAYERS SURROUNDING ENTIRE COMMUNITY ACCELERATION MOMENTUM CARRYING IT ATTAINMENT GOALS APPOINTED TIME.

SHOGHI

5 November 1949
Summer School Committee

Dear Bahá'í Sister:

Your letter of October 9 was received, and our beloved Guardian has instructed me to answer you on his behalf.

He was very glad to hear the School was such a success this year, and that—a very important factor—it placed no extra burden on the National Fund at this critical juncture.

Next year your School will be held after the end of your Plan, he hopes the victorious end! It would be suitable to hold some kind of review of how the goals were won and to remember the many sacrifices that have been made, for they have been very real and taxed to the uttermost the strength of the servants of Bahá'u'lláh in the British Isles.

Also he feels it would be good to have some course on the Covenant, the force that binds and strengthens the Bahá'í community and holds it together, when so many man-made institutions are disintegrating and going on the rocks of discord and lack of faith.

Likewise, discussion of the future needs of the community should be held. By next Summer you will know better what these are, and can formulate your points to be taken up and considered.

He will pray that a suitable place may be found for the friends to gather.

Every year your school is more representative and successful than the year before, and he feels sure this will continue to be so until that happy day comes when Summer School develops at last into a seat of Bahá'í learning....

May the Almighty bless your meritorious efforts, guide and sustain you in your activities, enable you to extend continually their range, and contribute to the consolidation of the newly-born institutions of the Faith.

Your true and grateful brother,
Shoghi

25 November 1949

DELIGHTED VICTORY OXFORD ASSURE PIONEERS DEEPEST APPRECIATION MERITORIOUS ACTION.

SHOGHI

4 December 1949

National Youth Committee of the
Bahá'ís of the British Isles

Dear Bahá'í Friends,

The Guardian approves of the policy your committee is pursuing, as outlined in your letter to him of October 27th, of devoting all the energies of the British Youth, active in the Cause, to assisting in the achievement of the goals of the Plan.

He was very happy to hear your part of the programme at Summer School was more successful than ever before, and that the Bulletin is being maintained and at the same time costing less.

Your determination, and the work you are doing, are admirable, and he is very pleased with you all. . . .

May the Almighty bless continually your high endeavours, aid you to extend the range of your meritorious labours, and win great and memorable victories in this vital sphere of Bahá'í activity in that promising country.

Your true brother,
Shoghi

12 December 1949

ADVISE HOLD 1950 CONVENTION DURING RIḌVÁN PERIOD.

SHOGHI RABBANÍ

21 December 1949

KINDLY MAIL FIFTY COPIES "GLAD TIDINGS BAHÁ'U'LLÁH" WISDOM EAST SERIES. PRAYING FERVENTLY SUCCESS FORTHCOMING CONFERENCE.

SHOGHI

23 December 1949

APPROVE SUBSTITUTION*.

SHOGHI

27 December 1949

DELIVER SIXTY POUNDS HAINSWORTH FROM NATIONAL FUND FOR PUBLICATION SWAHILI CHINYANZA LANGUAGES.

SHOGHI

29 December 1949 (Teaching Conference)

FEEL MOVED ADDRESS THIS ELEVENTH HOUR MY LAST FERVENT APPEAL ASSEMBLED REPRESENTATIVES BRITISH COMMUNITY SEIZE OPPORTUNITY TEACHING CONFERENCE AROUSE ENTIRE BODY FOLLOWERS FAITH BAHÁ'U'LLÁH BRITISH ISLES SAVE FORTUNES PLAN NOW HANGING BALANCE ENTREAT ONCE AGAIN ALL BELIEVERS ENGLAND WALES SCOTLAND IRELAND WHETHER YOUNG OLD MEN WOMEN NATIVE-BORN VISITORS OVERSEAS NEWLY-ENROLLED VETERANS BRACE THEMSELVES AS HOUR CENTENARY BÁB'S NOBLEST ACT SACRIFICE APPROACHES ONE LAST SUPREME SACRIFICIAL SUSTAINED EFFORT DESIGNED ENSURE TOTAL VICTORY NOW WITHIN REACH CONSTITUTING BEFITTING CULMINATION FINAL PHASE SIX YEARS HEROIC ENDEAVOUR AND WORTHY TRIBUTE COLLECTIVELY PAID BY BRITISH UPHOLDERS CAUSE BAHÁ'U'LLÁH IMMORTAL MEMORY DEARLY BELOVED MARTYR PROPHET THEIR FAITH ARRANGING TRANSMISSION £500 FURTHER CONTRIBUTION

---

*Substitution of Stockport for St. Ives as goal of Plan.

CONSUMMATION ENTERPRISE UNPRECEDENTED IN SCOPE SPIRITUAL POTENTIALITIES HALF CENTURY BRITISH BAHÁ'Í HISTORY.

SHOGHI

4 January 1950

GREATLY HEARTENED NEWS CONFERENCE PRAYERS CONTINUALLY ASCENDING THRONE BAHÁ'U'LLÁH TOTAL SUCCESS PLAN.

SHOGHI

19 January 1950

GREATLY HEARTENED ASSURE PIONEERS FERVENT LOVING PRAYERS ACCOMPANYING THEM. PARVINE HEARTFELT SYMPATHY LOVING PRAYERS CONTINUALLY OFFERED HER BEHALF.

SHOGHI

31 January 1950*

ADVISE DISREGARD PROCEDURE SUGGESTED LETTER JANUARY TWENTIETH. . . .

SHOGHI

25 February 1950

ASSURE PIONEERS HEARTFELT APPRECIATION CONVEY CONGRATULATIONS STOCKPORT NEWCASTLE PRAYING SOLUTION DIFFICULTIES CENTRE LONDON ENTREAT ENTIRE COMMUNITY SEIZE FIRMLY PRIZE FINGERTIPS CROWN EVERLASTING GLORY MIGHTIEST TASK UNDERTAKEN BRITISH FOLLOWERS BAHÁ'U'LLÁH.

SHOGHI

* Refers to a suggested new procedure for the recognition of Local Assemblies.

20 March 1950—National Teaching Committee

PRAYING FERVENTLY SUCCESS FORTHCOMING WEEKEND SCHOOL. DEEPLY APPRECIATE UNCEASING EFFORTS. RENEW THROUGH YOU IMPASSIONED PLEA ENTIRE COMMUNITY EXERT FLEETING FATEFUL DAYS AHEAD CONCERTED STRENUOUS UNRELAXING EFFORTS ENSURE NEEDED NUMBER PIONEERS FILL REMAINING GAPS IN NOBLY CONCEIVED LABORIOUSLY PROSECUTED HISTORICALLY UNIQUE SPITUALLY MOMENTOUS PLAN.

SHOGHI

28 March 1950

National Bahá'í Teaching Committee, England

Dear Bahá'í Friends,

Your letter of January 12th, written by Mr. Hainsworth, was received, as well as the material enclosed, and our beloved Guardian has instructed me to answer you on his behalf.

He was glad to learn the Manchester Conference was such a success, and appreciated the very generous offer of Mr. Leach†. If the believers all over the world were animated by such a spirit, there would scarcely be any necessity for "Plans".

These days, as Riḍván approaches, his anxious thoughts are with not only the British community, but other Bahá'í communities in different parts of the world. He longs to see them fully achieve their goals; for to do something for God 100 per cent has an attractive power, and brings future Divine confirmations.

His ardent prayers are with you all, you may be sure....

May the Spirit of Bahá'u'lláh sustain and guide you in your historic labours, aid you to extend the range of your splendid achievements, consolidate the victories you have won, and lend a still greater impetus to the progress and expansion of your unforgettable accomplishments.

Your true and grateful brother,
Shoghi

30 March 1950

DEEPLY APPRECIATE PARTICIPATION JOHN ROBARTS SPLENDID ACTION SCOTT† AND OTHER PIONEERS APPEAL FURTHER SACRIFICE GREATER HEROISM FIRMER RESOLVE NOBLER CONSECRATION ENSURE TOTAL SUCCESS PLAN NOW HANGING BALANCE FOR MY PART UTMOST CAN DO IS STRETCH PERIOD PLAN TO JULY NINTH DATE COMMEMORATION MARTYRDOM LAST REMAINING CHANCE OFFERED HARDLY PRESSED YET GLORIOUSLY STRIVING COMMUNITY SHOULD BE INSTANTLY SEIZED ERE IT IS IRRETRIEVABLY LOST.

SHOGHI

4 April 1950

DELIGHTED NEWS PRAYING ADDED FERVOUR TOTAL SUCCESS DEEPEST LOVING APPRECIATION.

SHOGHI

11 April 1950*

REJOICE EVIDENCES APPROACHING VICTORY PRAYING INCREASING FERVOUR.

SHOGHI

19 April 1950**

OVERJOYED DEEPLY GRATEFUL IMMENSELY PROUD SIGNAL VICTORY ACHIEVED BAHÁ'Í COMMUNITY BRITISH ISLES SHEDDING LUSTRE OPENING YEARS SECOND BAHÁ'Í CENTURY AIRMAIL LIST ASSEMBLIES GROUPS ISOLATED BELIEVERS ALSO MAP BRITISH ISLES SHOWING SAME.

SHOGHI

*In answer to cable of 10 April from N.S.A. "JOYFULLY TRANSMIT TEACHING COMMITTEE REPORT ARRANGEMENTS MADE COMPLETE PLAN BY RIḌVÁN EARNESTLY ENTREAT PRAYERS BAHÁ'U'LLÁH SEAL VICTORY."

**In answer to cable of 17 April from National Assembly. "TOTAL VICTORY ASSURED LOVING GRATITUDE BOUNTIES BELOVED GUARDIAN ASSISTANCE WHOLE BAHÁ'Í WORLD."

21 April 1950*

SHARE JOY RECIPROCATE NOBLE SENTIMENTS HEARTILY CONGRATULATE NATIONAL ELECTED REPRESENTATIVES TRIUMPHANT COMMUNITY INDEFATIGABLE NATIONAL TEACHING COMMITTEE ALL SUBSIDIARY AGENCIES PARTICULARLY SELF-SACRIFICING PIONEERS WHO SO OUTSTANDINGLY CONTRIBUTED SIGNAL VICTORY REVERBERATING BAHÁ'Í WORLD.

SHOGHI

---

*In answer to cable of 19 April from National Assembly. "JOYOUS RIḌVÁN GREETINGS BELOVED GUARDIAN FROM NATIONAL ASSEMBLY AND TWENTY-FOUR LOCAL ASSEMBLIES BRITISH ISLES."

"The threshold of a new and glorious epoch"

THE AFRICA PLAN
1950-1953

THE AFRICA PLAN (1950–1953) 245

Convention 1950

HEART FLOODED JOY STRIKING EVIDENCE BOUNTIFUL GRACE BAHÁ'U'LLÁH ENABLING VALOROUS DEARLY LOVED BAHÁ'Í COMMUNITY BRITISH ISLES TRIUMPHANTLY CONCLUDE FIRST HISTORIC PLAN HALF CENTURY BRITISH BAHÁ'Í HISTORY. HERALD AUTHOR FAITH CENTRE COVENANT CONCOURSE ON HIGH ACCLAIM SUPERB COLLECTIVE ACHIEVEMENT IMMORTALISING OPENING DECADE SECOND BAHÁ'Í CENTURY UNPRECEDENTED HISTORY FAITH BRITISH ISLES UNRIVALLED ANNALS ANY BAHÁ'Í COMMUNITY EUROPEAN CONTINENT UNPARALLELED PERCENTAGE MEMBERS COMMUNITY RESPONDING PIONEER CALL THROUGHOUT BAHÁ'Í WORLD SINCE TERMINATION APOSTOLIC AGE BAHÁ'Í DISPENSATION. HISTORIC PLEDGE BRITISH BAHÁ'Í COMMUNITY NOBLY REDEEMED. TRIBUTE MEMORY MARTYR PROPHET FAITH WORTHILY PAID. SPIRITUAL POTENTIALITIES PROSECUTE SUBSEQUENT STAGE UNFOLDING MISSION FULLY ACQUIRED. TRIUMPHANT COMMUNITY NOW STANDING THRESHOLD CATCHING FIRST GLIMPSE STILL DIMLY OUTLINED FUTURE ENTERPRISES OVERSEAS. HOUR PROPITIOUS GALVANISED FIRMLY KNIT BODY BELIEVERS BRACE ITSELF EMBARK AFTER ONE YEAR RESPITE YET ANOTHER HISTORIC UNDERTAKING MARKING FORMAL INAUGURATION TWO YEAR PLAN CONSTITUTING PRELUDE INITIATION SYSTEMATIC CAMPAIGN DESIGNED CARRY TORCH FAITH TERRITORIES DARK CONTINENT WHOSE NORTHERN SOUTHERN FRINGES WERE SUCCESSIVELY ILLUMINATED COURSE MINISTRIES BAHÁ'U'LLÁH 'ABDU'L-BAHÁ. HOUR STRUCK UNDERTAKE PRELIMINARY STEPS IMPLANT BANNER FAITH AMIDST AFRICAN TRIBES MENTIONED TABLET CENTRE COVENANT SIGNALISING ASSOCIATION VICTORIOUS BRITISH BAHÁ'Í COMMUNITY WITH SISTER COMMUNITIES UNITED STATES EGYPT DESIGNED LAY STRUCTURAL BASIS BAHÁ'Í ADMINISTRATIVE ORDER SCALE COMPARABLE FOUNDATION ALREADY ESTABLISHED NORTH SOUTH AMERICAN EUROPEAN AUSTRALIAN CONTINENTS. PROJECTED PLAN ITSELF PRELUDE DOUBLE TASK TO BE UNDERTAKEN COURSE FUTURE PLANS DESTINED SIMULTANEOUSLY BROADEN BASE OPERATIONS HOME FRONT AND PROSECUTE SYSTEMATIC CAMPAIGN DEPENDENCIES BRITISH ISLES. FIRST OBJECTIVE TWO YEAR PLAN CONSOLIDATION NINETEEN ASSEMBLIES PAINSTAKINGLY ESTABLISHED ENGLAND SCOTLAND WALES NORTH IRELAND EIRE. SECOND OBJECTIVE FORMATION NUCLEI THREE DEPENDENCIES BRITISH CROWN EITHER EAST WEST

AFRICA. THIRD OBJECTIVE TRANSLATION PUBLICATION DISSEMINATION BAHÁ'Í LITERATURE THROUGH PUBLISHING TRUST THREE AFRICAN LANGUAGES ADDITION THREE ALREADY UNDERTAKEN COURSE FIRST PLAN. SUCCESSFUL PROSECUTION CONTEMPLATED PLAN WILL PAVE WAY LARGE SCALE OPERATIONS CALCULATED LAY FOUNDATION PROMISED KINGDOM EARTH THROUGH ESTABLISHMENT ADMINISTRATIVE ORDER INFINITELY MORE GLORIOUS EMPIRE BUILT RULERS BRITISH ISLES THROUGHOUT THAT CONTINENT AND WILL ENABLE BRITISH BAHÁ'Í COMMUNITY SHARE HONOUR SISTER COMMUNITY ACROSS ATLANTIC PROSECUTING SUCCESSFULLY TWO SUCCESSIVE PLANS REGISTERING DOUBLE VICTORY LAYING TWICE REPEATED SACRIFICE ALTAR FAITH ANTICIPATION APPROACHING CELEBRATIONS COMMEMORATING CENTENARY BIRTH BAHÁ'U'LLÁH'S PROPHETIC MISSION. CONTRIBUTING ONE THOUSAND POUNDS FIRST CONTRIBUTION FURTHERANCE NOBLE PURPOSE.

SHOGHI

1 May 1950

GRIEVE PASSING DEAR DISTINGUISHED PROMOTER FAITH* HER SERVICES UNFORGETTABLE PRAYING PROGRESS SOUL ABHÁ KINGDOM.

SHOGHI

3 May 1950

DELIGHTED SUCCESS SESSIONS PRAYING MIGHTY VICTORIES.

SHOGHI

9 June 1950

Dear Bahá'í Brother,

At the instruction of our beloved Guardian I am forwarding you the enclosed material for possible use in connection with the centenary of the Báb's martyrdom.

* Mary Basil-Hall, "Parvine".

In America they are going to get out a pamphlet with this and other material, more complete, which the Guardian has asked them to forward you copies of as soon as printed.

He regrets the delay in answering your Assembly's letters. My father has been desperately ill for over 8 weeks and the worry involved and doctors, nurses etc. has been so distressing to us all that it has been temporarily impossible to attend to his mail. However, now he is improving, the Guardian hopes to shortly be able to get his letters answered....

15 June 1950

Dear Bahá'í Brother,

Your many communications dated August 20, 26; September 30; October 6, 7, 10, 26; November 7, 9, 14, 23, 25; December 8, 18, 22, 23 (two of this date), 24, all of 1949, and January 4, 20, 30; February 2, 22; March 1, 6, 18, 29 (two of this date); April 7, 18, 19 (two of this date), 24, 27; and May 2, 4, 8, 16 (three of this date) of 1950, have been received as well as their enclosures and other material, and our beloved Guardian has instructed me to answer you on his behalf.

He regrets very much the long delay in not only answering your Assembly's letters but those of other N.S.A.s' as well. The past winter, owing to the fact that large excavations had to be carried out behind the Shrine in order to permit construction to continue, was a particularly busy gruelling one for him. On top of this, at the beginning of April, Mr. Maxwell became dangerously ill and the constant worry and preoccupation of us all with doctors, nurses, etc., forced the Guardian to put aside his letters entirely for the time being. Thanks to the mercy of God Mr. Maxwell is now recovering slowly; but the past months were very difficult ones for everyone.

To now take up the various matters referred to in your letters.

The Guardian does not feel that a quorum of delegates is necessary in any sense for the convention. Under unusual circumstances National bodies can be elected by mailed votes of all the delegates; the primary function of the delegates is to elect the N.S.A. Suggestions from the Convention floor can be made by a majority of those present.

The Guardian is very pleased to see that Peter Esslemont is growing closer to the Faith. A friendly contact with him should always be maintained.

Regarding his cable concerning Hussein: he has been very surprised to note that the terms "low-born Christian girl" and "disgraceful alliance" should arouse any question: it seems to him that the friends should realise it is not befitting for the Guardian's own brother, the grandchild of the Master, an Afnán and Aghsán mentioned in the Will and Testament of the Master, and of whom so much was expected because of his relation to the Family of the Prophet, to marry an unknown girl, according to goodness knows what rite, who is not a believer at all. Surely, every Bahá'í must realise that the terms low-born and Christian are definitions of a situation and in no way imply any condemnation of a person's birth or the religion they belong to as such. We have no snobbery and no religious prejudice in our Faith. But the members of the Master's family have contracted marriages which cannot be considered in any other light than disgraceful, in view of what 'Abdu'l-Bahá wished for them.

Recently the Court of First Instance, in Karkúk, 'Iráq, has accepted to register a Bahá'í marriage certificate. This is the first time in the East (except for the British Mandate authorities and the Israeli Government), that a Bahá'í marriage has been recognised as being legal. The Guardian feels that this can form a very important precedent for the other Oriental countries, and he suggests you inform the Egyptian N.S.A. of his view and urge them to press for due recognition in Egypt, using this precedent as a lever.

There is nothing in our teachings about Freud and his method. Psychiatric treatment in general is no doubt an important contribution to medicine, but we must believe it is still a growing rather than a perfected science. As Bahá'u'lláh has urged us to avail ourselves of the help of good physicians Bahá'ís are certainly not only free to turn to psychiatry for assistance but should, when available, do so. This does not mean psychiatrists are always wise or always right, it means we are free to avail ourselves of the best medicine has to offer us.

The Guardian thanks you and the friends for your eagerness

THE AFRICA PLAN (1950–1953)   249

to contribute to the cost of the Shrine through the special edition of "Prescription for Living"; also he thanks the friends at Convention for the copy they sent him.

I need not tell you how immensely relieved, proud and gratified the beloved Guardian was when he knew the British community had achieved their Plan so successfully. During the last year he was often anxious as he shared with your Assembly and the National Teaching Committee the news of how acute the position was, and how great the obstacles still remaining to be overcome.

From the beginning, however, he felt confident that this dedicated and courageous community could and would drive through to victory, and his joy was very great when it did. He firmly believes this will exert a great influence on the future of the Bahá'í community there, and indirectly on the history of that country in the days to come. It is not possible, at close range, to understand the implications of what we do; but when we see things in historical perspective, we realise that what seemed small at the time was really a turning point in destiny.

The Guardian was delighted to receive the Welsh pamphlet, also the map you sent him. He is planning to have the map published in the next edition of "Bahá'í World", and he placed the pamphlet in the Mansion of Bahá'u'lláh.

He approves of the Investment Scheme of the Publishing Trust, and he trusts that the members of the community will respond and thus enable your Assembly to expand its publishing activities. He leaves the question of approaching Bahá'ís overseas, should the Trust be in need of further capital, to your Assembly's discretion.

The Guardian does not approve of your placing a condition upon recognition of local assemblies (mentioned in your letter of January 20); and he wishes in this connection to emphasise the fact that every possible care should be taken not to add to existing rules and regulations in the form of statements or otherwise. He has already advised the American and other National Assemblies to beware of adding more rules and regulations.

The death of Mrs. Hall, such a faithful and devoted servant of the Faith, is a great loss to the British community. The Guardian appreciated receiving a copy of her Will, which mirrors her solicitude for the interests of the Cause in England. He trusts that a Bahá'í Ceremony could take place at the graveside, which certainly would have been her own wish.

Regarding ..., if the financial response of the friends to the needs of the Faith there is not sufficient for your Assembly to continue to defray his expenses as a teacher and pioneer, then it seems inevitable that he will have to make some other plans. His services have been of real value, and his intimate knowledge of the teachings and steadfastness in the Covenant have enabled him to contribute much to the understanding of the friends.

The Guardian approves your resolution to keep Mr. Ferraby† as paid secretary of the Assembly. He deeply appreciates Mr. Ferraby's devoted services.

The Guardian wishes to assure you, one and all, of his prayers for the success of the new work your Assembly will be undertaking, and for the consolidation of all the recent goals achieved.

P.S. Also just received are a receipt for the Guardian's contribution, dated May 15th and your letter, with enclosure, of May 28th and May 24th. A photo of the Shrine will be mailed you very soon.

P.P.S. The Guardian will certainly pray for the progress and happiness of the soul of Mr. Manton. No doubt the selfless services his son has rendered the Cause of God, in an hour of great need, will be accepted and enable him to influence the state of his father through his own prayers.

Dear and valued co-workers,

On the occasion of the victorious consummation of the first historic Plan undertaken by the British Bahá'í community, I feel moved to reaffirm my feelings of exultation, joy and gratitude for the superb triumph that marks such a great turning point in British Bahá'í history. No single event, in the course of its half-a-century existence, with the exception of the twice repeated visit of the Centre of the Covenant to the British Isles, has proved as significant and momentous as this unique collective achievement, which may, in a sense, be regarded as the first and long-awaited fruit of that intimate and personal contact, established both in private and in public, by 'Abdu'l-Bahá with its members as well as with various representatives of the country to which it belongs.

THE AFRICA PLAN (1950–1953)

So magnificent an achievement has, no doubt, endowed the entire community, now representative of the peoples of England, Wales, Scotland and Ireland, with tremendous potentialities, empowering it to launch on the first stage of its historic overseas mission destined to bring that community into closer and more concrete association with its sister communities in North America and Egypt, for the purpose of promoting the Faith in the vast virgin territories where its banner is still unraised and which constitute an integral part of the territories of the British Crown beyond the confines of that community's homeland.

To the races and tribes inhabiting these territories throughout the vast African Continent 'Abdu'l-Bahá when His life was in imminent danger, specifically referred in a Tablet, addressed by Him to the cousin of the Báb and chief builder of the first Mashriqu'l-Adhkár of the Bahá'í world, in which He predicts, in moving terms, the awakening of the peoples of that dark continent and the ultimate triumph of His Father's Faith among its backward peoples as well as among the great masses inhabiting China and India.

To the accomplishment of the initial stages of this colossal task, envisaged by our beloved Master, the Bahá'í community of the British Isles, now greatly reinforced, resting on a far broader foundation, galvanised into action, qualified through its initial signal victory in its homeland—the base of its future operations overseas, is now summoned to direct its attention and its energies.

While, in the current and two succeeding years which separate us from the celebration of the centenary of the birth of Bahá'u'lláh's prophetic mission, close and sustained attention should be directed by the elected representatives, as well as by the rank and file, of that community towards the safeguarding of the prizes won throughout the length and breadth of the British Isles, and the consolidation of the newly born institutions, the preliminary steps, constituting the prelude to this prodigious systemic labour and soul-thrilling enterprise, destined to extend its ramifications, in the years that lie ahead, to the fringe and within the very heart of a vast continent, must be carefully and prayerfully taken.

Though the members of this community are still restricted in number, though its resources are as yet meagre, though its recent victories are as yet unconsolidated, though it has hardly recuperated from its recent labours, undertaken during a period of great national exhaustion and severe austerity, the mere act of launching upon so glorious, so fateful an enterprise, will, of necessity, create at this propitious hour the receptivity which will enable a swiftly marching, stout-hearted, virile community, now standing on the threshold of its mission beyond the seas, to attract a fresh measure of celestial potency adequate to its growing needs and its ever expanding responsibilities. The miracle its members have performed over so vast a territory, in so short a time, and under such adverse circumstances, cannot but augur well for the initial success of an enterprise infinitely more meritorious, of far greater promise, and endowed with vastly superior spiritual potentialities.

How great the honour with which the Bahá'í pioneers of the present generation of the subjects of the British Crown will be invested in the eyes of posterity within their island home and abroad! How great the debt of gratitude of those who will labour after them and garner the fruit of their present day assiduous exertions to those whose privilege is to blaze the trail and break the soil in the virgin territories destined, as prophesied by 'Abdu'l-Bahá, to acclaim the Faith of Bahá'u'lláh and establish the institutions of His embryonic World Order!

This community, laden with the trophies of so recent and splendid a victory, and summoned to brace itself for another exertion, so fate-laden in its consequences, stands too near the structure which its hands are now rearing to visualise the dimensions of its task, appraise its value, and appreciate its future glory. Alive to its inherent capacity, conscious of its high responsibility, aware of the sacredness of its mission, emboldened by its recent exploits, trusting fully in that reinforcing Power that guided and sustained it unfailingly in the past, this community can do no better than to gird up afresh its loins, turn its back upon the clamour of the age, its fears, confusion and strife, step resolutely forward on its chosen path, unshakably confident that with every step it takes, should it remain undeflected in its purpose and undimmed in its vision, a fresh outpouring of Divine grace will reinforce and guide its march on the highroad of its destiny.

Your true brother,
Shoghi

28 June 1950

Dear Bahá'í Brother,

Your letters dated June 6th and two of June 13th have just reached the Guardian, with their enclosures, and he wishes you

THE AFRICA PLAN (1950–1953)

to please regard this as a sort of postscript to the detailed letter to your Assembly which was mailed a short time ago. He thanks you for the copies of correspondence with the Official Solicitor, and trusts this matter is now satisfactorily settled.

He approves of the advice your Assembly has given. ... However, he does not approve of ... going to Canada or South America. He has been forced, owing to the very unfortunate influence of certain so-called Bahá'ís from Persia, to lay down a general rule that no Persians for the present proceed to North or South America. As many sincere souls have, through obedience to his instructions, given up trips to those territories, he feels he cannot permit any exceptions to be made, not even for so important a purpose as pioneering. This would be a manifest injustice to those who have obeyed him with an exemplary spirit. He feels sure ... will understand and accept this. There are a great many places where they can serve the Faith in the East, in Europe, or in Africa.

Whatever form of co-operation will get the best results your Assembly is free to decide upon in regard to the Egyptian and American N.S.A.s' extension teaching in Africa. He feels, however, that simultaneous activity is more practicable at present.

There are no specific tribes listed in the Master's Tablets; the pioneering should be directed at present towards the most feasible possibilities.

The Guardian feels that Kenya, as it already has a Bahá'í, should be excluded from your Plan. Uganda and Tanganyika would be much more suitable in conjunction with any other territory, but not Nigeria, which already has some Bahá'ís. However, it must not necessarily be these two.

Entirely aside from any additional literature it might be possible to get out in Hausa and Swahili he feels your objective must be to print at least a pamphlet in three languages other than those Philip Hainsworth has tackled. It must be borne in mind that printing in new languages kills two birds with one stone—not only does it enable the Faith to reach new elements, but it also enriches our literature and is excellent as a means of calling the attention of the public to the universality of our Cause and the extent of our world-wide activities!

He will be delighted to receive the reports regarding the progress of the British Bahá'ís' first overseas mission.

P.S. Regarding expenditures: the Guardian feels that the greatest effort should be made to curtail everything that is not essential; this is the primary responsibility of the N.S.A. The Guardian will be very pleased to receive copies of the reports of the Africa and Consolidation Committees and was pleased to read the first two reports.

24 July 1950

GOLD COAST ELIGIBLE DELIGHTED GRATEFUL PUBLICITY OCCASION CENTENARY.

SHOGHI

12 August 1950 (Summer School)

DELIGHTED SUCCESS WELCOME NOBLE RESOLVE ASSURANCE LOYALTY BELIEVERS URGE CONCENTRATION PERSEVERENCE COMPLETE DEDICATION NEWLY ASSIGNED EPOCH MAKING TASKS MARKING OPENING NEW CHAPTER WORLD WIDE EXPANSION FAITH SUPPLICATING BOUNTIFUL BLESSING PRIVILEGED PARTICIPANTS GLORIOUS ENTERPRISE URGING AMERICAN PERSIAN COMMUNITIES ARISE LEND ASSISTANCE ITS PROSECUTION DEEPEST LOVE.

SHOGHI

6 September 1950

WARN BELIEVERS AVOID PERDU OWING HIS CONTACT SOHRAB.

SHOGHI

11 September 1950

Dear Bahá'í Brother:

Under separate cover the Guardian is mailing two enlargements of the Shrine. He would like these to be shown as widely as possible to the friends and then hung in the London Bahá'í Centre.

THE AFRICA PLAN (1950-1953)

He has sent to America the negative of one of these enlargements with instructions that the friends can order copies for themselves. This applies to the British friends too, and if copies are desired you can enquire from the American N.S.A. what they cost etc.

He feels sure all the believers will be happy to see how beautiful the finished arcade is....

P.S. Please cable when you receive these two photos.

15 September 1950

APPROVE SENDING PIONEERS AFRICA IMMEDIATELY ALSO SEEK ASSISTANCE PERSIA AMERICA.

SHOGHI

2 November 1950

Dear Bahá'í Brother,

Some time ago I wrote you on behalf of the Guardian giving you the following information, but as I have heard a letter to Mr. Holley posted at the same time has not been received, I fear yours too may have been lost.

The beloved Guardian has sent each of the National Assemblies under separate cover, a couple of enlarged photos of the finished arcade of the Báb's Shrine. These are a little gift from him. He would like as many of the believers as possible to see them, and for them to then be hung wherever they would then be seen most, in some countries this would be the National Hazira.

He has sent two negatives to the American N.S.A., and instructed prints be made available for sale to the friends desiring copies. You can no doubt order some if desired.

Please cable the Guardian acknowledging receipt of these photos as soon as they reach you....

14 November 1950

KINDLY ARRANGE DEPARTURE LUṬFU'LLÁH ḤAKÍM HAIFA FOR NECESSARY SERVICE.

SHOGHI

14 November 1950

GRIEVE PASSING DISTINGUISHED INDEFATIGABLE PROMOTER FAITH★ ARDENTLY SUPPLICATING PROGRESS SOUL ABHÁ KINGDOM HER NOTABLE MERITORIOUS SERVICES UNFORGETTABLE.

SHOGHI

22 November 1950

URGE UTMOST ECONOMY APPEAL ENTIRE COMMUNITY ENDEAVOUR REDUCE DEFICIT FUND CONTRIBUTING FIVE HUNDRED POUNDS.

SHOGHI

22 December 1950

ASSURE CLAIRE GUNG FERVENT LOVING PRAYERS SURROUNDING HER MERITORIOUS HISTORIC JOURNEY SUPPLICATING BLESSINGS FORTHCOMING CONFERENCE DEEPEST LOVING APPRECIATION.

SHOGHI

10 January 1951 (Teaching Conference)

ASSURE ATTENDANTS SUPPLICATING ALMIGHTY BLESSINGS DELIBERATIONS MAY CONFERENCE LEND TREMENDOUS IMPETUS PROCESS CONSOLIDATION HOMELAND INITIATION PIONEER ACTIVITIES AFRICAN CONTINENT.

SHOGHI

16 January 1951

(Copy of a cable from the Guardian to the National Spiritual Assembly of the Bahá'ís of the United States dated 16 January 1951, sent also to the British National Spiritual Assembly.)

ASSISTANCE AFRICA PROJECT THROUGH FINANCIAL CONTRIBUTION PARTICIPATION PIONEERS WHITE COLOURED CLOSE CONSULTATION

★ Florence "Mother" George†.

CO-OPERATION BRITISH ASSEMBLY NECESSARY INDEPENDENT CAMPAIGN NOT INTENDED FERVENTLY PRAYING PARTICIPATION BRITISH AMERICAN PERSIAN EGYPTIAN NATIONAL ASSEMBLIES UNIQUE EPOCHMAKING ENTERPRISE AFRICAN CONTINENT MAY PROVE PRELUDE CONVOCATION FIRST AFRICAN TEACHING CONFERENCE LEADING EVENTUALLY INITIATION UNDERTAKINGS INVOLVING COLLABORATION ALL NATIONAL ASSEMBLIES BAHÁ'Í WORLD THEREBY PAVING WAY ULTIMATE ORGANIC UNION THESE ASSEMBLIES THROUGH FORMATION INTERNATIONAL HOUSE JUSTICE DESTINED LAUNCH ENTERPRISES EMBRACING WHOLE BAHÁ'Í WORLD ACCLAIM SIMULTANEOUS INAUGURATION CRUSADE LINKING ADMINISTRATIVE MACHINERY FOUR NATIONAL ASSEMBLIES EAST WEST WITHIN FOUR CONTINENTS AND BIRTH FIRST INTERNATIONAL COUNCIL WORLD CENTRE FAITH TWIN COMPELLING EVIDENCES RESISTLESS UNFOLDMENT EMBRYONIC DIVINELY APPOINTED WORLD ORDER BAHÁ'U'LLÁH.

SHOGHI

17 January 1951

INFORM MÚSÁ BANÁNI† HIGHLY APPROVE PIONEERING AFRICA WITH NA<u>KH</u>JAVÁNÍ† FERVENTLY PRAYING FOR HIS SUCCESS AND ENTIRE FAMILY.

SHOGHI

25 January 1951*

APPRECIATE SENTIMENTS BELOVED FRIENDS.

SHOGHI

25 February 1951

Dear Bahá'í Brother,
 Your letters of June 19th, June 22nd, July 18th, July 21st, July 26th, August 17th, August 29th, August 30th, September 6th, September 8th, September 27th (2 letters), October 3rd (2

* Reply to cable sent on the occasion of the appointment of the International Bahá'í Council.

letters), October 5th, October 17th, October 26th, October 30th (2 letters), October 31st, November 13th, November 24th (2 letters), December 10th, December 22nd, 1950, and January 2nd, January 25th and February 2nd, 20th, 1951, together with enclosures as well as photographs, have been received, and our beloved Guardian has instructed me to answer you on his behalf. (A postscript dated March 18th adds: "Your letters (two) dated March 8th have also been received with enclosures.")

He regrets that, due to pressure of work, he is not able to write more frequently, but feels that the cable communications between himself and your assembly attend to the essential work in between letters. . . .

Regarding your question about the communication with the King, as mentioned in Minutes 292 and 344, he feels that both contemplated approaches should be dropped for the present. By undertaking such action we call attention to ourselves in a very conspicuous manner, and investigation of who the senders are of such petitions would only expose the weakness of our numbers and detract from the prestige which the Cause is slowly beginning to acquire in the eyes of the world.

He thanks you very much for the map, showing the British Bahá'í community at the end of the Six Year Plan. He has placed it on a wall of the Mansion of Bahjí, where visitors and believers can enjoy it. It certainly marks the scene of one of the most historic victories of the Faith.

In regard to the question of the African campaign, the Guardian is immensely pleased with the way your assembly and the special committee you have appointed, have seized this project and are vigorously prosecuting it. He admires the evidences of careful planning and staunch determination which all the data regarding this important campaign, which you have forwarded to him, bear witness to.

He was very happy to receive the Chinyanza pamphlets which you sent to him, and also likes very much the "Africa News" which the committee is getting out and which is so alive with plans and news.

He is also delighted to see that the Persian National Assembly is vigorously co-operating with your Assembly and facilitating settlement of some devoted Persian pioneer there who no doubt will be of great help to the work. . . .

THE AFRICA PLAN (1950–1953)

He feels that, although it is preferable that the three pioneers to each virgin country should be in one town or at least as near each other as possible, it should not be considered the essential point at this juncture.

The most important thing of all is to get the pioneers out there and established if possible in some self-supporting work. Once this has been done, the work within the country itself can be gradually organised and plans made to consolidate it in a more practical manner.

He used the word "tribes" loosely to mean the peoples of Africa and not necessarily individuals still living under tribal system.

The Guardian does not feel that it is necessary to specify any particular prayer to be said for the Africa work. The main thing is that the Bahá'ís should pray for its success.

He approves of your getting out the edition of the "New Era" which you now have in the press; but feels very strongly that any future editions should strictly conform to the 1937 American edition, in order to preserve uniformity in this very important Bahá'í publication.

Regarding your question about military service, the Guardian sees no reason why the Bahá'í in question should not bring a test case, and press the matter. It is now, since he has become a follower of Bahá'u'lláh, against his conscience to kill his fellow-men; and he should have the right to explain his position and ask to be exempted from combatant service. During the hearing of such cases the Bahá'ís should make it absolutely clear that we do not fear being placed in danger, and are not asking to be given a safe berth in hours of national crisis—quite the contrary—any dangerous service the Bahá'ís can render their fellow-men during the agonies of war, they should be anxious to accept.

The work that the British Bahá'ís are accomplishing is very dear to his heart; and he wishes your Assembly to constantly encourage the friends (as of course they are doing) to go on with all phases of their Bahá'í work and maintain the tempo they achieved during the past few years. They have distinguished themselves so much that now their fellow Bahá'ís in other lands expect them to lead the way in new fields, and to continue being the pace setters for at least the British Empire, if not other countries as well! Success brings burdens; and the British Bahá'ís who were so miraculously successful at the last moment of their Six Year Plan, now find themselves in the sometimes difficult position of being a cynosure for all eyes.

He assures you, one and all, of his loving prayers for the work you are so faithfully carrying out on behalf of the believers in the British Isles. . . .

P.S.—I wish to call your attention to certain things in "Principles of Bahá'í Administration" which has just reached the Guardian; although the material is good, he feels that the complete lack of quotation marks is very misleading. His own words, the words of his various secretaries, even the Words of Bahá'u'lláh Himself, are all lumped together as one text. This is not only not reverent in the case of Bahá'u'lláh's Words, but misleading. Although the secretaries of the Guardian convey his thoughts and instructions and these messages are authoritative, their words are in no sense the same as his, their style certainly not the same, and their authority less, for they use their own terms and not his exact words in conveying his messages. He feels that in any future edition this fault should be remedied, any quotations from Bahá'u'lláh or the Master plainly attributed to them, and the words of the Guardian clearly differentiated from those of his secretaries.

Dear and valued co-workers,

The magnificent spirit of devotion and the initiative and resourcefulness demonstrated in recent months by a triumphant community, in its eagerness to launch, ahead of the appointed time, the enterprise destined to carry the fame of its members and establish its outposts as far afield as the African Continent, merit the highest praise. By their organising ability, by their zeal in enlisting the collaboration of their sister communities in the African, the American and Asiatic continents for the effective prosecution of this epoch-making enterprise; by the tenacity, sagacity and fidelity which they have displayed in the course of its opening phase; by their utter consecration and their complete reliance on the One Who watches over their destiny, they have set an example worthy of emulation by the members of Bahá'í communities in both the East and the West.

The despatch of the first pioneer to Tanganyika, signalising the inauguration of the African campaign, following so closely upon the successful termination of the Six Year Plan, will be recognised by posterity as the initial move in an undertaking designed to supplement and enrich the record of signal collective services rendered by the members of this community within the confines and throughout the length and breadth of its homeland. On it, however great the support it will receive from its sister communities in the days to come, will devolve the chief responsibility of guiding the destinies, of supplying the motive power, and of contributing to the resources of a crusade which, for the first time in Bahá'í history, involves the collaboration, and affects the fortunes, of no less than four National Assemblies, in both Hemispheres and within four continents of the globe.

On the success of this enterprise, unprecedented in its scope, unique in its character and immense in its spiritual potentialities, must depend the initiation, at a later period in the Formative Age of the Faith, of undertakings embracing within their range all National Assemblies functioning throughout the Bahá'í World, undertakings constituting in themselves a prelude to the launching of world-wide enterprises destined to be embarked upon, in future epochs of that same Age, by the Universal House of Justice, that will symbolise the unity and coordinate and unify the activities of these National Assemblies.

Indeed the birth of this African enterprise, in the opening decade of the second Bahá'í century, coinciding as it does with the formation of the International Bahá'í Council, should be acclaimed as an event of peculiar significance in the evolution of our beloved Faith. Both events will, no doubt, be hailed by posterity as simultaneous and compelling evidences of the irresistible unfoldment of a divinely appointed Administrative Order and of the development, on an international scale, of its subsidiary agencies, heralding the establishment of the Supreme Legislative Body designed to crown the Administrative Edifice now being laboriously erected by the privileged builders of a Divine Order, whose features have been delineated by the Centre of the Covenant in His Will and Testament, whose fundamental laws have been revealed by the Founder of our Faith in His Kitáb-i-Aqdas, and Whose advent has been foreshadowed by the Herald of the Bahá'í Dispensation in the Bayán, His most weighty Book.

To be singled out as the chief agency in the prosecution of a task of such dimensions, such significance, and the harbinger of events so glorious, is indeed at once an inestimable blessing and a staggering responsibility with which the British Bahá'í community, emerging triumphantly and in rapid succession from the ordeal of a world war and the struggles involved in the prosecution of an historic Plan, has been honoured at so critical and challenging an hour in the fortunes of mankind.

To labour assiduously for the despatch, in the coming year marking the official opening of the Two Year Plan, of pioneers to the chosen Territories of the African Continent; to ensure that its three sister National Assemblies will steadily reinforce its work through financial assistance as well as through the increase in the number of pioneers; to expedite the translation, publication and dissemination of Bahá'í literature in the three selected languages throughout these Territories; to enlarge the scope of the contacts established with representatives of the African peoples and with institutions designed to foster their interests; to cultivate cordial relations with, and secure the goodwill and support of, the civil authorities in the goal countries where the pioneers will reside; to maintain steady correspondence with, fan the zeal, seek the counsel and secure the assistance of the budding and scattered communities in the North, the South and the Heart of that vast, that promising and slowly awakening continent; to prepare for the eventual convocation, under its own auspices and following the example set, and the procedure adopted, by its sister American Assembly on the European Continent, of the First African Teaching Conference, representative of both the white and black races, constituting an epoch-making landmark in the evolution of the Faith among the African races and possibly synchronising with the centenary celebrations of the birth of Bahá'u'lláh's Mission, and adding another victor's crown to the laurels already won by the British followers of the Faith of Bahá'u'lláh in their own homeland—these stand out as the paramount and inescapable duties confronting the British National Spiritual Assembly as it stands on the threshold of a new and glorious epoch in British Bahá'í history.

Though the prospect of this new venture is indeed enthralling, though it demands careful planning, the allocation of substantial sums for its prosecution, and the exertion of strenuous efforts for its systematic development, the prizes so laboriously won at home must under no circumstances be jeopardised. The twofold obligation of preserving the status of the newly-fledged Assemblies in England, Wales, Scotland and Ireland and of propagating the Faith among the people dwelling in the British Isles through active teaching and the wide circulation of Bahá'í literature must be faithfully discharged. The necessary foundation for the proclamation of the Faith, at a later stage in the development of the British Bahá'í community, amidst the

British people and in the very heart of the British Empire must be carefully laid. Whatever measures will facilitate the future recognition of the Faith by the civil authorities in the localities where its followers reside, and eventually by the central government in Westminster, must, within the means at their disposal, and however tentatively, be adopted.

Then and only then will this community, carrying out faithfully the twofold duty incumbent upon it, both at home and abroad, be vouchsafed by Bahá'u'lláh the full measure of His grace which will enable it to traverse, speedily and successfully, the present stage in its evolution, and acquire still greater potentialities for the revelation of a still brighter aspect of its mission designed to illuminate with the light of Divine Guidance and in the course of the Formative and Golden Ages of the Faith all the Dependencies of the British Crown, and erect the administrative structure within these Territories, of an Order, incomparably mightier and more enduring than any which that Crown has ever established.

Shoghi

23 April 1951

DEEPEST APPRECIATION GREETINGS LOVING REMEMBRANCE SHRINES DELIGHTED SUCCESS.

SHOGHI

25 April 1951 (Convention)

REJOICE THANKFUL PROUD STERLING QUALITIES FIDELITY TENACITY INTREPIDITY BRITISH FOLLOWERS FAITH BAHÁ'U'LLÁH CONSPICUOUSLY DEMONSTRATED COURSE INTERVAL SUCCESSFUL CONCLUSION SIX YEAR FORMAL INAUGURATION TWO YEAR PLAN. HEARTILY CONGRATULATE DELEGATES ASSEMBLED OCCASION HISTORIC NUMERICALLY ENLARGED EPOCH MAKING CONVENTION. ONE YEAR RESPITE REGARDED BREATHING SPELL DESIGNED ENABLE TOILING TRIUMPHANT VALOROUS HIGH MINDED COMMUNITY RECRUIT FORCES WITNESSED UNEXPECTED DISPLAY VIGOROUS ACTIVITY RESULTING FIRST VICTORIES AFRICAN FIELD PRESERVATION LABORIOUSLY ESTABLISHED ASSEMBLIES LENGTH BREADTH BRITISH

ISLES. TWO YEAR PLAN NOW OFFICIALLY LAUNCHED DEMANDS CONTINUOUS UNSTINTED SYSTEMATIC SUPPORT NATIONAL ELECTED REPRESENTATIVES ALL LOCAL ASSEMBLIES RANK FILE ENTIRE COMMUNITY. AUSPICIOUS RAYS GOD'S DAWNING REVELATION WHICH FIRST STRUCK CORNER VAST DARK SPIRITUALLY DECADENT CONTINENT COURSE BAHÁ'U'LLÁH'S MINISTRY WHICH WARMED ILLUMINATED ITS NORTHERN SOUTHERN FRINGES CONCLUDING YEARS HEROIC AGE FAITH MUST NOW PENETRATE ITS HEART BRIGHTEN ITS JUNGLE FASTNESSES ENVELOP IT WITH SPLENDOUR THEIR RADIANCE COURSE PRESENT SUCCEEDING EPOCHS FORMATIVE AGE BAHÁ'Í DISPENSATION. CONFIDENT BRITISH BAHÁ'Í COMMUNITY WILL ARISE BEFITTINGLY MEET CHALLENGE NOW CONFRONTING IT ACHIEVE THREEFOLD PURPOSE PLAN. PRAYING ENERGETIC COLLABORATION PROSECUTORS 'ABDU'L-BAHÁ'S DIVINE PLAN WITH COMMUNITY BELIEVERS BELONGING NATION WHOSE DESTINY BEEN LINKED FORTUNES WORLD'S BACKWARD RACES REINFORCED ASSISTANCE SISTER COMMUNITY CRADLE FAITH NATIONAL ELECTED REPRESENTATIVES LEADING COMMUNITY AFRICAN CONTINENT MAY ENSURE SUCCESS CRUSADE CONSTITUTING SPIRITUAL LANDMARK PROCESS AWAKENING AFRICAN PEOPLES MARKING OPENING GLORIOUS CHAPTER EVOLUTION WORLD FAITH BAHÁ'U'LLÁH SIGNALISING INITIAL PHASE UNFOLDMENT MISSION COMMUNITY HIS FOLLOWERS BRITISH ISLES MIDST DOMINIONS COLONIES PROTECTORATES BRITISH CROWN. MAY PROJECTED CENTENARY BIRTH PROPHETIC MISSION BAHÁ'U'LLÁH BEFITTINGLY CELEBRATED CONVOCATION FIRST ALL AFRICAN TEACHING CONFERENCE REPRESENTATIVE BLACK WHITE RACES EMBRACING SEVENTEEN AFRICAN TERRITORIES NOW INCLUDED PALE FAITH. ARRANGING TRANSMISSION ONE THOUSAND POUNDS CONTRIBUTION FURTHERANCE GLORIOUS OBJECTIVE.

SHOGHI

2 May 1951

DEEPLY APPRECIATE GREETINGS HIGH RESOLVE ATTENDANTS CONVENTION DELIGHTED SUCCESS SESSIONS PRAYING SIGNAL VICTORIES.

SHOGHI

4 May 1951

OWING RECENT INSTRUCTIONS PERSIAN EGYPTIAN ASSEMBLIES TO DESPATCH PIONEERS FIVE ADDITIONAL AFRICAN TERRITORIES ADVISE UNDERTAKE TRANSLATION SMALL PAMPHLETS INTO ACOLI ADANWE EWE FANTA MENDE YORUBA.

SHOGHI

5 May 1951

ADD SOMALI TO LANGUAGES ALREADY CABLED.

SHOGHI

22 June 1951

NEWLY LAUNCHED HIGHLY MOMENTOUS AFRICAN CAMPAIGN CHIEF AUXILIARY MANIFOLD AGENCIES OPERATING FURTHERANCE 'ABDU'L-BAHÁ'S PLAN AMERICAN EUROPEAN CONTINENTS IRRESISTIBLY UNFOLDING GATHERING MOMENTUM THROUGH ADDED PARTICIPATION INDIAN BAHÁ'Í COMMUNITY ASSIGNMENT SPECIFIC SUPPLEMENTARY FUNCTIONS PERSIAN EGYPTIAN NATIONAL ASSEMBLIES CONTEMPLATED TRANSLATION BAHÁ'Í LITERATURE ADDITIONAL AFRICAN LANGUAGES MULTIPLICATION TERRITORIES NORTHERN EASTERN WESTERN FRINGES VAST AWAKENING CONTINENT. BRIEF SPAN TWO YEARS DESTINED WITNESS FIRST FRUITS HISTORIC CONTINENT-WIDE CRUSADE WILL ERELONG TERMINATE. VALOROUS BRITISH BAHÁ'Í COMMUNITY CENTRAL PIVOT MACHINERY NOW SET MOTION CHIEF AGENCY PROSECUTION MIGHTY DIVINELY PROPELLED ENTERPRISE MUST AWARE URGENCY TASK ACT SPEEDILY RESOLUTELY DESPATCH WITHOUT DELAY VOLUNTEERS, SETTLE PIONEERS DISSEMINATE LITERATURE INITIATE TEACHING ACTIVITIES ESTABLISH FRUITFUL CONTACTS ENSURE STEADY ENROLMENT FRESH RECRUITS AMONGST TRIBES RACES FARFLUNG VIRGIN TERRITORIES. TRANSMITTING ADDITIONAL CONTRIBUTION THOUSAND POUNDS ENSURE VIGOROUS PROSECUTION COLOSSAL SACRED TASK ENABLING WELL TRIED FOLLOWERS FAITH BAHÁ'U'LLÁH BRITISH ISLES WRITE WORTHILY FIRST PAGE HISTORY MEMORABLE UNDERTAKING CONSTITUTING OPENING PHASE THEIR GLORIOUS SPIRITUAL MISSION OVERSEAS.

SHOGHI

22 June 1951*

ASSURE DEPARTED PIONEERS FERVENT LOVING PRAYERS SURROUNDING THEM.

SHOGHI

4 July 1951

WORK NEWLY ASSIGNED EGYPT INDIA PERSIA SUPPLEMENTARY ANY ASSISTANCE EXTENDED THEM YOUR ASSEMBLY DEEPLY APPRECIATED. TWO FUNDS ESTABLISHED WORLD CENTRE SETTLEMENT BANÁNÍ NAKHJAVÁNÍ LEFT DISCRETION YOUR ASSEMBLY.

SHOGHI

15 July 1951

APPROVE IBO OR DAGBANE INSTEAD OF FANTA.

SHOGHI

20 July 1951

ASSURE SABRIS† LOVING FERVENT PRAYERS ACCOMPANYING THEM. GRIEVE PASSING PRESTON ASSURE WIFE LOVING PRAYERS APPROVE REINFORCE KENYA.

SHOGHI

21 August 1951**

OVERJOYED INITIAL VICTORY LOVE.

SHOGHI

---

* Músá and Samiyyih Banani, 'Alí and Violette Nakhjavání, and Philip Hainsworth.
** On receiving news of the first Declaration of the Africa project, in Tanganyika (Tanzania).

26 August 1951

CENTENARY CELEBRATIONS RIḌVÁN. TEACHING CONFERENCE MAY BE HELD ANY TIME BETWEEN JANUARY AND MARCH 1953 SUBSTITUTE ANOTHER LANGUAGE FOR SOMALI.

SHOGHI

2 September 1951

ASSURE ATTENDANTS SCHOOL ABIDING APPRECIATION NOBLE RESOLVE FERVENT PRAYERS.

SHOGHI

19 September 1951*

Dear Bahá'í Brother,

Your letter of August 27th has been received, and the beloved Guardian is sending you herein his receipt for the contribution of the British Bahá'ís to the Shrine. He noted with interest and appreciation that the Bank raised no objections to the transfer of this sum for such a purpose, and feels this indicates the slowly growing recognition of the Faith's nature and importance. Your own ever devoted services to the Cause are greatly appreciated by him, you may be sure. . . .

I gratefully acknowledge the receipt of the sum of three hundred pounds from the Bahá'ís of the British Isles, to be expended for the construction of the Shrine of the Báb on Mt. Carmel.

Shoghi

16 October 1951

Dear Bahá'í Brother,

Your letters dated March 26th (two); April 4th (three), 11th, 17th, 8th, 7th and 24th; May 1st, 4th, 12th and 24th; June 1st,

---

* To the Treasurer for this special fund—Arthur Norton†.

4th, 19th (two), 12th, 23rd and 27th; July 4th, 6th, 21st (two), 25th and 31st; August 8th, 9th and 15th; September 15th, 18th and 19th; have all been received, as well as their enclosures, and the photographs sent and material under separate cover, and the beloved Guardian has instructed me to answer you on his behalf.

It will no doubt make you happy to hear that the Guardian has really had a little rest this summer, much needed after the tremendous strain of last year's worries and burdens. He can now turn to his important N.S.A. letters somewhat refreshed.

To take up certain matters raised in your letters:

There are two Funds, that of the Shrine of the Báb and the International Fund; but at present it is more important for the friends to concentrate on completing the work in progress on the Shrine, which, thanks to the response of the believers from all over the world, is going forward uninterruptedly, in spite of the very difficult situation in the Holy Land which makes all kinds of building work frightfully complicated.

The Guardian would very much like to receive five copies of every publication brought out in England for the Bahá'í libraries in Haifa and at Bahjí and in Acre. He thanks you for the diaries you sent. . . .

For your information the Guardian does not want any believers to migrate at present to this country. It will not meet with his approval under any circumstances. The local problems, with a small group of Covenant-Breakers more or less active in stirring up trouble; the efforts, at present successful, which he is making to establish the most cordial relations with the Government; the upbuilding of the international institutions of the Faith; the consolidation of the International Bahá'í Council—all require that no complications arise and no further strain be added to the burden of work at the World Centre of the Faith.

Now we come to the part of your activities nearest to his heart at present—Africa Campaign. By all means any translation at present into Somali should be given up, as the advice of experts prove it both unnecessary and very expensive.

The Guardian feels that, in view of the fact that funds for sending out pioneers are limited, and that a good number of pioneers are available, it is better to choose those most qualified and not, for the time being at least, accept every offer, however devoted the spirit behind it.

He fully appreciates the fact that Somaliland is going to be somewhat difficult. In view of its peculiar status your Assembly should bear in mind the possibility of sending there a British subject, if this should prove feasible, and pending a time when the Persians can go there and make arrangements for someone to represent them.

The Guardian considers that your Assembly is the consultative body for all African territories, and that the other National Assemblies should keep in close touch with you. This does not mean, however, that the initiative for the places allotted to them by the Guardian does not lie in their own hands. Likewise, the planning of the African Conference should be handled by you, in close co-operation with the other N.S.A.s. He does not feel it is feasible for the other N.S.A.s to pool their finances for the African work and put it in your Fund.

The unfortunate crisis in Persia may hold up, for a time, their services in Africa, and he hopes you will do all you can to offset this most unfortunate setback to their work. The Persian believers, have, for over a hundred years, borne the brunt of persecution and are still doing so, being the unhappy victims of their country and their race. They merit the ardent sympathy of their fellow Bahá'ís the world over.

The Guardian is very anxious to know how the work is going in the British Isles: he feels that the Africa Campaign has been launched in a way far exceeding his hopes, is being visibly blessed from on high, and, with the same amount of perseverance shown so far, is assured of great and speedy victories. But the goals, so hard won and at such cost of sacrifice at home, must not be lost. He urges all the friends to not allow the dazzling prospect overseas to take their attention away from the steady work of consolidation still required at home! The work abroad rests on the foundation laid so well and so painfully at home; if one suffers, so will the other.

The British Bahá'ís have distinguished themselves in recent years to a degree which has given them great prominence in the entire Bahá'í World and inspired others to follow their example. They cannot and must not lose this hard-won prominence, but, on the contrary, must demonstrate that it was not a spurt of speed but the evidence of deep and hardy roots bearing their first fruits, after years of quiet growth.

He remembers all the members of your Assembly in his prayers, and prays that the community of believers you serve so devotedly may go on rising to ever greater heights and shoulder all their tasks with increasing vigour, faith and devotion. . . .

P.S. Regarding the forthcoming Centenary celebrations: the Guardian feels both national and local celebrations should be held very much as were those of the 1944 Centenary, but on a larger scale, with more publicity, if possible.

Dear and valued co-workers,

The auspicious launching of the first teaching Crusade undertaken by the British Bahá'í community beyond the borders of its homeland, marks yet another stage in the evolution of the Bahá'í Administrative Order in the British Isles, and signalises the opening of an epoch of the utmost significance in the Formative Age of the Bahá'í Dispensation. Though the operation of the Plan is of short duration, yet it constitutes a prelude to a series of successive campaigns which a firmly knit, vigorously functioning, clear visioned, intensely alive national community is destined to initiate, direct and control from its newly consolidated administrative headquarters in the heart of the British Isles, not only throughout the Dependencies of the British Crown within the African Continent, but eventually in the widely scattered Territories of an Empire whose ramifications extend into every continent of the globe.

A little over half-a-century ago, this community, now invested with a mandate of the utmost significance both at home and overseas, was called into being in the course of the opening years of the third and last epoch of the Heroic Age of the Faith. A decade later, the Appointed Centre of a Covenant, through the creative and potent energies of which so important a member of a steadily rising world community was conceived and nurtured, chose to infuse into that infant community through the impact of His personality in the course of a twice repeated visit to the heart and centre of that Empire, a measure of His own mysterious power, which, as He Himself prophesied, was destined to unfold its potentialities in the course of a later age. On the morrow of His passing, the earliest evidences of the unfailing promise He had made revealed themselves through the first stirrings of an Administrative Order—the Child of the Covenant, the Shield of that community and the divinely appointed Agency for the execution of the mandate with which that community was to be invested in the second epoch of

THE AFRICA PLAN (1950–1953) 271

the Formative Age of the Bahá'í Dispensation. A little over two decades later, that community, armed and equipped with the mighty, divinely conceived agencies of a laboriously erected, unassailably established Administrative Order, embarked upon a six-year enterprise that culminated in the erection of the institutions of that Order in the very heart and capital cities of its island home—the essential prerequisite for the inauguration of yet another stage in its unfoldment. On the morrow of the triumphant termination of the first collective enterprise launched by that community in British Bahá'í history, its jubilant members braced themselves, during a one-year interval, for the initial onslaught, which they were preparing to launch, unitedly and determinedly, far beyond the shores of their homeland amid alien, widely diversified, politically restless, economically backward, spiritually famished tribes and peoples, and in the course of one of the most critical periods in human history. On the morrow of the centenary of the martyrdom of the Prophet Herald of its Faith, this same community had already formulated its plans, initiated its programme of publications in various African languages, despatched its first pioneer to the heart of that continent, forged the necessary links with its allied sister communities participating in various enterprises in that same continent, and established its first essential contact with divers government agencies capable of giving their advice and assistance in the prosecution of its historic and arduous task.

This community, so young in experience, so richly endowed by the love and care of a departed all-powerful Master, so firmly entrenched in the stronghold of its Administrative Order, already so rich in prizes won in the course of the first collective enterprise undertaken in its history, so promising in the vigour, the zeal and devotion which it is now displaying, is faced, at the present hour, with a grave, a sacred and inescapable responsibility—a responsibility that will increase as the brief eighteen-month interval separating it from the termination of its Two Year Plan speeds to a close.

Upon the discharge of this weighty responsibility now resting upon it must depend the inauguration of yet another Plan, of longer duration, of greater scope, of a still more challenging character, and of greater consequence in the effect it must have on that community's destiny.

Time is running short. The present hour in the fortunes of mankind is critical. The centenary of the birth of the Revelation of Bahá'u'lláh is fast approaching. The British Bahá'í community must gird up its loins, redouble its exertions, undertake further sacrifices, demonstrate greater solidarity and rise to still greater heights of consecrated devotion.

The flow of pioneers to the African Continent must be noticeably accelerated. The provision of Bahá'í literature in all the selected African languages must be speeded up. The ties binding the community with its cooperating sister communities must be steadily reinforced. The prizes already garnered as a result of the operation of the Six-Year Plan in England, Wales, Scotland, Eire and Northern Ireland, must, at all costs, be safeguarded. The preparations for the forthcoming first African Teaching Conference must be carefully planned and meticulously carried out. Above all, the zeal kindled in the breasts of administrators, pioneers, teachers and supporters, jointly contributing to the success of this meritorious enterprise, must burn ever more brightly and be reflected in still more remarkable exploits.

Then, and only then, will this community be enabled to contribute its share of tribute to the memory of the Founder of its Faith, on the occasion of the centenary of the birth of His Prophetic Mission, in as befitting a manner as the share it already contributed, through the consummation of its first historic Plan, to the world-wide celebrations which commemorated the hundredth anniversary of the founding of its Faith. Then, and only then, will it be qualified to embark upon yet another Crusade, whose scope will transcend the limits of the vast African Continent, and the culmination of which might well coincide with the Most Great Jubilee that will commemorate the centenary of the formal assumption by Bahá'u'lláh of His prophetic office, a jubilee envisaged by 'Abdu'l-Bahá in His Tablets, and prophesied more than two thousand years ago, by Daniel in His Book.

So glorious a vision, now unfolded before the eyes of the British followers of the Faith of Bahá'u'lláh, cannot but galvanise them into action, at once swift, resolute and unrelaxing, and fire their souls with a spirit so consuming as to melt every obstacle that may intervene between them and the achievement of their present goal.

May they, one and all, prove themselves, in the crucial months immediately ahead, worthy of the blessings vouchsafed to them in the past, and of the high destiny which it lies in their power to achieve in the future.

Shoghi

28 October 1951*

ASSURE STEPHENS LOVING FERVENT PRAYERS ACCOMPANYING HER.

SHOGHI

11 November 1951

Dear Bahá'í Brother,

As I just recently sent you a long letter on behalf of the beloved Guardian to which he appended at some length, he wishes you to consider this reply to your letters of October 17th (three in number) as a postscript to the other.

As regards the questions you raised:

The ideal thing would be to have at least one Bahá'í from every territory in Africa attend the African Conference. This is the goal to be worked for, and attained if possible, as it will greatly stimulate the work and especially the inexperienced and isolated believers.

The solar calendar should, by all means, be adhered to in Africa.

He feels that your Assembly is responsible for the time being for the work in territories not under the charge of other N.S.A.s (Tunis, Sudan and Ethiopia are under Egyptian care).

You are not directly responsible for any work done in territories which have been allotted to other N.S.A.s. But you should correspond with them, and give them any help and advice you can, both the N.S.A.s and their African Committees. In the case of Eric Manton†, though he will be under Persia's jurisdiction you can keep him informed of your work, so as to cheer him up.

Only the five participating National Assemblies are responsible directly for financing the African work. No invitations should be extended to other bodies or individuals to contribute. Naturally if any one wants to, they no doubt will, but it would be, he feels, very inappropriate to broadcast any appeal. The Africa work is not an international undertaking but an inter-assembly one, confined to five national Bodies.

---

* When Ethel Stephens flew to the Gold Coast.

He is very pleased over the way the work is progressing, and sends you all his loving greetings. . . .

P.S. He thanks you for the Quarterly Report enclosed. He reads with great interest everything related to the African work.

23 November 1951*

CONFERENCE SHOULD BE HELD UGANDA.

SHOGHI

6 December 1951

Africa Committee

Dear Bahá'í Brother:

Your letters of November 5th and 22nd (enclosures were also received) have been received, and the beloved Guardian has instructed me to answer you on his behalf.

He was pleased to hear that Sir Ronald Storrs keeps up a friendly interest in the Faith.

Regarding . . . it is obvious that people like this, who have had in some cases a smattering of Bahá'í teaching are not fully aware of the implications of the Faith. However, this does not mean that we should not help them and hold on to them, in the hope of being able, as time and circumstances permit, to deepen them and produce from them really fine believers. This has happened on many occasions in the past, and the Guardian hopes that, through correspondence with him, your committee—and perhaps the Groups in Africa—will be able to accomplish this.

In response to his requests for money, you should point out to him that as we finance entirely our own activities as our gift to mankind, we have to harbour our resources and concentrate on the most important expenditures. You will know what these are; and they certainly don't include a headquarters in Nigeria. You might also encourage him to make an effort to attend the Africa Conference.

* Regarding the first Intercontinental Conference.

The Guardian also hopes that you will give ... every encouragement. She is a fine soul, and no doubt, if she had time devoted to her, would soon develop into an assured and active believer. You should encourage her also to make every effort to be present at the Africa Conference, and in the meantime to correspond with believers abroad, and do her best to teach the Cause there in spite of her handicaps.

The Guardian feels that the next step in Bahá'í literature might well be the publication of a more comprehensive work in Luganda and Swahili. However, he would like the Africa Committee to undertake pamphlets in other languages as well; let him know what languages the committee proposes.

He attaches, as you know, the greatest importance to the work of your committee and is tremendously impressed by the progress being made in Africa, and by the capacity, tenacity and enthusiasm the British Africa Committee is showing in handling its share of this extremely important campaign. His prayers are frequently offered on your behalf.

May the Almighty whose Cause you serve with such devotion, ability and faithfulness, reward you abundantly for your labours, guide you and sustain you and assist you to enrich continually the record of your meritorious service.

Your true brother,
Shoghi

19 December 1951*

DELIGHTED ASSURE THEM FERVENT PRAYERS HEARTY WELCOME BAHÁ'Í FOLD.

SHOGHI

30 December 1951

APPROVE PLAN CELEBRATION CENTENARY.

SHOGHI

---

* On 18 December 1951 the National Assembly reported to the beloved Guardian the acceptance of two African believers in Kampala.

8 January 1952 *(Teaching Conference)*

ASSURE ATTENDANTS TEACHING CONFERENCE DEEPEST LOVING APPRECIATION ASSURANCE LOYALTY. APPEAL FERVENTLY ARISE DETERMINEDLY STIMULATE PIONEER ACTIVITY SAFEGUARD HARD-WON PRIZES CONSOLIDATE HOME FRONT REINFORCE AGENCIES ADMINISTRATIVE BASE ON WHICH SUCCESS AFRICAN CAMPAIGN INAUGURATION FUTURE PLANS EMBRACING BRITISH TERRITORIES OTHER CONTINENTS ULTIMATELY DEPEND SUPPLICATING ABUNDANT BLESSING.

SHOGHI

16 January 1952*

DELIGHTED APPROVE TALKS HANDS LOVING APPRECIATION.

SHOGHI

13 February 1952

Dear Bahá'í Brother,

Our beloved Guardian has instructed me to write you the following:

He wishes the British National Assembly to please do all they can to watch over the two young sons of our dear friends, Mr. and Mrs. . . ., in view of the fact that the youngest boy is little more than a child, he needs particularly to have his spiritual welfare safeguarded through as much contact as possible with believers.

The wonderful services this devoted and self-sacrificing father and mother are rendering the Faith have forced them to be separated from their children, and hence the Guardian requests your Assembly to please take special care of the boys.

We are all very happy to have . . . here, and they have brought most heartening reports of the progress of the work in Africa with them. . . .

---

* Reply to National Assembly's enquiry whether Hands of the Cause could be invited to give talks at the Africa Conference.

20 February 1952*

GRIEVE TRAGIC LOSS PRAYING FERVENTLY BEHALF DEPARTED.

SHOGHI

29 February 1952

... ADVISE BUILD UP KENYA. URGE FORMATION ASSEMBLIES KAMPALA DAR-ES-SALAAM. APPROVE SPECIAL SESSIONS FOR NATIONAL ASSEMBLY REPRESENTATIVES OUTSIDE CONFERENCE.

SHOGHI

4 March 1952

Africa Committee of the National Spiritual Assembly.

Dear Bahá'í Friends:
Your letter of the 18th of February, with enclosures, has reached the beloved Guardian; and he has instructed me to answer you on his behalf.

He is very pleased over the progress being made, particularly in Uganda; and the recent pilgrimage of the dear Bánánis, he feels sure, will add a great impetus to the work there.

Regarding the matters of policy you raised in your letter, he sees no objection to the Persian Bahá'ís,—as long as there are so many of them, and it is unwise to concentrate too many applicants on one country at one time as you point out,—going to countries under the jurisdiction of other National Spiritual Assemblies, such as Egypt and India.

He considers that it is of the greatest importance that pioneers should have upright characters, as well as some considerable knowledge of the Teachings. We cannot expect that every pioneer will be a person of importance; but we must hope that each one will be a person of worth, in his own character. This should be pointed out to the Indian friends.

---

* Death of Marguerite Preston and eldest child killed in air crash returning to Kenya.

India should likewise make an effort to send pioneers primarily to the territories embraced in its own part of the Plan; but if they can make available to your committee for British territory, some qualified Indian Bahá'ís, who for some reason cannot go to one of the Indian National Assembly's assignments, then there is no objection.

The Guardian thinks that it is wise not to influence ... by sending him material which he does not at present wish to receive. He is, judging from his letter, a sincere but immature believer....

P.S. Your National Assembly is not responsible for Eritrea but you may encourage any believers there.

May the Almighty bless your high endeavours, guide and sustain you continually, and aid you to win great victories in the service of His Faith.

Your true brother,
Shoghi

8 March 1952*

APPROVE SHOMAÍS DEPARTURE AFRICA. 'ABBÁS RETURN PERSIA APPRECIATE DEEPLY SELF-SACRIFICE.

SHOGHI

12 March 1952

OWING RAPID PROGRESS AFRICAN CAMPAIGN ADVISE CONCENTRATION CONSOLIDATION HOME FRONT APPEAL UNITED RENEWED VIGOROUS EFFORT PRAYING FERVENTLY SUCCESS.

SHOGHI

18 March 1952

GOAL FULFILLED ANY PART SOMALILAND.

SHOGHI

---

* Regarding Dr. and Mrs. 'Abbás Afnán†.

16 April 1952*

OVERJOYED PRAYING SUCCESS BLACKPOOL LOVE.

SHOGHI

22 April 1952**

DELIGHTED APPRECIATE SERVICES PIONEERS.

SHOGHI

29 April 1952

DEEPLY TOUCHED PLEDGE BRITISH BAHÁ'Í COMMUNITY CONGRATULATE VALIANT MEMBERS MARVELLOUS PROGRESS AFRICAN CAMPAIGN CONSOLIDATION HOME FRONT OWING ATTAINMENT OBJECTIVES ADVISE CONCENTRATE NAIROBI AIMING ESTABLISHMENT ASSEMBLY LEADING PROMISING CENTRE BRITISH TERRITORIES HEART EAST AFRICAN CONTINENT FERVENTLY PRAYING STILL GREATER VICTORIES LOVING GRATITUDE.

SHOGHI

4 May 1952

National Bahá'í Youth Committee

Dear Bahá'í Friends,

Your letter of April 9, 1952, has been received, and the beloved Guardian has instructed me to answer you on his behalf.

He was most happy to see that so many of the Bahá'í youth and their friends had gathered together for the Youth Conference; and trusts that, from this consultation, a greater activity amongst the Bahá'í youth of the British Isles will result.

All over the Bahá'í world, we see that not an inconsiderable proportion of the most active and devoted pioneers are young

---

* The National Assembly cabled the Guardian on 14 April 1952: "KAMPALA DAR-ES-SALAAM NOW NINE ASSEMBLIES ASSURED. BELIEVE MAINTENANCE ASSURED ALL ASSEMBLIES EXCEPT BLACKPOOL WHERE TWO GAPS REMAIN. BEG SPECIAL PRAYERS".

** On news of maintenance of all Assemblies.

people. This is only right and proper, because they are freer, usually, to migrate to distant lands, embark on new projects, and withstand the trials and hardships, than older people, who have built up family ties and professional ties.

He will pray for all of you, for your success and the deepening of your capacities in the service of Bahá'u'lláh.

May the Almighty bless and sustain you in your meritorious activities and aid you to achieve great victories in the service of His Faith,

Your true brother,
Shoghi

3 June 1952

I gratefully acknowledge receipt of the sum of £200 Sterling from my dear Bahá'í co-workers, British Bahá'í community to be expended for the promotion of the international interests of the Bahá'í Faith.
Shoghi

3 June 1952

I gratefully acknowledge receipt of the sum of £300 Sterling from my dear Bahá'í co-workers, British Bahá'í community to be expended for the construction of the Shrine of the Báb.
Shoghi

4 June 1952

Africa Committee

Dear Bahá'í Sister:
Your letter of May 16th has been received, and the beloved Guardian has instructed me to answer you on his behalf.

He has read with great interest the reports which your committee sends him regularly, because as you know the work in Africa is to him one of the most important activities going on in the Bahá'í world, and very close to his heart.

He was very sorry to hear from the recent cable sent him that there is a question about the Kampala Conference, and whether arrangements can be made for it to be held there. Undoubtedly there is an increasingly negative attitude toward our work growing up amongst the officials, probably due to the lack of racial discrimination they are coming to realise is one of our fundamental teachings, a teaching carried into action, and not merely a pious hope.... He wishes you to keep him informed about this and the progress being made.

Your suggested souvenir booklet sounds interesting, and he urges you to consider the wisdom of including a photograph of Mr. Gregory, First Negro Hand of the Cause, in addition to the others.

As regards the latest progress photo of the Shrine Mr. Ted Cardell† took a great many pictures here, which the Guardian told him he could share with the Bahá'ís anywhere in the world; and it seems as if, exclusive of the work on the drum, which will begin showing distinctly in about two months' time, the best possible photograph you can obtain of the Shrine at present would be one of Ted's. You should therefore apply to him for one.

The Guardian is very anxious that, during the coming months, the Africa Committee and the Bahá'ís should concentrate their efforts on establishing an Assembly in Kenya, and hopes that you will be able to direct pioneers to Nairobi as soon as possible.

The Guardian considers that it is premature at this time to answer your question about consultation at the Africa Conference, between people from territories which will come under the jurisdiction of the East and Central Africa National Spiritual Assembly. He is so overworked and tired at the moment that he has not been able to go into the entire question of the Inter-Continental Conferences, the countries which will come under the jurisdiction of various future national bodies, etc. He hopes that he will be able, during the coming months, to do this, and if he feels it wise, will advise you by cable concerning a consultation such as you suggest, at the Conference.

He assures all the members of your committee of his deep appreciation of the work they are doing, and of his loving prayers for their success....

P.S. Your personal letter of May 17th was received, and he

assures you not only of how deeply he admires the spirit you and your husband have, and the work you accomplish, but of his loving prayers that you may be given strength to carry out this work.

Mr. . . . evidently is very immature and has no real concept of the Faith; this does not mean, however, that we should abandon him as a contact or let him become the prey of the New History Society. We should keep in friendly touch until someone can see him.

May the Almighty Whose Cause you and your co-workers are serving with such an exemplary spirit of devotion, fidelity and perseverance, reward you for your meritorious labours, remove all obstacles from your path and enable you to win great victories in the days to come,

Your true and grateful brother,
Shoghi

12 June 1952

Dear Bahá'í Brother:

The beloved Guardian has received your letters of October 3, October 27 (4), November 5, 9, 22 (2), 24 and 29, December 6, 19 (4) and 21, 1951, and January 1, 2, 7, 11, 16, 17, 20 and 29 (3), February 1, 16, 20 (3), 27 (2) and February 29, March 5 and 14, April 3, 15 and 24, May 5, 13, 19 (2), 27 and 31, and June 6th, 10th and June 12, 1952, and he has instructed me to answer you on his behalf. He also has received the various enclosures which you sent with these letters. . . .

The book you sent from the friends in Bahrein was received, and pleased the beloved Guardian very much, as the lines are written in the handwriting of Bahá'u'lláh at the beginning of the book. (This answers your question in your letter of June 6th.)

It brought great joy to his heart to see that you were able to maintain all assemblies in spite of the heavy odds against you. It demonstrates to him once more the tenacity and devotion of the British Bahá'ís, which is rapidly becoming one of the great assets of the Faith in its process of international expansion. . . .

The wonderful spirit shown by Dr. Afnán and his wife is

certainly an example to all pioneers. He hopes that Mrs. Afnán will settle herself successfully in Africa, and soon be able to have her husband join her.

He was very happy to hear that the Teaching Conference has been so successful. Undoubtedly the dedication of the friends to their tasks at that time facilitated the achievement of their goals in April. . . .

The Guardian would like to assure your Assembly of his loving prayers for dear Mr. Sam Scott, who pioneered at such a ripe age, and who is surely receiving his reward in the Abhá Kingdom.*

He considers it advisable that all believers living in Africa, even those who did so before the beginning of the Plan, should have some form of credentials. . . .

Your suggestion of inaugurating the Holy Year next Riḍván and continuing on until October, 1953, with celebrations, meets with his approval.

As regards the Africa campaign: this enterprise, so enthusiastically carried on, has been throughout this past year the greatest source of joy to the heart of the beloved Guardian. The visits of the dear Banánís and Ted Cardell, the news they brought and the general progress of the work, have made Africa seem right next door to Haifa! The formation of the Dar-es-Salaam and Kampala Assemblies was also a great satisfaction to him.

He urges you to now concentrate on an Assembly for Nairobi by next April. This should not be too difficult of achievement in view of the devoted efforts of Mr. Cardell and the pioneers eager to go there.

As regards your question about Somaliland: any one of the three Somalilands may be chosen as a goal territory.

In this connection, he feels that Persian pioneers should be accepted for any and all territories; they are arising in large numbers to offer their services, and it is a great pity that these dedicated and eager friends are so restricted as regards settlement. Your Assembly should do all in its power to facilitate placing them.

The Guardian feels that although the Conference planned for Kampala is primarily a Conference and in no sense a Convention

---

* From Leeds to Norwich at age 84 and died at age 86.

(having no delegates), there is no objection to the representatives of various N.S.A.s who may attend meeting in separate sessions for more special and concentrated consultation. Any Hands of the Cause attending could also be included in this private discussion.

He feels that now more than ever the British friends have every reason to feel proud of their accomplishments and happy over the very evident bestowals from the Throne on High. They have found, after half a century of development, scope for their abilities, and a field large enough to distinguish themselves in, and they are certainly taking advantage of it, much to the delight of the Guardian and their fellow-Bahá'ís.

You may be sure that he remembers you all in his prayers, and also the body of the faithful believers you serve to such good purpose.

He would like you to please thank, on his behalf, the friends who so devotedly contribute to the construction of the Holy Shrine....

P.S. As regards Bahá'í divorce as mentioned in your letters of June 12th: Bahá'ís (whether one party or both are believers) should follow the Bahá'í law of divorce, *i.e.* one year of waiting, and not neglect this divinely given law. Whether they were Bahá'ís when they married or not has nothing to do with it.

In connection with the budget, mentioned in your letter of June 10th, he feels, in the future, you should not set a budget which the resources of the community are unable to meet; however, owing to the crucial Africa work and the forthcoming Conference, he realises you had at this time no other choice. He is going to arrange for one thousand pounds to be sent to your Assembly in order to meet the needs of the Conference and the literature in African languages still to be published. The remaining translations should be pressed forward in order to be ready for the Conference next year.

Dear and valued co-workers,

The Two Year Plan on which the British Bahá'í community has embarked bids fair, as it approaches its conclusion, to eclipse, however short its duration, the exploits of that community throughout the length and breadth of the British Isles, in the course of the prosecution of the first collective enterprise undertaken in British Bahá'í history.

THE AFRICA PLAN (1950–1953)

This second historic undertaking marks the inauguration of the Mission entrusted to this community for the purpose of diffusing the Message of Bahá'u'lláh and of implanting its banner through successive stages, and in collaboration with its sister communities, not only in the territories of the British Crown in the African Continent, but throughout the dependencies of a widely scattered Empire in the remaining continents of the globe. It may well be regarded as a befitting prelude to the official participation of this community in the Ten Year, world-encircling Crusade, designed to signalise the celebration of the hundredth anniversary of the birth of Bahá'u'lláh's Mission, involving the systematic co-operation of no less than twelve National Assemblies throughout the Bahá'í world, and destined to culminate in the Most Great Jubilee that will, God willing, witness the introduction of the Faith into all the Sovereign States, the Chief Dependencies and Islands of the entire planet.

In the conduct of this world-encompassing task, so vast in scope, so thrilling in its possibilities, so formidable in its potentialities, the British Bahá'í community will be called upon to play a preponderating rôle, in conjunction with the American Bahá'í community, acting as the Chief Custodians of 'Abdu'l-Bahá's Master Plan, and seconded by its sister communities in the British Dominions in both hemispheres, in awakening the peoples, races and nations comprising the British Commonwealth and Empire to the redemptive Message of Bahá'u'lláh, and in establishing, on an unassailable foundation, the structural basis of His World Order.

The diversity of functions which the assumption of this task will involve; the privileges and bounties it will, of a certainty, confer on its prosecutors; the degree of dedication, the amount of preparation it will require for its proper discharge; the severe strain it must necessarily impose on all those who will shoulder its burdens; the gravity of the manifold problems it will raise; the severe challenge with which they who will arise to carry it out will be confronted—as witnessed by the delicate and complicated situation that has already arisen in the initial stage of this historic Mission in the heart of Africa, in connection with the holding of the projected inter-continental conference—all these must be carefully pondered in preparation for the launching, at its appointed time, of an undertaking that will constitute, not only a milestone of the utmost significance in the history of the Faith in the British Isles, but will also be hailed by posterity as a landmark of peculiar significance in British history.

Whilst the small band of wholly dedicated, patiently labouring, much admired, greatly promising followers and supporters of the Faith, in England, Wales, Ireland and Scotland, contemplate, from their respective homelands, the grandeur of their future task, dwell on its sacred character, and meditate on the wide range of its problems, possibilities, perils and glories, let them devote particular and sustained attention to the imperative needs, the urgent requirements of their no less important and vital mission at home, in their boroughs and counties, amidst their own people, and strain every nerve to reinforce, through a rapid increase in their numbers, through a steady multiplication of their administrative institutions, through a systematic consolidation of the structure of the edifice they are raising within the borders of their native land, their respective communities, which must be regarded as the base for the future operations that will be conducted by the members of these communities, under the guidance of their elected representatives, for the spiritual conquest and the ultimate redemption of the nations, tribes and races owing allegiance to the British Crown.

With every forward step taken by this stalwart community in the path of service to the Cause of Bahá'u'lláh, with every signal victory achieved for the promulgation of His Faith, a new revelation of the glorious Mission which this community is privileged to undertake is unfolded before the eyes of its members and a wider vista of the future range of its operations, both at home and overseas, opens before it. With every complication that arises in the course of its unfolding Mission, with even every seeming reverse it meets with, as its destiny unfolds, a clearer understanding of the character of its stewardship to the Faith of Bahá'u'lláh is vouchsafed to its members, a greater measure of His sustaining grace is poured forth from on high, a more compelling evidence of His all-conquering power is evinced, and a more majestic assertion of His mysterious purpose is demonstrated.

The potent seeds a loving and vigilant Master sowed with His Own hands, in the course of a twice repeated visit to the homeland of this community, are now, after having lain dormant for almost a quarter of a century, at long last, sprouting throughout the length and breadth of the British Isles, and are even revealing the potency of their regenerative power, through the instrumentality of those valiant pioneers, who, faithful to His Call and dedicated to His service, are leaving the shores of those islands to settle in the territories of a far-away and backward continent. Amidst their arduous labours, in their

Spiritual Assemblies, General (*cont.*)
members of, no substitutes for, 53; number of, 5, 6, 49, 70–1, 138; only nine to vote, 49, 59; qualifications of, 207; prime requisites of, 6, 7
nature of its minutes, 448
need to consult with, 4–6, 145
non-interference in election of, 72
not to allow creeds, 423
obedience to, 6
recognition of a vacancy, 224
to have, endowments, 221; Youth Groups, 204
to seek expert advice, 59
Spiritual Assemblies, Local,
boundaries, to be determined later, 185, 348; to observe civil limits (*see* Civil Limits)
Chairman of for Feast consultation, 450
co-operate with National Committees, 218–19
County assemblies prelude to proclamation, 209
in every locality where adults exceed nine, 5, 6
not to criticise, oppose N.S.A. policy, 125
status determined by National Assembly, 352
to be incorporated, 221, 339
to be maintained at all costs, 206, 209, 217, 222, 287
to ensure Feasts conform to Bahá'í spirit, 380
to have endowments, 221, 339
vigorously functioning, to be established at any cost, 182
Spiritual Assemblies, National, approves all Bahá'í publications, 382
basis for Universal House of Justice, 421
Convention to elect, 63
could be elected by mail votes, 247
decides on secondary matters not in *Bahá'í Administration*, 148; not in Constitution, 102, 184, 440
decides which matters local/national interest, 8
delegates, elect by secret ballot, 62; number of, 188, 194, 197
deals with inactive believers, 159, 184–5, 199
elected from whole body of believers, 62
formation dependent upon numbers believers, assemblies, groups, 345
indirect election of, 5

Spiritual Assemblies, National (*cont.*)
not to add to rules, regulations, 249, 440
not to create red tape, 440
their relationship with Hands of the Cause, 341–2
to curtail non-essential expenditure, 254
to give assistance to isolated, repressed assemblies, 231
to settle problems as they arise, 440
unified, co-ordinated by Universal House of Justice, 261
will elect directly Universal House of Justice, 455
Spiritual, awakening, 182, 430
edifice, 144, 286
contribution, 145
Council, 9
healing, 309, 434
potency provided, 431
potentialities, 245, 461
receptivity, 365
World Congress, Brussels, 182
Spiritually alive, potent, 227, 311
Spiritualists, 175
Splendid, beginning, 125
record services, 362
testimony, 66
Spokesmen, 340
Spontaneous and undiminished support, 10
Spontaneous, decision, 169, 171, 173, 220, 232, 234, 353, 386
response, 195
Spread of the Faith, 165–6, 173, 231, 410
St. Ives, 237
Stable world, 191
Stahler, Fred, 202, 479
Stamina from trials, testings, 453
Stammering, 446, 458
Standard bearers, 51
Standards for youth, 192–3
Stand on own feet, 121
Stannard, Mrs, 59, 429
Star of the West, 9, 12, 56
Star, The (U.S.A.), 42
Startling events, 75
Statements, disapproved, 324, 333
on Bahá'í administration vital in books, 435
Statistics, 165–6, 210, 216, 240, 289, 299, 359
Stature, true, 170, 196
Status as believer, *see* Refugees,
Staunch and unflinching adherence, 73
Staunchness, 88, 140, 144, 343, 362, 398
Steadfast, 115, 125, 133, 173, 410

INDEX 517

Significant, Phase, 211, 353
  undertaking, 178, 250
Signs of consummation, 385
  of success, 181
Simpson, George P., 9, 16, 18, 20, 23–5, 31, 44–5, 47, 53–5, 58, 61–2, 64, 70–4, 86–7, 96, 468
  his service to the Guardian, 32–3, 40, 44–5, 54–5, 59, 73–4
Sincerity, 10
Singled out, 261
Sister Communities, N.S.A.s, 198, 200, 210–11, 215, 226, 245, 254, 256–7, 260–2, 264, 269, 271–2, 285, 297, 337, 340, 353, 369, 385–6
Sites for Temples, 298, 325, 329, 353–4
Sitírih Khánum, *see* Lady Blomfield
Six Year Plan, India, 178, 185
Six Year Teaching Plan, 172, 174–5, 177–83, 185–6, 188–91, 193, 195–8, 200–1, 206, 208–12, 215, 219–20, 222, 225–38, 240, 245–6, 249–50, 258, 260–3, 271–2, 297, 372, 386, 391, 393, 408, 410, 443, 448, 455–6
  birth of, xvi, 169–71, 173, 220
  chief objectives of, 171, 182, 186
  critical stage of, 186, 188, 222, 225, 231–3, 237, 239–40
  direct and grave challenge, 178
  dynamic process, 187
  exertions youth vital, 188, 192–3
  greatest collective enterprise, 178, 180, 208, 226
  immediate destinies dependent upon, 171, 178, 188, 208, 229
  local assembly elections before April 1950, 228
  most acute phase, 230
  most important assemblies in, 219
  most significant undertaking any National Assembly, 178, 182
  must not, cannot, fail, 179, 232
  needs and requirements of, 171, 240
  offer to extend date of, to 9 July, 240
  pivotal year of, 187
  spontaneously conceived, 169, 171, 163, 220, 232, 234
  stepping stone for proclamation, 186–7
  subsequent plans, 201, 208, 221, 231, 233–4, 271
  unrivalled annals any European community, 245
  victory announced, 240, 245
Slade, Mrs Isobel, 61, 63, 94–6, 100–5, 470
Sleeping, 446

Slides, 141, 375–6
Slow progress, 178
Smallness of numbers, 134, 145, 198, 211, 214, 226, 251, 258, 287, 312, 353, 371, 386
Smyrna, 79
Social, forces, 75
  life, 457
Society, association, 91, 113
  rocking, 137
Sociologists, 435
Sohrab, 254
Solar calendar, for Africa, 273
Sole refuge, 151
Solicitude, 28, 133
Solidarity, 214, 226, 272, 364
Solid foundation, 399
Solomon, David, 387
Solomon Islands, 360
Somaliland, 269, 278, 283, 305, 325, 347
Some Answered Questions, 383
Sorrows, 422
Soul, influenced by prayers, 250, 256, 350, 363, 375
Sound, 211
Sound judgement, 369
South, 198, 338
South, Africa, 216, 262
  America, 253
  Rhodesia, 291
  West Africa, 297, 305
  West England, 116
Sovereign States, 285
Spanish, 331
Spark of truth, 6
Speaker, Reader, presentation, 21
Special meetings for Centenary, (1944), 159
Spectator, The, 366
Speech impediment, 446
Spirit, 129, 143–5, 153, 157, 183, 214, 222, 226, 229, 239, 272, 282, 301, 329–30, 366, 374, 379, 383, 393, 395–6, 399, 403, 407, 409, 413, 417, 422, 431, 438, 440, 447, 449–50
  of sacrifice, 422, 448
  of teachings, 129
Spiritual Assemblies, General, 5–8, 53, 145, 156–60, 181–2, 185–9, 194–5, 209, 263, 339, 343–7, 351, 353–4, 366, 371, 374, 382, 385
  all Bahá'ís to turn to, 145, 264
  dissatisfaction with officers of, 141
  duties of, 5–7; secretary of, 448
  evolve to Houses of Justice, 5–6
  majority voice, 7

Schools, Bahá'í, 78, 309; Summer, 97, 109–11, 118, 121, 127, 132, 147–8, 152, 154, 156, 162, 172, 179, 181, 188–9, 194, 203, 210, 217, 230, 235–6, 254, 267, 289, 340, 342, 357, 375, 382, 387, 447
  an institution, 98, 110, 147, 447
  a wonderful experience, 447
  believers from Continent to attend British, 200
  committee for, *see* Committees
  courses of study, 235
  during war time, 156
  important Bahá'í activity, 181, 200, 217, 235, 447
  inseparable part any teaching campaign, 110, 217
  seat of Bahá'í learning, 235
  Shetlands, 380
  to attract non-believers, 110
Schools, week-end, 239, 372, 396
Schopflocher, Fred, 333
Science, 445
Scope, 186, 313
Scotland, 169, 189, 192, 195–6, 201–2, 206, 209, 211, 215, 220, 237, 245, 251, 262, 272, 286–7, 297–8, 311–2, 339, 353, 377, 385, 399–401
  rôle of Edinburgh, 400
Scots, characteristics of, 399, 401
Scott, Samuel, 240, 283, 485
Scripture, Bahá'í, 208, 423
Secondary matters, 102
Second Bahá'í Century, 163, 166, 171, 179, 182, 208, 211, 214, 227, 234, 240, 245, 261
Second collective enterprise, 291
Second World War, xv, 133, 176–7, 420
  anticipated, 33
Secretary General, 288, 305
Secret Ballot, 62, 307
Seeds, 10, 58, 148, 211, 220, 286, 298
Seek best medical advice, 462
Seeming reverses, 286
Self-defence, 427
Selflessness, 421
Self-sacrifice, 88, 154, 172, 180, 182, 187, 209, 215, 217, 219, 223, 226, 241, 273, 313, 383
Self-supporting, 385
Semple, Ian, 411, 489
Sense of responsibility, 164, 353
Separation of Church/State, 76
Service, 15, 179, 180, 182, 188, 191, 198, 210, 256, 276, 279–80, 283, 286, 303, 321, 328, 375, 386–7, 391, 393–8,

Service (*cont.*)
  404–5, 407–11, 413, 415–16, 425, 446, 452, 461
  to one's country, 122–3, 129
Setbacks, 174, 182, 208, 339, 362, 453
Set example, 442
Set out to win goals, 177
Settlement (forerunner of pioneering), 156–7, 174, 283
Seven valleys, 453
Seven Year Plan (U.S.A.), 178, 185, 187, 225
Severest tests from each other, 454
Sex problems, 434–5
  laxity vehemently condemned, 435
Seychelles, 374
Sháh, 76, 423
  visit to West, 77
Sharples, Miss, 20–1, 24–5
Sháykh Faraj, Cairo, 8
Sháykh Ṭabarsí, 427
Sheffield, 127
Shetland Islands, 297, 305, 322, 380
Shí'ah Islám, 426
Shí'ites, 45
Shíráz, 348, 386
Shoghi Effendi, Guardian of the Bahá'í Faith, *see* Guardian, "Sign of God on Earth", ix, xi, xiii, xv, xvi, 15, 18–19, 22–5, 29, 31–2, 39–42, 44–8, 53–5, 58–9, 61–3, 71–3, 86–91, 93–5, 98–9, 103–4, 106, 112, 120, 127, 143–7, 149, 155, 195, 219, 367, 421–9, 438, 461
  to develop his full powers as Guardian, 461
Shortcomings, not to be source disunity, 442
Short obligatory prayer, 369
Shrewd, 207
Shrines, Holy, 134, 141, 249, 268
  of Báb, 166, 215, 225, 247, 250, 254–5, 267, 280, 281, 284, 292, 321, 374, 400, 455, 457; triple crowns of, 321
  of Bahá'u'lláh, 56, 306, 375; rug from, 324
  prayers in, *see* Prayers
  purchase of land, 39
  slides of interiors not to be shown, 375–6
Shun, 458
Sierra Leone, 297
Signal success, victories, 153, 169, 179, 187, 198, 209, 240–1, 251, 286, 400,
Significance, 182, 208, 215, 219, 261, 270, 285, 313, 338, 354–5, 369, 385, 394

INDEX 515

Religious community, 106
Religious conservatism, 433–4; more dangerous than apathy, 434
  leaders, 382
  rights of others, 200
  tribunal, 65
Remey, Charles Mason, 367
Removal of, obstacles, 110, 115
  voting rights, 159, 199
Reports required, 169, 171, 210, 305, 307, 324, 331, 344, 360
  quarterly, 274
Representative character, 394
Representatives, 340
Requirements of Six Year Plan, 188–9, 201, 208
  arise to serve, give generously, 179
  building primary institutions, 196
  dissemination literature, 171
  multiplication centres, 171–2
  proclamation, 196
Requisites, prime, 385
Resignation, 118, 141, 202
Resistless unfoldment, 257
Resolute, 211, 222–3, 227, 252, 272, 369, 384
Resolutely, relentlessly endeavour, 127
  safeguard prizes won, 198
Resolution, 133–4, 139, 201, 208, 234, 369
Resolve, 135, 158, 240, 264, 357, 363
Resourcefulness, 122, 134, 200, 260, 338, 369
Resources, 181, 183, 211, 215, 225–7, 251, 287, 309, 338–9, 369–70, 386
  limited in England, 110, 113, 288, 312
  sufficient in England, 121, 185
Responsibilities, 3, 5, 10, 70, 106, 115, 118, 133, 135–7, 140, 151, 154, 164, 177, 180, 185–7, 191, 193, 203, 208, 215, 227, 229, 252, 261, 271, 288, 309, 310, 331, 336, 341, 353–5, 371, 384–5, 433, 452
  of youth, 193
  overseas, 369–70
Rest assured, 111, 115, 204, 395, 397, 400
Resurgence, 226
Revelation pulsates, 454
Reverses, 208, 287
Reviewing, 38
  'Abdu'l-Bahá's example, 8
Revitalised, triumphant, dearly beloved, community, 198
Revolutionary reforms, 75–6
Reuters, 362
Rewards, 195, 233, 343, 392, 411–2, 459
Rhodesia, 382

Riḍván, 49, 239–1, 267, 283, 291, 367, 382, 417
  convention during, 63–4, 236
  date of, 64
  festivals suspended, 119
Right of Humanity, 148
Ring, 41, 143
Rise to the occasion, 384
Rising generation, 137, 210
Robarts, John, Hand of the Cause, 240
Rock-bottom requirements, 371, 385
"Roll of Honour", 303, 306
Rome, 335
Root, Miss Martha, 55–6, 58–9, 61
Rosenberg, Miss E. J., 11, 61, 63–4, 70, 86, 90, 130, 468
Rosen, Baron, 424
Roumania, 56
  Queen Marie of, see Queen Marie
Royalty, 56
Ruanda Urundi (Rwanda), 299, 305
Rug from Shrine of Bahá'u'lláh, 324
Ruḥíyyih Khánum, see Amatu'l-Bahá
Rules, regulations, not to add to, 249, 324, 368
Russia, 77, 424
Russian books, New Era, 182, 190

Ṣabrí, Ḥassan, 266, 487
Ṣabrí, Isobel, 266, 487
Sacred task, 151, 252, 271, 286, 340
  threshold, 404
Sacrifice, s, 113, 123, 170, 179–80, 183, 189, 195, 208, 211–12, 215, 224–7, 233–5, 240, 246, 269, 272, 312, 321, 333, 336, 338, 340, 353–4, 364, 369, 374, 377, 385, 393, 396, 398, 425, 428, 436–7, 441, 448, 457
  comfort, 177
Saint Petersburgh, 424
Saints, 453
Safeguard prizes won, 198, 215, 269, 272, 276, 354, 374, 376
Safety, 135, 437
Sagacity, 260
Salisbury, Rhodesia, 382
Samandari, Mrs. Ursula (Newman), 172, 191, 475
Same race, language, background, 370
Samuel, Sir H., 104, 162
Saying Grace, 446
Scale nobler heights, 166
Scholarship lacking, 439
Scholars, 445
School of Oriental and African Studies, 333

Prophecies, of 'Abdu'l-Bahá, 20, 56, 76, 78, 226, 251–2
of Bahá'u'lláh, 20, 75, 108
Prosecute energetically, 171
Protection, 135, 138–42, 144, 146–7, 151, 155, 157, 164, 178, 202, 330, 382, 391, 394, 437
Protectorates, 264, 297, 312
Protestant, 290
Provocative language, abstain from, 4
Psychiatric treatment, 248
Psychic forces, 178, 444
Publications, 11, 73, 86, 92, 97, 99, 115, 126–7, 130, 147, 158–9, 162, 165, 185, 213, 217, 224, 237, 246, 259, 262, 268, 271–2, 281, 287, 299, 300, 313, 330, 335, 337, 339, 344, 354, 365, 370–1, 377, 382–3, 423–4
alphabetical list of, see Annex "E"
books more needed than teachers, 431
five copies of each, to World Centre, 268, 351
in new languages, value of, 253, 262, 330
notice of review, 382
on Bahá'í procedure, 213, 260
on the Covenant, 224
quotation marks, 260
preserve uniformity in, 259
printing, 172, 253, 382
responsibility of N.S.A., 8, 9, 94
translations, see Translations
transliteration, see Transliteration
Publicity, 38, 50, 52, 55, 69, 79, 80, 91–3, 95, 100, 125, 135, 156, 159–60, 228, 230, 254, 270, 330, 348, 357, 362, 366, 370–1, 379, 383, 385
unfavourable, 300, 383
Public opinion, 309
Public to be attracted, 443
Publishing, letters to individuals, 212
Publishing Trust, Company, Bahá'í, 159, 163, 165, 246, 343, 441
aid other countries, 441
excerpts from, Meditations, 185
greatest asset of community, 114
great responsibilities of, 114
Investment Scheme, 249
not to have separate legal status, 343, 349
origins, N.S.A.'s project, 94, 114–5
related to teaching, 116, 441
royalties, 164
solicit subscriptions, funds for, 114
Punishment, s, 450–1, 455
Purest Branch, 134, 136

Purity of heart, 365
Put the past behind, 450

Qá'im, 425–6
Qualifications, assembly members, 207
believer, 444
delegates, 207
Qualities, 395
Quality of Bahá'í service, 154
Quddús, 426
Queen Marie of Roumania, 56–62, 423
Queen Victoria, 227
Quickening tempo of activity, 386
Quotation marks, 260
Qur'án, 432, 453–4, 456

Rabbaní, Hussein, 248
Rabbaní, Ruhiyyih, see Amatu'l-Bahá
Race against time, 232
Races, 251, 262, 264–5, 285–8, 299, 384
Racial discrimination, lack of, 281, 460
Radiance, 6, 449
Ramadan, 68–9
Rank and file, 264, 340
Reader, see Speaker
Reading, 418
Realisation cherished hopes, 181, 392
Receipts, 49, 267, 280, 374, 377
Reception, 30
Reciting "Greatest Name", 450
Recognise Bahá'u'lláh, 191
Recognised religious body, 99
Recognition, 123, 161, 230, 267, 382, 456
official, 72, 97, 263
universal, world-wide, 80, 191
Redemption of the world, 49
Refugees, Bahá'í, 126–7
Reincarnation, 451
Reinforcing new centres, 150
Regenerating power, 56, 60, 65, 215
Registration, as independent religious organisation, 116
as religious community, 106
of property, 97, 100, 103
Regional meetings, 217; Youth Conference, 196, 279
Regional National Spiritual Assemblies, 370, 385
Regional Teaching Committee, N. Ireland, 372
Rehabilitation National Fund, 385
Reliable, 10
Relic, 143
Relief fund, 36–7
Religion, new, independent, 65

INDEX

Plan (cont.)
   future, 245, 270–2, 276
   God's, for all mankind, 370
   Seven Year (U.S.A.), 178, 185, 187, 225
   Six Year, see Six Year Teaching Plan
   Six Year (India), 178, 225
   Two Year, see Two Year Plan
Plod on, 385
Poisoning of Bahá'u'lláh, 460
Poland, 234
Police service, 309
Political forces, 75
Politics, 180, 301, 351, 428, 444
   meddling in, forbidden, 8
Polygamists, 301
Portraits, 99
Portsmouth, 417
Portuguese, 331
Posterity, 210, 261, 321
Potentialities, 145, 186, 263, 288, 313, 385
Power, 60, 460
   from on high, 396
   on the, Revealed Word, 154; Teachings, 129
   to recreate us, 442
Praise, 122, 125, 143, 201, 204, 353, 449
Praiseworthy, 398
Prayer Book, 126, 133, 135, 368
Prayers and Meditations, 309
Prayers, for assemblies, 5
   for children, 154, 446
   for help and strength, 453
   for success, 73, 88, 93, 95, 100, 103, 107, 110–11, 117, 119–20, 124, 139–40, 145, 152, 157–8, 160, 164–5, 171, 174–5, 181–4, 186, 188–9, 192–3, 202–5, 209–10, 216–18, 222–4, 228–9, 237–40, 257, 259, 264, 278–81, 292, 306, 326, 330–1, 363, 369, 374–7, 383, 391, 395, 397, 400–2, 407, 409–10, 413–14, 416
   in shrines, 3, 14, 19, 26, 30, 54, 71, 73–4, 82, 85, 88–9, 92, 102, 117, 136, 145, 150, 166, 174, 182–3, 186, 200, 209, 219, 263, 299, 327, 352, 375, 383, 391, 399, 401, 403–4, 410, 415, 417
   not to be printed, 199, 357
   not to introduce a new set of, 446
   obligatory, 309, 369, 446
   pronouns not to be changed, 173
Preparation, 285
Prescription for Living, (Rabbaní), 249
Present status world order, 385
Press, see British Press

Prestige, 182, 200, 229, 232, 258, 310–11, 337, 339, 352, 354
   of summer school, 110
Preston, Mrs. Marguerite, 231, 266, 277, 484
Preston, Mr. Terence, 266
Priceless opportunities, 142, 191
Pride, 198, 208, 231, 240, 249, 284, 301, 307, 311, 326–7, 329, 355, 368–9, 381, 395, 398, 403, 407, 452
Prime requisities, 385; for assembly members, 6, 7
Primitive races, 213, 365
Principles, constructive, to be emphasised, 4
Principles of Bahá'í Administration, 260
Printing, 172, 253, 382
   N.S.A. approval may be omitted from, 382
Prisoners, Bahá'í, 352, 449–51
Privilege, s, 180, 233, 285
   of being Bahá'ís, 173, 193
   to lend a helping hand, 177
Prizes won, 209, 211, 215–16, 222, 227, 240, 251, 262, 271–2, 276, 313, 338, 354, 362, 376, 391
Problems, 23, 51, 140, 177, 203, 218, 285–6, 301, 343, 352, 384, 421–2, 429, 449, 459, 461
   solution of, 15, 145, 177, 222, 429, 449
Procedure, 141, 213, 238, 333, 348, 367, 423
   avoid on minor matters, 213
Proclaim courageously, 123, 173
Proclamation, 23, 186, 191, 196, 201, 209, 221, 262, 288, 371
Progress, 147, 171, 180, 239, 354, 370, 401, 411, 414, 417, 432, 441–2
Progressive, 123, 145, 384, 404
Revelation, 432, 451
Promised Day is Come, The, 456
Promise of All Ages, The, (Townshend), 92–6, 99, 135
   challenging, scholarly, timely, 93, 99, 100
   N.S.A. to undertake speedy publication of, 92, 94
   this brilliant production, 100
Promotion, 118, 171, 331, 392, 395–6, 402–3, 405, 409–10, 414, 427
Prompt action, 169
Promulgation of Universal Peace, 357
Promulgation, 141
Propagation, 290, 297, 394
Property, 97, 100, 146

Partisan or political, 213
Passing announced, mentioned, of, Aṣgháṛzadeh. Ḍ, 363; Basil-Hall, Mary, 246; Blomfield, Lady, 136; Challis, G, 218; Dreyfus-Barney, H. 84; Esslemont, Dr. J. E., 40; George, "Mother", 256; Hall, Mrs, 249; Langdon-Davies, C. 343; Marshall, J. L., 210; Mitchell, Dr. J. G., 375; Munírih Khánum, 119; Preston, Mrs. M., 277; Preston, T., 266; Rosenberg, E. J., 90; Scott, S., 283; Simpson, G. P., 96; Thornburgh-Cropper, 137; Townshend, Rev. G., 377
Passions, 129, 457
Path of, sacrifice, 406
  truth, 150, 451
Patience, patiently, 6, 196, 218, 286, 405, 411, 430, 449, 456, 462
Patient, efforts, 170
  in tribulation, 422
Peace, 15, 225
  Lambeth resolution on, 90
People, of the new creation, 350
  longing for an example, 445
  so divergent, 369, 384
Perdu, 254
Perfection, 453
Perils, 34, 133, 136, 143, 286, 339
Permanence of spiritual bonds, 460
Persecutions, 49, 52, 269, 336, 348, 362, 364–5, 425
Perseverance, 34, 102, 104, 107, 109–13, 115, 119, 122, 125, 131, 133, 136, 142, 148–9, 151–2, 154, 162, 172–4, 180, 182, 184, 192, 195, 204, 206, 214, 228, 254, 269, 282, 287, 338–9, 352, 367, 392–5, 397, 400, 404–5, 410, 430, 433, 439, 449, 457
Persia and the Persian Question (Curzon), 425
Persia, Írán, Persian Bahá'ís, 11–12, 27, 32, 36–7, 48–53, 55–6, 59–60, 66, 68–9, 75–8, 81, 84, 98, 101–2, 123–4, 219, 225, 231, 253–5, 257–8, 264–6, 269, 273, 277–8, 283, 301, 305, 348, 355–6, 360–2, 364–5, 371, 423–9
  avoidance of political, posts, 428
  claiming to be Bahá'ís, 190, 207
  crisis in, 269
  not to concentrate in one country, 277
  not to visit America, 207
  Sháh of, 76–7, 423
Persistent activities, efforts, 135, 142, 370, 417
Perspicacity, 288

Personalities to be forgotten, 402
Perversion of justice, 38
Petitions, 258
Phelps, Myron, book to be ignored, 127
Phenomenal progress, 370
Philosophy, 445
Photographs, 105, 171, 177, 183–4, 186, 250, 254–5, 258, 268, 281, 324, 382, 414
Physical, suffering, 434
  violence condemned, 128
Physicians, 248
Pilgrimage, 38, 160, 277, 403
Pilgrims, 76, 142, 326, 330, 332, 367, 379, 381, 444
  their notes not to be published, 323
Pinchon, Miss Florence, 72–3, 471
Pioneering introduced, 156–8
Pioneers, 35, 56, 84, 90, 158, 172–3, 181, 185–7, 189–91, 195, 198–9, 202–3, 210–11, 215, 217, 221–5, 227, 233, 236, 238–41, 250, 252, 255–60, 262, 265–6, 268, 271–2, 276–9, 281, 283, 286, 290–1, 297, 299, 301–4, 308–13, 323–4, 327–30, 332–6, 338, 340, 343, 347, 351, 353, 360, 362–3, 368–71, 373–5, 383, 395, 400–2, 413, 446, 451, 455, 458–9
  applications, not to get bogged down, 304
  choose most qualified, 268
  friends must disperse, 345
  listed, *see* Annex "B"
  Marion Jack their example, 336
  not abandon post, 327, 329, 336
  not to become public charges, 343
  qualifications of, 277
  settle easy areas first, 305
  soldiers of Bahá'u'lláh, 460
  their true function, 336
  to be, dispersed, 302, 304, 309, 313; financed temporarily, 185, 188, 233, 459; self-supporting, 259, 458–9
  to take precedence, 303–5
  unparalleled percentage community, 245
Pioneer work, 33, 81, 84, 156, 172, 185, 222, 253, 362, 365
Pivotal centre, s, 362, 376
Pivotal year, 189, 194
Places mentioned, *see* Annex "A"
Planet, 147, 285, 312
Planning, 258–9, 262
Plan, s, 271, 338, 394
  Africa, 163, *see* Two Year Plan
  Five Year, 225

North Africa, 12, 262
Northampton, 407
Northern Ireland, 169, 209, 245, 272, 339, 353, 372, 385, 391
North Sea Islands, 384-5
North Western outpost, 221
Norton, Arthur, 267, 487
Norwich, 217, 283, 408-9
No sacrifice too great for Cause, 455
Notable, achievements, activities, 126, 191, 197
  advantages, 171
  share, 138
Not agonise over the past, 441
Not a paid clergy, 185
Not become bitter, 450
Not by the force of numbers, 28
Notes and personal accounts imperfect, 89
No time to lose, 191, 287
Not the time to dwell on future, 385
Nottingham, 194-5, 222, 325, 409-10
Not to dwell on oneself, 447, 457
Not use psychic forces, 178, 444
Nuclei, 201, 220, 245, 382
  virgin territories, 192
Numbers, believers, active supporters, 150-1, 185-6, 197, 211, 251, 287, 345
Nyasaland, 301

Oaths, 368
Obedience, 6, 134
Objectives, 171, 182, 186, 245-6, 264, 271, 292, 302, 313, 338, 347, 365, 399, 433
  homefront, rockbottom requirements, 371, 385
Obligation, 115, 118, 172, 177, 201, 433
Obligatory prayers, 309, 369, 446
Obscurity, 35, 78, 385
Observer, The, 366
Obstacles, 94, 107, 110-11, 115, 125, 134, 147, 160, 166, 174, 182, 191, 193, 198, 200, 203, 205, 214, 222, 225, 232, 249, 272, 282, 291, 303, 308, 314, 321, 369, 385, 391, 397, 405, 409, 413, 418, 433-4
Officers, assembly, 71, 93, 108
  committee, 212
Official recognition, 72, 97, 263
  solicitor, 253
  title, National Assembly, 88-9
Officials, Board of Trade, 124
One spiritual family, 439
One thing and only one thing, 28

One year respite, 245, 263, 271
Onward march of the Cause, 112, 375, 405
  impeded, 4
Opportunities, 92, 102, 104, 112, 123, 126, 142, 150, 190-1, 201, 220, 229, 231, 233, 237, 310, 313, 355, 360, 381, 396, 450
Oppose National Assembly policy forbidden, 125
Opposition, 67, 287, 308, 334, 340, 379, 382, 436
Oppressive, 145
Optimism, 18, 181, 225, 452
Ordeal, 148
Ordered society, 137
Order of Bahá'u'lláh, 144
Organic union of all National Assemblies, 257
Organise work on new basis, 185
Organising ability, 369
Orient, 42
Oriental, s, 190, 207, 248
Orkney Islands, 297, 322
Orlova, Madam, 109, 118
Orthodox Christian, 131
Ostracism, 207
Our own inner life, 28
Out of hand, 454
Outstanding promoter, 123
Overseas campaigns, mission, territories, 196, 201, 208, 245, 251-3, 265, 270, 276, 285, 287, 297, 304-5, 314, 337-8, 353, 370, 379, 384-5
Oxford, 224, 230, 236, 331, 350, 411-17
  historic and promising city, 412, 414

Pace-setters, 259
Pacific Islands, 327, 360, 365, 383-4
  peoples of, 365
Pacifists, 435-6
Pagan, 290
Pain necessary, 434
Palestine, 97, 99-101, 103, 219
  Branch, (later "Israeli"), America, 97, 103; British Isles, 99-100, 215-16, 328, 354
Pamphlets, African, 237, 246, 253, 258, 265, 275, 290, 298, 306, 313, 321, 329-30
  for the clergy, 161
Paper, summer school, 127
Paramount and most urgent duty, 35
Parents, 335
Paris, 84, 99, 173, 177
Paris Talks, 164, 178
Parting of the ways, 226

National Spiritual Assembly (*cont.*)
  first meeting of, 9, 13, 163
  first order of business, 304
  incorporation of, 61, 97–101, 103, 116, 120–1, 124, 127, 132
  manifold and weighty obligations, 118
  minutes of, 31, 36, 61, 68, 71–3, 87–8, 108, 110–11, 115, 117–19, 130, 138, 140, 142, 144, 146, 148–9, 151, 154, 161, 163, 170, 198, 258, 387
  national endowment of, 221, 350
  official title of, 88–9
  quarter-acre land on Mount Carmel, 328
  refugees, Bahá'í, each individual case to be investigated by, 126–7
  responsibility for work in unallocated African territories, 273
  secretary of, 141, 222, 250, 448
  sets a noble example, 144
  should act with firmness, vigilance, wisdom, tact, 129, 174, 180
  to recognise local assemblies, 238, 249
  unity of, 189
  wise leadership of, 354
  zeal and wisdom of, 144
National Spiritual Assembly, (Regional National), Central and East Africa, 298, 355, 357, 367–9, 384
  Convention for, 358, 363, 367
  delegates, allocated to assemblies, 357–8
  endowment for, 298, 352, 355, 361
  Ḥaẓíratu'l-Quds, Kampala, 298
  incorporation of, 298
  its work dear to Guardian's heart, 368
  number of delegates for Convention, 357
  responsible for its Temple, 364
  token financial support only from parent N.S.A., 368
National Spiritual Assemblies, Australia and New Zealand, Egypt, Germany, India and Burma, Írán, 'Iráq, references to, (included in the index for each respective country)
National Teaching Committee, 106–7, 179, 186, 195, 206, 212, 216, 239–41, 393
National Teaching Conference (annual), 119, 136, 156, 181–2, 193–4, 196, 209, 222–3, 237–9, 254, 275, 283, 291–2, 324, 343, 361, 374
Nationhood, influence of Islám, 456
Nation-wide campaign, 186, 220, 229, 233
Nature of Scots, 399

Naw-Rúz, 157, 164, 400
Nayriz, Írán, 36–7, 425
Necessary uniformity, 102
Negative, existence of evil, 458; feeling, 447; teachings, 4
Negroes, 370
Neither vacillate not falter, 191
Never prefer own wills to the Will of God, 444
New age not born, 225
New and brilliant phase, 384
New basis, phase, for Six Year Plan, 185
Newcastle, 127, 235, 238
New centres, 171–2
New chapter, 254
New Commonwealth Society, 91, 113
New Day of God, 67, 148
New era of expansion, 114, 191, 311
New History Society, 218, 282
New religion, pronounced by tribunal, 65–6
Newly enrolled believers, 215, 220, 222–4, 227, 235, 237, 301, 308, 352
Newly fledged communities, 370
News, 180, 240, 258, 381, 391, 393, 398, 404, 409, 438, 445
  exchange of, 10, 51
  letters, 102, 258, 323, 409
  spreading the, 163
Newspapers, 80, 357, 413
New World Order, 124, 135
New York, 25, 73
New Zealand, 37, 96
Nicosia, Cyprus, 346
Nigeria, 253, 274, 298
Nineteen Day Feasts, 159, 190, 213, 380, 397, 450
  any Bahá'í (in good standing) may attend, 380
Nobility of purpose, 131
Noble, determination, 147, 171
  end, 174
  example, 144, 173, 202
  faith, 153
  perseverance, 142
  resolve, 135, 254, 267
  structure, 137
No end to time, 432
No higher call, 106
Non affiliation, 113
Non attendance at Feasts, 159
Non-combatant service, 122, 128–9, 134, 259
Non-political organisations, 91
No results from pessimistic approach, 199
North, 198, 221, 338

Mission (cont.)
  40, 353–5, 369–70, 379, 384–5, 416, 459
  the most spectacular phase of (British Bahá'í), 385
Missionaries, 300
Mitchell, Dr. John G., 307, 350, 361, 375, 488
Mitigation of suffering, 454
Moayad, Dr., 381
Moderation, 7, 129
Mogadiscio, Italian Somaliland, 346
Momentous stage, step forward, 128
Momentous verdict, 65
Monarchy, 335
Monogamy in Rosenberg Tablets, 131
Moore, Major, 17
Morocco, 299
Moses, 446, 448, 459
Most, Great Festival, 297
  Great Jubilee, 272, 285, 297, 313
  Great Name, 370
  memorable year, 195
  potent period, 214
  powerful pillars, 299
Mother assembly, 369, 386, 398
Motherland, 369
Mothers, 154, 440
Mount Carmel, 41, 43, 100, 103, 136, 141, 215–16, 328
Movement for World Government, 213
Mudaliar, Sir A. Ramaswami, 212
Muḥammad, the Prophet, 66, 426, 432, 451, 456, 459
Mullá Ḥusayn, 159, 426–7
Muníríh Khánum, wife of 'Abdu'l-Bahá, 119
Multiplication of centres, 339, 344, 347, 353–4, 371, 385
Multitudes, 196, 288
Murder, 129
Murray, Professor Gilbert, 366
Músá, Mírzá, 427
Muslim, 66, 68–9, 406
Myron Phelps book, 127
Mysterious Forces of Civilisation, 456
Mysterious power, 446
Mystery, 458
Mysticism, 407

Nabíl's, life, 427, 443
  narrative, 425–8, 433
  suicide, 406
Nairobi, 279, 281, 283, 287, 314
Nakhjavání, 'Alí (and Violette), 257, 266, 291, 301, 486

Nascent institutions, 191, 205, 221, 394
National, archives, 143, 350
  Bahá'í Centre, 193; Library, 130
National Convention, 146, 159, 264, 362
  delegates to, 62–4, 188, 194, 197, 207, 247–8, 297, 299, 325–6, 352, 363–4; their qualifications, 207; prior consultation with their own community, 193; their primary function, 247–8
  deliberations at, 183
  epoch-making, 263
  first British, 70
  greetings to, xvi, 70, 74, 89, 107, 117, 119, 126, 139, 142, 151, 157–8, 166, 183, 228–9, 245–6, 263, 293, 297, 299, 325–6, 347, 378–9, 381
  immediate action taken at, 395
  no exceptions for delegate allocation, 367
  quorum not necessary for, 247
  reports, recommendations, suggestions, 127, 130, 143, 147, by majority vote, 248
  statistics report to, 165
  time of, 63–4, 138, 159, 236
  tribute at, for George Townshend, 377
  venue for, 64
National endowments, 221, 298, 347, 350, 352, 354–5, 361, 367
  excitement, 129
  fund, *see* Fund, National
  headquarters, *see* Ḥaẓíratu'l-Quds
  secretary, 141, 222, 250, 448
  service, 122, 128–9
  state not city state, 456
National Spiritual Assembly, British Isles, xiii, xvii. 16–17, 21, 24–5, 27, 32–3, 37, 48, 62–4, 74–5, 85, 91–4, 97–8, 100–1, 104–6, 112, 114, 116, 121–2, 124–8, 131–5, 141, 145, 150, 152, 155, 158–61, 163–4, 170, 172–4, 178, 180, 183–4, 186, 190, 194–6, 200, 208, 212–13, 215–16, 218, 222–4, 227, 231, 237, 240–1, 247, 249, 251, 253–4, 257, 259, 262, 264, 266, 269–70, 273, 275, 288–9, 293, 297, 302–4, 306, 314, 326–7, 332, 334, 336–8, 340–3, 348, 350, 354, 358, 361, 364, 369, 380, 382–3, 385–6, 393–4, 416, 440
  annual reports, 117, 120, 130
  consolidation and distinction of, 215
  consultative body for all African territories, 269, 293, 308
  co-operation with other N.S.A.s, 245, 251, 253–4, 256–8, 285

Lustre, 128, 206, 240
Lynch, Mrs., 130, 181, 189

Madagascar, 291, 299
Madeira, 297
Magestic structure, 131
Magnet, 137, 204
Magnificent enterprise, 369
Maintain assemblies at all costs, 206, 209, 217, 222, 282, 382, 392, 394
Major, achievement, 170
  events, 96
  responsibility, 180
Majority voice, 7
Malta, 297, 305, 322, 324, 326–8, 333, 350
Manchester, xv, 9, 13, 24, 62–4, 85, 119, 142, 145, 160, 170, 181, 194, 239, 349, 404, 405, 407
Manchester College, Oxford, 412
Manchester Guardian, The, 366
Manifestation of God, 172, 405–6, 432, 443, 447–8, 451–3, 456, 458–60
Manifold anxieties, 145
Mankind, plight of, 33, 262, 447, 451–2
Mansion, Bahá'u'lláh's, Bahjí, *see* Bahjí
Manton, Eric, 250, 273, 487
Manton, Mr., 250
Man was always man, 458
Map, 240, 249, 258, 305
Maraghih, A<u>dh</u>irbáyján, Irán, 52
Marie, Queen of Roumania, *see* Queen Marie
Marriage, 66, 195, 215, 248, 301, 324, 333
  declaration, words used, 383, 435
  dependent upon parental consent, 435
  of Guardian, 115
  no minimum age for girls, 334
Marshall, George, 228, 484
Marshall, John L, 210, 480
Martyrdoms, 32, 48–9, 52, 56, 68–9, 177
Martyrdom of The Báb, 230–1, 234
Martyrs, 406–7
Masefield, Miss, 412
Ma<u>sh</u>riqú'l-A<u>dh</u>kár, Houses of Worship, 9, 43, 80–4, 87, 113, 156, 221, 251, 291, 298, 356–7
  no "chapels" in, 356
  significance of, 80
Ma<u>sh</u>riqu'l-A<u>dh</u>kár, Kampala, 298, 325, 329, 334, 356–9, 367
  decision to build, 356
  description of, 356, 359, 367
  drawings rejected, 359
Masses, 129, 174, 186, 191, 196, 201, 209, 221, 384

Materialism, 106, 447, 451
Mathews, Mrs. Loulie, 216
Matter of conscience, 170
Mauritius, 373
Maxwell, Miss Mary, *see* 'Amatu'l-Bahá Ru<u>h</u>íyyih <u>Kh</u>ánum
Maxwell, Mr. Sutherland, Hand of the Cause, 247, 402
Mázindarán, 425
McKinley, Hugh and Violet, 194, 178
Meaning obscure, 178
Medical opinion, 462
Medicine, 248, 462
Meditate, 406
Mediterranean Islands, 312, 353–4, 370, 383–4
Medium, spiritualist, 175
Members, of spiritual assemblies, 5, 6, 49, 70–1, 138
  no substitutes for, 53
  only nine can vote, 49, 59
  qualifications of, 207
  to seek advice, 59
Membership of, churches, synagogues, 150, 199, 200, 350
  freemasonry, 343, 350–1
  non-political organisations, 91
  spiritualist medium in Faith, 175
  The New Commonwealth, 91, 113
Memorial gatherings, 40, 90, 119, 136
Menace of social chaos, 33
Mental diseases, 462
Mesopotamia, 12
Messages, of affection, 410; Guardian's secretaries, 260
Message of Bahá'u'lláh (Esslemont), 45–6
Message of the New Day, 196
Messager Bahá'í, 59
Messages, Queen Marie, 57
Messages to America (1932–1946), 165, 175
  (items published in, not herein indexed)
Middle/Near East, 75, 142, 214
Mightier Crusades, 233
Mihdí, 426
Milestone, 214, 285, 349, 355, 369
Military service, *see* Active military service
Miller, Dr. Ernest S., 395, 489
Mills, Mountfort, 25–6, 31, 37, 44, 59, 61, 86
Mills, Mrs. M. Olga K., Knight of Bahá'u'lláh, 210, 218, 327–8, 480
Minorities, 395
Miracle, 252, 351
Mission, 191, 245, 251–3, 264–5, 285–8, 291, 297, 299, 311–12, 314, 338–

Kingdom of God, 246, 379
Kirmánsháh, 427
Kiss of Judas, 405
Kitáb-i-Aqdas, 6, 78, 195, 261, 424, 426, 455
Kitáb-i-Iqán, 424–6, 430, 432, 451
Knights, of Bahá'u'lláh, 303, 306, 336
of the Lord, 67
Kurdistán, 406
Kutendele, Dudley Smith, 301
Kuwait, 377

Labour continually, proclaim courageously, 123
Lady Blomfield, see Blomfield
Lambeth Conference, 90
Lammington, Lord, 120, 143
Landmark, 94, 97, 122–3, 173, 182, 189, 208, 211, 262, 264, 285, 368, 377
Land blessed with freedom, 355
Land, Mount Carmel, 328
Langdon-Davies, Mrs. Constance, 224, 324, 343, 350, 416, 484
Languages into which Bible is translated, 378
mentioned by Guardian, see Annex "D"
La Nova Tago, 48
Lantern slides, 141
Large centres of population, 345
Last minute appeal, 211
Latent potentialities, 145
Latin America eclipsed, 290
Laurels victory, 229, 262
Laws to be obeyed, 284, 301, 308, 311, 346, 369, 443, 450, 453, 455
Lea, Miss Elsie, 102
Leach, Bernard, C.H., O.B.E., 239, 484
Leaders of thought, 91, 100, 423
Leading outpost of Faith, 114
Leeds, 127, 283, 402
Lee, Joseph, 181, 476
Legal, -ly, 248, 354
Publishing Company, 116
Lend share assistance, 179
Lesson for Bahá'ís, 61
Lethargy thrown off, 200
Letter, and spirit, of teachings, 129
Liberal-minded parents, 205
Libraries, 78, 133, 170
Library, National, 130
Life a struggle, 450, 453–4
Light, absence of, 458
Limited numbers, resources, 113
Lindsay Hall, 73
Lion of confidence, 447

Lion's share, 180
Lists, areas, countries, places, see Annex "A"
individuals, people, see Annex "B"
languages mentioned, see Annex "D"
publications mentioned, see Annex "E"
qualities and descriptions of British Bahá'ís, see Annex "C"
Literature, not Scripture, 208
Liverpool, 235, 349, 395, 402
Lives protected, 142
Living Religions Conference, see Conferences
Living the life, 34, 452
Ljungberg, Eskil, Knight of Bahá'u'lláh, 321
Localities, centres, 158, 160–1, 210, 216, 287, 289–90, 298, 339, 344–5, 347, 353, 359, 366, 385
Local endowments, 221, 339, 341
Local people, nucleus of, 382
Local Spiritual Assemblies, see Spiritual Assemblies
London, xv, 9, 18, 23, 26–7, 31–2, 41–2, 44, 47–8, 53–4, 59, 62–4, 68, 72–3, 85–6, 88, 91, 94, 96, 98–9, 102–5, 110, 114, 123, 130, 135, 139, 142, 148, 150, 159, 163, 170–2, 174, 200–1, 214, 234, 238, 254, 308, 313–15, 331–2, 335, 338, 342–4, 349, 353, 357, 402, 443
archives to be removed from, in times of danger, 350
Centre, see Bahá'í Centres
Heart of British Empire, 114, 313, 338, 353
leading outpost of the Faith, 114
Spiritual Assembly of, 47–8, 53, 59, 62–4, 349; its area defined, 63–4; only one for London, 214
Youth Group, 110
venue for Convention, 64, 68
Loneliness, 336, 410, 442
Long obligatory prayer, 173
Lord Halifax, 127
Lord Lammington, 120, 143
Loss of assemblies, 366
Lou-Helen Ranch, U.S.A., 97
Love, 7, 15, 25, 34, 205, 218, 234, 311, 403–4, 408, 417, 439–1, 445, 447, 449–50, 457–8
understanding of, 406, 458
Lowliness, 6
Loyal citizens, 122
Loyalty, 110, 117, 122, 151, 153, 164, 204, 276, 291, 301, 410
of Assembly Officer, 141

Individuals, see Annex "B", 195
  even if bereft of every human knowledge and capacity, 436
  helping each other by suffering, 436–7
  insignificant, achieve remarkable things, 172–3
  letters to, extracts in chronological order, xvii, xviii, 420–462
  must arise, 120, 172
  thoughtful, 131, 133, 423
Indo-China, 85
Indomitable spirit, 145
Inflexible purpose, determination, resolve, 134, 311, 352
Influential people, to be contacted, 91, 100, 423
Inhospitable climate, regions, 287, 291, 371, 385
Initial phase, 201, 209–11, 214, 216, 220, 264
  stage, 182, 191, 208, 211, 229, 232
Initiative, 307, 347
Inner life and private character, 28
Inner meaning of life, 407
Innermost heart, 57
Institutions, 95, 98, 110, 133, 135, 147, 149, 151, 153–5, 174, 179, 186, 191, 196, 201, 206, 208, 215, 236, 251–2, 262, 268, 271, 286, 297–8, 312, 331, 350, 354, 364, 366, 375, 393–4, 397, 401, 403, 408, 412, 416, 441
Instructions for our own good, 443
Integrity, 129, 428
Intelligence, 288
Intensely alive, 270
Intercontinental conferences, see Africa, Europe
Internal consolidation, 371
International, Bahá'í Bureau, see Bahá'í Bureau
  Bahá'í Council, 257, 261, 268, 288, 305
  endowments, 215–16, 328
  institutions, 268
  scale, 261
  services to Faith, 196
  survey, 120
Interpretation of Scripture, 423
Intrepidity, 263
Investment scheme, 249
Invincible power of the Faith, 125
Ioas, Leroy, Hand of the Cause, 288, 300, 326
Íqán, see Kitáb-i-Iqán
Írán, see Persia
'Iráq, 37–8, 44, 80, 98, 101–2, 248, 427

Ireland, Eire, Irish, 62, 169, 189, 192, 195–6, 199, 201–3, 206, 209, 211, 215, 220, 237, 245, 251, 262, 272, 286–7, 297–8, 311–12, 339, 353, 377, 382, 385, 397–8
  Dublin, Mother Assembly of, 398
  to take Faith to other countries, 398
Ishqábád, Russia, 424
Ishráqát, 424
Islám, 66, 69, 78, 180, 426, 432, 442, 451, 456
Islands, 285, 297, 305, 310, 312–13, 326, 360, 370
  and archipelagos of the Seven Seas, 311
  bordering the British Isles, 312, 338, 358, 370–1, 376, 382–6
  Far East, 370
Isolated centres, see Localities
Israel Branch of British N.S.A., 328, 354
Israeli Government, 248
Italian Somaliland, 291, 346
Italy, 18

Jack, Miss Marion, 98, 336
Jahrum, 49, 52, 56
Janner, Lord Barnet, 358
Japan, Emperor of, 423
Jarrold Magazine, 409
Jehoveh, 432
Jenkerson, Cyril and Margaret, 217, 224, 230, 483
Jerusalem, 92, 364
Jews, 427
Jináb-i-Avárí, see Avárí
John the Baptist, 427
Joseph, Albert and Jeff, 146, 310, 474
Journal, see Bahá'í Journal
Joy, 241, 245, 249–50, 407, 461
Judaism, 432
Justice, 406

Kadiani sect, India, 27
Kampala, 275, 277, 279, 283, 290–2, 298, 309, 314, 325, 367
  temple site, 298, 325, 329, 334, 353, 354, 388–9
Karkúk, 'Iráq, 248
Kenya, 231, 253, 266, 277, 281, 287, 298–9, 303, 305, 309
Key assembly, 391
Khan, Dr., 199
Khochbine, A., 211
Kindness, 4, 49
King, 258

INDEX

High-minded, 263, 311, 345, 361, 384
High road leading to victory, 386
High road of its destiny, 220, 252
High-spirited, 210, 222
Hill, Mr. and Mrs., 152
Historical angle of philosophy, 445
Historical compilation, 37
Historic, achievements, 112, 203, 210, 336, 342, 398, 411, 418
  decision, 356
  endeavours, 174
  enterprise, 183, 393
  journey, 256
  process, 386
  service, 172
  success, 198
  victory, 258, 353, 416
  work, 145, 147, 186, 202, 271, 303, 377, 392–3
History, of the Cause in England, British Bahá'í, 97, 158–9, 173, 186, 189, 191, 195, 198, 201, 208, 211, 214, 219–21, 227, 234, 238, 245, 249–50, 262, 271, 285, 291, 297, 310–12, 355, 370, 377, 384
  new chapter in, 385
History of, humanity, a most critical period, 370
  the country, 249
  the Faith, 172, 180, 182; few references to individuals, 97; to be studied, 385
Hitching one's wagon to a star, 451
Hofman, David, xii, xiii, 108–9, 116–17, 119–20, 136–7, 139–40, 173, 179, 191, 222, 472
Hofman, Mrs. Marion, xiii, 179, 191, 206, 212, 216, 222, 476
Holley, Horace, Hand of the Cause, 53, 120, 216, 255
Holy days, 213
Holy land, 5, 11–12, 26, 51, 60, 78, 85, 133, 216, 268, 332, 337, 375, 445
  no migration to, 268
Holy Shrines, see Shrines
Holy Spirit, 150, 374
Holy Year, 283, 287, 289, 292, 297, 300, 311, 327
Home Front, 245, 256, 269, 276, 278–9, 286, 291, 298, 312, 326, 333, 336, 345, 362–3, 366, 370, 373, 379, 382–4
Homeland, 261–2, 270–1, 286, 297, 311, 337–8, 354, 362, 371, 386
Hong Kong, 298
Honour, 387
Hornell, Lady Kathleen, 172, 191, 475

Horrors of war, 145
Hostilities, 128
Host of Heaven, 304
Hour, critical, challenging, crucial, 262, 271, 362
  of greatest need, 314; of trial, crisis, 145, 381
  propitious, 245, 252, 340
House of Bahá'u'lláh, Baghdád, see Bahá'u'lláh
Houses of, Justice, 5–6
  worship, see Mashriqu'l-Adhkár
Howes, Miss Janet, 204
Ḥujjat, 426
Humanitarian work, 122–3
Humanity, more mature, 406
  motivation for love for, 458
  moving towards its destiny, 28
  must be unified, 452
  only way out for, 439
  tortured, confused, suffering, 177, 225, 350, 429, 437
Human passions, 457
Human society, 435
Humiliation, 451
Humility, 6
Hundred years respite, 456
Hungary, 80
Hurst, Frank, 126

Identified with Plan, 171
Ignite a fire, 371
Imperialistic, 213
Importance of, England, 164
  London, 114
  Some Answered Questions, 383
  summer schools, 97
Inactive believers, 159, 184–5, 199
Incompetence of an officer, 141
Incorporation, 61, 97–101, 103, 116, 120–1, 124, 298, 354, 373
  a pattern for, 93, 101, 382
Incorporated local assemblies, 289, 298, 339–40, 347, 354, 367, 371, 382, 385
  certificate of, 127, 349, 354
Incorruptible spirit, 153
Increase in membership, 150–1, 185, 286, 339, 345, 351, 354, 371, 385, 400–1, 410–11, 415, 441
Independent religion, 65–6
India, Indian, 12, 17, 19, 22, 27, 42, 67, 85, 98, 101–2, 178, 185, 215, 225, 251, 265–6, 277–8, 410, 424
  Kadiani sect of, 27

Guardian, The (cont.)
lemont, 41; service lonelier, more complicated, 410, 442; suffering on becoming Guardian, 459; tribute to Greatest Holy Leaf, 430–1; worries, problems, anxiety and pain, 225, 268, 334, 366, 402, 410, 455, 457; writings, 224
how to help him, 461
invited to attend Conference, 104
letters from individuals welcomed, 13–14, 16–17, 19, 145, 307, 332, 438
letters from Sir H. Samuel and Sir F. Younghusband, 104–5
likes to be provided with facts, 449
messages by his secretaries, 260
not able, attend London Conference, 26; visit London, 86
not omniscient at will, 449
not pronounced on Aqdas punishments, 455
opens all letters personally, 17
pledges every assistance, 171
source of constant encouragement, joy, to him, 28, 128, 283, 302, 410
translations by, 14, 17, 20, 22, 82, 195, 422
use of his full name on certain cables, 132
Guidance, 141, 146, 178, 203, 232, 287, 301, 392, 433
to a prisoner, 352, 449–51
Guide, 135, 141, 151, 160, 162, 178, 188, 197, 203, 211, 219, 235, 239, 252, 275, 278, 303, 314, 327, 375, 391–2, 395–6, 399–04, 407, 411–13, 416, 418, 441
Gung, Miss Claire, 211, 255, 321, 482

Haifa, 18, 25–7, 29–30, 32, 36, 40, 43, 47, 127, 130, 160, 169, 184, 187, 199, 216, 255, 268, 283, 350, 398, 414, 424
Newsletter, 29, 130, 182
personal accounts of visits to, not authoritative, 425
Hainsworth, Mrs. Lizzie F., 211, 482
Hainsworth, Philip, xiii, xviii, 187, 191, 237, 239, 253, 266, 303, 322, 477
Hájí, Mírzá Vakílu'd-Dawlih, 43
Ḥakím, Dr. Luṭfulláh, 195, 219, 255, 479
Halifax, Lord, 127
Hall, Edward, T., 9, 24, 404–5, 467
Hall, Mrs., 249

Hamburg, 48
Handicaps, 172
Hands of the Cause of God, 276, 284, 299, 308, 333, 377, 341–2, 382, 385, 387
Auxiliary Boards, 341
Dr. Esslemont announced as, 43
not to correspond with National Committees, 341
relationship with National Assemblies, 341–2
Happiness, prayers for, 178, 341–2, 450
through suffering, 434
Hardship, 123, 208, 336, 405
Harmony, 7–9, 15, 25, 179, 205, 404, 421, 445
essential between local/national assemblies, 8, 125
essential within, assemblies, 7, 8; Cause, 8, 85, 445
in procedure, 10, 53
the effect when absent, 28
Harvest, 131, 145, 147
Hasselblatt, Miss Brigette, Knight of Bahá'u'lláh, 322
Hate, 457
Hausa, 253
Haybittel, Mrs., 63
Hazards, 287
Ḥaẓíratu'l-Quds, 255, 301, 310, 313, 332
Kampala, 298, 334
London, national headquarters, 163, 221, 298, 314–15, 322, 324, 331–2, 335, 338, 342–4, 349, 353, 382
Healing, prayers, 173
spiritual, 309
Health, 440–1, 444, 462
Healthy social life, 457
Heart of Africa, 262
Heart of The Gospel (Townshend), 131–3
Hearts of humanity frozen, 439
Hebrides Islands, 297, 305, 323
Height to height, 340
Hejira, 432–3
Helping hand to Europe, 177
Hemispheres, 261, 285, 297, 337, 385
Heroes, 146
Heroic age, 264, 270, 290
example, 143
Heroism, 233, 240, 313
Hidden Words, 14, 23, 55, 86–7, 429–30, 456
High Commissioner, 91
Highest praise, 128, 143
Highly, challenging responsibility, 385
esteemed, 291
promising centre (Torquay), 116

INDEX 503

Giving to Fund a personal matter, 447–8
Glad Tidings of Bahá'u'lláh (Townshend), 237
Glasgow, 401
Globe, 288, 299, 340, 352–3, 371, 386
Gloom, 150, 448
Glory, -ies, 145, 252, 286, 313, 321, 385–6
Glorious chapter, 180, 182, 254
Goals, 107, 115, 140, 151, 169, 172, 177, 179–81, 189, 192, 198, 200, 209, 215, 217, 222, 225–6, 228–9, 231, 235–7, 239, 250, 262, 269, 272–3, 283, 290–2, 297–8, 302, 308–10, 313, 326–9, 331–3, 335–6, 345, 361, 372–4, 382–3, 387, 391, 403, 436, 448, 461
  request for, 169
  to be won quickly, 345
  Towns, 181–2, 185–6, 188–9, 194–5, 217, 219, 224, 331, 446
God-given strength, 147
God Passes By, 224
God's Plan, 370
God's sustaining grace, 287
Gold Coast, 254, 273, 297–8
Golden, Age, 57, 263
  dome of the Shrine, 321
  opportunity, 233
Good, 458
Goodwill, 4
Gospel in Many Tongues, The, 378
Gospel, the, 432
Governments, 334, 348, 444
  obedience to, 128
  of Írán, 366
  opposition from, 308
  recognition by, 263
  registration by, 101
  relations with, 268, 271, 444
Grace, abounding, 386
Grace, the saying of, 446
Gratification (of Guardian), 133, 249
Gratitude (of Guardian), 133, 137, 140, 143, 147, 189, 191, 197–8, 203, 210, 215–16, 240, 250, 254, 279, 392, 395, 400, 401
Grave matter—deprivation of rights, 213
Gravity hour, 139
Graves, Dr. J. E. Esslemont, 42, 46–7;
  design of, 46–7
Great Britain, *see* British Isles
Great change, 194
Great epoch, 191
Greater heights heroism, achievements, 223, 313, 386
Greatest asset (Publishing Company), 114

Greatest collective enterprise, 178, 180, 208
Greatest Holy Leaf (Bahá'íyyih Khánum), 25–6, 36, 328, 430–1
  follow her saintly path, 431; her memory will sustain, 431
Greatest Name, 369, 450
Great Jubilee, 313
Greatly promising, 286
Green Acre, U.S.A., 97
Gregory, Mrs., 98
Gregory, Mrs. Alma C., 191, 478
Gregory, Ernest W., 381, 399, 488
Gregory, Louis, first negro Hand of the Cause, 231
Greven, Mr. and Mrs., 98
Grinevskaya, Mde., 161
Groups, 195, 287, 289–90, 339, 344–5, 353–4, 371, 385, 428
Growing vitality, 146
Growth, 147, 269, 423
"Guardian" in *Seven Valleys*, 453
Guardian, The, Shoghi Effendi Rabbaní, *see also* Shoghi Effendi,
  absence from the Holy Land, 26–8, 87
  admiration for G. P. Simpson, 32–3, 44, 54, 73
  close association with Dr. Esslemont, 43
  contributions, gifts from, 23, 25, 100, 130, 142, 153, 155, 158, 160, 165, 175, 181, 188–9, 198, 206, 217, 228, 230, 237, 246, 255–6, 264–5, 300, 306, 314, 324, 348, 362
  co-operation with Rev. George Townshend, 86
  effect of unharmony on, 28, 421
  first letter received from West by, 11
  first letter to Great Britain from, 9
  heaviest load falls upon him, 307, 410
  his, concern for safety British believers, xv, 135, 139–45, 147, 171, 437–8, 449; dearest wish, 222; decisions guided by God, 449; grief at passing of Lady Blomfield, 136–7; hopes to attend London Conference, 25; hopes, 26, 30, 111, 114, 136, 151, 157, 288, 308, 314, 326, 340, 355, 365, 379, 397; last letter to British Isles, 380–386; letters to individuals, extracts from, xvii, 117, 212; marriage announced, 115; mental fatigue and strain, 71, 268; one joy, 29; overburdened heart, 170, 430, 442; regard for H. Dreyfus-Barney, 84–5; representatives, 104; responsibilities, 10, 135–7, 268; ring for Dr. Ess-

First (cont.)
  Spiritual Assembly in, Ireland, 398; Scotland, 399; Wales, 394
  Stage, noble enterprise, 182
  Stage, overseas mission, 251, 253, 287
  victories African field, 263
Focus on glory of Cause, 447
Followers of Faith not Moslems, 66
Footnotes, xvii, 178
Footsteps, early heroes, 146
Forbearance, 4, 48
Force, dynamic, latent, 50, 79
  new, 172, 423
  none can ignore, 60
Forces, 181-2, 456; sinister, evil, dark, 78, 436, 442
Forging ahead, 152, 198, 386, 409
Forgiveness, 449
Formative age, xi, 140, 261, 263-4, 270-1, 288, 380
Fortitude, 145
Fortunes mankind, 271
Forward marching, 338
Foundation, 16, 29, 125, 137, 144-5, 149, 151-2, 191, 196, 206, 245-6, 251, 269, 285, 297, 345, 352, 366, 392, 396, 399, 402, 405
France, 14, 80, 310
Freedom from prejudice, 291
Free love condemned, 435
Freemasonry, 343, 350-1
Free of the dross of self, 453
Free will, 447
French, believers, 173, 177
  Cameroons, 324
  Congo, Equatorial Africa, 299, 300
  Morocco, 291
  Somaliland, 299, 347
  Togoland, 324
French, Mrs., 120
Fresh conquests, 113
Freud, 248
Friends and foes, 145
Fulfil, 142
Fundamental verities, 371
Fund, International, 267-8, 321, 374; receipts, 49, 267, 280, 321
  international archives, 377
  for Publishing Company, to solicit for, 114-15
Fund, National, 127, 164, 181, 185, 201, 211, 219, 225, 235, 237, 250, 256, 310, 324, 348, 381, 385
  become self-supporting, 385
  budgeting, 211, 284, 307
  deficit, 256

Fund, National (cont.)
  economy urged, 256, 324, 335
  equilibrium achieved, 381
  not to support Central and East Africa N.S.A., 368
Funds, expenditures, 190, 254, 256, 325, 335, 381, 385, 447-8, 452
  at World Centre, 266
  economy urged, 256, 324, 335
  no conditions, 447
Funds for,
  Africa Plan, work, 256, 262, 269, 273, 300, 306-7, 309
  Africa Temple, 356
  delegates, 68, 352
  Dr. Esslemont's grave, 42
  expenses, 17
  Nayríz, 36-7
  pioneers, teachers, 185, 223, 233, 250, 262, 268
  relief, 201
  Shrines, 267-8, 280, 284, 321, 374
  summer school subsidy, 183
  Temple, 81, 83-4, 87
  Townshend, Rev. George, 218
Funds, from bequests, 350
Funeral ceremonies, Dr. Esslemont, 41; Mrs. Hall, 250
Future, epochs, 261
  glory, 233
  life, 157, 233, 461
  of the Cause, 102, 152-3, 221, 227, 326
  operations, 384
  plans, 245, 286
  so dark, 221, 437, 451

Gallant band, 385
Galvanised, 234, 245, 251, 272, 371
Gather momentum, 372
Generation tormented, 37
Genesis, 461
  of world order, 385
Geneva, 86, 98, 110, 130, 181
Genuineness, 131
George, Mrs. Florence, 256, 485
George, Mrs. Prudence, 202, 479
German, 180, 221, 335
Germany, 14, 18, 40, 47, 97-8
Geyserville, U.S.A., 97
Giddings, Mrs. Joan, 194, 478
Gilbert and Ellice Islands, 365
Ginman, Mrs. Louise, Madam Charlot, 63, 224, 471
Gird up its loins, 271-2, 311, 408

INDEX 501

Establishment, 138, 141, 145, 394
Ethiopia, 273, 323, 333
Ethnic elements, 215
Europe, European Continent, centres, peoples, 67, 77, 98, 177, 208, 221, 245, 253, 265, 292, 297, 298, 309, 311–12, 326–7, 338–9, 385, 433, 456
  and Asian Committee, 327
  influence of Islám in, 456
  Intercontinental Teaching Conference, Stockholm, 287, 308, 315–20 (message to Conference not indexed)
  war, 176–7
Events, of startling character, 75
  two major, in England, 97
Ever brighter beacon, 150
Every avenue, effort, sacrifice, 171
Evidences of growth, vitality, 147, 150, 223
Evil, 447, 458; forces of, 442
Evolution, 458
Example, 172, 210, 260, 321, 334, 366, 418; heroic, noble, 143
Example of our daily lives, 14
Exceptions not made, 253
Exchange of news, 10, 51
Exemplary, pioneers, 365; servants, 142
Exemption from combatant service, 122, 128–9, 134, 259
Exercise vigilance, 123
Exertions, 137, 144, 252, 272, 312, 345
Exhaustion, 226, 232
Exhibitions, exhibits, 20–1, 130, 171–2
Expansion, 113–15, 119, 158, 186, 189, 196, 205, 215, 223, 229, 239, 254, 287, 310, 314, 331, 360, 371, 377, 379–80, 384, 415
Expelled, 174
Expenses increasing, 324
Experienced, 10
Extension of activities, 139, 142, 145, 174, 204, 206, 299, 353, 392, 397, 399, 405, 410–11
Exultation, 250
Eyes of posterity, 252

Failures, 447
Faith, 34, 137, 164, 178, 214, 225, 235, 270, 353, 436, 438, 440–1, 452, 460
Faithfulness, 275
Faithful, 125, 352
Families, 191, 351
Fan flame pioneering spirit, 291
Far East, 370
Faroe Islands, 297, 321
Fasting, 440, 444, 457

Fearlessness, 139, 369
Fellow countrymen, 137
Fellowship, 119
Ferraby, Mrs. Dorothy, 184, 320, 332, 349, 381, 476
Ferraby, John, Hand of the Cause, 250, 320, 332, 341, 346, 348–50, 356–7, 359, 362–4, 378, 387, 485
Fervour, 288
Fidelity, 111, 133, 140, 260, 263, 281, 287–8, 307, 314, 370, 412
Final phase, 211, 215, 219–20, 224, 226, 229, 237
Finances, 381; difficulties, 112–13, 178, 452
  for pioneers, 173, 262
  for Publishing Trust, 114–15
  our gift to mankind, 274
Firm foundations, 16, 125, 206, 262, 312, 412
Firmly, grounded, 384–5
  knit, 210, 220, 245, 270
Firmness, of National Assembly, 129, 174, 180
First, African Teaching Conference, 257, 262, 264, 272
  Bahá'í Century, 157–162, 164–6
  British Convention, 70
  charter of liberty, 66
  collective enterprise, 173, 214, 219–21, 226, 231, 233–4, 245, 250, 271, 284, 287, 297, 310
  concepts of pioneering, 156–8
  crusade affecting four national assemblies, 261
  English Summer School, 110
  European country able to help, 177
  fires enkindled Uganda, 302
  fruit overseas mission, 355
  glimpses overseas enterprises, 245
  International Council World Centre, 257
  letter signed, "R. Rabbání", 143
  mention of, Africa Conference, 257; Assemblies of Scotland, Ireland, 189, Wales, 192; rôle throughout British Empire, 196; work in Africa, 163
  pioneer to Tanganyika, 261, 271, 459
  pioneers to arise, 172
  public meeting, Cardiff, 393
  references to, British National Headquarters, 163; collaboration of all National Assemblies (ten year Crusade), 257
  Regional Youth Conference (Nottingham), 196

Divine, -ly (cont.)
  blessings, 199
  confirmations, 178, 239, 436
  guidance, 133, 203, 263, 385
  Love, 406
  Message, 174, 201, 446
  outpourings, 169, 223
  promise, 57
  purpose, 58
  retribution, 53
  Revelation, xi, 454
  source, 173
  Station of Muḥammad, 66, 432
Divorce, 66, 284, 346, 361, 368, 435
Djibouti, French Somaliland, 346–7
Doctors, 446
Dominions, 264
Doors of servitude, 178
Do our part, 409
Double task, see two-fold
Drastic measures, 223
Dreyfus-Barney, H., 12, 84–5
Drinking, 308
Dublin, 202, 206, 211, 219, 394, 397; this historic assembly, 398
Dunning, Charles, Knight of Bahá'u'lláh, 211, 322, 481
Dutch Bahá'í, 182
Duty, 180, 187, 191, 196, 262, 287, 338–9, 355, 369–71, 385, 445, 447, 452
Dynamic principles, 4

Early heroes, 146
Earnestness, 29, 384
East, 12, 21, 34, 38, 51–2, 57, 79–80, 82–3, 100, 130, 145, 147, 176, 190, 198, 200, 208, 210–11, 226, 232, 234, 248, 253, 257, 260, 290, 297, 309, 353, 366, 369, 385, 424, 430
  regeneration of, 75
East Africa, see Africa
Eccles, 399
Ecclesiastical authorities, 65, 340, 379
Eden, Anthony, 127
Edifice, 29, 144, 149–50, 156, 286
Edinburgh, 195, 206, 210–11, 219, 394, 399, 400, 418
  Mother Assembly of Scotland, 400
  to assist all future Scottish assemblies, 400
Ego, 453–4
Egypt, 8, 12, 65–6, 80, 85, 98, 101–2, 245, 248, 251, 253, 257, 264–6, 273, 277, 323, 329
Eire, see Ireland

Elections, 5, 62–3, 72, 421, 455; Bahá'í, 72, 138
Eleventh hour, 232, 237, 293
Elston, Alan and Mary, 334
Emancipation, 61, 66, 67, 85
Embryonic, World Order, 386
Emergency, 122, 128
Emerge from obscurity, 35, 78, 366, 385
Emperor of Japan, 423
Empire, British, see British Empire
Empire more glorious, 246
Encourage by correspondence, 409
Endanger Faith, 174
Endowments, local, national, 221, 298, 339, 341, 347, 350, 352, 354, 361, 367
Enemies of the Cause, 34, 38, 67–8
Energetically prosecuting, 173, 384
England, English, 12, 14, 17–19, 22, 25, 31–2, 37, 39–40, 53, 61, 80, 88, 97–9, 104–5, 107, 109–10, 114, 118, 131, 134, 137, 140, 152, 154, 163–4, 169, 172, 177, 185–6, 191, 194–6, 201, 209, 214, 217, 219–20, 231, 237, 245, 250–1, 262, 268, 272, 286–7, 297–8, 310–12, 320, 328, 335, 346–7, 353, 357, 366, 373–4, 377, 403–4, 410, 434, 437–8, 441, 443, 445, 448, 451–2
  so important a country, 164
Enlarging numbers, 150
Enterprises, 128, 171, 178, 180, 182–3, 186, 197, 201, 206, 208, 221–2, 227, 232, 234, 238, 245, 251–2, 254, 257, 260–1, 265, 271, 283, 287, 297, 339, 355, 369–70, 384, 393
Enthusiasm, 126, 134, 181, 205, 275, 283, 346, 370, 404
Epistle to the Son of the Wolf, 456
Epoch, 191, 201, 211, 233, 254, 261–2, 264, 270, 288, 299
Epyeru, Enos, 301
Eritrea, 278
Esperanto, 48
Essays (Balyuzi), 122
Essential verities, 385, 447, 458
Esslemont, Dr. J. E., Hand of the Cause, 9, 12, 31, 36, 40–7, 54, 94, 130, 377, 467
  one of three luminaries, 377
Esslemont, Peter, 248
Esslingen, Germany, 97–8
Established religious systems, 65
Establish families, 191
Establishing assemblies, 181–2, 185, 187, 188–9

INDEX

Critical period, human history, 271, 370, 457
Critical stage/s of Plan, 186, 208, 221–2, 225, 232
Criticise, 125, 379
Cropper, Mrs., *see* Thornburgh-Cropper
Crucial year, 194–5, 198, 200, 384
Crusade for World Government Movement, 213
Crusades, 221, 229, 233, 257, 261, 264–5, 270, 272, 285, 290–2, 297–8, 312
Custodians of the Faith, 155
Customs of other Religions, 446
Curzon, Lord, 425
Cynosure, 260
Cyprus, 297, 305, 320

Daily sustenance, 386
Danger, personal, 144–5, 259
Dangerous, 139, 350, 434
Daniel, book of, 272
Dar-es-Salaam, 277, 279, 283, 314, 341, 460
Dark, and bright, side of life, 457–8
Dark Continent, 245, 251
Darkness, forces of, 33, 482
Daughter communities, 369, 386
Dauntless faith, 58
Dawn-Breakers, The, 425–8, 433
Daylight saving time disregarded, 170
Day, final phase, 224
Days, of anxiety, commotion, danger, ordeal, peril, storm, strain, stress, trial, turmoil, uncertainty, 122, 135, 137–8, 143, 146–7, 153, 157, 170, 405, 437–8, 441
Days dark yet historic, 173, 437
Dead Sea Scrolls, 387
Debt of gratitude, 146, 210, 252
Declaration, of intention at age 15, 335
of Trust, 98, 100–1
Dedication, 179–80, 186, 211, 226, 232, 234, 249, 254, 283, 285, 291, 324, 339, 371, 373, 381
Deeds, title, land Mt. Carmel, 328
Deepen knowledge, essentials World Order, 410
Deepen understanding of essentials, 410
Deep religious feelings, of Irish, 397–8 of Scots, 399
Defection, 174
Defence, 141
Delegates, *see* National Convention
Deliberations, 256, 402
Denison House, 171

Dependencies, 245, 263, 270, 285, 297, 299, 311–12, 338, 386
Depriving thirsty souls, 442
Deputisation implied, 179, 185–6
Despondent, 447
Destiny, 171, 180, 188, 196, 214, 220–1, 227, 229, 233, 249, 252, 260, 271–2, 286, 289, 313–14, 338, 353, 384
Detachment, 6, 338, 353, 384
Determination, 120, 131, 134, 141, 147, 161, 171, 174, 195, 200, 202, 214–15, 225, 229, 236, 258, 271, 311, 314, 333, 345, 361, 370–1, 385, 387, 393, 401, 408–9, 449
Development, 174, 191, 193, 196, 233, 262, 284, 312, 338, 340, 354, 360, 370, 400
Devonshire, 116
Devotion, 7, 10, 15, 113, 117, 123, 131, 133, 143, 151–3, 155, 164, 172, 174, 181, 198, 204–5, 214, 219, 232, 260, 270–2, 275, 282–3, 301, 306, 321, 331, 333, 343, 345, 351, 367, 369, 377, 384, 398, 408–11, 415, 431, 433, 438, 447
Diary, 163, 268, 364
Difference, between character and faith, 440–1
Difficulties, 74, 94, 110, 112, 124, 152, 164, 177, 202, 217, 222, 225, 238, 392, 394, 431, 446
in Egypt, 66–7
of teaching in England, 73, 92, 107, 434
Dignity, 4, 7, 412
Diligently, 331
Disappointments, 422
Discharge debts, 173
Disciples of Christ, 34
Dismissal, 141
Disobedience, 174
Dispensation of Bahá'u'lláh, 93, 224
Dispensation of Providence, 370
Disperse themselves, 34, 174
Displays, 130
Dissatisfaction with officers, 141
Dissemination Bahá'í literature, 171, 246, 262, 265, 339, 370–1, 385
Dissipation of resources, 211
Distant, field, 369; future, 452
Distinct mark, 128
Distinguished member British community, 382
Disunity deprives thirsty souls, 442
Diversity, 215; in secondary matters, 102
Divine, -ly, appointed institutions, 174, 261, 375

Commendation, 337
Committees, 190, 218–19; to elect own officers, 212
  Africa, 254, 258, 274–5, 277, 280–1, 300–1, 328–31, 351
  Asian, 298, 327
  Assembly development, 204–6
  Child education, 205
  Consolidation, 254
  European Teaching, 298, 327
  National Teaching, *see* National Teaching Committee
  National Youth, 187–8, 192–3, 197, 202, 204, 236, 279
  Reviewing, 126
  Summer School, 235
Commonwealth, 384
Commotion, 153
Communications, 190
Community, 205, 439, 445, 447; life enriched, 151, 215
Comoro Islands, 299
Company, Publishing, 114–16
Compensation, 233, 459
Compilation of Tablets, 163, 224
Complex tasks, 339
Concentration, 338
Concourse on High, 153, 201, 210–11, 245, 311
Condolences, 333
Conduct, 4, 52, 384; disapproved, 199; of Spiritual Assemblies, 6, 7
Conferences, Africa Intercontinental, *see* Africa
  European Intercontinental, *see* Europe
  County, 402
  "Living religions within the British Empire", 17, 19, 20, 24–7, 29
  National Teaching, *see* National Teaching Conferences
  "World Fellowship through Religion", 104–5, 109
Confidence, 135, 178, 225, 252, 288, 340, 436
Confirmation, 178, 345
Confusion, 141, 225, 252, 310
Congo, Belgian, 297, 299, 300; French, Equatorial Africa, 299, 300
Congratulations, 238, 241, 263, 279, 293, 325, 363, 369, 394, 416
Conquer, *see* Citadels
Conquerors, 456
Conquest, 286
Conscience, 170, 259
Conscientious, duty, 129; objectors, 435–6

Consecration, 121, 134, 214, 220, 227, 229, 232, 240, 260, 272, 287, 297, 312, 343, 369–70, 373–4, 385
Consideration, 49, 395
Consolidation, 113, 115–16, 118, 123, 125, 162, 173, 186, 189, 196, 206, 215, 221, 223, 236, 245, 251, 256, 259, 268–70, 276, 278, 286, 291, 297, 311, 314, 329–30, 336, 339–41, 353–4, 359, 362, 374–5, 379, 384, 397, 400–1, 405, 410–11, 417–18
Constancy, 117, 149
Constantinople, 78
Consultation, 5–7, 16, 194, 256, 284
Continents, -al, 261, 264–5, 276, 285, 288, 297, 299, 311, 352–3, 385–6
Convention, *see* National Convention
Conviction, 140, 401
Co-operation, 4, 179, 226, 231, 245, 251, 253, 257–8, 264, 269, 273, 285, 304, 308–9, 365, 408
  Britain, America, 86, 245–6, 253, 256–7
  Britain, Germany, 98–9
  Britain, Paris, 99
  local assemblies, 120
  sister communities, 245, 251, 253–4, 256–8, 285
  with World Congress of Faiths, 206–7
Co-ordination, 131, 208, 261, 308, 338
Copyright, 99
Cordiality, 421
Cormick, Dr., 428
Council, National, 9–11
Courage, 110, 125, 133, 137, 139, 142, 153, 195, 208, 212, 233, 249, 287, 369, 393, 422, 430, 452
Counties, 209, 286
Countries, list of, *see* Annex "A"
Courtesy, 7
Court of First Instance, 248
Covenant, 67, 235, 245, 250, 270, 337, 385, 461
  Compilation on, 224
  violators of, 149, 174, 180, 254, 268; Sohrab, Ahmad, 218, 254, 364–5, 383; their contaminating influence, 180, 218
Cradle of a civilisation, 221
Craney, Geraldine, Knight of Bahá'u'lláh, 323
Craven, John, 416, 490
Creativity, 461
Credentials, essential, 190, 283; not to those without rights, 213

INDEX

Canada, 22, 65, 81, 253, 335
Capable, 10, 386, 433
Capitals and chief cities, 209, 211, 271, 338, 353, 400
Caravan, 365, 383
Cardell, Edmund (Ted), 281, 283, 488
Cardiff, 184, 209, 219, 347, 393–6
Care, 7, 204
Carmel, Mount, see Mount Carmel
Carnegie, Andrew, 207, 212
Catastrophic trials, 454
Catholic, Roman, 290
Caucasus, 12
Caution with Orientals, 190, 207
Censure, conflicting discussions, cooling remarks, 4
Centenary celebrations, 386
   of Birth Bahá'u'lláh's Prophetic Mission, 246, 251, 264, 267, 270, 272, 275, 283, 285, 287, 297, 311, 352, 386
   of Declaration of the Báb, 158–66, 170–2, 220, 234, 311, 386; actions to be taken, 159; pamphlets for, 158–60, 162–3, 170, 272, 285
   of Declaration of Bahá'u'lláh, Baghdád, "Most Great Jubilee", 272, 285, 297–8, 386
   of Martyrdom of the Báb, 230–1, 234, 237, 240, 246, 254, 271, 386; offer to extend Six Year Plan to, 240
Centenary of a World Faith, The, 170
Central and East Africa, see National/Regional National Spiritual Assemblies
Central pivot, 265
Centre, new London Bahá'í, 86–8, 163, 403
Centres, new, 171–2, 196, 287, 289, 301
Challenge, 113, 178, 223, 225, 264, 285, 313, 339, 353, 361, 363, 371, 381, 384, 398
Challis, Sister Grace, 88, 216, 218, 471
Champions of the Cause of God, 146, 340, 437
Channel Islands, 297, 305, 322
Character, 438, 440–2
Charlot, Madam, see Mrs. L. Ginman
Cheek, Robert, 191, 222, 478
Cheer their hearts, 142
Cheyne, Canon, 416
Chicago, 5
Chief, Builders, 386
   dependencies and islands, 285, 311
   objectives, 171, 338
Child Education Committee, see Committees

Children, 154, 205, 335, 373, 440, 444, 446
   classes for, 205
   teaching by, 440
China, 8, 67, 251
Chinyanza, 237, 258
Chiríq, 427
Chosen Highway (Blomfield), 138, 141–2
Chosen ones of God, 80, 82
Chosen path, 252
Christ and Bahá'u'lláh (Townshend), 379, 382
Christ, Jesus, 405, 421, 426, 440, 456
Christian, 131, 135, 379, 421, 427, 446
   church membership, 350
   church officials, 135, 379, 382
   clergy, 442
   dispensation, 432–3
   missionaries, 300
   missions, 290
Citadels of mens' hearts, 371
Citizens, loyal and devoted, 122
City State, 456
Civil, authorities, 262–3, 287, 290, 340
   laws, in conflict, 346
   limits to be observed (boundaries), 348, 363, 366–7, 381
Civilisation, 70, 221, 330
Clamour, of the multitudes, 67
   of the age, 252
Clash of differing opinions, 6, 7
Clear visioned, 270, 352
Cling tenaciously, 123
Closed circles, 123
Clouds of war, 145
Coal, 203
Coherance, 385
Coleman, Mrs. Doris, 397
Coles, Mrs. Claudia, 88, 471
Collaboration all National Assemblies, 257, 264
Collecting Tablets, 89, 90
Collective enterprise, 173, 178, 180, 214, 245
Collins, Mrs. Amelia, Hand of the Cause, 98, 234
Collison, Rex, Mary, Knights of Bahá'u'lláh, 303
Colonial Office, 359, 365, 370
Colonies, 221, 264, 297, 308, 312
Colophenes, 424
Colossal responsibility, 385
Colour film, 292
Combatant, non-, 122, 128–9, 134, 259
Coming of the Glory (Pinchon), 72–3
Commemorations, time of, 170

Bounties, 285, 288
Bournemouth, 9, 13, 62, 64, 127, 161, 188, 224
Bradford, 126, 133, 156
Brahma Somaj, 19, 20
Breakwell, Thomas, one of three luminaries, 377
Brentano, 72
Brief an interval, 369
Brightness, 18
Brighton, 127, 217
Brilliant feat, 211
Bristol, 391–2
Britain, Great, British Isles, *see* British Isles
British Bahá'í History, *see* History
British Bahá'í Community, xii, xiii, xiv, xv, xvi, xvii, 20, 27, 29, 30, 49, 59, 109, 121, 133, 136, 138–9, 141–3, 152, 166, 170, 172–3, 178–80, 182, 186, 188–92, 196, 200–1, 203, 206, 208, 210–11, 215, 219, 221–3, 225–6, 229–30, 233–4, 237–41, 245–6, 249–51, 258–62, 264–5, 269–71, 279–80, 282, 284–5, 287–9, 291–3, 297, 299, 307, 310–13, 326, 332, 337, 339–40, 347–8, 351, 353, 355, 364, 366, 369, 371, 376, 379, 381, 384–7, 403, 410, 445, 448–9, 452
an example, 366
Champions of the Cause of God, 146
effect on sister communities, 198, 200, 210, 226, 232, 241, 245, 251
exemplary servants, 142
Guardian's concern for safety of, *see* Guardian
increasingly prominent position, 160
more pioneering per capita, 374
position occupied by, 288, 384
qualities of, *see* "Annex C"
registration of, 106
re-vitalised, triumphant, 198
the chief agency, responsibility, prosecution significant task, 261
their hard-won prominence, 269, 282, 366
their maturity, 355
their most distinguished collaborator, 371; member, 382
well tried, stout hearted, firmly knit, 166, 208
British Cameroons, 297
British Commonwealth, 285, 305, 384
British Crown, 245, 251–2, 263–4, 270, 285–6, 288, 292, 299, 311–12, 338, 353, 384, 386
British Dominions, 285

British Empire, 114, 187, 196, 201, 208, 220–1, 227, 246, 259, 263, 270, 285, 288, 297–8, 312–13, 338, 340, 353, 384
Exhibition, 20–21
British fairness and justice, 38
British Isles, British, Great Britain, 9, 11–12, 59, 62, 99, 103, 106, 109, 113–14, 119–21, 143, 145–6, 153, 155, 158, 160, 170, 178, 191, 195–6, 198, 201, 204, 207–8, 210–14, 216, 219–21, 225, 229–32, 234–7, 240–1, 245–6, 250–1, 253, 259, 262–5, 267, 269–70, 284–9, 291–2, 298, 302, 306, 311–14, 321, 331, 335, 339, 347–8, 351, 354, 359, 362, 367, 370–2, 374–5, 377, 379, 382, 384–6, 391–4, 398, 400, 402–3, 420, 429, 441, 452–3
Dependencies of, 245
land blessed with freedom, 355
people, shrewd, 207, slow to move, 351, spiritual re-awakening, 15
British mandate authorities, 248
British Press, 55, 59, 80, 230, 370
British Somaliland, 323, 347
British summer schools, *see* Schools
British Togoland, 297, 324
Broadcast the Teachings, 443
Broaden the base, 245
Browne, Prof. E. G., 423, 433
Brown, Kathleen, *see* Lady Hornell
Brussels, 181
Budapest, 458
Budgetting (N.S.A.), 212
Build for the future, 190
Building scheme, 146
Bulletin, national teaching committee, 103
Burdens, 157, 164, 285, 310
Burial ground, 341
Burma, 85
Burning bush, 448
Buxton, 154

Cairo, 8, 429
Calamity, 141
Calculations lunar solar years, 432
Calibre of Faith, 154
Caliphate and Sultanate, 78
Calm and determination, 10
Cambridge, 331, 381
Campbell, Miss Jean, 414, 489
Campaigns, Empire, overseas, 196, 245–6, 260, 262, 265, 268, 270, 288, 297–9, 333
Plans, Teaching, *see* Teaching

INDEX

Bahá'u'lláh, His, Administrative Order (*cont.*)
  commemorated, 56, 170; poisoning by His half-brother, 460; proclamation, 78; prophecies, 20, 75, 108; reinforcing power, 182, 286, 459; spirit to guide and sustain, 131, 179, 197, 205, 375, 396, 433; sustaining grace, 187, 229, 245, 263, 286, 300, 392; Tablet of the Holy Mariner, 462; Tablet of the Virgin, 336; Tablet of Visitation, 443; Tablet to the Christians, 226; unfailing assistance, guidance, 127, 200; wisdom, 406; Writings, quotations, 6, 82, 163, 224, 260
  inner sanctuary of His Tomb, 306
  lands associated with, 75
  Most Great Jubilee of, 272, 285, 298, 386
  only Bahá'ís can do His work, 444
  publication dates His Writings, 424, 429, 430
  put trust in Him, 191
  the greatest Manifestation, 448
  "the youth", in Tablet of Holy Mariner, 462
  unity with Revelation of The Báb, 426–7
  unsealed springs, 147
  watching over them, 141, 233, 260, 397, 400
  witness to the power of, 459
Bahá'u'lláh (Balyuzi), 122
Bahá'u'lláh and the New Era (Esslemont), 12, 43, 54, 97, 130, 259
  a real landmark, 97
Bahá'u'lláh The King of Glory (Balyuzi), 490
Bahjí, 95, 127, 132, 141, 170, 249, 258, 268, 349
Bahrein, 282
Baker, Mrs. Dorothy, Hand of the Cause, 210, 333, 413
Baker, Richard St. Barbe, O.B.E., 163, 216, 474
Balkans, 98
Balyuzi, Ḥasan M., Hand of the Cause, ix, 122, 363, 473, 490
Banání, Músá, Hand of the Cause (and Mrs. Samíḥih), 257, 266, 277, 283, 303, 347, 351, 356, 486
Barclays Bank, 189
Barred from the Path of God, 458
Basil-Hall, Mrs. Mary, "Parvine", 127, 164, 239, 246, 473
Basis, 201, 211, 245

Basis (*cont.*)
  of allocation of delegates, 197
  of ordered society rocking, 137
Baxter, Miss Evelyn, Knight of Bahá'u'lláh, 117, 211, 322, 472
Beacons of the Faith, 161, 173
Beginning, 125
Belfast, a key assembly, 211, 391
Belgian Congo, 297, 299, 305
Believers, numbers of, *see* Numbers
  dropped from voting list, 184
  love, patience, forgiveness, individually, 449
  qualifications of, 71, 335, 444
  relation to each other, 449
  those who cannot obey or accept, not considered Bahá'ís, 444
  to turn to Assemblies, 145
Benes, ex-President, 152
Bennett, Miss Irene, 321
Berry, Dr., 333
Bible translations, 378
Biggs. Rev., 71
Biographies, xvii, 467–490
Birmingham, 127, 194–5, 374
Bishop, Mrs., 98, 109–10, 112, 116, 118
Blackburn, 325
Blackpool, 205, 217, 279
Bless, 128–9, 135, 138, 141, 170–1, 188, 193, 197, 203, 205, 229, 236, 278, 280, 303, 391, 393, 395–7, 399, 401–2, 405, 407–8, 410–11, 413, 415–16, 418, 441, 446
Blessed, 227, 297, 330, 371
Blessings, 145, 147, 158, 162, 201–2, 208, 210, 223–5, 232–3, 254, 256, 269, 272, 276, 314, 326, 340, 380, 396, 410, 417–18, 438, 445
  in disguise, 51, 104
  of Bahá'u'lláh, 113, 137, 153, 170, 193, 394
  of God, 109, 199, 204, 223, 404
Blissful era, 385–6
Blomfield, Lady Sara, Sitárih Khánum, 30, 120, 136–9, 141–2, 469
Blum, Mr. and Mrs., 360
Board of Trade, 72, 103, 124
Bombay, 424
Book Exhibition, *Sunday Times*, 130
Booklet, 120, 281
Book of Acts, 290
  of Daniel, 2
  of Genesis, 461
Boroughs, 286
Boundaries, for local assemblies, 185, 348, 363, 366–7, 381

INDEX

Bahá'í Dispensation, 245, 264, 270–1, 290, 311
Bahá'í divorce, 284, 435
Bahá'í exhibition, 130
Bahá'í Faith, Movement, Cause, 12–13, 16, 23, 31–2, 35, 50–1, 56, 60, 66–7, 70, 75, 77, 80, 83, 85, 113, 143, 145, 152–3, 179, 186, 192–3, 196, 201, 205, 221–2, 227, 229–31, 234, 251–3, 264, 272, 285–6, 288, 290, 301, 309, 311–12, 329–30, 333, 337–8, 354, 366, 368, 370, 383–4, 386–7, 391, 394, 397, 399, 401–3, 411, 423, 426, 444, 447, 461
  basic principle of, 102
  declared "heresy", "new religion", "entirely independent", 65, 66, 231
  deepening in, 274, 280, 385, 415, 445, 452
  dignified presentation of, 21
  growing force for good, 423
  hesitation to embrace, causes of, 408
  its, essential verities, 385; healing message, 288; independence, 65, 66, 231; origins, 426; welding and assimilative power, 215
  needs, able devoted souls, 431; first class literature, 428, 431
  no creeds in, 423
  nothing to do with Caravan, 383
  one of its stoutest defenders, 377
  progress of, in Britain, 87–8, 93, 102, 116, 152–3, 194, 198, 210, 220–1, 226–7, 229, 234, 240, 245–6, 250–1, 262–3, 269–71, 284, 286–7, 298, 312, 314, 337–8, 359, 366, 394, 396–7, 441; assemblies, localities to be doubled, 298
  significant event in its evolution, 261
  to be, accepted in its entirety, 71; kept broad and progressive, 422
  upheld and attacked, 437
Bahá'í history, 97, 128, 158, 172–3, 180, 182, 189, 191, 195, 198, 201, 208, 211, 214, 227, 234, 238, 245, 250, 262, 271, 285, 291
Bahá'í International Council, 257, 261, 268, 288
Bahá'í Journal, 114–17, 119–20, 130, 135, 138, 144
Bahá'í laws, when in conflict with civil law, 346
Bahá'í libraries, 130, 268, 395
Bahá'í marriage certificate, 248
Bahá'í procedure, 190, 435
Bahá'í public relations, 228

Bahá'í Publishing Trust, *see* Publishing Trust
Bahá'í News, India, 12
Bahá'í refugees, 126, 127
Bahá'í Revelation, 426, 427
Bahá'í Schools, *see* Schools
Bahá'í Scripture, 208, 336, 462
Bahá'í Statistics, *see* Statistics
Bahá'í Youth, *see* Youth
Bahá'í Youth Bulletin, *see* Youth
Bahá'í wedding, 139, 383
Bahá'í world, 211, 214, 216, 230, 232, 240–1, 245, 251, 257, 261, 269, 279–80, 303, 306, 311, 321, 334, 354–5, 386
  announcement of "Knights" to, 306
Bahá'í World, originally *Bahá'í Year Book*, 64, 83, 98, 105–6, 120, 163
  contents, 98, 105, 106, 120, 127, 132, 135, 137–9, 183–4, 212, 249, 412, 416, 423
  International editors, 120
  its purpose, 83, 423
Bahá'ís and War, 135
Bahá'íyyih Khánum, *see* Greatest Holy Leaf.
Bahá'u'lláh, xi, 4–6, 9–12, 14, 16, 20, 22–3, 30, 32, 34–5, 43, 53, 56, 60, 65–6, 77–83, 85, 92, 106–8, 134, 140–2, 148–9, 151–3, 166, 170, 173–4, 177–8, 180, 185, 188, 191, 193, 201, 209, 211, 214–15, 221–2, 226, 229, 235, 237–40, 245, 248, 259–60, 262, 264, 272, 280, 282, 286, 291, 293, 306, 310–11, 330, 336–7, 355, 362, 366, 368, 369, 387, 392, 396, 400, 406, 411, 412, 424–8, 430–4, 436, 438, 440–4, 446–8, 450–1, 454, 456–8, 460–2
  almighty power of, 115
  blessings, confirmations of, 103, 108, 113, 170, 180, 182, 195, 197, 411
  booklet on, (Balyuzi), 122
  constructive, dynamic principles of, 4
  exalted Teachings of, 129
  force, mentioned by Him, not known, 456
  His, Administrative Order, xi, 131, 144, 261, 285, 338, 386, 408; army, 157; Baghdád House, 37–9, 44–6, 60, 85; claims greater, 406; creative, all-conquering power, 208, 400, 459; invincible Faith, 80, 145; Laws, 261; Mansion at Bahjí, *see* Bahjí; Message, 58, 83, 106–7, 173, 185, 288, 395; mysterious purpose, 286; Passing

INDEX 493

Anatolia, 79
Angola, 297
Anguish, 144
Answer, for everything in the Teachings, 439
Anti-Russian, 213
Anti-social conduct, 451
Anxiety, 137, 140, 145, 147, 402, 422
Apathy, 434
Apostolic age, 245
Appeals, 38, 50, 128, 157, 211, 222–4, 229, 237, 239–40, 256, 278, 293, 345, 347, 362, 376
Appeal to the masses, 174, 186, 191, 196
Appointed time, 196, 201
Appreciation, 146, 169, 174, 184, 189, 193–4, 196–7, 202, 206, 208–9, 211, 216–18, 222, 236, 238–40, 256, 263–4, 267, 276, 279, 289–92, 302, 320–4, 343, 346–7, 357, 361, 374, 379, 397, 401, 405, 407, 410, 412, 430, 447
Approval, 170
 of N.S.A. for all Bahá'í publications, 382
Aqdas, see Kitáb-i-Aqdas,
Arastu, Mírzá, 41
Archives, 143, 163, 350
Ardent, 384, 397
Ardibíl, Írán, 68
Areas mentioned, see Annex "A",
Arise, 177, 179, 182, 186, 191, 200, 222–3, 233, 333, 371
 as one soul, 227
 to pioneer, 172
 to teach, 35
Army, 134
Articles, of Association, 199
 on the Faith, essential features, 21
Ascension, of Bahá'u'lláh, 170
 of 'Abdu'l-Bahá, 170, 220
Asceticism condemned, 435
Aşgharzádih, Ḍiá'u'lláh, Knight of Bahá'u'lláh, 24, 72, 98, 322, 340, 363, 468
Ashanti Protectorate, 305
Asia, 85, 260, 298, 311–12, 327, 329
Assemblies, spiritual, general, see Spiritual Assemblies
 local, see Local spiritual assemblies
 national, see National spiritual assemblies
Asembly Development Committee, see Committees
Assiduously, 196, 198, 352
Assistance, 10, 171, 173, 177–8, 185, 195,

Assistance (cont.)
 209, 231–2, 254–6, 262, 309, 314, 323, 370, 394, 433, 436
Assistant secretary, 288, 364
Association not affiliation, 113
Association sister communities, see Sister communities,
Assurance, 152, 225, 452
Astonish Bahá'í world, 386
Atlantic Ocean, 354
Atrocities, 53, 55
Attacks, 301, 439, 457
Attendance at Feasts, 380
Attitude towards war, 128, 129
Audacity, 187
Auspicious stage, 115
Australia, 18, 37, 41, 96, 245, 453
Austria, 98, 221
Author, distinguished Bahá'í, 382
Authorities, London, 308
 obedience to, 128, 134
Ávárih, Jináb-i-, 13
Awakening of the masses, 384

Báb, The (Siyyid 'Alí-Muḥammad), 42, 68, 77, 234, 237, 245, 251, 271, 291, 359, 406, 425–8, 433
 Cormick, Dr., only Westerner to meet Him and make record, 428
 essay on, (Balyuzi), 122
 His, Declaration, time of, 159; Portrait, 291–2; Shrine, sepulchre, 166, 215, 225, 247, 250, 254–5, 267, 280–1, 284, 292, 321, 374, 400; Tablet to Bahá'u'lláh, 428; Writings, 224, 261, 357, 368, 426, 428
 Mde. Grinevskaya's play of, 161
 tribute to His memory, 245
 unity with Bahá'u'lláh, 426
Backwell, Richard H., xiii, 218, 228, 483
Baghdád, 37–9, 44–6, 60, 85, 386, 427, 430
"Bahá'í", name to be advertised widely, 438, 439
Bahá'í Administration, letters also printed in, xvii, 3, 27, 33, 38, 42, 49, 51, 56, 59, 65, 68, 75, 82, 84, 148
Bahá'í Bureau, Geneva, 98, 130, 182, 216
Bahá'í Centres (buildings), Africa, 301
 London, 86–8, 105–6, 130, 163, 183, 185, 238, 254, 443
 Manchester, 405
 Oxford, 415
Bahá'í conception of social life, 436
Bahá'í Council, first all-England, 9
Bahá'í declaration of children, 335

Administration (cont.)
  205, 207, 209, 213, 215, 257, 260, 298, 305, 310–11, 333, 335, 338, 341, 352–4, 367, 371, 384, 385, 400, 435, 441, 447, 449
  to be flexible, 213, 333
Administrative, agencies, base, 276, 311–12, 353–4
  headquarters, 163, 270, 310, 313, 371
  Order, xi, 102, 114, 131, 137, 148, 196, 201, 211, 215, 220–1, 245–6, 261, 263, 270–1, 290, 312, 314, 337, 339, 354, 366, 386; its significance to be included in written works, 435
Administrators, 198, 207, 272, 301, 303, 313, 339, 371, 375, 381, 438, 441
Admiration, of the Guardian, 137, 139, 140–7, 151, 155, 170, 191–2, 203, 210, 224, 286, 330, 337, 340, 349, 353, 366, 393, 399, 403, 407, 409
  of their brethren, 226, 288, 311, 352, 386
Adrianople, Turkey, 427
Adultery, 368
Advancement, 401, 438
Advent, 385
Adventures, 287
Advertise name "Bahá'í" widely, 438, 439
Advice to Bahá'ís in British Colonies, 359
Affiliation not permissible, 113
Afflictions, only remedy for, 172
  part of human life, 460
Afghánistán, 77
Afnán and Aghsán, 248
Afnán, Dr. 'Abbás and Shomais, 278, 282–3, 323, 333, 487
Afnán, Fuad, 144, 159
Africa, campaign inaugurated, launched, 260, 265, see Two Year Plan
  Committee, see Committees
  Continent, 67, 163, 216, 245–6, 251, 253, 255–60, 262–5, 268–71, 273–6, 278, 280, 283, 285, 287, 290–2, 297–305, 308–9, 311–13, 329–30, 332, 334, 348, 355, 363, 368, 370–2, 384, 453, 458, 459–60
  contribution to world civilisation, 330
  Conventions, 352
  East, 245, 265, 279, 281, 353–4, 370
  feats in, to be thrown into shade, 384
  Heart, 262, 264, 279, 285, 290, 311, 334, 353–5, 369–70
  North, 12, 262, 264–5
  South, 216, 262, 264
  Teaching conferences, 257, 262, 264, 267, 269, 272–5, 277, 281, 283–5,

Africa, Teaching conferences (cont.)
  287, 291–3, 300, 363; consultations at, 281; portrait of Báb exhibited at, 291–2; special sessions, N.S.A. representatives at, 277, 284
  teaching in, 458, 459
  truly awakening, 330
  vast, dark, spiritually decadent, 264
  West, 245, 265, 353–4, 370
Africa News, 358
African, Bahá'í community, 299
  languages, 237, 246, 253, 258, 262, 265, 271–2, 275, 284, 287, 290, 292–3, 298, 300–2, 306, 309, 313, 320, 323–4, 329–30, 333, 339, 349, 354, 360, 370, 378
  local assemblies to be incorporated, 339
  pamphlets, see Pamphlets
  pioneers, whole object to teach native Africans, 330, 458–9
  races, 371
  territories, 264–5, 269, 273, 279, 285–6, 290–3, 299, 305–6, 329, 331, 338–9, 347, 353, 362, 370; progress in, will be surpassed, 370, 371; newly-fledged communities in, 370; tribal system of, 334
  tribes, 245, 251, 253, 259, 264–5, 271, 287, 290, 306, 334, 458
Afrúkhteh, Dr. Yúnis, 217, 219
Age, apostolic, 245
  formative, xi, 140, 261, 263–4, 270–1, 288, 380
  for voting, 207
Ahmad, Mírzá, 427
Ahmadi, 19
Ahmadíyyih, 29, 424
Air raid precaution service, 122, 129
'Akká (Acre), 14, 47, 67, 84, 268, 424, 427
'Alá'í, Rahmatu'lláh, 123
Alcohol, 308
Alert, 384
Algeria, 299
'Alí, Dr., 135
Alien people, 370
Alive, 211, 311, 460
Alláh-u-Abhá, 369
Amatu'l-Bahá Rúhíyyih Khánum (Miss Mary Maxwell, R. Rabbání)
  Hand of the Cause, xvii, 115, 143
  illness of her father, S. Maxwell, 247
Ambulance Corps, 122, 129
America, see United States of America
  Continent of, 4, 72, 80, 245, 260, 265
Aminu'l-'Ulamá', 68
Anarchists, 435

INDEX

Aberdeen, 42
'Abdu'l-Bahá ('Abbás Effendi, Sir 'Abdu'l-Bahá 'Abbás, The Master, Centre of the Covenant), xvi, 3–6, 8–10, 12–15, 20, 22, 28, 32–5, 42, 48, 51, 56, 58, 64–5, 67, 75, 77–8, 81–2, 84, 90, 137, 161, 164, 166, 178, 190, 201, 203, 207, 245, 248, 250–1, 253, 261, 264, 270–1, 285, 288, 311–14, 337, 355, 368, 377, 386, 400, 410, 421–2, 424–5, 427–9, 433, 437–8, 440, 443–6, 448, 450, 455–8, 461
  anniversaries of His passing, 18, 33, 82, 170
  essay on, (Balyuzi), 122
  film and record of His voice, 9
  grave situation after His passing, 3
  His, attitude to psychic forces, 178, 444; British disciples, 227; carriage for Dr. Esslemont, 41; cherished desire, 81; first public appearance in West, 201, 313; great tact and wisdom, 458; letter to Andrew Carnegie, 207, 212; Mother, and Brother, Mihdí, 134, 136; Plan, 264, 265, 270, 272, 386, 437; portrait, 99, 414; prophecies, 20, 56, 76, 78, 226, 251–2; ring, 143; Sister, see Greatest Holy Leaf; statement on Greek philosophers, 445; Tablets to British Isles, 89, 90, 130; visits to England, Scotland, 89, 97, 170, 201, 211, 214, 220, 226–7, 250, 270, 286, 314, 337, 386, 400, 446; Wife, Munírih Khánum, 119; Writings, compilation of, 163, 224, 383, importance of originals, 89, 90, quotations from, 5, 6, 7, 34–5, 67, 224, 260, 433
  not pronounced on Aqdas punishments, 455
  personal accounts His visits not to be used, 89
  reflects qualities of the Manifestations, 440
  seeds sown, fire kindled by Him in Great Britain, xvi, 10, 13, 211, 220, 226, 286, 298
  to be turned to, 457

'Abdu'l-Bahá (cont.)
  watching from His station above, 4, 314
  Will and Testament of, 14, 174, 180, 218, 220, 248, 261
'Abdu'l-Bahá in London, 208
Abhá Kingdom, 153, 203, 227, 246, 256, 283, 343, 350, 363, 375, 377
Ability, 201, 260, 275, 284, 288, 346, 399, 412, 438
Abnormal state of world, 441
Abraham, 451, 461
Absence of light, 458
Absolute pacifists, 435, 436
Abstain from provocative language, 4
Abu'l-Faḍl, Mírzá, 451
Abundance of actions, acts, 34, 144
Acceptance of new believers, 352
Accomplishments, 109, 112, 113, 153, 155, 202, 215, 239, 251, 259, 282, 284, 326, 345, 349, 381, 392, 396, 457
  of national teaching committee, 107, 239
Achievements, 11, 15, 33, 110, 112, 126, 147, 153, 157, 169, 172, 189, 191, 194, 198, 200–1, 203, 210, 214, 216, 221, 226, 229, 231, 236, 239–40, 251, 283, 324, 326, 335, 337–9, 346, 353, 355, 366, 370–1, 385–6, 391–2, 394–5, 398–401, 409, 417, 449
  brightest, 226; in Britain when assessed in future, 449
  in Britain to offset losses in Írán, 355
  major, 170
Active military service, 122, 128, 129, 134, 259
Activities, 135, 140, 142, 144–8, 150, 153–5, 158, 162, 169, 180, 186, 188, 190, 197, 203–6, 223, 230, 233, 236, 253, 256, 274, 279, 280, 287, 321, 327, 338, 369, 372, 380–1, 386, 391–2, 396–7, 399–403, 407, 409, 411, 413–14, 418, 428, 439, 441, 450
Activity, 28, 88, 93, 102, 181, 183, 191, 311, 417
Acts, book of, 290
Ádhirbáyján, 52, 68
Administration, 59, 96–7, 101–2, 112, 115–17, 138, 144, 147–8, 159, 203,

INDEXES

Auxiliary Board for the Propagation of the Faith in November 1957. He was elected to the International Bahá'í Council at Riḍván 1961, and to the Universal House of Justice in 1963.

MISS JEAN M. CAMPBELL   *page 414*
Jean Campbell accepted the Faith in Oxford in 1949 in time to be on the first Spiritual Assembly there. She served as the Assembly secretary for some years, pioneered to Aberdeen in 1959 and then to Malta in February 1964 where she is still at her pioneer post (1979).

JOHN CHARLES CRAVEN   *page 416*
Was associated closely with E. T. Hall and Rebecca Hall from the earliest days of the Faith in Manchester, and remained a dedicated worker until his death, aged 80 in 1958. "Uncle John" kept up a wide correspondence with many of the early believers, and it was in a letter to him that Dr. T. K. Cheyne D.D. made his "Declaration" of belief in Bahá'u'lláh. He received three Tablets from the Master and was on the National Assembly for six of the first eight years. His teaching of the Faith was mostly in the Altrincham area and among his workmates.

ADDENDUM FOR Ḥ. M. BALYUZI   *page 473*
His crowning work, "Bahá'u'lláh—the King of Glory" was still at the binders when he passed away at his home in London on 12 February 1980. The Universal House of Justice cabled the Bahá'í world, "WITH BROKEN HEARTS ANNOUNCE PASSING DEARLY LOVED HAND CAUSE ḤASAN BALYUZI. ENTIRE BAHÁ'Í WORLD ROBBED ONE OF ITS MOST POWERFUL DEFENDERS MOST RESOURCEFUL HISTORIANS. HIS ILLUSTRIOUS LINEAGE HIS DEVOTED LABOURS DIVINE VINEYARD HIS OUTSTANDING LITERARY WORKS COMBINED IN IMMORTALISING HIS HONOURED NAME IN ANNALS BELOVED FAITH. CALL ON FRIENDS EVERYWHERE HOLD MEMORIAL GATHERINGS. PRAYING SHRINES HIS EXEMPLARY ACHIEVEMENTS STEADFASTNESS PATIENCE HUMILITY HIS OUTSTANDING SCHOLARLY PURSUITS WILL INSPIRE MANY DEVOTED WORKERS AMONG RISING GENERATIONS FOLLOW HIS GLORIOUS FOOTSTEPS."

BIOGRAPHIES 489

MISS DOROTHY WIGINGTON *page 362*
Became a Bahá'í at Summer School, Exeter in July 1954 and has been a staunch member of the Oxford Assembly from January 1955.

ERNEST WILLIAM GREGORY *page 381*
Responded to an experimental postal card advertisement in Sheffield and accepted the Faith there in March 1951. He was elected to the National Assembly in 1954 when John Mitchell pioneered to Malta. He served until 1963 when he became an Auxiliary Board Member. He left in April 1974 to serve at the World Centre and passed away there in April 1978. The Universal House of Justice cabled: "ANNOUNCE PASSING TO ABHÁ KINGDOM MORNING OF FIRST DAY RIḐVÁN DISTINGUISHED SERVANT BAHÁ'U'LLÁH ERNEST GREGORY. HIS OUTSTANDING CONTRIBUTION GROWTH BRITISH BAHÁ'Í COMMUNITY AS MEMBER MANY YEARS NATIONAL SPIRITUAL ASSEMBLY AND LATER MEMBER AUXILIARY BOARD ENSURE HIM HIGH PLACE THAT COMMUNITY'S ANNALS. HIS STIRLING QUALITIES ENDEARED HIM TO ALL AT WORLD CENTRE FAITH WHERE HIS LOSS KEENLY FELT. ADVISE BRITISH COMMUNITY JOIN PRAYERS THANKSGIVING HIS LIFE PROGRESS HIS SOUL."

DR. ERNEST SPENCER MILLER *page 395*
Became a Bahá'í in September 1951 in Liverpool and at great sacrifice left his medical practice to pioneer to Cardiff in 1955. For some years prior to his death in October 1976, he lived partly in Liverpool and partly in Anglesey, North Wales. The Universal House of Justice cabled: "GRIEVED LOSS DEVOTED BELIEVER ERNEST MILLER WHO RENDERED DISTINGUISHED SERVICES BRITISH HOME FRONT ENDEARED HIMSELF FELLOW BELIEVERS. EXTEND SYMPATHY FRIENDS ASSURE ARDENT PRAYERS SACRED THRESHOLD PROGRESS HIS SOUL ABHÁ KINGDOM."

IAN SEMPLE *page 411*
Heard of the Faith at the first public meeting organised by the Oxford Spiritual Assembly in 1949 and accepted it shortly afterwards. He was elected to the National Assembly in January 1955 and was a member until Riḍván 1961, serving as Secretary from January 1960 to January 1961. In 1956 he pioneered to Edinburgh for two and a half years, and was appointed to the

second Persian Bahá'í student to come to Northampton to train as a nurse and arrived in 1948. They married at Summer School, Cottingham, Yorkshire in 1951 and pioneered soon afterwards—Shomais to Ethiopia and 'Abbás to Persia. 'Abbás joined Shomais in Africa in 1953. They returned to England in 1958 and opened the town of Burnley where an Assembly was formed in 1961. In 1975 'Abbás pioneered to Newfoundland and Shomais joined him in July 1976. 'Abbás was a member of the National Assembly from 1964 until his pioneer move, and Shomais was active in United Nations' affairs. Shomais toured Persia in 1971 at the request of the Universal House of Justice, was one of the representatives of the Bahá'í International Community at the International Women's Year Convention in Mexico in 1975 and travelled extensively in the British Isles in 1978–1979.

EDMUND (TED) CARDELL,
Knight of Bahá'u'lláh *page 281*
Became a Bahá'í in Canada in 1948 and returned to his father's farm in England some time later. He pioneered to Kenya in October 1951 where he was a founder member of the first local Assembly in Nairobi. He became Knight of Bahá'u'lláh for South West Africa in 1953 and returned to England in 1963. He was elected to the National Assembly in 1973 and is still a member (1979).

DR. JOHN GEORGE MITCHELL,
Knight of Bahá'u'lláh *page 307*
Became a Bahá'í in 1950, was member of the National Assembly from 1952 to 1954 from which he pioneered as a Knight of Bahá'u'lláh for Malta. He had pioneered for a short while in Blackpool. He passed away on 19 February 1957 at the age of 50. ("Bahá'í World", Vol. XIII, p. 901.)

MISS IRENE BENNETT *page 321*
Became a Bahá'í in Kenya in 1953 and has been in pioneering posts since that time. She has served in Portugal, Switzerland, Scotland, Kenya, Uganda (where she was an Auxiliary Board Member), Nigeria, and is presently (1980) in the Central African Republic.

BIOGRAPHIES   487

International Council and finally as member of the Universal
House of Justice in 1963.

ḤASSAN AND ISOBEL ṢABRÍ   *page 266*
Ḥassan, a young Egyptian Bahá'í studying in England in 1945
met Isobel Locke, an American pioneer to England, and they
both served with distinction in the Six Year Plan, Ḥassan on the
National Youth and National Teaching Committees and the
Nottingham, Birmingham, Belfast, Liverpool, Cardiff and
Bristol Spiritual Assemblies, and Isobel on the Assemblies in
Edinburgh, Blackpool, Sheffield and Bristol, as well as on the
National Teaching Committee. They married in 1951 and
pioneered to Tanganyika and Uganda, where Ḥassan was on the
first National Spiritual Assembly of Central and East Africa.
Isobel became a Counsellor and Ḥassan Secretary of the
Continental Pioneer Committee for Africa. They subsequently
pioneered to Kenya where they still serve (1979).

ARTHUR NORTON   *page 267*
Was the Treasurer of the special fund for the Shrine of the Báb
when he received some letters and receipts. He and his wife
Marion were founder members of the Bradford Bahá'í community as well as being the first pioneers to Sheffield during the
Six Year Plan. He served on the National Assembly for seven
and a half years during the period 1938–1946, when he was
obliged to retire due to ill-health in December 1946.

ERIC MANTON   *page 273*
Became a Bahá'í in Northampton in 1946 where he was a
member of the first Spiritual Assembly. He later pioneered to
Edinburgh where he was also on the first Scottish Assembly and
to the virgin territory of Northern Rhodesia in 1951. He was
Chairman of the first National Spiritual Assembly of South
Central Africa in 1964 and of the National Assembly of Zambia
for nine years from its formation in 1967. He has remained at his
post and became a Zambian citizen in 1973.

DR. 'ABBÁS AND SHOMAIS AFNÁN,   *page 278*
'Abbás Afnán was a student in Paris and came to England as a
pioneer to Africa for the Two Year Plan. Shomais 'Alá'í was the

Land, it was Mother George who introduced the Faith to Dr. John Esslemont. For very many years she conducted Sunday afternoon meetings in her Chelsea home in London and she passed away on 4 November 1950 at the age of 91. ("Bahá'í World", Vol. XII, p. 697.)

MÚSÁ BANÁNÍ,
Hand of the Cause of God.   *page 257*
Pioneered with his wife Samíḥih to Uganda in 1951 and was elevated to the rank of Hand of the Cause in February 1952. The beloved Guardian also described him as the "spiritual conqueror of Africa". In spite of failing health he visited most African territories, served for some five years as the sole Hand of the African Continent, and finally, after many years of constant suffering, passed away at his pioneering post in Kampala, Uganda, on 4 September 1971. The Universal House of Justice cabled: "PROFOUNDLY MOURN PASSING DEARLY LOVED HAND CAUSE MÚSÁ BANÁNÍ RECALL WITH DEEP AFFECTION HIS SELFLESS UNASSUMING PROLONGED SERVICES CRADLE FAITH HIS EXEMPLARY PIONEERING UGANDA CULMINATING HIS APPOINTMENT AS HAND CAUSE AFRICA AND PRAISE BELOVED GUARDIAN AS SPIRITUAL CONQUEROR THAT CONTINENT. INTERMENT HIS REMAINS AFRICAN SOIL UNDER SHADOW MOTHER TEMPLE ENHANCES SPIRITUAL LUSTRE THAT BLESSED SPOT. FERVENTLY PRAYING SHRINES PROGRESS HIS NOBLE SOUL. MAY AFRICA NOW ROBBED STAUNCH VENERABLE PROMOTER DEFENDER FAITH FOLLOW HIS EXAMPLE CHEER HIS HEART ABHÁ KINGDOM. CONVEY FAMILY MOST TENDER SYMPATHIES ADVISE HOLD MEMORIAL MEETINGS ALL COMMUNITIES BAHÁÍ WORLD BEFITTING GATHERINGS MOTHER TEMPLES". ("Bahá'í World", Vol. XV, pp. 421–3.)

'ALÍ NAKHJAVÁNÍ   *page 257*
Left Persia in early 1951, after service for the Faith in youth and teaching activities and as a member of the National Assembly, to join his wife, Violette and her parents, Músá and Samíḥih Banání, in the British Isles, preparatory to their pioneering to Africa. His teaching activities in Africa took him to remote African villages, and, later, as assistant to Mr. Banání when he was appointed Hand of the Cause, to many countries on the African continent. Elected Chairman of the first Regional National Assembly of Central and East Africa, then as member of the first elected

Victoria and Albert Museum London. In 1919, when Bernard was about to leave Japan, the late Soetsu Yangi, the well-known Japanese art critic and philosopher and Bernard's friend for over fifty years, paid tribute: "When he leaves us we shall have lost the one man who knows Japan on its spiritual side . . . I consider his position in Japan, and also his mission in his own country to be pregnant with the deepest meaning. He is trying to knit the East and West together by art, and it seems likely that he will be remembered as the first to accomplish as an artist, what for so long mankind has been dreaming of bringing about. . . ."
He passed away in May 1979 and to the National Assembly the Universal House of Justice cabled:
"KINDLY EXTEND LOVING SYMPATHY RELATIVES FRIENDS PASSING DISTINGUISHED VETERAN UPHOLDER FAITH BAHÁ'U'LLÁH BERNARD LEACH. HONOURS CONFERRED UPON HIM RECOGNITION HIS WORLD-WIDE FAME CRAFTSMAN POTTER PROMOTER CONCORD EAST AND WEST ADD LUSTRE ANNALS BRITISH BAHÁ'Í HISTORY AND HIS EAGER WILLINGNESS USE HIS RENOWN FOR SERVICE FAITH EARN ETERNAL GRATITUDE FELLOW BELIEVERS. ASSURE ARDENT PRAYERS PROGRESS HIS SOUL."

SAMUEL SCOTT *page 240*
Became a Bahá'í when he was 76 years old and pioneered to Norwich at the age of 84. He passed away on 31 December 1951, at the age of 86.

JOHN FERRABY,
Hand of the Cause of God. *page 250*
Accepted the Faith in 1941 and was elected to the National Assembly almost immediately. He was Secretary from 1946 until December 1960 when he took up duties at the World Centre. He was also for a number of years manager of the Bahá'í Publishing Trust. On his passing in September 1973 the Universal House of Justice called for memorial meetings "ALL COMMUNITIES BAHÁ'Í WORLD" and referred to his "VALUABLE CONTRIBUTION BAHÁ'Í LITERATURE THROUGH HIS BOOK 'ALL THINGS MADE NEW'". ("Bahá'í World", Vol. XVI, p. 511.)

MRS FLORENCE "MOTHER" GEORGE *page 256*
Always proud of the designation "Mother" given to her by 'Abdu'l-Bahá when she was one of the early pilgrims to the Holy

MRS CONSTANCE LANGDON-DAVIES   *page 224*
Was one of the early believers in Torquay where she associated with Mark Tobey, Bernard Leach and other artists and writers at Dartington Hall. She accepted the Faith in December 1936 and served on the National Assembly for fifteen of the years from 1938 until her unexpected death in Oxford in December 1954. She had pioneered to help form the first Assembly there 1949.

GEORGE K. MARSHALL   *page 228*
Became a Bahá'í in 1949 although he had lived most of his life with his father, one of the early British believers, in Birmingham. (See "John L. Marshall".) George pioneered for a short while to Belfast and then in 1950 to Glasgow where he lived for seven years, except for a short pioneering project to maintain the Assembly in Edinburgh. He died at an early age on 30 March 1958.

MRS MARGUERITE PRESTON (née Wellby)   *page 231*
Became a Bahá'í in 1936, was a member of the National Assembly for three and a half years during the period 1939 to 1945. She married Terence Preston, a Kenya tea grower, in August 1945 and settled in Kenya where she was the only Bahá'í until the pioneers began to settle under the Two Year Plan. Her husband died unexpectedly in July 1951 leaving her with three young children and she and her eldest child were killed in an aeroplane crash when she was returning to Kenya after a short holiday in England, in February 1952.

BERNARD LEACH, C.H., C.B.E.   *page 239*
It was through Mark Tobey that world famous potter and author Bernard Leach became a Bahá'í in the early 1930's. He has through his works, his books, his press, radio and television interviews introduced the Faith with love, dedication and dignity to people in many spheres of society in Britain, Japan and America. He was honoured by Her Majesty the Queen and made a Companion of Honour. Even at ninety years of age, though blind, he was serving the Cause with distinction through his writings and interviews. In March 1977, he opened, with much favourable publicity, an exhibition of his works at the

BIOGRAPHIES 483

CYRIL AND MARGARET JENKERSON *page 217*
Became Bahá'ís in Bradford in 1940 and pioneered to Oxford to be members of the first Assembly there in 1949. (It is of interest to note that in 1938 there were only three Spiritual Assemblies in the British Isles—in London, Manchester and Bournemouth, and a total of about eighty registered Bahá'ís, yet in Bradford there were, during the course of about two years, so many new registrations that the first Assembly was elected there in 1939 and by 1949 that Community had sent out ten pioneers from its first twenty-five believers.) The Jenkersons pioneered to Cyprus in 1978 and are still there (1979).

RICHARD H. BACKWELL *page 218*
Became a Bahá'í in Ceylon in 1944 where he was an officer in the Royal Air Force. Returning to Britain in 1946, he pioneered in Nottingham, Newcastle, Glasgow, Edinburgh and Leeds; was a member of the National Spiritual Assembly from 1947 until January 1955 when he pioneered to British Guiana, now Guyana. He was for a time part-time manager of the Bahá'í Publishing Trust and Editor of the Bahá'í Journal. After his return from Guiana, he settled with his family in Northern Ireland in 1963 and again served on the National Assembly until 1968 when he was appointed an Auxiliary Board Member. His valuable contributions to Bahá'í literature include the compilations with which he was associated—"Pattern of Bahá'í Life", "Principles of Bahá'í Administration", "The Covenant of Bahá'u'lláh", "Guidance for Today and Tomorrow", "A Faith for Everyman", and his unique approach to the Christians, "The Christianity of Jesus". He passed away on 4 October 1972 at the age of 58 when the Universal House of Justice included in their cable: "GRIEF PASSING EARLY AGE RICHARD BACKWELL GREATLY ASSUAGED TERMINATION HIS SUFFERING CONTEMPLATION DISTINGUISHED RECORD SERVICE SOUTH AMERICA BRITISH ISLES SPIRITUAL RADIANCE EVENING EARTHLY LIFE . . ." ("Bahá'í World", Vol. XV, pp. 525–27.)

MISS ADA WILLIAMS *page 222*
Pioneered to Motherwell in 1948 and then to Blackpool in 1965. She has travelled widely to teach the Faith at home and overseas, visiting Malta, South Africa and Canada where her great spirit was most inspiring; she is still travelling (1979).

Assembly. After four years, broken by ill health and persecution, he was, for his own safety, sent back to Cardiff. After a bad fall in 1967 from which he never fully recovered, he passed away quietly in his sleep on Christmas Day, 1967 in Cardiff. ("Bahá'í World", Vol. XIV, pp. 305-8.)

MISS CLAIRE GUNG *page 211*
Born in Germany, became a Bahá'í in Torquay and later joined the small Bahá'í group in Cheltenham in 1940. She moved to Manchester and later pioneered to Northampton in November 1946 to become member of the first Spiritual Assembly there. In 1948 she again pioneered to help form the first Spiritual Assembly in the "Pivotal Centre" of Cardiff. In 1950, during the "Year of Respite", Claire became the first pioneer actually to move from the British community to settle in Africa. Hailed by the Guardian as the "Mother of Africa" she worked for some years in Tanganyika and then moved to Uganda where she established a multi-racial kindergarten; she is still at her pioneer post at the time of writing (1979).

MRS. LIZZIE FOWLER HAINSWORTH *page 211*
Became a Bahá'í in Bradford in 1946 after replying to her younger son Philip that she had not become a Bahá'í during his absence in the Armed Forces because "Nobody had asked me to". She pioneered to Nottingham in 1946, to Oxford in 1949 and, at the age of 72, was the first believer in the British Isles to offer to pioneer in the Two Year Plan to Africa. (Convention 1950.) She died in Bradford in September 1951 before she could join her son Philip in Uganda. The Guardian wrote of her through his secretary, "She has truly shown an exemplary Bahá'í spirit in every way.... He wishes more of the Bahá'ís would arise to such heights of devotion and sacrifice."

MISS MARGARET SULLIVAN (later MRS. MARGARET NELSON) *page 211*
Pioneered to Dublin and was on the first Local Assembly there in 1948. She was Caretaker of the National Ḥaẓí'ratu'l-Quds, London from December 1970 to August 1976, and then became a founder member of the Tameside Assembly, Lancashire.

BIOGRAPHIES

Ives, Brighton, and Bournemouth, making six moves in just over two years by a lady in her late sixties. In 1953 she responded immediately and was enrolled as a Knight of Bahá'u'lláh for Malta where, after numerous vicissitudes and a small but painful accident which affected her for many months, she was able, some twenty years later, to witness the formation of the first Spiritual Assembly in Malta. She passed away, after twenty-seven years of dedicated pioneering which covered four territories, in May 1974, when the Universal House of Justice cabled: "PASSING NOBLE SOUL OLGA MILLS GRIEVOUS LOSS BRITISH BAHÁ'Í COMMUNITY. HER LONG STEADFAST DEVOTION BAHÁ'U'LLÁH SHEDS LUSTRE ANNALS FAITH THAT COMMUNITY. ISLAND MALTA HISTORICALLY FAMOUS CLASSICAL CHRISTIAN ISLAMIC ERAS RECIPIENT NEW SPIRITUAL POTENTIALITIES THROUGH HEROIC SERVICE KNIGHT BAHÁ'U'LLÁH DEDICATED BAND PIONEERS. EXPRESS FRIENDS RELATIVES LOVING SYMPATHY ASSURE ARDENT PRAYERS PROGRESS SOUL." ("Bahá'í World", Vol. XVI, p. 531.)

ALFRED AND EDITH LUCY SUGAR *page 210*
After hearing of the Faith from her brother, E. T. Hall, Lucy Sugar accepted the Faith on 28 November 1921, but Alfred remained agnostic until about 1925. He became well known for his depth of knowledge of the Faith and for his cogent argument. He was a teacher of the highest order and was largely responsible for the development of the Faith around Lancashire and over the Pennines into Bradford and Leeds. Lucy was a member of the National Assembly in 1929 and Alfred was a member during eight of the following thirteen years.

Alfred died in December 1961 at the age of 92 (or 93) and was followed in March 1966 by Lucy aged 90.

CHARLES WILLIAM DUNNING,
Knight of Bahá'u'lláh *page 211*
Born in or near Leeds, March 1885. Met and embraced the Faith in 1948 and within a fortnight offered to pioneer to Belfast. After serious illness and a period of recuperation in Cardiff, he served in Sheffield until 1953. "Charlie" answered the Guardian's call to settle in unopened territories in the Ten Year Crusade and he arrived in Kirkwall, Orkney in September 1953, opening the way, "essentially . . . alone" for the founding of Kirkwall Spiritual

her young daughter in 1946 to settle in Blackburn, Lancs. From there to Norwich and Bournemouth in the Six Year Plan and then to Edinburgh and Portsmouth. In 1959 she pioneered to Luxembourg and then in the Nine Year Plan, to Guernsey, to Chelmsford, Essex and again overseas to the Canary Islands. In 1969 she returned to England to pioneer in Hereford and St. Austell and then back again to the Canaries where she was on the first Spiritual Assembly of Arucas. For over thirty years she served the Cause with utter consecration; carrying out at least sixteen pioneer projects in three continents. She passed away in Birmingham, England on 12 July 1974. ("Bahá'í World", Vol. XVI, p. 534.)

JOHN LUDLOW MARSHALL *page 210*
"Johnny" was a Scot, born in 1876, went to work as a tinsmith at the age of eleven and later, after marriage, settled in Birmingham to pursue his trade. He was confirmed in the Faith by the Master, Whom he met in 1911 and 1913, when he was, for many years, the only Bahá'í in Birmingham. Johnny kept excellent records of visits and lectures by some of the early visitors to Birmingham, including Martha Root, Dr. Esslemont, Mountfort Mills and Helen Bishop. At the age of 71 he retired from work and pioneered to Edinburgh where he died as a result of an accident in January 1948, only three months before the first Spiritual Assembly was formed there.

MARY OLGA KATHERINE MILLS,
Knight of Bahá'u'lláh *page 210*
Born in Germany in 1882 with a German father and English mother she grew up with an insatiable love for travel. In the United States she married an Englishman. It is not certain when she accepted the Faith but she was on pilgrimage in 1930 and stayed for a month as companion to Effie Baker. She was later a great help to the friends in Berlin and Leipzig and gave much support to Adam Benke who pioneered to Sofia. After suffering many privations during the war in Germany she wrote to the Guardian in 1947 and he encouraged her suggestion to pioneer to England. She arrived in early 1948 and settled in her first pioneer post in Nottingham. Within nine months she was again on the move in response to pioneer calls. Belfast, Edinburgh, St.

to the United Kingdom in October 1977. ("Bahá'í World", Vol. XVI, p. 512.)

DR. LUṬFU'LLÁH ḤAKÍM　　　　　　　　　*page 195*
Was born into a family of distinguished Jewish medical doctors in 1888. His grandfather was the first Jew to embrace the Cause and Bahá'u'lláh revealed a Tablet in his honour. Luṭfu'lláh came to study physiotherapy in England in 1910 and he was in constant attendance on the Master during His visit in 1911. He went to serve in the Holy Land and returned to England in 1920 when he accompanied Shoghi Effendi. He later served with distinction in Persia and returned, at the request of the Guardian, to Britain in October 1948, where he taught and travelled extensively until called to Haifa by the Guardian on 14 November 1950. He was appointed to the first International Bahá'í Council. He was elected to the first Universal House of Justice in 1963 but because of failing health and advanced age regretfully his resignation was accepted in October 1967 though he consented to serve until the 1968 election. He passed away in August 1968 and the House cabled the Bahá'í world: "GRIEVE ANNOUNCE PASSING LUṬFU'LLÁH ḤAKÍM DEDICATED SERVANT CAUSE GOD. SPECIAL MISSIONS ENTRUSTED HIM, FULL CONFIDENCE REPOSED IN HIM BY MASTER AND GUARDIAN, HIS CLOSE ASSOCIATION WITH EARLY DISTINGUISHED BELIEVERS EAST WEST INCLUDING HIS COLLABORATION ESSLEMONT, HIS SERVICES PERSIA BRITISH ISLES HOLY LAND, HIS MEMBERSHIP APPOINTED AND ELECTED INTERNATIONAL BAHÁ'Í COUNCIL, HIS ELECTION UNIVERSAL HOUSE JUSTICE WILL ALWAYS BE REMEMBERED IMMORTAL ANNALS FAITH BAHÁ'U'LLÁH." ("Bahá'í World", Vol. XV, pp. 430–4.)

FRED STAHLER　　　　　　　　　　　　*page 202*
Arose to pioneer shortly after accepting the Faith in Manchester in 1947. He pioneered first to Cardiff, then to Bristol, moved for varying periods to seven other cities and finally settled in Derby in 1965.

MRS. PRUDENCE GEORGE　　　　　　　*page 202*
Born in England in 1896 she moved to Canada in 1928 where she accepted the Faith in 1941. She first pioneered from St. Lambert to Moncton and then from Canada to England with

MRS ALMA CYNTHIA GREGORY   *page 191*
Although she remembers her mother, Louise Ginman, going from town to town in the United States trying to find the Master, but reaching the place shortly after He had left, and speaks with feeling of personal involvement as a Bahá'í youth, of many early meetings in London at the homes of Lady Blomfield, Claudia Coles, Ethel Rosenberg, "Mother" George and many others of that day, she did not formally register as a Bahá'í in the British Isles until 1942. She pioneered to Northampton in August 1946 and helped to form its first Assembly, leaving for Liverpool in 1949 for the same purpose. She subsequently pioneered to Bristol, Exeter and Stornoway; was the Secretary of the National Youth Committee when it launched its "Bahá'í Youth Bulletin" from 1946 to 1948; was Secretary of the Assembly Development Committee for some years and was a member of the National Assembly for seven years between 1948 and 1956.

ROBERT CHEEK   *page 191*
Became a Bahá'í in London on Naw-Rúz 1945, pioneered to Bournemouth in September 1946, to Bristol in 1947 to help form the first Assembly there, and to Norwich in 1948 where he has lived since except for a short special pioneer project in Blackburn in 1950–1.

MRS JOAN GIDDINGS (née BROWNE)   *page 194*
Accepted the Faith in Bradford in 1938. She pioneered first to Cardiff and later to York and Canterbury, and was active on Assemblies and on National Committees throughout her Bahá'í life. She passed away in Canterbury in 1978. (See also note about developments in Bradford under "Cyril and Margaret Jenkerson".)

HUGH AND VIOLET MCKINLEY   *page 194*
Hugh McKinley and his mother, Violet McKinley, pioneered from Torquay to Cardiff in 1947, serving on the first local Spiritual Assembly when formed there in 1948. Together they pioneered to Nicosia, Cyprus in 1953, moving to Famagusta in 1958. Violet passed away there in August 1959. In 1966 Hugh pioneered to Syros in the Cyclades Islands (Greece) and returned

British Bahá'í community was held together in the 1940's is generally recognised to have been due to the dedicated work of Dorothy as Secretary of the National Assembly working indefatigably in war-torn London. She became an Auxiliary Board Member in 1954 and was appointed to the European Board of Counsellors in 1968.

PHILIP HAINSWORTH *page 187*
Accepted the Faith in Bradford in 1938, and at the outbreak of War was the first British believer to register as a Bahá'í in the Armed Forces. He had to appeal in Court when seeking exemption from being involved in the taking of life and, being released from combatant service, was drafted into the Royal Army Medical Corps. Prior to his release from military service in 1946, he spent five weeks in Haifa and in the same year pioneered to Nottingham. He was appointed Chairman of the National Youth Committee and Secretary of the National Teaching Committee and was elected to the National Assembly in 1947. He subsequently pioneered to Oxford and Blackburn. In June 1951 he was one of the party of five pioneers who first went to Dar-es-Salaam and then on to Kampala, Uganda, where he became Secretary of the first local Spiritual Assembly in 1952 and of the Regional National Assembly in Central and East Africa in 1956. He returned to pioneer in the Leeds area in 1966, was elected to the National Assembly in 1967 and is still (1979) a member.

WALTER WILKINS *page 191*
Born in 1883 Walter embraced the Faith when he was about 40 years old. He was a keen Esperantist through which he learned of the Faith. He served for many years on the London Spiritual Assembly and was on the National Assembly for a year in 1934. Responding to the pioneer call of the Six Year Plan he moved to Birmingham in 1946, to Blackburn in 1947, to Norwich in 1948, and in 1961 at the age of 78 he pioneered to Canterbury. At the age of 82 he took a small flat in an old people's home where for the first time in his life he was able to entertain the friends and hold Feasts and even an assembly meeting. He passed away after an accident on 19 March 1973.

MRS MARION HOFMAN *page 179*
Came to Britain in 1945 to be married to David Hofman, after having served the Faith in America with great distinction as a teacher, writer and administrator. With her husband she pioneered during the Six Year Plan in Northampton, Birmingham and Oxford, and during the Ten Year Crusade in Cardiff and Watford. She served on the National Spiritual Assembly and National Teaching Committee and as an Auxiliary Board member. Since David's election to the Universal House of Justice, Marion was solely responsible for the family publishing business of George Ronald.

MISS UNA TOWNSHEND
Knight of Bahá'u'lláh *page 181*
Was the first of Hand of the Cause George Townshend's family to embrace the Faith which her father had espoused many years previously. She was an active Bahá'í youth and on 16 September 1946 became the first pioneer in Ireland where she opened the 'pivotal centre' of Dublin and was on its first Spiritual Assembly in 1948. She pioneered to Malta and was the first Knight of Bahá'u'lláh in that island in October 1953.

JOSEPH LEE *page 181*
Accepted the Faith in Manchester in 1932 and was active on committees and in the teaching work for over thirty years. He served on the National Spiritual Assembly from 1933 to 1940 and pioneered to Brighton, Torquay and Exeter, sacrificing material prosperity over many years in the interests of teaching and pioneering. He passed away in May 1966 at the age of 55 years.

MRS DOROTHY FERRABY (née Cansdale) *page 184*
Became a Bahá'í and was active in the London Youth group in the early 1930's. She was elected to the National Spiritual Assembly in 1941 and served continuously as either Secretary, Treasurer or Recording Secretary for the next twenty years. She retired when her husband, Hand of the Cause John Ferraby, left to serve at the World Centre. That the small and scattered

introducing or teaching the Faith in many lands and would be content to "lay down his bones in service to the Faith" in his beloved Africa.

MISS JESSICA YOUNG *page 172*
Historically was the first British pioneer to arise when she went for a short time to Bristol.

KATHLEEN BROWN (LADY HORNELL) *page 172*
Was elected to the National Assembly in 1936 and served until 1945. She pioneered to Nottingham in 1946 where she later married Sir William Hornell. Her next pioneer post was in Belfast in 1952, then to Venice (1960–1965) and later to Sardinia (1965–1968). She returned to London to live at the home of her son-in-law, Hand of the Cause, H. M. Balyuzi. She passed away in September 1977 and the Universal House of Justice cabled: "PASSING LADY HORNELL ROBS BRITISH COMMUNITY ONE OF FEW REMAINING LINKS EARLY DAYS FAITH. HER UNWAVERING FAITH CONSTANT DEDICATED SERVICES PIONEER TEACHING ADMINISTRATIVE FIELDS OVER SO MANY YEARS ASSURE HER HIGH STATION ANNALS CAUSE PROVIDE SHINING EXAMPLE PRESENT FUTURE GENERATIONS. ADVISE HOLD BEFITTING MEMORIAL MEETING. ASSURE ARDENT PRAYERS SACRED THRESHOLD PROGRESS HER LOVING SOUL ABHÁ KINGDOM."

URSULA SAMANDARÍ (née NEWMAN),
Knight of Bahá'u'lláh *page 172*
First served on the British National Assembly in 1945 and pioneered to St. Ives in the same year. Ursula became pioneer member of the first Dublin Assembly in 1948 and pioneered again, a year later, to Belfast. In Belfast she became member of the first Local Assembly and worked with pioneer Dr. Mehdi Samandarí, whom she married. They subsequently pioneered to Nairobi in 1953 and later to Somalia, where she was a Knight of Bahá'u'lláh and became a member of the first Spiritual Assembly of Mogadiscio, on which she served from 1954 until 1971. In addition to these experiences, she served on the National Assembly for North East Africa (1961–1970) and on the National Assembly of Cameroon since 1972, where she still serves (1979).

ALBERT AND JEFF JOSEPH *page 146*
Associated with the Faith from the very beginnings of the Administration in the British Isles, the Joseph brothers gave long and outstanding service to the Cause. Jacob (later "Jeff") was Chairman and Albert (then Ibrahim) a member of the first "Spiritual Council" of the Bahá'ís of Manchester. Jacob was a member of the first "All-England Bahá'í Council" in 1922 and of the first National Spiritual Assembly in 1923. Both were mentioned in and received some Tablets from the Master and both were warmly regarded by the Guardian for their services to the Faith. Jeff died in August 1969 in Manchester and Albert in August 1978.

RICHARD ST. BARBE BAKER, O.B.E., LL.D.,
FOR.D.I.P. (CAMBRIDGE) *page 163*
On his return from Kenya in 1924 where he had served as Assistant Conservator of Forests since 1920, R. St. Barbe Baker was asked to speak on the faiths of the Kikuyu under the title: "Some African Beliefs" at the 'Conference of Living Religions within the Empire', and was approached afterwards by Claudia Stewart-Coles who exclaimed "You are a Bahá'í". He subsequently accepted the Faith and has introduced it to many thousands of people in all walks of life in many lands, for more than half a century. The Guardian became the first Life Member of the Men of the Trees in Palestine in 1929. Later, for twelve consecutive years, he sent an official message to St. Barbe's World Forestry Charter Gatherings attended by Ambassadors from up to sixty-two countries each year. St. Barbe took an active part on the Committee celebrating the Centenary of the Declaration of the Báb in 1944. After his first Sahara University Expedition carrying out an ecological survey of 9,000 miles in 1953, and in response to the Guardian's desire, St. Barbe attended the First African Conference in Kampala. In 1975 St. Barbe was called upon to advise on tree planting of the site of the Ṭihrán House of Worship in consultation with Quinlan Terry, architect. Afterwards, in collaboration with architect Hossein Amánat, he recorded his observations for the Universal House of Justice for the landscaping of their site on Mt. Carmel and for tree-scaping at Bahjí. St. Barbe attended the Intercontinental Conference Nairobi, in October 1976 and still (1979) at almost 90 is

BIOGRAPHIES   473

and Cardiff. She died on 21 August 1969 and the Universal
House of Justice cabled: "DEEPLY GRIEVED PASSING KNIGHT OF
BAHÁ'U'LLÁH EVELYN BAXTER. AMONG FIRST PIONEERS SIX YEAR
PLAN HER LONG FAITHFUL SERVICE BRITISH BAHÁ'Í COMMUNITY
PROVIDES EXAMPLE DEVOTION FORTITUDE".
("Bahá'í World", Vol. XV, pp. 456–7)

ḤASAN M. BALYUZI,
Hand of the Cause of God   *page 122*
He was first elected to the National Spiritual Assembly of the
Bahá'ís of the British Isles in 1933 and served continuously until
1960, when he retired in order to devote his whole time to the
work of the Hands of the Cause. He served at the World Centre,
and travelled to South America and throughout Canada in 1961.
Mr. Balyuzi was Secretary of the first Summer School
Committee in 1936, on the National Teaching Committee in
1940 and Chairman of the National Assembly almost every year
from 1942 until his retirement. He was elevated to the rank of
Hand of the Cause in 1957, and has made invaluable contributions
to the literature of the Faith with his trilogy, "Bahá'u'lláh",
"'Abdu'l-Bahá" and "The Báb"; his "Edward Granville Browne
and the Bahá'í Faith", his pamphlet on "Bahá'í Administration",
and "Muhammad and the Course of Islám".   (*See page 490*)

FRANK HURST   *page 126*
An early worker in the Trade Union Movement in Britain,
Frank was an outspoken sympathiser of the Faith for over twenty
years before actually accepting it in Bradford in 1939. He died
in Leeds in 1949.

MRS MARY BASIL-HALL (PARVINE)   *page 127*
Daughter of Lady Blomfield, she was active in the Faith from
her youth, particularly during the visit to Britain of the Master
Whom she served with such devotion, and Who bestowed upon
her the name "Parvine" on His first visit in 1911. She served for
five years on the National Spiritual Assembly and for a short
time on the National Teaching Committee of the Six Year Plan.
At her passing the National Assembly cabled the Guardian,
"PARVINE GLORIED IN SUCCESS PLAN PASSED TO ABHÁ KINGDOM
MORNING 28TH" (April 1950).

Bournemouth Bahá'ís called to hear of the passing of the Master. Always an active teacher of the Faith, she also served on the National Assembly for fifteen of its first eighteen years, mainly as its Chairman. She passed away in Bournemouth in October 1948.

DAVID HOFMAN *page 108*
A member of the Universal House of Justice since its formation in 1963, he became a Bahá'í in the Maxwell home in Montreal in 1933, when he began corresponding with the Guardian. Returning to England in 1936, he was elected to the British National Spiritual Assembly and was the Secretary during some of its most crucial years. He was the first Manager of its Publishing Trust and played a vital rôle on the National Teaching and Africa Committees of the Six and Two Year Plans. He served almost continuously on the National Assembly until his election to the Universal House of Justice. David and Marion Hofman pioneered during the Six Year Plan in Northampton, Birmingham and Oxford and during the Ten Year Crusade in Cardiff and Watford. Throughout his years of devoted service to the British community he was always in demand as a most accomplished speaker and convincing teacher.

MRS. LILIAN STEVENS *page 116*
Was a founder member of the first Torquay Spiritual Assembly in 1938; was for many years its secretary and in spite of prolonged illness remained a great servant of the Faith. She passed away on 1 January 1958.

MISS EVELYN BAXTER,
Knight of Bahá'u'lláh *page 117*
Born around 1883 of missionary parents, accepted the Faith in 1923 and served with absolute devotion throughout the remainder of her life. She was for many years a member of the London Spiritual Assembly and served for six years on the National Assembly. Throughout her Bahá'í life she corresponded frequently with the Guardian and responded to his overseas pioneer call when she became a Knight of Bahá'u'lláh for the Channel Isles in September 1953. She had already pioneered in the Six Year Plan to Birmingham, Nottingham, Hove, Oxford

BIOGRAPHIES 471

98. The Universal House of Justice cabled: "PASSING ISOBEL SLADE SEVERS ONE FEW REMAINING LINKS EARLY CAUSE BRITISH ISLES DEPRIVES COMMUNITY OUTSTANDING BELIEVER STOP HER UNFLAGGING SUPPORT CAUSE GOD MORE THAN HALF CENTURY COMPRISING MEMBERSHIP NATIONAL SPIRITUAL ASSEMBLY PIONEER VISITING TEACHER SIX YEAR PLAN CONSTANT DEVOTION DUTY HIGH MORAL STATURE RENDER HER SHINING EXAMPLE FUTURE GENERATIONS STOP EXPRESS RELATIVES FRIENDS LOVING SYMPATHY ASSURE PRAYERS SACRED THRESHOLD AMPLE REWARD PROGRESS SOUL ABHÁ KINGDOM."

MRS. LOUISE GINMAN *page 63*
Also referred to later as "Louise Charlot". Became a Bahá'í in Burlingame, California about 1910, and came to England late in 1919. She served on the London Spiritual Assembly for a period; pioneered to Oxford, and then to Bristol where she died in February 1963 at the age of 92.

MISS FLORENCE E. PINCHON *page 72*
Little is known about Miss Pinchon's early life but she was mentioned as being active in the Faith with Dr. Esslemont and Major Tudor Pole during the First World War (See "Bahá'í World" Vol. XIV, pp. 370–2.). "Floy" had a most lucid pen and in addition to contributing to Bahá'í and non-Bahá'í magazines, wrote "The Coming of the Glory", and "Life after Death". She travelled as a Bahá'í teacher before the Second World War but suffered from indifferent health for many years before her death in Bournemouth in March 1966.

MISS CLAUDIA STUART COLES *page 88*
Having accepted the Bahá'í teachings in Washington, D.C. was one of its most loyal and enthusiastic adherents. Moved to London, England in 1920 and was for eleven years a member of the community, serving for a period as secretary of the National Assembly. She died in London on 25 May 1931. ("Bahá'í World", Vol. IV, pp. 263–4.)

SISTER GRACE CHALLIS *page 88*
Sister Challis was a Quaker when she heard of the Faith from Dr. Esslemont and she accepted it at the gathering of the

ones, the realisation of Bahá'u'lláh as Christ returned in the Glory of the Father. In spite of his important books, "The Heart of the Gospel" and "The Promise of All Ages", no one in the church responded and in 1947 the Guardian called upon him to resign from the church. He complied immediately and moved with his wife and two children to a small bungalow in Dundrum near Dublin. He was one of the founder members of the first Spiritual Assembly of the Bahá'ís of Dublin and in 1951 was elevated to the rank of Hand of the Cause. For many years he gave distinguished services to the Guardian, not least of which was the writing of the introduction to "God Passes By" and his presentation on behalf of the Guardian of his paper "Bahá'u'lláh's Ground Plan for World Fellowship" to the inaugural meeting of the World Congress of Faiths in 1936. The pamphlet he wrote to all Christians under the title "The Old Churches and the New World Faith" was sent out to 10,000 so-called "responsible people" in the British Isles on the occasion of his resignation from the church, and his last book "Christ and Bahá'u'lláh" was described by the Guardian as "his crowning achievement". He participated in the Inter-Continental Conference, Stockholm, Sweden in July 1953 and passed away in March 1957 at the age of 81. ("Bahá'í World", Vol. XIII, p. 841.)

MRS ISOBEL SLADE *page 61*
It has not been possible to trace exactly when Mrs. Slade became a Bahá'í but she did tell the story of how she heard of the Faith from a visiting American believer and wished to go on pilgrimage to see the Master. Before her plans were made she heard of His passing and she went in the early 1920s. In the year 1926 there is a record of her being a "substitute" member of the National Assembly elected to "represent" the London community. From the following year the delegates elected the National Assembly from the national electorate and Mrs. Slade served as a member for fourteen of the following nineteen years. She was, in different years, Chairman, Vice-President, Secretary, Treasurer and Assistant Secretary. She was a "last ditch" pioneer to Edinburgh to form the first Assembly there in 1948. To the end of her long life she would delight her visitors with fascinating stories of her experiences in the early days of the Faith in the British Isles and she passed away in September 1972 at the age of

seventeen years later, after which he settled in London, and his third was at the time of the passing of the Master when Shoghi Effendi gave him the task of making copies of the Master's Will from the original. He was a member of the National Assembly for various periods between 1925 and 1941 and settled in Jersey as a Knight of Bahá'u'lláh in 1953 at the age of 73. He passed away in Jersey in April 1956. ("Bahá'í World", Vol. XIII, p. 881.)

SARA, LADY BLOMFIELD (SITÁRIH KHÁNUM) *page 30*
For fuller details of her devoted services to the Cause it is necessary to refer to "The Chosen Highway" and "The Bahá'í World", Vol. VIII, pp. 651–6. Born in Ireland of a fearless Protestant mother and a strong Roman Catholic father, she understood from an early age the tragedy of religious intolerance which led her to search for Truth until she found the Bahá'í Revelation. She was held in high esteem in the London society of the late "nineties" but she herself was always looking for the Promised One. She was a great friend and admirer of Basil Wilberforce, Archdeacon of Westminster. Not only did she place her home in Cadogan Gardens at the disposal of the Master during His London visits but she accompanied Him to Paris. While He was in America she went to Mount Pelerin, in Switzerland, to edit the rough notes of "Paris Talks", had them sent to Him for correction and had the book published in time for His second visit when He signed and gave away many copies. She accompanied Shoghi Effendi when he returned to Haifa after the passing of the Master and wrote the letter which was later published as "The Passing of 'Abdu'l-Bahá". She was a member of the National Spiritual Assembly for eight of its first eleven years. She passed away on the last day of 1939 and a remarkably fine obituary in the magazine "The World's Children" of March 1940 was headed "Lady Blomfield—Apostle of World Unity".

GEORGE TOWNSHEND,
Hand of the Cause of God *page 55*
First corresponded with 'Abdu'l-Bahá about 1918. The Master wrote to him "It is my hope that thy church will come under the heavenly Jerusalem". For very many years he tried to bring to the clergy of the Church of Ireland and particularly the senior

Assembly for its first two years and it was in her house in Westminster that the first meeting of the "All-England Bahá'í Council" was held on 6 June 1922. She passed away on 15 March 1938.

GEORGE PALGRAVE SIMPSON *page 9*
Was associated with the Administration of the Faith in the British Isles from its earliest days. Elected as Chairman of the first "Spiritual Council" and President of the "National Spiritual Assembly" in 1923. He also served as the Assistant Secretary and the Treasurer for some years. All the early letters from the Guardian were addressed to him and the file copies of his letters to the Holy Land, some to the Guardian and others to the various secretaries, as well as the Minutes in his handwriting, give us our closest insight into the conditions obtaining in the 1920's. At one stage he felt obliged to resign from the National Assembly but was still called upon to remain as its Treasurer and attend the meetings! He served the Cause with great distinction until his death on 31 August 1934. (See letter 30 September 1934.)

MISS ETHEL JENNER ROSENBERG *page 11*
"One of the pioneers of the Bahá'í Cause in the Western World". Having first embraced the Faith in 1899 she soon afterwards went to 'Akká, subsequently visiting many times both 'Akká and Haifa for months at a time, learning from and assisting the Master in translating and transcribing the Teachings. Beloved by all the members of the Holy Family, her passing in November 1930 at the age of 72 evoked a cabled tribute from Shoghi Effendi, who knew her well in England and welcomed her in Haifa after the passing of 'Abdú'l-Bahá. She was the one entrusted to bring the robe of Bahá'u'lláh to England, and was a member of the National Assembly from 1923–1927. ("Bahá'í World", Vol. IV, p. 263.)

ḌIÁ'U'LLÁH AṢGHARZÁDIH,
Knight of Bahá'u'lláh *page 24*
Born in 1880 into a Bahá'í family which emigrated to 'Ishqábád when he was fifteen years old, Ḍiá'u'lláh was throughout his life an active Bahá'í. His first pilgrimage was in 1903, his second was

BIOGRAPHIES 467

DR. JOHN E. ESSLEMONT
Hand of the Cause of God page 9
Born in 1874 and accepted the Faith in early 1915, Dr. Esslemont was elevated to the rank of Hand of the Cause of God after his passing on 22 November 1925 and linked by the Guardian with George Townshend and Thomas Breakwell, on the passing of George Townshend, as "One of three luminaries shedding brilliant lustre annals Irish, English, Scottish Bahá'í communities". He was "Vice-President" of the first National Assembly from October 1923 until November 1924. For fuller details of his life and works read "Dr. J. E. Esslemont" by Dr. Moojan Momen. (Bahá'í Publishing Trust, 1975–B130.)

EDWARD THEODORE HALL page 9
First heard of the Faith in 1910 in the Salford, Lancashire area and with his wife Rebecca, her brother John Charles and his wife Hester Ann Craven, made contact with Sarah Ann Ridgway, one of the earliest British Bahá'ís, and later established the second Bahá'í Group in the British Isles. In 1912 Mr. Hall and Mr. Craven went to Liverpool and met 'Abdu'l-Bahá at the boat. Five Tablets from the Master were received. In 1922 the first Spiritual Assembly was formed in Manchester with E. T. Hall as Secretary. He also "represented" Manchester on the first National Spiritual Council in 1922, and was a member of the National Assembly until 1928. He was entrusted by Shoghi Effendi with part of his early diaries and later maintained a close correspondence with the Guardian for many years. His book, "The Bahá'í Dawn; Manchester" paints a vivid picture of the early days of the Faith in Lancashire. Through Mr. Hall's correspondence with the Editor of the 'John O'Groats Journal' (Mr. R. J. G. Millar) frequent reviews and letters were published for nineteen years until the Editor's retirement. He passed away on 5 December 1962 aged 82.

MRS. THORNBURGH-CROPPER page 9
One of the first Bahá'ís of the West and possibly the first Bahá'í resident in England. Her early Bahá'í life is described in "The Chosen Highway" and in "The Bahá'í World", Vol. VIII, pp. 649–51. She was a member of the National Spiritual

BIOGRAPHIES

These biographies appear strictly in the order the names first appear in the text of the book. Where a fuller report is published elsewhere, a summary only is given together with a reference to the other material.

NAME	PAGE	NAME	PAGE
Dr. John E. Esslemont	9	John L. Marshall	210
Edward T. Hall	9	Mrs. M. Olga K. Mills	210
Mrs. Thornburgh-Cropper	9	Alfred and Lucy Sugar	210
George P. Simpson	9	Charles N. Dunning	211
Miss Ethel J. Rosenberg	11	Miss Claire Gung	211
Ḍíá'u'lláh Aṣgharzádih	24	Mrs. Lizzie F. Hainsworth	211
Lady Blomfield	30	Miss Margaret Sullivan	211
Rev. George Townshend	55	Cyril and Margaret Jenkerson	217
Mrs. Isobel Slade	61		
Mrs. Louise Ginman	63	Richard H. Backwell	218
Miss Florence Pinchon	72	Miss Ada Williams	222
Mrs. Claudia Coles	88	Mrs. Constance Langdon-Davies	224
Sister Grace Challis	88		
David Hofman	108	George K. Marshall	228
Mrs. Lilian Stevens	116	Mrs. Marguerite Preston	231
Miss Evelyn Baxter	117	Bernard Leach, CH, OBE	239
Ḥasan M. Balyuzi	122	Samuel Scott	240
Frank Hurst	126	John Ferraby	250
Mrs. Mary Basil-Hall	127	Mrs. Florence "Mother" George	256
Albert and Jeff Joseph	146		
Dr. R. St. Barbe Baker	163	Músá Banání	257
Miss Jessica Young	172	'Alí Nakhjavání	257
Lady Kathleen Hornell	172	Hassan and Isobel Ṣabrí	266
Mrs. Ursula Samandarí	172	Arthur Norton	267
Mrs. Marion Hofman	179	Eric Manton	273
Miss Una Townshend	181	Dr. 'Abbás and Shomais Afnán	278
Joseph Lee	181		
Mrs. Dorothy Ferraby	184	Edmund Cardell	281
Philip Hainsworth	187	Dr. John G. Mitchell	307
Walter Wilkins	191	Miss Irene Bennett	321
Mrs. Alma C. Gregory	191	Miss Dorothy Wigington	362
Robert Cheek	191	Ernest W. Gregory	381
Mrs. Joan Giddings	194	Dr. Ernest S. Miller	395
Hugh and Violet McKinley	194	Ian Semple	411
Dr. Luṭfu'lláh Ḥakím	195	Miss Jean Campbell	414
Fred Stahler	202	John Craven	416
Mrs. Prudence George	202		

BIOGRAPHICAL NOTES

"THEIR DAILY SUSTENANCE"

In his last message to the British Bahá'í community as a whole the Guardian wrote:

May they, as they forge ahead along the high road leading to ultimate, total and complete victory, receive as their daily sustenance, a still fuller measure of the abounding grace, promised to the believers of an earlier generation by the Centre of the Covenant, the Author of the Divine Plan, Himself, on the occasion of His twice-repeated visit to their shores, and which has been unfailingly vouchsafed to themselves, in the course of over three decades, since the birth of the Formative Age of the Faith and the rise of its Administrative Order in their homeland.

Shoghi

Whatever happened, we Bahá'ís must follow the words in our own Scriptures as being the most authentic.

In the Tablet of the Holy Mariner, the Youth means Bahá'u'lláh, Himself.

12 January 1957

In the Bahá'í Teachings it is made quite clear that when one is ill, one should seek the best available medical advice. This naturally leaves a person free to choose what they consider good in medical opinion. If you and ... feel that she is improving under the care of your own doctor, and ... is willing to wait and be patient and see if she goes on making progress, there can surely be no objection to her doing this. There are a great many as you know mental diseases and troubles at present, and the one thing Bahá'ís must not do is take a defeatist attitude toward them. The power in the Faith is such that it can sustain us on a much higher level in spite of whatever our ailments might be than other people who are denied it. This however does not mean that we should ignore medical opinion and treatment. On the contrary, we should do our best to procure the opinion of specialists and competent doctors.

15 August 1957

You should not allow the remarks made by the Bahá'ís to hurt or depress you, but should forget the personalities, and arise to do all you can, yourself, to teach the Faith.

Bahá'u'lláh enjoins work on all. No one need ever be ashamed of his job.

5 October 1952

What the Master meant in the words you quoted is simply that joy gives one more freedom to create; if the Prophets, the Master Himself, and the Guardian, had less problems and worries, They could give forth a great deal more creatively to the Cause. When He said that "grow to be as a fruitful tree" he meant that, by lifting burdens from the Guardian and trying as much as possible to do our share of the work of the Faith, we would help Shoghi Effendi to develop his full powers as Guardian and, through the Covenant, the Cause would spread its shadow over all men. This we have seen happen in the last 30 years, but that does not mean we must not try to our utmost to help him by our lives and our services.

Teaching is an individual matter; one has to sense when it is right to go further in revealing the Source of our Message; no rules exist, really, for such things.

3 March 1955

As we almost never attain any spiritual goal without seeing the next goal we must attain still beyond our reach, he urges you, who have come so far already on the path of spirituality, not to fret about the distance you still have to cover! It is an indefinite journey, and, no doubt in the next world the soul is privileged to draw closer to God than is possible when bound on this physical plane.

6 March 1955

As regards the questions you have asked, as Bahá'u'lláh says categorically that God commanded Abraham to offer up Ismá'íl, as far as we are concerned, it is Ismá'íl who was the intended sacrifice.

In view of the great antiquity of Genesis, it is quite possible that at some period the names were changed, and the error was propagated.

upon to face, you must remember that these afflictions are part of human life; and, according to our teachings one of their wisdoms is to teach us the impermanence of this world and the permanence of the spiritual bonds that we establish with God, His Prophet, and those who are alive in the faith of God. You must always remember that the Manifestations of God, Themselves, were not immune to suffering of the most human nature; and that from the hands of their relatives, they drank the bitterest potions, Bahá'u'lláh even being proffered poison by His half-brother, Mírzá Yaḥyá. Beside their afflictions, our afflictions, however terrible for us, must seem small in comparison.

Regarding your personal affairs, the Guardian will pray that your cherished hopes may be fulfilled; and that the way may open, if you both desire it, for you to serve together the Faith you are so deeply attached to. Never lose heart, and always remember that the power in this Cause is of a nature not understood or accessible to those who have not our faith in Bahá'u'lláh.

30 August 1951

The progress being made in Africa is truly miraculous, as if a special benediction from on High is being extended to this work ... He (the Guardian) feels sure that the work in Uganda will now go forward rapidly. The news from Dar is wonderful too ... The racial question all over Africa is very acute, but, while being wise and tactful, believers must realise that their standard is far from that of the white colonials. They have not gone there to uphold the white man's supremacy, but to give the Cause of God to, primarily, the black man whose home is Africa.

11 November 1951

Many times the young Bahá'ís these days seem to be living the lives of soldiers, and in a way the pioneers are the soldiers of Bahá'u'lláh, going out to plant the banner of His dominion in far corners of the earth!

The first step is to get to Africa, and, in view of the cost involved, and the state of the Fund, the poineers should make every effort to get sent out there or at least get employment after arriving, thus relieving the Bahá'í Fund as much as possible. If this fails, then of course all the expense will have to be paid by the Fund.

11 January 1951

You have voiced the same suffering, the sign of the same mystery, as has been voiced by almost all those who have been called upon to serve God. Even the Prophets of God, we know, suffered agony when the Spirit of God descended on Them and commanded Them to arise and preach. Look at Moses saying, "I am a stutterer!". Look at Muḥammad rolled in His rug in agony! The Guardian himself suffered terribly when he learned <u>he</u> was the one who had been made the Guardian.

So you see your sense of inadequacy, your realisation of your own unworthiness is not unique at all. Many, from the Highest to the humblest have had it. Now the wisdom of it is this: it is such seemingly weak instruments that demonstrate that God is the Power achieving the victories and not men. If you were a wealthy, prominent, strong individual who knew all about Africa and looked upon going out there as fun, any service you render, and victories you have, would be laid to <u>your personality</u>, not to the Cause of God! But because the reverse is true, your services will be a witness to the Power of Bahá'u'lláh and Truth of His Faith.

Rest assured, dear sister, you will ever-increasingly be sustained, and you will find joy and strength given to you, and God will reward you. You will pass through these dark hours triumphant. The first Bahá'í going on such an historic mission could not but suffer—but the compensation will be great. . . .

10 February 1951

Whenever you see tremendous personal problems in your private lives, such as those the parents of . . . have been called attachment they have to another person, sacrifice principle or bar themselves from the Path of God.

We know absence of light is darkness, but no one would assert darkness was not a fact. It exists even though it is only the absence of something else. So evil exists too, and we cannot close our eyes to it, even though it is a negative existence. We must seek to supplant it by good, and if we see an evil person is not influenceable by us, then we should shun his company for it is unhealthy.

We must love God, and in this state a general love for all men becomes possible. We cannot love each human being for himself, but our feeling towards humanity should be motivated by our love for the Father who created all men.

The Bahá'í Faith teaches man was always potentially man, even when passing through lower stages of evolution. Because he has more powers, and subtler powers than the animal, when he turns towards evil he becomes more vicious than an animal because of these very powers.

Many Theosophists accept Bahá'u'lláh as a Prophet, but we have no special relation to theosophy. It would seem that the Master had some special reason for not mentioning Bahá'u'lláh specifically in His talk to the Theosophists in Budapest. What it was we do not know, but we can assume His great tact and wisdom impelled Him not to on that occasion.

20 October 1950

He (the Guardian) feels that in as far as possible the African pioneers should seek to get a job which will take them to one of the countries chosen and ensure employment for them there. It does not seem wise or necessary for a Bahá'í to stress the fact he or she is going to teach. A person's religion is their own business, and they can talk about it privately as much as they like without neglecting their employer's work.

Also, he feels no rules can be laid down about how to teach. Usually one teaches those receptive souls one finds. The same should apply to the beginning of the work in Africa. Any direct teaching work with the more primitive tribes would have to be done after finding out the best and most tactful way of doing it.

A healthy social life and Bahá'í work can go hand in hand, but not always in times of crisis, such as these days the Cause is passing through—and the world—when great sacrifice can alone meet the demands of the situation.

He urges you to persevere and add up your accomplishments, rather than to dwell on the dark side of things. Everyone's life has both a dark and bright side. The Master said: turn your back to the darkness and your face to Me.

18 February 1950

He (the Guardian) feels that if you consider it too much of a strain to keep the Fast you should not do so. Bahá'u'lláh has exempted people who are travellers at the time; if you could keep it the days you are not travelling, and thus partake of its bounty, it would be advisable, but it is not essential.

28 March 1950

The beloved Guardian, having been in touch with you by cable, and being more over-worked this year than ever, delayed answering. You know, from what you saw here, how inefficient—to under-state the matter—his servants are. The work at the Shrine has vastly increased and of necessity, for as the first part of the building will soon be finished, the grounds around it have been entirely remodelled to fit it better and show it off. All this he has been forced to superintend and plan personally. The attacks and status of the enemies you know about. So that in all he is very tired.

4 October 1950

We must never take one sentence in the Teachings and isolate it from the rest: it does not mean we must not love, but we must reach a spiritual plane where God comes first and great human passions are unable to turn us away from Him. All the time we see people who either through the force of hate or the passionate

25 July 1949

There are no quotations from the Qur'án to support the Master's statement that European thinkers acknowledge the influence of Islám in shaping the thought of Europe. In the "Gleanings", page 95 (third printing Jan. 1943) Bahá'u'lláh says:— "Of old it has been revealed: Love of one's country is an element of the Faith of God!" Here Bahá'u'lláh is quoting not the Qur'án but an Islámic tradition, and it is this statement which the Guardian has used as the basis of his argument in the "Promised Day" that nationhood grew out of the direct influence of Muḥammad's teachings, and was one of the great contributions to mankind's evolution of Islám. The building up of nations came after Muḥammad, and was a step forward in the direction of a unified world which the teachings of Bahá'u'lláh has provided for.

22 October 1949

We must not only be patient with others, infinitely patient!, but also with our own poor selves, remembering that even the Prophets of God sometimes got tired and cried out in despair!

The end of the Plan is in view, and a long last push will, he sincerely hopes and believes, bring success and a breathing space.

Regarding your questions: it is not the City State, but the National State which Muḥammad's teachings fostered. Christ had nothing to do with the City State concept in any direct manner.

The 100 years respite is only the phrase used by the Guardian to convey the idea that for a 100 years or so the Cause had not been recognised. It draws no parallel between this century and the last one, nor does it imply a repetition of events.

The Hidden Words have no sequence. They are jewel-like thoughts sent out of the mind of the Manifestion of God to admonish and counsel men. Unfortunately Bahá'u'lláh was never asked, and never, as far as we know, stated, what the force was mentioned by Him in the "Epistle". There is nothing in the "Mysterious Forces of Civilization" implying that these great conquerors were not blood thirsty.

things: in the first place, are you quite sure two years voice-training will really carry you where you hope it will? In other words, he presumes that your teacher's opinion has been backed up by the opinion of other professionals? It would be a great pity to, in any way, sacrifice your service to the Cause for a career which in the end might not prove a substantial one. And in the second place he advises you to remain in ... and continue your studies (once you are quite assured about the outcome), providing the Plan does not reach such a critical point that it is <u>imperative</u> for you to go as a pioneer in order to really help save the situation. If this need arises in such urgency, he certainly feels you should temporarily give up your singing lessons, for, of course, no sacrifice is too great for the Cause. What we put into serving it we know serves a useful and worthy purpose, whereas the outcome of our struggles in life is never assured completely, and is certainly insignificant compared to the Faith's importance.

22 July 1949

The work on the Shrine—now beginning to rise visibly at the corners—and the spread of the Faith which brings many communications from new places, and many problems too, keeps us all busy as never before, especially the Guardian. But to see the course going ahead so fast fills our hearts with gratitude and the work involved seems a small contribution to make to such a Holy Cause.

As regards to the question you asked me to put to the Guardian about the Aqdas and the House of Justice elections: as most of the laws of the Aqdas cannot at present be enforced anywhere he has not deemed it necessary or wise to translate and promulgate them. You can orally translate them for any of the believers anxious to know exactly what they are. The National Assemblies (or Houses of Justice) will elect <u>directly</u> the International House of Justice, but just what form this election will take must be decided in the future when the proper time comes. Neither the Master nor the Guardian have made any pronouncements about punishments stipulated in the Aqdas.

which would take years, unless they really want to. All Divine Revelation seems to have been thrown out in flashes. The Prophets never composed treatises. That is why in the Qur'án and our own Writings different subjects are so often included in one Tablet. It pulsates, so to speak. That is why it is "Revelation".

Life is a constant struggle, not only against forces around us, but above all against our own ego. We can never afford to rest on our own oars, for if we do, we soon see ourselves carried down stream again. Many of those who drift away from the Cause do so for the reason that they had ceased to go on developing. They became complacent or indifferent, and consequently ceased to draw the spiritual strength and vitality from the Cause which they should have. Sometimes, of course, people fail because of a test they just do not meet, and often our severest tests come from each other. Certainly the believer should try to avert such things, and if they happen, remedy them through love. Generally speaking nine-tenths of the friends' troubles are because they don't do the Bahá'í thing, in relation to each other, to the administrative bodies or in their personal lives.

No doubt to the degree we Bahá'ís the world over strive to spread the Cause and live up to its teachings, there will be some mitigation of the suffering of the peoples of the world. But it seems apparent that the great failure to respond to Bahá'u'lláh's instructions, appeals and warnings issued in the 19th century, has now sent the world along a path, or released forces, which must culminate in a still more violent upheaval and agony. The thing is out of hand, so to speak, and it is too late to avert catastrophic trials.

You should never be too depressed about your dissatisfaction concerning not finding a job you like, a place in the world that fits you. If you analyse it this general sense of mis-fit is one of the curses of your generation, one of the products of the world's disequilibrium and chaos. It is not confined to your life, it is pretty general.

20 March 1949

He (the Guardian) fully realises that some decisions are very hard to take in life, and he urges you in this case to do two

The Guardian urges you not to be discouraged by any setbacks you may have. Life is a process of trials and testings, and these are—contrary to what we are prone to thinking—good for us, and give us stamina, and teach us to rely on God. Knowing He will help us, we can help ourselves more.

He does not know how, in the present very chaotic state of the world, you could find just the kind of job you want of driving abroad. Positions are difficult to obtain and travel so complicated. Unless you can migrate out to Africa or Australia, in some regular government scheme, he would urge you to persevere in Great Britain and do the best you can. He urges you, in the next job you have, to pray whenever you feel the conditions at work are too much for you. You will find you are helped and strengthened and once you get established in some position you may work yourself up, or go on with good references to a better employment later on. . . .

8 January 1949

The only people who are truly free of the "dross of self" are the Prophets, for to be free of one's ego is a hall-mark of perfection. We humans are <u>never</u> going to become perfect, for perfection belongs to a realm we are not destined to enter. However, we must constantly mount higher, seek to be more perfect.

The ego is the animal in us, the heritage of the flesh which is full of <u>selfish</u> desires. By obeying the laws of God, seeking to live the life laid down in our teachings, and prayer and struggle, we can subdue our egos. We call people "saints" who have achieved the highest degree of mastery over their egos.

There is no contradiction between Gleanings p. 66 and p. 262. In one place He says the mirror will never be free from dross, in the other He says it will be "<u>so</u> cleared as to be able" etc. It is a relative thing; perfection will never be reached, but great and ever greater, progress can be made.

The word "Guardian" in the Seven Valleys has no connection with the Bahá'í Guardianship.

The Qur'án should be to some extent studied by the Bahá'ís but they certainly need not seek to acquire a mastery over it,

It is quite natural for anyone, observing the present state of the world, to feel very depressed and apprehensive of the future. Any intelligent person must be wondering what you are wondering. It is indeed hard to see what lies ahead of us in the near future—but we, as Bahá'ís, unlike most people, have absolute assurance that the distant future is serene and bright. We do not know if there will be another Great War; what we do know is this: that unless people become spiritually awakened in time, great suffering, maybe in the form of war, will come upon them, for humanity must be unified, must be redeemed. If men refuse absolutely to take the easier road of faith, of seeking out God's Manifestation for this age and accepting Him, then they will bring upon themselves a fresh crisis in human affairs and very great affliction. What we, as Bahá'ís, must do is our duty; we cannot do other people's duty for them, alas, but we can fulfil our own sacred responsibilities by serving our fellow-men, living a Bahá'í life, teaching the Faith, and strengthening its budding world order.

He urges you, just as you have surmounted the crisis in your own life, through faith and courage, to now go out and serve the Cause with that same faith and courage. We must leave to God the final reckoning with His creatures today—but meantime we must give them His Message.

17 October 1948

The Cause in England seems, in spite of financial handicaps, to be going forward in Seven League boots. He (the Guardian) is truly proud of the British believers, and this is more than he could say in the past, when the work for years seemed to be stagnating! Those days are now passed forever, he feels sure.

23 December 1948

He (the Guardian) is very glad to see you are now living the life of an active Bahá'í and keeping in close touch with dear ... who is a fine friend to have, with his devotion to the Cause and his optimism.

23 June 1948

He (the Guardian) encouraged him to face manfully the future, accept the legitimate sanction of society as punishment for his admittedly anti-social conduct, and realise that his very suffering, humiliation and punishment can—if he will let it—be the means of freeing him from many of his past weaknesses and mistakes, and making him a worthy member of society. He should look to the future, for there is in his power, with Bahá'u'lláh's help, to shape into a worthy and constructive way of life. . . .

The English Bahá'ís did gloriously succeed after all! Hitching one's wagon to a star, however impractical it may seem, does bring results, for man, with God to help him, does possess strengths far beyond the mere materialist's ken!

As regards your question about p. 41, Kitáb-i-Íqán; to say that, after 622 A.D., Christendom was Islám in disguise is a little misleading. The Sun of Truth, after the advent of Muḥammad, no longer shone from the Christian horizon. Islám was, from then until the Báb's advent, the Path of Truth.

We should never insist on teaching those who are not really ready for the Cause. If a man is not hungry, you cannot make him eat. Among the Theosophists there are, no doubt, many receptive souls, but those who are satisfied should be just associated with in a friendly way, but let alone. Once a seeker comes to accept the concept of progressive religion, and accepts Bahá'u'lláh as the Manifestation for this day, the reincarnation concept will fade away in the light of truth; we should try and avoid controversial issues in the beginning if possible.

Mírzá Abu'l-Faḍl was a very excellent and erudite Bahá'í teacher. Although he did err sometimes, yet in identifying Abraham with Zoroaster, he is not confusing the Prophet Abraham with the Prophet Zoroaster, as the name of Zoroaster was supposed to have been "Abram".

20 September 1948

He (the Guardian) is very happy indeed to see the change in your attitude and to hear that you are now not only a recognised member of our Faith, but a prospective Bahá'í pioneer!

proving, the testing, will surely consist of the way you determine to take your punishment.

Life is based on laws: physical, man-made, and spiritual. As you have broken the laws of the society in which you live, you will have to stand up like a man and take your punishment. The spirit in which you do this is the most important thing, and constitutes a great opportunity for you. He (the Guardian) advises you to turn your face towards the future, to realise that when you are set free you have loving and helpful friends to go to, an upright job awaiting you, and you can also become active in serving our glorious Faith. So really everything lies before you. But at present, until your sentence is up, you must live within yourself in a way not to spoil the new future awaiting you. You must not become bitter—for after all you are only reaping what you planted. Bahá'u'lláh and 'Abdu'l-Bahá, through no crime of their own, spent the better part of their lives in exile and imprisoned, but they never became embittered although they were the victims of injustice. You, on the other hand, are the victim of injustice which you have inflicted on yourself—therefore you certainly have no right to be bitter towards the world.

He urges you to grasp firmly the teachings of our Faith, the love of your family and many Bahá'í friends, to put the past behind entirely, realising that it can do you no more harm; on the contrary, through changing you and making you spiritually aware, this very past can be a means of enriching your life in the future! He will certainly ardently pray for your happiness, your victory over yourself, and that you may become an exemplary and active Bahá'í.

9 June 1948

"Reciting" the Greatest Name means to repeat it over and over, silently or out loud....

The chairman of the local assembly is, if present, the logical and appropriate person to take charge of the consultation period between the assembly and the community members at the Nineteen Day Feast.

state of their countrymen! It is a pity, and they should certainly try, as believers, to be cheerful and radiant; but he (the Guardian) feels the greatest sympathy for them, and considers that when their present achievements are assessed in future, people will give them a double measure of praise for having done so much when they were least fit to do it. The spirit of determination, and their perseverance, are truly outstanding.

Just because some people have lost their vision of the Cause, or never had a proper grasp of its implications before entering it, and leave the fold, should not cause undue discouragement. There are bound to be such cases, and although every moral support should be given them, if they still wish to withdraw, they fall off—as you said— like withered leaves from the Tree of the Faith, and do it no real harm.

He likes to be provided with facts by the friends, when they ask his advice, for although his decisions are guided by God, he is not, like the Prophet, omniscient at will, in spite of the fact that he often senses a situation or condition without having any detailed knowledge of it. . . .

26 March 1948

One of the greatest problems in the Cause is the relation of the believers to each other; for their immaturity (shared with the rest of humanity) and imperfections retard the work, create complications, and discourage each other. And yet we must put up with these things and try and combat them through love, patience and forgiveness individually, and proper administrative action collectively.

8 April 1948

We Bahá'ís firmly believe that it is possible, if we have the right spirit, to make our stumbling blocks stepping-stones to progress. You have already, through at last facing yourself and acknowledging that you have both failed and erred in managing your life so far, set your feet on the right path. But now this new and spiritual condition in you is going to be proved—and the personal matter, and each believer must act according to his own judgment and the needs of the Faith. In times of crisis, whether in the affairs of the Cause or in one's own family, people naturally behave differently from under normal circumstances. But decisions in these matters must rest with each individual Bahá'í.

Generally speaking the secretary of an assembly must be careful to convey exactly what the majority decision or advice of the body was. There can surely be no objection to his putting it in proper terms and clarifying the matter according to the decision or instruction of the assembly. But he should of course not introduce his personal views unless endorsed by the assembly.

The nature of assembly minutes is a matter for the body itself to decide. Naturally all important subjects brought up and notes must be recorded, but how detailed the record must be is for the members themselves to decide.

'Abdu'l-Bahá said we must sacrifice the important for the most important. The most important thing now for the English Bahá'ís is to accomplish their Plan. The sacrifice of other activities, cultural or otherwise, is not of very much importance compared to their goal. They can always return, when they have more time, to such pursuits. To serve any great Cause or purpose requires sacrifice....

Bahá'u'lláh is not the intermediary between other Manifestations and God. Each has His own relation to the Primal Source. But in the sense that Bahá'u'lláh is the greatest Manifestation to yet appear, the One who consummates the Revelation of Moses, He was the One Moses conversed with in the Burning Bush. In other words, Bahá'u'lláh identifies the glory of the God-Head on that occasion with Himself. No distinction can be made amongst the Prophets in the sense that They all proceed from one Source, and are of one essence. But Their stations and functions in this world are different.

4 March 1948

It is not surprising, in view of the gloom overhanging the entire world, and in conjunction with their run-down, exhausted state due to war conditions and present circumstances of life in England, that the British Bahá'ís should sometimes reflect the

13 October 1947

Regarding your own condition: he (the Guardian) strongly urges you not to dwell on yourself. Each one of us, if we look into our failures, is sure to feel unworthy and despondent, and this feeling only frustrates our constructive efforts and wastes time. The thing for us to focus on is the glory of the Cause and the Power of Bahá'u'lláh which can make of a mere drop a surging sea! You certainly have no right to feel negative; you have embraced this glorious Faith and arisen with devotion to serve it, and your labours are greatly appreciated by both the Guardian and your fellow-Bahá'ís. With something as positive as the Faith and all it teaches behind you, you should be a veritable lion of confidence, and he will pray that you may become so.

There is, unfortunately, no way that one can force his own good upon a man. The element of free will is there and all we believers—and even the Manifestation of God Himself—can do is to offer the truth to mankind. If the people of the world persist, as they seem to be doing, in their blind materialism, they must bear the consequences in a prolongation of their present condition, and even a worsening of it. Our duty as Bahá'ís is to build up such a love and unity within our own ranks that the people will be attracted by this example to the Cause. We also must teach all we can and strengthen the Bahá'í community in the Administration. But more we cannot do to avert the great sufferings which seemingly still lie ahead of the world in its present evil state.

14 October 1947

Summer School is, indeed, a wonderful experience, for at the present time it is the only institution that affords the Bahá'ís of England an opportunity of all living together, for however short a time, as a community, and this and the spirit it engenders, has a very inspiring affect.

19 October 1947

He (the Guardian) does not feel that it is desirable to lay down any conditions for giving to the Bahá'í Fund. This is an entirely countries of the West to hear the Divine Message, and was blessed by two visits from the Centre of the Covenant! Surely the older Bahá'ís must be astonished to see new centres springing up in a matter of months after years of an almost static condition! It shows that wherever and whenever the friends arise to serve, the mysterious power latent in this Divine Cause rushes in to bless and reinforce their labours far beyond their fondest hopes.

He is very happy to hear you are established as a pioneer, with a business of your own, and you may be sure he will pray for your material as well as spiritual success in this goal town....

27 September 1947

There is no objection to children who are as yet unable to memorise a whole prayer learning certain sentences only.

He (the Guardian) does not feel that the friends should make a practice of saying grace or of teaching it to children. This is not part of the Bahá'í Faith, but a Christian practice, and as the Cause embraces members of all religions we should be careful not to introduce into it the customs of our previous beliefs. Bahá'u'lláh has given us the obligatory prayers, also prayers before sleeping, for travellers, etc., we should not introduce a new set of prayers He has not specified, when He has given us already so many for so many occasions....

27 September 1947

He (the Guardian) does not feel you should permit your speech impediment to give you a sense of inferiority. Moses stammered! And what you are and what you believe as a Bahá'í give you a tremendous advantage over others. This does not mean that you should not make every effort to overcome it, and go to doctors for advice and assistance. He also assures you he will pray that you may overcome this difficulty entirely, also that wherever you are the way will open for you to teach and serve the Faith.

20 November 1946

The Master unceasingly emphasised the importance of unity among the friends, and, if anything, it is of even greater importance in this present chaotic state of the world than it was in His days. The people are longing for an example—proof that harmony and love can actually exist in a community—and it is one of the primary duties of the Bahá'ís to demonstrate these great principles in their relations with each other.

15 February 1947

Philosophy, as you will study it and later teach it, is certainly not one of the sciences that begins and ends in words. Fruitless excursions into metaphysical hair-splitting is meant, not a sound branch of learning like philosophy.

We have no historical proof of the truth of the Master's statement regarding the Greek philosophers visiting the Holy Land, etc. but such proof may come to light through research in the future.

As regards your own studies: he would advise you not to devote too much of your time to the abstract side of philosophy, but rather to approach it from a more historical angle. As to correlating philosophy with the Bahá'í teachings; this is a tremendous work which scholars in the future can undertake. We must remember that not only are all the teachings not yet translated into English, but they are not even all collected yet. Many important Tablets may still come to light which are at present owned privately.

18 February 1947

He (the Guardian) wishes he more often got such glad news in one letter! It seems that at last the Cause in England is really getting into its stride, and that the British community of believers are beginning to show forth the fruits of the many blessings showered on them—for England was one of the first

What 'Abdu'l-Bahá always pointed out in this matter is that these psychic powers were not to be used in this world, and that, indeed, it was dangerous to cultivate them here. They should be left dormant, and not exploited, even when we do so with the sincere belief we are helping others. We do not understand their nature and have no way of being sure of what is true and what is false in such matters.

If children are inclined to be psychic they should not be blamed for it too harshly, they should not be encouraged to strengthen their powers in this direction.

People who do not feel they can obey or accept the Teachings on a subject cannot be considered Bahá'ís, voting or otherwise. If a time comes when they feel ready to surrender their opinions to One we believe divinely guided, they should be joyously welcomed back into the Faith.

P.S. These friends you mention are being upset over this question should realise that if they reserve the right to disregard the Teachings on one subject, they must give the same right to other Bahá'ís, and obviously there can be no unity or strength in a Faith composed of individuals who only believe in part and not all of it. We must never prefer our wills to the Will of God.

19 March 1946

The Bahá'ís should refrain from signing petitions designed to bring pressure on the Government which may have any political character whatsoever. There are so many other people who can carry on progressive types of activity, but only the Bahá'ís can do the work of Bahá'u'lláh....

21 May 1946

Keeping the Fast is enjoined upon all Bahá'ís, regardless of nationality; it has a very salutary effect both physically and spiritually, and the friends should realise Bahá'u'lláh never would have instituted it if it were detrimental to the health. The Master referred to the Fast in talks to pilgrims, and some Tablets, but most material on this subject is not yet translated.

7 July 1945

What England needs is a higher percentage of people able to meet and attract the public on a large scale, and he hopes you will, in the course of giving the Message to every soul that yearns for it, make a special effort to confirm people who in their turn will be able to arise and broadcast the teachings.

The efforts of the friends are, of course, needed to accomplish the objectives of the Six Year Teaching Plan, and they should be encouraged to do their part, even though they may imagine themselves incapable of discharging such duties!

The Tablet of Visitation is a compilation of words of Bahá'u'lláh, revealed at different times for those who were far from Him, made by Nabíl, at the Master's instruction, after the Ascension of Bahá'u'lláh. . . .

3 March 1946

A city like London needs a really impressive, central and suitable room which will, on its own merits, create a favourable impression, and he hopes the friends will bear this in mind, and at the earliest possible date get quarters that are not in a basement.

As to attracting the youth; there must be a great number of serious-minded people coming back to civilian life. Of course youth attracts youth, and if once an active nucleus of young Bahá'ís could be formed, and conduct their own meetings no doubt they would soon get others interested.

4 March 1946

He (the Guardian) was very sorry to hear that . . . has left the Cause, and suggests that you point out to her, and to any other of the friends who are confused and upset over this matter, that the Manifestation of God only gives us teachings and instructions designed for our good and protection, and that if each person reserves the right to obey his own conscience, the logical conclusion is we don't need any spiritual authority to guide and protect us, the authority of our own consciences is sufficient!

believers but also are actively conducting fireside classes and hold public meetings. All these are evidences of progress, and you should feel happy and encouraged about them.

The believers, as we all know, should endeavour to set such an example in their personal lives and conduct that others will feel impelled to embrace a Faith which reforms human character. However, unfortunately, not everyone achieves easily and rapidly the victory over self. What every believer, new or old, should realise is that the Cause _has_ the spiritual power to re-create us if we make the effort to let that power influence us, and the greatest help in this respect is prayer. We must supplicate Bahá'u'lláh to assist us to overcome the failings in our own characters, and also exert our own will-power in mastering ourselves.

He will certainly pray for the work of the beloved Cause there and especially that new souls may be attracted and embrace the Faith. He will also pray that the believers may, for the sake of God, draw close to each other and not permit each other's short-comings to be a source of disunity and consequently a means of depriving thirsty souls of this life-giving Message! The world is full of evil and dark forces and the friends must not permit these forces to get hold of them by thinking and feeling negatively towards each other....

Undated

His (the Guardian's) burden is truly so heavy—no doubt in the future people will see his life in its proper perspective and be able to appreciate what he has done, to all intents and purposes entirely alone, for the Cause.

10 May 1945

Many of the most valuable, enkindled and erudite teachers the Cause has possessed were formerly members of the clergy, Islámic or Christian.

cause us suffering and are a test to us in our fellow-believers, most especially if we love them and have been their teacher!

The Guardian would advise you to leave your friend to himself, to associate with him, his wife and sister-in-law with love and forbearance in every way possible, but not to agonise over the past or let it cloud your Bahá'í life. You have given him the greatest gift in the world: the Faith. Now he must be responsible for his own soul. Your prayers and example can no doubt reach and help him.

It is true the Bahá'ís should try and live a normal healthy life. But we cannot for a moment overlook the abnormal state of the world. If there had not been believers ready to give their health, comfort, pleasure—everything, for the Cause in these dark days, the work would not have gone on. What are these sacrifices compared to keeping a beacon of the Light of Bahá'u'lláh burning in dark London all these war years?

The Guardian is very glad to hear you are so active, both in teaching and administrative work, and he will pray that Bahá'u'lláh may bless and guide you and enable you to serve the Cause in an ever increasing measure. He will also pray for your personal happiness. . . .

27 November 1944

The work in England has, indeed, progressed slowly from the standpoint of enlarging the Faith's membership and establishing new centres and assemblies. On the other hand, however, the British Bahá'ís have consolidated the administration and thus prepared the way for intensified teaching activities when conditions make life easier for the people in that country. They have also built up a very helpful institution in the Publishing Trust, one calculated to impress the public and aid greatly in their own and other countries' teaching programmes. The Faith there needs more active, devoted, young believers like yourself.

27 January 1945

He was very happy to hear of the marked progress the Cause has made in . . . and that you have not only a number of new

May 1943

If, however, you find your health affected by keeping the Fast the Guardian would advise you to consult a physician, and if he tells you you are unable to fast then of course, you should abstain from doing so.

26 May 1943

He (the Guardian) feels that Bahá'í children like you have a lot of wonderful work to do for others in the future. But you don't even have to wait until you grow up, you can help your dear Mother teach the Cause to others right now, and also tell your playmates about it. The Guardian is going to pray that you may grow up to be a shining light in the Cause of Bahá'u'lláh.

6 August 1943

The Master reflects the qualities of the Manifestations as if He were a mirror. He reflects not only those of Bahá'u'lláh but also of Christ as He is the exemplar of the spirit of the Prophet....

... These matters are left to the discretion of the N.S.A. The principle the Guardian has stated ... the addition of further regulations and rulings to those already laid down in the bye-laws he strongly discourages; he feels it is better, as far as possible, to settle problems as they arise rather than create too much red tape and hem in the spirit of the Cause into a rigid form.

17 October 1944

There is a difference between character and faith; it is often very hard to accept this fact and put up with it, but the fact remains that a person may believe in and love the Cause—even to being ready to die for it—and yet not have a good personal character, or possess traits at variance with the teachings. We should try to change, to let the Power of God help recreate us and make us true Bahá'ís in deed as well as in belief. But sometimes the process is slow, sometimes it never happens because the individual does not try hard enough. But these things remembrance of that word may aid some soul to seek and find the Faith.

At present people are too engulfed in hopes, events, desires, and various partizanships, to realise that there is no way out for humanity except to accept the Divine Plan for this Day, and put its healing principles and laws into practice. But gradually their eyes will be opened, and it is for this time that the friends must labour to bring the knowledge of the Cause before as wide a public as possible.

September 1942

He (the Guardian) fully realises how much strain you are subjected to, but he also feels that in so far as is compatible with your health you should persevere in all your Bahá'í activities, as your services could ill be spared in any field at this time.

25 September 1942

There is an answer in the teachings for everything; unfortunately the majority of the Bahá'ís, however intensely devoted and sincere they may be, lack for the most part the necessary scholarship and wisdom to reply to and refute the claims and attacks of people with some education and standing....

It is hard to foresee at present the way in which humanity is going to become spiritualised. At present it seems, the increased sufferings yet to be borne, combined with a far wider diffusion of the Divine Message, will bring about unbelievable changes in the days to come....

5 May 1943

Unless and until the believers really come to realise they are one spiritual family, knit together by a bond more lasting than mere physical ties can ever be, they will not be able to create that warm community atmosphere which alone can attract the hearts of humanity, frozen for lack of real love and feeling.

19 October 1941

The English Bahá'ís are being tested in both faith and character very severely, and the Guardian is deeply gratified to see the manner in which they are responding, a manner that proclaims to all who witness it that these souls are true Bahá'ís.

The Master longed so to see the believers perfect their faith in living. Now is the supreme hour of test applied, not only to the whole world, but to the Bahá'ís too; how they act, to the degree they adhere to the spirit and the letter of their Faith, will point the way to watching humanity and demonstrate the worth of being a follower of Bahá'u'lláh . . . the good news you convey of the spirit and devotion of the English friends greatly pleases Shoghi Effendi.

His hope and prayer is that during these times of danger, stress, and misery, the Bahá'ís will seek out amidst their fellow-countrymen those jewel-like souls that belong to Bahá'u'lláh and bring them the blessing and comfort of His Faith.

30 October 1941

He (the Guardian) feels that the great point is to confirm people of true capacity and ability—from whatever social stratum they may be, because the Cause needs now, and will ever increasingly need, souls of great ability who can bring it before the public at large, administer its ever-growing affairs, and contribute to its advancement in every field.

As the Guardian's thoughts are very often with the English friends, and he feels deeply conscious of both their trials and the wonderful Bahá'í spirit in which they are meeting them, he feels they have almost a special right to call on him, and he welcomes their letters and any news of them he receives. So you must feel free to turn to him whenever you feel the necessity of doing so. . . .

14 March 1942

He also approves of the idea of advertising the name "Bahá'í" as widely as possible, as we can never tell at what future date the results. This law of sacrifice operates in our own lives, as well as in the lives of the Divine Manifestations.

18 April 1940

In these stormy days his thoughts are often with you and our dear English believers, and his prayers continue to be offered on your behalf, that you may all be protected and remain safe, so that when this great ordeal of war which is threatening to engulf the whole world will have passed, you may all be able to continue serving our beloved Cause, and this time through more effective means and on a larger scale than ever before.

The immediate future, as clearly predicted by the Master, must necessarily be very dark for the Cause as well as for the whole world, but the promises He has repeatedly given us of a glorious future for the Faith and for mankind as a whole are of such character as should assuredly sustain and strengthen us amidst the trials and tribulations of the days ahead.

2 June 1941

There can be no doubt that after the present suffering of humanity many souls, who at present show only a mild interest in the Faith, will turn to it as the sole road which can lead them out of the valley of blindness and misery to the "green pastures" promised by their Lord....

1 August 1941

Wherever the Cause is being spread, as it grows in strength, people increasingly will take sides both for and against it. Therefore he (the Guardian) is not surprised to learn that you are finding yourself in the position, sometimes being upheld and sometimes being attacked! It is a great bounty from God that you have had a training in this world which so admirably suits you for a champion of His Faith and an exponent of His doctrines....

social life is essentially based on the principle of the subordination of the individual will to that of society. It neither suppresses the individual nor does it exalt him to the point of making him an anti-social creature, a menace to society. As in everything it follows the 'golden mean'. The only way that society can function is for the minority to follow the will of the majority.

The other main objection to the conscientious objectors is that their method of establishing peace is too negative. Non-co-operation is too passive a philosophy to become an effective way for social reconstruction. Their refusal to bear arms can never establish peace. There should be first a spiritual revitalisation which nothing, except the Cause of God, can effectively bring to every man's heart.

3 February 1937

Do not feel discouraged if your labours do not always yield an abundant fruitage. For a quick and rapidly-won success is not always the best and the most lasting. The harder you strive to attain your goal, the greater will be the confirmations of Bahá'u'lláh, and the more certain you can feel to attain success. Be cheerful, therefore, and exert yourself with full faith and confidence. For Bahá'u'lláh has promised His Divine assistance to every one who arises with a pure and detached heart to spread His Holy Word, even though he may be bereft of every human knowledge and capacity, and notwithstanding the forces of darkness and of opposition which may be arrayed against him. The goal is clear, the path safe and certain, and the assurances of Bahá'u'lláh as to the eventual success of our efforts quite emphatic. Let us keep firm, and whole-heartedly carry on the great work which He has entrusted into our hands.

31 March 1938

With reference to your question as to whether individuals can help each other by accepting to suffer for each other's sake. Surely such sacrifice for our fellow humans can have helpful condemns, in vehement language, all forms of sexual laxity, unbridled licence and lust. The Bahá'í standard of sex morality is thus very high, but it is by no means unreasonably rigid. While free love is condemned, yet marriage is considered as a holy act which every human being should be encouraged, though not forced, to perform. Sex instinct, like all other human instincts, is not necessarily evil. It is a power which, if properly directed, can bring joy and satisfaction to the individual. If misused or abused it brings, of course, incalculable harm not only to the individual but also to the society in which he lives. While the Bahá'ís condemn asceticism and all extreme forms of self-mortification they at the same time view with disfavour the current theories of sex ethics which cannot but bring ruin to human society. In the Bahá'í Cause marriage has been encouraged, but made somewhat difficult, conditioned as it is upon the consent of the four parents. Divorce, on the other hand, has been made relatively easy, and the sociologists are just beginning to realise the importance of this law. . . .

6 April 1936

He (the Guardian) is of the opinion, however, that while the secondary aspects of Bahá'í Administration should be left out, a comprehensive statement as to its origin and significance in the Bahá'í Dispensation is of vital importance in any work of the Cause, especially if it is written by a believer. The main thing is to properly present the subject so that the reader may be able to grasp it.

21 November 1936

With reference to the absolute pacifists, or conscientious objectors to war; their attitude, judged from the Bahá'í standpoint, is quite anti-social and due to its exaltation of the individual conscience leads inevitably to disorder and chaos in society. Extreme pacifists are thus very close to the anarchists, in the sense that both these groups lay an undue emphasis on the rights and merits of the individual. The Bahá'í conception of spreading the Message, and not until such an obstacle has been completely removed can the Cause effectively spread and establish itself in the West. This religious conservatism is in many respects far more dangerous and more difficult to wipe out than the religious apathy which is so rapidly invading all classes of society.

In view of that, it is, at least for the present, more advantageous to teach the Message in an indirect way, so as to gradually attract and confirm those who have the spiritual capacity of appreciating the Cause in its fullness.

29 May 1935

As to your question concerning the meaning of physical suffering and its relation to mental and spiritual healing. Physical pain is a necessary accompaniment of all human existence, and as such is unavoidable. As long as there will be life on earth, there will be also suffering, in various forms and degrees. But suffering, although an inescapable reality, can nevertheless be utilised as a means for the attainment of happiness. This is the interpretation given to it by all the prophets and saints who, in the midst of severe tests and trials, felt happy and joyous and experienced what is best and holiest in life. Suffering is both a reminder and a guide. It stimulates us better to adapt ourselves to our environmental conditions, and thus leads the way to self improvement. In every suffering one can find a meaning and a wisdom. But it is not always easy to find the secret of that wisdom. It is sometimes only when all our suffering has passed that we become aware of its usefulness. What man considers to be evil turns often to be a cause of infinite blessings. And this is due to his desire to know more than he can. God's wisdom is, indeed, inscrutable to us all, and it is no use pushing too far trying to discover that which shall always remain a mystery to our mind.

In connection with your question relative to the Bahá'í solution of sex problems. On the question of sex the Bahá'ís are, in most of their fundamental views, in full agreement with the upholders of traditional morality. Bahá'u'lláh, like all the other Prophets and Messengers of God, preaches abstinence, and

1 December 1933

One more European is reported to have seen Bahá'u'lláh from a distance, but Professor Browne was the only Westerner who actually met Him.

4 June 1934

You should, nevertheless, persevere in your efforts until your immediate objective has been fully attained. God cannot, indeed, withdraw from so devoted and so capable a Bahá'í like you all the guidance and assistance you need for the effective discharge of your responsibilities and obligations to the Cause. Be, therefore, confident in Bahá'u'lláh's help. His Spirit will lead you, and will feed your soul with that spiritual sustenance whereby you will be able to overcome the obstacles which seem to so hopelessly beset your path.

10 November 1934

When you quote the Báb, or anyone of His disciples you should make it clear that the words attributed to them are by no means their exact words. They constitute the substance of their message, and thus are not as definite as the quoted words of Bahá'u'lláh or the Master. So, the Guardian suggests that you should either omit the quotation marks, or to specify that the passages quoted are not the exact words used by the Báb and His disciples. In the future edition of Nabíl's Narrative a similar explanation will have to be inserted in the "Dawn Breakers".

You state that the Christian Dispensation "was six hundred and twenty-two years old at the time of the Hegira". The Guardian suggests that the words "at the time of the Hegira" be omitted as they may give the impression that the Revelation of Christ extended beyond the date of the Hegira.

8 February 1935

Religious conservatism, particularly in England, constitutes indeed a serious obstacle which the friends have to meet when or material, the Faith would have undoubtedly made a tremendous progress in the world....

12 November 1933

You use the expression "till time ends". This is misleading, for there is no end to time. The Guardian suggests that you should either use the term used in the Íqán "till the end that has no end", or express it in such a manner that would give the idea that time has no end....

Jehovah is a title of God, whereas Bahá'u'lláh is the title of the Manifestation of God.

... you count the period of the Christian Dispensation as having lasted for 1844 years. As in the Bahá'í teachings Muḥammad is considered as an independent prophet of God, you have to consider His Dispensation as having begun in 622 A.D. The Christian Dispensation must, therefore, end in 622 A.D. and from that date till 1844 is the era of Muḥammad. 1260 is the calculation based on the lunar system. In other words, it is the Hegira year or A.H. You should either specify this fact, or base your calculation on the solar year, in which case it will be less than 1260, as there is a difference of one year in every 33 years.

... you should point out that, only so far as it is recorded in the Gospel, Jesus gave two material ordinances only. Our knowledge of Jesus' life and teachings is rather fragmentary and so it would be more correct if you specify that these ordinances are only those recorded in the Gospel, and they may not be the only ones. There may be other teachings and ordinances too, of which no record is left.

... Muhammadanism is not only the last of the world religions, but a fuller Revelation than any one preceding it. The Qur'án is not only more authoritative than any previous religious gospel, but it contains also much more; ordinances, teachings and precepts, which taken together constitute a fuller Revelation of God's purpose and law to mankind than Christianity, Judaism or any other previous Dispensation. This view is in complete accord with the Bahá'í philosophy of progressive revelation, and should be thoroughly accepted and taught by every loyal ... Bahá'í.

You cannot imagine to what an extent our dear Guardian has, in this loss, been deprived for ever of the sustaining influence and kindness that this Most Exalted Leaf used to shower daily upon him. In this beautiful Tribute we can trace the life of this beautiful soul, witness with anguish all the sufferings and deprivations that she has endured. Now we should, all of us, try in turn to follow her saintly path and direct all our energy to serve the Cause which has been so dear to her.

6 May 1933

What the Faith needs, even more than teachers, is books that expound the true significance of its principles in the light of modern thought and social problems.

29 May 1933

He was deeply touched by the strong attachment of the friends to one who, besides being the beloved daughter of Bahá'u'lláh, exemplified perhaps more than any one the true spirit that animates His Teachings. His (the Guardian's) sincere hope is that your love for our departed Greatest Holy Leaf will attain such depth and intensity as to enable you to follow in her footsteps and to carry out with increasing devotion and vigour all that she cherished so much during the entire course of her earthly life. The memory of her saintly life will undoubtedly sustain and feed your energies and will provide you with that spiritual potency of which we are all in such a great need.

17 October 1933

How much the Faith is in need of able and devoted souls like you who are ready to suffer every possible deprivation for its sake. If every believer was ready to contribute his share, however humble and small, and through any means, whether intellectual generally believed that the Hidden Words was dictated by Bahá'u'lláh to His secretary as He strolled on the banks of the river in Baghdád—in sections rather than all at one time.

As to the date of the Íqán, I think it can be calculated from the actual text and I have it in my papers as 1278 A.H., i.e. 1861 A.D. You will find that in the text itself. It was written in answer to questions put by a distinguished Bábí.

16 May 1932

Even though outwardly the number of the friends has not been increasing so rapidly, yet the spirit has not remained idle. The leaven of spirituality has been working, and when the time will come it will manifest itself in a sudden awakening. All that we need is a little more courage, perseverance and patience. There are many important men that are attentively watching the progress of the Faith but are reluctant to come forward and extend a helping hand. In time they will, and then we shall see the Cause of God spread by leaps and bounds....

10 August 1932

Your touching words of condolence and sympathy in connection with the sudden removal of the Greatest Holy Leaf from our midst have greatly comforted (the Guardian's) aching heart and relieved the burden of sorrow that lies so heavily upon him.

In this great calamity which has seized the entire body of the followers of the Faith in both East and West our Guardian's loss is the greatest and the most cruel. His sole comfort, at this terrible hour, is to see the friends united and working together for the realisation of our departed Khánum's dearest wishes.

15 March 1933

He deeply appreciates your sincere, well-expressed reference to the Tribute he has written to the dearly beloved Greatest Holy Leaf.

7 November 1931

The present social and economic problems that are facing the British people are surely occupying their whole attention, but they should also operate as a reminder and draw them closer to spiritual matters. The people have to be made conscious of the fact that without a complete change in our outlook and a total reform of the guiding principles of our life, such as the Cause advocates, our social and economic problems cannot be solved nor our conditions ameliorated. Nothing short of the full message of Bahá'u'lláh can end the sufferings that are befalling humanity.

2 January 1932

It is strange how much suffering man has to put up with while on this earth. Our consolation should be however that it is part of a divine plan whose worth we cannot yet fathom....

... Shoghi Effendi wishes ... to encourage those who are talented to give expression to the wonderful spirit that animates them. We need poets and writers for the Cause.... Some of the poems are written by very youthful persons yet they ring so true and give expression to such thoughts that one should halt and admire. In Persia the Cause has given birth to poets that even non-Bahá'ís consider them as great. We hope before long we will have similar persons arise in the West.

10 January 1932

In Persia the Cause gave birth to many poets of national standing. Let us hope that the west will follow suit and produce similar talents.

23 February 1932

The exact date in which the Hidden Words was written you can find on the opening page of Mrs. J. E. Stannard's translation published in Cairo. She gives a line in the Master's own handwriting giving the date as 1274 A.H. (1857–8 A.D.). It is

Parts of his narrative were read in the presence of Bahá'u'lláh and approved by Him. 'Abdu'l-Bahá also went over sections of his narrative. . . .

Shoghi Effendi has found in the papers of 'Abdu'l-Bahá a complete set of the Báb's Tablets to the 18 Letters of the Living, all written in His own hand-writing and bearing His seal. In addition to these there are two other Tablets both written by Himself in exquisite hand-writing, the one addressed to the 19th Letter who was Himself and the other to "Him whom God will make manifest", i.e. Bahá'u'lláh. This last one has three seals and is written on blue paper. . . .

Regarding the question raised in your letter. . . . The Bahá'ís in Persia avoid political posts and positions, abstain from any interference in matters pertaining to the policy of the state, but fill the more important administrative posts that have no political character. They feel that in this manner they can best serve the interest of their country and prove by their action their integrity and attachment to Persia. . . .

Shoghi Effendi is enclosing an extremely interesting account given by a certain Dr. Cormick, an English physician long resident in Tabríz of his meeting with the Báb. He is apparently the only Westerner who has met the Báb and recorded his impressions . . . Shoghi Effendi thinks of adding it to his notes.

30 April 1931

. . . You could also in a quiet way speak to persons whom you think are ready for such a message and would appreciate the light when they see it. Try to form around you a group of Bahá'ís who are well versed in the teachings and who are ready to assist you in serving the Cause. In short try to form an assembly of pure and competent souls. Meanwhile you could write, for the Cause is in great need of first class literature and you are gifted along that line.

The Cause surely needs sacrifices, in fact it is only through sacrifice that it can progress, but such determined activity should be coupled with wisdom and caution if it is not going to be a temporary flare. Intimate talk and personal contact has proven the surest and quietest way for establishing a group. . . .

introductory to the advent of the latter. Just as the advent of John the Baptist—who according to various authorities was Himself the originator of laws which abrogated the teachings current among the Jews—forms part of the Christian revelation, the advent of the Báb likewise forms an integral part of the Bahá'í Faith. That is why Shoghi Effendi feels justified to call Nabíl's narrative a narrative of the early days of the Bahá'í revelation.

Shoghi Effendi feels that it should be explained that forbidding self defence by Bahá'u'lláh should not be taken too literally. To put it as bluntly as this, he fears that the question might be misunderstood. Bahá'u'lláh could surely have not meant that a Bahá'í should not attempt to defend his life against any irresponsible assailant who might attack him for any purpose whatever, whether religious or not. Every reasonable person would feel under such circumstances justified in protecting his life. . . .

Regarding Nabíl: He was born on the 18th day of the month of Ṣafar of the year 1247 A.H. in the village of Zarand in Persia. He was thirteen years old when the Báb declared Himself. Though still young he himself was preparing to leave for Shaykh Ṭabarsí and join the companions of Mullá Ḥusayn when the news of the treachery and massacre of the besieged companions reached him. He met Bahá'u'lláh in Kirmánsháh and Ṭihrán before the latter's banishment to 'Iráq. He was a close companion of the Báb's amanuensis Mírzá Aḥmad. He subsequently met Bahá'u'lláh in Baghdád, Adrianople and 'Akká and was commissioned by Bahá'u'lláh to journey several times to Persia in order to promote the Cause and encourage the scattered and persecuted believers. He was present in 'Akká when Bahá'u'lláh passed away in 1892 and soon after was so overcome with grief that he drowned himself in the sea. His body was found along the shore and was buried in the cemetery of 'Akká. 'Abdu'l-Bahá is reported to have been struck with deep sorrow at the manner of his death. He states in his narration that he met the maternal uncle of the Báb, Ḥájí Mírzá Siyyid 'Alí who had visited his nephew in the Castle of Chihríq and had recently returned to Ṭihrán. He started writing his narrative in 1305 A.H. four years before the passing of Bahá'u'lláh. It took him about a year and half to write it. His chief informants were Mírzá Aḥmad the amanuensis of the Báb and Mírzá Músá the brother of Bahá'u'lláh.

one, and not a material or political one ... His view of the sovereignty of the Qá'im confirms the various evidences given in the text of the narrative itself of the views held by those who actually participated in these events such as Ḥujjat, Quddús, Mullá Ḥusayn. The very fact that these disciples were ready and willing to emerge from the fort and return to their homes after receiving the assurance that they would be no more molested is itself an evidence that they were not contemplating any action against the authorities.

Shoghi Effendi is also sending you an account of the doctrines of Shí'ah Islám from which the Movement originally sprang. It will help you to connect the origin of the Movement with the tenets and beliefs held by the Shí'ahs of Persia. The Báb declared Himself at the beginning of His mission to be the "Báb" by which He meant to be the gate or forerunner of "Him Whom God will make manifest", that is to say Bahá'u'lláh, Whose advent the Shí'ahs also expected in the person of "the return of Imám Ḥusayn". The Sunnis also believe in a similar twofold manifestation, the first they call "the Mihdí", the second "the Return of Christ". By the term Báb, the Báb meant to be the forerunner of the second manifestation rather than, as some have maintained, the gate of the Qá'im. When He declared Himself to be the Báb, the people understood by the term that He was an intermediary between the absent Qá'im and His followers, though He Himself never meant to be such a person. All He claimed to be was that He was the Qá'im Himself and in addition to this station, that of the Báb, namely the gate or forerunner of "Him Whom God will make manifest".

There are many authorised traditions from Muḥammad stating clearly (as explained in the Íqán) that the promised Qá'im would bring a new Book and new Laws. In other words abrogating the law of Islám.

Shoghi Effendi feels that the Unity of the Bahá'í revelation as one complete whole embracing the Faith of the Báb should be emphasised ... The Faith of the Báb should not be divorced from that of Bahá'u'lláh. Though the teachings of the Bayán have been abrogated and superseded by the laws of Aqdas, yet due to the fact that the Báb considered Himself as the forerunner of Bahá'u'lláh we should regard His dispensation together with that of Bahá'u'lláh as forming one entity, the former being an reluctant to attribute to them much authority. Most of these are personal impressions and are to be valued only as such. Bahá'u'lláh definitely states that only His actual writings are to be relied upon. Such reports may be interesting but not authoritative, no matter who the reporter may be . . .

22 October 1930

. . . If those heroic deeds have made such an impression upon you, would not the reading of the narrative arouse the friends to greater sacrifices and stimulate them to more intensive service? It was not mere physical torture that the friends in Persia had to endure but also moral persecution for they were cursed and vilified by all the people, especially when they ceased to defend themselves . . . the Master used to say sometimes that the western friends will be severely persecuted but theirs will be primarily moral. . . .

30 November 1930

He (the Guardian) is enclosing extracts from Lord Curzon's "Persia and the Persian Question" giving a detailed and faithful description of the state of Persia in the middle of the 19th century. He thinks that references to the extracts . . . will be of great value in showing to the reader the contrast between the decadent state of the government and the people at that time and the heroism and nobility of character displayed by the early disciples of the Báb . . . Shoghi Effendi is also sending you . . . the Master's words concerning the situation which led to the defensive action which the early disciples of the Báb were compelled to take in Mázindarán, Nayríz and Zanján. From these words it is evident that a systematic campaign of plunder and massacre had been initiated by the central government. Bahá'u'lláh, Who Himself was an active figure in those days and was regarded one of the leading exponents of the Faith of the Báb, states clearly His views in the Íqán that His conception of the sovereignty of the Promised Qá'im was purely a spiritual

9 February 1930

The subject you had raised with regard to the date of the publication of the writings of Bahá'u'lláh is interesting as it is important. If I remember correctly the same issue was raised as an open challenge in India by some spokesman of the Ahmadiyya sect. The earliest published writings of Bahá'u'lláh date from the nineties of the last century. Over forty years ago the Aqdas, a volume of general Tablets including Ṭarázát, Ishráqát, and others were published in Ishqábád (Russia) and Bombay respectively and copies of these though rare are still procurable. Simultaneously with these, if not earlier, some of the writings of Bahá'u'lláh were published by the Oriental Department of the Imperial Russian University at St. Petersburgh under the supervision of its director Baron Rosen (and more particulars about these could be found in the books of E. G. Browne) and these of course are not undated like some of those published in Bombay.

The main bulk of the writings of Bahá'u'lláh however are to be found in manuscript form written by noted scribes after the fashion of orientals. These scribes did not leave all their manuscripts undated and Jinábi Zain, a very noted Bahá'í scribe, always dated his copies of the writings of Bahá'u'lláh at the end of the volume in what E. G. Browne calls 'colophenes' and the description of some of these colophenes could be found in the works of the Cambridge Professor.

The son of the above-mentioned scribe is still living in Haifa and does very much the same work as his father. He claims that as early as 1868 his father used to write copies of the Íqán for the Bahá'ís in Persia as a source of livelihood, and that after 1885 when he went to 'Akká to join Bahá'u'lláh's party his entire work and time was devoted to copying the sacred writings for sale among Bahá'ís. These copies are to be found all throughout the East and are almost invariably dated.

9 June 1930

Concerning the accounts of visits to Haifa, published by the friends during the Master's life-time, Shoghi Effendi is very thing in a certain way, and thereby become captive to prescribed forms. It should therefore be the duty of the assemblies everywhere to see that, though certain temporary measures are taken to further the Cause, they do not crystallise into hard and fast creeds.

6 April 1928

I feel that regarding such interpretations (of verses from the Scriptures) no one has the right to impose his view or opinion and require his listeners to believe in his particular interpretation of the sacred and prophetic writings. I have no objection to your interpretations and inferences so long as they are represented as your own personal observations and reflections. It would be unnecessary and confusing to state authoritatively and officially a dogmatic Bahá'í interpretation to be universally accepted and taught by believers. Such matters I feel should be left to the personal judgement and insight of individual teachers. . . .

12 December 1929

Ever since its inception (the "Bahá'í World") Shoghi Effendi has cherished the hope of making it a work that would prove interesting and illuminating to the reader. Destined mainly for the non-Bahá'ís, he has tried to attract through its pages the attention of educated and enlightened people and especially leaders in every country, with a view to aquaint them with the broad and fundamental principles of the Faith and to win their consideration of the Movement as a growing force for good and for peace throughout the entire world. It is therefore with lively satisfaction that he has seen the publication grow yearly in importance and this feeling has been lately enhanced very much by the words of interest or appreciation which he has received from many quarters and leading men, among which was a remarkably encouraging letter from Sir Herbert Samuel. Indeed Shoghi Effendi has made it a point to send copies to as many leading men as possible and copies of last year's issue were presented to the Emperor of Japan, the Sháh of Persia and Queen Marie of Rumania.

will increase the more they have to take courage and try to solve them. The Master has often said that sorrows are like furrows, the deeper they go the more productive the land becomes. If this problem of ... should be settled other problems will arise. Are the friends to become discouraged or are they to follow the footsteps of the Master and consider them more as chances to show their tenacity of belief and spirit of sacrifice? In short, Shoghi Effendi wishes you to keep on teaching the principles of the Cause no matter what problems may arise.

... Let not anxieties and disappointments overwhelm you or oppress your generous and sensitive heart. Turn to Him in prayer and remember that I am joining you in your supplications for guidance and strength. Be patient in tribulation and never relax in your efforts to promote the Divine Teachings.

28 March 1926

It must have been very distasteful to you to read some of the off-hand and ungrammatical translations that more out of necessity than choice won circulation and were even published. Furthermore, it was always the expressed wish and desire of 'Abdu'l-Bahá to have proper and adequate translations that would not only convey the true spirit of the original but also possess some literary merit. And for this he emphasised the necessity of a board of translators. Such a board it has unfortunately been impossible to form as yet.

Meanwhile Shoghi Effendi, realising the urgent necessity of the translation of some of the important writings, has translated some of the passages.

16 October 1926

We should, however, be careful, as you mention in your letter, not to make this system develop into a hard and fast creed or form. The Cause is pure and free from such things and it ought to be the task of the friends to keep it broad and progressive. Man is always apt to fall into the habit of doing a

28 September 1925

... I wish you, my dearest friend, to make once again a supreme effort to come to a full understanding with the friends outside.... Extend to them your generous and helping hand, approach them with a spirit of selflessness and cordiality and the result, I am confident will be indeed marvellous. My heart rejoices at the news of the growth of harmony among the friends and I feel paralysed in my work when I hear to the contrary. I am impressing on the friends in ... the absolute necessity of cultivating understanding and friendliness and consolidating the foundation of the National Assembly. For upon these National Assemblies will the Edifice of the Universal House of Justice be raised.

28 October 1925

Shoghi Effendi is much interested to hear of your literary work. He fully agrees with you that different people must be approached in different ways and that valuable work for the Bahá'í Cause can be done within the Christian Churches by promoting the "Christianity of Christ". 'Abdu'l-Bahá said that when people become true Christians, they will find themselves Bahá'ís. One or two of the best Bahá'ís I know were very earnest, sincere, devoted Christians and accepted the Bahá'í teachings with very little difficulty and without any intervening period of religious scepticism, as an amplification and fulfilment of the teachings and prophesyings of Christ and the prophets.

28 December 1925

He is very sorry that such undesirable things are every now and then cropping up in ... and discouraging you in your work, keeping you from devoting all your spare time in teaching the Cause and spreading its principles. He does not wish you, however, to lose heart from such things. As the Cause grows its difficulties will increase and its problems will become more numerous. The friends, especially the older ones, should therefore try and stand unmoved by them. In fact the more their difficulties

Over three hundred letters to individuals residing in the British Isles have been studied and passages selected which are of permanent value.

These excerpts were taken from the letters of no more than twenty believers of whom only seven corresponded regularly with the Guardian.

They have been arranged chronologically; for details of the subject matter the reader must turn to the Index.

Almost all these passages are answers given by the Guardian to questions asked in personal letters to him. It is possible therefore to catch a glimpse of the changing problems facing the Bahá'í community and these frequently reflected conditions in the country as a whole. This is particularly significant in the years immediately following the Second World War for as the Guardian, in a letter written on his behalf by his secretary, wrote of the British believers,

". . . he feels the greatest sympathy for them, and considers that when their present achievements are assessed in the future, people will give them a double measure of praise for having done so much when they were least fit to do it."

EXCERPTS FROM LETTERS
TO INDIVIDUALS

May the Beloved of our hearts, guide, bless and sustain you, remove every obstacle from your path, and graciously assist you to extend the range of your highly valued activities and consolidate your historic achievements,

Your true brother,
Shoghi

14 May 1957

Spiritual Assembly of the Bahá'ís of Reading

Dear Bahá'í Friends:

Your letter of May 8th has been received, and the beloved Guardian has instructed me to answer you on his behalf.

He was delighted to receive the news of your activities, and feels that Reading can be cited as a truly exemplary community in every way. He hopes you will maintain this enviable position as the years go by.

He will certainly pray that your teaching efforts may be richly blessed, and that you may not only continue to make Bahá'ís, but to export them, as you have done in the case of Edinburgh.

With warm Bahá'í greetings,

May the Almighty bless your highly valued activities, guide every step you take, remove every obstacle from your path, and graciously assist you to win great victories in the service of His Faith in the days to come,

Your true brother,
Shoghi

22 April 1950

APPRECIATE MESSAGE LOVING REMEMBRANCE SHRINES SUPPLICATING MANIFOLD BLESSINGS.

SHOGHI

26 October 1950

OVERJOYED NOTABLE INITIAL VICTORY INTRODUCTION FAITH UNIVERSITY UNDERGRADUATE CIRCLES ASSURE YOUNGEST PROMISING BELIEVER ARDENT PRAYERS CONCENTRATE CONSOLIDATION ACHIEVEMENT.

SHOGHI

21 April 1954

ASSEMBLY FRIENDS LOVINGLY REMEMBERED SHRINES.

SHOGHI

26 September 1957

The Bahá'ís of Portsmouth

Dear Bahá'í Friends:

Your letter of August 23rd has been received by the beloved Guardian, and he has instructed me to answer you on his behalf.

He was happy to learn of the spirit of active service which animates the friends in that city, and of the practical way you are approaching the teaching work.

Through love and unity among the believers, and the wise and persistent efforts of all the Bahá'ís, great results should be forthcoming.

He will certainly pray for the progress of the Faith there, and for the enrollment of a number of newly-declared believers by next Riḍván.

With warm Bahá'í greetings,

The Guardian assures you all of his loving prayers, and sends his greetings.

With warm Bahá'í love,

P.S. It is not necessary to send a detailed account of the funeral of Mrs. Langdon-Davies. A short biographical account of her life should be sent by the N.S.A. for "Bahá'í World".

May the Almighty bless, guide and sustain you, and enable you to achieve memorable victories in the service of our beloved Faith,
Your true brother,
Shoghi

21 March 1955

Spiritual Assembly of the Bahá'ís of Oxford

Dear Bahá'í Sister:
Your letter of February 27th with enclosure has been received by the beloved Guardian, and he has instructed me to answer you on his behalf.

He appreciates your thoughtfulness in sending to him the photostatic copy of Canon Cheyne's letter to John Craven†, in which he declared himself a Bahá'í, and is happy to have it.

He wishes you all a very happy New Year, and great success in your teaching activities during the coming year.

With warm Bahá'í greetings,

Assuring you of my loving, my continued and fervent prayers for your success in the service of our beloved Faith and of its nascent institutions,
Your true brother,
Shoghi

Cables to the Oxford Assembly

25 November 1949

HEARTFELT CONGRATULATIONS HISTORIC VICTORY ARDENT LOVING PRAYERS SURROUNDING YOUR NOBLE MISSION.

SHOGHI

received by the beloved Guardian, and he has instructed me to answer you on his behalf.

The news of the opening of the Oxford Bahá'ís' first Centre rejoiced his heart. He was particularly happy to know that this project was consummated and the Centre furnished and made ready for use almost entirely through the united efforts and devotion of the believers themselves.

As you know, the Guardian attaches great importance to Oxford. Now that the friends have a Centre, which in itself will be a means of attracting seeking souls to them to learn of the Faith; and also the Bahá'ís have made for themselves a teaching plan, he feels confident that the work will go forward there with great strides, and that your community will grow in numbers and in strength.

He will remember you all in his loving prayers in the Holy Shrines.

With loving Bahá'í greetings,

May the Almighty bless continually your highly meritorious efforts, and enable you to win great and memorable victories in the service of His Faith,

Your true brother,
Shoghi

28 February 1955

The Spiritual Assembly of the Bahá'ís of Oxford

Dear Bahá'í Sister:

Your letter of February 13th with enclosures has been received by the beloved Guardian, and he has instructed me to answer you on his behalf.

He is hoping that the fact that the believers now have their own Centre in Oxford will greatly stimulate the work there, and cause the more rapid expansion of the Faith in this difficult town.

The work done among the University students should be steadily pursued. Perhaps before long some among their number may determine to accept the Faith and arise whole-heartedly to serve it.

23 April 1954

The Spiritual Assembly of the Bahá'ís of Oxford

Dear Bahá'í Friends:

Your letter of April 9th has been received by the beloved Guardian, and he has instructed me to answer you on his behalf.

Mrs. Winsten invited the Guardian if possible to view in person her portrait of 'Abdu'l-Bahá. Needless to say, he thanked her for her kind invitation, but informed her this would be quite out of the question.

He is very pleased to hear that she has consented to forwarding a photograph through acquaintances of hers, and he will be very interested to see it. He will let you know if he considers the likeness sufficiently good to warrant any of the Bahá'ís purchasing it. It is a pity to own portraits of 'Abdu'l-Bahá which do not in any way resemble Him.

Some time ago you asked him to send you a copy of the description which Miss Campbell† brought to Haifa of how the artist made this drawing of 'Abdu'l-Bahá. Unfortunately this has been mislaid, and it is not possible for the Guardian to send you a copy. However, the original you may be sure is safe in his papers.

He is very happy to hear of the progress of the Cause in Oxford, such a very important centre from every standpoint. He assures you all of his loving prayers for the progress of your activities, and for each and all of you.

With warmest Bahá'í greetings,

Assuring you of my loving prayers for you all, and for the success of your efforts for the promotion of our beloved Faith,
Your true brother,
Shoghi

7 December 1954

The Spiritual Assembly of the Bahá'ís of Oxford

Dear Bahá'í Sister:

Your letter of November 30th with enclosure has been

wise association of the members of your Group with her, will feel moved to declare herself an active member of the Faith. He will pray that this may come about.

The Guardian will also pray for the success of the devoted labours of the believers in Oxford.

With warm Bahá'í love,

May the Almighty guide and sustain you always, remove all obstacles from your path, and enable you to win great and memorable victories in the service of His Faith,

Your true brother,
Shoghi

1 February 1954

The Spiritual Assembly of the Bahá'ís of Oxford

Dear Bahá'í Friends:

Your letter of January 16th with enclosure has been received by the beloved Guardian, and he has instructed me to answer you on his behalf.

He thanks you very much for the expression of your sympathy, and for the newspaper clipping you enclosed.

It has indeed been a great loss to the work of the Faith, to lose such a valiant, constant and distinguished Hand as dear Dorothy Baker. It will leave a gap in the pioneer field, as well. No doubt her noble spirit will be able to assist and inspire from on high, and this must be the consolation of all her friends and admirers.

He trusts the work in Oxford is progressing steadily; and he assures you all of his loving prayers in your behalf.

With warmest Bahá'í greetings,

May the Almighty bless your meritorious efforts, guide and sustain you in your activities, and enable you to win great victories in the service of His Faith,

Your true brother,
Shoghi

He was very pleased to hear of the progress being made; and that it has been possible to give the Message to some of the "undergrads". It is most important that the Faith should be conveyed with a sense of dignity at so important a university as Oxford; and better that the work should go forward slowly than that any mistakes should be made.

He assures you all that he deeply appreciates your devoted labours; and he hopes that you will fulfill your objective of increasing the number of believers there.

With warm Bahá'í greetings,

May the Beloved, whose Cause you are serving with such fidelity, ability and devotion, reward you abundantly for your meritorious labours, guide every step you take, and enable you to lay a firm and unassailable foundation for the future institutions of His Faith in that historic and promising City.

Your true and grateful brother,
Shoghi

25 December 1952

The Spiritual Assembly of the Bahá'ís of Oxford

Dear Bahá'í Friends:

Your letter of December 10th has been received by the beloved Guardian, and he has instructed me to answer you on his behalf.

He was very happy to see that you have held another meeting in Manchester College, and hopes that the attracted ones who attended may become real students of the Faith, and eventually join its ranks.

The poem by Miss Masefield was much appreciated by the Guardian. Please assure Miss Masefield that he liked it very much, and will consider using it for a future volume of "Bahá'í World". The only thing that he saw that seemed to need correction was that the word "Abhá", was spelled "Abba" instead of "Abhá".

He hopes that Miss Masefield, through the friendship and

Dear co-workers:
Your message cheered my heart, and I wish to assure you that I greatly value your noble sentiments, and will supplicate the Beloved to bless your efforts, guide every step you take in the path of service, enable you to extend continually the range of your activities, and consolidate the work you have so splendidly inaugurated, and are so devotedly prosecuting in the service of this glorious Faith,

Your true and grateful brother,
Shoghi

27 October 1950

The Spiritual Assembly of the Bahá'ís of Oxford

Dear Bahá'í Friends:
Your letter of September 14 with enclosure was received, and the beloved Guardian thanks you for it.

He was pleased to see the enterprising spirit shown by Mr. Semple†, and hopes his classes will produce many new contacts.

The progress made in Oxford is heartening, and he trusts still greater progress lies ahead.

With loving Bahá'í greetings,

May the Almighty abundantly reward you for your patient and splendid labours, sustain and guide you at all times and under all circumstances, enable you to extend the range of your meritorious activities, and aid you to consolidate your notable and indeed historic achievements,

Your true and grateful brother,
Shoghi

25 December 1951

Spiritual Assembly of the Bahá'ís of Oxford

Dear Friends:
Your letter of December 14th has been received; and the beloved Guardian has instructed me to answer you on his behalf.

He hopes your numbers will steadily increase and that many young people will be attracted to the Faith, as the part they have to play is very great and, also, their need of the Faith very great.

You may be sure his loving prayers will be offered for you, and for the success of your labours, in the Holy Shrines.

With Bahá'í love,

May the Beloved bless your efforts in the service of our beloved Faith, and you to deepen your knowledge of the essentials of His World Order, to increase your numbers, to extend the scope of your activities, and to fulfil every desire you cherish for its promotion and consolidation.

Your true and grateful brother,
Shoghi

30 May 1949

The Bahá'ís of Nottingham

Dear Bahá'í Friends:

Your letter to our beloved Guardian, dated May 4, has been received, and he deeply appreciates your message of devotion and affection.

His burden is indeed a heavy one, and after so many years of continuous responsibility he often feels very tired. But when he sees the loyalty of the friends and their steadfast perseverance in their tasks his heart is lightened and he feels greatly encouraged.

It is much easier to work when you see results being obtained under your very eyes, and, although in many ways his service to the Faith has been lonelier and more complicated than that of the beloved Master, yet he has had the great blessing of seeing the Cause spread out all over the world and greatly expand in many countries—such as England, India, the United States, etc.—as it never did in the days of 'Abdu'l-Bahá, Who worked so unremittingly towards this end, and Who planted what we now reap.

He feels the British believers can and will—indeed must—succeed in their Plan, and his thoughts and prayers are with them very often.

With Bahá'í love,

16 September 1956

Spiritual Assembly of the Bahá'ís of Norwich

Dear Bahá'í Brother:
 Your letter of July 29th with enclosures has been received, and the beloved Guardian has instructed me to answer you on his behalf.
 He was most happy to receive the July Jarrold Magazine and to see the article on the Faith; and also to learn from the copy of your News Letter of the activities of the believers in that locality.
 The Guardian greatly appreciates the spirit animating the friends there in the service of the Cause. He sends you all his loving greetings, and assures you of his prayers for the success of your devoted labours.

With warm Bahá'í greetings,

Assuring you of my abiding admiration of your devoted and constant endeavours for the promotion of our beloved Faith, and of my fervent prayers for the realisation of every hope you cherish for its promotion,

Your true brother,
Shoghi

8 April 1947

The Bahá'ís of Nottingham

Dear Bahá'í Friends:
 Your letter, dated February 16th, was received and read by our beloved Guardian with great joy, and he has instructed me to answer it on his behalf.
 The news of your group having reached Assembly status was a source of deep satisfaction to him, and demonstrates what the friends can do, once they put their shoulder to the wheel!
 You have every reason to feel proud of your achievement, and he hopes you will, through your correspondence and contacts with your fellow believers, encourage them to follow your example and forge ahead, in spite of every obstacle, with determination, confident that once we do our part, God is never failing in His.

hope you cherish in the service of our beloved Faith and of its nascent institutions.

Your true and grateful brother,
Shoghi

30 September 1949

The Bahá'ís of Norwich

Dear Bahá'í Friends,
Your letter of August 2nd has been received and our beloved Guardian has instructed me to answer you on his behalf.

He was very pleased to see that you are girding up your loins to do your utmost for the Plan in the critical months that lie ahead.

Nothing will further your ends more quickly than the greatest love, unity and co-operation amongst yourselves. These are the very soul of the order Bahá'u'lláh has come to establish in the world and when the people see these qualities and characteristics actively demonstrated in our midst, those who are receptive will hasten to join our ranks. Likewise when they see the lack of these virtues they will hesitate to embrace the Faith however much they may admire its teachings.

He will certainly pray that your Assembly may be maintained, your numbers increase, and your devotion be rewarded.

With Bahá'í love,

Dear co-workers,
I was pleased to hear from you and receive the assurance of your love, your devotion to the interests of our beloved Faith and your determination to serve its best interests.

I will pray from the depths of my heart on your behalf, that the Almighty may bless and sustain you and enable you to win memorable victories for His Faith.

Your true brother,
Shoghi

commune with Their Souls, and this is what the Martyrs seemed to have done, and what brought them such ecstacy of joy that life became nothing. This is the true mysticism, and the secret, inner meaning of life which humanity has at present, drifted so far from.

The Guardian will pray that this dear friend may deepen his understanding and arise and become a wonderful teacher of the Faith.

He will also pray for the progress of the work in Manchester and the success of your devoted labours.

With Bahá'í love,

May the Almighty bless your efforts, guide and sustain you in your activities, and enable you to promote effectively the best interests of His Faith.

Your true brother,
Shoghi

19 January 1950

Northampton Bahá'í Community

Dear Bahá'í Friends:
Our beloved Guardian thanks you not only for the good news you conveyed to him in your letter of January 6th, but for the spirit which prompted you to share it with him.

He admires greatly the services of your community and the unity amongst you, which no doubt is largely responsible for your success.

He will join his prayers to yours for the success of the labours of your two latest pioneering members.

With Bahá'í love,

Dear co-workers,
I feel truly proud of your notable services, and I wish to assure you of my profound appreciation of your labours, of my loving prayers for the progress of your meritorious activities, and the realisation of every

Souls seeing the future, but of what, in Their wisdom, They deem it necessary to accept in the Path of sacrifice. If we are going to question the wisdom of the Prophets we can question God's Wisdom too, and the advisability of the whole system we live in.

(2) Nabíl's suicide was not insanity but love. He loved Bahá'u'lláh too much to go on in a world that no longer held Him.

(3) The "sacrifice" of goats has nothing to do with the Faith. Bahá'u'lláh was surrounded by Muslim admirers and friends, and they merely followed the custom of their people on such an occasion, when many hundreds gathered to console His bereaved family.

(4) We cannot, not knowing the factors Bahá'u'lláh weighed in His own mind, judge of the wisdom of His withdrawal to Kurdistan. But, studying His life and teachings, we should see in it an act of wisdom, and not superficially measure Him by our standards.

(5) Love is certainly the attribute we associate par excellence with our Maker. But has He no justice and does not justice fall on the back of the evil doer as a scourge?

(6) This question seems to imply a lack of understanding of love. There is very little Divine love in the world to-day, but a great deal of intellectual reasoning, which is an entirely different thing, and springs from the mind and not the heart. The Martyrs—most of them died because of their love for the Báb, for Bahá'u'lláh, and through Them for God. The veil between the inner and outer world was very thin, and to tear it, and be free to be near the Beloved, was very sweet. But it takes love, not reason to understand these things. We must also remember the Martyrs were called upon to deny their faith or die, as men of principle they preferred to die.

(7) Bahá'u'lláh's claims are much greater because humanity is more mature and can afford to hear them. But He draws on the same Source that was accessible to all the Prophets, it is we who can now receive more.

(8) The Guardian feels . . . should study more deeply the teachings, and meditate on what he studies. We liken God to the Sun, which gives us all our life. So the Spirit of God reaches us through the Souls of the Manifestations. We must learn to

few lines expressing his heartfelt appreciation of the precious and most valuable steps taken by our Manchester friends towards a greater extension and consolidation of the Cause.

The Guardian was specially glad to hear that you have established a new Bahá'í Centre and he fervently hopes that as a result of this new move the interests of the Faith will be promoted and its teachings will succeed in comfirming some new souls.

The precious efforts so continuously exerted by our Manchester Bahá'ís and particularly by our beloved Mr. Hall and Mr. Sugar will undoubtedly yield their fruits in a not very distant future. But the friends should persevere in their task and not let any obstacle, however great, hinder their onward march. In these days of sufferings and hardships, patience and hope are indispensable for the success of any idea or plan.

In closing may I assure you of our Guardian's best wishes and ask you to extend to all our Manchester Bahá'ís the expression of his heartfelt thanks and appreciation.

Yours in His Service,

May the Beloved bless your high and unsparing efforts, enable you to extend the scope of your activities, and consolidate the foundations of the Faith in that great city.

Your true brother,
Shoghi

28 July 1950

The Manchester Spiritual Assembly

Dear Bahá'í Friends,

Your letter has been received, dated June 6th, and our beloved Guardian has instructed me to answer you on his behalf.

He feels that the questions of . . . could be answered by a better understanding of the teachings—however, for the sake of his sincere services to the Faith, he will answer them here:

(1) Christ received the kiss of Judas, in fact He said one of His disciples would betray Him. It is not a question of these Holy

25 January 1929

Manchester Spiritual Assembly

My Dear Friend,
I am directed by our Guardian to thank you for your welcome letter of January 11th.
He has been very pleased to learn of the more rapid progress of the Cause in Manchester and of a greater measure of unity among the friends. He is glad that Mr. Hall is taking this initiative and he sincerely trusts that you will all persevere in your endeavours, will keep dear the necessity for harmony and unity and thus make your group a progressive, enthusiastic and worthy Bahá'í centre in England. He appreciated your efforts and that of all friends in Manchester. He wishes you please to convey to them an expression of his heartfelt love and good wishes.
With best regards,
Sincerely in His Service,

My Dear co-worker,
I am delighted with the news you give me. The friends in Manchester occupy a warm and abiding place in my heart. The fragrant memory of my visit to them is still fresh and vivid in my mind. I will continue to supplicate at the Beloved's Shrine for each one of them the Almighty's richest blessings, that they may be guided and strengthened to render in the days to come inestimable services to the sacred Threshold.
With my best wishes to your dear relatives,
Your true brother,
Shoghi

20 July 1932

Manchester Spiritual Assembly

Dear Bahá'í Sister,
Shoghi Effendi was greatly pleased to receive your kind letter of June 24th, 1932, and he has requested me to address you these

The victory won in the British Isles filled his heart with pride, and encourages him to believe a brilliant future lies ahead of the community there.

With warmest greetings,

Dear co-workers:
Your most welcome message cheered my heart, and I wish to assure you in person of my sincere and profound admiration for the spirit that animates you in your activities, as well as of my ardent prayers for you, that the Beloved may guide and sustain you always, and enable you to win great and memorable victories for His Faith and its infant institutions.

Your true brother,
Shoghi

24 January 1952

To the believers who were present at the Feast of Sulṭán in London Centre, January 1952

Dear Bahá'í Friends:
The beloved Guardian was very happy to see that so many of you had gathered together and united in sending your love to him, with the first believer to come from England since the door of pilgrimage has been open.

He will remember you all in his loving prayers in the Shrines, and urges you to devote as much of your time individually as possible to the promotion of the goals of your present Plan.

With warmest Bahá'í greetings,

May the Almighty guide and sustain you in your high endeavours, bless and protect you always, aid you to extend the range of your valued activities, and win memorable victories in the service of His glorious Faith,

Your true brother,
Shoghi

14 March 1954

Spiritual Assembly of the Bahá'ís of Leeds

Dear Bahá'í Brother:

Your letter of February 20th has been received by the beloved Guardian, and he has instructed me to answer you on his behalf.

The Guardian was very happy to learn of your coming County Teaching Conference. He has been very happy over the large number of pioneers who have arisen in the British Isles and have gone to new territories, both in the British Isles and in foreign lands, and he considers this a fine record.

He hopes your deliberations will produce a still greater effort on the part of all the friends to implant more deeply and scatter more widely the seeds of the Faith, which are so greatly needed everywhere.

The Guardian assures you of his loving prayers for the abundant success of your endeavours.

With warm Bahá'í greetings,

May the Beloved bless, guide and sustain you, and enable you to promote the vital interests of His Faith,

Your true brother,
Shoghi

5 September 1950

Spiritual Assembly of the Bahá'ís of Liverpool

Dear Bahá'í Friends,

Your letter dated May 7 was received, and our beloved Guardian rejoiced over the news of the formation of your Assembly. He would have answered you sooner had he not been so overpowered with not only the work connected with the arcade of the Shrine's completion, but also anxiety caused by the long and serious illness of Mr. Maxwell, its architect.

He trusts your Assembly will enlarge its community during this year, and thus strengthen its foundations and ensure its future activities.

heart and he will continue to pray for its advancement, and for each and every one of you, in the Holy Shrines.
With warmest greetings,

May the Almighty bless, continually and abundantly, your high endeavours, aid you to add to your numbers, deepen your understanding of the essentials of His Faith, extend the range of your activities, consolidate your achievements, and win great and memorable victories for its institutions,
Your true and grateful brother,
Shoghi

9 September 1950

To the Glasgow Bahá'ís

Dear Bahá'í Friends:

Your letter dated 5.7.50 has been received, and the beloved Guardian has instructed me to answer it on his behalf.

The progress being made in spreading the Faith in Scotland pleases him immensely, and he feels the Cause will find many exemplary and wonderful servants among the Scotch people. They may be slow to be convinced, but once they embrace a thing they do so with full conviction and great determination to serve their belief.

He will pray that your assembly may confirm many new souls, and thus gradually free the devoted pioneers, who went there to teach, for services in new and maybe distant fields.

You may be sure he deeply appreciates all you have done.
With loving greetings,

Dear co-workers,

I was so pleased and grateful to receive your most welcome message, and I profoundly appreciate the noble sentiments you have expressed. I wish to assure you that I will pray for your success from the depths of my heart, that the Beloved may guide your steps, bless your high endeavours, and enable you to lend a tremendous impetus to the spread of the Faith in Scotland.
Your true and grateful brother,
Shoghi

in the British Isles, and, he hopes, later in the pioneer fields abroad.

He trusts that your Assembly, and especially those members of it who are natives of Scotland, will soon succeed in attracting many more serious minded truth-seekers to the Faith there. Now Edinburgh has become the mother Assembly of Scotland, and must, by its example, set the pace, and assist in the development of all future Scottish Bahá'í Assemblies.

He assures you all he will pray for your success, for your unity, and that Bahá'u'lláh may guide you all in administering the affairs of His Cause in that city.

He was particularly interested to hear that one of the new believers had met 'Abdu'l-Bahá on His visit to Edinburgh many years ago.

With loving greetings,

Dear and valued co-workers,

Your welcome message brought deep joy to my heart and filled me with gratitude for this latest evidence of the all-conquering power of Bahá'u'lláh, as well as for the magnificent efforts exerted by British believers in that historic and ancient city. I will, I assure you, pray from the depths of my heart for your success, the increase of your numbers, the multiplication of your activities, and the consolidation of your achievements. Persevere in your meritorious endeavours, and rest assured that the Beloved will watch over you and crown your high endeavours with signal success.

Your true and grateful brother,
Shoghi

9 April 1949

The Spiritual Assembly of the Bahá'ís of Edinburgh

Dear Bahá'í Friends:

As our beloved Guardian is at present very pressed for time in connection with the tremendous amount of work the building of the Shrine entails at this juncture, I am answering your loving Naw-Rúz Message very briefly on his behalf.

You may be sure the work in Edinburgh is very dear to his

27 January 1957

The Bahá'í Group, Eccles

Dear Bahá'í Friends:

Your letter of January 2nd was received, through the kindness of Mr. Gregory, and the beloved Guardian has instructed me to answer you on his behalf.

He will certainly pray in the Holy Shrines that you may succeed in attaining your objective; but, even should you fail to establish a spiritual assembly by April, you must not feel discouraged, because it is much more important to have a solid foundation in the beginning than to meet a date line—welcome as the assembly would be!

He admires very much the spirit animating you, and hopes that a flourishing community will develop there.

With warm Bahá'í greetings,

May the Beloved bless your efforts, guide your steps, aid you to extend the scope of your activities, and win great victories in the service of His glorious Faith,

Your true brother,
Shoghi

22 September 1948

The Spiritual Assembly of the Bahá'ís of Edinburgh

Dear Bahá'í Friends,

Our beloved Guardian was very happy indeed to receive your letter to him dated April 21st—which has taken a long time to reach him, as you can see—and he has instructed me to answer you on his behalf.

The formation of the first Assembly of the Faith in Scotland is a great and promising achievement. He has a profound admiration for the characteristics of the Scots; their deep religious feelings, their frank, open and friendly nature, their tenacity and abilities will enable them to greatly enrich the Faith

16 October 1948

The Spiritual Assembly of the Bahá'ís of Dublin, Eire

Dear Bahá'í Friends,
Our beloved Guardian was very delighted to receive your communication of April 21st, written to him from your newly elected body.

He was particularly pleased to read the signatures of three members of the Townshend family, as Mr. Townshend and his wife have truly sacrificed in order to stand forward as declared and active Bahá'ís and assist in the formation of this historic Assembly.

The task facing you is great, but very exhilarating. Eire lies before you, your territory, of which you are the Mother Assembly, and however difficult your conquest may be, it is a challenging and wonderful service you are called upon to render.

The Irish people, with their deep religious instinct, although they may be at first difficult to convert, once convinced of the truth, will make staunch believers and will, he hopes, convey this Faith, with all its promise and healing power, to other countries in the course of time.

He assures you his prayers are with you, for your progress and your success in every field of Bahá'í service.

With loving greetings,
P.S. The delay in answering your letter was due to the long time it took to reach Haifa.

Dear and valued co-workers,
The work achieved in Dublin during the last few months, culminating in the formation of the first Spiritual Assembly in Ireland, is indeed highly praiseworthy. Such a consummation is an event that will adorn the annals of the Faith, and is in itself a prelude to still greater victories in the days to come. I truly feel proud of the British and Irish believers who have collaborated so devotedly and strenuously, and won so conspicuous a victory. I will fervently supplicate on their behalf, and will await eagerly the news of the progress of their historic achievements.

Your true and grateful brother,
Shoghi

every obstacle from your path, and enable you to enrich the record of your deeply appreciated services to His Faith and its institutions,
Your true brother,
Shoghi

27 August 1947

To the believers who were present in Dublin at the 19 Day Feast of Kamál

Dear Bahá'í Friends,

Our beloved Guardian was very happy to receive your message and to see that the Cause is now gaining a firm footing in Eire.

He is particularly happy to welcome Mrs. Coleman into the Faith as the first new Bahá'í in Dublin, and he hopes that ere long you will be able to establish the first historic spiritual Assembly in that city.

The Irish are tenacious in their religious beliefs, and once convinced of the truth and significance of our glorious Faith should make ardent and devoted Bahá'ís.

He assures you all of his loving prayers for the success of your devoted labours.
With warmest greetings,

Dear and valued co-workers,

Your joint message rejoiced my heart. I cherish great hopes for the future of the work so splendidly initiated in that historic island. I will pray from the depths of my heart for the extension and consolidation of your meritorious activities to which I attach the utmost importance. Persevere in your glorious task, and rest assured that the Beloved, Who is watching over you, will bless your high endeavours and fulfil your dearest hopes.
Your true and grateful brother,
Shoghi

to his new post, which attract a reinforcing power from on High, and enable him to create in the hearts of those who meet him a longing to have what he possesses, and ignite in these new hearts the flame of the love of Bahá'u'lláh.

The Guardian feels sure his non-Bahá'í wife will likewise receive a blessing for her part in this sacrifice, which helped to make this move possible.

He is deeply appreciative of the Welsh translation; and is confident it will prove to be of great assistance in the promotion of the Teachings in Wales.

With warm Bahá'í greetings,

May the Spirit of Bahá'u'lláh guide you and your fellow-members, and enable you, in the days to come, to reinforce the foundation that has been laid, and to extend the range of your highly meritorious exertions and accomplishments,

Your true brother,
Shoghi

30 January 1957

Spiritual Assembly of the Bahá'ís of Cardiff

Dear Bahá'í Brother:

Your letter of December 29th was received, and the beloved Guardian was very happy indeed to hear that the week-end school had been a success.

He is delighted to see that the Faith is progressing in Wales, and he feels sure that the Welsh people will not only respond to the Message if given opportunity, but contribute to the Faith a distinctive share of their own, when they arise in its service.

He hopes that there will indeed be Welsh Summer Schools in the future.

Assuring you of his loving prayers,
With warmest greetings,

May the Almighty bless, guide, and sustain you and your dear co-workers in your constant and highly meritorious activities, remove wants twenty-five copies of it sent to him for distribution amongst various Bahá'í libraries here, and for our surplus stock. This booklet in their own language will do much to convince sincere Welsh truth-seekers of the respect and consideration with which we Bahá'ís approach all minorities, also of our devout desire to share with such a talented race the glory of Bahá'u'lláh's message.

He hopes there will be many new Welsh believers in the coming years, and he assures you all of his loving prayers for the success of your devoted efforts.

With Bahá'í love,

Dear and valued co-workers,

I was so pleased and grateful to receive your welcome letter, and the first fruit of your services and high endeavours for the promotion of our beloved Faith.

I feel proud of the spirit that animates you, and will supplicate the Beloved to bless, and sustain and guide you, and enable you to extend continually the range of your achievements. Persevere, and rest assured.

Your true brother,
Shoghi

16 September 1955

Spiritual Assembly of the Bahá'ís of Cardiff

Dear Bahá'í Sister:

Your letter of July 18th with enclosure has been received by the beloved Guardian, and he has instructed me to answer you on his behalf.

He is delighted with the way the work is progressing in Cardiff, and that there are now nine believers living there.

He particularly values the instant decision made during the Convention, and consequent action taken, by Dr. Miller† in leaving an excellent medical practice in Liverpool, to settle in Cardiff, with all it entailed of sacrifice in being separated from his wife, and in being obliged to accept a junior post in a hospital at Cardiff. It is qualities such as these, which the pioneer carries

17 October 1948

The Spiritual Assembly of the Bahá'ís of Cardiff, Wales

Dear Bahá'í Friends,

Your letter to our beloved Guardian of April 21st was received, after a long delay, and he was most happy to hear of the formation of your Assembly.

With an Assembly in Cardiff, in Edinburgh, and Dublin, the representative character of the Faith in the British Isles is fully established and the National body greatly re-inforced.

He fully realises the difficulties which have attended your work there, and which makes your victory all the more praiseworthy and precious. He urges you to now courageously persevere in your work and ensure that Cardiff has, by next April, a stable membership from which to call on for the Spiritual Assembly's maintenance.

You may be sure that he will assist you with his prayers, and pray that each and every one of you may be protected and assisted in your devoted services to the Faith.

With warm greetings,

Dear and valued co-workers,

The formation of the first Bahá'í Spiritual Assembly in Wales is an event of great historical significance. I congratulate you on this splendid achievement which, I trust, will be a prelude to still greater victories in the service of our glorious Faith. I will supplicate on your behalf, the blessings of Bahá'u'lláh, that your work may prosper, your plans bear abundant fruit, and your hopes realised for the propagation of the Faith and the establishment of its nascent institutions.

Your true and grateful brother,
Shoghi

15 February 1950

The Spiritual Assembly of the Bahá'ís of Cardiff

Dear Bahá'í Friends,

Your letter of January 20th has been received, and our beloved Guardian was simply delighted to get the Welsh pamphlet, he and aid you to render memorable services to His Faith and its institutions.

> Your true and grateful brother,
> Shoghi

1 November 1947

The Bahá'ís of Cardiff

Dear Bahá'í Friends,

Your welcome letter to our beloved Guardian dated Oct. 16th, has been received, and he has instructed me to answer it on his behalf.

He is well aware of the very real sacrifices you have made, and are making to establish the Cause in Wales, and he wants you to know he admires your courage and determination, and most deeply values the dedicated spirit which animates you.

The news of your first public meeting was good news indeed, and he feels sure your perseverance and the strong backing which you are receiving from the N.S.A. and the Teaching Committee, will crown your efforts with the success you so richly deserve.

His loving prayers will be offered for the speedy realisation of your hopes, and he urges you to persevere, conscious of the historical importance of what you are doing, and of how important your work is to the progress of the Plan in the British Isles.

> With warmest greetings to you all,
> Yours in His service,

Dear and valued co-workers,

I wish to add a few words in person and assure every one of you of my deep admiration of the spirit you manifest, the services you render, and the determination with which you are initiating the great historic teaching enterprise in Wales.

You are, I assure you, often in my thoughts and prayers, and I will supplicate the Beloved to bless continually your high and meritorious endeavours.

> *Your true and grateful brother,*
> *Shoghi*

He assures you that your devotion and services are very deeply appreciated.

With loving greetings,

May the Almighty bless your high endeavours, reward you abundantly for your historic accomplishments, guide your steps, and aid you to extend continually the range of your highly valued activities.

Your true and grateful brother,
Shoghi

22 September 1948

The Spiritual Assembly of the Bahá'ís of Bristol

Dear Bahá'í Friends,

Your letter of April 21st reached our beloved Guardian after a long delay, and he has instructed me to answer it on his behalf.

The formation of your Assembly, in the face of so many difficulties, was indeed a noble achievement, and serves to prove that our struggles as individuals, often handicapped by the sense of our own inadequacy, are reinforced by the grace of Bahá'u'lláh, Who enables us to achieve the seemingly impossible!

He urges you all to persevere in maintaining your Assembly, which forms one of the vital links in the Bahá'í chain, which will soon gird the British Isles, never to lose heart, and to redouble your teaching labours so as to ensure a broader foundation next year for your Assembly's election and thus guarantee its permanency.

His prayers will be offered for you, one and all, for your success and guidance.

With Bahá'í Love,

Dear and valued co-workers,

I was so pleased and grateful to receive your message, and I wish to assure you all of my loving and fervent prayers for the progress of your historic work, the extension of your activities and the realisation of every hope you cherish for the promotion of our beloved Faith. May the Almighty watch over you, sustain you in your valued endeavours,

23 April 1950

To the Spiritual Assembly of
the Bahá'ís of Belfast

Dear Bahá'í Friends,
   Your letter of April 12th, conveying such heartening news, was received by our beloved Guardian, and he has instructed me to answer you on his behalf.
   He feels your Assembly, a hard-won prize, and occupying an important position as representative of the Faith in Northern Ireland, is one of the key assemblies in the British Isles, and he is immensely proud of your achievement in at last forming it.
   You may be sure he will pray for your protection and success in the Holy Shrines, and that your numbers may increase in Belfast and your ship weather every storm triumphantly!
With loving greetings,

> *May the Almighty bless sustain and guide you in your meritorious activities, remove every obstacle from your path and enable you to win still greater victories in the service of His glorious Faith.*
> Your true and grateful brother,
Shoghi

14 November 1947

The Bahá'ís of Bristol,
England

Dear Bahá'í Friends,
   Your message of Oct. 21st reached our beloved Guardian, and he has instructed me to answer it on his behalf.
   Now that you are six there (judging by your signatures), a mere three is required to enable you to reach your Goal and have your Assembly next April.
   You may be sure that he will supplicate in the Holy Shrines that these three may be speedily found and the Assembly safely established in accordance with the present Plan.

*The Assemblies are listed
in alphabetical order
but their letters are chronologically
arranged.*

Belfast
Bristol
Cardiff
Dublin
Eccles
Edinburgh
Glasgow
Leeds
Liverpool

London
Manchester
Northampton
Norwich
Nottingham
Oxford
Portsmouth
Reading

THE GUARDIAN'S MESSAGES
To Local Spiritual Assemblies

7 September 1957

Dear Bahá'í Brother,
On behalf of our beloved Guardian I acknowledge with thanks the receipt of your letter of 17th August enclosing the minutes of the meeting of the British N.S.A. held at the Summer School on August 8th. . . .

14 September 1957

WELCOME DETERMINATION ASSEMBLED FRIENDS SUMMER SCHOOL PRAYING FERVENTLY FRIENDS ATTAIN GOALS SCALE NOBLER HEIGHTS PATH SERVICE CAUSE BAHÁ'U'LLÁH.
SHOGHI

2 October 1957

Dear John:
In "The Voice of Youth" for July, page ten, there is an article by David Solomon in which he quotes some very significant passages from the Dead Sea Scrolls. The Guardian would like to have the exact source of these passages, and the quotations in the paragraphs in which they occur, written out in full. . . .

11 October 1957*

CONFIDENT BRITISH COMMUNITY RICHLY DESERVES NEW HONOUR.
SHOGHI

---

*Sent in reply to a cable expressing gratitude for the appointment of two British Hands of the Cause of God.

faces not only the body of the elected representatives of this community, but each and every one of its members. As the world spiritual Crusade, to the successful prosecution of which the British followers of the Faith of Bahá'u'lláh have, singly and collectively, so markedly contributed, approaches its mid-point, the evidences of this indispensable quickening of the tempo of Bahá'í activity all over the British Isles and the islands situated in their neighbourhood and far beyond their confines, must become more manifest and rapidly multiply. The admiration and esteem in which a community, relatively small in numbers, strictly limited in resources, yet capable of such solid and enduring achievements, is held by its sister and daughter communities in every continent of the globe, far from declining must be further enhanced. The historic process originated as far back as the year which witnessed the formulation of the Six Year Plan on the occasion of the Centenary of the Declaration of the Báb in Shíráz, which gathered momentum, as a result of the inauguration of the Two Year Plan which followed the Centenary of the Báb's Martyrdom in Tabríz, which received a tremendous impetus, in consequence of the launching of the Ten Year Crusade, commemorating the centenary celebrations of the birth of Bahá'u'lláh's Mission in Ṭihrán—such a process must, as the centenary celebrations designed to commemorate the Declaration of that same Mission in Baghdád approaches, be so markedly accelerated, and yield such a harvest, as will astonish the entire Bahá'í world, and give the signal for the inauguration, by those who have so spontaneously set this process in motion, more than a decade ago, of a blissful era designed to carry the chief builders of Bahá'u'lláh's embryonic World Order, throughout the unnumbered, the diversified and widely scattered Dependencies of the British Crown, to still greater heights of achievements in the service and for the glory of His Faith.

May they, as they forge ahead along the high road leading to ultimate, total and complete victory, receive as their daily sustenance, a still fuller measure of the abounding grace, promised to the believers of an earlier generation by the Centre of the Covenant, the Author of the Divine Plan, Himself, on the occasion of His twice-repeated visit to their shores, and which has been unfailingly vouchsafed to themselves, in the course of over three decades, since the birth of the Formative Age of the Faith and the rise of its Administrative Order in their homeland.

Shoghi

years immediately ahead, acquire greater coherence, increase more rapidly in numbers, definitely emerge from obscurity, plumb greater depths of consecration, enrich its store of administrative experience, become definitely self-supporting, and associate itself more closely, through the body of its elected representatives and its future Hands, with the National and Regional Spiritual Assemblies on the European mainland and in all the other continents of the globe, and particularly with the Hands already appointed in both the Eastern and Western Hemispheres.

The sooner these prime requisites, so essential for a further unfoldment of the mighty potentialities inherent in so splendid a Mission, are fulfilled, the sooner will the call be raised for the opening of a new chapter in the history of British Bahá'í achievements overseas.

The rapid multiplication of isolated centres, groups and local assemblies, particularly in Scotland, Northern Ireland, Wales and Eire; the incorporation of firmly grounded local spiritual assemblies; a greater measure of publicity; a wider dissemination of Bahá'í literature; a quick and substantial rehabilitation of the vitally important national Fund; a firmer grasp of the essential verities of the Faith; a more profound study of its history and a deeper understanding of the genesis, the significance, the workings, and the present status and achievements of its embryonic World Order and of the Covenant to which it owes its birth and vitality—these remain the rock-bottom requirements which alone can guarantee the opening and hasten the advent, of that blissful era which every British Bahá'í heart so eagerly anticipates, and the glories of which can, at present, be but dimly discerned.

Now, of a certainty, is not the time for the members of this gallant band, so thinly spread over the length and breadth of its island home, and reaching out, so laboriously yet so determinedly to the inhospitable islands fringing its northern and western coasts, to dwell, however tentatively, on the nature of the tantalising task awaiting them in the not distant future, or to seek to probe into its mysterious, divinely guided operation. Theirs is the duty to plod on, however tedious the nature of the work demanding their immediate attention, however formidable the obstacles involved in its proper execution, however prolonged the effort which its success necessitates, until the signs of its ultimate consummation, heralding the launching of what is sure to be the most spectacular phase of their Mission, are clearly discerned.

A responsibility, at once colossal, sacred and highly challenging, spectacular success achieved by the firmly grounded, the progressive and alert British Bahá'í community in the heart of the African Continent—a success attested by the triumphant emergence of the Regional Spiritual Assembly of the Bahá'ís of Central and East Africa—has witnessed a progress throughout the length and breadth of the Homefront, as well as in the northern islands in the neighbourhood of the British Isles, which, though not spectacular, nevertheless testifies to the earnestness, the devotion and the exemplary tenacity with which the members of this community are conducting, in all its aspects, the noble Mission entrusted to their care, and are grappling with the manifold problems involved in its prosecution.

This present and crucial year must be signalised in the annals of British Bahá'í history by a substantial measure of internal administrative consolidation and a noticeable expansion in the all-important teaching field, which will enable the members of this community, now standing on the threshold of a new and brilliant phase in the unfoldment of their Mission in foreign fields, to reinforce and broaden the base of their future operations beyond the confines of their native land.

The splendid work achieved, in such a short space of time, in a field so distant, and amongst a race so alien in its background, outlook and customs, must, if the significance of that Mission is to be properly assessed, be regarded as only a prelude to the series of future campaigns which the privileged members of the British Bahá'í community, residing and firmly rooted in the heart of a far-flung Commonwealth and Empire, will, if faithful to such a Mission, launch, in the years ahead, in the islands of the North Sea and of the Mediterranean, as well as in the remote territories situated in the Pacific area—campaigns which, in their range and significance, must throw into shade the feats performed in the African Continent.

To be enabled to rise to this occasion, to ensure the energetic, the systematic and uninterrupted conduct of so vast and diversified an enterprise, amidst peoples and races fully as promising, and even more remotedly situated, and presenting them with a challenge more severe than any which has faced them in the past, the small band of the ardent, the high minded, the resolute followers of the Faith of Bahá'u'lláh, charged by Destiny and by virtue of the enviable position they occupy, with so glorious a responsibility for the future awakening of the great masses, living under the shadow of, or whose governments are directly associated with, the British Crown, must needs in the places the sooner will the pioneers be able to move on to new fields and to lend their assistance to the teaching work either on the Home Front or in the Pacific area.

Please assure the dear pioneers that he greatly admires their steadfastness of purpose, their self-sacrifice and their exemplary spirit, and that he particularly prays for them in the Holy Shrines.

As regards the future work in the Pacific: It is entirely premature at this time for your Assembly to think about the work there. The Home Front and the work in the neighbouring islands around Great Britain, as well as those allotted under the Ten Year Plan to your Assembly in the Mediterranean, must receive the concentrated attention of your Body, its Committees and the believers. When the time comes to become active in the Pacific area, you may be sure he will let you know!

He feels that the urgent need now is to get out "Some Answered Questions", which is one of the most important books for a proper study of the Faith. When this has been printed, the next publication of the Master's Works can be considered. . . .

As to your question about the words used in the marriage ceremony; the two versions mean practically the same thing, and either may be used.*

It is most regrettable that the Caravan should have gotten hold of . . .; if this situation is stirred up too much it will only enable Ahmad Sohrab to make a big fuss and get more publicity. In view of this the Guardian feels your Assembly should be watchful and seek out, if possible, a suitable person and a suitable opportunity to call to her attention the facts that the Bahá'í Faith, so widely spread and acknowledged, has nothing to do with the Caravan which is a purely opportunist organisation and so loosely knit together as to have almost no power of influencing people one way or another. To do the wrong thing in a situation such as this would be worse than to do nothing.

He assures you one and all of his loving prayers for your success in all you do for the Faith.

Dear and valued co-workers,
   The year that has just elapsed, following upon the swift and

---

*The two versions are: "We will all, verily, abide by the Will of God", and "Verily we are content with the Will of God".

He was pleased to hear from Rhodesia of the incorporation of the Salisbury Assembly, which seems to be in the nature of a foundation for the future incorporation of all Spiritual Assemblies throughout the Rhodesias. This is yet another valuable service which your Assembly has been instrumental in rendering the Faith in Africa.

He thanks your Assembly for the coloured photographs of the Ḥaẓíratu'l-Quds and also for the film of the Summer School which you sent him. He was very pleased also to receive copies of the Irish pamphlets, and hopes the Gaelic translation will soon be out.

As regards your question about printing in books the approval of the National Assembly, he thinks that, if in certain circumstances this seems inadvisable, there is no objection to omitting it. The approval of the National Body should be sought for all Bahá'í publications, so as to protect the Faith from unofficially disseminating information which may in some respects be false or inaccurate. Once this has been done, it is not so essential for the fact to appear in the book, if it will mitigate the effects of the book and decrease its sales. . . .

The death of the Hand of the Cause, George Townshend, is a great loss to the British community as it not only deprives them of their most distinguished member, their unique Hand, but also of a most inspiring and faithful co-worker and a distinguished Bahá'í author. His latest book has been read with great interest by the Guardian, and he hopes your Assembly is ensuring its wide distribution to various religious leaders in Britain. If opposition to the Faith can be aroused through this book, it will be the greatest service that dear George Townshend has ever rendered. It was always his hope that, through his pen, sparks would fly and begin the conflagration in whose light the Faith would shine forth in all its splendour. Let us hope that this last service of his will indeed prove to be the vital spark setting off this process of opposition which will inevitably lead to a wide recognition and acceptance of the Faith.

The Guardian hopes that during the present year the home Assemblies will not only be maintained and groups prepared for assembly status next Riḍván, but that it will be possible to reinforce the work in the islands off the shores of the British Isles. The sooner a nucleus of local people is established in these goal

Guardian has instructed me to answer you on his behalf and to acknowledge receipt of your letters dated: July 24, 27 and 31, August 24, 27, and 30, September 7, 26, 27, and 28, October 5, 13 (signed by all members), and 15, November 5 (signed by Dorothy Ferraby), and 28 (three), and December 14, 18, 27, and 28, 1956, and January 8, 16, 20 (one undated), and 22nd, February 4, 6, 8, 11, 19, 21, 23, and 27, March 7, 8, 13, and 18 (two), May 6, 9, 21, (two), June 3, 11, 14, 19 and 25, July 12, 16, (two), 19, 21, 26, and August 2, and 5 signed by Ernest Gregory†.

As a number of questions raised in your letters have been answered by cable or through the National Assembly Secretary, I will not go into those again here.

He was interested to see the Tablets which Dr. Moayad located in Cambridge, and appreciated having copies of them.

It has been a great pleasure to have had so many members of the British Bahá'í community here last winter and spring as pilgrims.

He is immensely proud of the work which has been accomplished during the last year, of the remarkable spirit of dedication which animates the entire community, and which invariably produces, at an hour of crisis, a strong and healthy reaction on the part of the community to rush reinforcements to its weak Assemblies, when they are in danger of dissolution.

He realises that the enforcement of the general rule that an Assembly must function within civic limits has caused considerable havoc in Britain, as well as other countries. However, it enables the friends, through splitting up into smaller communities, to have before their eyes the appetising prospect of forming yet another Spiritual Assembly, all on their own, so to speak. It gives more believers the opportunity to serve on these Administrative Bodies, challenges the teaching activities of them all, and stimulates them to fresh efforts in the hope of early victory.

The news of the success of your Convention this year; the fact that the community was able to manoeuvre its finances into a position of equilibrium, a position, incidentally, which it should make every effort to maintain; the large number of friends who attended the beautiful memorial meeting held for the dear Hand of the Cause, George Townshend, also pleased and encouraged our beloved Guardian.

27 May 1957

Dear Bahá'í Brother:
The beloved Guardian has instructed me to write about the ... situation raised in one of your recent letters. ...

It is inconceivable and wholly inadmissible that any Bahá'ís in a community should be permitted to hold a Feast in their home and refuse admission to another believer; and your Assembly should write accordingly in very strong terms to the ... Assembly, pointing out that the Guardian is not only surprised to learn of this situation, but disapproves of it in the strongest terms.

Any Bahá'í may attend a Feast, a local Bahá'í, a Bahá'í from out of town, certainly an isolated Bahá'í from the neighbourhood.

It is the duty of the ... Assembly to take strong measures to remedy this situation, and to ensure that the Feasts are held in a place and in a manner that conforms to the Bahá'í spirit. ...

7 June 1957 (Shetland Summer School)

SUPPLICATING ABUNDANT BLESSINGS DEEPEST LOVE.

SHOGHI

14 August 1957

DELIGHTED HISTORIC GATHERING ASSURE FERVENT PRAYERS UNPRECEDENTED EXPANSION ACTIVITIES.

SHOGHI

30 August 1957

Dear Bahá'í Brother:
Your communications with their enclosures and material sent under separate cover have all arrived safely, and the beloved

P.S. In order to gain time this is being mailed through a pilgrim from Rome.
P.S. No. 2. Will you please acknowledge receipt of this letter by cable to the Guardian.

19 April 1957

Dear Bahá'í Brother,
The Beloved Guardian has been very deeply impressed with the latest book of our dear departed co-worker, Hand of the Cause, George Townshend.

He feels that this Book should be used as the basis of a very active campaign of teaching and publicity throughout the British Isles.

Publicity regarding the book should be arranged, book reviews secured, if possible. Religious leaders should be sent copies, even the highest Ecclesiastical leaders. Many copies should be mailed to the important leaders of the Church of England, and other religious denominations of the British Isles.

This book very finely presents the relationship between Christ and Bahá'u'lláh, and outlines the manner in which the Bahá'í Faith is setting up the Kingdom of God, which the Christians are praying for.

The Guardian feels that very beneficial results will be achieved by this active public programme, with this book, "Christ and Bahá'u'lláh" even if it stirs up opposition and criticism for the time being.

He will pray for your Assembly, and for the success of your many labours in the Cause of God. . . .

30 April 1957

DEEPLY APPRECIATE CONVENTION MESSAGE REJOICE RECENT VICTORIES GREATLY VALUE SPIRIT ANIMATING ENTIRE BRITISH BAHÁ'Í COMMUNITY CHERISH BRIGHTEST HOPES FERVENTLY SUPPLICATING RAPID CONSOLIDATION HOME FRONT ESSENTIAL PRELUDE UNPRECEDENTED EXPANSION GLORIOUS MISSION BRITISH FOLLOWERS FAITH BAHÁ'U'LLÁH FOREIGN FIELDS DEEPEST LOVE.

SHOGHI

30 March 1957

Dear Bahá'í Brother:

The Beloved Guardian has directed me to write you concerning a list which he desires, showing the languages into which the scriptures, or parts of them have been translated.

He has the book entitled "The Gospel in Many Tongues" issued by the British and Foreign Bible Society, the Bible House, 146 Queen Victoria Street, London, E.C.4, (in 1948). This shows specimens of 770 languages in which this Society has published or circulated some portion of the Gospel.

In the preface, they state "If those versions published by other agents are included, there are now well over a thousand forms of speech represented in the Library at Bible House".

The Guardian would like to secure a list of the additional some 300 languages into which the Gospel has been translated, referred to in this quotation. Could you secure it for him, from the Bible Society, at the Bible House.

Is it fair to assume this would then be all the languages, from any source, into which the Bible or parts have been translated? Your early advice will be appreciated.

For your information, in the list of languages into which Bahá'í literature has been translated, there are some 20, not included in the published book of the 770 languages into which Christian Scripture has been published, as covered by the Book.

The question is, are these 20 included in the supplementary list, which makes the 1,000 or more into which Christian Scripture has been translated. Your sending the list will enable us to make the check here.

If you could secure this list and send it promptly, it might enable the Guardian to include this interesting point in his Convention message. . . .

12 April 1957

Dear John:

Enclosed please find the beloved Guardian's Message to the annual convention; it should be delivered to the Chairman to be read to and shared with the assembled friends. . . .

The Guardian has directed me to acknowledge your letter and the contributions on his behalf. Receipt is enclosed.

Will you please write the Bahá'ís of ... on behalf of the Guardian, and thank them for their contribution for the construction of the International Archives Building. Their sacrifices in that difficult area, at this time, shows their depth of spiritual consciousness. The Guardian will pray for them, and for the success of their work.

The Guardian also wishes to assure the Bahá'ís of the British Isles, of his appreciation of their sacrifice and devotion to the Cause of God. He is praying for them, for the success of their historic work, and for the rapid expansion of the Faith. He is sure the Blessings of the Beloved Master will rest on each and every one.

Please send the Friends in Kuwait the enclosed photo, showing the present stage of construction of the Archives Building.

He sends his loving Greetings ...

27 March 1957

DEEPLY MOURN PASSING DEARLY LOVED MUCH ADMIRED GREATLY GIFTED OUTSTANDING HAND CAUSE GEORGE TOWNSHEND. HIS DEATH MORROW PUBLICATION HIS CROWNING ACHIEVEMENT ROBS BRITISH FOLLOWERS BAHÁ'U'LLÁH THEIR MOST DISTINGUISHED COLLABORATOR AND FAITH ITSELF ONE ITS STOUTEST DEFENDERS. HIS STERLING QUALITIES HIS SCHOLARSHIP HIS CHALLENGING WRITINGS HIS HIGH ECCLESIASTICAL POSITION UNRIVALLED ANY BAHÁ'Í WESTERN WORLD ENTITLE HIM RANK WITH THOMAS BREAKWELL DR. ESSLEMONT ONE OF THREE LUMINARIES SHEDDING BRILLIANT LUSTRE ANNALS IRISH ENGLISH SCOTTISH BAHÁ'Í COMMUNITIES. HIS FEARLESS CHAMPIONSHIP CAUSE HE LOVED SO DEARLY SERVED SO VALIANTLY CONSTITUTES SIGNIFICANT LAND- MARK BRITISH BAHÁ'Í HISTORY. SO ENVIABLE POSITION CALLS FOR NATIONAL TRIBUTE HIS MEMORY BY ASSEMBLED DELEGATES VISITORS FORTHCOMING BRITISH BAHÁ'Í CONVENTION. ASSURE RELATIVES DEEPEST LOVING SYMPATHY GRIEVOUS LOSS. CONFIDENT HIS REWARD INESTIMABLE ABHÁ KINGDOM.

SHOGHI

9 March 1957

Dear Bahá'í Brother:

Your loving letter of March 4th, with regard to the Shrine of Bahá'u'lláh, interior view, slide; which was shown or to be shown at your Summer School.

The Guardian wishes me to see that all these slides are destroyed, and all informed that they should not be used. Therefore, can you send me the name of the person in America who sent the slide to the Bahá'í in England.

This will permit me to stop the exodus of these slides at the source....

14 March 1957

APPEAL VALIANT BRITISH BAHÁ'Í COMMUNITY FOCUS ATTENTION URGENT NEEDS PIVOTAL CENTRES STRENUOUS IMMEDIATE CONCERTED EFFORTS IMPERATIVE SAFEGUARD OUTSTANDING PRIZES LABORIOUSLY WON FERVENTLY PRAYING SUCCESS DEEPEST LOVE.

SHOGHI

16 March 1957

Dear Bahá'í Brother:

The Beloved Guardian has been greatly impressed by the number of Teaching Conferences held during the past year, especially in the virgin areas of the Ten Year Crusade.

My records are not complete concerning the Teaching Conference of the Northern Islands. Will you please cable me on receipt of this where this Conference was held, and the dates....

23 March 1957

Dear Bahá'í Friend,

Your loving letter of February 20th was duly received by the Beloved Guardian, and on March 20th, the contributions referred to therein.

He assures you one and all of his loving prayers for your success, and that he will remember you in his visits to the Holy Shrines....

May the Spirit of Bahá'u'lláh sustain you in your highly meritorious labours, guide every step you take in the path of service to His Faith, and enable you to lend a great impetus, in the days to come, to the onward march of our beloved Cause throughout the British Isles and to the consolidation of its divinely appointed institutions,

Your true brother,
Shoghi

26 February 1957

Dear Bahá'í Brother:

The Beloved Guardian has directed me to write your Assembly with regard to showing interior views of the Shrine of Bahá'u'lláh in slides.

The Guardian read in some minutes, or in a report of one of the Summer Schools, that slides were shown of the Holy Land, and among them one of the interior of the Shrine. He would like to know whether this is the interior Garden, or the Inner Shrine itself, and whose slides they are.

He feels that the Shrine of Bahá'u'lláh and the Báb are so sacred, it is improper for any slides to be shown of the Interiors. Thus, the slide which was shown at the Summer School should be destroyed, and if it forms a part of any sets of views of the Holy Land, this slide be removed from the set.

He sends you his loving Greetings....

27 February 1957

GREATLY DEPLORE LOSS MUCH LOVED JOHN MITCHELL STAUNCH CONSECRATED PROMOTER FAITH. REWARD HIS ADMINISTRATIVE PIONEER SERVICES GREAT ABHÁ KINGDOM FERVENTLY SUPPLICATING PROGRESS HIS SOUL.

SHOGHI

12 January 1957

Mr. Arthur Norton

Dear Bahá'í Brother,

Your loving letters concerning contributions to the Shrine of the Báb Fund, and the International Fund, have been received by the Beloved Guardian, and he has directed me to acknowledge them on his behalf. These contributions from the Friends in England, and the Friends in the Seychelles, are greatly appreciated by the Guardian. Receipt is enclosed. Will you please, on behalf of the Guardian express his appreciation to Mr. & Mrs. . . . and the devoted friends in the Seychelles.

The Guardian has been deeply touched by the continuing victories being won by the friends in the Seychelles.

The Beloved Guardian also wishes the dear Friends in England to know of his deep appreciation of their consecration, and their sacrifices for the Faith. This noble spirit cannot do other than attract the blessings of the Holy Spirit, which will assure victory. He assures you of his prayers in your behalf, and for the success of your many labours.

He sends you his loving Greetings. . . .

12 January 1957

To the Bahá'ís who were present at the Birmingham Teaching Conference, January 5th 1957.

Dear Bahá'í Friends,

The beloved Guardian has received your letter of greeting, and was very happy to hear that the Birmingham Teaching Conference had been such an outstanding success.

Undoubtedly the Faith in the British Isles is making steady and sound progress, and he hopes that during the coming months many of the Spiritual Assemblies which have been placed in jeopardy will be consolidated in time for the elections. He feels sure that the British Bahá'ís, who have done more pioneering per capita than any other Bahá'í community in the world, will do all in their power to safeguard the precious goals they have won at the cost of so much sacrifice and valiant endeavour.

8 December 1956

REGARDING CHILDREN FOLLOW AMERICAN PROCEDURE. APPROVE SUGGESTED METHOD INCORPORATION MAURITIUS.

SHOGHI

14 December 1956

Dear Bahá'í Brother:

The Beloved Guardian has directed me to write to your Assembly, with regard to the Tristan da Cunha Island.

Earlier in the Ten Year Crusade, one of the English Bahá'ís offered to settle in this Island, in order to establish the Faith there. At that time, the Guardian felt we must concentrate on the goals of the Crusade only. Now, however, the Friends have won so many victories, and the goals of the Crusade are being gained currently, early in the Crusade, he feels supplementary areas may be settled—and for that matter, supplementary activities engaged in.

Thus, if this friend still wishes to settle in the Island of Tristan da Cunha, he would welcome it being done.

If only the home front would surge ahead, then the Crusade would surely be moving ahead of the schedule. Let us pray those at home will arise with the same dedication, and consecration as the valiant pioneers, causing a new life to be manifest on all home fronts.

The Guardian sends the members of your Assembly his loving greetings. . . .

27 December 1956

AS NATIONAL AND FEW LOCAL ḤAẒÍRAS NOT YET RETURNED LETTER THANKS INADVISABLE.*

SHOGHI

---

* Proposed letter of thanks to a Head of State.

been vastly enriched. *The process set in motion and greatly accelerated through the successive formulation of the Six Year Plan, the Two Year Plan and the Ten Year Plan, must continue unabated and unimpaired. Nay with every passing day it must gather momentum. Every individual believer must, henceforth, encouraged and inspired by all that has already been achieved, contribute to its future and speedy unfoldment. That the entire community may befittingly respond to the call of the present hour and bring to a final consummation the Mission with which it has been entrusted is the deepest yearning of my heart and the object of my unceasing prayers.*
Shoghi

4 November 1956

Northern Ireland Regional Teaching Committee

Dear Bahá'í Brother:

Your letter of 16 Mashíyyat 113, with enclosures, has been received by the beloved Guardian, and he has instructed me to answer you on his behalf.

He is most hopeful that the second week-end school will prove as successful and fruitful as the one held in February apparently was.

The Guardian is delighted over the progress being made in Northern Ireland. He greatly admires the tenacity and spirit of dedication of the believers living in the British Isles, and is confident the friends in your region will unitedly bend all their energies toward the fulfilment of the goals they have set their hearts on attaining by next Riḍván.

Rest assured of his loving prayers for you all....

May the Beloved bless your efforts and those of your dear co-workers, and aid you to extend the range of your valued activities, and enable you to win memorable victories in the service of His Faith,
Your true brother,
Shoghi

to the Administrative Centre in the British Isles, provided that a determination no less unyielding, and a dedication no less wholehearted and complete, will be displayed by those who have already won such memorable victories in such far-off and inhospitable regions of the globe. He Who in recent years infallibly guided from His realms above the steps of the little band of pioneers and administrators under such difficult and challenging circumstances, Who galvanised their souls, blessed their handiwork, raised their status, and noised abroad their fame, can well enable them, if they but arise to the occasion now presenting itself, to conquer with no less rapidity and even greater effectiveness, the citadels of men's hearts, to tear down the barriers which now confront them, and ignite a fire in the hearts of their own countrymen as consuming as the one that has set ablaze, in so conspicuous a fashion, the souls of the African races over the length and breadth of an entire continent.

The rapid increase in the number of the avowed supporters of the Faith, the multiplication of groups, isolated centres and assemblies within the limits of the homeland and its neighbouring islands, must be accompanied by a marked acceleration in the process of internal consolidation, such as the incorporation of firmly established local Assemblies, expansion in the publication and dissemination of Bahá'í literature, and the adoption of carefully considered measures aimed at giving a still wider publicity, among circles hitherto unapproached, or as yet inadequately informed of the tenets, the aims and purposes, as well as the world-wide achievements of the Faith of Bahá'u'lláh in both the teaching and administrative spheres of its activities.

The highly gratifying and truly praiseworthy success which has attended, so unexpectedly, the energetic efforts exerted by your Assembly in connection with the campaign of publicity initiated for the purpose of safeguarding the rights of our oppressed brethren in Persia must be regarded as a most encouraging sign, and should constitute a prelude and a stepping-stone to a still wider undertaking, aimed at a more systematic presentation of the ideals animating our beloved Cause and of its fundamental verities, and an adequate proclamation of its God-given mission to this distracted, sadly erring, and increasingly tormented generation.

The annals of the British Bahá'í community, small in numbers, yet unconquerable in spirit, tenacious in belief, undeviating in purpose, alert and vigilant in the discharge of its manifold duties and responsibilities, have in consequence of its epoch-making achievements *fidelity, and the dogged determination that have characterised every stage in the rise, the development and fruition of the first collective enterprise embarked upon beyond the confines of the British Isles by the British adherents of the Faith of Bahá'u'lláh.*

Though much of the responsibility hitherto discharged by your Assembly, in both the heart of the continent and the territories situated on its Eastern and Western shores, will now devolve on the newly established Regional Spiritual Assemblies, the particular Mission you have been called upon, through the dispensation of Providence to fulfil, is by no means concluded. Every assistance within your power, particularly in matters requiring the aid, support and intervention of the authorities at the Colonial Office, and in connection with the translation of Bahá'í literature into African languages, their publication and dissemination, as well as with any publicity that can be given in the British press to the marvellous achievements of the numerous Bahá'í communities recently raised up in Africa, and now energetically discharging their manifold and sacred duties all over that continent—such assistance should be constantly and unstintingly extended to these newly fledged communities which the power of the Most Great Name has called into being at so crucial a period in human history, and at so auspicious a stage in the mysterious unfoldment of God's Plan for all mankind.

While this beneficent, slowly maturing, irresistibly advancing enterprise develops and gains momentum, through the concerted and tireless efforts of its original organisers in the British Isles and those in charge of its immediate destinies in Africa itself, a corresponding endeavour, no less consecrated, persistent and enthusiastic, should be exerted in the Islands of the Mediterranean and the Far East, where similar exploits must needs be achieved by those who have performed such unforgettable feats among the Negroes of the African continent.

Parallel with this highly vital and urgently needed exertion in foreign fields, a further intensification of effort is required on the homefront, and particularly throughout the newly opened islands bordering the homeland itself, now standing in such dire need of a flow of pioneers and a concentration of material resources unexampled in British Bahá'í history. There is no reason to doubt that the phenomenal progress achieved within the span of a few years, amidst an alien people, and in such distant and backward territories, will be duplicated, nay surpassed, among people of the same race, speaking the same language, of the same background, and living in such close proximity objection to Bahá'ís conforming to the requirements of the law court whatever they may be in such matters, as in no case would they constitute in any way a denial of their own beliefs as Bahá'ís.

Concerning the short obligatory Prayer: the Guardian does not wish to define these things at present; the time will come for it in future. The friends need not be too strict about it at present. The Greatest Name is Alláh-u-Abhá.

He remembers you and all the N.S.A. members in his prayers most lovingly, and supplicates for your success and that strength may be given you to discharge your many important duties.

Dear and valued co-workers,

The emergence of the Regional Spiritual Assembly of the Bahá'ís of Central and East Africa, under such auspicious circumstances, and after the lapse of such a short period of time since the inception of the Ten Year Plan, marks a milestone of far-reaching significance in the unfoldment of the great historic Mission entrusted to the British Bahá'í community in the vast and far-flung territories beyond the confines of its motherland. It is, moreover, a striking evidence of the exemplary and whole-hearted devotion of its members to that Mission, and of the vigour, the vigilance, the resourcefulness, the tenacity and the courage with which they have conducted this vast and magnificent enterprise launched in the heart of that continent, in the face of various obstacles and with such limited resources at their disposal. The entire community, now standing on the threshold of still greater and nobler enterprises in other parts of the world, and particularly its national elected representatives, who have so splendidly discharged their responsibilities overseas, and assumed with characteristic resolution, fearlessness and consecration the direction of the manifold activities of so dynamic an enterprise, must be heartily congratulated on so conspicuous a victory, won in such a distant field, within so brief an interval, at the cost of so much sacrifice, by so limited a number of pioneers, labouring amidst a people so divergent in language, customs and manners.

Its sister communities in both the East and the West, and particularly its daughter communities, now blossoming into new life, and marching forth, unitedly and resolutely, along the path traced for them in the Ten Year Plan, cannot but feel proud of the tremendous work first initiated in the heart of Africa by British Bahá'í pioneers, and of the organising ability, the sound judgement, the unquestioning upon their return, they carried back much of inspiration and encouragement to the friends at home.

Not the least of the landmarks reached on the international Bahá'í scene this year has been the formation of the three new National Bodies in Africa. Your Assembly and the community you represent have every reason to look with pride and affection upon the development of the Cause in the African continent, and upon the many spiritual children and grandchildren, and perhaps great-grandchildren you have over there. The record has been truly astonishing, and such as to gladden the heart of 'Abdu'l-Bahá Who so ardently longed, Himself, to go forth "on foot" and carry the Message to yet another of the far corners of the world.

No doubt although the Central and East Africa Assembly is a strong one, it will still welcome and need at least a large measure of moral support from its parent; and he feels sure that you will always be ready and willing to help in any way you can with advice and suggestions, and perhaps teachers and pioneers and other support as opportunity affords. (As he informed you when you were here, he does not feel the British National Spiritual Assembly can support financially its Central and East Africa one. However, a token contribution would be a kind and appropriate gesture.) In any case, you should keep in close touch with the work there, a work dear, not only to the Guardian's heart, but to all of yours as well.

As regards certain questions raised in your letters: There is no objection for the time being in going on including in Prayer Books the Prayer of the Báb: "In the Name of God, the Victor of the Most Victorious", etc.

As regards the question raised in Africa about divorce connected with adultery, these are matters for the future. No action of any new kind should be taken at present.

As regards strikes, the Guardian feels that your own understanding of the matter as expressed in your letter is quite correct, and he does not see the necessity of adding anything to it. We should avoid becoming rigid and laying down any more rules and regulations of conduct.

Regarding taking oaths, there is nothing in the Teachings on this subject. As a Bahá'í is enjoined by Bahá'u'lláh to be truthful, he would express his truthfulness, no matter what the formality of the law in any local place required of him. There can be no

He was sorry to refuse the request of the National Assembly to, under certain circumstances, permit the localities that would achieve Assembly status by next Riḍván, to have a delegate at the National Convention. He feels that, although this would no doubt have provided a great stimulus to the friends, it was an unjustifiable breach of the general administrative procedure. If there are too many exceptions, the rule has a tendency to lose its clearly defined character, not to mention encouraging other communities to want to be exceptions too, under various circumstances!

The Guardian hopes that during the coming year there will be more Assemblies incorporated, as he attaches great importance to this process.

He was delighted that the Irish translation had been completed, and also very happy to hear that the National Endowment for the British National Spiritual Assembly had been purchased. All these signs of life and vitality are greatly to be admired, and prove the intense virility and youthfulness of the British Bahá'í community.

He was sorry to have to disappoint Mr. ... who was so enthusiastic about his own design for the Temple. However, there was no possible question of accepting something as extreme as this. The Guardian feels very strongly that, regardless of what the opinion of the latest school of architecture may be on the subject, the styles represented at present all over the world in architecture are not only very ugly, but completely lack the dignity and grace which must be at least partially present in a Bahá'í House of Worship. One must always bear in mind that the vast majority of human beings are neither very modern nor very extreme in their tastes, and that what the advanced school may think is marvellous is often very distasteful indeed to just plain, simple people.

The Hand of the Cause, Mr. Remey, has now completed a design for the Kampala Temple which meets with the Guardian's approval. It will shortly be ready to be forwarded to the Central and East Africa National Assembly.

It was a great pleasure for Shoghi Effendi to have a number of pilgrims from the British Isles as his guests this winter. They brought with them the spirit of perseverence and devotion so clearly evinced by the British believers; and he feels sure that,

The Government has been forced to take action for the first time in its history to officially protect the Bahá'ís and their institutions and the Cause of God has received a publicity all over the world—entirely free of charge—which an expenditure of many thousands of pounds could not have secured for it.

In spite of the great anxiety and pain which the crisis of last summer caused the Guardian, he could not help being highly gratified that, for practically the first time, publicity of a weighty nature was given to the Faith in such papers as the "Spectator", the "Observer", "The Times" and the "Manchester Guardian", and that the voices of two such distinguished scholars as Professor Gilbert Murray and Professor Arnold Toynbee were raised in defence of the believers of Bahá'u'lláh and His Faith. This has opened the door on a new phase of the unfoldment of the Faith in the British Isles. However slow the process may seem, the first inklings of its emergence as a public force can now be discerned....

The loss of some of the Spiritual Assemblies in England this year need not be viewed as an unduly horrible experience. It was inevitable that the British Bahá'í community would have to get itself, once and for all, grounded on the same basis as all other Bahá'í communities, namely, that of having Spiritual Assemblies function within defined civil limits. Although this seems to have dealt a set-back to the work, it is purely temporary. The localities have perforce been increased, which is a step in the right direction, and which cannot but widen the foundation of the Administrative Order. In those islands more members of the community will be given the opportunity to serve on local Assemblies and their committees; and above all, the new crisis which developed because of this change-over once more demonstrated the truly extraordinary and exemplary steadfastness of the British Bahá'ís which had led them, over and over again, at great cost to themselves, to throw themselves into the breach. Although this is a well-known national characteristic, it provides nevertheless a great example to their fellow-Bahá'ís all over the world. The Guardian knows of no community, east or west, which so valiantly and so consistently, one might almost say ferociously, has arisen to defend its Home Front. He has the greatest admiration for the spirit which animates them and for their achievements.

manner, point out when occasion arises that the Caravan activities have nothing whatsoever to do with the Bahá'í Faith and are indeed unfriendly to it. Whatever he does cannot but end in failure, because he has cut himself off entirely from the living tree of the Faith and is wholly insincere in his motives.

In spite of the fact that Mr. . . . has been expelled from Gilbert and Ellice Islands, the remarkable progress of the Faith there has been a source of great satisfaction. It shows that a spiritual receptivity, a purity of heart and uprightness of character exists potentially amongst many of the peoples of the Pacific Isles to an extent equal to that of the tribesmen of Africa. It is indeed an encouraging and awe-inspiring sight to witness the spread of our beloved Faith amongst those whom civilised nations misguidedly term "savages", "primitive peoples" and "uncivilised nations". He hopes that your Assembly will do all in its power to ensure that Mrs. , . . remains in the Islands. Although for some period at least this may entail separation from her husband, he believes that these two dedicated and exemplary pioneers will be willing to accept this sacrifice in view of the extraordinary work they have accomplished and are accomplishing. The community there must not be abandoned, particularly by its "mother", so to speak. It must be well and profoundly grounded in the Faith before such a risky step can be taken. He hopes that you will deal most wisely and co-operatively with the Colonial Office officials in this matter and any others that may arise. Their esteem, their good-will, and their co-operation are practically indispensable for the future work in many islands throughout the Pacific area, and nothing but the frustration of our objectives can be gained through alienating them in any way. This should be impressed upon the pioneers and the local Bahá'ís as well.

The beloved Guardian regrets very much the entire situation in which the dear Hand of the Cause, Mr. Townshend, finds himself. He is much loved, and his services have been of a unique nature in providing the Faith with so many excellent books, the latest of which the Guardian hopes will soon be ready for publication. . . .

The persecution of the Faith last year in Persia, although no doubt a great trial to the Persian believers, can be regarded in no other light than as a triumph. The designs of the traditional enemies of the Faith, the mulláhs, have been entirely frustrated.

26 June 1956

REGIONAL ASSEMBLY RESPONSIBLE FOR TEMPLE.

SHOGHI

11 July 1956

Dear John,

As a number of questions raised in your communications addressed to the beloved Guardian have been answered by cable or through the Assistant Secretary, I will not go into these matters here, but merely acknowledge on his behalf receipt of the letters from your National Body, together with their enclosures and material sent under separate cover which were dated as follows: July 22, August 8, 9, 11 (two), 12 (two), and 18, September 7, 9, 10, 23 (three), 26 and 28, October 7 (two), 13 (two), 25, 26, 28 (two), and 29, November 3, 4, 9, 21 (two), 24 and 30, December 1, 2, 9 (three), 19 and 29 (two), 1955, and January 6, 10, 17, 23, 27, and 30 (two), February 10, 16, and 27, March 8, 9, 19, and 29, April 2, 10, 13, 16, 17, and 26, May 4, 14, 16, 31, and June 13, 19, 22, and 29, 1956.

He appreciated receiving copies of the Diary which your Assembly forwarded to him, and which is invariably gotten out efficiently and in a pleasing manner. He thinks the five copies you sent will be sufficient.

The generous spirit in which the British Bahá'ís, hard-pressed as they are to meet the requirements of the work in Great Britain, responded to the needs of their persecuted brethren in Persia, deeply touched him. These evidences of Bahá'í sacrifice and solidarity cannot but nourish the very roots of the Faith and strengthen its institutions.

As he advised you by cable, he felt it unwise to seek to clarify the relationship of the Bahá'ís to the advertised holding of Ahmad Sohrab's conference in Jerusalem. Having a very shrewd eye to his own advantage, it has become obvious that one of the means by which he hopes to promote interest in his conference is to arouse active opposition from the Bahá'ís and create a source of discussion in the press. In view of this, the Guardian has been very careful to have the friends avoid rising to this bait. They should, in their personal contacts with people, and in a quiet

10 April 1956

BALYUZI'S PRESENCE ESSENTIAL* UTMOST EFFORT NECESSARY IF ABSOLUTELY IMPOSSIBLE SUBSTITUTE JOHN.

SHOGHI

27 April 1956**

GRIEVED PASSING CONSECRATED PIONEER FAITH LONG RECORD SERVICES HIGHLY MERITORIOUS UNFORGETTABLE PRAYING PROGRESS SOUL ABHÁ KINGDOM.

SHOGHI

29 April 1956

ASSURE FERVENT PRAYERS HEARTFELT CONGRATULATIONS GREAT VICTORIES AFRICA URGE REDOUBLE EFFORTS HOME FRONT DEEPEST LOVE.

SHOGHI

2 May 1956

WELCOME RESOLVE MEET CHALLENGES LOVING FERVENT PRAYERS OFFERED SUCCESS DEARLY LOVED VALIANT COMMUNITY.

SHOGHI

10 May 1956

SUGGESTED DISPENSATION LETTER MAY FOURTH NOT POSSIBLE.***

SHOGHI

* As convening Chairman, Kampala Convention.
**Ḍíyá'u'lláh Aṣgharzádih.
***For allocation of delegates to Assemblies lapsing after civic limits rule imposed.

26 March 1956

APPEAL HIGHMINDED VIGILANT STAUNCH UPHOLDERS FAITH BAHÁ'U'LLÁH SCATTERED HUNDRED CENTRES BRITISH ISLES ARISE THIS CRUCIAL HOUR EXERT SUPREME EFFORT CONCLUDING MONTH SECOND PHASE WORLD CRUSADE MEET URGENT NEEDS HOMEFRONT VALIANTLY DEFEND HARD WON PRIZES ENSURE PRESERVATION PIVOTAL CENTRE. CONFIDENT HIS DEARLY BELOVED HIGHLY ADMIRED BRITISH FOLLOWERS WILL REFUSE ALLOW ANY SETBACK CONSOLIDATION WORK THEIR HOMELAND TARNISH SPLENDID RECORD PIONEER SERVICES ACHIEVED TERRITORIES AFRICAN CONTINENT PRAYING WHOLE HEARTED UNIVERSAL IMMEDIATE RESPONSE PLEDGING FIVE HUNDRED POUNDS MERITORIOUS PURPOSE.

SHOGHI

5 April 1956

Dear Bahá'í Brother:

Attached is a copy of a dispatch issued by Reuters in December, giving the conclusions of the persecutions in Persia.

The Guardian considers this a very fine statement, and urges you to have it given as widespread publicity as possible.

Dorothy Wigington† will have a copy, and she should be given the opportunity to read this at the British National Convention.

The Guardian would appreciate your sending copies of any publicity received on this important statement. . . .

6 April 1956

Dear John:

Enclosed please find the Guardian's long message to all the Conventions, to be shared with the friends and delegates at the National Convention soon to be held.

He hopes that it will be stimulating to the pioneer work at home and abroad. . . .

16 December 1955

Dear Bahá'í Friends:

The beloved Guardian has directed me to write you in connection with the purchase of an endowment for East Africa.

As you know, a contribution has been made by the Hand of the Cause, Mrs. Amelia E. Collins, of One Thousand Dollars for the purchase of the endowment for Kampala. The Guardian feels a small piece of property which can be bought for this One Thousand Dollars should be procured at once, so that this goal of the Ten Year Crusade can be concluded. He feels that you should at once buy a small plot of land in Uganda, at a cost of approximately One Thousand Dollars. The American N.S.A. will remit the funds as you direct.

Will you please let me know just what can be done in connection with this project?

The Guardian sends the members of the National Assembly his loving greetings, and assures them of his prayers in their behalf....

1 January 1956*

GRIEVED NEWS ASSURE JOHN DEAREST LOVE FERVENT PRAYERS.

SHOGHI

4 January 1956

DISREGARD PERSIAN STATEMENT REGARDING DIVORCE. ASSEMBLY'S UNDERSTANDING REGARDING STRIKES CORRECT.

SHOGHI

18 January 1956

DEEPLY APPRECIATE MESSAGE CONFERENCE WELCOME NEW DETERMINATION BEFITTINGLY RESPOND FRESH CHALLENGE PRAYING MIGHTY VICTORIES.

SHOGHI

*Refers to Dr. John Mitchell.

14 December 1955

Dear Bahá'í Brother:

Your loving letter of December 1st has been received.

The Guardian attaches the utmost importance to the development of the Faith in the Pacific Islands. Wherever an opportunity opens for expansion of the work in one of the Islands, he feels that opportunity should be seized and exploited to the fullest extent. Thus, if it is possible for anyone to proceed to the Solomon Islands to assist the Blums there, it would be very, very helpful.

As the Guardian understands the situation, the Blums have not left the Solomon Islands, but are expanding their business and service. Thus the work which Mr. Blum previously engaged in, of driving a taxi, is now open to someone else; and therefore the pioneer to go to the Solomons would find a position waiting for him.

The Guardian understands that the Blums are very well thought of and respected throughout the Solomon Islands.

I am sending a copy of this correspondence to the Persian N.S.A., and encouraging them to send pioneers to the Solomon Islands. You may wish to also correspond with them. . . .

15 December 1955

Dear Bahá'í Friends:

The beloved Guardian has directed me to write you in connection with the translation of Bahá'í literature into languages as called for by the Ten Year Crusade.

31 languages have been assigned to your Assembly; and of these, 24 translations have been made or are under way. The Guardian feels this is a very fine record, and one of which you may be proud.

At the same time he feels special effort should be made to complete the translations. He has no record of translations of 7 languages. Will you please send me a letter for him, indicating what the status of each of these languages is. . . .

Bahá'í Temple.... It seems to him that the modern influence is now so strong and widespread that it is out of the question to get a discreet and dignified building designed for our purposes.

... He is sorry to disappoint your Assembly, and regrets the time, trouble and expense which has been involved in finding a design.

As he cabled your Assembly he also feels that to seek a new Temple site is unwise; from descriptions received at the time of its purchase it seems satisfactory, and there is enough land around it for possible expansion in the future....

He feels therefore that until your hear from him you (had) better take no further steps as regards a design for Kampala.

8 December 1955*

CABLE NUMBER LOCALITIES BRITISH ISLES WHERE BAHÁ'ÍS RESIDE AIRMAIL LIST.

SHOGHI

13 December 1955

Dear John:

This is just a note on behalf of the beloved Guardian to answer the point raised in one of your recent letters.

You say that in Irish, the word "Báb" is not appropriate to be used; and as the word "Gate" is not as nice in translation in any language, he suggests that in place of the word "Báb", you use "Herald"....

P.S. The Guardian approves your sending "Advice to Bahá'ís in British Colonies" to other N.S.A.'s, but feels it is not necessary to send a copy to the Colonial Office itself. He feels teaching work in Uganda should now be concentrated on consolidation, primarily.

The Guardian's decision regard Mr. ... design is final; it is too extreme for any modification to render it possible as a temple....

* Replied "exactly 100".

He leaves an equitable distribution of the number of delegates to the Assemblies, to your Assembly to decide.

The British N.S.A. certainly has its work cut out for it in the near future, what with this historic convention in the offing and a Temple to be built! . . .

4 October 1955

LEAVE MATTERS REGARDING ASSEMBLIES LETTER SEPTEMBER 23 DISCRETION YOUR ASSEMBLY.

SHOGHI

28 October 1955

CABLE WHETHER TRANSLATION ERSE GAELIC STARTED.

SHOGHI

4 November 1955

DISAPPROVE CHANGE TEMPLE SITE.

SHOGHI

11 November 1955

APPROVE APPROACH JANNER EMPHASISE OCCUPATION ṬIHRÁN ḤAẒÍRA BY MILITARY.

SHOGHI

18 November 1955

The drawings for the Temple in Kampala have reached the beloved Guardian, and he has instructed me to answer you on his behalf regarding their suitability.

Frankly, he was very discouraged by these drawings, as he feels that such an ultra-modern style is wholly unsuitable for a

30 August 1955

The beloved Guardian has received the clippings from English newspapers and read them with keen interest; he attached much importance to such publicity in journals of such high standing....

Regarding your questions—

It is permissible to use selections from the "Promulgation of Universal Peace" in compilations.

Better omit the prayer of the Báb you mentioned.

The Guardian does not feel the present status of London, regarding its assembly, should be changed. Other cities should have their assemblies based, as usual, and already adopted in other countries, on the civil limits of the city in question....

6 September 1955

KINDLY EXPEDITE PREPARATION PLANS KAMPALA TEMPLE IMPORTANT.

SHOGHI

6 September 1955 (Summer School)

DELIGHTED GREAT SUCCESS. DEEPLY APPRECIATE RESOLVE LOVING PRAYERS.

SHOGHI

20 September 1955

Dear John:

The beloved Guardian has instructed me to write and inform your Assembly of the following:

The National Spiritual Assembly of Central and East Africa should be elected by 76 delegates, which is four times nineteen. This number should be apportioned amongst the spiritual assemblies within the countries the future N.S.A will represent.

22 August 1955

Dear John,

I am writing you this at the instruction of the beloved Guardian.

As you will have no doubt seen by his recent cable, he has come to the historic decision to build a Temple in Africa, in Kampala. He has been in communication with Mr. Bánání about this, and from reports received it appears there will be no objections. The land must be surveyed (this is being done), and design of the building submitted so as to meet health and building requirements.

The Guardian wishes your Assembly to please get busy at once and have a design, or designs, made for the building; it is not necessary to try in any way to copy the Wilmette Temple: the things that are essential are the following:

1. A nine-sided building.
2. A dome, in proportion to the building.
3. A seating capacity between 300 and 500; you could count floor space at 300 or 400 and provide a balcony around the auditorium for expansion in seating capacity.
4. No "chapels" or small rooms should be added; this was a misapprehension held in the old days.

As to materials your Assembly and architect can go into that, but brick or cement would be all right. Stone would seem to be out of the question.

It should not be too expensive or pretentious, but dignified and worthy.

There is no reason why the architect should be a Bahá'í—in fact your use of someone there would get it done faster, probably. The imperative thing is to send preliminary drawings to the Guardian within two months, if possible.

The terrible situation in Persia makes him most anxious to have this project go forward speedily. He feels funds will not be too much of a problem if great costs are not involved.

He sends you and all N.S.A. members his loving greetings. . . .

to the establishment of a similar endowment in the continent of Africa following the emergence of the National Spiritual Assembly of the Bahá'ís of Central and East Africa.

Above all, the most careful consideration should be given to the measures required to ensure the emergence of the afore-mentioned National Assembly in the heart of the African continent, marking the culmination of the efforts so diligently exerted, and the fruition of the enterprises so painstakingly inaugurated, since the formation of the Two Year Plan by the British Bahá'í community.

The emergence of this institution, signalising the erection of yet another pillar of the Universal House of Justice in the African continent, and constituting the first fruit, yielded on foreign soil, of the Mission entrusted to the British followers of the Faith of Bahá'u'lláh, and which may be hailed as a worthy counterpart of the central Administrative Institution established, on the morrow of 'Abdu'l-Bahá's Passing, in the heart of the British Isles, will be acclaimed by posterity as a milestone of far-reaching significance in British Bahá'í history. It will proclaim to the entire Bahá'í world the maturity of the swiftly rising, highly promising, steadily consolidating British Bahá'í community. Every British follower of the Faith, whether in his home islands or overseas, must feel proud and deeply grateful for the impending consummation of so superb and momentous a victory. Every energy must be lent to ensure a befitting celebration of such an enduring and magnificent achievement.

The efforts of the members of this community must indeed be redoubled, nay trebled, as they view with afflicted hearts the tragic trend of events transpiring with such dramatic and sudden swiftness in Bahá'u'lláh's native land. The tribulations suffered, over so wide a field, by so many of their co-religionists, under circumstances so appalling and harrowing in their nature, at the hands of redoubtable, pitiless, barbarous adversaries, should spur them on to still greater endeavours in a land blessed with freedom of religion and tolerance, and occupying so conspicuous a position among its sister nations.

Theirs is an opportunity which they must instantly grasp. Theirs is a responsibility which they cannot escape. Theirs is the duty to offset, by the quality of their achievements, the dire losses which are now being sustained in the cradle of the Faith. That they may in every field and at all times discharge their heavy responsibilities is my constant prayer and dearest hope.

Shoghi

Worship; the rapid advancement in the translation and publication of Bahá'í literature in the thirty-one African languages, allotted, under the Ten Year Plan to the elected national representatives of this same community; the steady progress made more recently in the incorporation of firmly established local assemblies; the formation of the Israel Branch of the British National Assembly at the world centre of the Faith in Israel—these stand out as the most prominent and significant evidences of the uninterrupted development of the Faith of Bahá'u'lláh under the wise leadership, and through the assiduous and incessant exertions, of the elected national representatives of this virile community.

The year that has recently opened, constituting the second and last year of the second phase of a Ten-Year global crusade, must witness a development and consolidation of the activities already initiated, in both the teaching and administrative spheres of Bahá'í endeavour, as swift and as notable as the progress already achieved in recent years. Time is indeed short. The responsibilities shouldered by the members of this community are manifold, pressing, sacred and inescapable. The eyes of the entire Bahá'í world are upon them, eager and expectant to witness feats as superb as those that have marked the birth and establishment of the Administrative Order of the Faith of Bahá'u'lláh in the British Isles, and exploits as meritorious and significant as those that have accompanied the inception and progress of the mission entrusted to His British followers, on the morrow of the emergence of that Administrative Order in their homeland.

The process aiming at the rapid increase in the number of the avowed and active supporters of the Faith must continue unabated in the months immediately ahead. A simultaneous multiplication in the number of isolated centres, groups and local assemblies must be ensured in order to reinforce the agencies on which the rising administrative structure of the Faith must ultimately rest. The process of incorporation must likewise be strenuously stimulated for the purpose of strengthening legally, and enhancing the prestige of, these rising institutions. The newly opened territories forming part of the British Isles, situated in the Mediterranean, in the Atlantic Ocean, along the western and eastern coasts of Africa, and in its very heart, must be continually reinforced, and the prizes won in those distant fields safeguarded, however great the sacrifice involved. The establishment of national Bahá'í endowments in the British Isles is yet another task which, ere the termination of the current year, must be accomplished, as a prelude whilst the variety and solidity of its administrative achievements have won the unstinted praise of its sister communities in both the East and the West. My own feelings of unqualified admiration for the tenacity of the faith of its members, for their unrelaxing vigilance, their unfailing sense of responsibility and their willingness to sacrifice in order to meet any challenges that confront them, have deepened with every advance they have made, and every victory they have won along the path leading them towards the fulfilment of their destiny.

The historic triumph achieved as a result of the successful prosecution of the Six Year Plan, spontaneously embarked upon by this numerically small yet richly endowed, spiritually resourceful community, on the morrow of the hundredth anniversary of the founding of the Faith of Bahá'u'lláh, followed immediately by the initiation of a Two Year Plan which marked the inauguration of this community's Mission beyond the confines of its homeland, culminated in the formal association of its members with their brethren in every continent of the globe for the launching and prosecution of a decade-long world-embracing crusade, destined to carry that same community through yet another stage, of the utmost significance, in the fulfilment of its worldwide and glorious mission among the widely scattered territories of the British Crown in no less than three continents of the globe.

The extension and consolidation, in the course of more than a decade, of the administrative base established so painstakingly for the prosecution of this community's far-flung mission, through the formation and multiplication of isolated centres, groups and local assemblies throughout the length and breadth of England, Wales, Scotland, Northern Ireland and Eire; the opening of the virgin islands lying in the neighbourhood of these territories and forming a part of the British Isles, constituting a most welcome and much needed reinforcement of the Administrative Structure raised so valiantly and patiently by its members in their island home; the magnificent success surpassing, in its quality and scope, the fondest expectations of the elected representatives of this community, which attended the spiritual conquest of a number of African territories, situated along the Western and Eastern shores of that continent and its very heart; the settlement of pioneers in two Mediterranean islands; the selection and purchase of a befitting national administrative headquarters situated close to the heart of the capital city of the British Empire; the acquisition of a plot in the outskirts of the capital city of Uganda, situated in the heart of the African continent, to serve as the site for a future Bahá'í House of friends always come up against this problem. He urges all the Bahá'ís, however, not to become discouraged, but to persevere and redouble their efforts, knowing that they can and must succeed in the end. He, on his part, will reinforce their efforts with his prayers in the Holy Shrines. . . .

As regards your question about depleted Assemblies, as there is nothing in the constitution of the National Spiritual Assembly covering these matters, every National Body is free to make its own decision as to what the status of an Assembly is from one annual election to the next, if they fall below nine for any reason.

As regards certain matters raised in your recent letters:

Your Assembly is free to choose the place for the endowment for the East and Central N.S.A. if you feel Uganda inadvisable.

The delegates reaching the Conventions in Africa is a matter for each N.S.A., from whose area of jurisdiction they are elected, to arrange and provide financial help if needed.

A prisoner, showing sincere faith in the Cause, may be accepted as a Bahá'í on the same basis of investigating his qualifications as to belief as any other individual outside prison. Each case should be carefully considered on its own merits. Naturally, a person in confinement cannot be active in any community and administrative work. When he gets out, he becomes part of the community in which he resides. No new ruling is required in this matter. All other details in relation to prisoners can be decided by the N.S.A. concerned as they arise.

The Guardian feels that, though it is naturally preferable, it is not essential for consolidation territories to have a group by Riḍván, 1956. . . .

Dear and valued co-workers,

The contribution made, since the inception of the world-wide Bahá'í Crusade, severally as well as collectively, by the assiduously striving, clear-visioned, inflexibly resolved, and unswervingly faithful members of the British Bahá'í community to the progress and development of the Ten Year Plan, inaugurated on the morrow of the centenary celebration of the birth of Bahá'u'lláh's Mission, has been such as to excite the heartfelt admiration of their fellow-workers in every continent of the globe. The prestige of this valiant community has soared rapidly, its annals have been notably enriched, the foundations on which its fortunes now rest have been considerably reinforced, such as Freemasonry may have been in the past entirely free from any political taint, in the state of flux the world is in at present, and the extraordinary way in which things become corrupted and tainted by political thought and influences, there is no guarantee that such an association might not gradually or suddenly become a political instrument. The less Bahá'ís have to do, therefore, with such things, the better.

He wishes you to thank ... on his behalf for the spirit of devotion to the Faith which he has shown in connection with this matter. He feels sure that he will see the necessity to sever himself from his previous association with Freemasonry. The older Bahá'ís, through their example in such matters, form rallying points around which the younger Bahá'ís, not so steady yet on their spiritual legs, so to speak, can cluster.

If you send him five copies of everything published in the British Isles, it will be sufficient for the libraries here at the World Centre. . . .

The Africa Committee should carefully consider such problems as that of the Negro pioneers being too long apart from their wives; and, if no other solution is feasible, the pioneer will have to return to his family. In the case of some of the very distinguished servants of the Faith who have arisen and gone forth from Uganda to pioneer, this would indeed be a loss to the work. If their wives could go and join them, it would naturally be preferable. This is a matter for the committee in consultation with your Assembly and the Hand of the Cause, Músá Banání, to decide.

Undoubtedly the most important task facing the British community at the present time, is to increase its membership. It has performed miracles during the past ten years, through shifting around devoted volunteers from one centre to another, in order to maintain or to create Spiritual Assemblies; but, efficacious as this has been in the past, it is certainly not a permanent solution to the problem. The only solution is to bring in more Bahá'ís. This requires patient, prayerful, ceaseless efforts on the part of, not only the Bahá'í teachers and pioneers, but every single member of the community. The British people are traditionally slow to move. Fortunately, once they do move, it's almost impossible to stop them; but to overcome the inertia requires great effort. In bringing new people into the Faith, the removing archives or other material from London. If, at a future date, the world situation reaches the point where it is obvious that things in London are in great danger, then your Assembly should consider the matter. Fortunately, that is not the case at present.

Any monies received from the sale of the property bequeathed by Mrs. B... can be used by your Assembly as it sees fit.

As he already pointed out to the Secretary, when he was in Haifa, a National Endowment is at the present time to be considered more in the nature of a token endowment. It need not be in the capital, and can represent a very small investment; indeed as little as one thousand dollars, if a suitable piece of property for that price should be found, would be acceptable.

He was very sorry to hear of the tragic death of Mrs. Langdon-Davies. She was a capable, staunch and devoted member of the community and of the National Assembly as well; and her services will be missed by her co-workers, and particularly the friends in Oxford. He prays for the progress of her soul in the Abhá kingdom, and that she may be rewarded for her labours in this world, performed with so much zeal and steadfastness.

He hopes that Mr. John Mitchell's condition has improved. He was very sorry indeed to hear that he had been forced to leave Malta. Please assure him of the Guardian's loving and fervent prayers on his behalf.

As regards the question of Bahá'ís belonging to churches, synagogues, Freemasonry, etc., the friends must realise that now that the Faith is over a hundred years old, and its own institutions arising, so to speak, rapidly above-ground, the distinctions are becoming ever sharper, and the necessity for them to support whole-heartedly their own institutions and cut themselves off entirely from those of the past, is now clearer than ever before. The eyes of the people of the world are beginning to be focussed on us; and, as humanity's plight goes from bad to worse, we will be watched ever more intently by non-Bahá'ís, to see whether we do uphold our own institutions whole-heartedly; whether we are the people of the new creation or not; whether we live up to our beliefs, principles and laws in deed as well as word. We cannot be too careful. We cannot be too exemplary.

There is another aspect to this question which the friends should seriously ponder, and that is that, whereas organisations

1954, and January 6 (two), 10 and 25, February 7, 11, 14, 21 and 28, March 11 (two), 16 and 23, April 4, 7, 15, 19, 22 and 27, May 9, 12 and 27, June 8 and 9, July 5 (four), 11 and 14, 1955, with enclosures, also the material sent separately, have been received by the beloved Guardian, and he has instructed me to answer you on his behalf.

The matters taken up by cable I will not go into again here in detail.

It has been a great source of satisfaction to him to receive here last winter two members of the National Body, Mr. and Mrs. John Ferraby, as well as more than one believer from England. The contact with the British Bahá'ís always pleases him greatly. As you know, he admires many of the staunch British qualities very much, and is proud of the accomplishments of this community during recent years.

He has been pleased over the progress made in the teaching field abroad and at home; in the publication of Bahá'í literature in African languages; and, above all, by the purchase of the National Headquarters in London, and the formal dedication of the building, recently held. He feels sure that, now that the National Assembly has a befitting seat for its national affairs—a building which at the same time will solve the problem of the London Spiritual Assembly, through giving them a meeting-place—the work in both London and throughout the country will receive a new impetus. With every important step forward there is a new release of spiritual energy; and the founding of the National Ḥaẓíratu'l-Quds is certainly a most important milestone in the progress of the Cause in the British Isles.

As regards various questions raised in your correspondence with him, he sees no reason why the Publishing Trust should have a separate legal status, as long as it is not essential for it to do so.

He approves of returning to Ronga as one of the languages into which Bahá'í literature should be translated, according to the provisions of the Ten Year Plan, and giving up Shangaan.

He would like very much to receive photostats of the actual Certificates of Incorporation issued to the London and Manchester and Liverpool Assemblies, to be placed in the Mansion of Bahá'u'lláh.

He does not think your Assembly need take any action about

2 June 1955

APPROVE PUBLICISING WORLD PROTEST DO NOT ATTACK GOVERNMENT APPROVE APPEAL AFRICAN COMMUNITIES.

SHOGHI

10 July 1955

The beloved Guardian has instructed me to inform you that he feels the time has come for the British N.S.A. to follow the procedure laid down by him as a general rule, namely that Spiritual Assemblies should adhere to the civil limits of their respective towns. All other National Assemblies are following this procedure and he feels yours should too.

The events in Persia have, naturally, distressed him greatly, particularly anxiety for the safety of the Holy House in Shíráz. However, the publicity will do the Faith a great deal of good....

26 July 1955

Dear John:

Just a line to inform you, and naturally through you the National Assembly, that the Beloved Guardian has instructed Varga to send you five hundred pounds for your National Fund, to be expended as the Assembly thinks best.

Regarding ... legacy he wishes your Assembly to hold this sum in trust for him until he gives directions for its use.

The beloved Guardian is most anxious that the representations to be made to UNO regarding the bitter and cruel persecutions in Persia at present should meet with success. I do hope all goes well....

5 August 1955

Dear Bahá'í Brother,

Your letters of July 7, 13 and 15, August 19, 20 (three) and 31, September 17 (two) and 27, October 13, 16 (two) and 26, November 4, 15, 16 and 20, and December 8 (four) and 18,

Somaliland. This leaves the only Somaliland without an Assembly as British Somaliland. The beloved Guardian would appreciate your Assembly giving consideration to this matter, to see if there is any way that a pioneer could go from England to British Somaliland, to firmly establish the Faith there. He understands fully the problems involved.

A copy of this letter is being sent to Mr. Banání, Hand of the Cause, so that he might give consideration to the possibility of having some native Bahá'ís from Uganda move to British Somaliland, and either teach or settle there.

The beloved Guardian assures your Assembly of his prayers on your behalf. He sends you his loving greetings. . . .

25 April 1955 (Convention)

DEEPLY APPRECIATE CONVENTION MESSAGE. APPEAL DELEGATES URGE ALL COMMUNITIES BRITISH ISLES CONCENTRATE ATTENTION ENERGIES INTENSIFICATION TEACHING ACTIVITIES MULTIPLICATION CENTRES STRENGTHENING ALLOTTED NEWLY-OPENED TERRITORIES INCORPORATION ASSEMBLIES ESTABLISHMENT NATIONAL ENDOWMENT PRAYING FERVENTLY ATTAINMENT OBJECTIVES COURSE SECOND LAST YEAR SECOND PHASE TEN YEAR PLAN.

SHOGHI

28 April 1955

REJOICE SPLENDID INITIATIVE ASSEMBLED REPRESENTATIVES VALIANT BRITISH BAHÁ'Í COMMUNITY ARDENTLY PRAYING FULFILMENT FONDEST HOPES.

SHOGHI

22 May 1955

CONSIDER CARDIFF MAINTAINED.

SHOGHI

ABILITY MAINTAIN STANDARD HISTORIC ACHIEVEMENTS FERVENTLY PRAYING SUCCESS.

SHOGHI

20 April 1955

Dear John:

In order not to keep the Assembly waiting for an answer, the beloved Guardian has instructed me to write you this letter in reply to yours of April 15th.

The principle is wherever the Bahá'í laws at the present time conflict with the civil law of the country, the believers living in it must obey the civil law.

The Bahá'ís in England, as regards divorce will consequently have to follow British law, and in conjunction with this, as far as possible, uphold the Bahá'í law of divorce as well. The way the details of this are to be worked out is left entirely to the discretion of your National Assembly....

21 April 1955*

DELIGHTED LOVING APPRECIATION. REGRET FORMATION NICOSIA ASSEMBLY IMPOSSIBLE.

SHOGHI

24 April 1955

Dear Bahá'í Friends:

The beloved Guardian has been greatly enthused the last few days with the reports that have been received of new Assemblies established in virgin areas. Of great importance and significance is the word that Spiritual Assemblies have been established in Mogadiscio, in Italian Somaliland and Djibouti in French

---

* On report that all Assemblies maintained; Nicosia had eight with ninth member en route to arrive 7 May.

During the past year, a great deal has been accomplished by the friends in their efforts to disperse from the large centres of population in order to build up the goal cities and establish new centres. However, we have not accomplished a great deal in the way of increasing the number of Bahá'ís, nor the number of Spiritual Assemblies.

The beloved Guardian sincerely hopes you will make it a point of major study and consideration on the part of your Assembly, so that the entire community may lend itself to the accomplishment of this great goal during the coming year. Foundations must be laid for many more Assemblies. The friends must disperse from the large centres of population. Our teaching work must become so sanctified and penetrating that many, many souls will be confirmed. The friends should go forward on this great task in a very determined manner in order to establish as many new Assemblies during the coming year as are possible.

In letters which have come to the beloved Guardian, he has noted the friends feel there is no need to establish new Assemblies until 1963.

The Ten Year Crusade ends in 1963; but as many of the goals should be won as quickly as possible. It should certainly be clear to all of the friends that we cannot hold off on winning the various goals of our tasks until the last year of the Crusade. They should be won just as quickly as possible. Furthermore, there are many tasks of the Crusade which the Guardian is not launching until preliminary goals have been won. For instance, it would be impossible to establish National Assemblies in all of the areas proposed until there are more Bahá'ís, more Groups and more Assemblies in those countries. On the home front, further tasks are dependent upon the winning of victories now. The Guardian hopes the keynote of the teaching work on the home front during the current year will be the dispersion of the friends on an unprecedented scale, and the winning of as many Assemblies as is possible....

9 April 1955

URGENTLY APPEAL HIGH MINDED DEVOTED BELIEVERS BRITISH ISLES EXERT SUPREME EFFORT FILL GAPS ASSEMBLIES DEMONSTRATE

20 February 1955

Dear Bahá'í Co-workers:

The beloved Guardian has instructed me to inquire of your Assembly what the situation is surrounding the translation and publication of Bahá'í literature into the following languages:

> Erso
> Gaelic

These are not languages of the Ten Year Crusade, but languages which have been translated prior to the opening of the Ten Year Crusade. He is very anxious to know what the status is of these translations and publications. If no work has been done on them, he would urge that you have the work undertaken at an early date....

8 March 1955

Dear Bahá'í Friends:

The beloved Guardian is very anxious to secure as quickly as possible data concerning the Ḥaẓíratu'l-Quds which have been acquired in connection with the goals of the Ten Year Crusade. To this end, he would very greatly appreciate your sending me by return air mail the information concerning the Ḥaẓíratu'l-Quds in London.

He would like to know the area of land involved, the size of the building, so far as number of rooms is concerned, the original purchase price of the Ḥaẓíratu'l-Quds, the expenses of the transaction, and then the total cost.

The Guardian asks that this be sent to me by return airmail....

29 March 1955

Dear Bahá'í Friends:

On April 21st we will enter the last year of the second phase of the Ten Year Crusade. As you know, one of the objectives of this second phase was the rapid multiplication of Assemblies, Groups and Centres throughout the world.

He sincerely hopes the problems surrounding Mr. ... have now been solved, as you seemed to think they have.

He advises that Bahá'í pioneers should not become public charges under any circumstances; and the Assemblies concerned should see that this does not occur in the case of Mr. ...

The beloved Guardian assures all the members of the National Assembly of his appreciation of their devoted services. He assures them of his prayers in their behalf, and sends them his loving greetings. ...

11 November 1954*

DISAPPROVE MEMBERSHIP FREEMASONRY.

16 December 1954

GRIEVE PASSING STAUNCH CONSECRATED PROMOTER FAITH LANGDON-DAVIES HER SERVICES UNFORGETTABLE REWARD GREAT ABHÁ KINGDOM.

SHOGHI

22 December 1954

PUBLISHING TRUST SHOULD NOT HAVE SEPARATE LEGAL STATUS. ANY BAHÁ'Í DETERMINED RETAIN MEMBERSHIP FREEMASONRY LOSES VOTING RIGHTS.

SHOGHI

17 January 1955**

SHARE JOY FRIENDS SUPPLICATING UNPRECEDENTED BLESSINGS.

SHOGHI

*See letter 5 August 1955 for references to status of Assemblies with fewer than nine members, use of bequests and Freemasonry.

**This was sent in reply to a cable from a meeting at 27 Rutland Gate, London, S.W.7, jointly to dedicate the new Ḥaẓíratu'l-Quds and to hold Teaching Conference.

Assemblies, but directly with the National Spiritual Assemblies themselves.

The beloved Guardian greatly values the outstanding work which your Assembly is doing. He will pray for your continued success. He sends you his loving greetings....

29 July 1954 (Summer School Committee)

DELIGHTED ASSURE ATTENDANTS LOVING FERVENT PRAYERS.

SHOGHI

29 August 1954

SUBSTITUTE FON FOR POPO COMMITTEES SHOULD NOT CORRESPOND HANDS WITHOUT EXCEPTION.

SHOGHI

*16 October 1954**

DELIGHTED HISTORIC ACHIEVEMENT.

SHOGHI

*27 October 1954***

FOLLOW AMERICAN POLICY REGARDING ASSEMBLY STATUS. USE PROCEEDS SALE HOUSE FOR ḤAẒÍRA.

SHOGHI

28 October 1954

Dear Bahá'í Brother:

The content of your letter of October 15th was given to the beloved Guardian.

---

*On signing of contract for Ḥaẓíratu'l-Quds, London.
**See letter 5 August 1955 for references to status of Assemblies with fewer than nine members, use of bequests and Freemasonry.

23 June 1954

Dear John:
Thank you for your letter of June 15th, with regard to Dar-es-Salaam.

The Guardian attaches very great importance to the "incorporation" and "exemption" of any Assembly; likewise the acquirement of any endowments.

Therefore, if you have not already sent directly to the Guardian a photostatic copy of the Exemption granted the Dar-es-Salaam Assembly, I would like to suggest that one be sent to him through me.

Likewise if anything constructive develops with regard to the burial ground at Dar-es-Salaam, please let me know as soon as possible....

22 July 1954

Dear Bahá'í Friends,
... The Guardian has instructed me to write your Assembly, calling attention to the manner in which questions of teaching activities in new areas and consolidation areas assigned to any Assembly, are carried out.

The National Spiritual Assembly is the Body which is charged with the administrative responsibility of the tasks of the Ten Year Crusade. Neither the Hands of the Cause nor their Boards have administrative responsibilities in connection with this work.

The members of the Boards are to report to the Hands of the Cause in the area regarding all situations, and of course in detail concerning any problem, so that the National Assembly may take appropriate action.

The Hands of the Cause themselves will correspond with the National Spiritual Assembly involved, calling their attention to the problem, so that the National Assembly may take appropriate action.

The Guardian has instructed that the Hands of the Cause are not to correspond with the committees of the National Spiritual *outposts of the Empire, the opposition which those responsible for its development and consolidation will encounter from those in authority, whether civil or ecclesiastic, will progressively hamper their efforts. The competition from its own sister communities, in various regions of the globe and in the course of the systematic prosecution of the same world-embracing task will, in the meantime, grow keener.*

Every ounce of energy its members can muster must unhesitatingly be expended to further the supreme end for which so sacred, so formidable and so momentous a Plan has been devised. With every sacrifice that is made, with every forward step that is taken along the toilsome and long road they are destined to tread, with every victory dearly and laboriously won by the champions, the representatives, the vanguard, the spokesmen, as well as the rank and file of this community, a measure of blessing from on high will undoubtedly be vouchsafed, in order to reinforce the exertions, cheer the hearts, and stimulate the march of all those enlisted in the service of so glorious a Cause.

The hour is propitious for a concerted effort which in its scope and intensity will surpass any united action of which the British followers of the Faith of Bahá'u'lláh have proved themselves capable in the past.

That they may ascend from height to height, go forward from victory to victory, is the fervent prayer of one who has invariably followed the course of their exploits with undiminished confidence and admiration, who has cherished the brightest hopes for the ultimate attainment of their Mission, and whose love and esteem for them has correspondingly increased with every revelation of the capacities and energies with which they have discharged, and are constantly discharging, their Mission.

Your true brother,
Shoghi

21 June 1954

APPROVE AṢGHÁRZÁDEH AND OTHER PIONEERS ISLANDS ATTEND SUMMER SCHOOL....

SHOGHI

Of no less importance is the responsibility to reinforce the structure of the Administrative Order throughout the British Isles, and particularly in the newly opened territories of Scotland, Wales, Eire and Northern Ireland, through a rapid and unprecedented increase in the number of the avowed supporters of the Faith, and a multiplication of isolated centres, groups and assemblies that constitute the warp and woof of the fabric of its evolving Order.

A no less urgent task, which will directly reinforce this fabric, and heighten the prestige of the Faith itself, and pave the way for the establishment of Bahá'í local endowments, is the prompt incorporation of firmly established local assemblies, a process which, as soon as it is initiated, must gather steady momentum throughout the length and breadth of the British Isles, and be ultimately reinforced by the incorporation of all local assemblies destined to be established in the virgin territories recently opened in the neighbourhood of the British Isles and in the African territories allotted to your Assembly under the provisions of the Ten Year Plan.

Special attention should, moreover, be paid to the no less vital duty of completing the translation, the publication and the dissemination of Bahá'í literature in the languages assigned to your Assembly, in accordance with that same Plan, an achievement which will greatly stimulate the work to be undertaken in the course of the future phases of this world spiritual Crusade as it unfolds itself in the African Continent.

Whilst these highly meritorious enterprises are being assiduously carried on, the inescapable and sacred duty of consolidating the nine African territories and the two additional ones in Europe and Asia must be adequately discharged, in order to enable the British Bahá'í community to bring to full fruition the noble mission entrusted so confidently to its care.

The tasks facing this community in the course of this second and future phases of a world-encircling Crusade are admittedly vast, complex and challenging. The resources at the disposal of its doggedly persevering, wholly dedicated members are, alas, circumscribed and inadequate. The Mission, however, to which its Founder is calling it, is unspeakably glorious. Many and divers will, no doubt, be the tests, the setbacks and trials which teachers and administrators alike within the ranks of its members, must necessarily experience. The times, during which the opening phase of its Mission overseas is to yield its fairest fruit, are fraught with great peril. Both at home and in distant the Orb of that same Covenant; enriched by the experience derived from the successful prosecution of two successive nationwide Plans formulated by its national elected representatives, this community finds itself, on the morrow of the termination of the opening year of the afore-mentioned Crusade, simultaneously firmly rooted within the soil of its homeland and vigorously branching out on the first stage of its mission in foreign fields, and exhibiting, both at home and abroad, evidences of a development that bids fair to eclipse any of its collective achievements in the past five decades since its inception.

In both the teaching and administrative spheres of its ever-expanding, swiftly unfolding activities, whether in the heart and capital city of the Empire to which it belongs, or in the chief cities recently opened by its pioneering members in the territories comprising its island home, or in the diversified and far-flung dependencies of the British Crown in the African Continent, this virile, forward marching, securely established community has amply demonstrated its capacity to be regarded as one of the chief strongholds of a divinely conceived Faith and one of the principal bastions sustaining the fabric of Bahá'u'lláh's world-encompassing Order.

Standing as it does on the threshold of the second phase of a Crusade with which its immediate destinies are inseparably linked, and to which it has voluntarily and enthusiastically pledged its combined resources, the tasks now confronting it demand a degree of concentration, dedication, co-ordination, resourcefulness and perseverance hitherto unequalled in any period of its career.

The prizes won in recent months, since the launching of the Ten Year Plan to which it stands committed, through the strenuous exertions and the shining example of its pioneers in the islands situated to the North, the West and the South of its homeland, as well as in the far away territories lying in the heart of the African Continent and situated on both its eastern and western shores, must, however great the sacrifices involved, be preserved. The acquisition of the national Ḥaẓíratu'l-Quds in a centrally located area in a city that ranks as the chief metropolis of a vast Empire is yet another task of the utmost urgency and of the highest significance, the consummation of which should be considered as the chief objective and pre-eminent duty of this community's elected national representatives, and one which is bound to exert, in the days immediately ahead, a far-reaching and pervasive influence on the growth and unfoldment of the Faith which it is their privilege to serve and promote.

to publish—the old translation is very poor and has many inaccuracies. However, the Guardian has no time at all to retranslate it or correct it himself.

He leaves it to the discretion of your Assembly as to whether you wish to include it in a compilation or not.

I am returning to you the list you sent with suggested corrections in relation to the pamphlet your Assembly published last year—"The Bahá'í Faith 1844–1952, Information Statistical and Comparative". The right hand column marked "Suggested", he considers quite acceptable. The places where you have put question marks are correct, with very few exceptions which the Guardian has corrected, in the column marked "As Listed", with the exception of the transliteration of the name Shu'á'u'lláh, (Number 12) which the Guardian has corrected.

Assuring you of the Guardian's loving prayers for the success of your devoted labours. . . .

P.S. July 28th. Your letter of July 7th has likewise been received.

Dear and valued co-workers,
The achievements of the members of the tenacious, the valiant and wide-awake British Bahá'í community, within the borders of their homeland and beyond its confines, in the course of the opening year of the Bahá'í World Crusade, deserve the highest commendation and have considerably heightened its prestige and deepened my own admiration for it as well as that of its sister communities in both Hemispheres.

Called into being through the dispensations of a watchful Providence, in the middle of the memorable decade that witnessed the introduction of the Faith of Bahá'u'lláh into the Western world; sharing with its sister community across the Channel the distinction of being the first to be quickened by the life-giving influences generated by the newly-established Covenant of Bahá'u'lláh in the Holy Land; the recipient of untold blessings showered upon it by the Centre of the Covenant in the days of its infancy; singled out among the newly-fledged communities in both Europe and the North American Continent through the twice repeated visits of 'Abdu'l-Bahá to the shores of its homeland; fully equipped with the agencies of a divinely conceived Administrative Order, patiently and laboriously erected by its stalwart members in the years immediately following the setting of which your own Assembly has been far from backward, are a source of great encouragement to all the believers as well as to him. The addition of one hundred countries during one year is certainly history-making.

Now that the back of the foreign pioneering work has been broken, so to speak, a greater measure of attention must be paid to the home fronts. The consolidation work, though far less spectacular, constitutes a very weighty task, and will require a constant measure of sacrificial effort if the goals are to be fulfilled. He thinks that during the coming year greater attention should be paid to the home front, while at the same time maintaining the pioneer posts at their present standard, at least.

The principle is, and it should be impressed on the minds of all pioneers, to hold their territory at any cost. Just because they have left their homes, and gone out and carried the Faith to one of these virgin areas, does not mean that the task is accomplished. On the contrary, nothing could be sadder than that these newly-won territories should be lost after a few months' effort. He hopes that in your correspondence with the pioneers you will impress this fact upon them and make them realise that to be a "Knight of Bahá'u'lláh" is not only a very high and pleasant position, but involves a truly tremendous responsibility. To remain at one's post, to undergo sacrifice and hardship, loneliness and, if necessary, persecution, in order to hold aloft the torch of Bahá'u'lláh, is the true function of every pioneer.

Let them remember Marion Jack, who for over twenty years, in a country the language of which she never mastered; during war and bombardment; evacuation and poverty; and at length, serious illness, stuck to her post, and has now blessed the soil of the land she had chosen to serve at such cost with her precious remains, every atom of which was dedicated to Bahá'u'lláh. Perhaps the friends are not aware that the Guardian, himself, during the war on more more than one occasion urged her to seek safety in Switzerland rather than remain behind enemy lines and be entirely cut off. Lovingly she pleaded that he would not require her to leave her post, and he acquiesced to her request. Surely the standard of Marion Jack should be borne in mind by every pioneer!

Regarding your question about including the Tablet of the Virgin in a compilation of "Bahá'í Scriptures" which you wish

Although the children of Bahá'í parents are considered to be Bahá'ís, there is no objection at the present time, for purposes of keeping a correct census, and also ascertaining whether the young people are, sincerely, believers, and willing to do their share in service to the Faith, to asking them to make a declaration of their intention at the age of fifteen or so. Originally, the Guardian understands, this was adopted in America to enable young Bahá'í men to make certain arrangements in connection with their application for non-combatant status upon their attaining the age of military service. There is really nothing about it in the Teachings or in the Administration. Your Assembly is free to do as it pleases in this matter.

Regarding the publication of a pamphlet on the Bahá'í Teachings on Monarchy, funds and circumstances permitting, the Guardian sees no objection to this whatsoever. It might appeal to a certain type of British mind very much, though he fears there are other minds to which it may not appeal! However, considering Bahá'u'lláh has taught these things, there is no reason why we should not share them with those interested in the subject.

He is very sorry that it has not been possible to purchase the National Ḥaẓíratu'l-Quds yet. In spite of the fact that he attaches great importance to this, he does not think that the cost should become exorbitant merely in order to accomplish a goal before a certain date. The Bahá'ís, not only in England, but all over the world, have embarked upon a Plan which will involve over a period of years a very heavy expenditure. Undoubtedly they will have to help each other; but they will scarcely have the financial strength to help each other to the tune of extremely expensive buildings, Temple sites, etc., in different parts of the world. He has given instructions to Canada, Germany, Rome, etc., to cut down on the proposals they made to him, because the price of these things in different parts of the world, when added up, would be well beyond the means of the Faith to meet at present. He feels sure that, however painful and toilsome the process may be, you will eventually find a suitable spot in London, and one that your Assembly, with the help of the British believers and other possible contributions from outside as well, can afford.

The remarkable achievements in the pioneer field, a field in your Assembly, and his friendly co-operation. You might also, at your discretion, extend his thanks to any other members of the Staff who have assisted you.

He is very pleased that the Temple land has been bought in Kampala. Mr. and Mrs. Elston are visiting here at the present time; and he has told them he feels that at present the Temple land should merely be held in trust, and all meetings continue in the Ḥaẓíratu'l-Quds building. Should this eventually prove too small, enlarging one of the rooms to accommodate more of the people at the meetings might be considered as a possibility; but any work carried out must be of a very economical nature, and he does not think it is pressing at present, anyway.

I need not tell you that the work in Africa, and more particularly in Uganda, is very dear to his heart. The progress made there during the last year has borne him up and encouraged him greatly when he was often weighed down with work. He feels that this country and its peoples, in the very heart of Africa, are a most precious trust. Their receptivity to the Teachings, their great desire to serve their new Faith, the number of them who have arisen to go out as pioneers, mark them as a people apart in the Bahá'í world, at least for the time being. May many others in neighbouring countries prove as worthy, and follow their example.

In dealing with people who are still backward in relation to our civilised standards, and in many cases guided by a tribal system which has strong orders of its own, he feels that you should be both tactful and forbearing. There is no specific minimum age mentioned in the Bahá'í teachings at which girls may marry. In the future, this and other questions unspecificed will be dealt with by the International House of Justice. In the meantime, we must not be too strict in enforcing our opinions on peoples still living in primitive social orders.

The difficulty of getting a Bahá'í into ... has now been temporarily solved. The Guardian does not see why Bahá'ís should have to state to any Government that the reason for their visit to a country is for the purposes of teaching the Bahá'í Faith. Most of the time, though not perhaps invariably, this is calculated to arouse suspicion and opposition. One has to deal with cases as they arise. A blanket rule could never apply over so wide a field as that in which Bahá'í pioneers are working.

campaigns carried on from different national bases will become absolutely unwieldy for lack of adequate able management.

The expression of condolences which your Assembly conveyed to him at the time of the passing of Fred Schopflocher and Dorothy Baker, two dear and trusted Hands of the Cause who could ill be spared from their work at this time, touched him very much. Others must now arise, and through their services seek to fill the gaps which such valuable workers have left in the vanguard of the Bahá'í host.

He would like you to express to the British pioneers on the home front, whose names you forwarded to him, his sincere thanks. Their arising to protect the goals which have been won by other pioneers at a cost of such sacrifice and effort was noble and highly meritorious.

Speaking of pioneers, he was very pleased to hear recently that Mrs. Shomais Afnán had succeeded in gaining entry into Ethiopia. Her perseverance in the face of a great deal of opposition is certainly exemplary.

As he already cabled you, he did not approve of the statements you had prepared for circulation amongst the Assemblies regarding Bahá'í marriage. Some of the remarks were incorrect in the first place, and in the second place he is strongly against Statements! He wishes the friends to keep as elastic as possible in administering the affairs of the Faith, while at the same time adhering to fundamentals. He knows that at times this inconveniences the National Bodies and makes their work more detailed, but believes it to be the lesser, so to speak, of two evils.

He was very sorry to learn that dear Mr. Townshend's health is in such a precarious state, and necessitated the return of his daughter from Malta. His devotion is so single-hearted and touching, and his determination to carry on at all costs is exemplary, and should inspire the young people to follow in his footsteps.

When compiling the list of African languages into which the Bahá'í Message should be translated, the Guardian realised that certain changes would probably be necessary—naturally the fewer the better. In this connection, if you feel it advisable and not otherwise, he would like you to convey to Dr. Berry, of the African Department of the School of Oriental and African studies, his personal thanks for the valuable advice he has given

Ten Year Crusade there are a total of 49 to be procured. 4 of them were procured during the first year of the Crusade.

At the Guardian's direction, I have written the National Assemblies involved, calling for the purchase of 17 Ḥaẓíratu'l-Quds of the 45, during this year. One of these 17 Ḥaẓíratu'l-Quds is the one in London.

The Guardian attaches the greatest importance to the fulfilment of this aspect of the Ten Year Crusade; and sincerely hopes your Assembly will concentrate on the purchase of the Ḥaẓíratu'l-Quds for London, so that it may be consummated as soon as possible....

17 June 1954

Dear Bahá'í Brother,

Your Assembly's letters dated June 10 (2), 17, 22 and 26, July 3, 7, 8, 9 (2), 16 and 24, August 17, 19 (2) and 24, September 17, 21, 24 and 25, October 1, 8, 12, 22 and 28, November 13 (4) and 18 (2), December 10 (2), 12 and 23, 1953, and January 7, 20 (2), 21 and 22, February 17 (3), 19 (3), 21, 23 (2) and 25, March 1, 23, 24 and 25 (3), April 13 and 28, May 12, 21 and 25, June 1 (4) and 15, 1954, with enclosures, have been received by the beloved Guardian, and he has instructed me to answer you on his behalf.

He regrets very much the long delays in answering the National Spiritual Assemblies, but is finding it increasingly difficult to keep abreast of his work. He feels sometimes that he will soon be forced to give up correspondence with individuals, although he is reluctant to do so, because so many of the new believers brought in during the present teaching activities in Africa and other far goals are writing to him. However, he has attended to a great many of your questions by cable, and the visits of a number of English pilgrims have enabled him to send you messages and to keep the British community in contact with the work in the Holy Land.

He greatly appreciated the desire of John and Dorothy Ferraby to go out as pioneers, but considered that it would weaken the work of the National Assembly altogether too much. Important as the pioneer field is, if all the most able workers go out, the difficult places to settle. The Portuguese and Spanish territories seem to be the hardest of all to gain access to. Any help your committee can give along this line would certainly be rendering a great service to the Cause.

He deeply appreciates the work you have done, and your committee achievements, during the past year, and assures each and all of you of his loving prayers on your behalf. . . .

Assuring you of my loving and constant prayers for the success of the efforts you are so devotedly exerting for the promotion of our beloved Faith and its institutions,
Your true brother,
Shoghi

6 June 1954

Dear Bahá'í Friends:

The beloved Guardian has been greatly pleased with the reports he has received of the progress of the teaching work in Oxford. He feels the friends in that city have undertaken their responsibility diligently and successfully.

It is his feeling that the Faith should be firmly established in Cambridge, which is also one of the great centres of learning in the British Isles. He understands that Cambridge is a goal city of the Crusade, and he feels that the time has now arrived for the opening of that city and the expansion of the teaching work there.

He would appreciate a report from you as to the progress of the Faith in that important city. This report should be addressed to me, and I will inform him of its contents. . . .

11 June 1954

Dear Bahá'í Friends:

The beloved Guardian has directed me to write you in connection with the purchase of the Ḥaẓíratu'l-Quds for the city of London. The Guardian is very hopeful that your Assembly will be able to complete this important matter in the near future.

In connection with the purchase of Ḥaẓíratu'l-Quds, under the

... and not give any wide publicity for the time being, than to spend money translating a lopsided presentation of the Teachings. However, he believes that, with sufficient effort and good judgment, a pamphlet could be gotten out that would neither stress too strongly the racial teachings, nor minimise them too much, and could discreetly be used for teaching purposes in. . . .

He has spoken very strongly to some of the pilgrims here about the teaching work in that country, and impressed upon them that the whole object of the pioneers in going forth to Africa, is to teach the coloured people, and not the white people. This does not mean that they must refuse to teach the white people, which would be a foolish attitude. It does, however, mean that they should constantly bear in mind that it is to the native African that they are now carrying the Message of Bahá'u'lláh, in his own country, and not to people from abroad who have migrated there permanently or temporarily and are a minority, and many of them, judging by their acts, a very unsavoury minority.

He hopes that every effort will be made to get out a pamphlet in each of the languages chosen, or those that you have substituted for a chosen language. He fully realises that, in many cases, the people who speak the language are illiterate, and, strictly speaking, do not require a printed pamphlet in their own tongue. He considers however the psychological values of having something translated into their own language, the compliment implicit in it, so to speak, of great importance, sufficient to offset the time, effort and expense involved.

He would like your committee to convey to all the pioneers, most particularly the negro ones, the expression of his deep admiration of the wonderful spirit that animates them, his feeling of affection for them, and the assurance of his ardent prayers for their success.

Africa is truly awakening and finding herself, and she undoubtedly has a great message to give, and a great contribution to make to the advancement of world civilisation. To the degree to which her peoples accept Bahá'u'lláh, will they be blessed, strengthened and protected.

He hopes that, whilst concentrating on the consolidation of the work under your jurisdiction, you will give every assistance within your power to the other National Assemblies who have beloved Guardian and he has instructed me to answer you on his behalf. As he has been in constant cable communication with you during the past year, I will not go into many of the matters which have already been attended to.

Of all the places in the world where the Bahá'í Faith exists and is spreading, the Guardian is definitely most pleased with Africa, and most proud of Uganda. He feels that the spirit shown by white and negro pioneers alike in that continent, presents a challenge to the Bahá'ís everywhere in the world, and that old and staid communities may well learn from, and emulate the example of, the believers of Africa, many of them scarcely a year old in the Cause of God!

He feels that your committee and the British N.S.A. have every reason to be proud of the work you have accomplished, and grateful for the blessings you have received from on High.

It has particularly rejoiced his heart to see the way almost every goal was attained at the last minute, before the end of the first year of the Ten Year Crusade, many of these goals through the immediate whole-hearted response of some of these new African Bahá'ís, themselves the spiritual children of other African Bahá'ís—young in the Faith, but old in their understanding of it.

The main task, now that the back of the pioneer settlement work has been broken, so to speak, is the consolidation of these territories and the maintaining of the pioneers at their posts. He is constantly urging all National Assemblies to impress upon those who have gone forth to settle virgin territories, the importance of staying there, and of only abandoning their posts if they are forced to do so by the Government in question, and not for some other reason. The friends have had such difficulty in gaining access to some of these countries,—visas, housing, expenses have all been such a problem—that once they get there, they should really move heaven and earth to remain.

He is very happy that two of the Temple sites on the African continent have been purchased, and feels that this will release a tremendous spiritual impetus. He hopes that the Egyptian Bahá'ís will soon decide on a site, and that will complete the chain for the time being.

Concerning the various questions you have raised regarding literature and translations, he thinks that it is perhaps better to have a proper introductory pamphlet on the Faith translated into is serving there very actively. The beloved Guardian had been informed by someone that she had left.

However, the intent of the letter of April 24th still remains—that no pioneer should leave their goal unless for very urgent reasons. In the case of Malta, this is a country which can only be settled by English Bahá'ís, and therefore the Guardian feels it of great importance that any pioneer who goes there should remain. It is hoped that it may be possible for Una Townshend to return in due course, to carry on her work there.

The Guardian asks that you convey to Olga Mills his loving appreciation of her devoted services, and assure her of his prayers in her behalf.

If Una Townshend finds it impossible to return to Malta, then the Guardian hopes you can send some other pioneer to that important post....

16 May 1954

I am enclosing, at the instruction of our beloved Guardian, the original title-deed of one-quarter of an acre of land recently purchased near the resting-place of the Greatest Holy Leaf on Mount Carmel; and registered in the name of the Israel Branch of the National Spiritual Assembly of the Bahá'ís of the British Isles.

The cost of this property was six thousand dollars.

He feels sure that the British Bahá'ís will rejoice to know that they now have a part of the International Bahá'í Endowments in the name of their own special Israel Branch....

4 June 1954

British Africa Committee

Dear Bahá'í Sister:

The various letters of your committee dated June 8 and 25, July 6, August 13, September 23, October 8, November 25 and December 31, 1953, and January 27 (3), March 6 and 30 and April 20, 1954, with their enclosures, have been received by the

3 May 1954

European and Asian Committee

Dear Bahá'í Friends:
Your letter of the 9th of Nur, 110, was received by the beloved Guardian.

As he has been tremendously busy during this Holy Year—and indeed his work is increasing all the time—and there was nothing urgent that required an immediate reply—he has delayed in answering you until he had more time.

He hopes that your committee will be able to gradually assist in the work allotted to the British National Spiritual Assembly during the Plan.

The most important thing of course is to get the believers out into wholly virgin areas, and keep them there. So far, England has done nobly, and he is proud of their efforts.

The Pacific area is also of great importance. If there is any possibility of British subjects going out to territories that are under the jurisdiction of other National Bodies, but difficult to get into, he feels that they should be referred to the committees concerned, or the National Spiritual Assemblies concerned, because of the importance of achieving all the goals of the Plan, regardless of which Assembly has certain goals under its immediate jurisdiction.

He assures you he will pray for the success of your devoted labours, in the Holy Shrine.

May the Almighty bless your meritorious activities, guide and sustain you always, and enable you to lend a great impetus to the splendid work now being accomplished in Europe and in Asia.

Your true brother,
Shoghi

6 May 1954

Dear Bahá'í Brother:
Your loving letter of April 30th has just come to hand, calling attention to the fact that Olga Mills, one of the pioneers in Malta,

Convention Message which was mailed you a short time ago. As there is a pilgrim leaving, he is taking the precaution of having this mailed in Europe.

I hope it reaches you in time for the Convention. . . .

24 April 1954

Dear Bahá'í Friends:

The beloved Guardian has directed me to write you concerning the Island of Malta. He attaches great importance to this Island, and wishes your Assembly to see that the teaching work there progresses as rapidly and efficiently as possible.

At the present time, it has again become virgin, according to our records. Do you know if Miss Townshend intends to return? If not, your Assembly should undertake to fill the post just as quickly as possible, with someone else.

As you have become aware through the Guardian's Convention Message, he is very happy with the result of the first year of the Ten-Year Crusade. He is hoping that the second year will witness even more glorious victories, and this time on the home front, as well as in foreign fields.

He would appreciate a report of the plans for Malta, as soon as possible. In order to save him work, it is suggested it be sent to me. (Mr. L. Ioas)

The Guardian sends you his loving greetings. . . .

25 April 1954 (Convention)

ASSURE ASSEMBLED DELEGATES ARDENT PRAYERS ABUNDANT BLESSINGS DELIBERATIONS PROUD RECENT ACHIEVEMENTS BRITISH BAHÁ'Í COMMUNITY CHERISH GREAT HOPES FUTURE HISTORIC ACCOMPLISHMENTS DEEPEST LOVE.

SHOGHI

29 April 1954

WELCOME PLEDGE DELEGATES PRAYING SUCCESS ATTAINMENT GOALS.

SHOGHI

HUNDRED POUNDS SOMALILAND INADVISABLE. PURCHASE SITE INSIDE KAMPALA OR WITHIN THREE MILES.

SHOGHI

7 April 1954

FOLLOW LAWYER'S ADVICE REGARDING TEMPLE LAND OUTSIDE KAMPALA.

SHOGHI

13 April 1954

ASSURE PRAYERS BLACKBURN NOTTINGHAM.

SHOGHI

17 April 1954*

Dear Bahá'í Brother:
At the instruction of our beloved Guardian, I am forwarding you herewith his Convention Message.
He wishes you to have it read aloud to the assembled delegates, and then published and circulated among the believers. ...

20 April 1954**

HEARTFELT CONGRATULATIONS GREAT VICTORY.

SHOGHI

21 April 1954*

Dear Bahá'í Friends:
I am forwarding you herewith a copy of the Guardian's

---

*Joint Convention Message to all National Assemblies. Published "Bahá'í Journal" No. 114 and "Messages to the Bahá'í World 1950–1957", p. 60.
**On report that all overseas territories opened and all home Assemblies assured.

PRIORITY. REGRET OWING INCREASING EXPENSES UNABLE EXTEND FINANCIAL ASSISTANCE EXERCISE STRICT ECONOMY.

SHOGHI

29 November 1953

DISAPPROVE CIRCULATION STATEMENT MARRIAGE OWING GENERAL PRINCIPLE ALREADY ESTABLISHED.

SHOGHI

12 January 1954

TRANSMITTING FIVE HUNDRED NATIONAL FUND SENT THROUGH LANGDON-DAVIES RUG FROM BAHÁ'U'LLÁH'S SHRINE AND PHOTOS FOR NATIONAL ḤAẒÍRA LOVE.

SHOGHI

12 January 1954 (Teaching Conference)

DEEPLY APPRECIATE NOBLE SENTIMENTS DEDICATION ATTENDANTS CONFERENCE. ARDENTLY SUPPLICATING FULFILMENT HOPES ACHIEVEMENT UNPRECEDENTED VICTORIES. DEEPEST LOVE.

SHOGHI

9 March 1954

CABLE NAMES LANGUAGES ALREADY TRANSLATED UNDER TEN YEAR PLAN SPECIFY ALSO WHICH LANGUAGES PROCESS TRANSLATION.

SHOGHI

24 March 1954

ADVISE SEND PIONEERS PROMPTLY BRITISH TOGOLAND FRENCH TOGOLAND FRENCH CAMEROONS. ORME SQUARE TOO EXPENSIVE. ADVISE TOWNSHENDS ABANDON PLAN MALTA. EXPENDITURE

10th October 1953

ASSURE CRANEY LOVING APPRECIATION. (Knight of Bahá'u'lláh to Hebrides.)

SHOGHI

10 October 1953

ADVISE ASSIST EGYPT BY PIONEER BRITISH SOMALILAND.

SHOGHI

16 October 1953

APPROVE SHOMAIS DEPARTURE ETHIOPIA.

SHOGHI

16 October 1953

ASSURE BATTAH LOVING APPRECIATION.

SHOGHI

9 November 1953

Dear Bahá'í Friends:

In your recent News Letter the beloved Guardian noted some quotations from the pilgrims notes of . . ., and he wishes me to tell you that he feels it is wiser, in such official organs as our News Letters, not to publish such notes as, unfortunately, they often contain errors. He has recently had occasion to call the American N.S.A.'s attention to this too. . . .

His loving thoughts and prayers are often with you all.

21 November 1953

APPROVE SUBSTITUTION LANGUAGES REFERRED LETTER DATED NOVEMBER THIRTEEN SENDING SECOND PIONEER HAS NO GREATER

6 September 1953

ASSURE AṢGHARZÁDÍH LOVING APPRECIATION FERVENT PRAYERS. (Knight of Bahá'u'lláh to Channel Islands.)

SHOGHI

8 September 1953

ASSURE BAXTER LOVING APPRECIATION. (Knight of Bahá'u'lláh to Channel Islands.)

SHOGHI

11 September 1953

ASSURE DUNNING DEEPEST LOVING APPRECIATION. (Knight of Bahá'u'lláh to Orkney Islands.)

SHOGHI

22 September 1953

ASSURE HASSELBLATT DEEPEST LOVING APPRECIATION. (Knight of Bahá'u'lláh to Shetland Islands.)

SHOGHI

4 October 1953

ADVISE TAKE NO RISK OWING POSSIBILITY HIGHER OUTLAY. URGE SEARCH OTHER PLACES AS NEAR AS POSSIBLE.* APPROVE HAINSWORTH SIX MONTHS LEAVE.

SHOGHI

7 October 1953

ASSURE UNA LOVING PRAYERS. (Una Townshend, Knight of Bahá'u'lláh to Malta.)

SHOGHI

*Refers to purchase of National Ḥaẓíratu'l-Quds, London.

Guardian, and he has instructed me to answer you on his behalf.

The contributions made by the British Bahá'í community to the Shrine of the Báb Fund and to the Bahá'í International Fund are greatly appreciated. Receipts are enclosed herewith.*

The beloved Guardian deeply values the unique and outstanding services of the Bahá'ís of the British Isles. Through their devotion and sacrifice, they are setting an example for posterity.

He wishes me to assure you that he prays fervently for the spiritual confirmation of all of the friends of the British Isles; for their material and spiritual welfare, and that every obstacle may be removed from their paths of service, particularly during the Global Crusade.

The Shrine of the Báb is rapidly nearing completion. Its beauty and splendour are difficult to portray. Certainly the Guardian very aptly described the octagon, the drum and the dome as the triple crowns on the Shrine of the Báb. Now that the glory and splendour of the golden dome is revealed by the removal of all of the scaffolding, it is truly a golden crown for the Shrine, and each time one looks at it, one becomes more and more impressed that it is a symbol of the manner in which the Bahá'ís of the world, led by the beloved Guardian, are crowning the Bahá'í activities of the past one hundred years by spreading the knowledge of the Glory of the Lord throughout the world.

The Guardian sends his loving greetings to you all. . . .

31 August 1953

APPROVE RETAIN YAZDIS BENNETT† GUNG. FIVE THOUSAND WORD PAMPHLET ADVISABLE INFORM AMERICA.

SHOGHI

31 August 1953

ASSURE LJUNGBERG DEEPEST APPRECIATION PRAYERS. (Knight of Bahá'u'lláh to Faroe Islands.)

SHOGHI

---

* £600 on this occasion.

ultimate unification of the divers and conflicting peoples, races and classes dwelling within the borders of a travailing, a sorely-agitated and spiritually-famished continent.

May all the privileged participators, enlisting under the banner of Bahá'u'lláh for the promotion of so pre-eminent and meritorious a Cause, be they from the Eastern or Western hemisphere, of either sex, white or coloured, young or old, neophyte or veteran, whether serving in their capacity as expounders of the teachings, or administrators, of His Faith, as settlers or itinerant teachers, distinguish themselves by such deeds of heroism as will rival, nay outshine, the feats accomplished nineteen hundred years ago by that little band of God-intoxicated disciples who, fearlessly preaching the Gospel of a newly-arisen Messiah, contributed so decisively to the illumination, the regeneration and the advancement of the entire European continent.

Shoghi

22 July 1953

ADVISE FERRABYS REMAIN ENGLAND MORE MERITORIOUS.

SHOGHI

23 July 1953

APPROVE SUBSTITUTION LINGALA LUBA MBUNDO TONGA FOR BUA WONGO LUIMBI SENA RESPECTIVELY.

SHOGHI

23 August 1953

ASSURE VAKÍL PRAYERS APPRECIATION. (Knight of Bahá'u'lláh to Cyprus.)

SHOGHI

30 August 1953

Dear Bahá'í Brother,

Your letter of 5th August has been received by the beloved

members who will, in conjunction with the four National Spiritual Assemblies participating in the European campaign, assist, through periodic and systematic visits to Bahá'í centres, in the efficient and prompt execution of the Plans formulated for the prosecution of the teaching campaign in the European continent.

A continent occupying such a central and strategic position on the entire planet; so rich and eventful in its history; so diversified in its culture; from whose soil sprang both the Hellenic and Roman civilisations; the mainspring of a civilisation to some of whose features Bahá'u'lláh Himself paid tribute; on whose southern shores Christendom first established its home; along whose eastern marches the mighty forces of the Cross and the Crescent so frequently clashed; on whose south-western extremity a fast evolving Islamic culture yielded its fairest fruit; in whose heart the light of the Reformation shone so brightly, shedding its rays as far as the outlying regions of the globe; the well-spring of American culture; whose northern and western fringes were first warmed and illuminated, less than a century ago, by the dawning light of the Revelation of Bahá'u'lláh; in whose heart a community, so rich in promise, was subsequently established; whose soil was later sanctified by the twice-repeated visit of the appointed Centre of His Covenant; which witnessed, in consequence of the rise and establishment of the Administrative Order of His Faith, the erection of two of the foremost pillars of the future Universal House of Justice; which, in recent years, sustained the dynamic impact of a series of national Plans preparatory to the launching of a world spiritual crusade—such a continent has at last at this critical hour, this great turning-point in its fortunes, entered upon what may well be regarded as the opening phase of a great spiritual revival that bids fair to eclipse any period in its spiritual history.

May the elected representatives of the National Bahá'í communities entrusted with the conduct of this momentous undertaking launched on the soil of this continent, aided by the Hands of the Cause and their auxiliary boards, reinforced by the local communities, the groups and isolated believers sharing in this massive and collective enterprise, and supported by the subsidiary agencies to be appointed for its efficient prosecution, be graciously assisted by the Lord of Hosts to contribute, in the years immediately ahead, through their concerted efforts and collective achievements, in both the teaching and administrative spheres of Bahá'í activity, to the success of this glorious Crusade, and lend a tremendous impetus to the conversion, the reconciliation and the

Part of a letter in Shoghi Effendi's handwriting from the later days of his Guardianship (*reduced size*)

Albania, Crete, Estonia, Finno-Karelia, Frisian Islands, Greece, Latvia, Lithuania, Moldavia, Rumania, White Russia, assigned to the National Spiritual Assembly of the Bahá'ís of Germany and Austria; Channel Islands, Cyprus, Faroe Islands, Hebrides Islands, Malta, Orkney Islands, Shetland Islands, assigned to the National Spiritual Assembly of the Bahá'ís of the British Isles; Andorra, Azores, Balearic Islands, Lofoten Islands, Spitzbergen, Ukraine, assigned to the National Spiritual Assembly of the Bahá'ís of the United States of America; Liechtenstein, Monaco, Rhodes, San Marino, Sardinia, Sicily, assigned to the National Spiritual Assembly of the Bahá'ís of Italy and Switzerland. Fifth, the translation and publication of Bahá'í literature in the following ten languages to be undertaken by the National Spiritual Assembly of the Bahá'ís of the United States of America, through its European Teaching Committee: Basque, Estonian, Flemish, Lapp, Maltese, Piedmontese, Romani, Romansch, Yiddish, Ziryen. Sixth, the consolidation of Belgium, Denmark, Finland, France, Holland, Italy, Luxembourg, Norway, Portugal, Spain, Sweden, Switzerland, allocated to the National Spiritual Assembly of the Bahá'ís of the United States of America; of Austria, Bulgaria, Czechoslovakia, Hungary, Poland, Russian S.F.S., Yugoslavia, allocated to the National Spiritual Assembly of the Bahá'ís of Germany and Austria; of Eire, allocated to the National Spiritual Assembly of the Bahá'ís of the British Isles; of Iceland, allocated to the National Spiritual Assembly of the Bahá'ís of Canada; and of Corsica, allocated to the National Spiritual Assembly of the Bahá'ís of Italy and Switzerland. Seventh, the incorporation of the thirteen above-mentioned National Spiritual Assemblies. Eighth, the establishment by these same National Spiritual Assemblies of national Bahá'í endowments. Ninth, the establishment of a national Ḥaẓíratu'l-Quds in the capital city of each of the countries where the National Spiritual Assemblies are to be established, as well as one in London and one in Paris. Tenth, the formation of a National Bahá'í Publishing Trust in Frankfurt, Germany. Eleventh, the formation of Israel Branches of the National Spiritual Assemblies of the Bahá'ís of the British Isles and of Germany and Austria, authorised to hold, on behalf of their parent institutions, property dedicated to the Holy Shrines at the World Centre of the Faith in the State of Israel. Twelfth, the conversion to the Faith of representatives of the Basque and Gypsy races. Thirteenth, the appointment during Riḍván 1954, by the Hands of the Cause in Europe, of an auxiliary board of nine above all, in the convocation of the historic Convention in Florence, culminating in the emergence of the National Spiritual Assembly of the Bahá'ís of Italy and Switzerland, the third in a series of institutions destined to play their part in the eventual establishment of the Supreme Legislative Body of the Administrative Order of the Faith of Bahá'u'lláh.

The hour is now ripe for these communities, whether new or old, local or national, already functioning on the northern, the western and the southern fringes of that continent, as well as those situated in its very heart, to initiate befittingly and prosecute energetically the European Campaign of a global Crusade which will not only contribute, to an unprecedented degree, to the broadening and the consolidation of the foundations of the Faith of Bahá'u'lláh on the continent of Europe, but will also diffuse its light over the neighbouring islands, and will, God willing, carry its radiance to the eastern territories of that continent, and beyond them as far as the heart of Asia.

The privileged prosecutors of so revolutionising, so gigantic, so sacred and beneficent a campaign are, on the morrow of its launching, and at such a crucial hour in the destinies of the European continent, summoned to undertake: First, the formation, under the aegis of the National Spiritual Assembly of the Bahá'ís of the United States, of one National Spiritual Assembly in each of the Scandinavian and Benelux countries, and those of the Iberian Peninsula, and one in Finland, as well as the establishment, in collaboration with the Paris Spiritual Assembly, of the National Spiritual Assembly of the Bahá'ís of France, the establishment under the aegis of the National Spiritual Assembly of the Bahá'ís of Germany and Austria, of the National Spiritual Assembly of the Bahá'ís of Austria, and the establishment, under the aegis of the National Spiritual Assembly of the Bahá'ís of the United States, and in association with the National Spiritual Assembly of the Bahá'ís of Italy and Switzerland, of independent National Spiritual Assemblies in Italy and Switzerland. Second, the construction of the first Ma<u>sh</u>riqu'l-A<u>dh</u>kár of Europe in the city of Frankfurt, the heart of Germany, which occupies such a central position in the continent of Europe. Third, the purchase of land for the future construction of two Ma<u>sh</u>riqu'l-A<u>dh</u>kárs, one in the north in the city of Stockholm, and one in the south in the city of Rome, the seat and stronghold of the most powerful Church in Christendom. Fourth, the opening of the following thirty virgin territories and islands:

on the morrow of His Father's ascension. I recall the slow eastward spread of that infant Light which led to the gradual emergence of the German and Austrian Bahá'í communities, during the darkest period of 'Abdu'l-Bahá's incarceration in the prison-fortress of 'Akká. I am reminded of His subsequent epoch-making visit, soon after His providential release from His forty-year confinement in the Most Great Prison, to these newly-fledged struggling communities, of His patient seed-sowing destined to yield at a later age its first fruits, and constituting a landmark of the utmost significance in the rise and establishment of the Faith of Bahá'u'lláh in that continent.

I, moreover, call to mind, on this occasion, the successive episodes which, on the morrow of 'Abdu'l-Bahá's ascension, in the course of the initial Epoch of the Formative Age of the Bahá'í Dispensation, signalised the emergence of those administrative institutions, both local and national, which proclaimed the germination of those potent seeds which had lain dormant for more than a decade in these newly-opened European territories, and which culminated in the construction of the framework of the Administrative Order of the Faith of Bahá'u'lláh and the erection of the first two pillars destined to sustain in that continent the weight of the final unit of that Order.

Nor can I fail to acclaim, as a further milestone in the irresistible evolution of that Faith, the launching, following the creation of the administrative agencies designed to provide the effectual instruments for its propagation, of the Six Year Plan of the British Bahá'í community followed successively by the European Teaching Campaign, inaugurated in accordance with the provisions of the second Seven Year Plan of the American Bahá'í community, the Five Year Plan conceived by the German and Austrian Bahá'í communities and the Two Year Plan later initiated by the British Bahá'í community—Plans which, within less than a decade, succeeded in laying the structural basis of the Administrative Order of the Faith in Wales, in Scotland, in Northern Ireland and in Eire, in multiplying and consolidating Bahá'í institutions throughout the British Isles, in broadening and strengthening the foundations of that same Order in Germany and Austria, in erecting the National Administrative Headquarters of the Faith in the city of Frankfurt, in establishing Spiritual Assemblies in the capital cities of no less than ten sovereign states in Europe, in reinforcing the administrative foundations of that Faith in those territories, in providing the means for the convocation of four European, and a series of regional, Teaching Conferences, and

18 July 1953*

IF LESS EXPENSIVE NOT AVAILABLE APPROVE.

SHOGHI

21 July 1953

To the Hands of the Cause, the members of the National Spiritual Assemblies, the pioneers, the resident believers and visitors attending the European Intercontinental Teaching Conference in Stockholm, Sweden (July 21/26, 1953).

Well-beloved Friends,
With a glad and grateful heart I welcome the convocation, in the capital city of Sweden, of the third of a series of Intercontinental Teaching Conferences associated with the world-wide festivities commemorating the Centenary of the Mission of Bahá'u'lláh and destined to exert a profound and lasting influence on the immediate fortunes of His Faith in all continents of the globe.
I look back with feelings of wonder, thankfulness and joy upon the chain of memorable circumstances which, a little over a century ago, accompanied the introduction of the Faith into, and marked the inception of its nascent institutions within a continent which, in the course of the last two thousand years, has exercised on the destiny of the human race a pervasive influence unequalled by that of any other continent of the globe.
I feel impelled on this historic occasion, when the members of the American, the British, the German and the newly formed Italo-Swiss National Spiritual Assemblies, as well as representatives of the Bahá'ís of the United Kingdom, of Eire, of Germany, of Austria, of the Scandinavian and Benelux countries, of the Iberian Peninsula, of Italy, of Switzerland, of France and of Finland are assembled, to pay a warm tribute to the valiant labours of the early British and French Bahá'í pioneers, who at the very dawn of the Faith in Europe, strove with such diligence, consecration and resolution to fan into flame that holy Fire which the hand of the appointed Centre of Bahá'u'lláh's Covenant had kindled in the north-west extremity of that continent

* Refers to purchase of Ḥaẓíratu'l-Quds, London.

conferred upon it the inestimable blessings of personal contact with its members, Who sustained, from His station on high, its development in the course of no less than two decades, within the framework of a rising Administrative Order, Who enabled it to expand and consolidate itself within its island home, Who launched it, subsequently, on its mission overseas, will, if its members prove themselves worthy of His trust, continue to shower His manifold blessings upon them, at this hour of their greatest need, and will enable them to traverse, speedily and successfully, the second and momentous stage in the progressive unfoldment of that same Mission.

That they may, guided and assisted by the vigilance, the wisdom and devotion of their elected national representatives, forge ahead with undiminished vigour, with exemplary fidelity, and with inflexible determination, along the path of their high destiny, overcome every obstacle that stands in their way, achieve signal success in the course of the opening phase of this world-girdling Crusade, and crown eventually their Ten Year Plan with a victory unexampled in the annals of the Faith in the British Isles, is my cherished hope for them and my fervent and constant prayer.

Shoghi

28 June 1953

ADVISE PROMPT MEASURES OUTRIGHT PURCHASE ḤAẒÍRA LONDON CONTRIBUTING TWO THOUSAND POUNDS ENCOURAGING NATIONAL ASSEMBLIES.

SHOGHI

30 June 1953

GUARDIAN URGES PROMPT HANDLING VOLUNTEERS KAMPALA NAIROBI DAR-ES-SALAAM FOR IMMEDIATE SETTLEMENT. . . .

IOAS

9 July 1953*

ADVISE FREEHOLD PURCHASE.

SHOGHI

*Refers to purchase of Ḥaẓíratu'l-Quds, London.

of the community living in the British Isles, including administrators and teachers, as well as the band of self-sacrificing pioneers who have already forsaken their homes and are labouring in distant fields in the African Continent, must, at whatever cost, disperse more widely and direct their footsteps to the virgin territories and islands assigned to their National Assembly, contributing thereby, directly and effectively, to the speedy and successful termination of the initial phase of a Crusade on which the immediate destinies of the entire community so largely depend.

While this supreme effort is being exerted special and immediate attention must, likewise, be directed to two other objectives which constitute a vital part of the work now confronting the members of this community. The selection of the site of the Ḥaẓíratu'l-Quds in the city of London, the heart of the British Empire, and the national administrative seat of the Bahá'ís of the British Isles, and the adoption of effective measures for its immediate purchase, as well as the preparation of a suitable pamphlet and its prompt translation and publication in the thirty-one languages assigned to the British Bahá'í National Assembly, are matters of such urgency as to be given precedence, during the coming two years, over all the other objectives of the Ten Year Plan.

The Plan on which the British Bahá'í community has embarked, unique in its significance, unprecedented in its scope, so vast in its potentialities, so meritorious in its objectives, so challenging in its features, will, if consummated, at the appointed time, open a further vista, before the eyes of its victorious prosecutors, of such transcendent glory as none of them can as yet even dimly imagine. The path leading to the discovery of this brilliant yet at present distant goal, at which a triumphant community will be enabled to catch a glimpse of its ultimate destiny, revealed in the plenitude of its splendour, is long, steep and thorny. The prizes to be won by those who must tread this path, in the years immediately ahead, are not to be easily secured. The challenge will be prolonged and severe. The opportunities they now have to scale loftier heights of heroism, and achieve still mightier victories during the interval separating the Great and Most Great Jubilees, will if missed never again recur.

He Who, in His infinite love and mercy, called into being this community, more than fifty years ago, at the time of the inception of His Father's Faith in the West, Who tenderly and vigilantly nursed it and guided its footsteps in the early years of its infancy, Who twice chapter in British Bahá'í history that will illuminate the annals of the Faith of Bahá'u'lláh and eclipse the splendour of the feats already accomplished in the past fifty years by the adherents of His Cause in their native land.

The twofold process, already set in motion, which has been attended by such conspicuous success, must, in the course of the coming decade, be not only fully maintained but steadily accelerated. While the structure of the Administrative Order of the Faith within the British Isles is being steadily reinforced and enlarged, through the multiplication of the administrative institutions of the Faith in England, Scotland, Wales and Ireland and the consolidation of the newly-fledged assemblies already established, an effort, unprecedented in scope and intensity, must be continually and determinedly exerted to lay the administrative basis of this Order not only in the islands bordering the British Isles, but in the Dependencies of the British Crown in the Mediterranean, and in the African and Asiatic Continents.

This vital aspect of the Mission committed to the care of the British Bahá'í community, must, in the course of the Crusade upon which it has embarked, receive a tremendous impetus, and gather such momentum as to justify the trust 'Abdu'l-Bahá so confidently placed in this community and the distinctive functions with which its members have been invested since His passing. The development of the institutions of the Faith on the home front must be supplemented by, and afford a constant stimulus to, the rise of similar institutions, first in the limited number of territories and islands assigned to the elected representatives of this community, and eventually throughout the colonies and protectorates comprising the British Empire.

The opening phase of the Ten Year Plan so auspiciously inaugurated on the morrow of the memorable victories already achieved, covering a period of no less than two years, must be distinguished by the opening, in rapid succession, of the eleven virgin territories in Europe and Africa and the laying of a firm foundation for the future erection of a rapidly rising Administrative Order whose ramifications are destined to encircle within the coming ten years the entire planet.

The exertions required to consummate the first stage of this Ten Year Plan are admittedly arduous, and demand the utmost attentiveness, and a degree of sacrifice and consecration unequalled in the entire course of British Bahá'í history. In spite of the smallness of their numbers, and the limited resources at their disposal, the members the morrow of the centenary celebrations of the Founding of the Faith of Bahá'u'lláh, and on the other, the successful termination of the Two Year Plan, marking the inauguration of the community's historic Mission beyond the confines of its homeland, have immensely enhanced its prestige throughout the entire Bahá'í world, have won for it the abiding gratitude and profound admiration of all who labour for our beloved Faith, and entitled it to assume a prominent share in the conduct of the world spiritual Crusade launched amidst the festivities signalising the climax of the celebrations of this Holy Year commemorating the centenary of the birth of the Mission of the Author of the Bahá'í Dispensation.

Much has been achieved in the course of the past nine years, both within the borders of this community's island home, and throughout the widely scattered Dependencies of the British Crown, on the shores as well as within the heart of the vast and far-off African Continent, to merit the pride that fills the hearts of its staunch and stalwart members, to deserve the applause of the Concourse on High, to evoke the fondest hopes for the steady unfoldment and ultimate consummation of the historic Mission entrusted to the care of the British followers of the Cause of Bahá'u'lláh, and to befittingly usher in a new Era in British Bahá'í history—an Era that will for ever remain associated with the systematic introduction of God's triumphant Faith, through the concerted efforts of the heroic band of Bahá'í pioneers, dwelling within the British Isles, into the Chief Dependencies of the British Crown scattered throughout the European and Asiatic continents and the islands and archipelagos of the Seven Seas.

The entire community, now firmly entrenched within the Administrative strongholds, recently and so laboriously established in England, Wales, Scotland and Ireland, must rise as one man to the occasion that now presents itself. With hearts brimming with the love of Bahá'u'lláh, with souls entirely dedicated to His Cause, with minds attuned to the laws and precepts underlying His teachings, steeled with an inflexible determination to utilise, to the fullest extent, the administrative agencies which their hands have fashioned since the passing of 'Abdu'l-Bahá, and deriving fresh hope and sustenance from the rapid and remarkable victories won in both the teaching and administrative spheres of Bahá'í activity, both at home and abroad, the members of this high-minded, tenacious and spiritually alive community must gird up their loins, intensify their efforts a hundredfold and, through their combined and sustained efforts, write yet another possible. Not only will spiritual strength accrue from this settlement of so many new lands, but the prestige it gives us in the eyes of the non-Bahá'ís is great. He fully realises heavy burdens have been placed upon the shoulders of all the Bahá'ís, and particularly upon the members of the twelve N.S.A.s directing this great crusade. But who else except the believers can do the work of Bahá'u'lláh? And short of accomplishing His work, where else lies hope for this confused and sorely-tried world?

In spite of your many problems, he feels confident that you will find amongst the valiant members of the British Bahá'í community sufficient volunteers to enable you to fill your virgin territories and islands with at least one pioneer per place. As he has already pointed out, there can be exchange; in other words, one Assembly can make use of volunteers for its goals from amongst believers under the jurisdiction of another N.S.A. if such are available.

In spite of your financial position and the work that lies ahead, the Guardian has felt it wise and necessary for you to take steps to purchase a national headquarters. When we remember that England is one of the oldest Bahá'í countries, so to speak, in the West, and that in spite of her distinction she is still without a suitable seat for her national Bahá'í administration, we see how important it is for her, on the eve of this great period of expansion, to have a National Centre. France, without any N.S.A. as yet, now has one, and it is high time England had one too. You will receive aid from others in this undertaking, as well as from the Guardian. He was pleased that Mr. Joseph took the first step in enabling you to fulfil this objective.

His loving thoughts and prayers are with each and every one of you, as you face your great responsibilities and rise to meet your priceless opportunities. . . .

P.S. The Guardian wishes your Assembly to express to Mr. Albert Joseph his deep appreciation of the assistance he is giving you in connection with the purchase of a National Headquarters.

Dear and valued co-workers,
　　The successive victories won, in recent years, by the British Bahá'í community, proclaiming, on the one hand, the triumphant conclusion of the first collective enterprise undertaken in British Bahá'í history on

As he has cabled, he considers that, at this stage in the development of the Faith in Africa, it is not necessary for so many people to congregate in one centre, such as Kampala, when there is such a tremendous need in neighbouring territories for pioneers, whether native or European.

He considers that the formation of a school at this time is premature. It would involve us in heavy responsibilities which for the sake of public opinion would have to be discharged efficiently and in an exemplary manner, and he does not consider that we have the resources or the facilities at present to embark on such a project. There is no reason why the subject cannot be reconsidered at a future date.

He considers that the attitude of your Assembly regarding police service which might be required of the Bahá'ís in Kenya at this time is correct, and that it is not war, so far. As it seems that ... situation with his employer, for the present at least, prevented him from having to do police duty, the subject does not arise for the moment. He does not think that any general rule can be laid down in such matters. Events must be watched, and, when situations such as these arise, fresh consultation with him will be necessary. ...

As he has already informed you, and the National Spiritual Assembly of America as well, there is no objection to your receiving co-operation from them and financial assistance which they might be able to give you in publishing some of the literature in the African languages.

He thinks your Assembly's decision regarding spiritual healing being demonstrated at a Bahá'í meeting was quite sound. We should try not to have the Faith identified with such things in the eyes of the public, officially. What the believers do privately, which in no way contravenes the Teachings, is their own affair.

As regards the Obligatory Prayers, the friends in the West should continue to use them exactly as they have been doing, and as is set forth in the remarks in parentheses which accompany the prayers in the book "Prayers and Meditations". The Guardian himself will, whenever he sees fit, and considers the time is ripe, inform the friends in such matters in greater detail.

Of all the work being undertaken by the believers, East and West, at the present time, undoubtedly the most urgent is that of getting the pioneers out to the goal countries during this year, if the Stockholm Conference, where his presence will be welcomed by all the other Hands attending, and the believers as well. . . .

The letters which your Assembly wrote at the request of the . . . Bahá'ís to certain officials there, he thought were excellent. What he did not think was excellent was the almost insulting reply you received as regards . . . from the authorities in London and signed by. . . . The letter was a mass of contradictions, and the excuses transparent, to say the least. It shows that there is no doubt going to be a stiffening opposition from certain colonial governments, as the Bahá'í work progresses.

Your Assembly will undoubtedly continue to press the matter as best you can with the authorities, without causing too much opposition. . . .

The question of impressing upon the Africans who are seeking enrolment the necessity of not drinking is a delicate one. When enrolling new believers, we must be wise and gentle, and not place so many obstacles in their way that they feel it impossible to accept the Faith. On the other hand, once accorded membership in the community of the followers of Bahá'u'lláh, it must be brought home to them that they are expected to live up to His teachings, and to show forth the signs of a noble character in conformity with His laws. This can often be done gradually, after the new believer is enrolled.

Now that the African work has entered upon an entirely new phase, indeed the work all over the world, the position your Assembly held as the more or less co-ordinating body for the work in Africa has been changed. However, the closest co-operation will be necessary between all the National Assemblies concerned with the Africa teaching work, if the Plan is to go ahead swiftly; and exchange of information, especially as regards pioneer possibilities and posts, is essential, in order to get the believers out to the goal countries during this year, which is the Guardian's ardent hope, and to which he attaches the greatest possible importance. There is no objection to British pioneers going into the territories of other Assemblies, or believers under other jurisdiction being used by your Assembly. The most important thing is to open up the virgin countries; and of course whoever works in a country under the jurisdiction of a specific Assembly, no matter where their origin may have been, would be under the orders of that Assembly.

The Guardian wishes you to budget the necessary funds to cover this work and to see that it is actively pursued, so that the literature will be available at an early date.

He wishes you to send current reports of activities in connection with this matter to the Secretary-General of the International Bahá'í Council, so that the data may be assembled with all the necessary information in connection with the Ten Year Crusade, for the Guardian.

He sends his loving greetings to you.

25 June 1953

Dear Bahá'í Brother,

Your letters of July 8, 12 and 16, August 5 and 13, September 16, 20 and 26, October 13, 14 and 26, December 12 (3) and 17, 1952, and January 4, 6, 13, 15, 20, 27 (2) and 29, February 3 and 6, March 12, 17, 22, 23 and 26, April 1, 17, 20, 24 and 29, May 5, 11, 14, 15 (2), 28 and 30, 1953, with their enclosures, have been received by the beloved Guardian, as well as material sent under separate cover, and he has instructed me to answer you on his behalf.

As you are all aware, the pressure of work is constantly increasing all over the Bahá'í world, and of course the heaviest load falls upon the Guardian. That is why he is finding it increasingly difficult to keep up with his letters, not only to individuals, but also to national bodies, important as they are. He regrets this delay, but sees no remedy for it.

It was a source of great pride to him that the British Bahá'ís succeeded with their Plan, in spite of the fact that it was a long, hard struggle, and in some instances the odds seemed very much against them. He feels sure that their qualities of tenacity of purpose, fidelity and initiative will carry them on to even greater distinction during the coming ten years, as they execute their portion of the Global Crusade, an important portion.

It was very nice to have dear Dr. Mitchell† here; the Guardian hopes that gradually more British Bahá'ís will be able to make the pilgrimage.

He was very relieved to hear that dear Mr. Townshend has recovered his health to such an extent that he will be attending

"Roll of Honour" on which will be inscribed the names of the "Knights of Bahá'u'lláh" who first enter these 131 virgin areas, will be placed inside the entrance door of the Inner Sanctuary of the Tomb of Bahá'u'lláh. From time to time, the Guardian will announce to the Bahá'í World the names of those Holy Souls who arise under the conditions outlined in his message, and settle these areas and conquer them for Bahá'u'lláh.

Now is the Hour for the Friends everywhere to demonstrate the spiritual vitality of the Faith, and of their devotion. There is no time after this moment, to settle the unconquered areas. The Guardian is sure the Friends throughout the world, and particularly the staunch Bahá'ís in the British Isles, will arise as one soul in many bodies, and surging ahead, cover the face of the Earth with the Glory of the Lord.

The Guardian will pray fervently for the Bahá'ís of the British Isles for the success of their efforts.

The Guardian will pray for the members of your Assembly, whose sacrificial efforts he greatly values. . . .

8 June 1953

Dear Bahá'í Brother:

The beloved Guardian has asked me to write to you following my letter of June 5th in connection with the great importance of settling one hundred and thirty-one virgin areas, during the next few months.

Naturally it will be difficult for the Faith to be established in the new territories or amongst the new tribes if they do not have at least a pamphlet for distribution to the new contacts.

He therefore feels that along with the sending of pioneers into the virgin areas, the translation of literature into the languages assigned to the British National Assembly should take place. He has cabled you direct concerning this very important matter, and has informed you in his cable that he is arranging for a gift of 1,000 Pounds to assist you in this most important work.

The Guardian feels that one of the existing pamphlets would be satisfactory, or a new one, which you may feel it desirable to prepare. At this time, it is not necessary to enter into the question of translation of Bahá'í books, simply a pamphlet, which can be used for teaching purposes.

areas of the Commonwealth which are not under your assignment.

The specific suggestions of the Guardian are:

(a) Areas close at hand and easy of settlement should be filled first. Then the areas more difficult, and finally those which will be quite difficult.

(b) Whenever a pioneer enters a new territory, a cable should be sent at once to the Guardian, giving the name, place, and any pertinent information.

(c) A monthly report of progress is to be sent by your Assembly to the Secretary-General of the International Bahá'í Council. Special matters of report nature, for the Guardian, in connection with the plan should be sent to the Secretary-General of the Council also.

This does not mean that any administrative matters in connection with the settlement of pioneers, etc., should be handled with the Council. Such matters should continue to be handled with the Guardian direct. The Council is simply to co-ordinate reports, consolidate them, keep maps up to date, etc., for the Guardian, and your reports will enable them to do this.

(d) The Guardian feels the following areas are not difficult to settle, and he thinks you should arrange for their settlement at once; and he will appreciate cable advice of each settlement as they take place.

Channel Islands   Malta
Hebrides Islands   Cyprus
Shetland Islands

(e) The Guardian has cabled you, and at his direction I have written the Friends in Uganda, Kenya and Tanganyika of the importance of their spreading out, and if possible sending pioneers into the surrounding areas in Africa, such as Belgian Congo, Ruanda Urundi, Somaliland, and even South West Africa. He wishes you to follow up this matter closely. The Guardian attached great importance to the Ashanti Protectorate, and if any of the Friends can go there, particularly any Persians you may be assisting in getting located, he will appreciate it.

As the Guardian's dramatic cable indicates, an illuminated

There are some general observations which the Guardian shares with you, and then some specific suggestions which are enumerated below:

1. Every individual who has offered to pioneer, must be encouraged in every way by the National Assembly.

2. The National Assembly should assist each pioneer, so they may be placed in their post just as quickly as possible.

3. The handling of each application for pioneering service must be expedited, and not allowed to be bogged down for any reason, or in the hands of committees.

4. The National Assembly should make it their first order of business to follow up actively this most important task. They must make it the first order of business at each Assembly meeting to see that each application is being progressed rapidly. This does not mean the special committees should not handle the details, but it does mean the Assembly itself must review each application at each meeting and see that the pioneer gets into the field as soon as possible.

5. A large number of pioneers should not be sent to any one country. One, or even two, will be sufficient for the time being. Later on, if supplementary assistance is needed, that of course can be taken care of. The all important thing now is to get at least one pioneer in each of the 131 virgin areas.

6. The National Assembly may exercise its prerogatives and suggest to applicants where their services are most needed. This, of course, applies particularly to pioneers who might wish to settle in one area.

7. Because there have been so many applicants in America, the Guardian has written them that they may place their pioneers in any virgin area in the world. His objective now is to fill these lands yet unconquered by the Hosts of Heaven and he feels the initial impact must be made now. Thus, from whatever sources they come, they should be placed in the field at the earliest possible moment. Furthermore, as the Chief Executors of 'Abdu'l-Bahá's Divine Plan, He expects the Americans to bear the brunt of the load everywhere. He has instructed the American N.S.A. to communicate with your Assembly with regard to pioneers to be settled in territories coming under your assignment, as well as territories not under your assignment, but where your Assembly can aid them in settling, particularly in

has for the wonderful spirit shown by Mr. Banání and his wife, as well as by Philip Hainsworth and Mr. and Mrs. Collison. The services of all of those friends cannot be overestimated, nor those of the devoted pioneers in Kenya and Tanganyika.

May the Almighty bless, sustain and guide you in your highly meritorious endeavours, remove all obstacles from your path, and enable you to lend a great impetus to the historic work being achieved in the African Continent.

Your true and grateful brother,
Shoghi

5 June 1953

Dear Bahá'í Friends,

Our Beloved Guardian has been greatly encouraged by reports reaching him from all parts of the Bahá'í World, of victories, already gained, and plans being laid for the prosecution of the Ten Year Crusade. He was particularly pleased to learn that some 150 people have offered to pioneer in virgin overseas areas at the American Convention.

These reports have evoked his awe-inspiring and soul-stirring cablegram of May 28th*, calling for the immediate settlement of all the 131 virgin areas of the Plan, just as quickly as possible. He is convinced the Friends will arise and translate their enthusiasm into Action, because the Keynote of the Crusade, must be Action, Action, Action.

The Beloved Guardian has directed me to write your Assembly to amplify some of the aspects of his dynamic message.

The settlement of these virgin areas is of such an emergency nature, that he feels pioneering in one of them takes precedence over every other type of Bahá'í service—whether it be in the teaching or administrative fields of the Faith. So important is it that the National Assembly may delay initiation of steps to fulfil other phases of the Plan, until all these areas are conquered for the Faith. Nothing, absolutely nothing, must be allowed to interfere with the placing of pioneers in each of the 131 goal countries.

---

*Announcing "Roll of Honour" for "Knights of Bahá'u'lláh" published in "Messages to the Bahá'í World, 1950–1957", p. 48.

THE GUARDIAN
The last photograph of Shoghi Effendi taken a few months before he passed away

first fires in the hearts of the believers in that land, and which have spread so swiftly and have been the cause of such joy to our beloved Guardian.

The Guardian considers that the settling of all the virgin territories all over the world is the most important of the goals given to any of the National Assemblies, and that it should be given precedence. Indeed, he is hoping that the one hundred and thirty territories still unopened may all be settled by pioneers this year, if possible.

It is not necessary for a National Assembly to confine itself to the placing of pioneers from its own community in its goal areas—it may draw on other Bahá'í communities for pioneers for its goal territories, as well, and vice versa. In other words, pioneers from the British Isles may be sent to territories under the administrative jurisdiction of other National Bodies than the British National Assembly, and pioneers may be accepted for British posts who are not members of the British community. The important thing is to achieve the goals.

The Guardian is urging the bodies associated with the work in Africa to disperse their forces, and not endeavour to build up large communities. Otherwise, there will be a large number of pioneers in one place, while other goal countries may be left entirely without a pioneer.

As regards the translations for Africa, he has urged the American National Spiritual Assembly, in connection with the printing of Bahá'í literature in the languages allotted to that continent, to give you any help it can.

The Guardian feels confident that, by proper concentration of effort and exchange of information between the committees responsible for getting the pioneers out to Africa, the ways and means will be forthcoming to achieve our objectives this year.

You may rest assured that his prayers will continue to be offered for the work you are performing, and that he most deeply appreciates the conscientious and tireless devotion of all the members of your committee, a devotion which has enabled the Conference to take place with such success.

With loving Bahá'í greetings. . . .

P.S. In reading over this letter, I see that I have not done justice to the deep feeling of appreciation our beloved Guardian

Your committee will no doubt face, in the days to come, many grave problems; but the Guardian feels sure that, whatever happens, and whatever attacks are made upon the Faith and its pioneers, the net result cannot but be good for us in the long run, and can only serve to hasten the spread of the Cause.

He feels that your committee has every right to feel immensely proud, and grateful to God, for the success of your unremitting labours over such a long period of time.

He was most happy to hear that Mr. Dudley Smith Kutendele is planning to go and teach the Faith in Nyasaland, and will pray that his efforts may meet with success in the end.

Your understanding of the treatment of polygamist converts to the Faith is quite correct, but of course if anyone who is a Bahá'í wishes to marry more than one wife, he cannot do so. If they should disobey this law, then the cases must be handled in the same way as the Persians do, which is that these persons who become polygamists, break the laws of marriage.

As regards your question about the proper designation for the huts which will be used by the believers in villages, as Bahá'í Centres, he thinks that, for the time being, until a more dignified structure can be erected, they should be called "Bahá'í Centre", and not Ḥaẓíratu'l-Quds—the correct name is Ḥaẓíratu'l-Quds and not Ḥaẓíra.

He was immensely pleased over the example shown by Enos Epyeru, in withdrawing from political affiliation, and feels that some of the African friends are showing a most exemplary spirit of devotion and loyalty. He feels that a great potential strength lies in these new African believers.

No doubt your committee will be faced with problems, due to the inexperience of some of these people in administrative matters, but, through loving guidance, and the wisdom of those who are associated with them on the spot, these minor things can be satisfactorily taken care of, and the main thing, the establishment of assemblies and groups, be carried out successfully.

The Guardian was indeed delighted over 'Alí Nakhjavání's trip to the Teso district. The purity of his spirit, the intensity of his devotion, and the longing in his heart to bring the Faith to his African brothers, all of which he so clearly showed forth in his actions, were no doubt the great factors which enkindled the

1 June 1953

URGE IMMEDIATE STEPS PUBLICATION PAMPHLETS AFRICAN LANGUAGES. APPROVE APPROACH NATIONAL ASSEMBLIES FINANCIAL ASSISTANCE. MYSELF CONTRIBUTING THOUSAND POUNDS MERITORIOUS PURPOSE.

SHOGHI

4 June 1953

Africa Committee

Dear Bahá'í Sister:
Your letters of June 27, August 4, August 18, September 19, October 9 and November 27, 1952, with enclosures, have been received, and the beloved Guardian has instructed me to answer you on his behalf.

Your letter of May 25th has also been received. He of course meant French Equatorial Africa, but condensed it for the sake of the cable. The Belgian Congo is naturally separate.

As many of your questions and reports dealt with pre-Conference complications, which, thanks to the grace of Bahá'u'lláh, were all satisfactorily removed, I will not touch upon them in this letter.

The Guardian was immensely pleased and relieved when it became clear that the Bahá'ís had obtained visas for Uganda, and were attending in large numbers, and that hotel accommodation was available.

From the report he has received from Mr. Ioas and pilgrims, the Conference was undoubtedly a tremendous success, and befittingly inaugurated the round of celebrations during this Holy Year.

It is a great pity that there should have been so much unfavourable publicity connected with the public meeting associated with the Conference, and its attendance. One cannot, however, help but feel that such an attitude was inevitable sooner or later, because there is no doubt that the missionaries are beginning to feel the keenest resentment and a certain degree of alarm, due to the success of our teaching methods in Africa.

RÔLE IN TEN YEAR CRUSADE (1953–1957) 299

TRIUMPHANT CONCLUSION INITIAL EPOCH UNFOLDMENT WORLDWIDE MISSION ENTRUSTED BRITISH BAHÁ'Í COMMUNITY AMIDST PEOPLES RACES DWELLING DEPENDENCIES BRITISH CROWN SCATTERED THROUGHOUT FIVE CONTINENTS GLOBE.

SHOGHI

28 April 1953 (Convention)

GREATLY VALUE NOBLE SENTIMENTS HAND CAUSE DELEGATES FRIENDS FERVENTLY PRAYING SHRINES VALIANT BRITISH BAHÁ'Í COMMUNITY PLAY MEMORABLE PART WORLD CRUSADE FULFIL HISTORIC MISSION. DEEPEST LOVE.

SHOGHI

13 May 1953

URGE FULL FLEDGED BAHÁ'Í ASSEMBLIES BRITISH TERRITORIES UGANDA TANGANYIKA KENYA NOW REGARDED MOST POWERFUL PILLARS SWIFTLY EMERGING STEADILY CONSOLIDATING HIGHLY PROMISING AFRICAN BAHÁ'Í COMMUNITY SET GLORIOUS EXAMPLE THROUGH PROMPT MEASURES INITIATION EXTENSION WORK THROUGH DESPATCH SURPLUS MEMBERS LOCAL COMMUNITIES INCLUDING AFRICANS NEIGHBOURING TERRITORIES FRENCH SOMALILAND RUANDA URUNDI MADAGASCAR FRENCH BELGIAN CONGO COMORO ISLANDS EVEN ALGERIA MOROCCO ACCELERATING THEREBY PROCESS FORMATION LOCAL ASSEMBLIES ESTABLISHMENT NATIONAL ASSEMBLY CENTRAL EAST AFRICA ADDING FRESH LAURELS CROWN ALREADY WON PIONEERING FIELD AFRICAN CONTINENT.

SHOGHI

17 May 1953

MAIL FIFTY COPIES STATISTICAL PAMPHLET.

SHOGHI

	COAST, KENYA, NIGERIA, SIERRA LEONE, TANGANYIKA, UGANDA, ZULULAND; EUROPE—EIRE; ASIA—HONG-KONG.
THIRD	ESTABLISHMENT NATIONAL SPIRITUAL ASSEMBLY BAHÁ'ÍS CENTRAL EAST AFRICA.
FOURTH	PURCHASE LAND ANTICIPATION CONSTRUCTION MA<u>SH</u>RIQU'L-A<u>DH</u>KÁR KAMPALA.
FIFTH	ESTABLISHMENT NATIONAL ḤAẒÍRATU'L-QUDS LONDON.
SIXTH	CONVERSION INTO NATIONAL INSTITUTION LOCAL ḤAẒÍRATU'L-QUDS KAMPALA.
SEVENTH	INCORPORATION NATIONAL SPIRITUAL ASSEMBLY BAHÁ'ÍS CENTRAL EAST AFRICA.
EIGHTH	ESTABLISHMENT NATIONAL ENDOWMENTS BRITISH ISLES.
NINTH	ESTABLISHMENT NATIONAL ENDOWMENTS BY NATIONAL SPIRITUAL ASSEMBLY BAHÁ'ÍS CENTRAL EAST AFRICA.
TENTH	TRANSLATION BAHÁ'Í LITERATURE THIRTY-ONE AFRICAN LANGUAGES: ACCRA, AFRIKAANS, ALADIAN, ASHANTI, BANU, BEMBA, BUA, CHUANA, GIO, GU, JIENG, JOLOF, KUANYAMA, KRONGO, KROO, LIUMBI, MALAGASY, NUBIAN, PEDI, POPO, RONGA, SENA, SHILHA, SHONA, SOBO, SUTO, WONGO, XOSA, YALUNKA, YAO, ZULU.
ELEVENTH	DOUBLING NUMBER SPIRITUAL ASSEMBLIES LOCALITIES BRITISH ISLES.
TWELFTH	INCORPORATION NINETEEN ASSEMBLIES ENGLAND, SCOTLAND, WALES, IRELAND.
THIRTEENTH	ESTABLISHMENT ISRAEL BRANCH NATIONAL SPIRITUAL ASSEMBLY BRITISH ISLES.
FOURTEENTH	FORMATION EUROPEAN, ASIAN TEACHING COMMITTEES, DESIGNED STIMULATE, CO-ORDINATE TEACHING ACTIVITIES PLAN.

ARDENTLY PRAYING DECADE LONG CRUSADE CULMINATING HUNDREDTH ANNIVERSARY DECLARATION FAITH BAHÁ'U'LLÁH MAY WITNESS BOTH ADMINISTRATIVE TEACHING FIELDS HOME FRONT AS WELL AS BEYOND CONFINES BRITISH ISLES FRUITION SEEDS HAND CENTRE COVENANT SO LOVINGLY PATIENTLY SOWED COURSE TWICE REPEATED VISIT HEART BRITISH EMPIRE. MAY IT LIKEWISE CARRY

RÔLE IN TEN YEAR CRUSADE (1953–1957) 297

1953 (Convention)

WARMLY CONGRATULATE ASSEMBLED DELEGATES BAHÁ'Í COMMUNITY BRITISH ISLES CELEBRATING MOST GREAT FESTIVAL HOLY YEAR ON MAGNIFICENT VICTORIES ACHIEVED AFRICAN CONTINENT EXCEEDING HIGHEST HOPES PLAN FORMULATED TWO YEARS AGO ORIGINALLY CONCEIVED MERE PRELUDE AFRICAN CAMPAIGN ASSUMED SUCH PROPORTIONS YIELDED SUCH FRUIT DESERVE BE REGARDED DISTINCT STAGE CAMPAIGN LAUNCHED BRITISH BAHÁ'Í COMMUNITY BEYOND BORDERS HOMELAND SIX YEAR PLAN FIRST COLLECTIVE UNDERTAKING BRITISH BAHÁ'Í HISTORY LAID BROADENED FOUNDATIONS ADMINISTRATIVE INSTITUTIONS DESTINED DIRECT OPERATION FUTURE OVERSEAS ENTERPRISES BRITISH BAHÁ'Í COMMUNITY TWO YEAR PLAN INAUGURATED WITHIN AFRICAN CONTINENT GLORIOUS MISSION SAME COMMUNITY CALLED UPON ACCOMPLISH THROUGHOUT BRITISH DEPENDENCIES EASTERN WESTERN HEMISPHERES HOUR PROPITIOUS TRIUMPHANT RICHLY BLESSED BRITISH NATIONAL SPIRITUAL ASSEMBLY PARTICIPATE ELEVEN SISTER NATIONAL ASSEMBLIES EAST WEST IMPENDING WORLD SPIRITUAL CRUSADE THROUGH LAUNCHING TEN YEAR PLAN EMBRACING THREE CONTINENTS GLOBE CALCULATED CARRY STAGE FURTHER THEIR OWN PARTICULAR CRUSADE THROUGHOUT NUMEROUS WIDELY SCATTERED HIGHLY DIVERSIFIED COLONIES PROTECTORATES BRITISH EMPIRE HASTEN DAY BE ABLE ASSUME PREPONDERATING SHARE SUCH VAST HIGHLY MERITORIOUS PIONEERING ENTERPRISE.

MOMENTOUS PLAN WHICH COURSE COMING DECADE SEPARATING THEM MOST GREAT JUBILEE WILL DEMAND COMPLETE SUSTAINED CONSECRATION TWOFOLD TASK CONSOLIDATION FAITH ENGLAND SCOTLAND WALES IRELAND ITS PROPAGATION BEYOND ISLAND HOME INVOLVES

FIRST OPENING FOLLOWING VIRGIN TERRITORIES: SEVEN EUROPE—CHANNEL ISLANDS, CYPRUS, FAROE ISLANDS, HEBRIDES ISLANDS, MALTA, ORKNEY ISLANDS, SHETLAND ISLANDS; FOUR AFRICA—BRITISH CAMEROONS, BRITISH TOGOLAND, MADEIRA, SOUTH WEST AFRICA.

SECOND CONSOLIDATION FAITH FOLLOWING TERRITORIES: NINE AFRICA—ANGOLA, BELGIAN CONGO, GOLD

"World wide mission entrusted British Bahá'í Community"

THE BRITISH RÔLE IN THE TEN YEAR CRUSADE
1953-1957

THE AFRICA PLAN (1950–1953)   293

25 March 1953

YOUR ASSEMBLY HENCEFORTH CONSULTATIVE BODY ONLY FOR BRITISH TERRITORIES IN AFRICA.

SHOGHI

3 April 1953

Dear Bahá'í Brother:
Enclosed please find the Guardian's Convention Message.
As there are a great many African languages enumerated, and the spelling is very involved, the Guardian has decided to Air Mail you this message, rather than have it cabled, which was his original intention.

Please cable immediately you receive this letter, acknowledging it, so that the Guardian will know his Convention Message is in your hands. Otherwise he will of course have to cable it from here.

He is eagerly awaiting the report of the African Conference, which he has not received to date. . . .

P.S. Your letter regarding a rug supposedly owned by Bahá'u'lláh coming up for sale, has just been received, and the Guardian feels that he cannot possibly authenticate this rug as having belonged at any time to Bahá'u'lláh. It may of course be quite true that it did. He leaves it to the discretion of your Assembly to decide whether you wish to purchase it or not.

8 April 1953

APPEAL ENTIRE COMMUNITY EXERT SUPREME EFFORT ELEVENTH HOUR SEAL SUCCESS PLAN ASSURE LOVING FERVENT PRAYERS.

SHOGHI

18 April 1953

HEARTFELT CONGRATULATIONS DEEPEST LOVE.

SHOGHI

LOYAL BRITISH BAHÁ'Í COMMUNITY WORLD WIDE CELEBRATIONS HOLY YEAR PAVE WAY EFFECTIVE PARTICIPATION ITS MEMBERS IMPENDING TEN YEAR CRUSADE MARKING OPENING THIRD COLLECTIVE ENTERPRISE INAUGURATED SINCE INCEPTION FAITH BRITISH ISLES SIGNALISING SECOND MEMORABLE STAGE THEIR UNFOLDING MISSION FOREIGN FIELDS DESTINED EMBRACE TERRITORIES BRITISH CROWN BOTH AFRICAN EUROPEAN CONTINENTS. PRAYING FERVENTLY ATTAINMENT OBJECTIVES ULTIMATE ACHIEVEMENT DISTANT GOALS.

SHOGHI

15 January 1953 (Teaching Conference)

DEEPLY TOUCHED MESSAGE APPRECIATE REDEDICATION PRAYING GLORIOUS SUCCESS.

SHOGHI

28 January 1953

ADVISE MODIFY LIST LANGUAGES. KINDLY AIRMAIL IMMEDIATELY EXPLANATION AMERICAN NATIONAL ASSEMBLY FOR MODIFICATION THEIR MANUSCRIPT.

SHOGHI

1 February 1953

ADVISE ASSEMBLY'S REPRESENTATIVES ATTENDING KAMPALA CONFERENCE ENSURE NO ONE PHOTOGRAPHS BÁB'S PORTRAIT DURING DISPLAY. SENDING COLOUR FILM SHRINES ARRANGE PROVIDE PROJECTOR SIXTEEN MILLIMETRES.

SHOGHI

13 March 1953

ASSURE YOU LOVING FERVENT PRAYERS.

SHOGHI

THE AFRICA PLAN (1950–1953)

ATTAIN COMING RIḌVÁN ASSEMBLY STATUS WITHIN SINGLE TERRITORY LONG-SLUMBERING CONTINENT. ZANZIBAR MADAGASCAR FRENCH MOROCCO SOUTH RHODESIA ITALIAN SOMALILAND ALREADY OR SOON BE OPENED FAITH. DESIRE PAY SPECIAL TRIBUTE STRENUOUS EFFORTS EXERTED 'ALÍ NAKHJAVÁNÍ SETTING EXAMPLE DEDICATION FREEDOM PREJUDICE FELLOW PIONEERS LABOURING INHOSPITABLE SURROUNDINGS CONFRONTED MANIFOLD FORMIDABLE OBSTACLES.

PLANNING ENTRUST SPECIAL REPRESENTATIVE DELEGATED ATTEND APPROACHING KAMPALA CONFERENCE PORTRAIT HOLY BÁB REPLICA ONE DEPOSITED BENEATH DOME MASHRIQU'L-ADHKÁR WILMETTE TO BE EXHIBITED ASSEMBLED ATTENDANTS HISTORIC OCCASION CONFIDENT UNVEILING MAY DRAW NEWLY RECRUITED VANGUARD EVER-SWELLING HOST BAHÁ'U'LLÁH AS WELL AS ALL PARTICIPATING VISITORS ITINERANT TEACHERS SETTLERS CLOSER SPIRIT MARTYR-PROPHET FAITH BESTOW EVERLASTING BENEDICTION ALL GATHERED MEMORABLE SESSIONS EPOCH-MAKING INTERCONTINENTAL CONFERENCE DEDICATED PROSECUTION LATEST MOST GLORIOUS CRUSADE LAUNCHED COURSE ELEVEN DECADES BAHÁ'Í HISTORY.

SHOGHI

8 January 1953 (Teaching Conference)

MOVED PLACE RECORD EXPRESSION ABIDING APPRECIATION NOTABLE CONTRIBUTION BRITISH BAHÁ'Í PIONEERS MAGNIFICENT SUCCESS HISTORIC ENTERPRISE LAUNCHED AFRICAN CONTINENT COURSE TWO YEAR PLAN FORMULATED BRITISH BAHÁ'Í COMMUNITY. GOALS FIRST EPOCH-MAKING STAGE GLORIOUS OVERSEAS MISSION FOLLOWERS BAHÁ'U'LLÁH BRITISH ISLES NOBLY ACHIEVED. APPEAL ATTENDANTS CONFERENCE FOCUS ATTENTION FLEETING MONTHS AHEAD CONSOLIDATION HOMEFRONT CONSTITUTING NO LESS VITAL PHASE SECOND COLLECTIVE ENTERPRISE BRITISH BAHÁ'Í HISTORY. URGE PARTICIPANTS RESOLVE UPON RETURN RESPECTIVE COMMUNITIES EXERT UTMOST FAN FLAME PIONEERING SPIRIT UTILISE EVERY AVAILABLE MEANS ENSURE ALL ASPECTS TRIUMPHANT CONSUMMATION PLAN. TOTAL SUCCESS INTERNAL EXTERNAL PHASES PRESENT UNDERTAKING WILL CONSTITUTE BEFITTING CONTRIBUTION STEADFASTLY LABOURING HIGHLY ESTEEMED TENACIOUSLY

20 November 1952*

DELIGHTED LOVING APPRECIATION.

SHOGHI

28 December 1952

MAINTENANCE GROUPS ISOLATED CENTRES ADVISABLE THOUGH NOT ESSENTIAL PART PLAN.

SHOGHI

To Entire Bahá'í World, 5 January 1953

REJOICE SHARE BAHÁ'Í COMMUNITIES EAST WEST THRILLING REPORTS FEATS ACHIEVED HEROIC BAND BAHÁ'Í PIONEERS LABOURING DIVERS WIDELY-SCATTERED AFRICAN TERRITORIES PARTICULARLY UGANDA HEART CONTINENT REMINISCENT ALIKE EPISODES RELATED BOOK ACTS RAPID DRAMATIC PROPAGATION FAITH INSTRUMENTALITY DAWN-BREAKERS HEROIC AGE BAHÁ'Í DISPENSATION MARVELLOUS ACCOMPLISHMENTS SIGNALISING RISE ESTABLISHMENT ADMINISTRATIVE ORDER FAITH LATIN AMERICA ECLIPSED EXPLOITS IMMORTALISING RECENTLY LAUNCHED CRUSADE EUROPEAN CONTINENT SURPASSED GOAL SEVEN-MONTH PLAN INITIATED KAMPALA ASSEMBLY AIMING DOUBLING TWELVE ENROLLED BELIEVERS OUTSTRIPPED NUMBER AFRICANS CONVERTED COURSE LAST FIFTEEN MONTHS RESIDING KAMPALA OUTLYING DISTRICTS PROTESTANT CATHOLIC PAGAN BACKGROUNDS LETTERED UNLETTERED BOTH SEXES REPRESENTATIVE NO LESS SIXTEEN TRIBES PASSED TWO HUNDRED MARK.

EFFULGENT RAYS GOD'S TRIUMPHANT CAUSE RADIATING FOCAL CENTRE FAST AWAKENING CONTINENT PENETRATING ACCELERATING RATE ISOLATED REGIONS UNFREQUENTED WHITE MEN ENVELOPING THEIR RADIANCE SOULS HITHERTO INDIFFERENT PERSISTENT HUMANITARIAN ACTIVITIES CHRISTIAN MISSIONS CIVILISING INFLUENCE CIVIL AUTHORITIES NO LESS NINE LOCALITIES QUALIFIED

---

* On completion of nine African Pamphlets, a goal of the Two Year Plan.

'Information Statistical and Comparative' be brought up to date as of May 1 1952, and sent to him here by the first possible air mail post.

One of the features of the Holy Year will be the re-issuance of this important book; inasmuch as the Holy Year is fast approaching the Guardian wishes the information as quickly as possible.

Briefly, the information which your N.S.A. is to provide, brought up to date of May 1, 1952, is as follows:

Incorporated local spiritual assemblies in the British Isles.

Bahá'í Centres in the British Isles, showing, if possible, the division between local spiritual assemblies, Groups and Isolated Believers.

Any information not immediately available should be handled by telegraph, but such information as is available should not be delayed for any one or two delinquents. You can appreciate that if the booklet is to be published early in the Holy Year, the information should reach the Guardian at a very early date.

The Guardian sends his loving greetings to the National Assembly and its devoted members. . . .

29 August 1952*

DEEPLY TOUCHED PROFOUNDLY APPRECIATE NOBLE SENTIMENTS PRAYING FULFILMENT HIGH DESTINY DEEPEST LOVE.

SHOGHI

15 October 1952**

PROFOUNDLY APPRECIATE MESSAGE ARDENTLY PRAYING BRITISH COMMUNITY MAY ARISE BEFITTINGLY DISCHARGE GREAT TASKS AHEAD.

SHOGHI

---

* Reply to Summer School.
** Reply to greetings of N.S.A. at beginning of Holy Year.

be meagre, though the cares and preoccupations of the peoples amidst whom they live are such as to often blind them to the Faith and its healing message, yet the position they occupy and the responsibilities devolving upon them in the heart and centre of a world-wide empire, the manifold tokens of esteem and loving-kindness showered upon them during the infancy of this community by the Centre of God's Covenant; the inherent qualities of tenacity of purpose, of exemplary fidelity, of perspicacity that distinguishes the race to which they belong, must inspire hope and confidence in their future, and fully entitles them to play a leading role in the future proclamation of the Message of Bahá'u'lláh to the multitudes that live beneath the shadow of the British Crown.

That they may become increasingly conscious of the sublimity of their task; that they may address themselves to it with their characteristic zeal, ability, intelligence and fervour; that they may speedily acquire the spiritual potentialities for the initiation of a still more momentous stage in the unfoldment of their historic Mission; that they may earn increasingly, through their superb feats, the unqualified admiration of their brethren in every continent of the globe and prove themselves worthy of the bounties already received and those which, we may well believe, are held in store for them, is my cherished hope and constant prayer.

Shoghi

*15 June 1952**

Dear Bahá'í Friends,

The beloved Guardian has instructed me to write you in his behalf, to request that information relating to the British Isles and their activities, contained in the booklet "The Bahá'í Faith"

---

* On 9 January 1951 the Guardian announced the formation of the first International Bahá'í Council, hailing it as "the greatest event shedding lustre upon second epoch of Formative Age ..." and on 8 March 1952 he enlarged it and named its eight members. Hand of the Cause Leroy Ioas was appointed Secretary General and as such wrote frequently to the British National Spiritual Assembly. He wrote more frequently, however, conveying messages from the Guardian, requesting information, sharing news, etc., signing his letters "Assistant Secretary". This was the first letter of this kind. His letters are now included wherever he indicates that he is writing on behalf of the Guardian.

contact with the heterogeneous tribes and races dwelling in that continent, in their dealings with the civil authorities of divers countries and states within whose jurisdiction they will labour, in their struggle with an inhospitable climate, in the hazards to which they will be inevitably exposed, in the adventures they may experience, in the reverses they may temporarily suffer, in the opposition they will meet with, in the tests and trials they will undergo, His unfailing guidance will be vouchsafed to them in direct proportion to the degree of their consecration to their task, and the perseverance, the courage and fidelity they will display as they discharge their duties.

The remarkable success that has attended their high endeavours since the initiation of their first collective enterprise within the confines of their native land, the still more notable evidence of God's sustaining grace that has accompanied the opening of the first stage of their Mission overseas, are sufficient proof of the tremendous potency of the forces at work for the purpose of ensuring the unrestricted expansion of their future activities within and beyond the frontiers of their island home, and the ultimate consummation of their magnificent enterprise.

In the months immediately ahead, the strongholds of the Faith erected, in the form of local assemblies, and already established in Ireland, Scotland, Wales and England, must be maintained at all costs in their present strength; the groups and isolated centres already brought into being must, under no circumstances, be allowed to decrease in number or be lost to the Faith; the translation and publication of pamphlets in the languages already selected must be vigorously pushed forward and completed; the centre in the capital of Kenya must be assiduously expanded; the preparations for the projected intercontinental Conference must be carefully carried out; the effective participation of the representatives of the British Bahá'í community in the Stockholm inter-continental Conference must be ensured; and all the preparatory steps, required for the effectual collaboration of the members of this community in the global crusade, destined to be launched on the morrow of the world-wide celebrations of the approaching Holy Year, should, to whatever extent possible, be undertaken.

There is no time to lose. The issues at stake call for immediate action, demand unrelaxing vigilance, undivided attention, and a consecration unexampled in the annals of the Faith in the British Isles. Though the number of those summoned to shoulder so immense a task be dishearteningly small, though the resources at their disposal

I gratefully acknowledge receipt of the sum of £200.0.0 Sterling from my dear Bahá'í co-workers British Baháʼí Community to be expended for the promotion of the international interests of the Baháʼí Faith.

Haifa, Israel.
June 3, 1952.

Shoghi

I gratefully acknowledge receipt of the sum of £319.12.3 Sterling from my dear Bahá'í co-workers The British Baháʼí Community to be expended for the construction of the Shrine of the Báb.

Haifa, Israel
August 25th 1953

Shoghi

Examples of receipt cards given to the British Bahá'í community by Shoghi Effendi

INDEX

Steadfastness, 141, 153, 181, 217, 291, 350, 366, 383
Stepping-stone, 187, 371, 449
Step resolutely forward, 252
Steps guided, 142, 188, 392
Stevens, Ethel, 273
Stevens, Mrs. Lilian, 116, 472
Stimulate, 186
Stockholm, 287, 308, 315
Stockport, 237–8
Storrs, Sir Ronald, 152, 162, 166, 274
Stout-hearted, 252
Strain, of responsibility, 154
  physical, nervous, 148, 198, 285, 439
Strength, 141, 178, 180, 310
Strengthen, 172, 330, 354, 364, 404, 437, 447, 452
Stress, 122, 133, 135, 137–8, 140, 146–7
Strikes, 361, 368
Struggle of life, 454–5
Studies, 445, 455
Sublime heroism, 69
Sublimity of, character, 58
  their task, 288
Subordinate all activities to teaching, 119, 183
Success, 169, 171, 179–80, 182, 192, 195–8, 200–1, 203, 205, 209, 214, 225, 227, 232–3, 235, 239–40, 254, 259, 261, 263–4, 272, 287, 291, 293, 300–2, 307, 312, 348, 353, 357, 371, 374, 381, 384–5, 392–3, 396, 398, 405, 407, 416, 436, 446, 456
  and failure, wide repercussions of, 232
  prayers for, *see* Prayers
  rapidly-won, not the best, 436
  secret of, 35, 107–8, 182, 302, 407
  signal, 153, 169, 179, 187, 209, 314
Sudan, 273
Suffer deprivations, 431
Sufferings, 80, 102, 125, 141, 144, 148, 177, 214, 405, 429, 431, 434, 437, 441, 447, 451, 459–60
Sugar, Alfred and Lucy, 210–11, 405, 481
Suicide of Nabíl, 406
Sullivan, Margaret, 211, 482
Sultanate, 78
Sun, 406
Sunday Times, Book Exhibition, 130
Sunnis, 426
Sunset as base time for commemorations, 170
Supplications, 422
Support, 10, 185–6, 195, 210, 223, 368
Supreme, legislative body, 261
  obligation, 114

Survey outstanding events, 158–9
Sustain, -ed, 135, 138, 150–1, 162, 178, 180, 182, 186, 203, 206, 211, 219–20, 227, 229, 235, 239, 251–2, 275, 279, 286, 297, 302, 311, 314, 327, 391–2, 395–6, 402, 407–8, 411, 413, 416, 418, 431, 437
Swahili, Kiswahili, 237, 253
Swiftly marching, 252
Swiftness, 128
Switzerland, 336
Sympathy, 413
Synagogue, membership in, 150, 199–200, 350
Syria, 80
Systematic, systematised effort, 9, 115, 131, 174, 186, 191, 201, 209, 215, 220, 227, 245, 251, 262, 285–6, 311, 340, 371, 384
System of Transliteration, 39

Tabríz, 386
Tablet, of the Holy Mariner, 426
  of the Virgin, 336
  of Visitation, 443
  to the Christians, 226
Tablets of 'Abdu'l-Bahá, not all collected, 445
  not notes taken or personal accounts, 89
  only those signed, in original language, 90
Taking oaths, 368
Tanganyika, Tanzania, 253, 260, 298–9, 303, 305
Tarázát, 424
Task colossal, 182, 265
Teachers, 198, 213, 272, 313, 339, 351, 407, 423, 441–2
  good lesson for, 61
  travel, *see* Travel
Teaching, 10, 14, 17, 29, 35, 60, 102–3, 106, 110–12, 116–23, 127, 131–5, 139–40, 142–5, 147–8, 150, 153, 155–9, 161–2, 171, 185–8, 195–6, 203, 210, 213, 217–19, 253, 262, 265, 270, 298, 303, 306, 308, 311, 326, 330–2, 334, 338, 341, 345, 347, 349, 351, 368, 371, 379, 381, 383–4, 392–3, 401, 405, 416–17, 422, 431, 434, 441, 416–17, 451, 458, 461
  'Abdu'l-Bahá's example, 35
  achieve new victories in, 143
  arise to teach, 35
  Bulletin, 106
  by children, 440
  Campaigns, plans, 80, 106, 110, 127,

Teaching, Campaigns, plans (*cont.*)
    134, 136, 145, 169, 185, 196, 210, 245–6, 260, 262, 265, 268, 270, 297–8, 379, 415
    difficulties in, 18, 73, 107
    enjoined by Bahá'u'lláh, 185
    essential pre-requisites, 35
    every believer to be involved in, 118, 186, 195
    find receptive souls, 458
    in Africa, 163, 262, 458
    indirect, 91, 434
    methods, 35, 130, 155, 300
    no rules laid down for, 458, 461
    opportunities, 92, 102, 104, 142
    paramount duty, 35
    related to Publishing Trust, 166
    sanctified and penetrating, 345
    subordinate all activities to, 119
    young people, 155, 187–8, 191–3, 195
    unity of Bahá'í revelation to be emphasised in, 426
    value of summer school to, 98, 110
Teaching Committee, *see* National Teaching Committee
Teaching Conferences, 376
    Africa, *see* Africa
    British Isles, *see* National Teaching Conference
    county, 402
    Europe, *see* Europe
    Northern Islands, 376
Teachings, 70, 77, 110, 129, 193, 248, 277, 281, 308–9, 311, 330, 334–5, 368, 396, 405–6, 408, 439, 443, 445, 450, 453–4, 457, 460, 462
    upheld, 128, 437
Temple, Wilmette, 80, 113
Temporary support, not a paid clergy, 185
Tenacity, 10, 28, 133, 137, 231, 260, 263, 275, 282, 288, 307, 311, 337, 353, 369, 371, 384, 397, 399, 422
Ten Year Crusade, Plan, Global, 285, 292, 297–8, 303–5, 307–10, 312–14, 321, 324, 326–7, 329, 331–3, 335, 338–41, 344–5, 352, 354, 360–1, 369–70, 372–3, 376, 383, 386
    action the keynote, 303–5
    approaching its mid-point, 386
    exchange of information essential, 308
    future phases, 339, 369, 384
    goals of, 297–9, 302–4, 313, 344–5; objectives, 360
    opening, initial phase of, 312–14, 337
    pioneering to take precedence, 303–5
    second phase, 338–9, 344, 347, 354, 362

Ten Year Crusade (*cont.*)
    supplementary goals, 373
    systematic co-operation twelve N.S.A.s, 285, 297, 310
    third collective enterprise, 292, 370
Termination European War, 175–6
Territories Dark Continent, 245, 270, 285–6
Teso, Uganda, 301
Tested, 438
Testings, 452
Thankfulness, 208, 210
The Bahá'í Faith; Information, etc., 289, 337
Theosophists, Theosophical Society, 20, 451, 458
Thornburgh–Cropper, Mrs., 9, 16, 63, 137–8, 163, 467
Thoroughness, 36
Three-fold, Crusade, 221
    purpose, 264
Threshold, 384, 404
Ṭihrán, 77, 217, 358, 386, 427
Time, for commemorations, 170, 272
    running short, 271, 354
Time and Tide, 92
Times, The, (London), 29, 366
    Literary Supplement, 100
Times of Crisis, 448
Tireless Efforts rewarded, 150
Toiling, 143, 263
Tokens of esteem, 288
Torbay (Torquay), Devonshire Group, 116, 126, 133, 161, 170, 188
Torch of divine guidance, 133
Tortured humanity, 177
Too late to avoid catastrophic trials, 454
Towers of strength, 173
Townshend, Rev. George, Canon, Hand of the Cause, 55, 86, 89, 92–6, 99, 100, 104–5, 111–12, 131, 135, 161, 199, 201, 203, 218, 307, 324, 333, 365, 377, 379, 381–2, 398, 469
    his, stirling qualities, scholarship, high ecclesiastical position, 382; writing ability, knowledge, zeal, 199, 365, 377
    one of three luminaries, 377
Townshend, Miss Una, Knight of Bahá'u'lláh, 181, 191, 322, 324, 326, 328, 333, 476
Toynbee, Professor Arnold, 366
Tragic, days, 140
    events in Írán, 355, 365
Transforming spirit, 144
Translations, 246, 262, 265–8, 287, 298, 302, 306, 313, 324, 329–30, 336, 339,

INDEX 521

Translations (cont.)
344, 354, 359–60, 367, 370, 378, 394, 422, 429
Esslemont's book, 130, 182, 190; German, 130; Icelandic, 130; Russian, 182, 190
Guardian's, 14, 17, 20, 22, 82, 195, 422
necessity for a Board of Translators, 422
of the, Bible, 378; word "Báb", 359
to be faithful and presentable, 163
Transliteration, 39–40, 46–7, 337
Travel teachers, 121, 161, 182, 188–9, 210, 234, 272, 291, 301, 446
circulating, 186
projects assigned to, financed, 185, 188, 250
Trembling, 137
Trials, tribulations, 140, 151, 280, 355, 365, 437, 453
Tristan da Cunha Island, 373
Triumphant conclusion, 211, 245, 261, 263, 291, 297, 299
Triumph,-ant, 80, 146, 174, 178, 183, 250, 313, 365, 391
Troubles, cause of, 454
True, mysticism, 407
stature, 170
upholders, 155
Trusted ones of the Merciful, 6
Trust in, Bahá'u'lláh, 191
God, 173
Truthfulness, 368
Truth, of the Teachings, 129, 137
Tudor-Pole, Major, 120, 162, 171, 230
Tunis, 85, 373
Turkestan, 12
Turkey, 12, 67, 77–9
Turmoil, 80
Turning point, 181, 189, 250
Turn to Spiritual Assemblies, 145
Two-fold, double, task, duty, process, 158, 196, 245, 262–3, 297, 312
Two Year Plan, "Africa Plan", xvi, xvii, 163, 245–6, 251, 253, 257–8, 260–5, 268–72, 276, 278–9, 283–4, 290–1, 293, 297, 311–12, 353, 355, 372, 386, 403
demands continuous, unstinted, systematic support, 264
eclipse exploits Six Year Plan, 284
enterprise, unique, epoch-making, soul-thrilling, meritorious, 251–2, 257, 260–1, 265, 272, 283, 287
exceeded highest hopes, 297
independent campaign not intended, 257

Two Year Plan, "Africa Plan" (cont.)
inter-assembly, not international, undertaking, 273
mandate of utmost significance, 270
objectives of, 245–6, 264, 271
opening, initial phase, 260, 264–5, 285, 287
prelude to future plans, 245, 270–2, 276, 285, 297
victory announced, 297

Uganda, 253, 274, 277, 290, 298–300, 305, 329, 334, 347, 351–3, 359, 460
a people apart, 334
Ultimate triumph, 140
Unabated persecution, 49
Unassailable foundation, 137
Unbelievable changes in days to come, 439
Uncertainties, 136
Unconquerable spirit, 183
Understanding, 123
Undertakings, mighty, collective, historic, 182, 187, 232, 245, 257, 261, 285, 291
Undeviating in purpose, 371
Unexampled harvest, 131
Unfailing protection, 133
Unfolding mission, 245, 292, 311, 314
Unified world, 456
Uniformity in essential principles, 102
United effort, 180, 206, 278, 340, 415
United Kingdom, 128, 211, 220, 221
United labour, 113
Unitedly, 181, 186, 189, 196, 211, 218, 232, 271, 369, 372, 403, 430
United Nations Organisation, 190, 348
United States, North America, 5, 9, 14, 17, 19, 22, 42, 55, 63, 72, 80–1, 96–8, 101, 113, 139, 150, 156, 169, 178–9, 185–7, 199, 203, 207, 214–15, 221, 225–6, 232, 245–7, 249, 251, 253–5, 264, 285, 304, 321, 335, 373, 376, 410
chief custodians 'Abdu'l-Bahá's Master Plan, 285, 304
send pioneers to any virgin area, 304
United States National Spritual Assembly, 5, 17, 19–21, 49, 65, 81, 83, 86, 96–7, 99, 101–3, 161, 253, 255–7, 264, 292, 302, 304, 309, 323, 361
Unity, 9, 88, 106, 119, 121, 151, 153, 182, 185, 261, 400, 404, 407–8, 417, 444
in diversity, 102
of the Bahá'í Revelation to be emphasised, 426

Unity (cont.)
    of the Believers, 11, 13, 26, 110, 123, 140, 162, 164, 205, 445, 447
    of the Cause, 8, 15
    prayer for, 5, 6
Universal, carnage, 145
    destruction, 147
    recognition, 35, 58, 66, 80, 191
Universal House of Justice, 257, 261, 334, 355, 421, 455
Universality, 77, 253
University undergraduates, 412, 415, 417
Unprecedented, 186, 261, 313
    achievements, 123, 198, 211
    developments, 113
Unquenchable spirit, faith, 142, 171
Unreserved, acceptance, 71
Unsavoury minority, 330
Unspeakably glorious mission, 339
Unswervingly faithful, 352
Unworthy, 447, 459
Unyielding determination, 171
Uprightness of character, 365
Urgency, acute but temporary, 231, of task, 265
Utmost economy, 256, 324

Vacancy recognised, 225
Vakíl 'Abbás, Knight of Bahá'u'lláh, 320
Vakílu'd-Dawlih, Hájí Mírzá, 43
Valiant British Community, 146, 211, 222, 279, 299, 310, 337, 347, 352, 363, 376
Valley of spiritual death, 143
Valour, -ous, 145, 245, 263, 265
Vanguard, 340
Varqa, Valíyu'lláh, Hand of the Cause, 219, 348
Vast, 339
Verbatim reports required, 171, 208
Verities, 385
Veterans, 237
Vicissitudes, 49, 141
Victories, Victory, 143, 155, 157–8, 164, 166, 171, 181, 183, 196, 198, 200–1, 203, 211, 214, 220, 225-6, 229, 231–3, 235–7, 239–41, 245–6, 249–52, 258, 264, 266, 269, 278–80, 282, 286, 297, 303, 310–14, 324–6, 340, 345, 353, 355, 361, 363, 369, 371–2, 374, 379, 381, 386, 391, 394, 398, 399, 401, 403, 408, 413, 415–18
    achieved by God not men, 459
    over self, 441–2, 450
Victoriously advancing, 206, 217
Victor's crown, 262

Vigilance, of N.S.A., 129, 174, 180, 231, 287, 314, 353, 362, 371, 431
Vigour,-ously, 115, 131, 133, 149, 162, 182, 258, 263, 265, 270–1, 278, 287, 314, 369
Vindication of Faith, 123
Violence, worst form of, 128
Virgin territories, Homeland, Ireland, Scotland, Wales, 192, 209, 353–4
    overseas, 251–2, 259, 265, 278, 286, 290, 297, 302–6, 308, 310, 312–13, 327, 329, 336, 353–4, 369
    posts to be kept open at any cost, 336
Virile, 203, 229, 252, 338, 367
Virtues, qualities, British believers, *see* Annex "C"
Vision, 252, 272, 449
Vista of vast dimensions, 220, 313
Vitality, 150, 170, 200, 306, 367, 385, 454
Voice of Youth, 387
Volunteers, 185, 310, 314, 351
    in times of emergency, 122–3
Vote for World Government representatives, 213
Voting age, 207
Voting for oneself, 170
Voting list, 184, 199
Voting rights, 159, 199, 207, 213, 225, 343, 444

Wales, Welsh, 169, 192, 196, 201, 206, 209, 211, 215, 217, 220, 237, 245, 249, 251, 262, 272, 286–7, 297–8, 311–12, 339, 353, 388, 393–6
    a talented race, 395
    pamphlet in, 394, 396
    will respond, 396
Walmar House, Regent St., London, 86–88
Walsh, Dr., 30
War, xi, 128–9, 133, 141, 150, 154, 156, 160, 173, 176–7, 179, 181, 185, 190, 259, 261, 309, 356, 435, 437, 448
Warman, Zara, 217
Warm community atmosphere, 439
Warp and woof, 339
Weak instruments demonstrate God's power, 459
Wedding, 139
Welfare, 321
Well tried, 265
West, 12, 18, 21, 23, 34, 38, 49, 51, 56–7, 59, 65–6, 69, 75, 79, 80, 82–4, 93, 100, 138, 145, 147, 156, 164, 176, 190, 198, 200, 208, 210–11, 234, 257,

West (*cont.*)
260, 290, 297, 309–10, 337–8, 353, 366, 369, 377, 385, 429–30, 434, 446
will seize the Cause, 51
West Africa, 245, 262
Western World, 145, 215
Westminster, 263
Whole-hearted immediate response, 362
Wholly dedicated, 286
Wide, awake, 210, 337
  recognition, 382
Wigington, Miss Dorothy, 362, 488
Wilful murder, 129
Wilhelm, Roy, 12, 25
Wilkins, Walter, 191, 217, 224, 477
Williams, Miss Ada, 222, 483
Will-power, 442
Wilmette, U.S.A. 80, 113, 291, 356
Winsten, Mrs., 414
Wisdom, 131, 140, 144, 212, 217, 219, 301, 314, 406, 417, 428, 434, 439, 459–60
  of suffering, 459–60
Wisdom of God, of His Prophets, 406, 434, 459
Wisdom of the East series, 237
Withdrawals, 449
Wives, 351, 395
Work, chosen for themselves, 177, 186, 221
  enjoined on all, 462
Workings of World Order, 385
World, Bahá'í Community, 211, 214, 261, 270
  centre, 225, 266, 268, 351
  civilisation, 330
  condition of, 177, 190, 310, 437, 445, 447, 452–4, 457
  Congress of Faiths, 105, 109, 144, 206–7; inaugural meeting, blessings to whole community, 109
  encircling crusade, 285, 314, 339, 353; empire, 187
  encompassing task, 285, 340
  fellowship through religion, 104
  Government, 213
  on path towards upheaval, agony, 454
  order, 143, 191, 252, 257, 285, 338, 385–6, 410, 452

World, Bahá'í Community (*cont.*)
  protest, 348
  religion, Faith, 170
  situation, 33, 221, 445, 454
  spiritual crusade, 297, 299, 311, 352, 386
  unity, 456
World's disequilibrium and chaos, 454
World-wide, activities, 253–4, 353, 371
  attacks, 67
  enterprises, 261
Wren, Mr., 90
Writers and poets needed, 428–9

Yaḥyá, Mírzá, 460
Yazdí, 'Azíz (and Soraya), 321
Year, crucial, 194–5, 198, 200
  most memorable, 195
  pivotal, 189, 194
Yool, Robert, 160
Young, Miss Jessica, 172, 475
Younghusband, Sir Francis, 104
Youth, Bahá'í, young believers, 110, 126, 187–8, 191–13, 195, 197–8, 202, 204, 207, 236, 279–80, 332, 335, 351, 410, 441, 443, 460; their declaration of intention, 335; their only hope, 191
  Bulletin, 188, 192, 197, 203–4, 236; contents of, 188, 192; firm inovation, 192
  Groups, 110, 204
  National Committee of, *see* Committees
  Regional Conference, 196, 279
  work, 192
Youthfulness, 367
Yunis Khán, 41

Zain, Jinábi, 424
Zanján, 425
Zanzibar, 291
Zarand, Írán, 427
Zeal, 110, 121, 123, 144, 185, 198, 260, 262, 271–2, 288, 350
Zía'iyyih Khánum, (Ḍíyá'íyyih), Mother of Shoghi Effendi, 115
Zoroaster, 451
Zululand, 298.

ANNEX "A"

COUNTRIES, PLACES, AREAS MENTIONED

Aberdeen
A<u>dh</u>irbáyján
Adrianople
Af<u>gh</u>ánistán
Africa
'Akká (Acre)
Algeria
Anatolia
Angola
Ardibil, Írán
Ashanti Protectorate
Asia
Australia
Austria

Ba<u>gh</u>dád
Bahjí
Bahrein
Balkans
Belfast
Belgian Congo
Birmingham
Blackburn
Blackpool
Bombay
Bournemouth
Bradford
Brighton
Bristol
British Cameroons
British Isles
British Somaliland
British Togoland
Brussels
Budapest
Burma
Buxton

Cairo
Cambridge
Canada
Cardiff
Caucasus
Central, East Africa
Channel Islands
Chicago
China
<u>Ch</u>iríq
Comoro Islands
Constantinople

Cyprus
Czechoslovakia

Dar-es-Salaam
Devonshire
Djibouti
Dublin

Eccles
Edinburgh
Egypt
Eire (Ireland)
England
Eritrea
Esslingen (Germany)
Ethiopia
Europe

Far East
Faroe Islands
France
Frankfurt
French Cameroons
French Congo
French Morocco
French Somaliland
French Togoland

Geneva
Germany
Geyserville (U.S.A.)
Gilbert and Ellice Islands
Glasgow
Gold Coast
Great Britain
Green Acre (U.S.A.)

Haifa
Hamburg
Hebrides Islands
Holy Land
Hong Kong
Hungary

Iceland
India
Indo-China
Írán
'Iráq
Ireland (Eire)

ANNEX

Italian Somaliland
Italy
I<u>sh</u>qábád, Russia

Jahrúm, Írán
Jerusalem

Kampala
Karkuk, 'Iráq
Kenya
Kirmán<u>sh</u>áh
Kurdistán
Kuwait

Lambeth
Leeds
Liverpool
London
Lou-Helen Ranch, U.S.A.

Madagascar
Madeira
Malta
Manchester
Marághih, Írán
Mauritius
Mázindarán, Írán
Mediterranean
Mesopotamia
Middle, Near East
Mogadiscio
Morocco
Mount Carmel

Nairobi
Nayriz, Írán
Newcastle
New York
New Zealand
Nicosia, Cyprus
Nigeria
North Africa
Northern Ireland
Northampton
Norwich
Nottingham
Nyassaland

Orkney Islands
Oxford

Pacific Islands
Palestine

Paris
Poland
Portsmouth

Reading
Rhodesia
Rome
Roumania
Ruanda Urundi
Russia

St. Ives
St. Petersburgh
Salisbury, Rhodesia
Scotland
Seychelles
Sheffield
Shetland Islands
<u>Sh</u>íráz
Sierra Leone
Smyrna
Somaliland
South Africa
South America
South Rhodesia
South-West Africa
South-West England
Stockholm
Stockport
Sudan
Switzerland
Syria

Tabríz
Tanganyika
Teso, Uganda
Țihrán, Írán
Torbay (Torquay)
Tristan da Cunha Island
Tunis
Turkestán
Turkey

Uganda
United Kingdom
United States of America

Wales
Wilmette, U.S.A.

Zanján, Írán
Zanzibar
Zarand, Írán
Zululand

ANNEX "B"

INDIVIDUALS MENTIONED; PIONEERS IN ITALICS

Abu'l-Faḍl, Mírzá
Afnán 'Abbás
Afnan Fuad
Afnán Shomais
Afrukhteh, Yunis
Aḥmad, Mírzá
Alá'í, Rahmat'u'llah
'Alí, Dr
Aminu'l-'ulamá
Arastu, Mírzá
Aṣgharzádih, Ḍiá'u'lláh
Avaríh, Jináb-i-

Backwell, Richard H.
Baker, Dorothy
Baker, Richard St. Barbe
Balyuzi, Ḥasan M.
Banání, Músá
Banání, Samíḥih
Basil-Hall, Mary
Baxter, Evelyn
Benes, ex-President
Bennett, Irene
Biggs, Rev.
Bishop, Mrs.
Blomfield, Lady
Blum, Mr., Mrs.
Breakwell, Thomas
Bronne, E. G.

Campbell, Jean
Cardell, Edmund
Carnegie, Andrew
Challis, Sister Grace
Cheek, Robert
Cheyne, Canon
Coleman, Doris
Coles, Claudia
Collins, Amelia
Collison, Mary
Collison, Rex
Cormick, Dr.
Craven, John
Craney, Geraldine

Dreyfus-Barney, H.
Dunning, Charles

Eden, Anthony
Elston, Alan
Elston, Mary

Emperor of Japan
Epyeru, Enos
Esslemont, John E.
Esslemont, Peter

Ferraby, Dorothy
Ferraby, John
French, Mrs.

George, Florence
George, Prudence
Giddings, Joan
Ginman, Louise
Greatest Holy Leaf
Grinevskaya, Mde.
Gregory, Alma C.
Gregory, Ernest W.
Gregory, Louis
Gregory, Mrs.
Greven, Mr., Mrs.
Gung, Claire

Hainsworth, Lizzie F.
Hainsworth, Philip
Ḥakím, Dr. Luṭfulláh
Halifax, Lord
Hall, Edward, T.
Hall, Mrs.
Haybittel, Mrs.
Hasselblatt, Brigette
Hill, Mr., Mrs.
Hofman, David
Hofman, Marion
Holley, Horace
Howes, Janet
Ḥujjat
Hurst, Frank

Ioas, Leroy

Jack, Marion
Jenkerson, Cyril
Jenkerson, Margaret
Joseph, Albert
Joseph, Jeff

Khán, Dr.
Khochbine, A.

Lammington, Lord
Langdon-Davis, Constance
Lea, Elsie

Leach, Bernard
Lee, Joseph
Ljungberg, Eskil
Lynch, Mrs.

Manton, Eric
Manton, Mr.
Marie, Queen of Roumania
Marshall, George K.
Marshall, John L.
Masefield, Miss
Mathews, Loulie
Maxwell, Sutherland
McKinley, Hugh
McKinley, Violet
Miller, Ernest S.
Mills, Mountfort
Mills, Olga M. K.
Mitchell, John G.
Moayad, Dr.
Mudaliar, Sir A. R.
Mullá Ḥusayn
Munirrih Khánum
Murray, Prof. Gilbert

Nakhjaváni, 'Alí
Norton, Arthur

Orlova, Madam

Perdu
Phelps, Myron
Pinchon, Florence
Preston, Marguerite
Preston, Terence
Purest Branch

Quddús

Robarts, John
Root, Martha
Rosenberg, Ethel J.

Ṣabrí, Hassan, A. F.
Ṣabrí, Isobel

Samandarí, Ursula
Samuel, Sir H.
Scott, Samuel
Schopflocher, Fred
Semple, Ian
Sharples, Miss
Shaykh Faraj
Simpson, George P.
Slade, Isobel
Sohrab, Ahmad
Stahler, Fred
Stannard, Mrs.
Stevens, Ethel
Stevens, Lilian
Storrs, Sir R
Sugar, Alfred
Sugar, Lucy
Sullivan, Margaret

Thornburgh-Cropper, Mrs.
Townshend, George
Townshend, Una
Toynbee, Prof. Arnold
Tudor-Pole, Major

Vakíl, 'Abbás
Vakílu'd-Dawlih, Hájí Mírzá
Varqa, Valíyu'lláh

Walsh, Dr.
Wigington, Dorothy
Wilhelm, Roy
Wilkins, Walter
Williams, Ada
Winsten, Mrs.
Wren, Mr.

Yaḥyá, Mírzá
Yazdi, 'Azíz, (Soraya)
Yool, Robert
Young, Jessica
Younghusband, Sir F.

Zain, Jinábi
Zía'iyyih Khánum

ANNEX "C"

QUALITIES, VIRTUES, OF BRITISH BELIEVERS

ability
activity
alert
alive
ardent
assiduously striving

blessed
brightness

care
clear visioned
confidence
consecration
consideration
constancy
co-operation
courage
courtesy

dedicated
detachment
determination
devotion
dignity

earnestness
energy
enthusiasm

faith
fervour
fidelity
firmly grounded
firmly knit
forbearance
forward marching

galvanised
genuineness
goodwill
greatly promising

harmony
high minded
high spirited
highly esteemed

incorruptible spirit
initiative

inflexible purpose
inflexibly resolved
intelligence
intensely alive
intrepidity

kindness

love
lowliness
loyalty

moderation
much admired

nobility of purpose

obedience
optimism

patience
patiently labouring
peace
perseverance
perspicacity
progressive
purity of motive

radiance
resolution
resolve
resourcefulness

sagacity
self-sacrifice
sense of responsibility
service
sincerity
solicitude
solidarity
sound
sound judgement
spirit
spirit of faith
spiritually potent
staunchness
steadfastness
stout hearted
swiftly marching

tenacity

toiling
triumphant

unconquerable spirit
understanding
undeviating purpose
unity
unquenchable faith
unquenchable spirit
unswervingly faithful

valiant

valorous
victoriously advancing
vigour
vigorously functioning
virile
vitality

well tried
wholly dedicated

zeal

ANNEX "D"

LANGUAGES MENTIONED

African
Accra, 298
Acoli, 265
Adanwe, 265
Afrikaans, 298
Aladian, 298
Ashanti, 298

Banu, 298
Bemba, 298
Bua, 298, 320

Chinyanza, 237, 258
Chuana, 298

Dagbane, 266

Ewe, 265

Fanta, 265, 266
Fon, 342

Gio, 298
Gu, 298

Hausa, 253

Ibo, 266

Jieng, 298
Jolof, 298

Krongo, 298
Kroo, 298
Kuanyama, 298

Lingala, 320
Liumbi, 298, 320
Luba, 320
Luganda, 275

Malagasy, 298
Mbundo, 320
Mende, 265

Nubian, 298

Pedi, 298
Popo, 298, 342

Ronga, 298, 349

Sena, 298, 320
Shangaan, 349
Shila, 298
Shona, 298
Sobo, 298
Somali, 265, 267, 268
Suto, 298
Swahili, (Ki) 237, 253, 275

Tonga, 320

Wongo, 298, 320

Xosa, 298

Yalunka, 298
Yao, 298
Yoruba, 265

Zulu, 298

Others
Arabic, 14
Erse, 344, 358, 369, 382
Esperanto, 48
Gaelic, 344, 358, 382
German, 130
Hebrew, 46
Icelandic, 130
Persian, 14, 130
Russian, 182, 190
Welsh, 394, 396

ANNEX "E"

PUBLICATIONS MENTIONED

'Abdu 'l-Bahá in London
Advice to Bahá'ís in British Colonies
Africa News

Bahá'í Administration
Bahá'í Journal
Bahá'í News (India)
Bahá'í Year Book
Bahá'í Youth Bulletin
Bahá'í World
Bahá'ís and War
Bahá'u'lláh (Balyuzi)
Bahá'u'lláh and the New Era (Esslemont)
Bahá'u'lláh-The King of Glory (Balyuzi)
Bulletin, Teaching Committee

Centenary Pamphlet
Chosen Highway, The (Blomfield)
Christ and Bahá'u'lláh (Townshend)
Coming of The Glory (Pinchon)

Diary
Dispensation of Bahá'u'lláh

Epistle to the Son of the Wolf

Glad Tidings of Bahá'u'lláh (Townshend)
Gospel in Many Tongues, The

Haifa Newsletter
Heart of the Gospel (Townshend)
Hidden Words

Ishráqát

Kitáb-i-Aqdas
Kitáb-i-Iqán

La Nova Tago

Message of Bahá'u'lláh (Esslemont)
Messager Bahá'í
Mysterious Forces of Civilisation

New World Order

Paris Talks
Persia and the Persian Question (Curzon)
Prayer Book
Prayers and Meditations
Prescription for Living (Rabbaní)
Principles of Bahá'í Administration
Promised Day is Come, The
Promise of All Ages, The (Townshend)
Promulgation of Universal Peace

Seven Valleys
Some Answered Questions
Star of the West

Tarázát
The Bahá'í Faith: Information Statistical and Comparative

Voice of Youth